The Internet Power Toolkit

Cutting-Edge Tools & Techniques for Power Users

The Internet Power Toolkit

Cutting-Edge Tools & Techniques for Power Users

Sean Carton
Gareth Branwyn

VENTANA

The Internet Power Toolkit: Cutting-Edge Tools & Techniques for Power Users
Copyright © 1996 by Sean Carton and Gareth Branwyn

Library of Congress Cataloging-in-Publication Data
Carton, Sean
    The Internet power toolkit : cutting-edge tools & techniques for power
users / Sean Carton, Gareth Branwyn.
       p. cm.
    Includes index.
    ISBN 156604-329-8
    1. Internet (Computer network) I. Branwyn, Gareth. II. Title.
TK5105.875.I57C37 1996
004.6'7—dc20   96-6196
                                     CIP

First Edition 9 8 7 6 5 4 3 2 1
Printed in the United States of America

Ventana Communications Group, Inc.
P.O. Box 13964
Research Triangle Park, NC 27709-3964
919/544-9404
FAX 919/544-9472

About the Authors

Sean Carton is a writer, interactive media designer, and Webmaster. He's currently VP, Director of Interactive Media Development for RMD Interactive—Baltimore, Maryland's largest interactive agency. His book credits include *Mosaic Quick Tour Special Edition* (Ventana), *Internet Roadside Attractions* (Ventana), and *Internet Virtual Worlds Quick Tour* (Ventana). He contributed subversive materials to The *Happy Mutant Handbook*, and has also written for *bOING bOING*, *Link*, *Cape-X*, and *Stim*. When he's not writing or working, Sean enjoys spooking the neighbors by creating crop circles in their front lawns.

Gareth Branwyn is a freelance writer whose main beat is the intersection of culture and technology. He is a contributing writer to *Wired*, the senior editor of *bOING bOING* (a pop culture humor mag) and a contributing editor to *Stim*, Prodigy's new webzine. His book publishing credits include *Mosaic Quick Tour* (Ventana), *The Happy Mutant Handbook* (Riverside) and chapters in *Mondo 2000's User's Guide to the New Edge* (HarperPerennial), *Flame Wars* (Duke University Press), *Virtual Reality Casebook* (Van Nostrand Reinhold), and *The Millennium Whole Earth Catalog* (Harper Collins). He is also co-creator of Beyond Cyberpunk, the critically-acclaimed HyperCard compendium of early '90s cyberculture.

Acknowledgments

I would like to thank my wife Lorna for her unwavering support, love, and patience during the creation of this book. I never would have made it without you! I'd also like to thank my parents, Bob and Christy Carton, for all their love and support over the years. To all *my* friends who I've not called during the course of this book, I just want to say one thing—I'm back! To my friend and partner, Chuck Donofrio, thanks for being patient with me. I'll be back at the salt mine early Monday morning. Finally, I want to extend my deepest thanks, love, and appreciation to my co-author Gareth. You are truly an inspiration to me. Thanks, bud!
—*Sean*

I would like to thank my wife Pam and son Blake whose constant help, moral support, and good humor got me through. You are a constant reminder that the physical world will always outshine the virtual one. To all my friends and family who took the hint and left me alone so that I could finish this thing: OK, I'm done, you can call me now. Thanks also to my good pal Alberto who was always there at 2 AM when I needed to road test one piece of software or another. Thank goodness he's on vampire time, too! And of course, most of the yahoos go to my partner in crime, Sean Carton, who kept me laughing even during the most exhausting and tedious moments of this project.
—*Gareth*

Our very special thanks also go to Arthur Griffith and Elizabeth Lipson, who went to bat for us late in the game and wrote several chapters after we got mouse elbow and needed to call in reinforcements. We'd like to thank all the fine folks at Ventana who were involved, especially Sherri Morningstar, Tim Mattson, Eric Edstam, Brian Little, JJ Hohn, Judy Flynn, Jaimie Livingston, John Cotterman, and Lois Principe. We appreciate your patience while the deadlines kept whizzing by. We'd also like to thank our agent, the ubiquitous Matt Wagner.

Dedication

Sean would like to dedicate this book to his wife, Lorna. Without you, all this means nothing.

Gareth would like to dedicate this book to his son, Blake. The future's yours, little buddy!

Contents

Part II
Windows Power User's Tools

Part III
Macintosh Power User's Tools

Part IV
UNIX Power User's Tools

Part V
The Power User's Guide to E-Mail

Part VI
The Power User's Guide
to Usenet News

Part VII
The Power User's Guide to the Web

Part VIII
Netsearching: Unleashing Your
Code Hound

Part IX
Miscellaneous Power Tools

Appendices

Introduction

Is this you? You've been online for a while now; you've learned a few things. You know how to fire up the modem, check your e-mail, participate in some newsgroups, and do a little Web browsing. Maybe you spend your time chatting, or checking up on the daily news, or staying in touch with a few far-flung friends. You've figured out how to download files, but have a hard time finding the exact files you want. Now that you've gotten your feet wet, you're probably starting to realize that there's a huge amount of stuff out there—resources you can use to improve your business productivity, your ability to communicate, and your ability to stay on top of late-breaking news, information, and entertainment. Trouble is, you're no techno-wizard and you don't have the time to become one. But you do have lots of questions about how all this works and how you can make the most of it. You want answers . . . now! Well, read on dear friend, read on.

Or maybe this is you. You've read all the beginner Net books you could get your hands on. You now check your e-mail every few hours (and usually find messages each time you do). You gobble down newsgroups by the domain. You surf the Web with aplomb. You subscribe to an ever-growing list of e-mailed publications and reports. You're never at a loss for new software now that you've mastered grabbing files with FTP. Archie isn't just a cartoon character to you anymore, and you know how to talk Veronica into being your Gopher. You amaze your friends and confound your family by tossing off terms like Web robots and TCP/IP. The Net has stopped being a novelty for you; it's become an important part of your life. But, you want to learn even more, to move on to the next level. You want to be able to filter that growing e-mail queue. You want to start your own e-zine or Web site. You want to learn all the secrets of the Net gurus so that you too can be on top of the information mushroom. You've collected a long list of question about how the Internet works, and now you'd like some answers. This book's for you, too.

The *Internet Power Toolkit* is for anyone who wants to get the most out of the Internet. There is a plethora of beginners books out there, and free trial memberships to online services arrive in the mail weekly. Every day, more and more people crack open the doors of cyberspace. They establish an e-mail address, poke around a bit, and then get intimidated by the overwhelming task of actually figuring out how to use everything. This is a book for anyone who wants to expand their Net horizons, communicate more effectively, find valuable information on demand, and stay abreast of new sites, services, and breaking technologies.

Since the "superhighway" metaphor hasn't been flogged enough, let's use it *one more time*. Have you ever gone on a trip with someone who seems to live for the road? They know how to pack the right provisions and have AAA Triptiks and other useful information close at hand. They remember to get the car serviced and even know what all those little symbols on the roadmap mean. They seem to be totally organized and able to get the most out of their trip. (And you can't remember to bring your toothbrush). The computer equivalent of this seasoned traveler is a "power user." Regardless of your current level of expertise, this book will turn you into an Internet power user.

WHAT THIS BOOK IS (& ISN'T)

So what exactly are you going to learn once you dive headlong into this tome?

❐ This book is not about how to get started with e-mail; it's about how to use advanced e-mail tools and techniques to communicate more effectively and to manage the flow of your e-mail.

❐ This book is not a beginners' guide to Usenet news; it's a guide to making better use of newsgroups to find the information and discussions you want (when you want them), and learning how to filter out the "noise" in these groups.

❐ This book is not about how to use FTP; it's about how to make use of *all* the features that FTP and other file search and retrieval systems can offer. With this knowledge, you can have almost instant access to the documents and software that are stored throughout the Net.

❐ This book is not about how to browse the Web; it's about how to use the Web as a "front end" to all of the Internet's resources, how to manage your time on the Web, and what tools are available to you for creating your own Web presence.

❐ This book is not about how to get on the Net; it's about traveling deeper into it to mine its vast resources.

❐ This book is not a directory of yesterday's interesting Net sites. It will teach you how to stay on the crest of the information wave and how to use the latest Web and Net technologies to create a "living directory" that will not go out of date. It's about knowing where to look.

❐ This book is for anyone who wants to stop using their computer as a toy and start using it as a serious information appliance.

❐ This book is not for a new user; it's for the intermediate user who wants to learn more about the way the Internet works and the software and hardware that sustains it. It's everything you wanted to know about the Internet but were afraid to ask.

WHAT'S INSIDE

So join the ranks of the Internet power users, those industrious Net citizens who've learned all the tips, tricks, and well-kept secrets that make online life easier and more productive. There's a lot of information between these pages, but if you follow along closely you'll master the Net in no time. Or, if you have short attention spans like we do, you can skip around to the sections that interest you.

Part I: Expanding Connectivity

One of the first things that's important in trying to expand your mastery over the Internet is understanding how the Net itself works and the various options for how you can connect to it. In Part I, we'll look at modems and how they work, the TCP/IP protocols on which the Internet is based, and local area networks and how they're connected to the Net. We'll also take a peek at the future of home and office connectivity through options like ISDN, ADSL, and cable modems. Finally, we'll cover making connections on the road and how you can stay wired regardless of whether you're moving around a building, a city, or the whole blue planet. We'll even tell you how to create your own inexpensive "road warrior" travel kit so that you'll always have what you need to connect, no matter where you are.

Part II: Windows Power User's Tools

For Windows users, we'll cover all the latest tools and techniques for getting connected, with a special focus on Windows 95. We'll look at Microsoft's TCP/IP tools (that come built into Win95) and other vendors' packages for connecting to the Internet, and we'll give you some tips for troubleshooting your connections, and managing your time online. We'll also cover the latest and greatest in Windows e-mail software, Usenet newsreaders, Web browsers, and miscellaneous Net power tools. Along the way, we'll give you lots of advanced techniques for using the software and pointers to online resources where you can go for even more information and cool tools.

Part III: Macintosh Power User's Tools

For the Macintosh users, we'll cover all of the latest tools and techniques for getting connected with your Mac. We'll look at Apple's MacTCP tools (now built into the Mac OS) and other vendors' packages for connecting to the Internet, troubleshooting your connections, and managing your time online. We'll also cover the latest and greatest in Macintosh e-mail software, Usenet newsreaders, Web browsers, and miscellaneous Net power tools. Along the way, we'll give you lots of advanced techniques for using the software and pointers to online resources where you can go for even more information and cool tools.

Part IV: UNIX Power User's Tools

Next stop, UNIX. For those of you who only have UNIX shell account access to the Net, or who have a shell account as part of their PPP or SLIP service, we offer all the basics (and beyond) of UNIX Internet. Until now, this operating system may have been a mystery to you, and you've avoided it like the plague. Even though UNIX can be intimidating to even an experienced computer user, we're here to guide you through, from getting connected to using UNIX e-mail, news, World Wide Web, and other powerful tools. As an added bonus, we've included a UNIX boot camp (Appendix D) for those who need a quick tour of the UNIX OS.

Part V: The Power User's Guide to E-Mail

Since communication is one of the most important aspects of the Internet, and e-mail is the hub of that communication, we've devoted an entire section to helping you get the most out of e-mail. Although Parts II, III, and IV have chapters covering the specific e-mail tools for Windows, Mac, and UNIX, in Part V we look at e-mail issues that affect all users. First, we'll look at all the features that most people never use; features that can make your communications faster and more efficient. We'll unravel the most overlooked part of e-mail—the header information—and discover what all that arcana means. Next, we'll examine just how to get your message to where you want it to go, looking at all the ways you can send e-mail from the Internet to any of the online services (and back again). And, for those of you who get the sweats whenever you have a MIME attachment on your mail or you have to encode files to send with your mail, we've come to your rescue (do you like our big white hats?). Security is becoming an important issue as we communicate online more and more. We address this by giving you a crash course in data encryption, anonymous remailers, password do's and don'ts, and a look at network security in general. After all, your e-mail is only as secure as the system it's on. It's important that a power user knows something of basic security issues.

Part VI: The Power User's Guide to Usenet News

You probably already know Usenet to be a furious, frolicking, free-for-all of shot-from-the-hip opinions, socially-created news, and flame wars. But there's a whole lot more out there than just those MAKE.MONEY.FAST messages and arguments over Windows vs. Macintosh. In this section, we'll give you a brief history of Usenet, tell you what it is and isn't, and reveal some secrets for how to use it to its fullest extent. We'll put a posting under a microscope to examine its parts and functions. We'll even tell you what you need to know to start your own newsgroup. Then we'll delve into the world of binary newsgroups with their wealth of pictures, programs, and clip art. You'll learn where they are, how to get at them, and how to decode what you find there. Your hard drive will never be empty again. You'll also learn how you can get your stuff onto these newsgroups.

Part VII: The Power User's Guide to the Web

Of course, the place where all the action is in cyberspace (at least for the next 15 minutes) is the World Wide Web. We'll run through all of the latest plug-ins and helper applications that you can add to your Web browser to make it an even more powerful multimedia viewer—from movie players to real-time audio/video plug-ins to the many "virtual reality" (VRML) plug-ins and stand-alone clients. We'll tell you what they are, how they work, and where you can get them. Much of the software in this section is available on the CD-ROM in the back of the book, so you don't even have to bother downloading it! Next, we'll consider some of what goes into setting up shop on the Web. We'll look at HTML editors and how they can be used to streamline your Web-page design and implementation. In our HTTP server tools section, we'll discuss several server packages you can use to create your own island in the Net.

Part VIII: Netsearching: Unleashing Your Code Hound

"What the heck is a Codehound?" you ask. Codehound is a mythical artificial intelligence program conceived by Mark Frauenfelder of *bOING bOING* and *Wired* magazine fame. Codehound is the ultimate data sniffer, a state of the art software agent. He can seek out and retrieve whatever information his owner requests. If you want to find something online, Codehound is the digital pooch to ask. He's so good, in fact, that he's developed quite a snooty attitude. He's the best in the business *if* you can pull him away from all the mischief he likes to cause online (ever wonder why some of your mail gets routed via Lithuania?).

We can't guarantee that you'll ever reach Codehound's level of proficiency, but we'll bet that we can get you close. In Part VIII, we'll examine all the ways and means for tracking down data and people on the Net. First, we'll cover the myriad tools available for finding those info needles in the vast silicon haystacks of cyberspace. We'll cover Web search engines, indexes, libraries, and other information repositories. After that, our data-surfing acumen will turn to four of the weirdest-named utilities on the Net: Archie, Veronica, Jughead, and Gopher. Before we're through learning the game of data tracking, we'll even cover some of the more under-utilized resources, like WAIS and Netfind. Next, we'll move into real bloodhound territory as we learn some real-life people-finding skills. You'll learn what it takes to track friends, relatives, business associates, and others you want to locate, even if they're not online! We'll cover how to use commands such as finger and whois to get the goods on someone. You'll learn how to use the Internet White Pages and X.500 to search e-mail addresses. We'll also look at how two valuable resources—Usenet indices and postmasters—can be used as tools of last resort. No matter what, if anyone's on the Net, you should be able to find them by the end of this section.

Part IX: Miscellaneous Power Tools

In this section, we'll move along the cutting edge of cyberspace, investigating the current state of real-time audio and video and what the future may hold for them. More and more media outlets, businesses, and amateur media-nauts are beginning to make use of "live" netcasting technologies. Radio stations are online, classrooms are conducting inexpensive video teleconferences with other students and teachers in far away places, and a growing community of people are using Internet telephones to make free international phone calls. That's right, the Net can send and receive audio "packets" from one computer to another, anywhere in the wired world! All you need is the right software and hardware. We'll also consider the implications of these technologies on the future face (eyes and ears) of the Net.

Appendix A: About the Online Companion

To stay abreast of developments covered in this book, visit our *Internet Power Toolkit Online Companion*. There you'll find updates, late-breaking news, valuable links to some of the key power tool sites mentioned in this book, and updates of the software contained on the CD-ROM. Drop on by and pay us a visit—we love company. The address is http://www.vmedia.com/updates.html.

Appendix B: About the Companion CD-ROM

You may have been wondering what that shiny silver disk in the back of this book is. That little disk is actually the heart of this book, the "Toolkit" in the title. We've assembled a bundle of software, our picks for some of the coolest tools available. Armed with this book and its software toolkit, you'll not only have the resources you need to catch up with today's Internet technology, they in turn will help alert you to what's ahead.

Appendix C: Field Guide to File Types

From UNIX compress to LHARC, SIT, CPT, GZIP and ZIP file formats, this handy chart will tell you what they are, what they do, and what type of software you need to handle them.

Appendix D: UNIX Boot Camp

For those of you who are tired of hearing about UNIX and feeling vaguely inferior because you don't know, we're here to whip you into shape. We've done our best to get to the heart of what you need to know in dealing with a UNIX shell account. We'll familiarize you with the UNIX file structure, how to move around directories, and how to move and copy files. The heart of our boot camp training is our UNIX Command Survival Kit, our take on the 14 most useful UNIX commands. We'll wrap things up with common problems and their solutions.

Shop Talk: A Glossary of Common Internet Terms & Slang

A handy guide to technical terms and online argot. Once you know what something is called, and what it means, you're halfway toward mastering it.

HOW TO USE THIS BOOK

If you're holding this book in your hands, one thing is immediately apparent: It's big and heavy! As you start thumbing through it, another thing will become apparent: it's jam-packed with intimidating amounts of information and scary-looking commands and procedures. Don't fret! This book wasn't designed to be read cover to cover (although you'll get one heck of an education if you do!). In creating the mother-of-all-Net books, we had to cover a lot of territory: different types of networks, platforms, and programs. We wanted to cover all the aspects relevant to the power user. The best way to use this book is to scan the table of contents and index to zero in on the topics that interest you. If you're like us, you might get antsy and want to start playing with the software right away. Once you see which programs look right for you, you can find the section in the book that explains how the software works.

We know that reading computer books, especially one the size of a waffle iron, can be a chore. Who has time to read books these days? We tried to write a fun and readable computer book, the kind of book that we'd want to read. Why not drop a line and tell us how we did? Let us know what tools and tricks you find most useful.

Gareth Branwyn
gareth@vmedia.com

Sean Carton
carton@vmedia.com

Expanding Connectivity

Part 1

1

Expanding
Connectivity

## Chapter 1

Inside Modem Connections

If you've had any experience at all with modems, you probably know that getting a connection up and running is not always easy. Physically connecting the computer, the modem, and the phone line isn't so bad. It's getting everything to work together and getting your computer to talk to another computer by whistling tones across a phone line that can drive you crazy. No sooner do you make all the connections than you're confronted with the joys of configuring "initialization strings," "flow control," "terminal emulations," "stop bits," "handshaking," and all the other obscurities that modems seem to thrive on. Even though you manage most of the important modem settings through your communications software (discussed in the next chapter), there are some low-level modem settings that have little to do with the software you'll be using. This chapter includes a discussion of those settings, prefaced by a short primer covering how and why modems work the way they do.

HOW (& WHY) DO MODEMS WORK?

Your computer is a digital device, a slave to ones and zeros. Whenever you put data in or take data out, it arrives or leaves as a string of bits. The ones and zeros in these bits represent one of two electrical states, either on (1) or off (0).

Phones, on the other hand, are analog devices. The sounds you hear when you pick up the phone are the result of electrical signals varying in intensity. When you talk into the phone, the microphone takes the sound waves (which are analog signals of varying volumes) and transfers them into electrical signals of varying voltages. These signals are then transmitted across the phone lines to a receiver (the earpiece), which takes the varying voltages and converts them from electrical signals to sound again—what you hear coming out of the speaker in the phone.

So, if a computer is digital and a phone line is analog, you'd think there would be trouble hooking one to the other. You'd be right. To get your computer to talk to another computer over analog phone lines, you need a device to translate the digital information to analog signals that can be transmitted over a phone line. Then, at the other end of the line, you need a device that translates the analog phone signals back to digital ones. Introducing: your modem!

The word *modem* is an acronym for what the modem actually does—*mo*dulates digital signals to analog ones and then *demo*dulates them back to digital. If you've ever picked up an extension in your home when someone was using a modem, those weird tones you heard were the sounds of data beeping and squawking its way over the wires. See Figure 1-1.

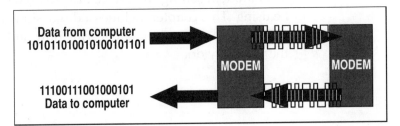

Figure 1-1: A modem at work.

Modem Basics

If you've ever looked at all the modems in a computer catalog, you probably wondered why there are so many types. After all, if all the modem is doing is translating digital to analog and back again, shouldn't all modems be the same? Not at all.

In the old days of modems, this digital-to-analog conversion was all the modem did. However, straight translation of bits to noise only works up to a point. In fact, if all your modem did was straight encoding, it would be limited to a speed of only 1,200 bits per second. At that rate, a 200Kb file (about the size of a chapter of this book) would take over 22 minutes to transfer to another computer! That's pretty slow. For a long time, that's what people put up with. Then someone had a bright idea. Why not use four separate tones to represent the possible combinations of two bits? That way, you could transmit information twice as fast! Confused? Let's look at an example:

Bit one	Bit two	Frequency
0	0	440 Hz
1	0	880 Hz
0	1	1320 Hz
1	1	1760 Hz

In the older scheme, 440 Hz represented a 1, and a tone of 880 Hz represented a 0. To encode a stream of 8 bits, you'd have to use 8 different tones. Using this new method, we only need 4 tones to represent those same 8 bits. Each tone representing a chunk of bits is called a baud. Half as many tones means twice the speed!

Baud or BPS—What's the Difference?

A lot of people get confused when it comes to describing modem speeds. Often, you'll hear a modem described as being "2400 baud" or "14,400 baud." Actually, what people mean is not "baud" but bits per second (abbreviated bps). The two terms aren't interchangeable.

➡

Baud describes a chunk of data sent across a modem line. It can mean 4 bits, but it can also mean more or less, depending on the transmission scheme. Bits per second, however, is an accurate measure of raw speed—how many data bits can be pumped through the wires.

Remember, too, that a character is actually made up of 8 bits (one byte). That means that a 28,800 bit-per-second modem actually transmits 3,600 characters per second.

Of course, things are a little more complicated than this in real life. Modems not only use amplitude shifting as we just described, but they also use changes in phase to modulate the data. Using phase, we can crunch 4 bits into each baud. This is known as Quadrature Amplitude Modulation (Quad=4), and it was used to create the first standard for modern modems. This standard was called V.22bis, a name given to it by the International Telecommunications Union, an international body that approves standards for telecommunications. Table 1-1 shows some of the more commonly recognized modulation schemes.

Modulation Scheme	Transfer Speed
V.22bis	2400 bps
V.32	9600 bps
V.32bis	14,400 bps
V.34	28,800 bps

Table 1-1: Modulation schemes and transfer speeds.

Since this early standard was developed, modem speeds have moved far beyond the old 2400 bps. In fact, the explosion of the Internet and the World Wide Web over the past few years probably would not have been possible without today's faster modems. While 2400 bps modems were the norm three or four years ago, today you shouldn't settle for anything slower than 14,400. And with the prices of 28,800 bps modems dropping rapidly, faster speeds are much more affordable.

These faster speeds are made possible by advances in modem technologies called data compression and error correction. These two features allow modems to communicate at much higher speeds while also making sure that the data stays intact during its trip over the phone lines. If you've ever used a program like Stuffit or PKZIP, you've already had some experience with data compression. These programs take big files and compress them into smaller ones, enabling you to transfer them more quickly over a modem connection. While many of the compression programs you may have come across use their own special "compression algorithms," they all basically do the same thing: scan a file for redundant data and then reduce the redundancy to make the file smaller.

For example, let's say that your data looked like this:

AAAAABBBBBBCCCCCFFFGHHHHIIIIKKKKK   (33 characters)

Because there are multiple characters, the simplest way to reduce the redundancy would be to "encode" the data into a letter (standing for the letter that repeats) and a number (indicating the number of repetitions). Using this method, our data stream now becomes:

A5B6C5F3GH4I4K5   (15 characters)

We now have to send only 15 characters instead of 33! That's over a 50 percent file size reduction, resulting in half the file transfer time. In real life, compression is much more complicated than this, but the idea's the same.

To help increase the apparent transfer speed of a modem, many newer modems have data compression built in to the modem itself. The modem compresses data on the fly, effectively sending bits more quickly. That's why you'll see modem ads claiming astronomical "throughput" numbers such as 115,200 bits per second. The modem doesn't actually send data that quickly; it just acts as if it does.

■ ■

Built for Speed—A Brief Note on Modem Transfer Rates

In a perfect world, every modem would operate at its fastest speed, over perfect phone lines, transferring data in the quickest possible way. Unfortunately, not all modems are created equal; some are faster than others. What happens when you try to connect a fast modem to a slower one?

When two modems try to connect, one of the first things they do is "negotiate" a speed at which they can both converse. If a faster modem is calling a slower one, it must step down its speed to connect.

Even if modems are already connected, sometimes line conditions deteriorate and force them to lower their speeds to make sure that no data is lost. Slower speeds allow for more accurate data transmission.

Luckily, modem manufacturers have agreed upon standards for speed negotiations. Each modulation protocol has its own way of "stepping down" its speed when it needs to:

Protocol	Speeds
V.32	9600, 4800
V.32bis	14,400, 12,000, 7200
V.FC	28,800 to 14,400 in seven different steps
V.34	28,800 to 4800 in many steps

As you can see, the faster protocols (V.FC and V.34) are able to use more steps in reducing their speeds than the other protocols. This allows them to maintain a more efficient connection, always staying closest to the optimum transmission speed.

■ ■

Data compression sounds great in theory, but in practice, it often doesn't increase speed that much. In fact, if a file is already compressed (such as a SIT or ZIP file), transferring it using data compression can actually make it take longer than an uncompressed file! If you use an online service and download a lot of files, you'll run into this problem all the time because most of the files you'll find online are already compressed, including the popular GIF and JPEG image formats.

How can you tell if your modem uses data compression? Look on the box or in the manual that came with it. If you see that the modem includes something called MNP-5 or V.42bis, your modem uses compression—most modems sold today do.

Even though compression is a mixed blessing, modems with error correction can really make your life a lot easier. By constantly checking the integrity of the data during each transmission, error-correcting modems can make sure that you have clean transfers all the time, regardless of static or other "noise" on the line. In fact, if you live in an older house or building with noisy phone lines, you may not be able to get a connection at all unless you have an error-correcting modem.

Error-correcting modems utilize the V.42 and MNP-4 protocols to "filter" the data and make sure that it's correct. Error correcting has several benefits. First, as we discussed above, it can make up for a lot of your phone line ills. Second, it can sometimes increase transmission rates by giving you more efficient transfers. Finally, error correction can actually reduce the size of your files. Because it "packetizes" the data, the modem doesn't have to send extra information called "start" and "stop" bits as overhead.

And there you have our modem primer. By using modulation, bit encoding, compression, and error correction, these handy little boxes perform the miracle of getting data from one place to another. Now let's take a look at how to set up and use your modem.

MODEM SETUP

The physical setup of a modem is pretty straightforward. If you've got an external one, you simply need to use the cable that came with it to attach it to the serial port on your computer (labeled with a telephone icon on the Macintosh and usually labeled either COM1 or COM2 on your PC). Connect a phone cord from the line jack on the modem to the phone socket in the wall. If you want to use a telephone with your modem, plug it in to the phone jack in the back of the modem. Finally, plug the modem cord or power supply into an electrical outlet, and you're ready to go.

If you've got an internal modem, setup is even easier. If it's already installed, just plug the phone cords into the appropriate places. If you need to install your internal modem, stop reading this and go read the installation manual! Once you've read it twice and have a good grip on what you need to do, take a deep breath, open your computer's case, and follow the instructions in the modem installation manual. Once you have the modem board installed, double-check to make sure that it's fully seated in the slot, close up the case, and then plug the phone cables into their respective receptacles, turn on the computer, and get ready to start modeming.

Basic AT Commands

Most modems accept commands prefaced by AT. These commands can mean anything from "Hey modem! Dial this number," to "Hang up the phone line," to "These are the settings you should use." By using a cryptic combination of letters, numbers, and characters, you can get your modem to behave any way you want it to (within reason).

To see how the AT commands work, why not fire up your communications program and take a peek. If you're using Windows, the Windows terminal program will work just fine. If you're on a Mac, try using Z-Term or the communications program that came with your modem. If you need help setting up your communications program, see Chapter 2, "The ABCs of Communications Software."

As long as your communications program is configured correctly, when you first start it up, you'll have a direct way to "talk" to your modem. Any commands that you type into the terminal window of your communications software go directly to the modem and can be used to control its behavior. Let's test it out. Type the command **AT** in the terminal window, and press Enter. OK should appear on the screen. See Figure 1-2.

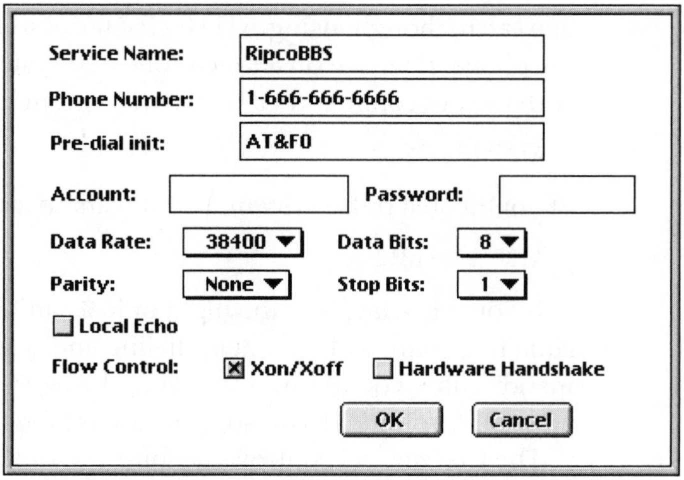

Service Name:	RipcoBBS
Phone Number:	1-666-666-6666
Pre-dial init:	AT&F0

Account: _____   Password: _____

Data Rate: 38400 ▼   Data Bits: 8 ▼
Parity: None ▼   Stop Bits: 1 ▼
☐ Local Echo
Flow Control: ☒ Xon/Xoff   ☐ Hardware Handshake

[OK]   [Cancel]

Figure 1-2: Saying hello to your modem with the AT command.

If you don't get an OK, then it may be that your communications program has not been configured correctly. See Chapter 2, "The ABCs of Communications Software," for some tips on setting up your communications program, and then return to this chapter. The AT command means "Attention! Here come some commands" and must precede any command you want the modem to use. Using it by itself is a good way of checking to see if the modem is turned on and ready to roll.

But let's do something useful. One of the most commonly used commands is the dial command: D. Remember, all commands must first be preceded by the AT command, so in real life, the D command looks like this:

```
ATD <phone number>
```

For example, if you wanted to dial the number 555-1212, you'd type the command:

```
ATD 555-1212
```

and press Enter. The modem then dials that number using touch-tones. You can use this command when you want a quick and dirty way of dialing the modem without having to choose a number from a menu in your communications program. There's one catch, though: using ATD by itself doesn't specify how to dial the phone. If you're on a touch-tone dial system, you'll need to add another command (T) to the dial command:

```
ATDT 555-1212
```

If you're on a pulse system, you'll want to add a P to the string:

```
ATDP 555-1212
```

If you work late into the night or just can't stand the bizarre squalling sounds of a modem dialing and connecting, AT commands allow you to turn the dialing speaker on and off or even to adjust the volume. To do so, you can use the L and M commands.

The L command controls the loudness of the modem speaker. Not all modems support this feature, but if yours does, you have four levels to choose from—0, 1, 2, 3. L0 commands the modem to turn the volume down all the way, effectively silencing the speaker. As you can probably imagine, L3 is the loudest setting. To set the loudness of your modem speaker, use the command:

```
ATL<number>
```

Besides controlling the loudness, you can also turn your modem's speaker on and off entirely, using the M command. Like L, the M command takes 4 values: 0, 1, 2, 3. Using M0, you can shut the speaker off entirely, while M1 keeps the speaker on until a connection is made. M2 activates the speaker during dialing and for the duration of the connection, and M3 activates the speaker only when the modem is dialing.

Sometimes you may want to set up your modem so that another person can call in to your computer to exchange files. However, to do this, you need to be able to set your modem so that it "answers" the phone when it detects an incoming call. To do so, you can use the A command. When you're setting your modem up for an incoming call, first type the following in the terminal window of your communications software:

```
ATA
```

This will put your modem into "answer" mode. Then, when a call comes in, your modem will pick up the line, make the connection, and you're ready to go from there.

You can issue many other commands using AT settings. The following table provides a brief overview of some of the more useful AT commands.

Command	Description	
A	Set answer mode	ATA
	Makes modem available to answer incoming phone calls. Modem waits the number of rings specified in register S0 before answering. (A *register* is an area of your modem's memory that it uses to store settings. For more information, see the section "S Registers" later in this chapter.) If S0=0, modem attempts to answer call immediately.	
D	Dial telephone number	ATDS=#, ATDT <phone number>, ATDP <phone number>
	Dials specified telephone number. If modifier S is included, (ATDS=#), the phone number stored in register # is dialed. To use tone dialing, include T in the string: ATDT <number>. If using pulse dialing, include a P: ATDP <number>. To use alpha characters in the number, enclose them in quotes: ATD "DEAD-CAT" dials the number 332-3228.	
I	Display modem speed	ATI
	Shows the last speed dialed by the modem.	
L	Set speaker volume	ATL#
	Sets the volume of the internal modem speaker to value #. Not all modems contain this feature. Speaker values are: 0 - Speaker off 1 - Low volume 2 - Medium volume 3 - Loud volume	
M	Set speaker behavior	ATM#
	Use this command to turn your modem speaker on and off. To turn the speaker off, use ATM0. To turn the speaker on during dialing and handshaking, use the command ATM1. If for some reason you want the speaker to be on all the time (even during the connection), use ATM2. If you just want to hear the speaker when the modem is dialing, use ATM3.	
P	Pulse dialing mode	ATP, ATDP
	Puts the modem in pulse dial mode. This command can be used by itself or in conjunction with the D dialing command.	
S#?	Display value of register	S#, ATS#?
	Displays the value stored in S register specified by #. For example, to display the number of rings the modem waits until answering the phone, type the command ATS0?.	

➡

Command	Description	
S#=value	Set register # to value	ATS#=value

Sets S register to the value specified. See Table 1-3 for a description of S register values and uses.

T	Tone dialing mode	ATT, ATDT

Places the modem in touch-tone dialing mode. Like P, this command can be used by itself or in conjunction with D.

V	Error code setting

Sets how the modem displays error codes. If V is set to 0, errors are displayed as numbers only. If V is set to 1, errors are displayed as text.

W	Connect code settings	ATW#

Controls how connection codes are displayed. Working in conjunction with S register 95, W displays the following information:

> If W=0, then the modem reports the speed at which it is communicating with your computer (the DTE speed).
>
> If W=1 and S95=0, only CARRIER and PROTOCOL are displayed.
>
> If W=2, disable all connect codes.

To use register S95 to get extended information on your connection, use the command: ATS95=47. Upon connection, your modem displays speed, PROTOCOL, and COMPRESSION information.

X	Call status	ATX#

Controls the display of call status:

> X1 = disables busy and dial tone check.
>
> X2 = disables busy detect.
>
> X3 = enables busy signal, disables dial tone detection.
>
> X4 = enables both busy and dial tone detection.

Z	Resets modem	ATZ#

Resets modem to profile #. (The *profile* is a stored configuration; most modems can store two profiles. For more information, see the "S Registers" section later in this chapter.)

&F	Reset factory settings	AT&F

Restores modem to factory settings.

Command	Description
&K	Set flow control options AT&K#

Sets options for modem flow control based on the following options:

> K0 = disables all flow control.
>
> K3 = enables RTS/CTS (hardware) flow control. Most high-speed connections require this type of flow control.
>
> K4 = enables XON/XOFF flow control.
>
> K5 = enables transparent XON/XOFF flow control.
>
> K6 = enables bidirectional XON/XOFF flow control.

Command	Description
&Q	Communications type select AT&Q#

Allows you to select various types of communications options. You can use several different settings, but in practice these are the most useful:

> Q5 = enables error control.
>
> Q8 = enables MNP error control.
>
> Q9 = enables V.42bis/MNP2-4 error control.

Command	Description
&V	Display stored profiles AT&V

Displays all stored profiles, S registers, and stored phone numbers.

Command	Description
&W	Store current setup in profile AT&W#

Stores the current modem configuration in the profile specified. Settings stored in this way are permanent, unless changed by using this command again.

Command	Description
&Y	Select startup profile. AT&Y#

Selects the stored profile to be used by the modem when it is turned on.

Command	Description
&Z	Store phone number AT&Z#=*phone number*

Stores a telephone number in non-volatile memory. If you wanted to store the number 555-1212 in phone number slot 1, you'd use the command AT&Z1=555-1212. You can check the stored phone numbers by using the AT&V command. To dial a stored number, use the command ATDS# where # indicates the stored number you want to dial. If we wanted to dial the number in the previous example, we'd use ATDS1.

Command	Description
,	Pause

Inserts a pause into the dialing string. The number of seconds that the modem waits is controlled by the value in S register S8. As an example, if you had to dial a 9 before the number you want to call, you'd use the command ATD9,555-1212.

Table 1-2: Hayes AT commands.

Initialization Strings

Modems are snobs. They only like to speak with others of their kind. Most claims made by manufacturers about their modems' performance are based on testing two of their modems connected together in a laboratory, not in the real world where you're likely to hook your Brand X modem into God-knows-what when you dial out. That's where the tweaking comes in.

Most modems come preconfigured with some set of configuration options that seems to work well a good part of the time for a good many modems. In many cases, you can get away with using the factory settings. You'll know as soon as you try to connect (and try and try and try . . .) and don't get connected. When that happens, it's time to check the initialization string.

For your modem to behave correctly, it needs a correct initialization string before it starts dialing. Luckily, most modem manufacturers are nice enough to include a sample initialization string (also known as an *init string*) in the documentation that comes with the modem or preset into the communications software that came with the modem. This string should work in most situations. The simplest initialization string is:

```
AT&F0
```

This string tells the modem to reset itself to its "factory" (that's why there's an F in there) settings. Basically that's all the initialization string does—it sends a stream of commands (in this case, &F0) to the modem. You can string as many commands as you want after the AT; just don't leave any spaces between them. If all else fails, try the factory presets.

Initialization strings can look hideously complicated, especially if you don't know what you're looking at. Unfortunately, as big as it is, this book doesn't have nearly enough space to go into how to configure your particular modem with your software. However, if you want some help, bop on over to gopher://gopher.hooked.net:70/11/hooked/modems for an extensive listing of popular modems and the initialization strings that seem to work best with each of them.

S Registers

In addition to the commands that you can use to control your modem, many of the internal workings are controlled by values stored in special areas of the modem called *registers*. You can access this area of your modem's memory by reading and storing values in S registers. These S registers act like little boxes that can hold various values. When you use AT commands, your modem determines what to do first by looking at the value of the appropriate S register and then using the parameter stored there. Setting values in the S registers is easy. If you looked at Table 1-2, you may have noticed the command:

```
S#=
```

When you issue this command, you tell the modem to store the value after the equal sign in the register you've specified (the pound sign—#). If you want to check the value of a certain register, use the S#? command, which tells the modem to read back the value of the register # you've asked for.

So, what can you use registers for during your modeming? Well, one of the most useful registers is S8, which tells the modem how long to wait for each comma that you put in your dial string. For example, let's say that you're dialing out of an office phone system where you have to dial a 9 to get an outside line. If you wanted to dial the number 555-1212, you'd use the command:

```
ATDT 9,555-1212
```

This command tells the modem to use tone dialing, dial a 9, wait for the amount of time specified in register S8, and then dial 555-1212. In some office phone systems, there's a delay of a few seconds between dialing 9 and getting an outside line. If your modem doesn't wait long enough, it'll start dialing before you get a line, and your call won't go through. In many modems, S8 comes set to wait for two seconds for each comma. If this isn't long enough, you can change the amount of wait time with the command:

```
ATS8=number of seconds to wait
```

The number of seconds that the modem waits can be anywhere from 0 to 255 seconds.

Another useful S register is S0, which specifies how many rings to wait until your modem answers the phone. This register may be useful if your modem shares a phone line with your regular telephone and you leave your modem on all the time. If you don't want your modem always answering the phone before you, you can set the S0 register to make it wait until six or so rings before it picks up the phone and answers the call.

To set the number of answer rings to six, use the command:

```
ATS0=6
```

If you don't want your modem to ever answer the telephone, just set the S0 register to 0:

```
ATS0=0
```

If you've set your registers to the settings you'd like them to have, you can store them permanently into your modem's memory by using the ATW# command, where # stands for the profile number you want to store your settings in. Most modems have two profiles, with profile 1 being the one that's used on modem startup. So if you wanted to store your register values in profile 1, you'd use the following command after you've set the registers to the values you want:

```
ATW1
```

Stored profiles are kept in your modem's "non-volatile memory," which stores the values permanently, even if the modem is shut off or disconnected from its power source. If you ever want to set profile 1 back to the way it was when you bought the modem, first reset the modem to its factory settings:

```
AT&F
```

Then store the settings back in the profile:

```
ATW#
```

where # is the profile number you want to reset.

If you want to check the profiles that you've stored, you can use the command:

AT&V

This command "dumps" the values of the stored profiles to the screen, complete with AT settings and S register values.

Many registers are available on modems, and your modem may use all of them or its own special set. Use AT&V to check your registers. If you want to start experimenting with the registers on your modem, remember this—unless you store the values in the profiles, all the settings will return to their original states as soon as you shut off your modem.

For the adventurous types reading this, the following table describes some of the more useful S registers and the modem behaviors they control.

S Register	Description	Use
S0	Rings before answer	Sets the number of rings the modem should wait before answering. If S0=0, the modem does not answer incoming calls. Values can be from 0-255.
S8	Seconds to wait on comma	Sets the number of seconds the modem should wait when it encounters a comma in the dialing string. Values can be from 0-255.
S10	Hang-up time delay	Defines how much time (in tenths of seconds) the modem should wait after it has lost a carrier before beginning to hang up. Values can be from 1-255.
S30	Time-out delay	Defines (in tenths of seconds) how long the modem must wait until it begins to hang up once any transmission activity has ended. Values can be from 0-255.
S37	Modem speed	Locks in a modem speed. Values can be set as follows:

Value	Speed (in bps)
0	Use Last AT Speed
3	300
5	1200
6	2400
7	4800
8	7200

➡

Command	Description	Use	
S37 (cont.)	Modem speed	**Value**	**Speed (in bps)**
		9	9600
		10	12,000
		11	14,400
		26	16,800
		12	19,200
		33	21,600
		29	24,000
		34	26,400
		15	28,800

S46	Compression settings	Enables or disables data compression during modem transmission. S46 is used with the &Q AT command to determine how compression is used. S46 can be set to the following values:

Value	Result
S46= 2	Enables compression.
S46= 16	Disables compression.

S70	Number of times to retransmit after error	Sets the number of times that the modem tries to retransmit data when a transmission error is encountered. If you're using a noisy line, you may want to try setting S70 to a higher value. Value can be from 1-255.
S86	Connection failure code	Displays a number indicating why a connection was terminated. Useful when trying to determine modem connection problems. Error codes are as follows:

Code	Error
1	Normal FAX disconnect.
4	Carrier lost.
5	Did not detect error-correcting modem at other end of line.
6	Error-correcting modem at other end did not correct transmission errors properly.
7	The other modem only operates in synchronous mode.
8	Modems could not find a common connection method.
9	Modems could not agree on a common protocol.

➡

Command	Description	Use		
S86 (cont.)	Connection failure code		Code	Error
			10	Other modem's connection message incorrect.
			11	Synchronous data needed was not received from other modem.
			12	Normal disconnect.
			13	Other modem did not respond to retransmission of data after error.
			14	Protocol violation.
			15	Compression failed.
			16	Desired speed did not match selected carrier speed.
			17	Timed out.
			18	Inactivity time out.
			19	A long space hang up.

Table 1-3: S registers and settings.

MOVING ON

Now that you've gotten a good peek at the guts of your modem and you understand the concepts behind how it works, it's time to put the darn thing to work. In the next chapter, we'll cover everything you need to know about how to configure communications software, beginning with an overview of what all the obscure settings mean and how you can use them to make your online life easier. Once you've got all that under your virtual belt, you'll be more than ready to dig in to all the gory platform-specific details of setting up communications software on Windows and Macintosh machines later on in the book.

## Chapter 2

The ABCs of Communications Software

Well, now you know all about modems and the settings that make them work, but that's really only half the story—the hardware half. Regardless of the type of connection to the Internet you have, your modem will work closely with some sort of communications software to make sure the data flies right.

In this chapter, we'll cover all the communications software settings you need to know in order to make a connection to the Internet. At first, we aren't going to get into the "what button do I push?" details—you'll get the background that you'll need to become a well-rounded Net power user. Understanding *why* things happen is the first step before we get into the details of *how* to do things. But then it'll be time to get your hands dirty and set up your software, and we'll walk you through the steps. And since things don't *always* go as planned, we'll wrap up the chapter with a handy troubleshooting guide to get you through the tough parts.

CONNECTION BASICS

You can use two types of communications software for connecting to the Internet: TCP/IP dialer software and terminal software. The type you use depends upon the kind of connection you want to make; a SLIP/PPP connection requires TCP/IP dialer software, while a shell connection calls for a terminal program.

The major difference between a shell connection and a SLIP / PPP (Serial Line Internet Protocol and Point To Point Protocol, in case you're wondering!) connection is the extent to which you're computer is *actually* connected to the Internet. A shell connection simply gives you remote control over the host you dial into. Technically, the computer connected to the Internet is the host computer, *not* your computer. As far as the host computer is concerned, as soon as you dial in with a terminal program, your computer becomes a terminal. It doesn't matter if you've got the latest super-fast scream machine or a 10-year-old clunking high-tech paper weight. Both become mere conduits for information between you and the host. A SLIP/PPP connection, on the other hand, connects your computer directly to the Internet and relies on your computer for processing resources.

With the explosion of TCP/IP connectivity, brought about by the popularity of the World Wide Web, shell accounts aren't nearly as common as they used to be. In fact, many people on the Net today don't use a shell account, even if one is available to them.

Saved by the Shell: A True Story

Even if you're very happy with your SLIP/PPP connection, it's still useful to be able to connect with a terminal program into a shell account. If your service provider's SLIP or PPP connectivity capabilities ever go down, you still can probably still get on the Net through your shell connection.

For a good example of how knowing how to use a shell account can be used to save your virtual butt in a pinch (no pun intended!), you need to look no further than one of your humble authors.

Sean's a Web developer. He was under deadline, putting the finishing touches on a WWW site for one of his customers when the FTP services for the service provider went down for a major software overhaul.

He was in big trouble. The client was breathing down his neck, anxious for the site to be finished. Unfortunately, with the FTP server down, he had no way to transfer the last parts of the Web site up to the server.

Then, right at the last moment (just like in the movies), his good ol' shell account came to the rescue. He dusted off his terminal program, dialed into the service provider, and was able to upload the last parts of the site using the Zmodem transfer protocol. Within minutes, the pieces were there, the site was up, and everyone was happy. His shell account was last seen riding into the sunset.

▪ ▪

The communications software settings you'll need to figure out are basically the same regardless of whether you're using TCP/IP dialer software or terminal software. The next section outlines these settings. If you don't want to bother with the whys and wherefores of communications software configuration, you can skip ahead to the how-to section for your type of connection. If you have a SLIP/PPP account, you're already in the right chapter, just flip ahead to "Setting Up Your Communications Software." If you have a shell account, skip ahead to Chapter 16, "Getting Connected With a Shell Account." But make a little dog-ear at the top of this page (or make an imaginary one in your head), because you may want to return later to look up specific details about your modem's connections and settings.

COMMUNICATIONS SETTINGS

When you fire up any communications program, the first thing you're going to have to do is configure some settings. Most terminal programs really live up to their "dumb" reputation—they don't have a clue about how to connect themselves until you specify the needed settings. If you are lucky enough to enter all the right settings, you'll be rewarded with flawless connections and smooth file transfers. The wrong settings will send you off into a quagmire of garbage characters and a modem gone haywire. Getting the connection settings right is even more important with a SLIP or PPP connection. A wrong setting could give you problems that take days (or even weeks) to resolve. We know, we've been there!

The first logical step in determining the right settings is asking your service provider. Knowing *why* the settings work the way they do is a different story, one your ISP doesn't really have time to tell you. But we do. Once upon a time. . .

When you ask your service provider for the communications settings that you should use, they'll probably rattle off something like "14,400, 8, N, 1" or maybe they'll be a bit more verbose and tell you "14,400 bps, 8 data bits, no parity, one stop bit." Either way, this information will probably leave you scratching your head unless you know what these settings mean.

Baud

The first setting, 14,400 bps (or 28,800, or whatever) is the easy one. It refers to the connection speed you should be using. If you remember from our discussion in Chapter 1 about the ins and outs of modems, you'll know that this speed refers to how many bits of information your modem can pump across the phone line at any given second. 14,400 bps means that your modem can send and receive *up to* 14,400 bits of information every second.

For the best results, you should set your communications program to the same bps setting as your service provider uses. If you have a faster modem than your service provider, you can probably get away with leaving your communications program set to the higher speed—most modems "negotiate down" to a slower speed. If you have a modem that transmits at a slower speed, set the communications software bps setting to the speed of your modem. If you aren't sure what speed your modem uses, drag out the manual and check the documentation.

Of course, there are exceptions to these rules. (Aren't there always?) Because the bps setting actually tells the modem at what speed to expect data traffic, if you're using a modem with error correction and compression and the modem you're connecting to has the same features, you should set your bps rate 2 to 4 times faster than the speed your modem actually transmits.

"Why on earth should I do that?" you ask. Because compression can theoretically quadruple the throughput of your modem, setting the bps rate to a higher speed allows your computer to pump the information through the serial port fast enough to get this kind of throughput. Generally you won't get this kind of performance unless you're transferring huge chunks of redundant data, but it doesn't hurt to try!

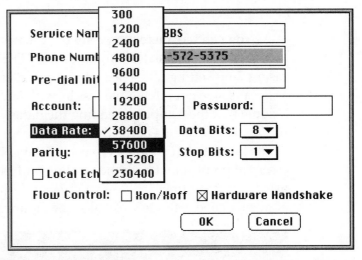

Figure 2-1: Setting the correct baud rate with Z-Term on a Macintosh.

Data Bits

The next setting, such as 8 data bits, refers to number of bits your communications program expects each ASCII character to be composed of. When data is transmitted across a phone line, it's merely transmitted as a stream of ones and zeros. If you communications program doesn't know how to break up that data stream into the appropriate characters, you'll end up with garbage on your screen.

Let's take a look at an example. Say the following binary information came over the modem:

1010100010001010101001101010100

If we break this up into 8-bit chunks, the stream looks like this:

```
10101000  10001010  10100110  1010100
   T         E         S         T
```

However, if we were to break the data stream into 7-bit chunks, the result would look like this:

```
1010100   0100010   1010100   1101010   100
  T          "         T         J       ^H
```

As you can see, there's a pretty big difference! In the first case, an 8-bit setting translates into the string "TEST." In the second case, a 7-bit setting translates into meaningless babble: "T"Tj^H."

Because we got intelligible results with an 8-bit setting, we can assume that the computer sending the data was using an 8 data bit setting. However, it's perfectly reasonable for a computer to use a 7 data bit setting (CompuServe used 7 data bits for years). The essential point is that both the sending and the receiving computer use the same settings. In case you're wondering what a full screen of mismatched settings looks like, see Figure 2-2.

```
Connecting to port 58 on annex7.clark.net.

   Welcome to ClarkNet!

Log in as "guest" for ClarkNet info and registration.

ClarkNet Username: M-eM-lM-rM-oM-dM-^MM-^MM-^M
```

Figure 2-2: What your screen might look like if you don't match data bits correctly.

Stop Bits

Modems can speak to each other in one of two ways: synchronously or asynchronously. When they're communicating synchronously, each computer politely takes turns sending and receiving data, kind of like talking to someone else on a radio. When communicating asynchronously, the computers don't have to take turns. They can send and receive data whenever they feel like it, regardless of whether the other computer is sending or receiving.

As you can imagine, synchronous communication requires the least amount of hassles. One computer talks. The other listens. Then they switch off. Simple.

However, most modems today use asynchronous communication, mainly because synchronous communication requires a special communication port with its own "clock line" to time the communications. Asynchronous transfer simplifies the process of connecting, but it does make keeping track of who's sending what a little more complex.

That's where stop bits come in. Stop bits are bits inserted by the sending modem at the end of a chunk of information that tells the receiving modem that the chunk has ended. Usually, this chunk consists of one character of data, but it can change depending on the information being sent. If you want to see the results of incorrect stop-bit settings, see Figure 2-3.

Almost without fail, when you need to connect to a modem these days, you'll have to set your communications program to expect one stop bit.

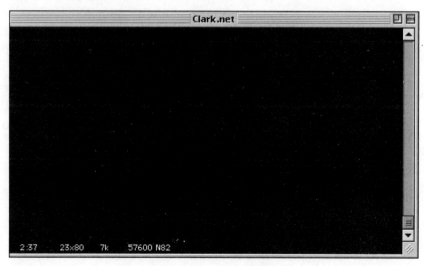

Figure 2-3: The results of incorrect stop-bit settings.

Parity

A lot can go wrong between the time that the digital data leaves your computer, travels through your communications port, gets transmogrified into analog data in your modem, travels across miles of copper wire through the phone line, and finally arrives at the modem on the other end. During this process, if one stray bit of information gets into the stream of data or some static comes over the line, you can end up with garbage.

To combat this problem, modem designers were forced to come up with a way to make sure that the data leaving one modem was the same data entering the modem at the other end. This process is called *error correction* or *error checking*.

One form of error checking performed by your modem is a parity check. Parity checks make sure that the unit of data being transmitted is the same one being received. By using a *check bit* in the information stream to make each chunk of data an even or odd number, the modem at the other end of the line knows whether it received the data correctly. If one chunk of data is 8 bits long (a common occurrence with 8-bit ASCII encoding), it is said to have *no parity*. If a chunk uses 7 bits to get its point across, it is considered to have *even parity* because the parity bit gives the chunk an even 8 bits.

Because most of the information coming across the wires these days comes over in 8-bit chunks, you'll usually set your communications programs for no parity. Figure 2-4 shows what'll happen if you set your parity incorrectly.

Figure 2-4: The results of incorrect parity settings.

Flow Control

One thing that's easy to forget when we start mucking around with modem-to-modem settings is that the most important connection for your modem is its connection to your computer. You might have the wang-dang zippiest modem in the entire world, but if your computer can't communicate with it, it's not going to do you any good.

One of the problems that computers have with communicating over modems is that the average personal computer "talks" to the modem much faster than the modem can talk across the phone lines to another modem. If we left the whole situation alone, without trying to account for the speed difference, one thing would happen pretty quickly: data overload.

To make sure that a speedy serial port doesn't overload a slower modem, modems employ flow control to tell the computer when to start and stop sending data. Here's how it works.

Most modems contain a special memory chip that's used specifically for buffering the information coming in from the serial port. As soon as the buffer fills up, the modem must send a stop command to the computer, which then halts the flow of information until the modem has transferred the data in the buffer. Once the buffer's clear, the modem sends a start command to begin the process again. This stop-start stuff is called *flow control*.

A modem can tell the computer when (and when not) to send data in two ways. The first method is called *hardware flow control*, sometimes known as *hardware handshaking* or *RTS/CTS flow control*.

In RTS/CTS flow control, the modem sends signals over two parts of the modem line—the RTS (Request To Send) pin and the CTS (Clear to Send) pin. By signaling when it can accept data or not, the modem can control the flow of information by directly interacting with the serial port hardware. This speeds up transfers and also keeps from having the data affect the connection because the flow control takes place over a completely separate set of wires. See Figure 2-5 for a description of a typical modem cable setup.

RS-232 DB25

Pin#	Signal
2	Transmit Data (TxD)
3	Receive Data (RxD)
4	Request to Send (RTS)
5	Clear to Send (CTS)
6	Dataset Ready (DST)
7	Ground
8	Data Carrier Detect (DCD)
15	Transmit Clock
17	Receive Clock
20	Data Terminal Ready
24	Auxilliary Clock

Figure 2-5: Standard RS-232 serial cable layout.

Hardware flow control is always the best choice if your computer is capable of using it. However, many older computers aren't, especially older Macintosh computers. In that case, your communications program and modem have to rely on *software flow control*.

Software flow control works by checking the stream of data for stop and start information. Stop commands are indicated by a special character XOFF and start commands are initiated with an XON character. By using these special characters, your modem can communicate with your communications program to make sure that no data gets lost in a backup.

There are two problems with this method. First, because your computer has to look for start and stop characters, which means it has to do more work, transmission speeds are a lot slower. Second, because the flow control of the modem is achieved by using special ASCII characters, most binary files cannot be transferred with XON/XOFF flow control. If you have a choice, always use hardware flow control.

Hardware versus Software Flow Control

Hardware Flow Control
- ❏ Requires a special hardware handshaking serial cable.
- ❏ Works by directly accessing serial port data lines (the "hardware" in "hardware handshaking").
- ❏ Works best with high-speed, error-correcting modems.
- ❏ Allows high-speed transfers with YMODEM/G.

Software Flow Control
- ❏ Works with nearly all types of serial cables.
- ❏ Uses special characters to control transmission.
- ❏ Only allows reliable transfers up to 2400 bps.
- ❏ Unsuitable for binary file transfers.

Echo

One of the other options you might notice when you're setting up your communications program is the echo function, sometimes called *local echo*. When you use this command, your modem types back every character that you type into it.

If you use your modem for the first time and notice double characters on your screen, that's echo at work (See Figure 2-6). Most of the time you don't need to worry about turning it on because most computers that you connect with echo your typing back to you.

Check with your service provider to see if you need to have echo turned on.

```
explorer:[/homeh/elrod] IIthintkhinkthattihatshouldi tshoulurndturnttheheechecoho
offoff_
```

Figure 2-6: Time to turn echo off!

Terminal Emulations

As you can probably guess, terminal emulation settings pertain almost exclusively to terminal software. It's important to make sure that the host computer you're connected with and the terminal program you're using speak the same language. Even if you're using a SLIP or PPP connection to get on the Net, you still have to worry about this whenever you telnet in to a host.

There were no personal computers in the old days of computing. Computers occupied humongous rooms hidden away in air-conditioned buildings. Most people who used the computer never even really saw it. If they wanted to use it, they used a terminal connected to the main computer system.

Even though a terminal looks a lot like today's PC—small box, monitor, and keyboard—it really couldn't do anything by itself. Terminals had no internal computing power on their own. Consequently, they were known as *dumb* terminals.

Dumb terminals really didn't do graphics. Instead, the on-screen interface was generated from some fancy manipulation' of ASCII characters. The host computer and dumb terminal used various ASCII codes to design menus, lists, and other user interface elements.

This situation worked pretty nicely until you wanted to use a terminal with a different host computer than it was designed for. Even if you got the cabling right, you'd most likely end up with a wacky display because the terminal and the host computer didn't use the same codes to generate the display. To remedy this problem, some terminals were designed so that they could be set to "emulate" other terminals.

And that's where today's terminal emulation comes in. PC terminal programs are designed so that they can emulate the functions of several of the more popular dumb terminals. By using the correct terminal emulation, you can make sure that your computer is speaking the same display language as the computer you're connecting to.

Over the years only a few of the many different terminal types have risen to the top and become more or less de facto standards for computers on the Internet. Let's take a look at some of the more popular types.

VT100

This is the major one, the one terminal emulation that you can use probably 95 percent of the time. In fact, it'd probably be safe to say that whenever you're in doubt about what terminal emulation to use, try this one first.

Many UNIX shells give you the choice (or you can set it up yourself—see Chapter 16, "Getting Connected With a Shell Account") of using either a straight TTY terminal emulation (see the "TTY" section later in this chapter) or VT100. Unless you're a glutton for punishment or your terminal program doesn't allow it, you should always choose VT100 because it allows full-screen editing and supports full-screen cursor movement.

Why would you want that? Well, for starters, it's probably what you're used to on your PC. When you edit a document in a typical word processor, the word processor functions as a full-screen editor, allowing you to use the arrow keys (or cursor keys) to move the cursor anywhere on the screen that you want it to go. And as you change, delete, or add text, everything moves nicely out of the way to make space for your changes

The same is true if you're using a full-screen editing program on your shell account. While many full-screen UNIX programs still can be used (in a limited fashion) with a command line,

VT100 emulation allows you the freedom to use fancy menus, editing features, and even inverse and blinking text. Table 2-1 lists some popular UNIX programs that work best in VT100 mode.

Program	Function
Elm	E-mail
Pine	E-mail
Tin	Usenet News
Trn	Usenet News
Rn	Usenet News
Gopher	Gopher Client
Lynx	WWW Browser
Pico	Editor
Vi	Editor

Table 2-1: VT100-savvy UNIX Net Tools.

Besides allowing you to use programs with full-screen capabilities, VT100 emulation also allows you to use the numeric keypad on your keyboard (available on most extended keyboards) to issue various commands to the UNIX programs. These commands can be anything from moving the cursor up and down to complicated macro triggers.

ANSI

If you've ever logged onto a local bulletin board system and have been . . . er . . . treated to whole screenfuls of blocky color graphics, even blockier animations, or wildly colored menus, then you've already been exposed to the wonderful world of ANSI.

Don't worry, most people recover . . . eventually. Take a tour of some local BBS systems that cater to high-school kids, and you'll see how the ANSI virus can spread rapidly. Heavy metal bands, blocky pictures of pin-up calendars, and elaborate cartoon characters seem to be the subjects of choice. Yikes!

If you've never been exposed to ANSI, you may wonder what the heck we're talking about. Let's explain.

ANSI is another common form of terminal emulation. To be perfectly geeky about it, we do have to point out that technically ANSI is not a true terminal emulation by itself—it's actually a subset of VT100. For all intents and purposes though, ANSI and VT100 are usually treated as separate emulation types.

One of the nifty features of ANSI is that it allows you to make blocky "graphics" out of characters by using special color control codes that paint blocks of color on any screen using ANSI terminal emulation. Some resourceful folks have used ANSI color control codes to vent their artistic talents by drawing pictures with these blocks of color. See Figure 2-7 for an example.

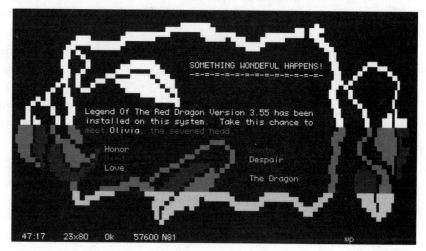

Figure 2-7: ANSI art. You be the judge.

However, if you spend most of your online time on the Internet, you probably will miss out on the crude charms of ANSI art. If your terminal program can display it, you may occasionally run into some colored text, but even that's rare. Generally, you should stick with VT100 terminal emulation.

TTY

At the bottom of the terminal emulation heap is TTY or ASCII terminal emulation. While VT100 and ANSI terminal emulations turn your computer into a relatively sophisticated full-screen color terminal, the TTY emulation type basically turns your computer into a teletype machine.

A long time ago, before there were video screens, if you wanted to type information into a computer and you were lucky, you'd get to sit down at the teletype to do your computing. The unlucky people had to make punch cards and submit them in stacks to a computer operator who would run them through a reader. You returned a few hours later to see what happened—not very user friendly.

A teletype is basically a big electric typewriter that prints onto a continuous strip of paper. When you sat down to interact with the big computer through a teletype terminal, you'd type a command into the keyboard. The teletype would print your command on the paper. Then, when the computer responded to the command, the response would be printed on the paper.

If you sat down at a TTY terminal to edit a file, you'd have to print the file on the paper one line at a time, enter the command to edit that line, and then print the corrected line. This method was called *line editing*.

The same thing went for e-mail or whatever else you wanted to do. To read your mail, you'd print a list of all your incoming messages, type a command to read the one you wanted, wait for the computer to print the message, read it, and then repeat the process for the next one.

When video terminals came along, the first big change was that people used less paper. However, since the terminals were basically video-teletype machines, there was no fancy editing or color features. Text appeared on the screen line by line and then scrolled away when it reached the top of the page. Not until a few years later did people begin programming for the video screen, developing full-screen editors and the other niceties we're so used to today.

However, TTY terminal emulation still survives. In fact, most command-line interaction is still very similar to the early days: type a command at the cursor, read what the computer spits out, and type the next command.

Most of the time you won't ever have to contend with the TTY or ASCII terminal emulation, but nearly every communications program still includes it as a choice. If you leave your terminal set to TTY, dial in to your shell account, and see weird characters, chances are you'll need to switch to VT100 emulation. Figure 2-8 shows what you'll see if you are using TTY when you should be using VT100.

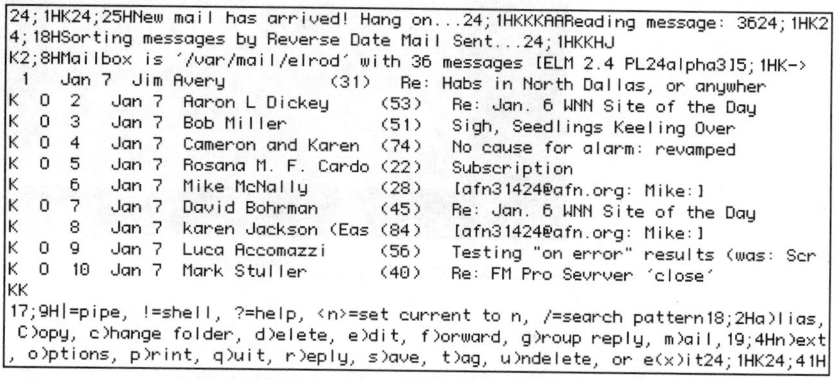

```
24;1HK24;25HNew mail has arrived! Hang on...24;1HKKKAARReading message: 3624;1HK2
4;18HSorting messages by Reverse Date Mail Sent...24;1HKKHJ
K2;8HMailbox is '/var/mail/elrod' with 36 messages [ELM 2.4 PL24alpha3]5;1HK->
  1   Jan 7  Jim Avery          (31)   Re: Habs in North Dallas, or anywher
K 0 2   Jan 7  Aaron L Dickey     (53)   Re: Jan. 6 WNN Site of the Day
K 0 3   Jan 7  Bob Miller         (51)   Sigh, Seedlings Keeling Over
K 0 4   Jan 7  Cameron and Karen  (74)   No cause for alarm: revamped
K 0 5   Jan 7  Rosana M. F. Cardo (22)   Subscription
K   6   Jan 7  Mike McNally       (28)   [afn31424@afn.org: Mike:]
K 0 7   Jan 7  David Bohrman      (45)   Re: Jan. 6 WNN Site of the Day
K   8   Jan 7  karen Jackson (Eas (84)   [afn31424@afn.org: Mike:]
K 0 9   Jan 7  Luca Accomazzi     (56)   Testing "on error" results (was: Scr
K 0 10  Jan 7  Mark Stuller       (40)   Re: FM Pro Sevrver 'close'
KK
17;9H|=pipe, !=shell, ?=help, <n>=set current to n, /=search pattern18;2Ha)lias,
C)opy, c)hange folder, d)elete, e)dit, f)orward, g)roup reply, m)ail, 19;4Hn)ext
, o)ptions, p)rint, q)uit, r)eply, s)ave, t)ag, u)ndelete, or e(x)it24;1HK24;41H
```

Figure 2-8: Time to use VT100!

Odd & Sundry Terminal Types

Some of the more complicated (and usually expensive) terminal programs offer many other emulations settings besides VT100, ANSI, and TTY. If you take a peek at the list, you may see ones that we haven't mentioned here. Don't worry about them. Between VT100, ANSI, and TTY, you're covered for about 99.9 percent of all your terminal emulation needs. There are exceptions, though, and here's a brief overview.

RIP

The RIP terminal emulation was developed in an effort to bring more user friendliness to terminal connections (particularly with BBSes). RIP occupies a strange middle ground between true graphical user interfaces and pure text-based interfaces. Generally, you won't ever see this type of interface unless you call a BBS. In case you're curious, Figure 2-9 shows an example of a RIP terminal.

Figure 2-9: Connected with RIP.

Miscellaneous VT Emulations

While trying to bring even more functionality and graphic whiz-bangery to terminal communications, the Digital Equipment Corporation (originators of VT100 terminals) brought out several variations on the original VT100 theme, VT102 being the most popular. Generally, though, unless you find yourself calling some *very* obscure systems, VT100 should suit you fine.

IBM Terminal Emulations

The granddaddy of all mega-mainframe manufacturers, IBM developed several terminal types of its own. In IBM's grand tradition of keeping things as obscure as possible, many of these terminal emulations were given cryptic numeric designations. Most of these are not in use any more, but occasionally you may find a system that uses either the IBM3278 or IBM7171 emulation type. However, if you're using systems that use these types of emulations, you probably don't need this book.

SETTING UP YOUR COMMUNICATIONS SOFTWARE

Whew! Now that you know what all of the different settings mean, it's time to get down to business. Even though some of the information we've covered so far may seem a little obtuse, don't worry—most of the time your service provider will tell you all the settings that you need to know in order to connect correctly to their system. If you sign up and they don't tell you, give 'em a call.

One important thing to remember about setting up communications software is that the computer you're connecting to doesn't give a hoot what kind of system you're using. It does, however, care about all the settings we've covered so far.

Every communications program is a little different, but they all have a way for you to specify the configuration information we've discussed. Access the configuration dialog boxes for the program you're using, and enter the information you got from your ISP. It's as simple as that.

Here's a recap of the settings that you'll be dealing with:

❐ Baud rate. Make sure that you set your baud rate to match both the speed of your modem and the speed of the modem that you're connecting to. An exception is if both your modem and the one at the other end use error correction and compression In that case, you should set your baud rate to be two to four times *faster* than the actual speed of the modem you're using.

If your modem is faster than the modems your service provider uses, you have two options. First, you can leave your communications program set to the speed of your modem. Most modems will "negotiate down" to match the speed of the slower of the two modems. Of, if you really want to be a perfectionist about it, go ahead and set the speed of your modem in your communications program to match the speed of the modem that you're connecting to.

If your modem operates at a slower speed than the modem you're trying to call up, then set the speed of your communications program to the highest speed that your modem's capable of. The other modem should slow down to match the speed of your modem.

- ❐ Data Bits. Make sure that you've found out how many data bits you need to use to connect properly. In most cases, if you don't know whether to use 7 or 8, choose 8. Eight data bits is more common.

- ❐ Stop Bits. As with the data bits setting, you can be pretty safe by picking the most common stop bit setting—1. However, check with your service provider to determine the correct setting.

- ❐ Parity. The wrong parity setting is one of the leading causes of screen junk. If your communications program is looking for a different type of parity than the one that your service provider's using, you'll usually end up with annoying problems, including a screenful of garbage and a disconnected modem. Check before you dial.

- ❐ Flow control. This one you'll have to determine for yourself. The modem that you're making a connection to doesn't care what kind of flow control you use. That's between your modem and your computer. Generally, if you're using a modem at connection speeds faster than 9600 bps, you'll want to use hardware flow control. This is usually indicated in your communications program as either RTS/CTS flow control or hardware handshaking.

- ❐ Echo. It's pretty easy to tell if you've set this incorrectly. You'll see double of everything or nothing at all. If you're seeing double, turn the local echo off. If you're not seeing anything when you type, try turning echo on.

- ❐ Terminal Emulation. Check with your service provider first, but most of the time you can't go wrong by choosing VT100 terminal emulation. This will cover both ANSI and TTY if VT100 isn't available.

Keeping these settings in mind, you should be able to set up and run about any communications program that you come across. While many programs come with a lot more bells and whistles than we've looked into here, most of that stuff isn't necessary if you merely want to get connected.

Even though all of the communications programs you come across should have similar settings, the type of computer that communications programs run on *does* make a difference. Let's look at what you'll have to deal with in setting up a Windows or Macintosh machine.

Setting Up Communications Software in Windows

Windows' ability to let you fiddle with the inner workings of your system is both a bane and a blessing. In configuring communications software and a modem for Windows (especially Windows 3.1), you have to consider a number of settings.

Windows 3.1 System Modifications

Most Windows 3.1 communications problems with high-speed modems involve a little something called *data overrun*. In a data overrun, the data that your modem is receiving isn't being handled fast enough by the system. When this happens, you are most likely to see missing characters, lost data, or slow connections. While some of these errors might be caused by an older or insufficient UART chip in your serial port (see the section "Setting the Right Speed or UART Quite a Problem Sometimes" later in this chapter for more info on UARTs), the best place to turn to eliminate errors is the system software itself.

First, open up your system.ini file (found in the Windows directory), and go to the section marked [386enh]. As you scan down the lines, look for two lines similar to these:

```
MinTimeSlice=20
WinTimeSlice=100,50
```

These two settings control the amount of time that Windows gives programs while multitasking, or running several programs at once. By giving certain time slices to each program, Windows is able to play traffic cop, dishing out processor time as needed. However, high-speed modems demand more processor time than slower ones, so you may need to modify these values if you're having problems.

If your system.ini file already has these two lines and you aren't experiencing any problems with your modem, you probably should leave these lines as they are. However, if your system.ini file doesn't contain these lines, you should add them.

TIP

You can really, *really* munge things up in a hurry if you make a mistake when you're editing any system configuration files, such as system.ini. Before you edit, it's a good idea to make a backup of the old file by saving it with a .BAK suffix. In this case, name your backup file system.BAK. This way, if you make a mistake and have a problem with Windows, you can replace system.ini with system.bak and all will be well again.

Besides configuring for the proper time slices, you'll also need to add a few more lines to your system.ini file to make sure that your serial port is operating at peak efficiency. After the two lines you added above, add the following two lines:

```
COMxFIFO=1
COMxBuffer=1024
```

In both cases, you should replace x with the number of the COM port your modem is connected to. For example, if your modem is connected to COM port 1, the lines would read:

```
COM1FIFO=1
COM1Buffer=1024
```

Adding these lines to your system.ini file helps you in two ways. First, COMxFIFO=1 activates the "first-in, first-out" buffer in your 16550 UART serial port controller chip, allowing it to work at higher speeds. COMxBuffer=1024 tells the serial port to allow 1024 (1 KB) characters into its internal buffer, allowing it to process data in more efficient groups.

NOTE: If you aren't sure if you have a 16550 UART or want more information about what the heck a UART is, read the section "Setting the Right Speed or UART quite a problem sometimes."

Next, check the system.ini file for a line in the [BOOT] section that looks something like this:

```
COMM.DRV=COMM.DRV
```

Don't panic if this line reads a little differently in your system. If you already have a modem installed in your computer, this line may have been modified for another driver. If it is, leave it as is.

If the line looks like COMM.DRV=COMM.DRV and you're running Windows 3.1 with a high-speed (14,400 bps or above) modem, you may want to try replacing the standard Microsoft comm driver with a third-party driver. You can get one at ftp://ftp.smc.com/pub/chips/superio/serial.zip or ftp://ftp.best.com/pub/malch/serial.zip. Once you download serial.zip, unzip it, read the readme file, and install it according to the directions.

Common Windows 95 Settings

Setting up Windows 95 to operate correctly is much easier than Windows 3.1 — you don't have to do anything. Just set up the modem using the Modems Control Panel and you're pretty much ready to go. Windows 95 communications drivers are a big improvement over their Windows 3.1 counterparts, so you don't have to worry about editing INI files or any other techie fiddlin'.

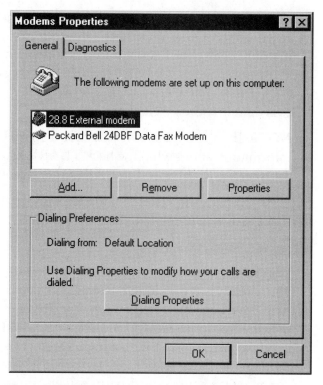

Figure 2-10: The Windows 95 Modems Control Panel.

However, a few settings seem to work well with most Windows 95 modem applications. These aren't hard and fast rules here, but they do seem to work for nearly everyone:

❏ Auto Baud should be OFF.

❏ Port Speed Locked should be ON.

❏ Carrier Detect should be ON.

❏ Hardware flow control (may be indicated as RTS/CTS flow control) should be set to ON or YES.

❏ Software flow control (may be called XON/XOFF) should be set to NO or OFF.

Picking the Right COM Port & Avoiding IRQ Conflicts

The first thing that you have to do when setting up your communications program is determine which COM port your modem is attached to. If you have Windows 95, this isn't a problem. It's been configured correctly as long as you have set up your modem with the Modems Control Panel. Since we're assuming that you're already online, we don't need to go into detail here. If you're having trouble finding the Modems Control Panel or are having trouble setting it up, consult your Windows 95 documentation.

Windows 3.1 isn't quite as easy. Because no integrated plug and play architecture is in the system, each program has to be set up separately in order to function correctly.

It's essential that you pick the right COM port for your communications program. Since your PC communicates with the modem through this port, if it doesn't know what port to use, it can't talk to the modem.

Most PCs have two serial ports—COM1 and COM2. However, many new machines have up to four COM ports as standard equipment—COM1, COM2, COM3, and COM4. Unfortunately, just because you have four ports doesn't mean that you can necessarily plug in four devices.

The flow of data from programs through the serial COM ports is controlled by interrupt requests (IRQs), special signals that tell a port to accept information. (Actually, this is not *exactly* how interrupt requests work, but for our purposes it's close enough). Unfortunately, the original designers of the PC didn't expect that anyone would want to have more than two serial devices hooked up at one time. (They also thought that no one would ever need more than 512 KB of memory!) What this means to you is that they only assigned two interrupt request numbers to the four ports. Table 2-2 shows the COM ports and their IRQ numbers.

COM Port	IRQ
COM1	IRQ4
COM2	IRQ3
COM3	IRQ4
COM4	IRQ3

Table 2-2: COM ports and IRQs.

Notice a pattern here? COM1 & COM3 share IRQ4. COM2 & COM4 share IRQ5. This means that you can use a modem and another serial device (like some mice) in the following configurations: COM1 & COM2, COM1 & COM4, COM2 & COM3, COM3 & COM4.

When two devices share the same IRQ, all sorts of funky things can happen, not the least of which is a big ugly system crash. You probably won't damage the hardware, but IRQ conflicts do make for nasty software problems.

The most common symptoms of IRQ conflicts are:

❏ Your communications program can't find the modem.

❏ Your system freezes when you try to use your communications program.

❏ You can connect, but you can't maintain a connection.

❏ Everything appears to work, but when you try to use your modem, nothing happens.

❏ Any combination of the above.

So what can you do to avoid IRQ conflicts when setting up your communications program? Simple. Look at the hardware you've installed in your computer, consult Table 2-2, and make sure that you're not using a COM port that conflicts with what you have installed.

TIP

If you can, always try using COM2 or COM4 (IRQ3). Your computer automatically gives this port the highest interrupt priority.

If you already have two serial devices installed, you're probably out of luck unless you want to try and fool with buying a serial port expander card. Some of these let you add more ports by assigning COM3 and COM4 to different IRQs. However, this doesn't always work. It depends on your software.

The best solution is not to have more than two serial devices hooked up to your machine at a time. If you have more than two serial devices (including your modem), try unhooking one and plugging your modem in when you need to use it. This isn't always convenient, but it does work. Or, you can buy an A-B switchbox that allows you to manually switch between devices without unhooking them.

Internal Modems & PMCMCIA Cards: IRQ Lowdown

Just because you use an internal modem board or a PMCMCIA *PC card* modem doesn't mean that you're out of the woods when it comes to IRQ conflicts. Even though these devices don't technically attach to a COM port, they still function as if they did. Most come configured to COM2. Even if you have a free COM4 port on the back of your computer, you can't use it.

If you have to change your internal modem COM port designation, check the documentation that came with the board. Most good internal modem boards use either DIP switches (small switches mounted on the circuit board) or jumpers (little plastic doohickies that connect 2 pins together) to set the COM port designation.

However, if you're using a PMCMCIA card, you may be out of luck unless your driver software allows you to change the COM port. Check your documentation.

Setting the Right Speed or UART Quite a Problem Sometimes

This can be confusing. Logic would dictate that you set the baud rate in your communications program to the baud rate of your modem, right? Wrong.

As we mentioned near the beginning of this section, if you're using a modem with data compression, you should set your communications program baud rate to a speed 2 to 4 times higher than your modem is rated. This insures that your computer is pumping data into the modem as quickly as possible.

TIP

Many people running Windows 3.1 think that by setting the communications port speed in the Control Panel is enough. Not so. Most communications programs ignore this setting. You need to set the COM port speed in each program.

However, if you have a three-year-old (or older) computer or are still using a version of Windows earlier than Windows 3.1, you may have to experiment. Older versions of Windows had modem drivers that aren't all that good at talking to high-speed modems and often can't handle the higher transfer rates. The best solution is to upgrade your system software.

If you have an older computer, you may not be able to use higher transfer rates because your hardware won't be able to handle it. Earlier PCs were equipped with UART (Universal Asynchronous Receiver/Transmitter) serial port chips, which could only transfer data one byte at a time. This was fine when a blazing fast modem topped out at 2,400 bps, but these days, when 9600 bps modems are considered slow, these older UARTs just don't cut it.

So how do you know what kind of UART you have in your PC? If you've got Windows, use Microsoft Diagnostics (msd.exe) to get a reading of your UART type (see Figure 2-11).

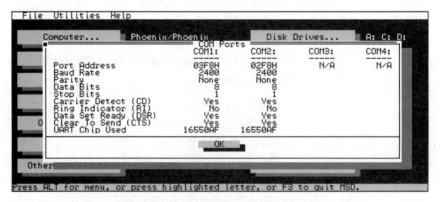

Figure 2-11: Using Microsoft Diagnostics to check the UART.

If Microsoft Diagnostics reports that you don't have at least a 16,550 UART, you may need to upgrade your system. Many systems use a 8250 or 16,450 UART, which may not be able to keep up with Windows when transferring data. You can tell when this is happening because you'll notice characters or groups of characters missing when you download text online. This is particularly true with older, slower systems running Windows (systems slower than a 486/66).

TIP

Quit Windows and go to DOS before running Microsoft Diagnostics. It's the only way to get a correct reading.

So what do you do if your UART is old and you want to use a high-speed modem? You have three options. First, if the UART on your motherboard is socketed (plugged in to a socket rather than soldered to the board), you may be able to pull it out and replace it with a newer, faster chip (a 16,550A UART or better) . However, if your UART is soldered, the best you can do is plunk down about a hundred dollars or so for a newer, faster serial card. Finally, you can buy a good internal modem. Internal modems use their own onboard UARTs, and any new internal modem should include an updated UART. Check the documentation before you buy.

New UART Problems: PCI Bus PCs

Having a spanking new computer doesn't necessarily mean that you're immune to UART problems. Some newer computers (PCI bus—equipped Pentiums, particularly) don't even use UARTs. Instead, they use SMC 655 controllers, which more or less emulate a 16,550 UART. *More or less* is the operative term here.

Because the UART is only emulated, some users have encountered problems with Windows 3.0, Windows 3.1, Windows 3.11, or Windows for Workgroups 3.11. They've reported system hangs when using computers with SMC 655 controllers. Fortunately, there's an easy fix:

➡

❏ If you have Windows 3.0, upgrade to Windows 3.1, 3.11, or Windows 95.

❏ If you have Windows 3.1 or 3.11, you need to replace your comm.drv file (located in the Windows/System directory).

❏ If you have Windows for Workgroups 3.11, you need to replace your serial.386 file (located in the Windows/System directory).

Both of these files (comm.drv and serial.386) can be found in a file called serial.zip, located at ftp://ftp.smc.com/pub/chips/superio/serial.zip or ftp://ftp.best.com/pub/malch/serial.zip.

▪▪

Setting Up Communications Software on a Macintosh

Generally, with Macs, you only need to plug in the modem, install the software, and get to it. Things have been designed to be as plug and play as possible. However, you need to know some information about configuring (or at least checking) your modem software in order to insure that everything works properly.

▪▪

Fax Software + Communications Software = Trouble!

If you're using FAX software on your Mac, you should probably disable it before using any other communications software. Even though a lot of FAX software developers try to deny it, the FAX software often conflicts with your other communications software. This conflict can cause problems that range anywhere from dropped connections to system lockups.

Why does this happen? Mainly because the FAX software likes to listen to the modem port all the time, waiting for incoming FAX calls. Sometimes, when you try to use your communications software, the FAX software won't realize that it should stop trying to listen to the modem port. It likes to make trouble!

As a quick and easy solution, disable the FAX software. Often this involves turning it off from a control panel or a configuration program. Check your documentation.

▪▪

Picking the Port

The Macintosh has two serial ports, handily called *modem port* and *printer port*. Even though they have different names, they generally serve the same function—a place where serial devices (modems, printers, and other peripherals) can attach to send and receive data.

In most cases, it doesn't matter which port you connect your modem to. Most Macintosh serial hardware functions equally well in either the modem or the printer port. The trick is that most communications programs (and other software using a modem) expect to find the modem attached to the modem port, and most printing software expects the printer to be attached to the printer port.

Even though most well-designed software allows you to choose which port you want to use, it's probably best to keep your modem connected to the modem port. This protects you from poorly designed software that doesn't give you a choice and saves you from having to dig around the back of the computer to switch cables later on.

You must remember, no matter which port you choose, that for your modem to function correctly, you *must* use a hardware hand-shaking cable to connect your modem to your Mac (See Figure 2-12). Most modems come with a cable, but if you happen to get a modem that isn't bundled with a cable, don't let some know-it-all sales droid tell you that "all the cables are the same." They aren't. Without a hardware handshaking cable, you won't be able to use hardware flow control, on your modem and you'll probably be limited to speeds below 9600 bps. Check before you buy.

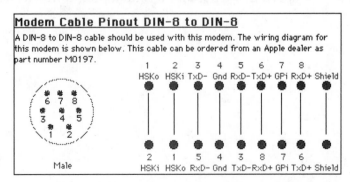

Modem Cable Pinout DIN-8 to DIN-8

A DIN-8 to DIN-8 cable should be used with this modem. The wiring diagram for this modem is shown below. This cable can be ordered from an Apple dealer as part number M0197.

1	2	3	4	5	6	7	8
HSKo	HSKi	TxD-	Gnd	RxD-	TxD+	GPi	RxD+ Shield

2	1	5	4	3	8	7	6
HSKi	HSKo	RxD-	Gnd	TxD-	RxD+	GPi	TxD+ Shield

Male

Figure 2-12: Pin designations in a Macintosh hardware handshaking cable.

Some people find that two serial ports are not enough. If you end up with three or more serial devices, you have two options. First, you can replace your modem with Apple's GeoPod, a special adapter that attaches to a GeoPort on the back of your computer (most newer Macs come with a GeoPort), and frees up the two serial ports. GeoPods are nice because they are software-upgradable: when a faster speed comes on the market, you don't have to ditch your Pod—you just upgrade the software. Unfortunately, at the time of this writing, Apple still hadn't released the 28,800 bps GeoPort software.

Your other option is to buy a DIN8A/B switch box, which allows you to connect two serial devices (such as a modem and a Connectix QuickCam) to the same port, and then manually switch between them when you need to. They cost about $20, so it's not too much of an investment if you want to get more from your machine.

Setting the Right Speed

When you set your communications port speed on your Mac and you're using a high-speed modem, you should set the speed to a number at least twice as fast as the actual rating of your modem. You may not be able to select a speed that's actually twice as fast, but choose the one that's closest to the number you need. For example, twice 28,800 is actually 57,600, but many communications programs only let you select 57,000 or 58,000. Either one will do. Figure 2-13 shows an example of setting the communications speed in the popular terminal program Z-Term.

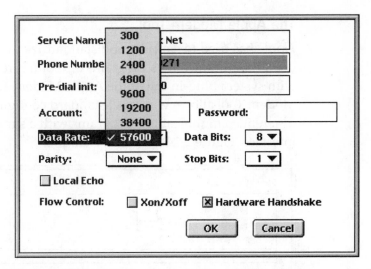

Figure 2-13: Setting the communications speed in Z-Term, a popular Macintosh shareware terminal program.

If you have an older Macintosh—a Mac II, MacClassic, MacPlus, or older—you may not be able to use a high-speed modem reliably. Many of these older machines aren't fast enough to handle the flow of data required by a 14,400 or 28,800 bps modem. You may be able to connect and use communications programs, but when it comes to uploading and downloading, you may find that you constantly have problems with dropping connections or lost data.

TIP

Remember, if you're using a modem speed of 14,400 bps or higher, you *must* use hardware handshaking flow control and a hardware handshaking cable.

The Apple Modem Tool

Apple has tried to simplify and standardize the way that Macintosh communications programs are configured by coming out with system plug-in called the Apple Modem Tool. The Apple Modem Tool allows you to set standard configurations across different communications programs with a simple, easy-to-use interface. Figure 2-14 shows an example.

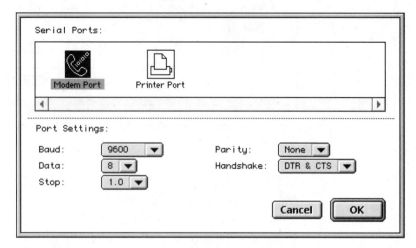

Figure 2-14: Configuring communications parameters with the Apple Modem Tool.

One of the major advantages of using the Apple Modem Tool is that it allows easy customization of many communications features. If a communication program uses the Apple Modem Tool interface, all you need to do to add a new service or protocol is drop a new "tool" into the System folder. Tools are available for nearly every transfer protocol—Xmodem, Ymodem, and Zmodem—as well as tools that even let you use other communications protocols, such as TCP/IP.

MODEM TROUBLESHOOTING

While we can't cover every contingency for what might go wrong with a persnickety modem, we'll cover some of the troubleshooting basics. Many of these problems can be cured by knowing how to configure your communications software correctly—

something that we'll cover in the next chapter. However, if you're already online, this guide may be exactly what you need to see your way through any problems.

Here are the top five modem problems and some suggestions for solving them. If none of these situations match your problem, or none of the solutions seem to help, try calling the technical support number that came with your modem. And remember to be nice to the tech support people. They really do want to help you solve your problem.

Problem 1: My modem doesn't seem to do anything when I try to dial out with it!

❒ First of all, make sure that your modem is connected to the computer. If you've got an external modem, make sure that it's on and connected to the correct port on the back of your computer. If you're using a Mac, the modem port is marked with a little phone icon (Figure 2-15). If you're using a PC, the modem port should be labeled COM1 or COM2 (Figure 2-16).

Figure 2-15: A Macintosh modem port.

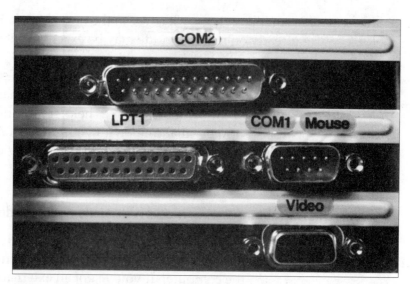

Figure 2-16: COM ports on the back of a typical PC.

❏ Next make sure that your modem is turned on (the switch is usually in the back of an external modem) and is connected to a power source. If your modem has an external power supply (one of those little black boxes that plugs into the wall socket), make sure that it's connected to the modem. If the modem is on and plugged in, you should see some lights on the front of the modem. If you don't, you may have a faulty power supply. Call the manufacturer to find out what to do next.

❏ Okay, if the modem appears to be on and functioning correctly and is connected to the right port on the computer, the next step is to check to make sure that the phone line is connected properly. If you have an internal modem, you should try this, too.

Most modems have two phone jacks in the back. One is usually labeled "line" and the other is labeled "phone." If yours are unlabeled, check your modem documentation to find out which jack is which.

You should have a telephone cable connected from the line jack in the back of the modem to the phone jack in the wall. If you want to use a telephone with your modem, the phone should be connected to the jack labeled phone on your modem.

If all the phone cords are hooked up correctly, it's time to check the phone line itself. Unplug the telephone cord from the "line" jack and plug it into an extra phone that you have lying around. You should listen for two things:

1. First, do you hear a dial tone? If you don't then the line is dead. Call the phone company, or check it out yourself.

2. If you do hear a dial tone, do you also hear a lot of static or interference on the line? If you do, this line noise may be preventing your modem from operating correctly. Fixing line noise is a bit beyond what we're covering here, but for a quick fix, Radio Shack (or other electronic hobby stores) carry "line noise suppressers," which can be helpful in filtering out noise. For really severe line noise, you may want to contact the telephone company.

   ❐ If all the phone connections check out, then maybe you have your communications program set incorrectly. We'll go into setting up communications programs in the next chapter, but for now, make sure that your communications program has been set to the right port for your modem. If it is, check to see if your modem is responding at all by typing the following in the terminal window of your communications software:

   AT

   If the modem is alive, it should respond with OK. If you don't get an OK, don't panic. As a final resort (before calling the manufacturer), reboot the computer, turn the modem on and off, and recheck the communications program settings. If everything checks out and the modem still doesn't work, call the manufacturer—you may have a bad modem.

Problem 2: I can connect with my service provider without a problem, but my connection quit when I was in the middle of something.

This problem can be a toughie if you aren't getting any error messages from your software. Modems don't really give you much feedback about their internal workings, so finding the cause of a constant problem can be kind of difficult if you don't know where to look.

- ❐ One of the most common reasons for hang-ups in the middle of a session is line noise, either natural or accidental "human error" noises. Natural line noise occurs when wind, rain, ice, and snow cause the telephone wires to move or become more susceptible to electrical signal crossover. These two conditions can induce static into the line and kill your connection. If you're experiencing this kind of natural line noise, there's really not a heck of a lot you can do except call the phone company.

- ❐ The second type of line noise, the human error kind, is most likely caused by the most dreaded hazard of all—the extension phone. If someone picks up the extension when you're on the line, your connection is likely to get cut. Maybe it's time to think about another phone line.

- ❐ Another human-related modem problem is call waiting. If the line that you're using has call waiting and you don't turn it off before you go online, any incoming call will trash your connection. To turn off call waiting, just type your phone company's call waiting disable code (usually ***70** or 1170) before calling out.

- ❐ If you're connecting using a TCP/IP dialer such as MacPPP, InterSLIP, Trumpet Winsock, or the Microsoft Internet Dialer, the problem may be related to your TCP/IP settings. Go back to the "Communications Settings" section of this chapter, and see if you can find the answer there.

Problem 3: My communications software can't find my modem!

You've determined that your modem is Okay. All the cords and cables are connected in the right places. The modem lights are on. But when you try to do anything, you get an error message telling you that your computer can't find the modem. What do you do?

❐ The most common reason for this type of error is not telling your communications software which port your modem is plugged into. On a Macintosh, the answer's pretty easy: double-check to make sure that the modem cable is plugged into the modem port.

On a PC, things can get a bit hairier. Most PC configurations give a choice of 4 COM ports to attach the modem to: COM1, COM2, COM3, and COM4. Most internal modems come preconfigured to work as if they're connected to COM2, and most external modems can be plugged into COM1.

The problems begin to arise if you already have a device plugged into either COM3 or COM4. Because of the wacky way that IBM originally designed their computers, if you've got a device connected to COM1 and COM3 or COM2 and COM4, you can't use them at the same time. So, if you have a mouse, a scanner, or even a video camera attached to COM3 or COM4 and you plug a modem into COM1 or COM2, you may have a conflict. Why? Your computer keeps track of which device is sending data by way of tracking IRQs (interrupt requests) from the devices. IRQ conflicts can arise between serial devices (like modems, mice, and scanners) that use COM ports sharing the same IRQs. In our case, COM1 and COM3 share IRQ4 and COM2 and COM4 share IRQ3. Figure 2-17 shows an example of how to set the COM port in Windows95.

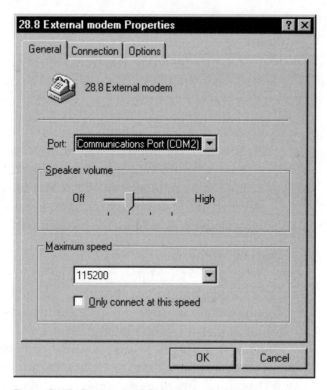

Figure 2-17: Setting the COM port in the Windows 95 Hyperterminal program.

The best way to solve this problem is to make sure that you're not using ports sharing the same IRQ. If you have a mouse plugged into COM2, don't install your new modem into COM4; install it in COM1 or COM3. If the modem is internal and already configured to COM2, check the documentation to determine how to change the COM port configuration before you install it. In most cases, you can do this just by changing a few switches.

If you're a gadget junkie and all your COM ports are filled up, there may be hope. Just make sure that the devices you have plugged into the conflicting COM ports are turned off when you use your modem.

❐ If you must use COM3 or COM4, make sure that your software can recognize these ports. If it can't, you won't be able to use your modem.

❏ If you're running Windows 95, you may need to run the Modems Control Panel again and check to be sure that a modem has been configured for your machine. If it hasn't, click the Add button, and follow the directions on the screen for adding a new modem profile. See Figure 2-18.

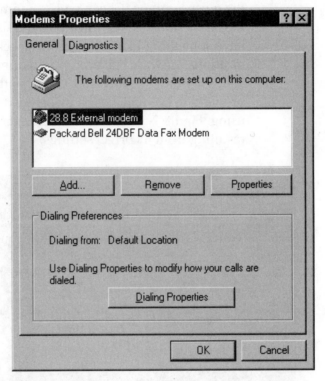

Figure 2-18: Setting up a new modem with the Modems Control Panel in Windows 95.

Problem 4: When I dial into my shell account, all I see is garbage.

❏ If you're seeing lots of random characters on the screen followed by a sudden disconnection, you're probably experiencing some pretty hefty line noise or someone picking up the extension phone. See the preceding sections for solutions to these problems.

❏ If the "garbage" that you're seeing seems to follow a pattern: brackets around weird characters, strange line breaks, or letters following ^ symbols, you may have terminal emulation problems. We'll cover terminal emulation in a lot more depth later on, but for now, you should probably be aware that VT100 and ANSII emulations are the most common. Check your communications software settings to make sure which one you have selected. If you have something like none or TTY checked, your communications software has been put in dumb terminal mode and will not work correctly. Check with your service provider to see which terminal emulation you should be using. Figure 2-19 shows a typical example of "garbage" resulting from incorrect settings.

Figure 2-19: Typical results of not using the correct terminal emulation.

❏ If you're seeing double characters (or no characters at all) when you type, you need to check the Echo and Duplex settings in your communications software. If you're seeing double, you'll need to set Echo to OFF and Duplex to FULL. If you aren't seeing anything at all, then you'll need to change Echo to ON.

❏ If your communications settings don't match the ones for the computer you're trying to connect to, you'll get meaningless junk on the screen. If this is happening, you need to check to see what your Data Bits, Stop Bits, and Parity settings are. Nine times out of ten, they should be set to 8 Data Bits, 1 Stop Bit, and No Parity. However, check with your service provider to make sure.

❏ Sometimes "garbage" is not too many characters, but not enough. If you're missing characters on the screen and you're connecting at a speed greater than 9600 bps, you need to check the Flow Control or Handshaking settings in your software. At high speeds, software flow control (XON/XOFF) doesn't work fast enough. You need to use what's called hardware handshaking, also known as *RTS/ CTS flow control*. Check your communications software settings to make sure that you're set up correctly.

❏ If you're using a high-speed modem (greater than 9600 bps), make sure that you've set the speed in the communications software to a number higher than the speed of your modem. For example, if you're using a 14,400 bps modem, set the Data Speed to 19,200. If you're using a 28,800 modem, set the speed to 57,600.

❏ Your modem may not be connecting at a high speed because of line noise or because the modem you're trying to connect to is a lower speed modem. Try calling back at a slower speed.

❏ Finally, check the initialization string to make sure that it's correct. If you don't know what init string to use, check your modem documentation. You'll often find that the modem manufacturer has helpfully provided a general-purpose init string for you. Try it. If that doesn't work, try setting the init string to AT&F. This will restore the modem to its factory settings.

■■■

TIP

If you need a good init string, check out America Online.

America Online does a remarkable job of getting almost every modem to work correctly. One of the reasons AOL excels at this is because they've been able to develop really good initialization strings for just about every modem on the market.

If you have AOL installed on your machine, you can find out what init string to use with your modem. If you have AOL for Windows, press the Setup button at the first screen, go to the Setup Modem section, and select Edit Commands. The init string is in the box labeled Setup Modem String. Write down the appropriate string, and use it with your other modem software

If you're using a Macintosh, you'll have to do a bit more digging. Using a text editor that lets you read any file type (such as Bare Bones Software's BBEdit Lite), go to the Online Files folder in the America Online folder, and open the file for your brand of modem. Look for a section starting with CONFIG=. The text following CONFIG is the init string you should use. However, when you add it to your other communications software, make sure to put an AT at the beginning of the line.

■■■

Problem 5: My uploads and downloads seem to be taking an awfully long time (when they work at all).

❏ Make sure that you're using the right transfer protocol. We'll get into this more in the next chapter, but for now, remember this—Zmodem is probably your best bet if it's available. It's fast, it works well, and, as an extra added bonus, it'll let you resume your transfer later if it conks out in the middle of a transfer.

❏ If you have a modem that uses data compression, make sure to use either Zmodem, Ymodem, or Kermit to transfer files. The Xmodem protocol contains its own data compression algorithms and can conflict with your modem's own compression scheme.

64

❒ Using FTP to transfer files with a TCP/IP connection can have its own set of problems.Remember this: FTP can be slowed down considerably if the site that you're transferring files from is very busy, far away, or on a slow machine. If any of these conditions apply, be patient. There's really nothing you can do about it.

❒ If you're using an older PC and an external modem, your UART chip may be old. Check your computer documentation to see which one you have. If you don't have a 16550AFN UART (or newer), you're going to need one. Try upgrading the chip, if possible. If not, you may need to buy a new serial controller board.

MOVING ON

Now that we've covered what you need to know when configuring your modem and your communications program, it's time to move on to the next level —TCP/IP communications.

In the next section, we'll take a look behind the scenes of the Internet, at its networking protocols. We'll explore the way that the Internet handles data traffic and assigns addresses, how these addresses work, and the ins and outs of getting your computer hooked directly into the Net's great datastream.

Even if you've already set up your PC for a SLIP or PPP connection, we'll explain what all those strange settings were that you had to contend with. We'll cover everything from domain name servers to subnet masks, and when we're finished, if you've paid attention, you'll be able to amaze your friends and coworkers with your new mastery of TCP/IP connectivity.

So, let's get ready to peel away some of the layers of mystery and find out how the Internet really works (and how it can work better for you)!

## Chapter 3

TCP/IP Primer

From modems and communications programs, we move another rung up the ladder to TCP/IP connectivity. While technically, TCP/IP connections include hard-wired LANs (local area networks) and WANs (wide area networks), we'll save the details of those branches of networking for Chapter 4. Here, we'll cover the basics of TCP/IP, which are pertinent no matter what platform or network you're running.

In keeping with our general tack, the purpose of this chapter is not to tell you what buttons to push or which switches to throw in connecting your PC or Mac to the Internet. Instead, we're going to let you in on some of the inner workings of TCP/IP and explain how it is used to get computers on the Net to talk to one another. Once we're finished, you'll have a much better understanding of how TCP/IP works and a few handy tricks under your belt to boot.

WHAT THE HECK IS TCP/IP & WHY SHOULD I CARE?

After all, isn't life cluttered with enough acronyms without adding another one—with five letters, no less?!

Well, yes it is, but TCP/IP is not just a meaningless techie term to file away and toss out every once in a while to impress fellow nerds and confound newbies. It stands for Transmission Control Protocol/Internet Protocol, and it's the essential lifeblood of the Net and the Holy Grail of Internet Power Userdom.

Everything that happens on the Net—every program you use, every message you send, and every picture you download—is brought to you by this amazingly simple and flexible communications protocol. Just like the Universal Translator in *Star Trek*, TCP/IP provides a way for the incredibly diverse constellation of computers that make up the Net to communicate with one another. Basically, without TCP/IP networking, there'd be no Internet.

A Completely Unrelated Aside on *Star Trek's* Universal Translator

While we might buy into the notion of a tiny computer powerful enough to translate alien languages, wouldn't it make living in the *Star Trek* universe a little bit like being trapped inside of a badly dubbed Japanese monster movie? Someone's lips move to a weird alien cadence while all you hear is the out-of-sync voice of your translator. And, how is it that you don't hear the alien's native tongue at the same time? Is this handled by some advanced sound-canceling technology?

Oh well . . . just something to distract you while you're trying to bone up on TCP/IP.

A Little Background

We're sure by now that you've heard the story about how the Internet was originally developed by the military to survive a nuclear attack. What you may not know is that the TCP/IP protocol is what made the Net nuke-proof.

Before TCP/IP, most computer networks were centralized. One main computer (a hulking mainframe) was usually surrounded by smaller "dumb" terminals or perhaps a few smaller satellite computers. All network data traffic went through the main computer. Knock the central computer out, and all the computers on the network were cut off from each other. See Figure 3-1.

Obviously, this configuration wouldn't do in a nuclear war. All the enemy would have to do is vaporize the central computer and the entire network would be kaput.

TCP/IP was developed to provide a "packet-switched" network. Packet switching was a radical idea for its time: eliminate the central computer, and let each computer on the network function as a peer of every other computer on the network. Each computer would take care of receiving network traffic, deciding where it should go, and sending it on its merry way. See Figure 3-2.

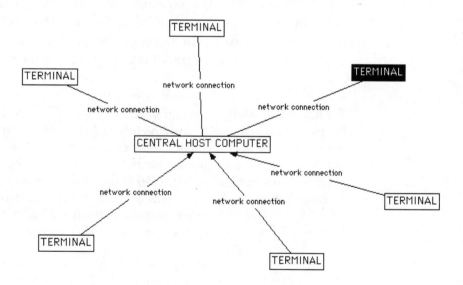

Figure 3-1: A centrally controlled network.

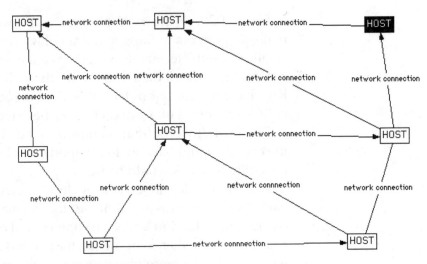

Figure 3-2: A packet-switched network.

The major advantage of a decentralized system like this is that there is no central controller to be knocked out. Wipe out one computer (or group of computers), and the others simply route network traffic around the damaged computers.

Packet-Switched Networks' Trial by Fire

During the Persian Gulf War, Allied forces had a difficult time wiping out Iraq's command and control networks. A lot of bombs hit their marks, but in the end, most of the network still functioned. Why? Because the Iraqis were using TCP/IP and other forms of packet-switched networks. And, as the original designers intended, the network was able to function, even after taking incredible damage.

Packet-switched networks began to come into their own with ARPANET, an experiment by the Defense Advanced Research Projects Agency (DARPA). Eventually, ARPANET was combined with several other government and military networks—the Internet was born and TCP/IP was well on its way toward becoming the popular protocol it is today.

TCP/IP was designed from the ground up to be modular, not to care what kind of hardware it was running on, and to allow for complete decentralized operations. The Internet was able to grow so quickly because whoever wanted to connect to it could, provided he or she had a computer to connect.

From the beginning, TCP/IP protocols were "open standards." No one owned the technology, and no company had a patent or other corporate hold on its development. TCP/IP was a network-wide effort.

The one major feature of TCP/IP that set it apart from other networking protocols was that it allowed each computer on the Net to have its own unique address. As long as you knew the address, anywhere in the world, of the computer you wanted to send information to, TCP/IP could get it there.

PEELING BACK THE LAYERS: NETWORK COMMUNICATIONS

TCP/IP is actually a set of several protocols, not just the Transmission Control Protocol and the Internet Protocol. These protocols define how data is packaged, transmitted, and received across the network; they guarantee that any computer speaking with the same protocol can communicate with any other computer using the same protocol.

One feature that sets TCP/IP apart from other forms of networking protocols, such as AppleTalk on the Mac or the Novell IPX protocols, is that TCP/IP is hardware independent. Any computer that can run TCP/IP doesn't have to worry what kind of computer it's going to talk to down the line. As long as they're both running TCP/IP, the hardware doesn't matter. And, because TCP/IP is an open standard developed by a community of users, the nuts and bolts of how it works are available to everyone.

The Communications Model

A lot of times, when discussing a particular piece of hardware or software, it's fairly easy to visualize how it works: disk drives store information as magnetic bits on a platter, scanners translate images into data, and a CD-ROM drive bounces a laser beam off little pits that stand for ones and zeros. Even though you may not know the nitty-gritty of how it works, you can at least feel comfortable understanding it on a conceptual level.

Networking protocols are a little bit more convoluted. Probably the best way to describe how network communications work is to use the metaphor of a *stack* made up of layers. This metaphor was first proposed by the fine folks over at the International Standards Organization who defined an "Open Systems Interconnect Reference Model" (known also as the *OSI model*).

Open Systems Interconnect Reference Model

The OSI model doesn't represent any real data or operational structure. Instead, the OSI model is an abstraction of the process that must occur to successfully transmit and receive data. As we peel back the layers of the OSI model, keep in mind that there's no actual one-to-one correspondence between parts of the model and actual communications—the OSI model just serves as a simpler way of conceptualizing the process.

The OSI model divides the different events and functions that occur during data transmission into separate layers of functionality. The layers are then grouped into a "stack" (Figure 3-3) representing the entire communications process.

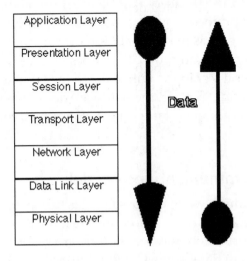

Figure 3-3: A communications stack.

In the OSI model communications stack, each layer performs a different function:

- Application Layer: This level encompasses all the applications that you use to access the network. For example, Telnet and your e-mail program reside in the Application Layer.

- Presentation Layer: This layer handles how the data coming down from the Application Layer is presented to the lower levels. Data coming in from the Application Layer (what you type when using Telnet, for example) arrives at the Presentation Layer as any one of several formats. This layer then takes that data and translates it into a standard format.

- Session Layer: The Session Layer maintains the communication connection. Here's where a connection is made and maintained during the course of data transfer.

- Transport Layer: After the data's been entered in the Application Layer, transformed in the Presentation Layer, and a connection has been made via the Session Layer (whew!), the Transport Layer makes sure that the data gets to where it's going. Error correction and retransmission of garbled data take place in this layer.

- Network Layer: This layer is where the actual connection is maintained across the network. The Network Layer also serves as a type of barrier between the lower-level protocols (the Data Link Layer and the Physical Layer) and the upper-level protocols (Application, Presentation, Session, and Transport Layers).

- Data Link Layer: When data passes through this layer, the Data Link Layer makes sure that the actual physical delivery of data takes place. Unlike the Transport Layer, which handles data integrity, the Data Link Layer makes sure that packets actually go out across the network by providing the necessary functionality needed for moving the packets across the network.

❏ Physical Layer: The real hard-core hardware wizardry takes place here. In the Physical Layer, "real-life" concerns come into play, including what kind of wires (copper or fiber optic) carry the information, how those wires plug into the computer (RS232 or coax), and what kinds of electrical signals are going to carry the data.

Every layer in the communications stack of one computer communicates with its peer layer in the other computer's stack. For example, when you use FTP to send a file across the Net, the FTP program you're using (in the Applications Layer) talks to the FTP server program on the remote computer you're transferring files to and from. When you start up that connection, each layer takes care of its task by communicating with the appropriate layer on the remote system's stack.

As data originates in the Applications Layer, it moves down through each level of the stack, getting transmogrified as needed. In the remote computer receiving the data, the data enters the Physical Layer (through the wires or other physical connection) and then moves up through each layer of the stack until it reaches the Applications Layer.

Now, it might sound like we're doing two things at once here—sending data down the sending stack and then up the receiving stack while also allowing corresponding layers to talk to each other directly. How can we do both?

Here's how: Data does have to move down through the stack to the lower layers before moving out, but when it arrives at its destination, it only moves up the stack far enough to deliver its data to the corresponding layer. If the Transport Layer in communications stack A has to send data to the Transport Layer of stack B, the Transport Layer-specific information originates in the Stack A Transport Layer, passes down through the Network, Data Link, and Physical Layers of Stack A and then back up the layers in Stack B until it reaches the Transport Layer.

The TCP/IP Communications Stack

TCP/IP doesn't exactly conform to the OSI model, but it comes pretty close. It's even a bit simpler. Figure 3-4 shows a simple diagram of a TCP/IP stack. Even though no one agrees on how many layers TCP/IP actually has or what they're called, one of the best representations of it uses four layers:

❏ Application Layer: Programs that use the network.

❏ Host-to-Host Transport Layer: Makes sure that data is delivered monitoring the integrity of the data received and properly addressing outgoing data.

❏ Internet Layer: Puts together the communications packets and oversees the routing of the packets.

❏ Network Access Layer: Handles the actual interface with the physical network.

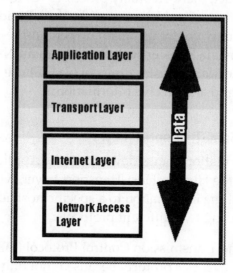

Figure 3-4: The TCP/IP stack.

As with the OSI model, data starts at the Application Layer and moves downward through the layers until it moves across the network to the receiving computer. Along the way, the data picks up control information. Once at the Network Access Layer, the packet heads off to its destination. On arrival, it moves up through the stack again until it reaches the application that's receiving it. As the data moves up the stack, the control information is stripped off layer-by-layer until it arrives at the Application Layer in its original format.

Application Layer

As far as you're concerned, the Application Layer is where all the action is. The programs that you use to interact with the Internet, Telnet, FTP, e-mail, and so on, all function within the Application Layer.

But, in fact, there are many processes residing in the Application layer that are transparent to the user. Besides the programs that you know you're using, many behind-the-scenes components of Internet data transfer such as the Domain Name Services (DNS) and Simple Mail Transfer Protocol (SMTP) use the Application Layer to send and receive information.

Host-to-Host Transport Layer

Once information comes down from the Application Layer, it's passed to the Host-to-Host Transport Layer, which handles the delivery of the information to a specific host address across the network using two different protocols:

❐ The Transmission Control Protocol (TCP): TCP is known as a *reliable* protocol because it not only arranges for the delivery of data to the remote computer, it also provides error correction to make sure that the data arrives intact. While this method does a good job of insuring the integrity of the data, it also adds a significant amount of overhead to the information. Figure 3-5 shows a simplified diagram of the information contained in a TCP packet.

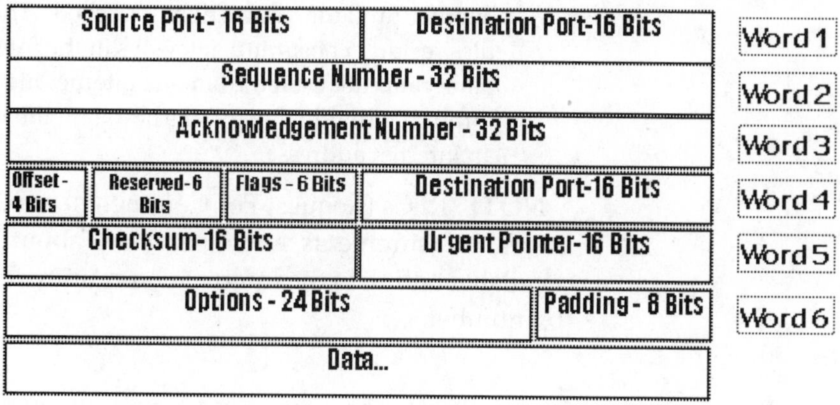

Source Port- 16 Bits	Destination Port-16 Bits	Word 1
Sequence Number - 32 Bits		Word 2
Acknowledgement Number - 32 Bits		Word 3
Offset - 4 Bits · Reserved-6 Bits · Flags - 6 Bits	Destination Port-16 Bits	Word 4
Checksum-16 Bits	Urgent Pointer-16 Bits	Word 5
Options - 24 Bits · Padding - 8 Bits		Word 6
Data...		

Figure 3-5: A TCP packet.

❏ User Datagram Protocol (UDP): UDP is known as an *unreliable* protocol because it does no error checking. UDP provides a direct line for applications in the Application Layer to send messages over the network without having to deal with all the overhead data that must go along with an error-corrected packet, allowing for more efficient data transfer. Compare Figure 3-6 (the UDP packet) to Figure 3-5 (the TCP packet). Quite a difference, eh?

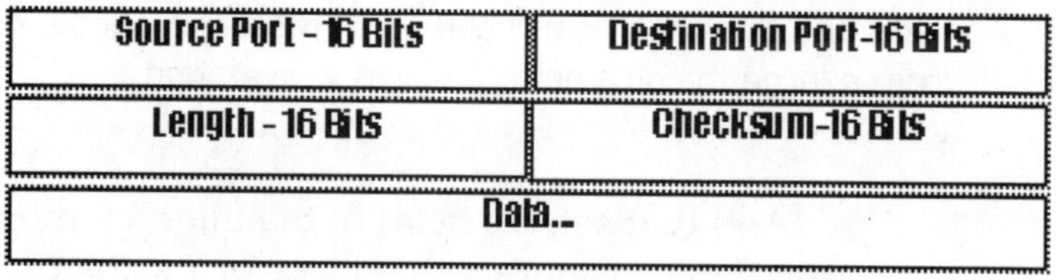

Source Port - 16 Bits	Destination Port-16 Bits
Length - 16 Bits	Checksum-16 Bits
Data...	

Figure 3-6: A UDP packet.

Internet Layer

The Internet Layer *is* the IP—Internet Protocol—of TCP/IP. It is the delivery department. As defined in RFC* 791 "Internet Protocol":

> The function or purpose of Internet Protocol is to move datagrams through an interconnected set of networks. This is done by passing the datagrams from one internet module to

another until the destination is reached. The internet modules reside in hosts and gateways in the internet system. The datagrams are routed from one internet module to another through individual networks based on the interpretation of an internet address.

*NOTE: RFCs (Request For Comments) are a series of technical notes, measurements, and discussions about TCP/IP that are available online to the Internet community. They are referenced by number.

Geekspeak Alert!

If you're confused by some of the terminology in the above quote from RFC 791, you're not alone. Most RFCs are written by computer scientists for computer scientists, so they often assume that you know what they're talking about. In case you're a little hazy on some of the terms, here's a brief glossary:

A *datagram* is the unit of data that a protocol uses. It's different from a *packet*, which is a physical group of electrons transmitted by the actual networking hardware.

A *gateway* is a computer used to connect a network to the Internet. Gateways handle the interface between the network and the Internet at large.

A *host* is a single computer with a unique IP address directly connected to the Internet using TCP/IP protocols. Hosts can be anything from a large mainframe to a single workstation.

And that's it, the heart of the Internet: moving data from one computer to another thanks to an attached address.

IP is called a *connectionless* protocol. It doesn't have to actually care about establishing a connection with the remote computer it's communicating with. It slaps an address on the data and sends it off. Internet Protocol uses two different data-moving methods—addressing and fragmentation. Since we're having so much fun peeling back these layers of net.arcana, let's take a peek at both of these.

Addressing

Data makes its way across the Internet by being transformed from its original state into packets of information called *datagrams*. The information in this datagram functions as an "envelope" for the information coming down the pipe from the layers above. Figure 3-7 shows a diagram of an Internet datagram.

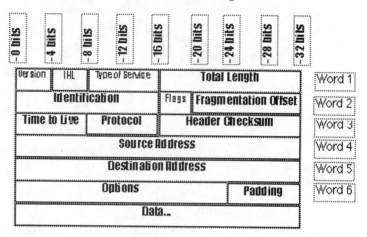

Figure 3-7: An Internet Protocol datagram.

As you can see, a datagram is a pretty complex little beast, but basically it's made up of a header containing five (sometimes six) 32-bit words and then a variable amount of data. The most important part of the header is word five—the destination address of the datagram.

As a packet goes off through the Internet and gets passed through several gateway machines (also known as routers), each gateway takes a look at the destination address and then passes the packet off to the next machine. After any number of hops from gateway to gateway, the packet finally arrives at the destination computer, which then passes the packet "up" the TCP/IP stack layers to the Application Layer (or whichever layer needs the information).

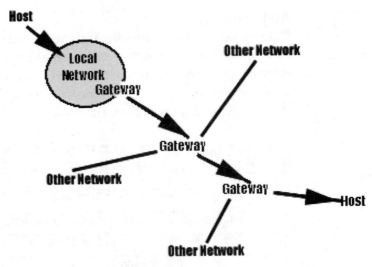

Figure 3-8: Routing an addressed datagram across the Internet.

Fragmentation

Because the Internet Protocol was designed to pass packets through a whole variety of networks, it also has the ability to break data into fragments that can pass through any network it comes across.

Internet vs. internet: What's the Difference?

When TCP/IP was originally developed as a way of passing information through a variety of networks, the word *internet* (lowercase *i*) simply referred to any packet-switching network running the Internet Protocol. Since then, the word (with a capital *I*) has come to mean the vast network of networks connected to form the global information and communication exchange system we all know and love ('til things go wrong).

If you look at Figure 3-7, you'll notice that header Word 2 contains several pieces of information: the Identification field, the Flags field, and the Fragmentation Offset field. These fields allow the datagrams to be broken into smaller segments for transmission across networks that might not be compatible with large chunks of information allowed by the Internet Protocol. The Identification field tells the network which fragment a particular header belongs with. The Flags field contains a bit that indicates whether or not the entire datagram has been reassembled properly. Finally, the Fragmentation Offset field identifies which packet a particular fragment belongs to. Using all this information, data can fly through whichever network it's handed off to and be reassembled correctly once it reaches its destination.

Network Access Layer

The Network Access Layer handles the actual interface with the physical network. Most of the time, you'll never have to worry about what goes on in this layer. Because this layer interfaces so closely with the hardware its running on, most of the action takes place within protocols specifically designed for that hardware. Since TCP/IP was designed to be hardware independent, the upper layers of the protocol stack (the Application, Host-to-Host Transport, and Internet Layers) are isolated from the Network Layer.

But even though you may never be aware of what's going on in this layer, a lot of important stuff is happening. The Network Access Layer takes care of a broad range of functions including IP datagram encapsulation, IP address mapping, and actually transmitting data across the network by interfacing with the physical infrastructure of the Internet.

COMPONENTS OF TCP/IP NETWORKING

It's fine to know the theory of how TCP/IP networking works at the protocol level, but in real life, you have to contend with a lot of details if you're going to get your connection up and running correctly. See Figure 3-9.

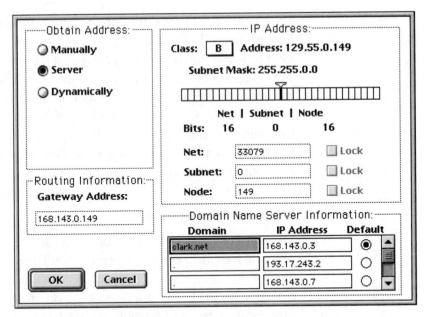

Figure 3-9: Some of the TCP/IP settings you have to contend with in MacTCP.

Most people fill in the information they need by following a FAQ or checklist provided by their service provider without having any idea what it is that they're filling in. Usually, the settings work, but sometimes they don't. If they don't, you're left scratching your head, trying to figure out what the problem is.

In this section, we'll look at all these obscure-sounding settings and how (and *why*) they work. When we're done, you may not be ready to be a network administrator, but you'll at least know what things like IP addresses and domain name servers are so you can intelligently tackle problems when they arise.

IP Addresses

Every computer connected to the Internet through a TCP/IP connection has its own address. In the TCP/IP protocol stack, the Internet Protocol uses this unique address (called an *IP address*) to move data between hosts. The address is assigned based on what other computers the host is attached through to get to the Internet.

When data is sent across the Internet, the address of the destination computer is put into Word 5 of the Internet datagram as a 32-bit number. As the datagram travels across the Internet, each computer checks the address in the datagram and then either sends it up the protocol stack to the Application Layer (if the datagram has arrived at the correct host) or passes it along to the next computer in line.

Classes, Hosts & Networks—The Magic Behind the Numbers

Even though we ordinarily write out IP addresses as four number groups separated by periods (129.55.0.149, for example), computers on the Net don't see them that way. In fact, those dots separating the numbers are there as a convenience to us humans for easily reading the address. To computers, the address is really a 32-bit number. Each number group (as we see it) represents one of four 8-bit "octets" in the 32-bit address.

Bytes vs. Octets

Most of the time when we're talkin' computer lingo, we refer to groups of 8 bits as a *byte*. However, when you're talking about the Internet, you can't make that assumption. Some computers on the Net have "bytes" that are more than 8 bits. For that reason, groups of 8 bits are called *octets*.

Separating the four octets makes sense for more reasons than just clarifying the address. IP addresses are grouped into classes based on the number in the first octet of the address. How do you tell what class an IP address belongs to? Check out Table 3-1—a handy-dandy chart we've whipped up for you.

First Octet Value	Class
0	Default Route: used for debugging purposes only.
1-128 (except 127)	Class A
127	Loopback Address: used for debugging and network testing.
128-191	Class B
192-223	Class C
224-254	Reserved: not normally used.

Table 3-1: IP address classes.

IP addresses work by identifying both the host computer and the network that the host is connected to. Because addresses work this way, the number of hosts a computer can have connected to it is dependent on the class of the address. Why? Read on.

Class A addresses use the first octet to indicate the network of the host and then use the next three octets to indicate the particular host. A network machine with a Class A IP address can have 16,777,215 host computers attached to it. Class B computers use the first two octets to identify the network and the last two octets to indicate the various hosts on the network. Class B computers can have 64,516 computers attached to them. Finally, Class C IP addresses use the first three octets to identify the network and only one octet to identify the computer. This allows for only 256 hosts attached to a machine with a Class C address. See Figure 3-10.

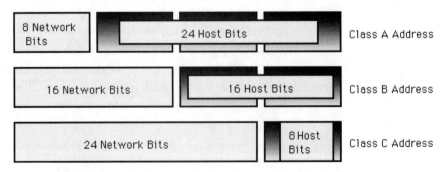

Figure 3-10: IP Address classes.

All right, so this is a little confusing—let's try an example. Say your IP address is 129.55.0.149. By looking at the first octet, we can determine that it is a Class B IP address. Because Class B addresses use the first two octets to indicate their network identities, this computer is attached to network 129.55. In short, a computer with the IP address 129.55.0.149 actually is identified as computer 0.149 on host 129.55.

Subnet Masks

Sometimes an organization may want to divide its network into several different subnets or smaller networks. By doing so, several Class C networks can be created without the "overhead" associated with having to administer several different Class C nets. Subnetting allows a larger network to "hide" the complexities of its internal networks from the rest of the world, saving its network neighbors the trouble of having to deal with yet more addresses in their routing tables.

Let's take our theoretical IP address 129.55.0.149. Imagine that 129.55 is actually the network IP number owned by KataCorp, a large software conglomerate. Because it's so large, it needs a Class B address to handle the thousands of computers networked within the company.

There are 16 departments within KataCorp, each with its own network of a hundred or so computers. (See Figure 3-11.) Theoretically, you could connect them on the entire 129.55 net, but that would cause a lot of administrative headaches. Instead, KataCorp "splits" off the third octet of the Internet address and uses it to indicate which internal network (i.e., subnet) a computer is attached to. Splitting off the third octet is roughly the same process as splitting the first octet into network classes. By assigning certain ranges within the octet to certain subnets, you create a net of nets.

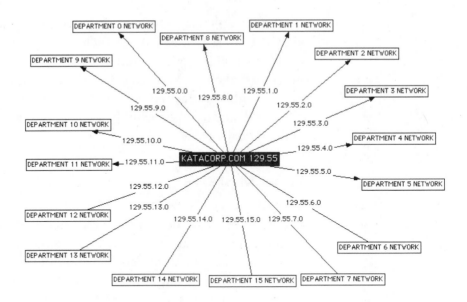

Figure 3-11: Applying subnets to KataCorp's internal networking structure.

So, let's say computers in the Design and Control Department are indicated by a number between 0 and 15. Looking at our theoretical IP address, we'd know right away if a given computer was part of the Design and Control Department network by seeing if the third octet of its IP address contains a number between 0 and 15.

Subnets are defined by placing a *subnet mask* on top of an IP address. Remember that an IP address is really a 32-bit binary number. A subnet mask is another 32-bit binary number that looks like an IP address but really functions as a kind of template which fits "over" a 32-bit IP address to change the values of the IP addresses' bits.

For example, if a bit is "on" (a one) in the subnet mask, that bit is considered to be a network address bit in the IP address. If our IP address was 146.45.21.1 and the subnet mask was 255.255.0.0, you would interpret the address as referring to host 21.1 on the subnet 146.45.0.0. See Table 3-2.

Note: 0=off, 1=on	Decimal IP Address	Binary IP Address
Host Address	145.45.21.1	10010001.00101101.00010101.00000001
Subnet Mask	255.255.0.0	11111111.11111111.00000000.00000000
Subnetting Result	net=145.45	host=21.1

Table 3-2: How a subnet mask works.

Routing

Now that you know more about IP network addressing than you probably care to, the question still remains—how do those datagrams get to where they're going? The answer is *routing*.

When the Internet Protocol deals with a datagram, it assumes those packets are going to another computer attached to a local network—it just sends it out to the network. Sending a datagram to another computer on the same network is easy. It passes it over to the next computer on the local net until the datagram reaches its destination. However, if you want to send a datagram to another computer on a different network, things get a little hairier.

For incoming data, IP treats each datagram as an entity unto itself. It doesn't look to see if the packet "belongs" with any others. All the IP cares about is: "Does the datagram go to this computer, another computer on this network, or a computer on another network?" If the datagram belongs on the computer that the IP is running on, it passes it up the protocol stack for reassembly into the correct block of data. If the datagram is supposed to be on another computer on the same network, it passes it along. However, if the datagram belongs on another computer on a different network, the datagram is passed to a gateway.

In theory, a gateway can be any computer with more than one network port. One network port is for the local network and the other network port allows the gateway to be attached to a gateway at another network. In practice though, gateways are usually dedicated to overseeing Internet traffic. Figure 3-12 shows a small corner of the Internet consisting of several local nets and their gateways.

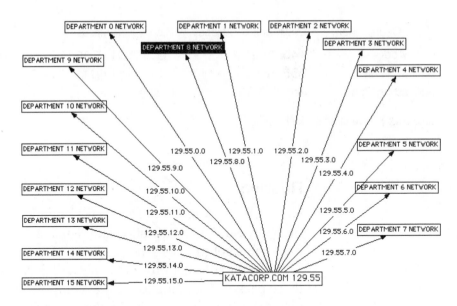

Figure 3-12: Several local networks linked by gateways.

When the IP on a local network host recognizes that a datagram belongs on another network, it shuffles the datagram off to the gateway. The gateway then decides which network to pass the datagram to.

One of the really cool things about how TCP/IP works is that the gateway that a datagram arrives at doesn't have to be directly connected to the destination network for that datagram—it just has to be on the way. If the remote gateway isn't the datagram's final destination, the gateway looks at a file called a *routing table* to see which nearest network the datagram should be forwarded to. By using this pass-along method, datagrams eventually arrive at their destination where they are reassembled (using the information in the IP header) into the correct block of data.

Individual computers on a local network *can* have their own routing tables that tell them where to send datagrams, but they don't have to. In fact, given the size of the Internet, these tables would get way too big, too fast if each individual computer on the

Net had to keep track of all its routing. Instead, most computers on a local net never have to worry about routing—they let the gateways handle the tough work. The gateway is placed on the network of computers and routes packets destined for the Internet as they come along the net.

For example, if we use a local area network, the gateway may be just another computer on the LAN. However, as traffic passes over the network and is identified as being destined for a computer on the Internet, the gateway sends it out. In many situations, the main file server for the LAN also functions as the gateway.

If you're attached to the Internet through a service provider and a dialup TCP/IP connection (SLIP or PPP), then a computer on your ISP's network functions as the gateway to get your packets out to the Internet.

MBONE: Internet Audio, Video & the Next Generation of Routing

You may have heard some buzz lately about "Internet Radio" or "Internet TV"—live audio and video "broadcasts" across the Net. Now that you know a little bit about how TCP/IP works, you might begin to wonder how one host could "broadcast" to many people at the same time. After all, since datagrams are addressed to only one specific receiver, how could a broadcast to many computers occur?

Enter the MBONE. Designed as a "virtual multicasting network" on the Internet, the MBONE uses a new type of addressing—Class D—to create datagrams that can be received by more than one computer. When these special multicast datagrams cross the MBONE to routers equipped for multicasting protocols, they duplicate themselves at every host set up along the way to receive multicast datagrams. One datagram goes to the receiver and another gets passed along. Figure 3-13 illustrates how these datagrams get moved through the MBONE.

If this sounds a little too complicated, it is. Right now, TCP/IP protocols are not very well suited for multicasting and real-time audio/video applications. Several solutions are in the works as we speak. Watch for the MBONE to become a very hot topic in the next year or so.

➥

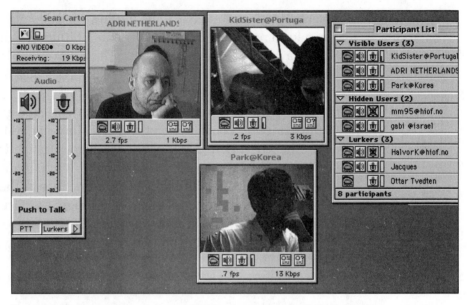

Figure 3-13: Live video over the MBONE using a CU-SeeMe "reflector."

Domain Names & Name Servers

At this point, you may be saying to yourself, "Uh, all this is very interesting, guys, but most of the Net addresses *I* use are made up of words and letters, not a series of numbers. What's up?"

The Internet addresses that you use most of the time are represented as words and letters. However (isn't there always a *however*?), those words are actually translated into IP address numbers for use on the Internet. When you try to access a remote host with an Internet address name (such as www.cooltool.com), the name is converted to a number that computers on the Net can understand (205.160.235.85).

Names are attached to numeric IP addresses for one reason—humans have a much easier time remembering names than they do remembering numbers: elrod-ppp.clark.net is much easier to remember than 129.55.0.149.

Most of the time you can substitute a numeric IP address for its corresponding IP address name (or hostname). If you wanted to FTP a file from elrod-ppp.clark.net, you could type the UNIX command: **ftp elrod-ppp.clark.net** or **ftp 129.55.0.149.** Either one would do. The only exception to this rule is that some domain names don't have a corresponding *unique* IP address. Why? Because in the interests of corporate appearances, many companies want their "Internet Address" to make people think they're running their own server. Instead, the host that their domain name is attached to aliases the name. If megacorp.com was actually an alias on serviceprovider.com, both would have the same IP number.

- -
TIP

If you want to find out the IP number for a particular host, most UNIX systems have a command called nslookup. (See, we told you that learning UNIX would come in handy!) If you want to find out an IP address, type the following, and press Enter:

```
nslookup <hostname>
```
- -

So how does this all work? When you use a hostname instead of an IP address, your system converts the host's name into a IP number using either a "host table" or (in most cases) what's called a *domain name server* to handle the translation.

A host table looks something like this:

```
#
#
# ServiceProvider Host Table
#
#
123.55.23.1      mega.serviceprovider.com  megacorp.com
123.55.18.2      design.megacorp.com doodles elrod
123.55.21.2      engineering.megacorp.com propeller hardhat
123.54.18.256    lunchroom.megacorp.com burger
123.55.234.1     spies.megacorp.com spy
123.55.215.2     jolt.megacorp.com soda
```

TIP

If you're curious about how the host table is set up on the computer system you use, go look at the /etc/hosts file. If you need help finding this file, check out Appendix D, "UNIX Boot Camp."

As you can see, each IP address is associated with a particular hostname and alias. When a host on the local network has to send information to another host, it consults the host table to translate the alias or the hostname to the correct IP address. It looks at the first column to find the numeric IP address and then looks in the next two columns to the right of the numeric IP address to match up the hostname and the alias.

In practice, most systems have done away with using host tables except for looking up hosts on the local network. As you can imagine, maintaining a host table for more than a few hundred computer systems can get unwieldy.

As the Internet grew, a better system had to be found for keeping track of all those addresses and hostnames. For a while, the Defense Data Network Information Center maintained a huge host table called the "NIC Host Table." However, even this method got unwieldy. That's when the Domain Name Service system was developed.

The beauty of the DNS approach is that it doesn't use a central database of names. Instead, the DNS uses a distributed database served by hundreds of different systems. When a DNS database server gets a request for a host that it doesn't have any information on, it hands the request off to a special server responsible for maintaining name information on its particular domain. This "authoritative server" then sends the new name/IP address information to the local domain name server, which saves the information in its table. That way, an information request only has to occur once. If the DNS can't find a match anywhere, it returns an error.

The big-daddy of all domain name services is InterNIC, an organization that keeps track of domain name assignments. Once the numeric IP address/domain name combination is entered into the InterNIC database, it "propagates" out through the domain name servers on the Net until every domain name server has a record of it.

When you're setting up a TCP/IP connection, you'll have to specify one or more domain name servers. It's best to list as many domain name servers as you can—that way if one server goes down or is unavailable due to an overload in network traffic, your TCP/IP connection can look somewhere else for the information it needs. See Table 3-3 for a list of domain name servers to use. These are all root-level domain name servers (they function as the "first-level" of all domain name servers, getting new DNS information first), which should work in a pinch, though slowly if your ISP's or local network's DNS goes down. To use them, just add them to your DNS setup table in your TCP/IP software (Winsock , MacTCP control panel, or Open Transport network setup).

198.41.0.4	a.root-servers.net
128.9.0.107	b.root-servers.net
192.33.4.12	c.root-servers.net
128.8.10.90	d.root-servers.net
192.203.230.10	e.root-servers.net
192.5.5.241	f.root-servers.net
192.112.36.4	g.root-servers.net
128.63.2.53	h.root-servers.net
192.36.148.17	i.root-servers.net

Table 3-3: Some root-level domain name servers.

Numeric IP Address	Domain Name
com	Businesses and other commercial entities.
edu	Schools and educational institutions.
gov	Government bodies and agencies.
mil	Military organization.
net	Network operations centers, some service providers.
org	Organizations separate from all of the above. Includes most nonprofits.

Table 3-4: Top-level domain name categories.

Seven Steps to Registering a New Domain Name

Hey, want to be a big shot in Cyberspace and register your own domain name? If so, you might want to hurry. Domain names are hot property these days as companies around the world scramble to snatch up the good ones. So far, no legal precedents have been contested over who "owns" a domain name, but you can be sure that there'll be plenty of "my lawyer can out-bill your lawyer" battles in the next few years.

Here are seven steps to following when registering a domain.

1. Come up with a name. Check Table 3-4 to find out what category of name you qualify for.

2. Check to see if the name you want is already taken. You can do this by either using the whois command in UNIX or by going to the InterNIC whois server at: http://rs.internic.net/cgi-bin/whois and typing in the domain name you wish to look up.

   If you get a bunch of information about the domain name you're trying out with whois, tough luck—the name's taken. Go back to Step 1. However, if you get something like:

   ```
   No match for "NEOWOBBLY.COM"
   The InterNIC Registration Services Host contains only
   Internet information (networks, ASNs, domains, and POCs).
   Please use the whois server at nic.ddn.mil for MILNET
   information.
   ```

   You're in luck! No one has your domain name. Go on to Step 3.

3. Fill out the Domain Name Registration form. It contains complete instructions on what information to fill out, why you need to fill it out, and where you need to send the form once it's completed. You can find this handy form at: ftp://rs.internic.net/templates/domain-template.txt.

4. Wait patiently. A lot of people are registering domain names these days. While you'll probably get confirmation right away that the form's been received, you may have to wait several weeks for the registration to actually take place.

5. Break out the checkbook. When you get notice that your name has been registered, you'll need to pay InterNIC a $100 registration fee to cover two years' administrative costs. In the old days it was free. See what you get for waiting?

6. Go wild printing up business cards, letterheads, T-shirts, caps, pens, PEZ dispensers, and key rings with your new domain name on them! You're somebody in Cyberspace now!

7. Defend your domain name. Hire a legal team to defend your company against a) another company who thinks they deserve the name or b) any trademark you may have infringed on with your domain name. If you lose, go back to Step 1.

TCP/IP ON YOUR HOME PC

Even though TCP/IP can run on nearly every type of network architecture, TCP/IP translates to a SLIP or PPP connection for most home users on PC or Macintosh computers. For those of you who are going to be running a TCP/IP connection via a LAN or other high-speed connection, we suggest that you turn ahead to Chapter 4, "Above & Beyond 28.8 Kbps," for a more in-depth look at the special considerations of direct Net connectivity.

When TCP/IP was originally developed, the assumption was that all the connections between the computers on the TCP/IP network would be hard-wired, dedicated network lines. Since most personal computers at the time were pretty wimpy (by today's standards) and most modems extremely slow (a fast modem in the early '80s was 2400 bps), the whole idea of a dial-up TCP/IP connection was ignored.

It wasn't until fast modems became cheaper and more easily accessible to home users that people started wondering how a home computer could be networked into the growing Internet over a regular telephone line using the TCP/IP protocols. Most of the earliest experiments with telephone line (serial) TCP/IP were run by frustrated hackers who wanted to bring their work home with them.

No one even seriously looked into the problem until 1984 when three researchers (Farber, Delp, and Conte) published RFC 914. This document laid the groundwork for all the "thin wire" (telephone line) TCP/IP networking protocols that were to come later.

SLIP (Serial Line Internet Protocol) and PPP (Point to Point Protocol) were both developed as ways of pumping TCP/IP packets through a telephone line. If you remember our discussion of the TCP/IP protocol stack, you already know what layer of the stack they belong in. But in case you were snoozing during that part of the chapter, we'll refresh your memory. SLIP and PPP run at the Network Access Layer of the TCP/IP stack, handling the actual network hardware (modem and phone lines) for the upper layers of the stack. Now that you've absorbed that general idea, let's take a look at how SLIP and PPP work. This background knowledge will help you when we discuss how to get your SLIP or PPP connection working in Chapter 6, "Getting Connected With TCP/IP in Windows," and Chapter 11, "Inside MacTCP Connections."

SLIP (Serial Line Internet Protocol)

From our earlier discussion of the ins and outs of modems and communications software, you may recall that digital information coming through your computer's serial port must be modulated into an analog information stream to be sent across the telephone lines. Typical modem-to-modem communications protocols use stop bits, parity, and other error-correcting protocols to make sure that data goes across the lines smoothly. SLIP works in much the same way.

As TCP/IP information comes from your computer (or into it from the host you've connected to), SLIP packages the TCP/IP datagram into "frames" by appending data flags to the beginning and the end of the TCP/IP datagram. Figure 3-14 shows the structure of a SLIP packet.

Figure 3-14: SLIP packet format.

That's one byte at the beginning, the TCP/IP datagram in the middle, and one byte at the end. If SLIP encounters a data byte with the same value as one of the "flag" bytes at the beginning or end of the packet, it translates the data byte into a pair of characters before transmitting them. That way the connection doesn't get "confused" by misinterpreting data bytes as flag characters.

One of the major features of SLIP is that it keeps protocol overhead to a bare minimum. SLIP has no error control, no link-level authentication, no data compression, and no data integrity controls. Either SLIP is up or it isn't. The SLIP protocol assumes that everything is hunky dory and being taken care of "up the stack" somewhere.

Because SLIP doesn't do any checking or link negotiation, you have to be *very* careful when setting up a SLIP connection to make sure that your settings are the same ones your service provider's using. If you decide to go with SLIP, make sure that either you have a configuration file preloaded with your software or you get instructions on variables such as frame size, VanJacobson compression, IP addresses, and any other blanks that need filling in.

What do you need to get SLIP going on your home computer? Check out Table 3-5 for the lowdown on SLIP software. The details about using this type of software to get your SLIP connection working are presented in Chapter 6, "Getting Connected With TCP/IP in Windows," and Chapter 11, "Inside MacTCP Connections."

Software	Platform	Features	Source
Trumpet Winsock	Windows 3.1 and Windows 95	SLIP, PPP, CSLIP (compressed SLIP)	http://www.trumpetcom.au
Chameleon Sampler	Windows 3.1 and Windows 95	SLIP, PPP	http://www.netmanage.com/ netmanage/products/chamsamp.html
InterSLIP	Macintosh	SLIP	ftp://ftp.intercon.com/InterCon/ sales/Mac/Demo_Software/ InterSLIP.sit.hqx

Table 3-5: SLIP software and sources.

PPP (Point to Point Protocol)

While SLIP is a model of simplicity, PPP is a study in how flexible and robust protocols are made and why simpler isn't always better. Figure 3-15 shows a diagram of a typical PPP packet.

Flag Byte	Address	Control Info	Protocol Data	FCS Data	Flag Byte	Interframe Fill or next address

Figure 3-15: PPP packet structure.

Big difference, eh? PPP appends a lot more information to a serial packet, including addressing, control, protocol, and frame information. It's a lot more than SLIP's "flag" bookends.

In fact, PPP does everything that SLIP doesn't—error checking, link control, IP address negotiation, and data compression. Unlike SLIP, PPP is able to negotiate nearly every networking variable at the time of connection. As one person on the Net once said, PPP "distill[s] the wisdom of a link-level guru into an algorithmic process." That may be a geek's overstatement, but most of the time, networking with PPP is much easier than getting a SLIP connection up and running correctly.

Another nice feature of PPP is that other types of networking protocols—AppleTalk or Novell's IPX/SPX, for example—run at the same time as PPP . . . across the same line! These networking packets don't have to be "encapsulated" into IP datagrams. This means that with PPP, you can actually run two networking protocols at the same time on one serial line! For example, with the right software, you could dial in to your office LAN, hook up using your LAN's protocol, and still send TCP/IP packets through the LAN to the Internet.

Take a look at Table 3-6. It outlines the different PPP packages you can use. As far as getting your PPP connection up and running, we'll cover that in Chapter 6, "Getting Connected With TCP/IP in Windows," and Chapter 11, "Inside MacTCP Connections."

Software	Platform	Features	Source
Trumpet Winsock	Windows 3.1 and Windows 95	SLIP, PPP, CSLIP	http://www.trumpetcom.au
Windows 95 Dial-up Networking Adapter	Windows 95	PPP	Comes with Windows 95
MacPPP2.2	Macintosh	PPP	ftp://igc.org//pub/STAFF/anthony/ MacPPP2.01cm3.sit
MacPPP2.11sd	Macintosh	PPP, Support for ISDN connections	ftp://wuarchive.wustl.edu//systems/ mac/umich.edu/util/comm/ macppp2.11sd.sit.hqx

Table 3-6: PPP software and sources.

SLIP vs. PPP: Choosing a Connection

Over the years, there's been some debate that PPP, despite its robustness and flexibility, was a slower, bloated protocol and that SLIP was actually better for maintaining a home TCP/IP connection. This debate has lead to the inevitable Net flame wars on comp.protocols.tcp-ip, comp.protocols.slip, and comp.protocols.ppp as the different camps wage endless word battles over which protocol is better.

Want our advice? Of course you do! Otherwise you would never have made it this far in the book. First, whenever you see a high-level technical flame war going on, it's probably a good idea to ignore it. The real question isn't which protocol is faster in *theory* but rather which protocol is going to let you get the job done at the fastest overall speed with the least amount of hassles. There's one answer to this question: PPP.

Even though PPP puts a lot more "overhead" on the data going through the line, it tends to actually get data into and out of your computer faster because it uses its own error checking to insure the integrity of the data. Rather than forcing the TCP/IP stack to check and retransmit incorrect datagrams, PPP nips the problem in the bud with its own error correction at the Network Layer.

But, on top of all the technical mumbo jumbo that PPP does, the big overall difference really crops up when you consider how much easier a PPP connection is to set up and maintain. Since PPP takes care of so many of the details itself, it's a much easier protocol for the average networking Joe (or Jane) to set up and actually *use* every day. So, if you have a choice, we recommend you use PPP.

TCP/IP INTERNET RESOURCE GUIDE

As you can imagine, there's a treasure trove of resources on the Net for anyone who's itchin' to learn more about TCP/IP. This small resource guide is a good place to start in exploring what's out there.

Web Sites

An Introduction to TCP/IP
http://pclt.cis.yale.edu/pclt/comm/tcpip.htm
A very nice, brief introduction to TCP/IP networking, including some helpful diagrams and definitions. Useful if you want a refresher course after reading this chapter.

The PC-Internet Connection Update Page
http://www.zilker.net/users/internaut/update.html
Even if you aren't using a PC, stop over here for the absolute latest in information about TCP/IP, networking, and all types of Internet connectivity. FAQs, software, service providers . . . it's all here. The newest TCP/IP FAQ, comp.protocols.tcp-ip.ibmpc faq, link is provided. It's a must-read for anyone who wants to stay on top of personal computer TCP/IP networking.

Network Development—PC/TCP
http://www.net.cmu.edu/pctcp/faq-index.html
Sure, it's written specifically for getting a TCP/IP connection working with Carnegie-Mellon's computer system, but beyond these specifics, it's a great general document about setting up and configuring TCP/IP connections.

RFC Archive

http://nic.noaa.gov/RFC/Rfc.html

Why not go to the source? The RFC (Request for Comment) archive, maintained by the nice folks at NOAA (National Oceanic and Atmospheric Administration)—your tax dollars at work, is a great place to go if you want to read the original working "specs" on the Internet.

FAQs

The PC-Mac TCP/IP & NFS FAQ List

http://www.rtd.com/pcnfsfaq/faq.html

Networking guru Rawn Shah has assembled a mighty fine FAQ that deals with just about everything you could ever want to know about hooking up your Macintosh or PC with TCP/IP or NFS (network file system) software. Though a lot of the information deals with NFS issues, this site is absolutely *huge* and a great place to stop if you're in search of TCP/IP info.

The comp.protocols.tcp-ip.ibmpc FAQ

http://www.cis.ohio-state.edu/hypertext/faq/usenet/ibmpc-tcp-ip-faq/top.html

Pretty much a book itself (over 180-page printout), this must-read FAQ covers everything from what software you need to what network card works with which computer. An incredible reference.

Newsgroups

If you have any questions about TCP/IP, check these newsgroups. You'll find hundreds of knowledgeable networking gurus ready and willing to answer your questions, often within a hours of posting them. A word to the wise: read the appropriate FAQs *before* you post a question to any of these groups. Most of these seasoned Net vets have no tolerance for questions like "What do I need to connect Windows 95 with a SLIP account?"

bit.listserv.ibmtcp-l   An IBM TCP/IP mailing list also available on Usenet.

comp.os.ms-windows.networking.tcp-ip   Getting TCP/IP to work with Windows.

comp.os.os2.networking.tcp-ip   Using OS/2 with TCP/IP.

comp.protocols.tcp-ip   Technical discussions on TCP/IP.

comp.protocols.tcp-ip.domains   Questions and answers about domain names and domains.

comp.protocols.tcp-ip.ibmpc   TCP/IP networking with PC-compatible computers.

comp.sys.mac.comm   Communications using a Macintosh. You can ask Mac-specific TCP/IP questions here.

Other Resource Documents

RFC 1055: A Nonstandard for Transmission of IP Datagrams over Serial Lines: SLIP

http://www.cis.ohio-state.edu/htbin/rfc/rfc1055.html
Here's the Holy Grail of source info on SLIP. In HTML format for easy reading, it'll give you the lowdown on all the technical aspects of using SLIP over a modem.

RFC 1661: The Point to Point Protocol

http://www.cis.ohio-state.edu/htbin/rfc/rfc1661.html
This site contains a nicely HTML-ized version of the RFC that first defined PPP.

Introduction to Internet Protocols
http://www3.umdnj.edu/~som/library/tcp.html
A great overview of all the Internet protocols, how they work, and how to get the most out of them. Kinda old but useful none the less.

MOVING ON

Now that we've had a crash course in TCP/IP fundamentals, it's time to put some of our knowledge to practical use. Until now, the connection types that we've discussed have had one thing in common—they all take place over a modem. That's fine if you're an average home user, but what if you're one of the growing number of people who are accessing the Net via a high-speed ISDN line or from work via a LAN? If you look at most Internet books, they leave people like you out in the cold. But we wouldn't do that to you!

In the next section, we'll examine what it means to move beyond modems and into the burgeoning world of high-speed Internet connectivity. We'll delve into the sometimes uncharted and scary waters of ISDN connectivity. Then we'll move on to the corporate world of Internet LAN connections. We'll examine what it is that makes getting on the Net through a LAN so different than jacking in at home and what kinds of office networks work best. Then, we'll spend some much-needed time on security issues, delving into such things as firewalls and proxies. Finally, we'll help you decide if direct, high-speed Internet connectivity is something your company should be considering. We'll give you a breakdown of connection types, speeds, issues in working with service providers, and what kinds of hardware you'll need to get your high-speed connection working.

So, if you're ready to kiss your old modem and slowpoke connection good-bye, read on. We're going to explore the next generation of Internet connections.

## Chapter 4

Above & Beyond 28.8 Kbps

Several years ago, the Internet escaped from the office and the university and came home with everybody. Home connections are normally through a dial-up modem. It wasn't that long ago that a 1200 baud modem was considered a breakthrough in lightning fast communications. In the early '90s, a 9600 baud modem was a coveted device. The increase in popularity of the Internet seems to have occurred because of two events: the advent of inexpensive 14,400 baud modems and the growth of the World Wide Web. (Nobody expected it to happen. The Web came out of left field. Here we have a combination of the slowest-to-transmit form of information—graphical display—and the slowest form of data transmission—a modem—combining to change the face of computing!) In the mid '90s came the 28800 modem, and several things are happening now that might mean speeds for the home user are about to increase by an order of magnitude. Because of the volume, existing technologies for bringing high-speed connections into the home are getting cheaper, and there are new technologies warming up in the wings.

Of course, the dial-up link is only part of the story. Schools, businesses, and government offices, where there are a number of computers in direct and constant communication, have ways of connecting that do not limit data transmission to the speed of a modem. Some of this technology has been around for a quite a while, some is just beginning to spread, and there is always new stuff on the horizon. We have LAN (Local Area Network) technology for high speed communications among a group of directly connected computers. We also now have WAN (Wide Area Network) technology being used by companies to connect widely dispersed computers over high speed links. Connecting to a host on a WAN can make it seem like the connection is in the next room instead of across the country.

At the software level, anywhere above the lowest level device drivers, all of these Internet connection methods look pretty much the same. One of the really nice things about TCP/IP is its internal architecture, which is constructed like a stack of pancakes with the applications as the butter and the network as the plate. From the viewpoint of your Web browser, e-mail client, FTP file transfer utility, or any other application, it makes no difference whatsoever which of the communications technologies is being used to send and receive datagrams. The only place the medium makes a difference is at the bottom of the TCP/IP stack where the data hits the highway. Of course, no system is perfect, not even TCP/IP, but the isolation of each TCP/IP layer is fairly clean.

The software (known as device drivers) at the lowest layer of the TCP/IP stack is written with the capability to control a specific type of hardware interface. It will only work with one specific type of communications equipment. In fact, most diagrams and descriptions of the TCP/IP stack will show the two bottom layers (driver and hardware) as a single entity called "Layers 1 & 2." Layer 1 is the physical network. The purpose of layer 2 is to write packets to and read packets from the physical network. These two layers are very tightly coupled. The software of layer 2 must be written specifically for the hardware of layer 1. The data packets (sometimes called frames) are blocks of bit streams that carry all the transmitted data and enough information about both the sender and receiver to get the message through to the right place. The IP layer (the layer just above the driver layer) will package the datagram and pass it down to the layer below. Layer 2 may or may not put a header block on the data (depending on the requirements of layer 1) before transmitting it to its counterpart on the receiving end. The receiving layer 2 passes what it gets up to its corresponding IP layer. Here's where the nifty part of the architecture comes in. The IP layer doesn't care if layer 1 sent it by modem, fiber optics, on camel back, or a stiff wind—it's all the same. Conversely, at the bottom layers, the packet is just so many bits to be shoved over the connection.

In this chapter, we are going to take a look at some of the higher speed methods of connecting to the Internet; methods that exist now and that will exist in the near future. The LANs that will be discussed are used primarily by industry to connect office computers together. However, LANs are beginning to make their way into the home as they become easier to install. Besides existing LAN systems, we'll take a look at some of the emerging technologies for both LAN and cross-country connections.

INTERNET CONNECTIONS VIA A LAN

A LAN is a group effort. It's basically a bunch of computers all banding together to share things like printers and an Internet connection. They can share each others' facilities to the point that an entire disk drive on a machine in the next office can look and act just like it's on the machine on your desk. In many ways, a group of computers on a LAN act as if they are one computer. As a matter of fact, many LANs have their computers connected together so tightly that if one of the important ones goes down, all the others become useless. It's reminiscent of the good old days when we all worked on a mainframe and, during a system crash, there was a sudden social gathering in the hall.

What is a LAN?

The acronym LAN stands for Local Area Network. It is so common today that a LAN is usually called just the network, as in "Is the network down?" and "When will the network be up again?" Also, since the Internet has become so popular, sometimes a local group of one or more LANs is referred to as an intranet.

A LAN is a local network of computers directly wired together over some sort of link that is usually very fast. While there are several types of links, the most common technologies are Ethernet, Token Ring, and (more recently) fiber optic. A LAN may or may not be connected to the outside world. If it is, that connection is known as an internet (with a lower-case I) connection, since it is the connection between two networks. Normally, there is one computer on the LAN that is connected to an internet and the other computers talk through it. This one computer is a gateway. Large or complex LANs can have multiple gateways. This is how the whole world is becoming linked.

Every computer on the LAN must have an address that is unique in relation to any computer with which it can communicate. If there is no connection to the outside world, the system administrator can just make up any old addresses he or she feels like. If, however, the gateway is going to communicate over the Internet, the gateway must have a world-wide unique address. Further, if each computer on the local network is going to be addressable over the Internet, they all must have unique addresses. In these cases, your system administrator must contact the NIC and request an address range for the network.

One of the most commonly shared facilities on a LAN is the connection to the outside world via the Internet. This is normally a high-speed connection of some sort, since a dial-up link would just not be adequate for multiple users. Under normal circumstances, there is only one computer in the LAN that's responsible for this connection. This computer is called the gateway, since it acts as the digital doorway to the outside world. As you might suspect, this opens up all the computers on the LAN to the possibility of intrusion from the outside. To increase the safety of the LAN, there are often restrictions placed on the type of things that can be passed through the gateway. While these limitations do increase safety, they also limit somewhat free and easy Internet access.

Types of LANs

There are several different types of LANs. The most common are Ethernet, Token Ring, and FDDI. In reality, there is a lot of commonality among them. Ethernet is a run of coaxial cable with the computers all contending for time to communicate. A Token Ring is pretty much like an Ethernet in its wiring, but each computer has its own unique method of contending for time on the wire. FDDI is a fiber optic version of Token Ring. Let's take a closer look at each of these types.

Ethernet

Ethernet is the most common of all the LAN technologies. It is a cable with a terminator on each end (as shown in Figure 4-1). The computers tap onto the line using special interface cards. Its protocol is known as MAC (Media Access Control). MAC is a sort of sub-layer protocol hanging off the bottom of the TCP/IP stack.

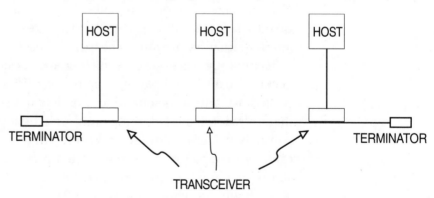

Figure 4-1: Ethernet LAN topology.

A Beginning, Middle & End

Having an Ethernet LAN is sort of like having a long rope stretched across a pasture and pulled tight. All of the computers stand along the length of the rope and hold on to it with one hand. (OK, so computers don't have legs and hands, but bear with us while we stretch an analogy.) If one of the computers wants to send a message, it starts shaking the rope—the message travels along in the form of waves in the rope. The other computers, with their silicon mitts on the rope, notice the pattern of the message and, if they find their own address in the pattern, read the message. Before a computer starts to send a message, it makes sure the rope is not already waving with a message from somewhere else. If two (or more!) computers start to send a message at the same time, they can tell immediately that things aren't working right because the waves in the rope are all messed up. When this happens, they all stop, wait awhile (a random amount of time), and then, if the rope is not waving, try it again.

If you've ever worked with Ethernet, you've probably heard the term "terminator." For Ethernet to work, there must be a terminator on each end of the line. In our analogy, these are our two cyborgs holding the rope tight. You can see that if the rope goes slack, nothing will work.

The original Ethernet cable was a chunky half-inch in diameter. This was later reduced to a quarter-inch, and now it is even smaller. The thinner wires (called ThinNet) have some advantages and some disadvantages. The original half-inch wires are now sometimes called ThickNet. Although the thinner wires are more sensitive to interference, they are much cheaper and easier to install.

Technology has gone even further and reduced Ethernet connections to a twisted pair instead of coax. This reduces wiring costs drastically. It is sometimes possible to use telephone wiring that's already installed in the building. The topology of a twisted pair network is a bit different. Where ThinNet and ThickNet are cables with a pair of ends, the twisted pair cables are arranged in a star with a hub (or concentrator) at the center and one computer on each wire (as shown in Figure 4-2).

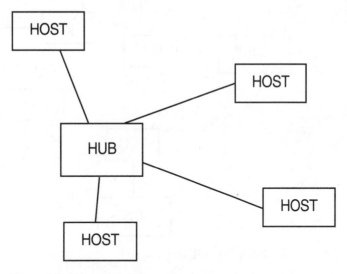

Figure 4-2. Ethernet LAN star topology.

Ethernet has its own protocol and addressing that have nothing to do with TCP/IP. The Ethernet software driver will take an IP datagram and package it into its own framing protocol for transmission. This has the interesting side effect of making it possible (and common) for multiple protocols to operate over the same Ethernet at the same time, with TCP/IP being only one of them.

Token Ring

Token Ring is another type of LAN technology. It's fairly similar in hardware and configuration to Ethernet, but does have a couple of major differences. First, since it runs in a circle, there's no terminating end to the connecting medium. Second, there's a difference in the way communications are established and maintained. In the ring arrangement, the computers are attached in a circle so that every computer has another computer on both its left and right. Signals are passed around the circle from one computer to another (as opposed to Ethernet, where the signals effectively appear everywhere at once). Figure 4-3 is a diagram of Token Ring topology.

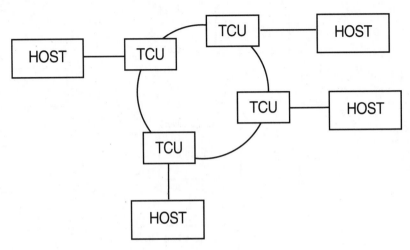

Figure 4-3. Token Ring topology.

The lowest level technology of a Token Ring is quite similar to Ethernet, except that the actual connection is made with a simple device called a TCU (Trunk Coupling Unit). There are several TCUs connected in a circle (one for each host) and each has the job of detecting whether it has an active host attached to it. If there isn't a host attached to the TCU, or if the attached host is inactive, the TCU allows all signals to pass through unmolested. If there's an active host, the signals are sent to the host instead of passing on around the ring. There is a special frame, called a "token," that is sent from one host to the next. Only the host in possession of the token will transmit frames over the LAN. Now, are you good and confused? We suspected as much—check out the sidebar on Token Ring for an English-language translation of all this geekspeak.

Token Ring (or What Goes Around Comes Around)

OK, time to lighten things up with another goofy analogy.

Imagine the computers on a Token Ring net as King Arthur's knights at the Round Table. They all want to talk, but if they were to talk all at once, there would be nothing but babble. Since it's a round table, nobody seems to be in charge of deciding who's going to talk next. There's a small token on the table that is embossed with the words from Merlin, "You may speak, but only for a short time." The knights all start scrambling to grab the token, and one of them gets it. He gets his say until he either finishes or his time runs out. Then he passes the token to the knight on his right. If the new possessor of the token has nothing to say, he simply passes the token to the next knight. This continues around the circle until each knight has had a chance to speak. If the remarks of one knight are prefaced by the name of another knight at the table, the two have a one-on-one conversation; all the knights but the two speaking ignore what's being said (they are, of course, being chivalrous). Often, one knight will make a general statement for all to hear, but they will each wait their turn before responding. An empty seat is simply skipped when the token comes around to it. If a knight dies while he holds the token, the others all wait politely for a few moments before scrambling for it as they did in the beginning. And if a new knight arrives, he takes his seat and waits for the token to come around to him.

FDDI (Fiber Distributed Data Interface)

FDDI (or "fuddy") is fiber optic LAN technology. Fiber optic is quite different from other LAN hardware since it uses light pulses along an optical fiber. Its topology and protocol are Token Ring. It's actually a dual ring made up of two rings with the data rotating in opposite directions. One of the rings is called the primary; the other is the secondary. Data normally passes around in the primary direction, but the secondary is always there if light goes out in the primary direction.

There is one station on the ring where the two rings are connected together, called the "dual-attached rooted" station. It has one port to receive from the primary ring and send to the secondary, and another to receive from the secondary and forward to the primary. This dual ring construction is for robustness and enables the LAN to continue to operate even after some degradation in signals. If the secondary ring is better than the primary, the LAN will switch to it.

The Cylindrical Mirror

The "conductor" in FDDI is a thin glass fiber, which works for a couple of reasons. First, glass drawn into a thin fiber this way turns out to be quite flexible, allowing us to build cables and run them around like any other kind of wire. Second, there's a peculiarity with light and glass that causes the light beam to stay in the fiber. Light that strikes the surface of glass (from the inside or outside, the effect is the same) at a very shallow angle does not penetrate the surface of the glass. It reflects. Within the thin FDDI fiber, there is no opportunity for the light to strike the outer surface at a sharp enough angle to make it escape. You can demonstrate this for yourself. Look out of a window. Slowly move your head closer to the surface of the wall next to the window so that the light you observe coming through it is passing at a sharper and sharper angle through the window pane. As you get very close to the surface and the angle becomes very shallow, the glass becomes a mirror and the only light you see is from inside the room. Don't try this at the office. If you're like us, your workmates already think you're strange enough.

The transmitted data is encoded differently than it is in electrical pulsing. The 1s and 0s are sent as changes of state instead of "on" for 1 and "off" for 0 as in most digital transmission. The signals are transmitted by pulsing the light on and off. A one is sent by changing the state, and zero is sent by not changing the state. In other words, if the light is on and stays on, or if it is off and stays off, a 0 bit is being sent. If the light changes from on to off, or from off to on, a 1 bit is being sent. The receiver reads the value of the incoming light at timed intervals (about every 8 nanoseconds or so) and compares the results to the last reading. Any sort of change is a 1 bit.

Firewalls & Security

Once a LAN is connected to the Internet, there's a security problem. The very software that makes things work so well also increases your LAN's vulnerability. There are basically three types of threats to a LAN:

- ❒ Unauthorized access
- ❒ Disclosure of information
- ❒ Denial of service

Unauthorized access is a break-in by a person that has no business inside your system—hacking or cracking, as it is more commonly know. This is often accomplished by someone using an existing account, divining the password through one method or another. If this is as far as it goes, the principal damage can be adverse publicity (if you're a company whose security is an issue to outsiders). For the most part, it is well-known systems that get broken into—large universities, government systems, and military sites are frequent targets.

Disclosure of information is a concern since, in the information age, information is obviously of great value. An intruder can cause considerable damage to a company by gaining access to proprietary information. A single technical paper can represent years of expensive research.

Service can be denied when files are altered in such a way that the normally operating software just doesn't work or does something completely unexpected. Modification of executable programs, as well as the modification or deletion of data, is likely to occur, which can be very expensive to a business that needs to halt operations and recover the status quo.

What is a Firewall?

A firewall is a computer that's connected to a LAN and also has an external connection. The external connection can be a neighboring LAN (or LANs) and/or the Internet. Figure 4-4 shows LANs being protected by a firewall. All communications to the outside world pass through the firewall, and all communications from the outside come in through the firewall.

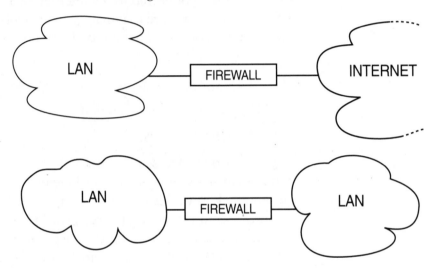

Figure 4-4: Firewalls isolating LANs.

There is no standard configuration or specific list of duties for a firewall. Its abilities and limitations are chosen according to the requirements of the system and the needed level of protection. Usually, one thinks of a firewall as the protection of a LAN from the outside world of the Internet, but protection can also exist from one department to another by having two LANs interlinked by a firewall.

As far as the topology of the connections are concerned, a firewall looks very much like a router. A firewall, however, handles things very differently. The inner workings of a firewall are shown in Figure 4-5. In a router, a datagram is received and forwarded to its recipient by the IP layer of the TCP/IP stack. In a firewall, the IP layer doesn't forward anything. All datagrams are passed on up the stack to the application layer. It's the application layer that makes the decisions about what should go where. This gives the firewall the ability to refuse to forward certain (or all) packets in or out and to make any necessary changes to those that it does pass through.

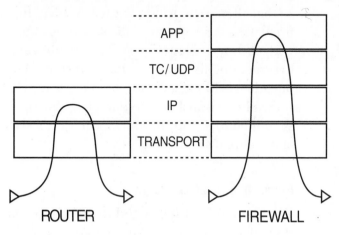

Figure 4-5: Datagrams in a router and in a firewall.

Firewalls are like snowflakes—no two are alike—but there are certain basic services that they have in common. Your basic show-room stock firewall has three applications: sendmail, Telnet, and FTP. We will discuss how each operates in a firewall shortly. There are other applications that can be used in a firewall, but care must be taken so as not to breach the security of the firewall. There was the famous "Internet worm" years ago that caused all sorts of devastation by using a loophole in the finger daemon. This loop-hole has since been plugged and fingerd now appears to be safe. The point is that if one of the simplest networking applications had enough complexity to open a dangerous loophole, it must be true that more complicated applications will certainly have loop-holes somewhere in them. There's danger any time a program or a script can be executed remotely.

Firewall Sendmail

Mail sent from a host on the LAN will pass through the firewall and have the name and address of the sender modified. The name is changed to prevent the actual LAN user names from being broadcast. The LAN address is replaced with that of the firewall, so that all mail returning to the LAN will first be routed to the firewall. Say, for instance, the sender is dabigboss@wedgie. widget.com. The outgoing message will have its name translated to something like grumpy@widget.com. Mail coming in from the outside world will be addressed to grumpy@widget.com, and the firewall will translate it to dabigboss@widgie.widget.com and send it on to the appropriate local host. See Chapter 21 for more about e-mail security.

Firewall Telnet & rlogin

The two services, Telnet and rlogin, allow remote logins to the firewall. The logins can be from the outside world or from another host on the locally protected network.

Login accounts can be set up allowing the outside world direct access to the firewall host. The capabilities of the remote login can be limited to specific actions. One such configuration is to have a special login for a specific application; when a remote user logs in, the application begins execution, and when the application ceases, the user is automatically logged out. This is the sort of thing that's done in a client-server configuration. For example, whenever a remote user logs in, a database access program could start running and act as the only interface available. Common scenarios are for the remote user to communicate with the firewall via Telnet, rlogin and FTP. While the firewall host provides these services to the remote user, it prevents the services from being available from any other computer on the LAN. You might say that the firewall steps into the line of fire and takes the bullet for all the computers on the LAN.

The users on the LAN (those behind the protected firewall) can also use the facilities of the firewall. This way data can be transferred in and out of the LAN in a two-stop hop requiring human intervention from within the LAN. E-mail works the same way. The firewall can act as a mail server. All incoming mail is stopped and the firewall and the e-mail users inside the LAN pick it up from there. Remember that there are an infinite number of ways to configure firewalls and gateways. The only thing consistent is that they are all different.

Any remote login accounts on the firewall should have certain restrictions. For example, on UNIX systems, it's possible to disallow a remote super user login (a super user in UNIX is basically someone with access to the entire network, much like an administrator on a NetWare LAN). There are special restricted shells on UNIX systems to make it simpler to configure this type of login—many of the normal capabilities are simply missing from the shell programs. By preventing users from gaining access to the root levels of the firewall, the shells prevent them from gaining unlimited access to the network.

Firewall FTP

Computers are networked primarily to transfer files. To ensure that files are transferred in relative safety, the firewall can act as an intermediary. Simply set up a directory (or a set of directories) on the firewall to act as an intermediate stop for the files. Users log in via FTP to the firewall to copy files in and out of these directories. There are some things built into FTP to help with security. First, there are login names and passwords (Yes, Virginia, there are FTP sites that reject anonymous logins). There is another little trick. The FTP server will allow certain files and directories to be "hidden." The FTP software will never display these names, so the user must already know the names and request them specifically. It's sort of like a secret passageway in a haunted house. If you know it exists, you can do magic things.

Servers, Proxies & Programs

So far, we've discussed LANs in terms of a group of computers all wired together with one (or more) of them having the responsibility of communicating with the outside world. There is a bit more to it than that. All of these computers need to know each other's addresses so they can send messages to one another. To make this possible, there are hosts on the LAN that are responsible for keeping track of things for all the others. These are called servers.

A server is a host that sits waiting for a request before it takes an action. Its action is usually to return some sort of data to the requester, and there are all kinds of servers serving up all kinds of data. A Domain Name Server (or just "name server"), for instance, serves up addresses of networked computers.

Whenever a host needs to know the address of another host, a broadcast request is sent. This request goes to every host on the local network. If the requested host is on the local LAN, it will answer, "Here I am!" If it's not on the LAN, there will be no answer at all unless there is a name server on the network. If the name server happens to already have the address, it will respond with the information. The name server is normally connected to the outside world, which enables it to send out a query and thus answer address requests for any host on the planet. The request goes higher up the hierarchy until it finds the answer.

Remember that we are dealing with different forms of addresses here. First, there's the form that we humanoids see, which is something like "elephant.animals.com". The human form is the one that goes out in the query. The second form is the IP address, the 32-bit number used by TCP/IP. The third form is the hardware address on the LAN. This is a 48-bit hardware address of the Ethernet, Token Ring, or whatever type of technology is used for the LAN connection. In order to send a datagram to a host on the LAN, we must know the 32-bit form (for TCP/IP) and the 48-bit form (for the LAN), and we keep track of them in host tables that also contain the human form. The name server is responsible for maintaining these tables. If the host being addressed is not on the LAN, then the 48-bit address is that of the network router that takes on the responsibility of passing the datagram to wherever it needs to go.

Who Has the Authority Here?

There are two kinds of addresses listed in a name server's host table. If the network is configured by the system administrator and the addresses are entered into the table by a human, there's no way this address can be changed by incoming messages. This name server is said to be an authority for this address, and so it is "authoritative" for the address in question. If, through regular communications with other name servers, the local name server discovers a new host address, it will tell users who query it. Even though it now knows this new address, the address could have changed and so the newfound host name is considered "non-authoritative." An address considered authoritative will remain the same until a human changes it. A non-authoritative address will "age" and eventually disappear from the table.

A name server can be connected to two or more LANs and resolve the addresses among them. In this case, the server also acts as the router, passing datagrams from one LAN to another. LANs of completely alien technologies can be hooked together this way. All they need is a common connection to get the addresses resolved and a router to communicate from one to the other. An example of a connection between an Ethernet and a Token Ring is shown in Figure 4-6. Since this computer is on two networks, it has a different address on each. This is called "multi-homing," since there's more than one way of addressing the same host.

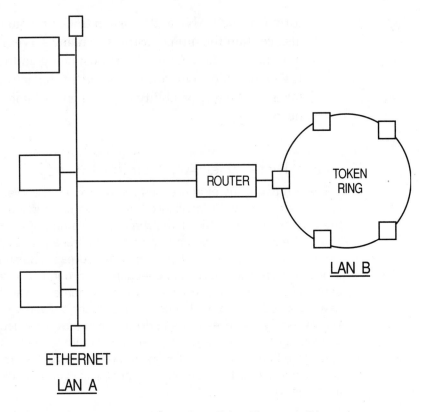

Figure 4-6: Ethernet meet Token Ring; Token Ring meet Ethernet.

Whenever a name server connects LANs together, as in Figure 4-6, it will act as a proxy. A proxy is sort of a computerized liar and busybody. Whenever a host on LAN A requests the address of a host on LAN B, the proxy pipes up and says, "Here I am!" claiming to the host on LAN B. It does this by responding with its LAN A version of the 48-bit LAN hardware address. Whenever the hosts on LAN A sends datagrams to the proxy, the proxy looks at the IP address and determines that it should go to a host on LAN B. The LAN A 48-bit hardware address is replaced in the message with the appropriate LAN B hardware address and the datagram passed on to the intended receiver. The proxy handles the return addresses the same way so that throughout the conversation, neither host knows it's been lied to. This way, two LANs connected through a proxy can act just as if it were one big LAN.

DIRECT INTERNET CONNECTIONS

We're all familiar with dial-up links to the Internet. You dial into a provider using a temporary IP address that allows you to act like a big-shot Internet computer until you hang up the phone. Not all connections are that transient. If you have the need to be permanently connected, or if you have a large volume of data to be transmitted, you should consider a full-time direct Internet connection. It's a bit more work, and the connection cost goes up, but with high-speed, direct access, you can connect to remote computers just as if they were right next to you.

There are several ways to construct high-speed links. The largest (the one with the widest bandwidth) is X.25, which is normally reserved for massive connections where entire databases are being shared. There is also the T1 link, which can be set up to operate at high enough speeds to link together LANs that have a good bit of traffic. A newcomer to this group is ISDN, which is basically a high-speed link designed for an individual.

X.25

X.25 is a digital service provided by telephone companies worldwide. The X.25 standard, and its addressing standard, is a product of the International Telegraph and Telephone Consultative Committee. This technology has been around for several years. It's on the expensive side and is usually reserved for establishing connections that require a lot of data transfer.

Because it is its own complete communications networking system, X.25 has its own addressing scheme along with protocols and routing. It is like TCP/IP in that it has an internal logical protocol stack. The address is a string of fourteen base 10 digits. It's sort of like a telephone number, which isn't surprising coming from the phone company. Probably the most significant difference between an X.25 network and a TCP/IP network is that X.25 communications are based on a virtual connection between the two points (again, that telephone company heritage). Once the connection is established, communications proceed unfettered until the connection is terminated. A connection can be set up and left in place as a permanent virtual circuit, and all the messages will follow the established path. This differs from the framing packets that are the basis of TCP/IP, which can follow different paths even to the point of having different parts of the same message select different paths.

To use X.25 to transmit and receive TCP/IP data, a technique known as *tunneling* is used. Tunneling is simply slipping one protocol inside of another. On the sending end, the IP address and its frame is packaged inside the addressing and protocol of X.25 for transmission and then unpacked back to TCP/IP on the receiving end. X.25 has its own protocol stack, so the tunneling is achieved by placing the IP layer of TCP/IP on top of the X.25 stack. This is effectively stacking a layer 3 protocol on top of another layer 3 protocol. All that is needed is some address translations to go from one to the other, and communications proceed through a great multilayer cake.

T1

The telephone company has developed a standard method of combining 24 voice circuits into a single link. T1 links are digital links that move along at a total rate of 1.5 megabits per second. This is common technology for phone companies. They use it for establishing connections with their service areas. The result is that the phone company is willing and able to connect one of these links between any two locations in their service area—for a fee, of course. This kind of link is often used by companies to create a WAN. It won't carry the heavy load of an X.25 link, but it will do a fine job of connecting up to about 25 users, depending on how heavily they load the system.

All that is required is a method of combining the 24 circuits in such a way that they all work together as one high-speed link. Of course, the 24 lines can be divvied up in various ways. Also, it is not uncommon to combine multiple T1s to construct an even faster link. When they are combined together, each user can get the benefit of the high-speed data rate whenever he or she uses the link.

To make the link into a T1 link, there is a device called a bridge. A bridge has an Ethernet connection on one end and a serial interface on the other. The serial side of the bridge connects to a high speed modem specially designed to communicate over a T1 link. This type of arrangement has become so common that the bridge and the modem are often combined into a single hardware unit. The devices have become quite sophisticated in their ability combine and split T1 links in all sorts of ways.

ISDN (INTEGRATED SERVICES DIGITAL NETWORK)

ISDN is the name of a digital networking service that the telephone industry is beginning to offer to both companies and individuals. Although it isn't universally available, it is available in most major cities in the United States. The service stems from a new technology for transmission over standard telephone lines. Well, most standard phone lines, anyway. The cost of this service is low enough for a home user to consider it, and many Internet providers are willing to connect you up through an ISDN modem. We've seen prices as low as $25 a month quoted, but there is usually some sort of per-minute connection fee along with this. If this technology proves to be viable, the price will almost certainly drop even further.

The technology is very much like the existing phone service. An ISDN connection can carry dial-up voice traffic as well as digital information, so it can be used in place of your existing telephone service. It does require a special modem-like interface with a special type of modulation that will handle the higher speeds.

To find out about the costs, contact your phone company. The costs vary from one community to the next. They are divided up among initial equipment purchase, the phone company installation fee, the monthly base charge, and possibly a per-minute of use charge. You may also want to consider some sort of power backup if you're going to use it for voice. Since you must supply your own power to the phone (as opposed to the regular telephone having the power supplied over the line), the line will be disabled during power failures.

The interface to the connection is such that existing telephone switching equipment and most wiring that's already in place can be used for ISDN. It has been estimated that 90 percent of all existing wiring in North America will not need to be conditioned. All existing equipment (telephones, fax machines, and such) can be connected by using adapters. There are also special modems and other devices designed to communicate over ISDN. These are called terminal adapters and they adapt ISDN to RS-232 and other protocols.

ISDN is a point-to-point digital connection. This is a change from the analog signals currently passed over the telephone service wires. The way it works now is that the analog audio signal is transmitted from your home to the telephone switching office where it is converted to digital signals. ISDN is a digital connection directly from the phone company to your location. The conversion between analog and digital signals is done locally instead of in the phone company switch. The ISDN modem is the device that performs this little trick.

A Basic Rate Interface (BRI) has three channels that communicate over a single link. Two of these are 64k *bearer* channels (the B channels), one is the *delta* channel (the D channel). A Primary Rate Interface (PRI) will have one D channel and either 24 or 30 B channels. The B channels are used in the same sort of ways that Plain Old Telephone Service (POTS) is used now for both data and voice. The D channel can also be used to transmit data. For higher transmission rates, the B channels can be used together.

Just like the existing telephone service, the link can be dedicated (always up and connected) or switched (connected on command). Since TCP/IP already includes a successful Point to Point Protocol with PPP; it is well suited for operation over ISDN. PPP presents a stream of octets to ISDN in the same way that it does with a dial-up modem.

ISDN is certainly not the do-all and end-all of data links, nor does it seem to be the wave of the future. It is what the existing infrastructure can support until a better system is put in place. It was the best that technology could provide to run over the existing wires. No one knows how fast newer and better technology will be devised and installed to replace it, but for right now, it is the best link that a small amount of money can buy. Keep reading to take a look at the future.

THE FUTURE OF HOME DATA COMMUNICATIONS

There are a lot of speculative plans for the future—neighborhood transceivers, fiber at the curb, and new areas of the radio spectrum opening up for cellular data. A lot of this technology still resides with Buck Rogers, but some of it is coming out of the realm of speculation and beginning to appear on the Information Superhighway.

There has been a lot of talk about cable companies using their video wiring to carry data. All cable companies are planning to do this, and some are installing pilot projects. It is already happening commercially in Canada. There is also the Asymmetric Digital Link (ASDL) system that runs over existing copper telephone wires using a little trick of signal modulation that reduces interference and increases the data rate.

Cable Modems

Cable television is wired into millions of homes across the country. This is now a one-way communication link, but the existing structure is proposed to be the basis of the construction of a high-speed, two-way link. The telephone companies are also wired into houses, but they're largely using an open pair of copper wires. As they exist, neither wire is suited to carry high-speed, digital data.

There is a completed and agreed-upon specification to connect households with high-speed data (IEEE specification 802.14, for you engineers in the audience). The equipment already exists that will put it into operation. Once it becomes established, the cable TV companies and/or the telephone companies will be able to provide high-speed Internet access at a low cost. The new telecom legislation from Washington is designed to let this happen by removing the restrictions on competition that existed in the past. The cable company and the phone company are going to meet head on. Will we see convergence . . . or a train wreck? Only time will tell.

A cable modem is a special modem that hooks directly to the cable TV coax cable. It is used very much like your regular telephone modem to send and receive data. What can cable modems be used for? According to the IEEE 802.14 specification, just about anything. Here's a quote from the specs:

> The end users using the service are likely to be either in home or commercial environments, under diverse ownership. In this respect the network differs from a LAN, which is generally under the ownership or control of the same enterprise throughout.
>
> In the home, it is likely that some connections will be to computers for such applications as telecommuting and retrieval of information from service providers, other connections will be to set-top equipment which will interface to users via a TV set, and still others could be telephone for traditional voice services. *No reasonable communication appliance should be precluded by the standard.* [our emphasis]

People are hooking up their coffee pots, hot tubs, and vending machines to the Internet with the links they have now. What next? Will the doors and windows of your house notify you over your cell phone that they have just been opened? Will your dog's empty food dish track you down in cyberspace to alert you that the pooch is hungry?

Speed Kills

If you don't have a high-speed link and can't afford one, we suggest you don't try out anybody else's. Once you see the Web pages snapping into place on the screen and the zippiness of on-demand video and downloading, you'll never want to go back to your "World Wide Wait" at 28.8.

What if all this high-speed access by everybody causes major gridlock on the Infobahn? If everyone were to sign onto the Internet tomorrow, that's exactly what would happen. The growth of the Net has already caused periods of slowness due to the number of modems on the phone lines and jam ups at major routing points. With these new 28.8 higher speed modems, the load will be even heavier. Look for virtual highway shoot-outs and angry traffic snarls as everyone heads for the on ramp.

There are some factors that keep us all from getting fancy wires immediately. Almost all of the existing cable installed for video is not up to the task. It's good enough for analog video signals where boops, beeps, and sparkly spots are sort of expected. Also, the existing equipment along the line (signal boosters and so forth) all have amplifiers and splitters that only work in one direction. And then there's "fan-out." Experiments have shown that the noise injected into the cable can mount up to the point that a returning signal is drowned out. Whenever you watch cable TV, the signal comes to you along one single traceable line from the cable office through amplifiers and splitters. All along this line, little noises, such as motors and electronic devices, are injected into the signal. They usually stay at a low enough level that the picture remains basically undisturbed. However, passing a signal along this same network back to the central hub is a different matter all together. Signals come in from a huge web that's spread out in all directions. Noises from every foot of cable in the entire system add up to completely overwhelm any of the signals coming in.

The only solution cable companies have come up with is to completely rewire the system with better insulated cable and two-way amplifiers. The telephone company needs to rewire with the same kind of technology. And, they're both doing just that as you read this. One of the largest cable companies, Time-Warner, has set a goal to be completely rewired by the year 2000. The regional Bells across the country are running Hybrid Fiber/Coax (HFC) or Fiber To The Curb (FTTC).

When will this happen? That depends on where you are. Right now, it looks as if it will be almost universally available by 2000. As we write this, the phone company is laying fiber cabling just a few blocks away. Sales of hundreds of thousands of cable modems have been signed and the assembly lines are buzzin'. So, get ready to have to be at home between the hours of 8:00 AM and 2:00 PM for the cable guy to show up at 2:20 to install your new box.

ASDL (Asymmetric Digital Link)

ASDL is high-speed data transmission over existing copper-based wiring now used for POTS (Plain Old Telephone Service). This is new technology (the second generation is supposed to hit the streets sometime during 1996).

There can be problems when attempting to cram high data rates through copper wiring. The unshielded pair of copper wires is simply lying in wait for any kind of noise that comes along. This causes the signal to degrade rapidly, even under ideal circumstances; and there are almost no ideal circumstances. Because of this degradation, ASDL is limited to being a short-distance service. Exactly how short varies according to the surrounding environment and the condition of the wiring. The length, 3.5 kilometers, is bandied about a lot, and 5.5 kilometers appears to be some sort of maximum.

It is asymmetric in that data goes much faster in one direction than in another. The first generation transmits 8.192 mbps downstream (from the connection point to the house) and 640 kbps upstream (from the house to the connection point). This is not as silly as it may seem at first. At the client end (that's your house and mine), a lot of data is normally received while very little is sent. This isn't a universal absolute, but it fits most of the time. A television signal is 100 percent downstream traffic; there is no upstream data at all. A regular telephone conversion is symmetric (same data rate in both directions), but the data rate is very low and the upstream speed of ASDL will handle it nicely. A Web browser receives large quantities of data for graphical display after sending out only a tiny little URL, so it's virtually all downstream. None of the regular Internet utilities (such as e-mail, FTP, and Telnet) normally transmit great gobs of data upstream. There are occasions when they do, but these are fairly rare.

Let's talk about bandwidth and modulation for a moment. To facilitate different types of service, the available ASDL spectrum is divided according to the needs of each type of service. The voice transmissions are kept at the lowest end of the band, the bottom 4 kHz. Optionally, instead of POTS at the bottom of the spectrum, it is possible to put ISDN (which can quite easily be tunneled right through ASDL) in at the bottom, in which case it would take everything up to about 50 kHz. This could carry a basic rate ISDN that is capable of carrying two voice channels and one low-speed data channel. Most of the bandwidth (from about 50 kHz to the maximum of 1 mHz) is used for downstream digital traffic. Typically, the available spectrum of the connection is divided into 256 sub-channels of 4 kHz each and allocates power to each of these depending on the noise and loss found in each.

One advantage this system has over the existing system for the transmission of video is the simple fact that you don't need to receive all the video at once. The cable TV company sends every channel to every TV set every minute of the day and night. There is no need to send something that is not being received. The tuner can be at the upstream end of the digital link, and only the requested channel (or channels) need to be transmitted.

Astute readers must now be saying, "Wait, if this ASDL stuff works, and it works over the wires I have now, why don't I have it?" First, it's still quite new, and anything new takes a while to percolate. Second, the market pressures just haven't been there. Third, a lot of people don't seem to know about it as an option.

Actually, this technology could spring up at any moment. With the opening up of competition and the rapid expansion of the Internet, ASDL could be used like the pony express was used to connect the two ends of the unfinished intercontinental railroad. Fiber trunks could be laid to central neighborhood junction points and ASDL equipment could be installed there for local distribution. Then, as time marches on, the ASDL could be slowly replaced by fiber (since fiber is really, really fast, and is just as fast in one direction as the other).

MOVING ON

If you've followed along in this chapter like a good little power user, you just got a basic education on current and near future high-end connectivity options. As more businesses, and even households, connect their multiple computers into local networks connected to remote networks, knowing what your options are becomes increasingly important. Also, learning now about the next generation of data delivery options (such as cable modems) will give you a leg up as these technologies are rolled out and everyone else is scratching their heads trying to figure out what they're all about.

In the next chapter, we'll complete our section on expanding connectivity by covering mobile computing. Laptop and hand-held computers are allowing us to move beyond what's been called "the tyranny of the desktop." Lots of people now work as they travel; on planes, in cars, and in hotel rooms. "Road warrior" is the term given to the new breed of wired business traveler. Let's take a peek at some of the concerns of computing on the road.

## Chapter 5

Leaving the Desktop

This chapter is going to be disconnected and wander around a lot. No, we haven't lost our train of thought or been nipping the sauce on the job again; it's *supposed* to be that way! This chapter is about leaving the desktop and taking the Internet with you out into world. Since the Internet covers much of the planet at this point, it's possible to plug in to it from just about anywhere. The Internet's not the problem. It's always there, buzzing away 24 hours a day, 7 days a week. The problem is staying connected to the global information matrix as you move around.

There are different degrees of mobile . . . ah . . . disconnectedness. The most extreme case is one in which you take a trip and want to connect to the Net from the other side of the world, or the country, or the state. Then there's the problem of wanting to make a wireless connection from across town or within the same building. There are a number of solutions that address the many levels of connectivity problems.

Mobile and wireless connectivity is one the fastest growing areas of digital technology in the world right now. The traveling salesman of old is fast becoming today's road warriors—people who carry their office around with them on planes, in their cars, and in remote hotels and office buildings. The commercial potential of this virtual office trend has generated lots of really neat (and some totally useless) gadgets that allow one to process and communicate all types of data from a distance. This is an area of almost completely new technology, with anything a year or two year old already obsolete. Did you know, for instance, that there's a replacement technology for the cellular phones we're all just now getting?

This chapter includes a brief survey of technologies currently available, some that are just emerging, and others that are expected in the near future. Given the fickle nature of digital technologies, we won't bother making any predictions about how the world of mobile and wireless computing is going to turn out.

THE PORTABLE PROVIDER

All Internet providers are not equal. They may provide you with local access, but they won't necessarily provide access when you travel. A local phone number is known as a Point of Presence (POP). Large providers have POPs in several major cities. A good provider will supply you with an 800 number that you can use to connect when you travel. However, there's always a fee for the 800 number (usually at, or slightly above, the provider's cost).

There are national Internet service providers, too—large services with local phone numbers in several cities. Normally, they all have a monthly fee and charge by the minute. The largest is America Online. There is one national provider, Netcom, that charges a low flat rate and offers unlimited monthly access. They can be found at http://www.netcom.com. Netcom is not in every city in the United States, but they are in all the larger ones, and they are expanding constantly. A newer national provider is Netcenter (http://www.netcenter.com). Netcenter has a flat rate for local access and an hourly rate for a traveling account. Of course, with the deregulation of telecommunications, the telephone companies are getting into the act and will soon be wiring every square inch of the United States for Net access.

One solution to the current situation is to have a local flat-rate provider as your basic service and use one of the pay-by-the-minute subscriptions services for travel. CompuServe, America Online, and Prodigy have phone numbers in most major regions of the United States. You will simply need to figure out how much time you're going to be spending online while traveling and compare that against the costs and convenience of having multiple services or, possibly, going exclusively with a national service.

For international travelers, there are a number of providers that offer worldwide Internet service. Table 5-1 lists several of them and their Web sites.

International ISPs	Internet Address
CompuServe	http://www.compuserve.com/
EUNet (Europe Only)	https://traveller.eu.net/
GeoAccess Network	http:// globalexpo.com/geoaccess/ grasp2.html
IBM Global Network	http://www01.ny.us.ibm.net/ phoneint.html
Sprint's Global One	http://www.si.net/

Table 5-1: International Internet services.

CONNECTING FROM THE ROAD

What follows is a short primer on how to connect your modem while you're on the road. Whether you're a business person that needs that vital link to the Net and the home office while you travel, or a globe-trotting vacationer who wants to stay connected to your e-mail and newsgroups from different ports of call, this section should prove useful to you.

Hotel Phone Systems

When you make a hotel reservation, and you're going to need data communications, the first thing to do is ask what sort of provision they make for connecting from your hotel room. Many hotels now cater to wired travelers, making it easy and safe to plug in and go to work. If they don't, the easiest thing to do may be to find another hotel. After reading this section, however, you'll have many other options available to you.

There is more to this hotel and pay phone thing than just variations in how the connections are made. Some of the phone systems have modulation methods that are totally alien to your modem. Telephone systems are designed to carry audible sounds. Modems are designed to convert the digital data from the computer into analog, and, on the other end of the line, convert the analog back into digital data. That is, they modulate on the sending end and demodulate on the receiving end. (Remember, that's where "MoDem" comes from.) Other than providing audio of a certain minimal quality, there are no basic requirements for how a telephone system should operate internally in order to connect your modem to it. The bottom line is there are many variations on the theme of connecting a modem to a phone line. Knowing how to determine what type of line you have is the first step to overcoming any incompatibility problems.

TIP

You need to be very careful when connecting a modem to an unknown hotel (or other) phone system. Modems are manufactured to connect to the traditional analog lines. Most phone systems being installed in hotels (and offices) today are digital. You can't tell which is which by looking at the plug. Plugging a modem into a digital connection can destroy the circuitry in your modem. Even worse, if you're using a laptop with an internal modem, you can fry the internal circuitry as well. We know; we saw it happen recently. A friend came to town on a book tour, checked himself into the Ritz-Carlton, went to plug in his modem and zappo—his Hayes was history. See below for information on safe connection options for digital phone systems.

If you travel a lot and need to telecommute from your hotel room frequently, you need to know what type of phone system your hotel uses and if they have facilities (called data ports) that allow you to easily jack in from your room. Data ports are little phone jack boxes that look similar to a conventional phone jack.

They are usually marked with "Data Port," "Modem Port," or some other identifier. Many hotels and businesses now use digital public branch exchanges (PBXs) that are *not* modem-friendly. There are hotels that recognize this problem, and more and more are starting to make it very easy to safely connect to their phone system. The vast majority, however, are not doing anything yet. If you do a lot of traveling, especially internationally, you'll need to familiarize yourself with the various ways you can connect to hotel, office, and pay phone systems. Luckily, there are devices and tricks that can help overcome almost any connection obstacle.

Travel Tips for Budding Road Warriors

Before we get into some specifics, let's take a look at some general tips for connecting from the road:

- ❏ Plan your trip. This might seem obvious, but when traveling with a modem and a laptop (or PDA), you have a lot of considerations (type of connectivity, power supply, and Net access points, to name a few). The more you plan for contingencies, the fewer surprises you'll be faced with.

- ❏ Always call your hotels, businesses, and any other place where you plan to use your modem to find out what type of phone systems they have and what provisions they make for modem connectivity.

- ❏ Make sure you have all of the phone numbers you'll need for international access, tech support, and back-up plans if your preferred provider doesn't work out.

- ❏ Make backup copies of all essential modem files, such as software and address books. If you can't afford to lose it, be overly generous with the backups.

- ❏ Know the code . . . no, not *that* code. Know your Hayes modem commands. You may be in situations where you'll need to blind dial (to overcome a foreign dial tone), manual dial, switch to pulse dial, and set up the modem software up to accept long number strings, to name a few.

137

❐ Practice your connections at home. Learn how to use the various connection tools (plug adapters, acoustic couplers, phone clips) and connection methods. If you can't get everything to work in your own neighborhood, it's not going to get any better halfway around the world.

❐ Before you spend hours of frustration trying to connect your modem, make sure you have the right number and that there's a modem tone on the other end of it. To check, manually dial with the regular phone and listen for the tone. This is the road warrior's equivalent to making sure the device is plugged in. (Oh yeah . . . don't forget that too.)

❐ Use an international phone credit card to avoid sometimes exorbitant hotel and international surcharges on calls.

❐ If getting through is really important to you, make sure you have high-quality equipment on your end. International phone connections can vary greatly in quality. You may need all the help you can get if, say, you're trying to connect using an acoustic coupler on a Czech pay phone.

❐ Don't forget power considerations. You may need a power adapter. Don't forget to bring as much battery power as you can carry and a recharger. And check to make sure that your recharger works under the power conditions you'll be faced with. If you do need power conversion, extension cords, or surge suppressors, it's best to get them in the country you're connecting from, rather than buying them in the United States. Of course, this can get too expensive if you do a lot of country hopping.

❐ Always travel with your handy dandy connectivity kit (see below).

❐ Finally, read, read, *read* (no, not just this book). Lots of people travel with their computers, and they write to newsgroups, magazine columnists, and just about any other knowledgeable source for help with problems. Scour newsgroups, personal websites and the online back issues of computer publications for help. You'll be amazed at how much information you can glean from another person's tale of woe regarding their attempt to telecommute while on their honeymoon in Bali—although it's hard to feel sorry for someone in that predicament.

Gareth & Sean's Handy Power User's Travel Kit

If you're going to be using a modem on the road, and under different circumstances each time, you'll need a connectivity kit that contains the tools and hardware that can address different phone types. What follows is a basic kit that should cover most situations. You don't necessarily need to carry all this stuff. Do your research beforehand and carry only the tools and equipment you'll need for the country you're traveling to.

❐ A simple set of tools, including a small flashlight (with extra batteries), several small sizes of both Phillips and flathead (slotted) screw drivers, and a small pair of wire cutters/pliers. You can get inexpensive computer toolkits that come in a zipper case for under $20. You can remove the tools you won't need on the road (like chip inserters and extractors) and replace them with stuff you do need, like the flashlight and a phone line tester.

❐ An assortment of RJ11 adapters, extenders, and couplers. RJ11 is the standard type of phone plug used in the United States and 50 percent of the rest of the world (see Figure 5-1).

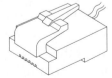

Figure 5-1: A standard RJ11 phone plug.

❐ If you're going to be traveling to Europe or elsewhere abroad, you'll need a set of adapters to connect the RJ11 plug from the phone cable coming out of your modem to the wall jack. Radio Shack sells a set of three adapters for Britain, Germany, and France. TeleAdapt (http://www.teleadapt.com) sells 40 different foreign phone adapters.

❐ A phone line tester. This is a small device that either plugs into the phone jack or clips onto the phone wires inside the junction box and tells you if the jack is wired correctly or if the polarity of the clips is correct. They usually have little lights on them that indicate a correct connection (green), reverse polarity (red) or non-operational (no light). The one that Radio Shack sells (for around $6) is meant to be plugged into an existing outlet and cannot be used if you need to bypass a foreign plug or a hardwired phone. You can hack this little device and attach alligator clips so that you can clip it directly onto the wires inside the junction box. TeleAdapt sells a set of clips with a female RJ11 adapter on the other end that can accept a line tester. They're a bit pricey at $15. You can easily make one for about half that.

❐ A small coil of RJ11 phone cable with male RJ11 plugs on both ends (for normal connections). Make sure you have a decent length of cable. The location of the phone jack may be far away from where you're working. You know the common setup in a hotel room: the phone is on the nightstand between the two beds and the desk is way over in the corner of the room.

❐ A small spool of RJ11 phone cable with a male RJ11 plug on one end and two alligator clips on the other. You can easily make this yourself by screwing two alligator clips to the red and green wires of the phone cable. Alternately, you can make a simple clip adapter by attaching the alligator clips onto a short length of phone cable with a female RJ11 adapter on the other end. This way, your clip adapter can do double duty—use it as an adapter for the line tester and for directly connecting to a hardwired junction box.

TIP

Make sure you get large alligator clips (not microclips). Different phone junction boxes have different-sized screws and different wiring schemes. You need a big jaw on your clip so you can get a good, solid connection.

❐ An extension cord and a three-prong to two-prong adapter. Sometimes the power outlets are not conveniently accessible.

❐ You may also need a power converter and surge suppressor. Some laptops' power supplies can now negotiate different types of power. If yours can't, you'll need an AC foreign power converter/adapter. TeleAdapt also sells a set of power plug adapters that will adapt from three-prong U.S. to the socket of whatever country your trying to get juice from.

❐ There are a number of different connection methods available to you even if you can't plug your modem directly into a wall jack. One option is a modem doubler (Figure 5-2). It's available from a company called Road Warrior Outpost (http://warrior.com/). It turns out that even though the internal structure of phones and the wall jacks vary all over the map, the handsets (that's the phone company word for that thing you pick up and stick in your ear) are mostly the same. You simply unplug the handset from the phone and plug this little doo-dad in. You then connect your modem to the doubler and you're off and running.

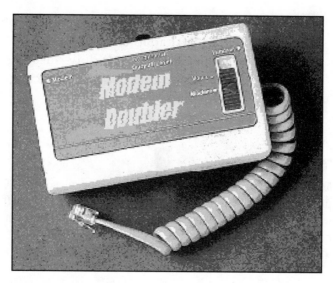

Figure 5-2: The modem doubler.

❐ A modem doubler only works if the handset is not hardwired into the phone. There are some phone systems that just won't be bothered by having a standard handset jack, or any other type of standard tomfoolery. Well, technology never sleeps. Figure 5-3 shows an acoustic coupler that will work with probably every phone on the planet. That's right, an acoustic coupler, just like the old days. The first modems were acoustic couplers that topped out a screaming 300 baud. This new device will allow for data rates of up to 28.8K baud (your speed will vary according to phone line conditions). Since this device is audio based, it will perform just as well internationally as it does domestically.

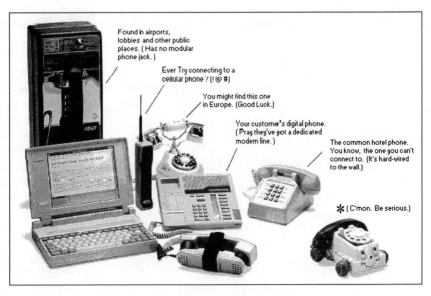

Figure 5-3: TeleAdapt's versatile TeleFast acoustic coupler sells for $150. (Photograph ©1996 TeleAdapt, Inc. Used with permission.)

Troubleshooting

There are a lot of things that can go wrong on the road, but most of the problems are common and easily overcome. Table 5-2 outlines a number of common connectivity snarls and their solutions:

Problem	Likely Solution
Digital phone system	If the hotel or office has a digital Public Branch Exchange (PBX), don't plug in your modem directly! You'll need an acoustic coupler or a special digital switch you can get at stores catering to mobile computing. IBM sells a Modem Saver that can test for a digital phone line (or you can just ask the hotel!). Some hotels have special wall jacks called data ports.

Problem	Likely Solution
Foreign phone jack.	Use a special adapter, an acoustic coupler, or phone clips at the junction box.
The phone is hardwired to the wall, but the handset has a standard RJ11 jack.	Use a modem doubler, an acoustic coupler, or try using phone clips to connect to the wires inside the phone's mouthpiece (if you can do this without damaging the wires).
The phone is hardwired to the wall and to the handset.	Use an acoustic coupler or remove the junction box with one of your screw drivers. Find the two hot wires with a phone tester and then use phone clips to connect your modem phone cable. Be careful not to touch the wires and connectors. You can get shocked.
Pulse-only dial tone.	Select the Pulse switch on your modem (if it has one) or enter a "P" before your Hayes dialing sequence in your terminal program.
Foreign dial tone.	Select the blind dialing option in your modem program (if it offers one) or insert "X1" before the "D" in your Hayes dialing sequence.
You're in a country that uses tax impulsing, a high frequency signal that's used to meter local phone usage. Austria, Germany, Spain, and parts of Eastern Europe have this.	You'll need a special line filter. TeleAdapt sells one (the TeleFilter) for $60.
If you're in the United Kingdom or Hong Kong, you need to adjust your "pulse ratio" or your connection won't work.	Enter the following Hayes modem command: AT&P1&W in your modem program's terminal window. To return it to U.S. pulsing, switch the "P1" with "P0"

Problem	Likely Solution
You hear a strange sizzling sound as smoke rises from your modem.	Retire to the backyard of the hotel and conduct a short and sweet funeral for your modem. It's history. Consider passing the collection plate among the congregation to pay for a new modem, since you've probably jacked into a digital PBX. Just pray that you didn't damage your computer. (Return to troubleshooting tip #1.)

Table 5-2: Mobile office connection troubleshooting.

Road Warrior Resources

There are a number of useful online publications and Web sites for wired travelers. TechnoTravel's Web site (http://www.dk-online.dk/users/anders_a/) has lots of travel tips, hotel phone hacking info, a Cyber Cafe guide, and links to International ISPs and other travel-related resources. TeleAdapt has a series of Web pages offering advice and information on different countries' phone services and how you should prepare to deal with them. The table of contents is located at http://www.teleadapt.com/regions/regions (see Figure 5-4). Mobile Office and mobilis are two online publications dealing with all aspects of wireless and mobile computing. They can be reached at http://www. mobileoffice.com and http:// www.volksware.com/mobilis/, respectively.

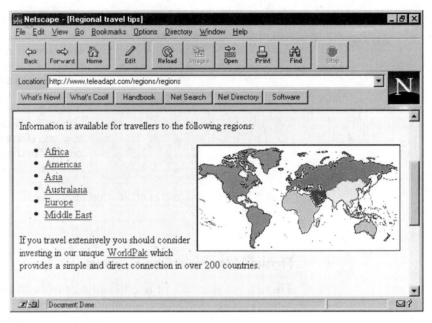

Figure 5-4: TeleAdapt's Regional travel tips page.

Free Swanky Office Space!

Those of you who conduct business from a laptop and a briefcase are often faced with the problem of where to hold that all-important meeting or where to set up shop so that people can drop by without having to go to your hotel room. Increasingly, the answer is hotel lobbies and lounges. Many hotels have caught on to this and have embraced it as a way of getting more food and beverage business. Some have even gone so far as to install data ports and offer laptops and cell phones for rent. You don't even need to be staying at that particular hotel. You can check into the fleabag motor lodge down the street and set up your virtual office at some plush five-star up the street. Of course, you'll have to pay the higher food and beverage prices while you're there, but it's probably worth the impression you'll make holding court in such high-toned surroundings. And, you can make the bellhop carry your laptop!

THE INFORMATION SUPERSKYWAY

One can think of the Internet as a giant webwork of computers, cables, and optic fibers blanketing the globe. But there's more to it than that. It also permeates the atmosphere, via cellular modems and satellite transmitters. There is an entire parallel industry (to desktop computers) that handles the equipment and services related to mobile connectivity. And what is the principal product of this industry? Acronyms. Every new idea that comes along seems to need its own acronym. There's one exception: cellular. It's an honest-to-goodness, full-blown English word!

Cellular

Cellular telephones have become so popular that they're starting to become a traffic hazard. It used to be that a driver had to take care to watch out for the few cell phone users who might be distracted by in-car calls. Now, everybody's yakking as they drive (in Brazil, for instance, the problem is so persistent that they have gone so far as to outlaw use of a cellular phone while driving). A recent study conducted at the State University of New York found that there was a 34 percent greater chance of having an accident while driving and talking on the phone. If you're doing something else as well (such as tuning the radio or eating a ham sandwich) that number rises even higher. So be careful out there!

The principal of the cellular phone is quite simple. It works just like the cordless telephone you probably have at home. The handpiece has a small transceiver that's capable of communicating with the nearest telephone company transceiver. You've seen the cellular towers with the triangular tops as shown in Figure 5-5. The triangle at the top is an array of antennas. The receiving antennas stick up above the triangle, and the transmitting antennas are below. (You can't hook the receiver to the same antenna as the transmitter. Receivers are very sensitive about that.) From one place to another, you will see slightly different antenna configurations. This is for what's called "pattern shaping." The area covered by one cellular station needs to fit snugly up against the area covered by its neighbor antenna array. The surrounding terrain can vary the signal strength in any given direction, so it's necessary to do some shaping so the cells all fit together.

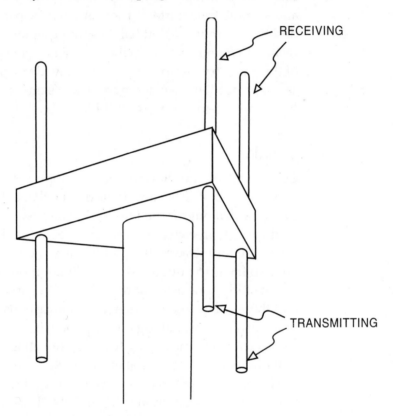

Figure 5-5: A cellular antenna.

A cellular phone is one smart cookie. Whenever you light one up, it scans around to find the strongest signal available and latches onto it. It will use that signal for its communication, but it is not married to it. In fact, it's quite fickle. If the signal starts to fade, it will switch to another to continue communications. The switched-to signal could be on the same cellular station or on an adjacent station. By switching signals, the phone will continuously stay connected to a nice strong signal as you travel along. (Well, underpasses are an exception to this.) This channel switching is called a *hand-off*. Whenever a signal is handed off, the land-based system must keep track of it. All this signal tracking is maintained by using the ESN and MIN. (Oops, acronyms.) The ESN (Electronic Serial Number) uniquely identifies the phone; it's like the phone's fingerprint. The MIN (Mobile Identification Number) is what you and I would call the phone number. These numbers (and some station ID numbers) are used by the cellular system to track the connection and keep it alive. The audio portion of the communication is frequency modulated (FM). Frequency modulation is what keeps the communications quality high.

Like all new technologies, there is no accepted universal standard. The cellular phones in the U.S. will not work in any other country in the world. Some countries use the same standard, but even then they have a tendency to use it in a different part of the spectrum. Each country seems to have its own set of frequencies with different bandwidths and channel spacing. They basically don't talk to each other. If you plan to travel to another country, you might as well leave you cellular phone at home.

There is one thing to remember about cellular hand-off. Under normal circumstances, it's not a problem. It is completely inaudible in a phone conversation. The same is *not* true of data. Hand-off is quite noticeable to a modem. The higher the speed of the modem, the more noticeable it becomes. Of course, you only have this problem if you're moving while you're telecommunicating, since sitting still would rarely cause a hand-off. And, if you're using your cellular modem to answer your e-mail while you're tooling down the highway, you need to stop and smell the roses! Your life has become far too hectic.

If you'd like another argument against using your cellular phone while you're in transit, consider this. For a reasonable sum, a less-than-honest person can purchase a *sniffer*, a device designed to intercept cellular transmissions and extract the ESN and MIN.

Then, using a special device to create a set of control chips for a "blank" or unassigned phone, this person can fool the phone system into thinking that the "blank" phone is, in fact, registered with the system. Badabing badaboom—instant free cellular time, courtesy of the sniffed account! Your best protection? Stay in one place when you use your cellular phone, whether for data or voice calls. And make that place a private one, if possible.

Personal Communications Services (PCS)

In 1993, the Federal Communications Commission authorized the use of the frequencies from 1850 to 2200 MHz for what was termed "emerging technologies in personal communication." The commission later specified the lower part of this block, 1850 to 1990 MHz, to be used solely for PCS. They then placed some usage restrictions on the band, and auctioned it off in pieces. One chunk of the band, 1910 to 1930 MHz, was not auctioned off. It was allocated for low-power, unlicensed PCS usage. The unlicensed portion of the band is to be used for the wireless local area networks (WLAN). This range of frequencies can also be used for very short distance communications using transmitters that have a maximum output power of 3 milliwatts. This is meant to operate in a range of 50 feet or less.

There is a variety of things that can be done with these PCS frequencies. One characteristic that all the PCS frequencies have in common is that they operate over short distances. The lower end of the band (the part that was auctioned off) is going to be used as a micro-cellular service. It will operate on the same concept as the existing cellular telephone system, but with some basic differences. One antenna will service a single office complex, or a single street intersection, or a single building. It will be a good deal cheaper to use than the existing cellular (macro-cellular?) system because it will be so much cheaper to install and maintain.

Will Your Refrigerator One Day Have an IP Address?

Conceivably, short distance wireless service can be used to disconnect the printer, mouse, and keyboard from the wires on your desk. The printer can then be connected via Internet Protocol to your desktop computer. This means that the printer will have its own IP address—so will the mouse, and keyboard, and anything else you want to "connect" to your computer.

This has two implications. First, an IP address of four octets is not going to work. We will need to start using the longer IP addresses. In fact, the system is already set up and will be in use some time in the near future. Second, since everything will be connected and have its own IP address, every object will be addressable. A keyboard in Sri Lanka could directly address a printer in Memphis. The advantage of this is not totally obvious now, but somebody will come up with a brilliant application soon, and we'll all say, "Hey, why didn't I think of that?" But sheesh, can you imagine the headache for your sysadmin? "Hey Bob, I'm trying to print to the HP in Pago-Pago, and it's giving me a 'paper-out' error. What should I do?"

Because of a history of anarchy in the area of cell phone standards, an attempt is now being made to have an international standard for PCS. The Telecommunications Industry Association (TIA) and the Alliance for Telecommunications Industry Solutions (ATIS) have formed the Joint Technical Committee (JTC). The JTC was formed to constantly review and coordinate the PCS developing technology and bring the world to one set of standards. Do you think this is going to work? Neither do we, but it's certainly worth a try and the world will be a better place if such a standard did exist. If it does work, you'll be able to yak on your cell phone in Paris, Texas and Paris, France; Moscow, Idaho and Moscow, Russia; Lima, Ohio and . . . well, you get the idea.

Billions have been spent on PCS already. The FCC auctioned off the frequencies for $7 billion just for starters. There are also projects going on in several countries around the world. To make PCS generally available, billions more will have to be spent to build the transceiver stations. PCS has several advantages over cellular. One is that the signal is more consistent and it's interference-free. Another is the (eventual) lower cost. If the standards thing works, it will become the hands-down favorite. (Oops, there we go predicting again.)

Some Mobile Connectivity Options

Here is a sampling of some of the types of hardware available for mobile computer communications. Keep in mind that this is only a representative sample of the products that are out there, or will be soon.

Wireless Modems

Wireless modems were originally designed to be used in automobiles. There have been quite a few changes since those first designs. The newer modems are operating at speeds up to 19.2K, which is almost as fast as the fastest wired modems. Figure 5-6 is a picture of a Motorola wireless modem that plugs into a type II card slot on a laptop computer. This amazing little device will even receive e-mail, just lying there on the table, not even connected to your computer. You can have something else plugged into the computer slot and not miss an incoming message (it has a light on it that indicates when e-mail arrives).

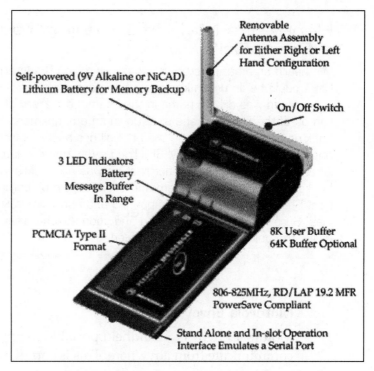

Figure 5-6: A Motorola wireless modem.

There's an interesting twist on the wireless modem from Xircom—their CreditCard Ethernet+Modem. This is a two-in-one, credit card size add-in. It is a 28.8 kbps modem, an ethernet adapter, and a fax modem. Without any change in hardware, the computer can be connected directly into a LAN or be connected to a telephone line for a dial-up connection.

Honey, It's Me. I'm E-mailing You From a Snow Drift.

We heard an amazing story this past winter on the Internet. It sounds like it could be an urban legend, but it is entirely plausible.

A woman was driving home in the infamous blizzard of '96. Her car ran off of the road and she slide down an embankment. Unable to get back up to the highway, she tried to call her husband from her cell phone. The phone was busy. She tried a few minutes later. Still busy. After a while, it dawned on her that he was probably online. She hooked up her cellular modem and used her laptop computer to e-mail him. She told him what had happened and approximately where she was. Sure enough, he was online and soon saw her message. He called the police and she was rescued.

Motorola Envoy

Motorola Envoy is a handheld portable computer system that can communicate from anywhere. This is sort of the next step in the sequence from pager to cellular phone. It is primarily a communications device instead of a computer, but it does its communications with fax, e-mail, and file transfer.

Envoy is completely wireless. It has a built-in wireless modem that is effectively connected whenever you turn it on. There is no dialing—you just start, send, and receive. Of course, there's no Web browser or anything . . . yet. You have the option of connecting it to a modem for dial-up connections. It can also be connected directly to a PC for transferring files.

Wireless LANs

There are several companies producing wireless LANs. Among them are AT&T, Proxim, Xircom, and Solectek. A wireless LAN is set up with a number of wireless access points installed around the building. The computers are all equipped with adapter cards and antennas. Any other device that wants to communicate over the LAN (printer, laptop, or whatever) is also equipped with a card and an antenna. There are even building-to-building connections that can be established with directional antennas.

The transmission method most often used is called "spread spectrum frequency hopping packet radio." There doesn't seem to be an acronym for this name, but they sure missed a good opportunity. Let's see, that would be: SSFreHoPRad. Wireless LANs operate in the 902 to 928 MHz range and up in the 2.4 gHz range. (In the 2.4 gHz range, microwave ovens can interfere.) Even considering the cost of running the cables, a wireless LAN costs several times as much as a wired LAN. It now looks like the wireless LANs will be used in special places where it's impractical or impossible to run cables.

The TAL Wireless Router

A company called TAL (Tetherless Access Limited) has developed, and is producing, a device they call the SubSpace 2001 Wireless Router. This is a wireless router to be used in a wireless LAN. It provides full TCP/IP routing at data rates averaging 64 kbps over distances of up to 19 miles. (At that distance, it would be something of a WAN instead of a LAN.) It is a full-blown router that can be "multihomed" (that is, act as a server to several LANs simultaneously). It also has a 10BASET ethernet interface. TAL can be contacted at http://www.tetherless.net.

The transmitters and receivers for this technology use part of the spectrum that doesn't require licensing in the United States; and in countries where licensing is required, it is normally quite simple. It presently operates in both the L-band and S-band. The L-band system operates in the 902 to 928 MHz frequency range and has five channels. The S-band system operates in the 2400 to 2483.5 MHz range and has 15 channels.

Richochet

The Richochet system has been designed as a group of repeaters to be mounted on top of light poles along a city street. This would effectively create a meshlike web of interconnected nodes. Each node communicates with its adjacent nodes and with any device equipped with a special transceiver modem.

Richochet's hardware topology fits perfectly with Internet topology. Any single message block is broken up, and the parts follow different paths to their destination. Any point on the network can fail and not have a negative effect on any other part of the network. The topology is also similar to that of a cellular network. The hand-off is too slow for continuous data communications while in motion, but any particular computer would be quite portable connected with this method.

Richochet is a product of Microcom, which can be reached at http://www.microcom.com. The company will be deploying the pole-top networking transmitters and then selling monthly subscriptions. Once this system becomes widespread, it will be another option for the road warrior.

Access Point & Netwave

Xircom has a matched pair of products that will allow you to move around the building connected to a network even though you've disconnected your laptop from the network connection. You just connect the Netwave Access Point where your laptop is connected, and pop the CreditCard Netwave into your laptop. You can then roam the building at will.

My, What a Nice Computer You're Wearing.

As we move farther and farther away from the desktop, we begin to wonder how far we will go. One likely direction is toward the wearable computer. Imagine monitors as eyeglasses, computers as back and hip packs, and input devices on your finger tips. These, or some variation on them, are sure to be in our near future. But imagine going further still.

In a 1993 article in *Mondo 2000*, sci-fi writer and cyber-pundit Bruce Sterling posited the "Computer as Furoshiki." Furoshiki is a Japanese word for a piece of decorative fabric that's used "as a grocery bag, a book tote, and a decorative wrapper for ceremonial gifts." Sterling's futuristic version is a weave of optical fibers interwoven with other as-yet-developed "smart materials." These various fibers would hold power and memory while serving as an antenna and a display. One portion of the "fabric" computer might even stiffen to become a speaker diaphragm. One can take off from this point and imagine full suits of clothes made from this computer-capable clothing. The woven, color-emitting fiber optics could create video-like images across its surface. Imagine being able to change the styles and colors of your clothing by broadcasting images along their outer surface. Your clothing could respond to voice commands, touch, and gesture. And, of course, the communications grid threaded throughout your zoot suit would allow you to log *into* the Internet in an entirely new way. This might be pure fantasy . . . but maybe not. Just remember, in 1949, *Popular Mechanics* predicted that "computers in the future may weigh no more than 1.5 tons."

MOVING ON

Now that we've looked at modems, delved into the inner workings of TCP/IP, and offered some solutions for staying connected to the Net when you just can't stay in your seat any longer, it's time to look into Net tools (which, after all, is the reason you bought this book).

Our Windows friends are invited to join us in Part II as we start with a basic primer on getting connected with Windows 95 and move on to examining some tools and techniques for serious Netheads. Our Mac pals should tiptoe around Part II (don't want to disturb the classes there) and join us in Part III where we give that smiley Mac machine the same treatment. UNIX purists are invited to turn their noses up at these two platforms with all the pretty pictures and menus, and get command line with us in Part IV.

## Part II

Windows Power User's Tools

## Chapter 6

Getting Connected With TCP/IP in Windows

Chances are, if you're reading this book, you're already on the Internet using TCP/IP with SLIP or PPP. If you're like most of us, you probably got your connection up and running by following step-by-step instructions you got from your service provider or by using Windows' setup wizards. Those directions may have gotten you connected in a snap (if you were lucky), but they probably left you in the dark about how all of this stuff works.

In this chapter we hope to shed some light on this subject. There's a lot more to that little Network control panel and the Dial-Up Networking folder than meets the eye. It's important to know what everything is and how it works if you want to get the most out of your Internet travels. The same thing goes whether you're using PPP or SLIP protocols—they can be cantankerous beasts if you don't know how and why they work.

TIP

We're not trying to run your life, but if you haven't done so already, you may want to go back to Chapter 3, "TCP/IP Primer," and bone up on the basics of TCP/IP before you go any further. We're going to cover a lot of stuff in this chapter, stuff that'll probably sound like gobbledygook if you aren't prepared. So go back if you need to, bone up, and return to this chapter. We'll wait.

First, we'll look at how the TCP/IP protocols work under Windows. Even if you're already running Microsoft TCP/IP (which came with Windows 95), you still may want to look over the sections of this chapter covering TCP/IP basics, Microsoft TCP/IP software, and the information on creating and installing login scripts. We also take a peek at Trumpet Winsock, a popular shareware TCP/IP protocol stack, favored by many experienced Netheads. Last, but not least, we look at a number of monitoring and diagnostic tools that can help you troubleshoot problems and insure optimal network performance. We'll also tell you where you can get help if you're having trouble with your TCP/IP connection.

TIP

In this chapter, we're primarily going to cover dial-up TCP/IP connections. If you're connecting with TCP/IP over a LAN, read over the section on TCP/IP, skip the SLIP and PPP stuff, and then jump ahead to the "Monitoring Your TCP/IP Connection" section. You may also want to go back to Chapter 4, "Above & Beyond 28.8 kbps" and brush up on some of the concepts that make LAN connectivity unique.

Just like everything else with computers, getting a good TCP/IP connection up and running doesn't involve magic, unattainable skills, or secret knowledge—just a basic understanding of how things work. Oh yeah, and did we mention a lot of knuckle biting, hair pulling, and colorful use of language? Welcome to the magic of TCP/IP!

WINDOWS TCP/IP BASICS

For a computer to be connected to the Internet, it has to be able to speak the TCP/IP protocols. The TCP/IP stack you run on your Windows PC allows your computer to do just that. To refresh your memory, a TCP/IP communications protocol stack is composed of four basic layers:

- ❏ Application Layer
- ❏ Host-to-Host Transport Layer
- ❏ Internet Layer
- ❏ Network Access Layer

Each of these layers is responsible for a different function: the Application Layer takes care of the user interface and the different programs used on the Internet, the Transport Layer carries the information generated by the Application Layer onto the Net, the Internet Layer makes sure the data arrives at its destination, and the Network Access Layer provides the medium on which the information travels.

The TCP/IP stack that comes with Windows 95 (Microsoft TCP/IP) provides the Transport and Internet Layer functions for your PC with the following protocols:

- ❏ Internet Protocol (IP)
- ❏ Internet Control Message Protocol (ICMP)
- ❏ Gateway-to-Gateway Protocol (GGP)
- ❏ Transmission Control Protocol (TCP)
- ❏ Exterior Gateway Protocol (EGP)
- ❏ PARC Universal Packet Protocol (PUP)
- ❏ User Datagram Protocol (UDP)
- ❏ Host Monitoring Protocol (HMP)
- ❏ Xerox NS-IDP (XNS-IDP)
- ❏ Reliable Datagram Protocol (RDP)
- ❏ MIT's Remote Virtual Disk (RVD)

Trumpet Winsock's TCP/IP stack (see the section "Trumpet Winsock" later in this chapter) uses a slightly different set of protocols. It uses all of the protocols listed above that are followed by an asterisk, and it adds IGMP (Internet Group Multicast Protocol). If you're interested in finding out the nitty-gritty details of what part these protocols play in the functioning of your TCP/IP stack, you'll want to check out the RFCs that discuss them. RFCs

(Request for Comments) are the standards documents that define how the Internet works. The library of them located at http://www.cis.ohio-state.edu/hypertext/information/rfc.html allows you to search on key words. By searching on any of the protocols above (use their names, not their abbreviations or acronyms), you can learn more (a lot more!) about them. Table 6-1 lists the Internet software and hardware components used with Windows 95 and what each of them does.

Software/Hardware Layer	Description
Application	Your Internet client software: Netscape, Eudora, Telnet, etc.
Winsock (winsock.dll)	The .DLL file that translates communications between your Winsock-compliant applications (above) and your PC's TCP/IP stack (below).
TCP/IP protocol stack (the Transport and Internet Layers)	Translates communications between your PC applications and the Internet. Includes SLIP and/or PPP support.
Modem hardware or network interface card (The physical network connection)	Translates incoming/outgoing communications into binary data that can travel through network cables and phone lines and on to the Internet.
The wild and woolly Internet	The constellation of TCP/IP-speaking computer networks, routers, bridges, and gateways that make up the Internet.

Table 6-1: The TCP/IP in Windows chain of command.

The crucial link in this chain is the Winsock .DLL. Probably 75 percent of the problems users have when setting up a PC for Internet connectivity involves problems with Winsock. Winsock ("Windows Sockets") was originally developed as a standard that would allow different vendors' Net software to be plugged into this "universal" socket, thus minimizing software conflicts and allowing smooth communications between your Windows Net software, your computer's TCP/IP stack and operating system, and the Internet. Unfortunately, it's not that simple. There are now a number of different Winsocks. AOL has one, Trumpet Winsock is another, and Windows 95 uses yet another. There are also 16-bit Winsocks and 32-bit Winsocks. If you end up with more than one winsock.dll and wsock32.dll in your Windows directory, it can cause trouble. Most TCP/IP stacks come with their own Winsocks. Before you install a new stack, make sure that you remove your old version to a backup disk (or simply give it a new extension, such as winsock.old).

MICROSOFT TCP/IP

Windows 95 comes with Microsoft TCP/IP, which includes a TCP/IP stack, Winsock, the Dial-Up Adapter, and a variety of tools for using and monitoring your connection. If you have Windows 95, you have everything you need to connect to the Internet. Table 6-2 lists the crucial networking and client software that comes with Windows 95.

Software	Description
Client for Microsoft Windows (and various other clients for Novell, Sunsoft, etc.)	The main network client that lets you connect to other computers over a LAN or WAN.
TCP/IP	Microsoft's version of the suite of Internet protocols.
Dial-Up Adapter	The adapter software that allows you to access an Internet service provider via a dial-up connection.
Network Adapters (for computers on a LAN)	The adapter software that allows you to connect your PC to a LAN.
FTP	A text-based FTP client that allows you to download files and programs from the Internet.
Telnet	A Telnet client that lets you log on to remote computer hosts. Text-based.
Ping	A Net utility program that lets you send an echo over the network to see if you get a signal bounced back (letting you know that you have a legitimate Net connection). Text-based.
Dial-Up Scripting Tool	Allows you to create login scripts for your dial-up connections.
Windows IP Configuration (winipcnfg)	A tool that allows you to check your basic TCP/IP settings. Useful in troubleshooting.

➡

Software	Description
Netstat	Diagnostic tool for displaying protocol stats and current TCP/IP connections.
Nbstat	Diagnostic tool for displaying protocol stats and current TCP/IP connections using NetBIOS.
Arp	Diagnostic tool for displaying and modifying IP to Ethernet and IP to Token Ring address translation tables.
Route	A tool for manipulating network routing tables.
Tracert	A route-tracing tool that sends ICMP (Internet Control Message Protocol) echo packets along a network to count hops and trace the route.
Windows 95 Resource Kit Help File	The main Help files on Windows 95 have precious little information on TCP/IP networking. The real info is hidden away in the admin\reskit\helpfile\win95rk directory on the CD-ROM.

Table 6-2: Microsoft TCP/IP software and tools.

As Windows 95 started to make its way into the world, feedback on the Net was harsh about its TCP/IP tools and its convoluted setup procedure. Microsoft has made it very easy to connect to its own ill-fated Microsoft Network (MSN), but if you want to go your own way, using another service provider, things get weird. When I called Microsoft Support with a question about TCP/IP, the "engineer" I reached knew less than I did! He encouraged me to use MSN and Internet Explorer (their Web browser). After this frustrating call, I had a much better understanding of why several online services initially threatened to sue Microsoft, claiming that Windows 95 disabled their services. The heart of this controversy is—you guessed it—the Winsock. When you install Windows 95's TCP/IP stack, it renames your existing Winsock to winsock.old (without so much as a howdy do!). If you were previously using a different Winsock, all of a sudden, it stops working. If you don't know a lot about computers and such things as Winsock. DLL files, this can be a very unnerving occurrence. As of this writing, many online services have not yet released a

Winsock that's compatible with Windows 95's TCP/IP stack. This means that you can't use multiple browsers if they have incompatible Winsocks. So much for universality.

Your Microsoft TCP/IP stack provides you with a not-terribly-easy interface to configure all the settings you need to get your connection running. If you have the Microsoft Plus! for Windows 95 CD-ROM, getting yourself set up will be a lot easier. Using the Internet Setup Wizard, you simply need to answer questions in a series of dialog boxes (about your connection method, service providers, username, password, etc.) If you have the disk-based or CD-ROM version of Windows 95, you'll need to configure your network setup manually. All of the basic information about your network connections are entered into the Network Control Panel (see Figure 6-1).

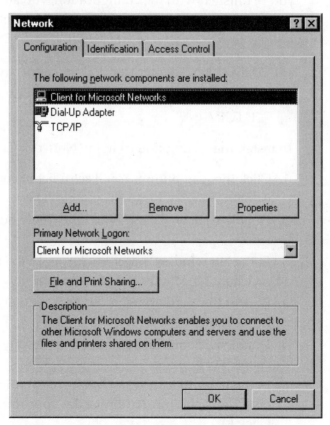

Figure 6-1: The Windows 95 Network Control Panel.

Normally, we wouldn't go into the nitty-gritty details of setting up for Internet connectivity, but because of all the problems people are reporting in setting up TCP/IP in Windows 95 (and because many people are still switching from 3.1 to Windows 95), we thought we'd include some quick and dirty setup instructions.

Configuring Dial-Up Networking for TCP/IP

The TCP/IP setup for Windows 95 is configured in the Network section of the Windows 95 Control Panel. You'll also want to make sure that your modem settings are correct for the type of network you're on. See Chapters 1 and 2 for more information on modems.

First, let's go to the Network dialog boxes (found in the Control Panel). You'll see that the network components list is blank. When you're finished with the configuration, you should end up with the following components installed in this components box:

- ❑ Client for Microsoft Networks
- ❑ Dial-Up Adapter (for dial-up connectivity)
- ❑ Network Adapter (for LAN connectivity)
- ❑ TCP/IP

To install these components in the Network Control Panel:

1. Click the Add button. You'll see a list of component types (Client, Adapter, Protocol, and Service).
2. Double-click on Client. When the Client box pops up, choose Add.
3. In the left window, select Microsoft. In the right window, click on Client for Microsoft Networks, and then click OK.
4. Back at the Network window, click Add again. You'll see the list of component types.
5. Double-click on Adapter. When the Adapter box pops up, choose Add.
6. In the left window, select Microsoft. In the right window, click on Dial-Up Adapter (or the appropriate LAN adapter). Click OK.

7. Back at the Network window, click Add one more time. You'll see the list of component types.

8. Double-click on Protocol. When the Protocol box pops up, choose Add.

9. In the left window, select Microsoft. In the right window, click on TCP-IP, and click OK.

TIP

At this point you may notice that there are more adapters and protocols in the Network box than you've selected. This is because Windows 95 adds the components it thinks you will need based on other choices you made. Remove everything except Client for Microsoft Networks, Dial-Up Adapter (or the appropriate LAN adapter), and TCP/IP.

---

10. Now, at the Network box, click on Client for Microsoft again, and click on the Properties button. Check with your systems administrator or ISP as to what should be configured here. If you're on a Windows NT network, you'll need to check the Log on to Windows NT Domain box and enter in the name of the NT server. If you're configuring for SLIP or PPP, you have nothing to fill in on this dialog box. (You can leave it set to "Logon and restore network connections" and nothing else, since one of these options must be selected. Click OK.

11. Back at the Network box, select Dial-Up Adapter, and then click on Properties. Under the Driver Type tab, Enhanced Mode should be checked. Under the Bindings tab, TCP/IP should be checked. Under Advanced, Property: Record a log file should be set to No, and Use IPX header compression should be Yes.

Important Note: You should check with your systems administrator or ISP about these settings. We've just given you the most common ones. Your mileage may vary.

12. Back at the Network box, select TCP/IP, and then click on Properties. The information for this section is specific to your network connections. Consult your systems administrator or ISP about these settings; the sections "Your IP Address," "Gateway," and "Domain Name Server" below also provide you with some information about these settings. When finished filling everything out, click OK, and then click OK again at the Network dialog box. You'll be asked to restart your machine, or you may be prompted to insert the Windows 95 CD-ROM or floppies.

Once your computer is finished booting up, you'll be ready for the final step: making a "connectoid." You can find out what a con-nectoid is and why you need to make one in the section "Creating a Connection Icon."

IP Address

It's important to understand how your IP address is assigned. Depending on the IP address assignment scheme used in your system, your IP address will be specified in one of three ways: manually, by the server, or dynamically. When you know how your address is assigned, you can configure your system accordingly, using the IP Address tab of the TCP/IP Properties dialog box (see Figure 6-2).

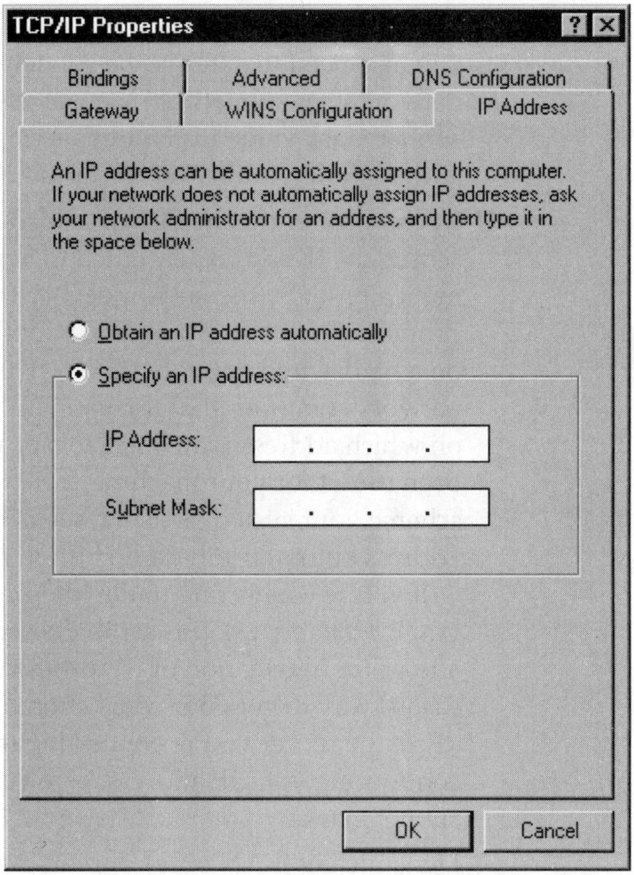

Figure 6-2: The IP Address tab in the TCP/IP Properties dialog box.

Let's take a closer look at these three types of IP address assignment schemes:

☐ Manually: In a manually assigned IP address scheme, your machine's IP address is assigned by your system administrator (or your service provider) and never changes. In this case, you must enter the IP address in the Specify an IP address section in the IP Address tab. If you're using a PC on a preconfigured network, this address may already have been entered for you.

Don't forget, when entering in a manual IP address, you also need to enter in the subnet mask (providing your network uses subnetting). You should get the correct subnet mask value from your service provider or systems administrator—don't try to guess.

❏ By the Server: If your PC's IP address is obtained by the server, the IP address assigned to your computer is automatically set by the network every time you make a connection (or every time you boot the computer if you're on a hard-wired network). TCP/IP talks to the main network computer that then assigns an IP address based on which addresses are available or which address has been preset for your machine. If this is the IP address scheme your system is using, select the Obtain an IP address automatically radio button in the IP Address tab.

If you're connecting to the Internet via a PPP account, you'll probably use this setting because the PPP protocol allows for negotiation of IP addresses. This is by far the easiest way to get your connection up and running because the server you're connecting to does all the work, configuring your IP address, gateway numbers, and subnet mask.

❏ Dynamically (LAN only): Servers running the Dynamic Host Configuration Protocol (DHCP) lease an IP address to your machine for a specified period of time. Before that time expires, the server will release the old address and lease you a new one. Currently, DHCP addressing does not work over a router, so it's only a LAN thing. If you need to "release" and "renew" your IP address before it expires, you can do so by running winipcnfg and pressing the appropriate buttons. For more information on DHCP, look in the Windows 95 Resource Kit Help File on the CD-ROM.

Know Your Address

It's important that you know the numerical IP address of your machine if you want to use any programs that enable you to directly connect your PC to another machine across the Internet. For example, if you want to use the popular video conferencing software CU-SeeMe to hold a video-chat with your friend in Malaysia (more on how to do that in Chapter 28, "Audio/Video Power Tools"), you'll need to know your IP number (as well as your friend's IP number) in order for the two computers to connect to each other. You can easily find IP addresses (if you know the hostnames) by searching with a NSLookup utility. (See "Monitoring Your TCP/IP Connection" below.)

In some TCP/IP application interfaces (such as MacTCP), you see the address "class" (A, B, or C) for your IP number as you enter it. Microsoft TCP/IP does not display the address class. If you're interested in knowing anyway, see Table 6-3 (and go back to Chapter 3, "TCP/IP Primer," to find out what these classes mean). Don't worry, you won't be tested on this. It's only for the "deep geeks" in the audience.

Class	First Octet Value	Subnet Mask
A	1—127	255.0.0.0
B	128—191	255.255.0.0
C	192—254	255.255.255.0

Table 6-3: TCP/IP address class assignments.

Gateway

The term "gateway" is used in two different ways in TCP/IP networking. On a LAN, a gateway can be a device or software program that communicates between different network protocols. For instance, a Novell network may use a gateway to translate network traffic into TCP/IP for transport onto the Internet. In SLIP and PPP type connections, a gateway is a server computer that connects your computer to the Internet services available through your service provider. This gateway is represented by a "gateway IP address," which is either assigned to you when you set up your Internet account or is automatically assigned by the server (so you do not have to enter a specific gateway IP address). If you're not sure how your network is set up, don't experiment—ask someone. Knock on the ol' sysadmin's door (or contact your ISP), and verify the settings you should use before entering anything. It also never hurts to bring gifts of coffee, Jolt Cola, or Cheetos if you must disturb the local net guru.

If you do require a gateway IP address, it is entered under Properties in the TCP/IP section of the Network Control Panel. Click on the Gateway tab and enter the specified gateway IP address in the New Gateway box. You can enter more than one gateway (if you were given more than one). This way, if one gateway server is down, your computer will use the next available gateway.

If you have a network setup that does not require a specified gateway, leave this tab in the TCP/IP Properties blank. Now, go to the connectoid for your service provider in the Dial-Up Networking folder and right-click on the connectoid icon to reveal its menu. Choose Properties, then Server Type, then TCP/IP settings. Make sure that Use default gateway on remote network is checked.

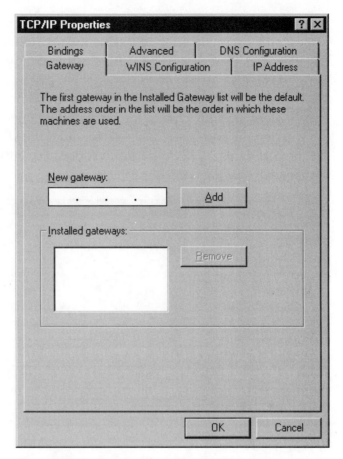

Figure 6-3: The Gateway tab in the TCP/IP Properties dialog box.

Domain Name Server

The Domain Name Server, or "System"(DNS) setting in TCP/IP is one of the most misunderstood parts of getting a connection up and running. The DNS is a service available on your LAN host or ISP that is used to match up IP addresses with domain names. This way, to access an Internet address, you only have to enter the name of the site (say www.cooltool.com), and the DNS will match that name to the correct IP address. If you set the DNS information correctly, you'll be rewarded with a smooth, consistent TCP/IP connection. Set it incorrectly, and you'll be tearing your hair out wondering why your TCP/IP software can't seem to connect to anything. Some network setups require that you enter the DNS IP address(es), while others assign them dynamically. As usual, check with your ISP or sysadmin to find out which configuration is right for your type of connection. If you need to manually assign the addresses, that's done under the DNS Configuration tab of the TCP/IP Properties box (located in the Network Control Panel). See Figure 6-4.

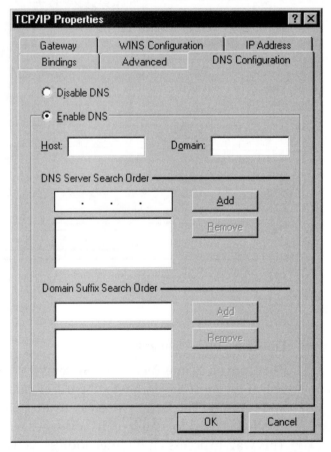

Figure 6-4: DNS Configuration tab in the TCP/IP Properties dialog box.

NOTE: If you have more than one connectoid in the Dial-Up Networking folder, you'll need to specify the DNS information for each Internet service you set up. To do this, right-click on the connectoid and selected Properties from the menu. Click on Server Type and then TCP/IP Settings. If your connection requires no DNS addresses, click on the Server assigned name server addresses radio button. If DNS information is required, enter those in the Primary and Secondary DNS boxes.

The DNS address for the main domain name server should be entered first. This will make sure that you at least have one name server. You were probably also given a secondary DNS address from your ISP or sysadmin, which will be used should the first one become too busy or disabled. One good thing to know is that the DNS addresses do not have to be on your host's server. You can use any DNS address located on any Internet-accessible server. It may take a bit longer for a look-up (in the unlikely event that both the primary and secondary DNS don't work), but at least you'll stay up and running. Most systems administrators and ISPs provide you with a list of multiple DNSes.

Some networks may use the WINS (Windows Internet Name Server), which is another name service popular on Windows NT systems. If your network does use WINS, you will be given a primary and secondary WINS address to enter in WINS Configuration tab of the TCP/IP Properties dialog box.

The Hosts File

If you want to bypass the DNS all together (or if you have an unreliable DNS) and you know the IP addresses of the computers you frequently need to communicate with, you can do what the UNIX guys and gals do: create a hosts table. The hosts table is a file that lives in your Windows folder that has a list of domain names mapped to IP addresses. Think of it as a sort of local cache or shortcut for the domain names/IP addresses you frequently access.

When you install TCP/IP, it creates a file called Hosts.sam. If you have TCP/IP installed already, you'll find it in the Windows folder. Table 6-4 shows what you'll find.

```
# Copyright (c) 1994 Microsoft Corp.
#
# This is a sample HOSTS file used by Microsoft TCP/IP
# for Chicago
#
# This file contains the mappings of IP addresses to
# host names. Each entry should be kept on an individual
# line. The IP address should be placed in the first column
# followed by the corresponding host name.
# The IP address and the host name should be separated by
# at least one space.
#
# Additionally, comments (such as these) may be inserted
# on individual lines or following the machine name denoted
# by a '#' symbol.
#
# For example:
#
#    102.54.94.97     rhino.acme.com          # source server
#     38.25.63.10     x.acme.com              # x client host

127.0.0.1        localhost
```

Table 6-4: The Microsoft TCP/IP Hosts file.

Just like the Hosts file that your network host or ISP has on their server, your PC's Hosts file allows you to directly map names to IP addresses. Then, if your domain name server goes down, Dial-Up Networking will look directly into the Hosts file to find the IP address for the machine you're trying to reach. The Hosts file can be used to provide quick access for commonly accessed Internet hosts and as a back-up option should your DNS become inaccessible.

In mapping names to IP addresses in the hosts file, use the following syntax:

```
ip address    domain name  #comment
```

For example, say you frequently use the following hosts (listed with their corresponding IP addresses). By entering them in your hosts table, they will be readily available for lookup regardless of whether your DNS is functional. (These are for example only—any correspondence between real domains and IP addresses is purely coincidental.)

```
128.45.222.123   natty.boh.com            #source server
132.32.33.1      nigel.linux.com
144.22.21.128    boingboing.com           #@emerald.net
122.22.45.21     seansa.slacker.com       #unreliable
```

Make sure each entry is on a line by itself and that the IP number goes in the first column and the hostname in the second. You can also put comments on lines by themselves if preceded by a pound sign (#).

Creating a Connection Icon

You've configured your Dial-Up Networking, you've rebooted your machine, and now you're ready to create a connection icon (or "connectoid"). On your desktop, you should now see a folder called Dial-Up Networking. Open that folder, and choose Make A New Connection.

1. In the Make New Connection Wizard, type in the name of your new connection (i.e., the name of your ISP or the LAN machine you are calling). Click Next.

2. Enter the phone number of your ISP, click Next, and then click Finish.

3. Right-click the new icon that you've just created in the Dial-Up Networking folder. Select Properties.

4. Click on Configure. Set up your modem's General and Connection properties according to the type of modem you have. If you have questions about these settings, see Chapters 1 and 2.

5. It's very important that you select the Options tab and check the Bring up Terminal Window After Dialing box. Click OK. You can de-select this option after you have your connection and dial-up script working.

6. Back at the General tab, click on Server Type. Your likely selection will be PPP: Windows, Windows NT 3.5, Internet. If you're trying to set up a SLIP connection, skip ahead to the section "Installing SLIP Support," and then return to this point. The option SLIP: Unix Connection will be available once you have added SLIP support.

7. When you're finished filling out all of the appropriate properties, click OK in the General properties box. You'll be returned to the open Dial-Up Networking folder.

8. Double-click on your newly created Connection icon. Enter your username, password, and the number of your Internet provider. Press the Connect button, and your modem should begin dialing.

9. When your modem connects, the Post-Dial Terminal Screen will pop up. For some connections, you may have to press Continue at this point before the Service Provider login screen will appear. For others, it will appear right away. Enter the information your service provider requires at login; it will probably be your username and password, the type of connection you're trying to make (PPP, for example), and whatever else you're asked to enter. When you've finished filling in the required information, press Continue (or F7). The Connection Indicator box should pop up and begin counting your time online. When you see this box, you know you're jacked in!

Once you have one connection working, it's easy to make connectoids for other services. Just choose New in the Dial-Up Networking folder, fill in the connection information in the setup wizard and the Properties section of the connectoid. Don't forget to fill out the server information and TCP/IP settings. Each new connectoid needs new ISP information.

TIP

It's an unfortunate fact of net.life that your service providers are often not there when you need them. Sometimes, you can get mouse cramp pressing that connect button only to hear a constant busy signal. To save a few moments of your time, you can automate your redials in the Dial-Up Networking folder under the Connections menu. Choose the Settings item, check the Redial box, and fill in the number of retries you want and the amount of time delay between tries.

If you're the forgetful type and have a bad habit of falling asleep in your overstuffed executive chair when you're still logged on, ask Windows 95 to disconnect your Net connection after a specified interval of time. This is done by right-clicking on your service's connectoid and choosing Properties. Select the Configure button and then the Connection tab. Under Call Preferences, check the appropriate box, and enter the time-out value. The default (after you check the box) is 30 minutes.

On the other hand, some ISPs have their own idle daemons set to break your connection should it be idle for some interval of time (say 30 minutes). This can be a problem if you want to maintain a connection but you're not actually doing anything over it. There are a number of shareware programs, such as Ponger, that keep your connection alive while you do other work. They "ping" the ISP at intervals you specify, thus keeping the connection alive

Unless you just enjoy typing your login information every time you connect , you'll want to create a script to automate the login procedure. See the section "Creating a Login Script" for instructions.

Installing SLIP Support

Windows 95 comes with the capability to connect your PC to the Internet using a SLIP account, but the SLIP program is not automatically installed. It can be found on the Windows 95 CD-ROM or the Microsoft Plus! CD-ROM. You can easily install it using the Add/Remove Programs utility found in the Control Panel folder. On the CD-ROM, the SLIP program is in the admin\apptools\dscript directory. The file is called rnaplus.inf. To install SLIP and the Dial-Up Scripting Tool, choose Windows Setup in the Add/Remove Programs Properties box. Click the Have Disk button. Browse through the CD-ROM along the following path: admin\apptools\dscript\rnaplus.inf. Once you've located the rnaplus.inf file, click OK—and OK again. Now, in the Have Disk box, check the component SLIP and Scripting for Dial-Up Networking. Click Install. SLIP support and the Scripting Tool are now installed on your hard drive. Now, when you go to the Server section of your Connectoid (in the Dial-Up Networking folder), SLIP: Unix Connection will be a selectable server type.

SLIP support is available on the CD-ROM version of Windows 95, the CD-ROM Extras for Windows 95 upgrade, and the Internet Jumpstart Kit component of Microsoft Plus! SLIP support and the Dial-Up Scripting Tool are not available on the floppy version of Windows 95.

TIP

You can also get SLIP support and the Windows 95 Dial-Up Scripting Tool from Microsoft's web site. It's http://www.microsoft.com/WINDOWS/SOFTWARE.HTM—there's a link labeled "Windows 95 CD ROM Extras—Additional files that are on the CD-ROM version of Windows 95 but not on the floppy disk version."

Creating a Login Script

Login scripts are used to automate the process of establishing your Net connection. Instead of having to enter in your username, password, and connection type every time you log in, you can assign a script to your connectoid, giving you one-button connectivity. What follows is an introduction to the Windows 95 scripting tool and the scripting language that it uses.

Using the Dial-Up Scripting Tool

Windows 95 Dial-Up Networking comes with a Dial-Up Scripting Tool (also called Scripter on the CD-ROM). It allows you to create automated login scripts and link them to your dial-up connectoids. The scripting language is fairly straightforward. Windows 95 comes with several example scripts, including one for establishing a PPP connection via CompuServe (Figure 6-6). This script is typical of those used for SLIP and PPP connections..

All of the scripting files are located in the admin\apptools\dscript directory on the Windows 95 CD-ROM. The Dial-Up Scripting Tool may already be on your hard drive (in the Accessories folder). If not, you can copy it (using the Add/Remove utility) from the Windows 95 disk directory above.

NOTE: Before you do any scripting, check with your ISP/sysadmin. They may already have a script set up that you can modify with your name, password, and other information. If so, you'll only need to download it, edit it, put it in the Accessories folder (make sure it has a .SCP extension), and link to your Dial-Up Connection with the Dial-Up Scripting Tool.

To create a script file, follow these steps:

1. Open Notepad (or any other text-editing program).
2. Type the scripting commands necessary to access your ISP. To see what's required (how the login procedure runs), log on with a terminal program first, and then print out the login screen. By comparing this screen with the scripting commands found in Table 6-5, you should be able to block out the script.
3. Save the script as a text file, using the extension .SCP, in the Accessories folder.

To assign a script to your dial-up connectoid:

1. Launch the Dial-Up Scripting Tool (the default location is your Accessories folder). See Figure 6-5.

2. Click on the service you want to assign the script file to (located in the Connections box on the left).

3. Enter (or Browse to find) the location and filename of the script you want to link to the connectoid.

4. The first time through, you'll probably want to check the Step through script box, which will allow you to check/troubleshoot the script line-by-line on login.

5. Click Apply.

6. Now double-click on the Connection icon in the Dial-Up Networking folder. Click on Connect. When the Post-Dial Terminal Screen pops up, press Continue.

7. The Automated Script Test window will appear with your script in it. Step through each line of the script and watch what happens in the terminal window. Tweak as needed until the script works successfully.

8. Don't forget to go back to the Scripting Tool, and uncheck the Step through script option.

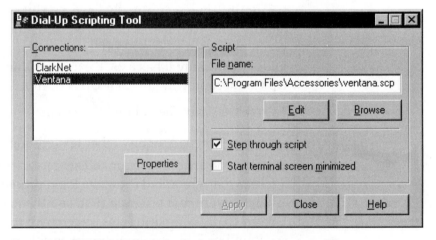

Figure 6-5: The Dial-Up Scripting Tool dialog box in Windows 95.

```
Cis
;
; This is a script file that demonstrates how
; to establish a PPP connection with Compuserve,
; which requires changing the port settings to
; log in.
;
; Main entry point to script
;
proc main
     ; Set the port settings so we can wait for
     ; non-gibberish text.

     set port databits 7
     set port parity even

     transmit "^M"

     waitfor "Host Name:"
     transmit "CIS^M"

     waitfor "User ID:"
     transmit $USERID
     transmit "/go:pppconnect^M"

     waitfor "Password: "
     transmit $PASSWORD
     transmit "^M"

     waitfor "One moment please..."

     ; Set the port settings back to allow successful
     ; negotiation.

     set port databits 8
     set port parity none
endproc
```

Figure 6-6: Sample CompuServe Script that comes with Windows 95.

Scripting Commands

The commands in Table 6-5 can be used in building a script file to automate your logins.

Command	Description
proc main	Goes at the beginning of the script. All scripts must begin with this command.
delay <n seconds>	Pauses for the number of seconds specified as *n*.
waitfor "<string>"	Waits for the data specified in quotes to be received from the computer you are connecting to. Case sensitive.
transmit "<string>"I$ USERIDI$PASSWORD	Sends the data you specify in quotes. If you use $USERID or $PASSWORD, it will send those as specified in your Dial-Up Networking connectoid box. You do not need the quote marks for these.
set port databits <integer>	Allows you to change the number of bits in your bytes. That is, a number between 5 and 8 bits. If this is not contained in your script, it will default to the number of databits you assigned in the Properties tab in your Dial-Up Networking connectoid box. For example, CompuServe requires 7 databits.
set port stopbits <integer>	Allows you to select the number of stopbits (1 or 2). If this is not contained in your script, it will default to the number of databits you assigned in the Properties tab in your Dial-Up Networking connectoid box.
set port parity <none>, <odd>, <even>, <mark>, <space>	Guess what this does? That's right, allows you to select your parity (none, odd, even, mark, space). If this is not contained in your script, it will default to the number of databits you assigned in the Properties tab in your Dial-Up Networking connectoid box.
set ipaddr	Sets the IP address.
set screen keyboard <on>, <off>	Allows you to enable (or disable) keyboard input in the terminal window.

➡

Command	Description
getip <optional index>	Gets an IP address and uses it as the workstation's address. <optional index> allows you to specify which IP address to use if the remote computer sends more than one.
halt	Causes the script to stop running. The terminal window will appear onscreen so you can enter data and commands manually.
endproc	Ends the script. When this command is reached in the script, Dial-Up Networking will launch PPP or SLIP (as you've specified in Server Type).
;	Sets off a comment. Any lines of text preceded by a semicolon will be ignored by the script.
"^M"	Sends (or receives) a carriage return. For example, transmit "^M".
<cr>	Can be used to indicate carriage return.
<lf>	Used to send or receive a linefeed.

Table 6-5: The scripting commands for the Microsoft Dial-Up Scripting Tool.

TIP

If, for some reason, you do not have the Windows 95 Scripting Tool, there is a freeware program called RoboDUN (Robotic Dial-Up Networking) that basically does the same thing. Look for it at your favorite Winsock Apps site (such as http://WWW.NetEx.NET:80/w95/windows95/internet/robodun61.zip).

TRUMPET WINSOCK

Trumpet Winsock (see Figure 6-7) is a shareware Windows Sockets-compliant TCP/IP stack created by Peter Tattam. Over the years, it's become the most popular TCP/IP shareware stack for the Windows platform. Now that Windows 95 comes bundled

187

with a Winsock-compliant TCP/IP stack, Trumpet Winsock's place
in the grand scheme is uncertain. Many loyal Netheads are sticking by it, waiting patiently for the full release of Trumpet Winsock
for Windows 95. As of this writing, you can use the 16-bit Trumpet
Winsock (and 16-bit Internet applications), or if you want to use
32-bit TCP/IP applications, there's something called the 32-bit
"Thunking" Winsock. It's not really a full implementation of 32-bit
Winsock but rather a layer that patches 32-bit applications into the
16-bit Trumpet Winsock. If you already have the 16-bit version
(known as Trumpet Winsock 2.1*x*), you should have little trouble
upgrading to the new version. If you don't already have version
2.1*x*, you should download it and follow the instructions for
replacing old files with new ones as outlined in "Installing and
Configuring Trumpet Winsock" below.

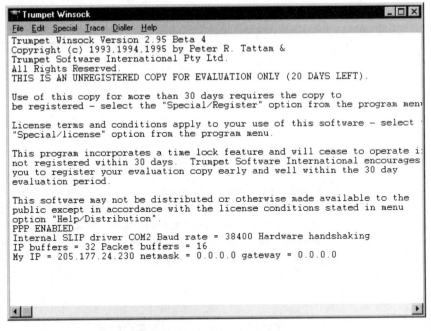

Figure 6-7: Trumpet Winsock.

There are several advantages of Trumpet Winsock (TWSK) over the Microsoft Winsock. It's quicker to install and seems a bit peppier in operation (although we didn't do any benchmark tests). It does give you more control over settings that affect your Winsock performance, such as Maximum Transmission Units (MTU), Maximum Segment Size (MSS), Receive Window (RWIN), and Retransmission Time Out (RTO Max). If you know what you're doing, you can tune your Winsock for peak performance by tweaking these settings. TWSK has the protocol tracer tools built right into it to allow you to do this. Another advantage of Trumpet Winsock over the Microsoft Winsock concerns how it handles packet drivers. The TCP/IP driver (i.e. the protocol stack) in Trumpet Winsock is written in such a way that it can interface with a packet driver. This means that its TCP/IP stack can be used with any network card's packet driver, thus eliminating the need for software companies to have to include hardware drivers for every possible card. Microsoft TCP/IP does not use a packet driver interface and therefore must include the drivers for popular network cards.

Where to Get It

Both versions of Trumpet Winsock are widely available on many FTP servers and Web pages dedicated to TCP/IP and Winsock. The makers of Trumpet Winsock, Trumpet Software International, have their own Web site located at http://www.trumpet.com.au/wsk/winsock.htm.

Installing & Configuring Trumpet Winsock

Trumpet Winsock doesn't have the most warm and fuzzy inter-face, but its no-nonsense approach to TCP/IP connectivity and its many advanced performance and troubleshooting features make it attractive to the power user. What follows is the basic installation and configuring information for both the 16-bit and 32-bit version.

16-bit Trumpet Winsock

Setting up the 16-bit version of Trumpet Winsock is fairly easy. All you need to do (after you've downloaded it and set it up in its own folder) is to add its directory path to your autoexe.bat file's path statement. Also make sure that there are no other active Winsocks on your system. The Trumpet Winsock is kept inside of the Twsk folder. After you've modified the path statement, restart your computer. Double-clicking on the TWSK icon will launch the program. The first time you launch the program, the Trumpet Winsock Setup box will appear. Here's where you'll enter in the network information provided by your sysamin or ISP. Most of these settings should be familiar to you (IP address, name server, domain). Here are a few things to keep in mind:

1. If your IP address is dynamically assigned, enter 0.0.0.0 in the IP address field.

2. If you were not assigned a subnet mask, leave the Netmask box defaulted to 0.0.0.0.

3. If you were assigned a Default gateway, enter its IP address in this box, or set to 0.0.0.0.

4. If you're already familiar with advanced modem and network tweaking, you can add the appropriate numbers in the Demand load timeout, MTU, TCP RWIN, TCP MSS, and TCP RTO MAX boxes. If this all looks like Greek to you, start with the following numbers:

   ❏ MTU: 576

   ❏ TCP RWIN: 2048

   ❏ TCP MSS: 512

   ❏ TCP RTO MAX: 60

   ❏ Demand load timeout: 10

   For more information on how you can use these features to get optimum performance, see the Tips and Tricks section below.

5. Select either Internal SLIP or PPP.

6. Set SLIP port to the number of your modem's comm port.

7. Set the Baud rate (and remember to set the rate higher than your modem's capability). For example, if you've got a 28.8k modem, enter: 38400.

8. Click on Hardware handshaking (if your modem supports it).

9. If you're using a SLIP connection that uses Van Jacobson CSLIP compression, check this box.

10. Select the kind of Online status detection your modem supports. This is defaulted to none.

11. When you are done, click on OK and if all goes well, the Trumpet Winsock will be initialized.

To run Trumpet Winsock successfully, you need to have a login.cmd and bye.cmd script installed. The program comes with sample scripts and there are complete scripting instructions in the Help file. Most service providers have TWSK scripts available that have been custom configured. Save yourself a lot of hassle by trying to locate a script tailored to your provider.

32-bit Thunking Winsock

If you're installing Trumpet Winsock for the first time and you want to use the 32-bit Thunking version, make sure that all other winsock.dll and wsock32.dll files have been renamed. First download the old 16-bit version to get the login.cmd and bye.cmd scripts and other support files (twsk95b4.zip only comes with the files listed in item 1 below). Unzip everything into a Trumpet Winsock directory. Then, follow the instructions below for adding the Thunking Winsock files. When you're done, launch the tcpman.exe, and fill in your ISP information in the Setup box (as described in the section "16-bit Trumpet Winsock").

If you are upgrading from an earlier 16-bit version of Trumpet Winsock to the 32-bit Thunking Winsock (currently called twsk95b4.zip), you need to:

1. Add/Replace the following files:
   - ❏ tcpman.exe
   - ❏ winsock.dll
   - ❏ twsk16.dll (the 16-bit interface)
   - ❏ wsock32.dll (that's your Thunking Winsock!)

2. Make sure the Trumpet Winsock directory is in the path statement in your autoexec.bat file. You can leave the .DLL files in the Trumpet directory, you do not need to move them to \windows\system (where other Winsocks reside). This is very important.

3. Also, make sure that all other winsock.dll and wsock32.dll files have been renamed (do a Find on them). You can rename the Microsoft files with an .ms or .old extension.

4. That should do it. Launch tcpman.exe and enter your ISP information in the Setup box. Also, look at Edit Scripts under the Dialler menu item. You should have both a login.cmd and bye.cmd script for TWSK to work properly. These scripts do not come with twsk95b4.zip. You can use the ones that came with the 16-bit version or are available from your ISP.

Tips & Tricks

If you want to tune Trumpet Winsock for maximum efficiency, you've got to check out Al's Winsock Tuning Page (http://www.cerberus-sys.com/~belleisl/mtu_mss_rwin. html). Al has done an amazing job of describing how the data flows in and out of your machine and what you can do, using the TWSK trace tools and TCP/IP settings, to make that baby hum. For most people, trudging through 15 pages (printed out) on Winsock/modem communications might not be worth the trouble. But, if you stick with Al, he'll turn you into a Winsock speed demon.

If you want to switch back and forth between two different Winsocks, you can . . . sort of. (You just can't have more than one running at the same time.) To switch from one Winsock to another, simply rename the Winsock files you want to "turn on" winsock.dll and wsock32.dll and turn off the others by giving them another extension, say .TWS (Trumpet Winsock). Remember, if you're "turning on" Trumpet Winsock, you need to add it to your autoexec.bat path statement (and comment it to turn it off). Don't forget to restart your machine. Obviously, not many people are going to need to switch Winsocks like this, but if you do (say you're writing a chapter on TCP/IP in Windows), this will work. If you get confused as to which Winsock is which, here's a hint: the Microsoft Winsock .DLL file is around 40K in size while the Trumpet Winsock file is around 160K.

One drawback of Trumpet Winsock is that it doesn't make it very easy to have multiple logins. There are several fixes for this:

- ❑ You can create separate copies of tcpman.exe in different directories and put login scripts for the services you wish to contact in each directory. You only need to point your autoexec.bat path statement to the one directory that contains the Winsocks.

- ❑ You can also use a command-line statement that switches between trumpwsk.ini files (each with the different appropriate settings). The command would be:

```
tcpman.exe -inipath=<directory path>\<filename>
```

- ❑ Winsock wizard Al Belle Isle has created a TWSK script that allows for multiple ISPs. You can download it at his page (http://www.cerberus-sys.com/~belleisl/ mtu_mss_rwin. html) under the "Links" section.

MONITORING YOUR TCP/IP CONNECTION

One problem with TCP/IP networking in Windows is that it's tough to tell what's going on. The lazy way of checking your connection is launching a TCP/IP client and trying to connect to a server someplace. If it connects, it's working. But what if it doesn't? Or what if things are running amazingly slow. Is everything working properly? Is it a traffic jam on the Information Highway or do you have water in your gas tank? Wouldn't you like to know just what the heck is going on behind the interface? Let's take a look at a few tools that can help.

Windows 95 Connection Indicator

The most basic tool for monitoring your connection is the Connection box that pops up as soon as you establish a Net connection (see Figure 6-8). If your Dial-Up Networking is set up incorrectly, this box will not appear. As soon as it does show up, it will start a clock running, counting off how long you've been online. It also shows you what baud rate you're connected at. This can be a useful clue in checking to make sure that your modem is properly configured. If the bps is significantly lower than it should be, you might want to check your Modem Control Panel and make sure the settings are correct. Check Chapters 1 and 2 for information about modem settings. The Connection box also tells you what protocols you're using. Click on the Details button to expand the box. Here you will see the Server Type you are using and a list of protocols. Of course, if you're capable of reading this box, it means you're online, and everything is hunky dory.

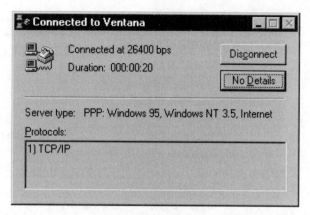

Figure 6-8: The Windows 95 Connection box.

Windows IP Configuration Tool

The next tool in the set is the Windows IP Configuration program. It's named winipcnfg and located in the Windows directory. To access winipcnfg, enter its name in the Run box under Start. The IP Configuration window that appears displays your current TCP/IP settings in two parts: Host Information and Ethernet Adapter Information. (Click the More Info button to display the full box.) Figure 6-9 shows what type of information is provided. Let's look at some of the info this tool provides.

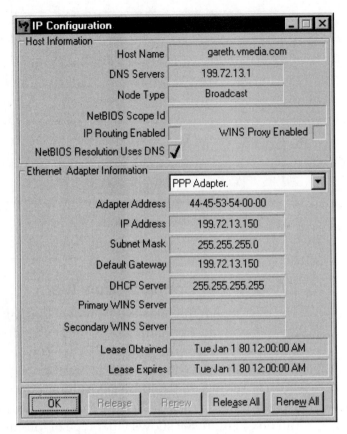

Figure 6-9 The Windows IP Configuration window.

Adapter Address

If your computer is part of a LAN, the number that appears in the Adapter Address box is the identification number that was hardwired into your network adapter card by the manufacturer (see Chapter 4, "Above & Beyond 28.8 Kbps" for more information on these Adapter address numbers). If you have a PPP or SLIP connection, the number that appears in this box is randomly chosen and meaningless.

IP Address

This is *your* IP address. If you have a manual IP address, what appears here should be what you entered in the Network Control Panel and/or the connectoid for this ISP. If you have a server-assigned address, the currently assigned IP number will appear here.

The Servers

The IP addresses for the DHCP (Dynamic Host Configuration Protocol) Server and WINS servers will show up if you're on a local network using them. The DHCP number is dynamically assigned when you log on. If you're on a LAN using DHCP, you can use the Release and Renew buttons to return an IP address to the host and get a new address assignment. The WINS server is the lookup service for a LAN. It translates the network's NetBIOS names (the alphanumeric names of each computer on the LAN) to their IP addresses. Lease Obtained and Lease Expires indicate the date when your DHCP was assigned and the date it's due to expire, respectively. You can manually expire an IP and lease a new one by using the Release and Renew buttons. Under normal circumstances you do not have to do this. The DHCP client will do it automatically before the expiration date.

TIP

If you make any changes to your TCP/IP information while winipcnfg is running, the change is not automatically updated. You need to close the IP Configuration window and re-launch it for the change to take effect.

WS_Watch (Windows Sockets Net Watch)

This incredibly cool piece of freeware (see Figure 6-10) lets you monitor your network (from a LAN to a WAN) on a graphical map. You are alerted to problems by color designations and sounds. Selecting Properties on any of the map icons (representing hosts, servers, routers, bridges, hubs, LANboxes, workstations, and printers) brings up a Host Information dialog box (see Figure 6-11). This dialog box shows the IP information, the protocol being used, and preferences for monitoring items on the network. There's even the capability to connect to an external digital beeper to report network trouble. Table 6-6 shows the connection monitoring tools that are available in WS_Watch.

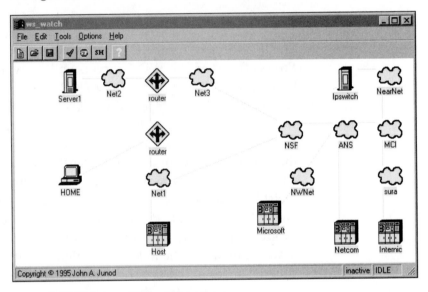

Figure 6-10: Windows Sockets Net Watch.

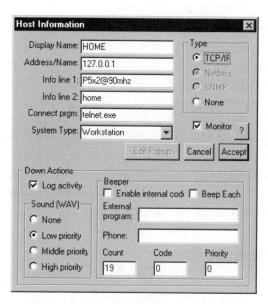

Figure 6-11: The Host Information dialog box.

Tool	Description
ping	A utility for measuring the round-trip time a packet travels from a remote host and back. Also lets you know if a host is reachable.
Traceroute	Allows you to view the path taken between you and a remote host. Shows the IP addresses and names of the computers on the route.
NSLookup	Lets you look up either a hostname or its IP address. Great for finding IP numbers when you know only the domain name (i.e., clark.net).
whois	Provides the ability to search through whois databases for information on users and systems.
finger	Lets you look up user information on remote systems.

Table 6-6: The suite of cool tools available in WS_Watch.

You can also launch an FTP or Telnet client from within WS_Watch. You can even Telnet into a host just by clicking on its icon on the network map! The program uses colors to indicate network performance. When you run a check on the network, the colors of each component change to reflect packet performance. Initially, all the hosts appear in yellow. A green icon means that the contacted machine has responded to a data packet. Varying intensities of light green to yellow to dark red indicate the number of lost packets. It's a fun and visual way of troubleshooting a network. The quick-click Telnet feature is also handy if you need to remotely login to various hosts.

NetScanTools

If playing with little colored maps that beep isn't your speed, we've also included NetScanTools 2.1, a shareware suite of essential Net tools (see Figure 6-12). In addition to the tools that come with WS_Watch (listed in Table 6-6), NetScan also includes the goodies listed in Table 6-7.

Tool	Description
WinSock Info	Tells you what Winsock is on the machine, maximum allowed sockets and UDP datagrams, and supported socket types.
Socket Services	Checks to see (and lists) all of the sockets utilized on the machine. Includes port number, service name, and protocol used.
Socket Protocols	Lists all of the protocols on this machine understood by Windows Sockets.
NetScanner	Another routing tool that lets you trace the route between two IP addresses.
DayTime	Displays the current time at the remote host you specify. A handy way of finding out busy (or idle) times of the day to access a host. What time *is it* in Denmark when it's 2:51 a.m. (Yikes!) here?
Quote	Returns a quote of the day (if the host is in the mood). Today's quote (at www.rmm.com): "Man can climb to the highest summits, but he cannot dwell there long" –Shaw

Table 6-7: Additional tools available in NetScan.

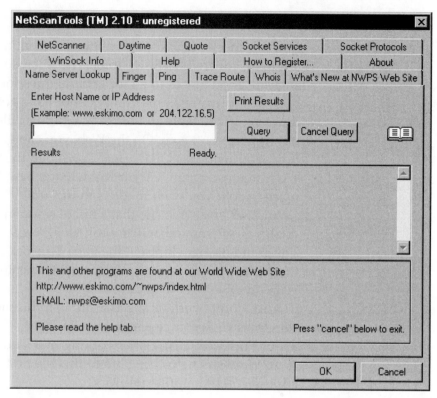

Figure 6-12: NetScanTools.

Other Monitoring Tools

Windows 95 comes with a number of other tools to help you monitor, troubleshoot and maintain network connections on both dial-up and LAN setups. See Table 6-1 at the beginning of this chapter for a list of them and what they do. Most of them are located in the \windows directory. Complete help information on them is available in the Windows 95 Resource Kit Help File, located on the Windows 95 CD-ROM.

HELP!

You can check out a number of excellent online sites for help on anything covered in this chapter. The Microsoft Web and FTP sites are good places to go for general questions, troubleshooting tips, and software extras you may not have gotten with Windows 95. If you have an idea of what file or files you want, check out ftp.microsoft.com. On the Web, you can get a lot of information about what's available *and* download the files—it's http://www.microsoft.com/. Their Knowledge Base Library is a handy place to go if you want to looks things up.

Another great Web site that's full of setup instructions and oodles of awesome shareware is http://www.windows95.com. The grand ole man himself, the Papa Winsock FTP is king of Winsock application sites. FTP to papa.indstate.edu/winsock-l/Windows95/.

Also, don't overlook the TCP/IP help files located in the Windows 95 Resource Kit on the CD-ROM. There's tons of stuff about Microsoft TCP/IP networking that's not covered in the main Windows help. The path to this file on the CD-ROM is admin\reskit\helpfile\win95rk.

TIP

If you want to get your hands on the latest and greatest power tools and techniques for Windows 95, check out Mansfield and Petroutsos' *Windows 95 Power Toolkit* (Ventana). It's jam-packed with information on getting the most out of Windows 95 and your frequently-used applications (such as Word and Excel). The chapters on The Registry and Tuning Up Windows are especially useful. This book makes an excellent companion volume to the *Internet Power Toolkit*. It also comes with a CD-ROM full of useful applications and utilities. We can't recommend this book highly enough.

MOVING ON

Now that you've gotten your TCP/IP connection running smoothly (we hope!), it's time to move on to actually using it. In the next four chapters we'll examine some of the most popular Windows Internet power tools. These chapters won't be primers on how to set up your e-mail account, newsreading software, or Web browsers—we're assuming that you already know how to do that. What you will learn are tips and tricks for effective use, along with obtaining handy quick-reference guides to all of the features and concise explanations of functions that may have been glossed over in the documentation. And, while we're at it, we'll throw in some information on cutting edge ways to extend your programs and make the most out of your connections with the coolest power tools we could find.

We're going to start with the one function of your online life you probably use the most—e-mail. We'll take a look at several of the most popular and useful Windows Internet e-mail tools.

## Chapter 7

Windows E-Mail Power Tools

Undoubtedly, e-mail is the most commonly used and arguably the most useful service on the Internet. It allows us to keep in touch with far-flung friends and to get publications and lively discussions delivered to our e-mail boxes. It's also had a tremendous impact on global business communications.

E-mail provides an entirely new wrinkle on communications by enabling us to communicate in a quick, casual, and often, spontaneous way. Just think of all the people you talk to via e-mail (many whom you've met online) who you wouldn't stay in such close contact with by snail mail or telephone.

Unlike the phone, e-mail doesn't interrupt and demand our immediate attention. It waits patiently for us to answer it. Unlike Usenet newsgroups, e-mail is private, allowing us to have conversations free of the self-editing that comes with public message posting. E-mail is point-to-point communications, offering relative privacy in an increasingly public world.

Windows users with TCP/IP connections are blessed with some excellent e-mail packages. (Some of them are even free!) Pick any of the programs discussed in this chapter, and you'll find them easy to use with lots of useful features. All of them are available online and can be used (at least for a trial period) without charge.

We'll also look at some e-mail power tools. These aren't mail readers, but e-mail extensions that allow you to check your mail without having to fire up your e-mail program or run an incoming mail server on your PC.

We assume you already know the basics of how to read and send your e-mail. In this chapter, we're going to focus on handy tools and tricks that can expand your e-mail options and improve your e-mail management.

SENDING & RECEIVING E-MAIL

Since you spend so much time using e-mail, it's important that you're comfortable with your e-mail program and knowledgeable about what it does. A good e-mailer, properly configured, can make information glut easier to deal with. A bad e-mail program can make your life miserable. Since e-mail is so important to the power user, we've assembled the best e-mail shareware and freeware programs we could find—Eudora Light, Pegasus Mail, and E-Mail Connection. They offer well-designed graphical interfaces, information-organizing functions, and file attachment features. The following table provides a brief comparison of these programs. Since each program has strengths and weaknesses, we'll also look at each of them in more detail in the sections that follow.

	Eudora Light	Pegasus Mail	E-mail Connection	Comments
Filtering	No	Yes	Sort of	Auto-sorting mail
Address Book	Yes (& aliasing)	Yes (& aliasing)	Yes (& aliasing)	Place to keep e-mail addresses and names. Aliasing allows you to subscribe to mailing lists.
Spell Checker	No	Yes	Yes (a good one!)	A Dan Quayle must-have!
Helper Apps	No	Yes	No	External viewers (GIF, JPG, MIME, etc.).
Customizable	No	Yes	No	Can functionality be extended beyond "stock" model?

➡

	Eudora Light	Pegasus Mail	E-mail Connection	Comments
Special Features	Ph & finger server access	Workgroup-accessible discussion folders over a LAN	Nice local mail search capabilities, swank-o-rama interface.	See sections below on each program for more info on special features.
Mac Version	Yes	Yes	Coming soon	Good for two-party families and businesses.
Ease of Use	Easy	Moderate	Easy	Level of ease for experienced users.
Cost	Freeware	Freeware	Freeware	Can't beat the price.
Comments	Commercial version with filtering available.	Not the most elegant interface in the world.	A lot of the real goodies are disabled in the freeware version.	

Table 7-1: E-mail programs.

Eudora Light

Originally a shareware program written by Steve Dorner, Eudora is now a full-fledged, powerful e-mail program published by Qualcomm as Eudora Pro. Luckily for us budget-conscious Netheads, Qualcomm distributes a freeware version called Eudora Light. Even though Light doesn't have all of the power features of Pro (such as automatic mail filtering), it's still a great program that will fulfill most people's e-mail needs.

Since you may already have this program (and if you don't, it's fairly easy to install), we won't go into the basic setup procedure here. What we will do is cover the options of the program that you might have overlooked in setting it up or that may have been unclear.

Getting Eudora

If you don't already have Eudora Light, it is available from Qualcomm's Web site at http://www.qualcomm.com/ or direct at http://www.qualcomm.com/ ProdTech/quest/light.html. Just follow the directions on the screen to download it. Once you've downloaded and unzipped it, double-click on the Eudora icon. The multiscreened Settings dialog box will appear. This is the same dialog box that's available as the Options item in Eudora's Tools menu. If you have any questions about the basic setup, check the Eudora help file. Qualcomm also has a free 136-page manual that you can download at the light.html Web page.

NOTE: The version that was available when we were writing this book was labeled 154b11. It is this version that is discussed below. Beta software can change during its journey to a full-blown release. If you get a later version of Eudora Light that is slightly different than what is discussed here, that's probably why. Consult the help file that comes with the program.

Eudora Light Options

Eudora Light offers many different options for setting it up and customizing it to your needs. While you may already know the bare-bones stuff (POP, SMTP, password, and username), we thought we'd run through these options with an eye toward those things that may not be apparent to you.

Getting Started

Under the Getting Started icon (see Figure 7-1), the POP Account text box refers to your e-mail address (e.g., binky@lifeinhell.com). Eudora uses this information to get both your username (everything that comes before the @) and the name of your system's POP mail server (everything after the @).

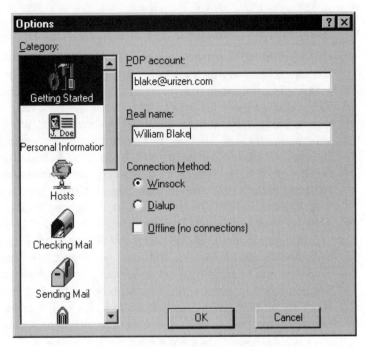

Figure 7-1: The Getting Started dialog box in Eudora.

If you don't want to enter your real name into the Real name text box, you don't have to. If you leave it blank, no name will appear in the From: mail header.

Finally, make sure that the Winsock radio button is checked if you're using TCP/IP. Select the Dialup button if you're making a connection directly from your machine to a host's POP mail server. (See the "Dialup" section later in this chapter.) Offline (no connections) allows you to open Eudora without it trying to launch your PPP or SLIP connection. Unfortunately, you have to select this button before you exit a session to have it work for the next session.

Acronym Alert! POP & SMTP

Uh oh, dreaded acronyms again! POP and SMTP are the names for the two protocols that your computer uses to receive and send mail.

POP (first proposed in RFC 918) stands for Post Office Protocol. No, it doesn't describe how to keep from annoying disgruntled employees at the U.S. Postal Service. POP describes how workstations (i.e., your computer) can receive mail from a host computer. The exact details aren't terribly important, but you should know that POP servers are designed to be secure, only allowing users with valid passwords to get their private mail. When mail comes in from across the Net to the host where the POP server is located, it's stored until you dial in and give the right password. Then the mail is forwarded to your machine.

On the other hand, SMTP (Simple Mail Transport Protocol) was designed to pass mail back and forth between UNIX hosts, as well as a way for you to pass mail between your computer and the host computer. When you send a message out to the Net from your machine via Eudora (or another e-mail program), it goes to the SMTP server, which packages it up and sends it to its destination.

Personal Information

In Personal Information (see Figure 7-2), you can enter optional information about your account. You'll notice that your POP account and name have been transferred from the Getting Started section and that there are two empty boxes: Return Address and Dialup username. If you use a different address for returned mail, enter it in the Return Address text box.

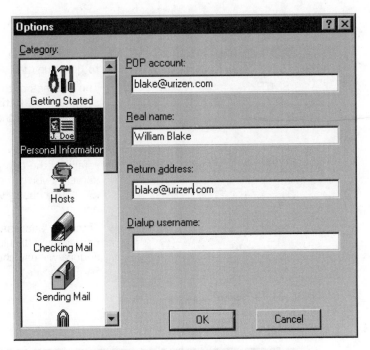

Figure 7-2: The Personal Information dialog box in Eudora.

TIP

Take care when entering a return address. If you make a mistake typing the address, no one will be able to reply to your messages. Not a good thing.

If your username is different from your e-mail name, and you're using the Dialup Connection Method option, enter your username in the Dialup username text box.

Hosts

The Hosts dialog box (see Figure 7-3) is where you tell Eudora about the different host computers you'll be using for your various online tasks. Table 7-2 describes the function of each of these options.

Option	Description
POP account	The name of the POP server you use to get your mail.
SMTP	The address of the SMTP server used to send mail. If this field is left blank, Eudora will use the same address as the POP server.
Ph	No, that's not for a phone number. Ph refers to the campus phonebook server. If you're using a commercial ISP, you probably won't need this option.
finger	Enter the address of your finger server here. If this field is left blank, Eudora will use the address for your SMTP server.

Table 7-2: Hosts dialog box options.

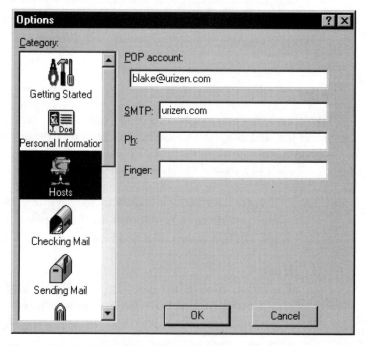

Figure 7-3: The Hosts dialog box in Eudora.

Checking Mail

The interesting options under this icon bear some looking into. (See Table 7-3.) By selecting the various options in this dialog box, you can control how (and when) Eudora checks your mail, and what it does with it after it checks it. See Figure 7-4.

Option	Description
POP Account	Address of POP server used for getting mail.
Check for mail every...minutes	Specifies the interval at which Eudora logs onto the POP server and checks for new mail.
Skip big messages	Leaves messages over 40K on the server, and downloads only the first few lines.
Send on check	Sends mail queued in Out mailbox after logging on to check for new mail.
Save Password	Saves password for POP server so you don't have to enter it every time you check your mail.
Leave mail on server	Does not delete mail from POP server after checking.
Authentication Style: Passwords	Uses plain-text password for user authentication on POP server.
Authentication Style: APOP	Uses APOP protocol (encrypted secret password and timestamp) for authentication when logging on to server. See RFC 1460.

Table 7-3: Checking Mail dialog box options.

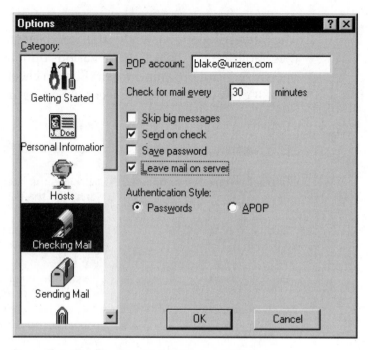

Figure 7-4: The Checking Mail dialog box in Eudora.

Sending Mail

Eudora offers a whole slew of options for sending mail (Table 7-4). In general, Eudora should work fine if you use the default options, but if you have any special preferences, you may want to fiddle with these settings.

Option	Description
Return address	Specifies the address that message replies go to. This must be a valid e-mail address or you won't get any replies to your messages.
SMTP server	Specifies the SMTP server address used for outgoing mail.

Option	Description
Immediate send	Sends mail immediately to the SMTP server (via the Send button in the message composition window). If this is unchecked, button in message window will read "Queue."
Send on check	Sends mail queued in Out mailbox after you log on to check for new mail.
Word wrap	Toggles outgoing text word wrap, usually at 76 characters.
Fix curly quotes	Changes curly quotes into straight quotes for compatibility with 7-bit e-mail systems.
May use Quoted-Printable	Allows the use of 8-bit (foreign and special characters) in e-mail messages. This option is useful for corresponding with people not using the Latin alphabet.
Keep copies of outgoing mail	Places a copy of each outbound e-mail message in the Out mailbox. Useful if you tend to drink while writing e-mails and can't remember the next morning what you wrote the night before.
Use signature	Appends signature file (defined with Signature option in the Windows menu) to outgoing mail messages.
Tabs in body of message	Turns on tabs for use inside e-mail messages.

Table 7-4: Sending Mail dialog box options.

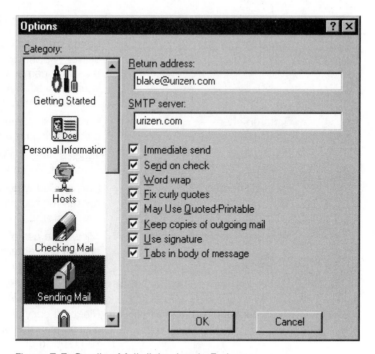

Figure 7-5: Sending Mail dialog box in Eudora.

Attachments

Here's where things can really get fun. Eudora offers several options for attaching files to your e-mail (see Table 7-5). Unfortunately, there's no hard and fast standard (though MIME is getting there) for sending and receiving files via e-mail, so you'll have to know what type of computer and mailer the recipient of your files has before you decide how best to send them. These options allow you to tailor your attachments so that the people getting them (hopefully) receive them in one piece. This dialog box also allows you to specify the destination folder for any incoming attachments as well as the file creator for any e-mail you save. See Figure 7-6.

Option	Description
Encoding Method: MIME	Encodes attachments into MIME format. Choose this option to send attachments to recipients who have MIME capability.
Encoding Method: BinHex	Encodes attachments into BinHex for compatibility with older versions of Eudora and non-MIME e-mail systems.
Encoding Method: Put text attachments in body of message	Sends attachments in body of e-mail message.
Attachment Directory	Pressing this button presents you with a directory dialog box in which you can specify where you want incoming attachments to be saved.
Delete attachments when emptying Trash	Deletes attachments when mail message is deleted.

Table 7-5: Attachments options.

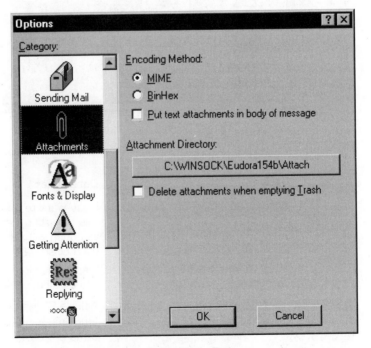

Figure 7-6: Attachments dialog box in Eudora.

Fonts & Display

The Fonts & Display options allow you to customize the look and feel of Eudora. Choose the font you want to use to view your messages and the font you want to use when printing mail. Table 7-6 lists some of the other available options.

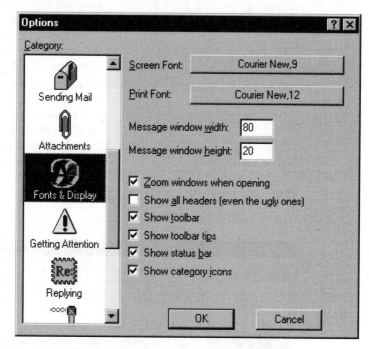

Figure 7-7: Fonts & Display dialog box in Eudora.

Option	Description
Zoom windows when opening	If you want to add some pizzazz, check this box. All message windows that you open will zoom open to their correct sizes.
Show all headers (even the ugly ones)	Displays full Internet mail header info on all messages.
Show toolbar	Toggles toolbar in main window on/off.
Show toolbar tips	Toggles pop-up descriptions of toolbar items on/off.

➡

Option	Description
Show status bar	Toggles status message bar at bottom of main window on/off.
Show category icons	Toggles between list of options and option icons in Options dialog boxes.

Table 7-6: Fonts & Display options.

Getting Attention

In case you fall asleep at your keyboard (we don't know about you, but we do that a lot) or tend to forget that you left Eudora running in the background, this dialog box (see Table 7-7) lets you specify how you want Eudora to wake you up and tell you about your new mail. See Figure 7-8.

Option	Description
Use an alert dialog box	Displays dialog box when mail arrives. See Figure 7-8.
Open mailbox	Displays In box with new message list.
Play a sound	Plays a sound to alert you to incoming mail. Click on the Directory button to choose a sound that you want played.

Table 7-7: Getting Attention options.

Figure 7-8: Mail call in Eudora!

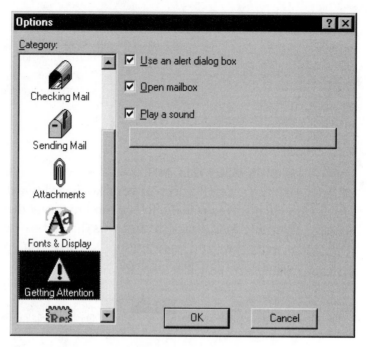

Figure 7-9: Getting Attention dialog box in Eudora.

Replying

Eudora gives you several options (see Table 7-8) for replying to mail, not the least of which are options for controlling who on a list your replies goes to. Many a relationship has been nipped in the bud when someone on a mailing list replied to the whole list instead of just the person(s) they intended. Some unfortunate e-mail newbies have even lost their jobs by sending whiny letters about the boss *to* the boss! Don't let this happen to you. See Figure 7-10.

Option	Description
Reply to all (otherwise when Shift is down)	Sends reply to all the recipients of a message. If this option is not checked here, you'll need to depress the Shift key while replying in order to reply to all.
When replying to all: Include yourself	This way you get to read your scintillating prose all over again!
When replying to all: Put original To: recipients in Cc: field	Puts the original recipients in the Cc: field; only the original sender is placed in the To: field.
Copy original's priority to reply	Applies the priority status of the original message to your reply.

Table 7-8: Replying options.

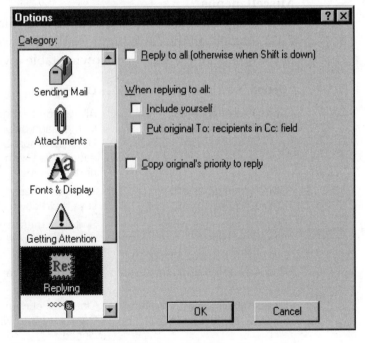

Figure 7-10: Replying dialog box in Eudora.

Dialup

Eudora for Windows allows you to dial in to a host computer to get your mail without the need of a TCP/IP connection. Eudora Light comes with a number of dial-up scripts (called Navigation or .NAV files). If your provider is not on this list, ask them if they have the appropriate script. If they don't, you may need to hack one yourself using one of the scripts in the Eudora Scripts folder. Unfortunately, getting this feature to work is *not* trivial. The .NAV scripts are difficult to configure, and you need to have a program called srialpop installed on the UNIX machine you'll be connecting to (which allows you to Telnet into the host's POP server port–port 110). This is a dying form of connectivity (thanks to PPP and SLIP), and we found it almost impossible to get any help in setting this up on our ISP's hosts.

Miscellaneous

True to its name, the Miscellaneous settings dialog box (see Figure 7-11) contains all the configurations that just wouldn't fit into any of the other categories. The following table gives a breakdown.

Option	Description
Switch messages with: Unmodified arrow keys	Allows you to move from message to message by using the arrow keys. Up or Left opens the previous message while Down or Right opens the next message.
Switch messages with: Ctrl+arrow keys	To switch messages with the arrow keys, hold down the Control key, too.
Switch messages with: Alt+arrow keys	Switches messages using the arrow keys while you're holding down the Alt key.
Require confirmation for deletes	Asks for confirmation before deleting messages.
Close messages with mailbox	Closes all currently open messages from a mailbox when that mailbox is closed.
Empty Trash when exiting	Automatically empties Trash when you quit Eudora.

➡

Option	Description
Say OK to alerts after 2 minutes	Automatically presses the OK button if an alert on the screen is not responded to after two minutes.
Automatically open next message	Automatically opens the next message after you have deleted or transferred the current message.

Table 7-9: Miscellaneous configuration options.

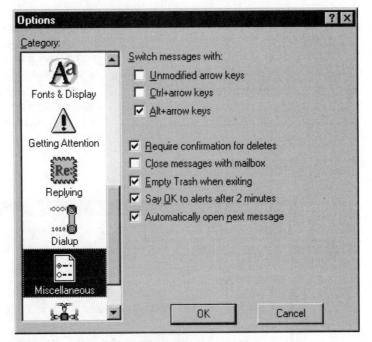

Figure 7-11: The Miscellaneous options in Eudora.

Advanced Network

The Advanced Network settings, listed in Table 7-10, control various aspects of how Eudora communicates with your Winsock and your network at large. If you're on a LAN, you shouldn't change any of the settings without first talking to your systems administrator.

Option	Description
Use asynchronous Winsock calls for: All non-database functions	Asynchronous Winsock calls is the most desirable connection between Eudora and your TCP/IP stack. Try unchecking if you're having trouble with Winsock.
Use asynchronous Winsock calls for: Database functions	Same as above but used for database functions only.
Network timeout after...seconds	Designates the number of seconds that elapse before network times out when connection is idle.
Network buffer size of...bytes	The buffer size that Eudora can use to transfer data between you and the server. Try *decreasing* this amount if you're having trouble transferring large messages.
Cache network info	Allows Eudora to store a session's internal database functions. This setting can enhance program performance.

Table 7-10: Advanced Network options.

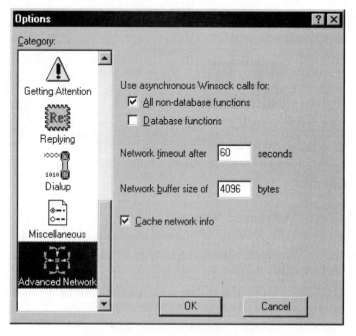

Figure 7-12: The Advanced Network dialog box in Eudora.

Sending Mail With Eudora Light

Sending e-mail with Eudora is easy. First, choose New Message from the Message menu, or type **Ctrl+N**. A window will appear (see Figure 7-13) containing spaces for the address of who you want to send the message to (the To: field), for the subject of your message (the Subject: field), for who you want to send a carbon copy to (the Cc: field), for who you want to send a blind carbon copy to (the Bcc: field), and for a list of your attachments.

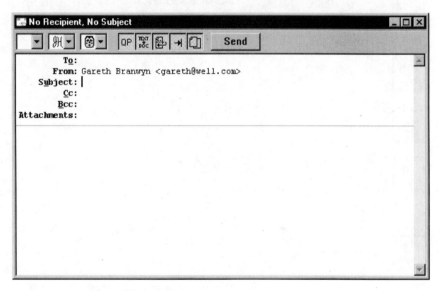

Figure 7-13: The New Message window.

The message bar icons that appear just below the title bar are a bit on the on the cryptic side. Table 7-11 will straighten things out.

Icon	Type	Function	Choices	Description
⌄ ▼	Pull-down menu	Sets priority level	Highest, High, Normal, Low, Lowest	Assigns a priority level (Highest, High, Normal, Low, or Lowest) to a message so the recipient knows the importance you attach to a message.

Icon	Type	Function	Choices	Description
	Pull-down menu	Appends signature	Signature/None	Appends signature defined in Signature menu (under Windows menu) to outgoing message.
	Pull-down menu	Applies encoding	MIME/BinHex	Encodes attachments into MIME or BinHex format.
QP	Toggle icon	Applies Quoted-printable encoding	On/Off	Enables MIME quoted-printable encoding for 8-bit message compatibility.
TEXT + DOC	Toggle icon	Text As Attachment	On/Off	Sends plain text attachments in message box.
	Toggle icon	Word wrap	On/Off	Wraps words at approximately 76 characters per line.
	Toggle icon	Tabs in body	On/Off	When on, inserts eight space characters for every tab. When Off, returns cursor to To: field.
	Toggle icon	Keeps copies	On/Off	Keeps a copy of each outgoing message in Out mailbox.
Send	Button	Sends message	Send	Sends message to SMTP server.
Queue	Button	Queues message	Queue	Adds message to mail queue in Out mailbox.

Table 7-11: New Message icons.

Remember, the default values for these message bar options were set when you configured Eudora in the Options dialog box. Use these icons only when you need to change a default value.

Once you've completed your message, all you have to do to press the Send button. If you chose Send on check in the Sending Mail dialog box, the Send button will read Queue instead. Pressing it sends your message to the Out mailbox where it'll wait to be sent until Eudora checks for new mail.

If you want to attach a document to your message, select Attachments from the Message menu. Eudora will provide you with a File dialog box where you can select the file you wish to attach to your message. If you want to learn about attaching files, we'll cover more in Chapter 20.

What the Heck is Eudora?

Almost everyone, when first exposed to Eudora, asks "Why Eudora?" Creator Steve Dorner says he couldn't help thinking about Eudora Welty's short story "Why I Live at the Post Office" while he was working on this Post Office Protocol program. Thing is, when you respond to a new user's question with "He named it after Eudora Welty," you've still got some explainin' to do. If you want to read the story that inspired the software, it's in a collection called *A Curtain of Green & Other Stories*.

Receiving Mail With Eudora Light

To check to see if you have any new mail messages, select Check Mail from the File menu (or press **Ctrl+M**). A dialog box will prompt you for your password. Then Eudora will make the connection to your POP account and download your new messages. To let you know what's going on, a status box appears as downloading occurs. If you don't have any new mail, nothing happens after the status box disappears. After your new mail is downloaded, it is listed in the In window. See Figure 7-14.

TIP

If you want Eudora to check your mail automatically when you first start it up, or you want to leave Eudora open as you work to periodically check for new messages, select the Save Password option in the Checking Mail section of the Options dialog box.

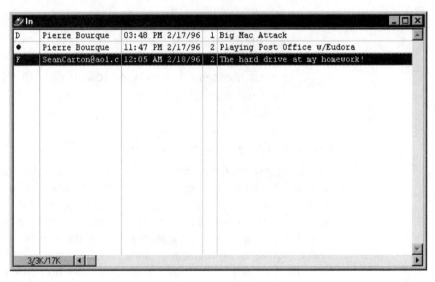

Figure 7-14: In mailbox in Eudora.

As you can see, the In mailbox window is divided into six sections. These are listed in Table 7-12.

Field	Values	Description
Status	•	Unread message.
	<nothing>	Read message.
	D	The message has been redirected.
	F	The message has been forwarded.
	R	The message has been replied to.
Priority	<<	Sender has assigned highest priority to the message.
	<	Sender has assigned high priority to the message.
	<nothing>	Normal message priority
	>	Sender has assigned low priority to the message.
	>>	Sender has assigned lowest priority to the message.
Sender	Name or e-mail address	Name appearing in the From: field of the incoming message header.
Date	Date & time	Date and time message was sent.

Field	Values	Description
Size	Integer	Size in kilobytes of incoming message text. This does not include the size of the attachment.
Subject	String	String appearing in the Subject: field of incoming message header.

Table 7-12: In mailbox fields.

To read a message, double-click on the line in the In mailbox that lists the message you want to read. A message window will open (Figure 7-15), containing the message.

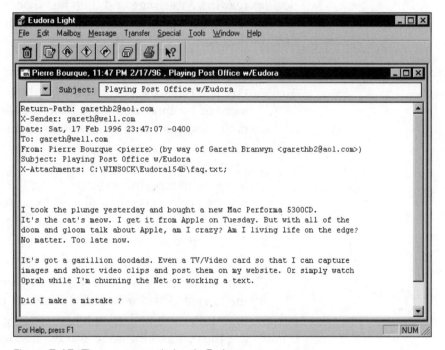

Figure 7-15: The message window in Eudora.

The title bar of the message window contains the name of the sender, the time and date the message was delivered, and the subject. The pop-up menu to the left of the subject box icon is the priority setting. Just as with outgoing messages, you can set the priority of the message from this menu. For messages you receive, this can be useful to remind yourself which incoming messages are important and which ones aren't.

Receiving Attachments

If the message you received includes an attachment, you'll see a line at the end of the message indicating the name of the attachment. You don't have to do anything more to get the attachment—it's already in the directory you specified for attachments in the Attachments section of the Options dialog.

Replying, Forwarding & Redirecting Incoming Mail

Besides reading a message and then just discarding it once you're done with it, you can send it to someone else in one of three different ways:

- ❏ Replying: While you've got the message window open, you can reply by pressing the Reply button (the U-turn icon) or by choosing Reply from the Message menu. A new message window will open containing the text of the message you're replying to, each line of which will be preceded by a greater than symbol (>). You can delete the text you're replying to by pressing the Delete key, edit the text by clicking on it, or just add your own words to the message and send it as is. You can edit any of the header information so if you want to change the subject, send copies to some people, or add attachments, go ahead.

- ❏ Forwarding: If you want to forward a message, click on the Forward button or select Forward from the Message menu. Eudora will open a new message window containing the original message and the header information from the original message. Your name will be in the From: field in the header of the message, and the cursor will be in the To: field so that you can indicate who you wish to send the message to.

❐ Redirecting: Redirecting (the Right Turn icon) is almost like forwarding. When you redirect a message, the original message is copied directly into the new message window (without the header information) and the address in the From: field stays the same, with the addition of information that indicates that the message comes "by way of" you.

Managing Your Mail With Eudora Light

The major difference between Eudora Light and Eudora Pro (the commercial version of Eudora) is the mail-handling features. Eudora Pro contains a slew of features for automatically filtering and organizing your e-mail. With Eudora Light, you'll have to do most of the work yourself.

Filing E-mail

If you get a lot of e-mail, the best way to keep track of it is to organize it into different folders or mailboxes. Eudora Light comes with two preconfigured mailboxes: In and Trash. You're already familiar with the In mailbox; it's the directory that mail is delivered to when it arrives on your machine. The Trash mailbox contains all the messages you want to delete. If you have selected Empty Trash when exiting in the Miscellaneous section of the Options dialog, Eudora will delete all the messages in the Trash when you quit the program. Otherwise, you'll have to remove them yourself by selecting Empty Trash from the Special menu.

If you want to organize your e-mail into folders, begin by selecting a message you want to file by clicking on it once in the In mailbox so that it's highlighted. Then go to the Transfer menu and select New. Eudora will then present you with the dialog box as shown in Figure 7-16.

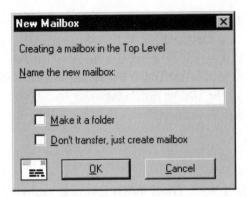

Figure 7-16: The New Mailbox dialog box in Eudora.

First, enter the name of the folder that you want to create in the text box at the top of the New Mailbox dialog box. Give the new mailbox a name that pertains to the messages you're putting in it.

Next, you have three choices: Make it a folder; Don't transfer, just create mailbox; or nothing at all. If you don't select any of the choices, but you've typed a name in the Please name the new mailbox text box, Eudora will create a new mailbox with the name you specified and place the message you've selected into that mailbox. The name of the mailbox will appear on the Transfer menu. When you want to send another message to that mailbox, just select the message in the In window, and then select the destination mailbox from the Transfer menu.

If you want to create a new mailbox but not put any messages into it, type the name of the new mailbox in the text box, and check "Don't transfer, just create mailbox." A new mailbox name will show up under the Transfer menu.

You can also organize your mailboxes into folders. While you'll never see any folder icons, you'll get a hierarchical menu on the Transfer menu labeled with the name of the folder you've created. You can then create mailboxes within that folder transfer to messages to.

Using Nicknames

Anyone who frequently uses e-mail will soon assemble a hefty pile of e-mail addresses. Keeping track of them isn't easy, unless you use Eudora's Nickname feature. Nicknames allow you to assign a shortcut name to someone's e-mail address, so that, for instance, we could assign "sean" as a nickname for seancarton@vmedia.com. Then, to e-mail Sean, we'd only have to enter "sean" in the To: field of our mail message.

To start your nickname file, select Nicknames from the Tools menu. The Nicknames window (shown in Figure 7-17) will then appear. You can store and annotate your nickname list in this window.

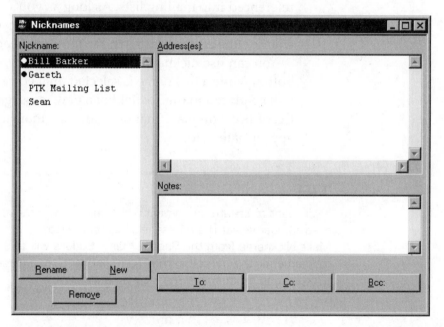

Figure 7-17: Creating a nickname in Eudora.

To add a new nickname, click the New button. Enter the word you want to use as the nickname for the person's e-mail address. Click OK, and you'll be placed back in the Nicknames window with the cursor in the Address(es) list box. Type the e-mail address of the person into this box.

If you need a reminder of who a person on your list is, enter your notes in the Notes text box. These notes are never sent with a message, so feel free to fire at will! Nicknames can be cross-referenced into mailing lists. As long as you've already defined a nickname, you can use it in the Address(es) list box instead of entering the entire address in the message header.

You can use nicknames in several ways. If you press the To: button while a nickname is selected, that corresponding address will be placed in the To: field of a new message. Likewise, pressing Cc: or Bcc: will place that nickname's e-mail address into the appropriate field.

Quick Recipients

If you frequently correspond with certain people (or lists of people that you've set up with nicknames), you may want to add them to the Quick Recipient list. If a nickname has been selected as a Quick Recipient, you can send, reply, forward, or redirect a message to that nickname by selecting it from the hierarchical menus (New Message To, Reply To, Forward To, and Redirect To) under the Message menu.

When you select one of these menu items, another submenu will appear to the right of the menu selection, allowing you to select a nickname you wish to send a message to. Selecting a nickname will cause a new message window to appear, addressed and ready to go.

To add a nickname to your Quick Recipient list, open the Nicknames window, click on the nickname you wish to add to the list, and then right-click the mouse button. A bullet next to the nickname (as shown in Figure 7-18) indicates that the nickname has been added to the Quick Recipient list.

Figure 7-18: Adding a nickname to the Quick Recipient list.

Eudora Light Quick Reference

Eudora Light has many features, and keeping them straight is important if you want to get the most out of the program. Here's a handy quick reference to ease you through your e-mail travels. Don't forget your AAA TripTicks!

The File Menu

The File menu contains many of the options you're used to seeing (Save, Close, Print), and it's also where you send mail and check your online mailbox. See Table 7-13 for a description of the options in the File menu. Figure 7-19 shows you what the File menu looks like.

Option	Keyboard Shortcut	Description
Close	Ctrl+W	Closes current message window.
Save	Ctrl+S	Saves changes to the current window.
Save As		Saves the current message as a text file.
Send Queued Messages	Ctrl+T	Sends all messages in Out mailbox.
Check Mail <time>	Ctrl+M	Checks POP server for mail. If you have instructed Eudora to check for new mail at regular intervals, the time of the next mail check will appear.
Print	Ctrl+P	Prints current message to the printer.
Print Preview		Displays a fit-to-window view of the page to be printed. A zoom feature is included.
Print Setup		Allows you to configure print options.
Exit	Ctrl+Q	Um...you can probably figure this one by now.

Table 7-13: The File menu options.

Close	Ctrl+W
Save	Ctrl+S
Save As...	
Send Queued Messages	Ctrl+T
Check Mail	Ctrl+M
Print...	Ctrl+P
Print Preview	
Print Setup...	
Exit	Ctrl+Q

Figure 7-19: The File menu in Eudora.

The Edit Menu

The Edit menu contains many of the options you're used to (Undo, Cut, Copy, Paste) as well as some options for text and nickname handling. See Table 7-14 and Figure 7-20.

Option	Keyboard Shortcut	Description
Undo	Ctrl+Z	Reverses most recently completed action.
Cut	Ctrl+X	Cuts selected text and places it in the clipboard.
Copy	Ctrl+V	Copies selected text to clipboard.
Paste	Ctrl+W	Pastes text in the current message window.
Paste as Quotation	Ctrl+'	Pastes text in clipboard into the current message, placing a greater than symbol (>) at the beginning of each line.
Clear		Deletes selected text.
Select All	Ctrl+A	Selects all the text (including headers).
Wrap Selection		Initiates word wrap, breaking each selected line with a carriage return.

➡

Option	Keyboard Shortcut	Description
Finish Nickname	Ctrl+,	No, this has nothing to do with Laplander terms of endearment. This option instructs Eudora to complete any partial nicknames you have entered in the To:, Cc:, or Bcc: fields of a new message.
Insert Recipient		Inserts another nickname into a new message header.
Find		Allows you to find a string in the current message or any other messages.
Sort		Sorts e-mail messages in current In mailbox by Status, Priority, Date, Sender, or Subject.

Table 7-14: The Edit menu options.

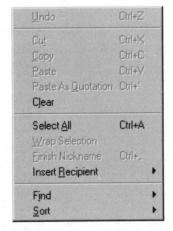

Figure 7-20: The Edit menu in Eudora.

The Mailbox Menu

The Mailbox menu is where you manage your incoming, outgoing, and discarded e-mail messages. See Table 7-15 and Figure 7-21.

Option	Keyboard Shortcut	Description
In	Ctrl+I	Opens In mailbox.
Out		Opens Out mailbox.
Trash		Opens list of items waiting to be discarded.
New		Displays New Mail dialog box for creating new mailboxes.
<user defined mailboxes>		Selects a user-defined mailbox from this menu.

Table 7-15: The Mailbox menu options.

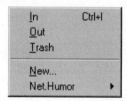

Figure 7-21: The Mailbox menu in Eudora.

The Message Menu

The Message menu is where you create new mail messages, as well as reply to, forward, redirect, and resend mail you have received. See Table 7-16 and Figure 7-22.

Option	Keyboard Shortcut	Description
New Message	Ctrl+N	Opens a new message window.
Reply	Ctrl+R	Replies to currently selected message.

Option	Keyboard Shortcut	Description
Forward		Forwards the current message.
Redirect		Sends current message to another e-mail address.
Send Again		Resends message returned from mail server. Reformats and removes the error headers from the returned message.
New Message To		Same as New Message but allows you to choose recipient from Quick Recipient list.
Reply To		Replies to current message, allows you to access Quick Recipient submenu.
Forward To		Forwards message to user(s) specified in the Quick Recipient list.
Redirect To		Redirects message to user(s) named in Quick Recipient list.
Send Immediately	Ctrl+E	Sends mail directly to SMTP server or queues it for later delivery (as specified in the Sending Mail section of the Options dialog.
Attach File	Ctrl+H	Accesses a standard file dialog box so you can choose what file you wish to attach to your message.
Change		Allows you to change the outgoing message priority as well as how the message should be sent from the queue to the SMTP server.
Delete	Ctrl+D	Deletes current message.

Table 7-16: The Message menu options.

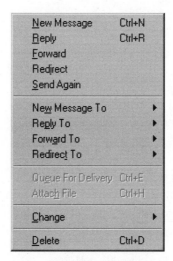

New Message	Ctrl+N
Reply	Ctrl+R
Forward	
Redirect	
Send Again	
New Message To	▶
Reply To	▶
Forward To	▶
Redirect To	▶
Queue For Delivery	Ctrl+E
Attach File	Ctrl+H
Change	▶
Delete	Ctrl+D

Figure 7-22: The Message menu in Eudora.

The Transfer Menu

The Transfer menu allows you to move messages to the In and Out boxes and the Trash. It's also where you can create new, user-defined mailboxes. See Table 7-17 and Figure 7-23.

Option	Keyboard Shortcut	Description
In		Transfers message to In mailbox.
Out		Transfers message to Out mailbox.
Trash		Transfers current message to the Trash.
New		Creates a new mailbox and saves current message in it.
<user defined mailboxes>		Selects a user-defined mailbox from this menu.

Table 7-17: The Transfer menu options.

Figure 7-23: The Transfer menu in Eudora.

The Special Menu

The Special menu is where you create nicknames, add addresses to your Quick Recipient list, and change your password. See Table 7-18 and Figure 7-24.

Option	Keyboard Shortcut	Description
Make Nickname	Ctrl+K	Creates nicknames for addresses in the current window.
Add as recipient		Adds currently selected e-mail address to the Quick Recipient list.
Remove Recipient		Removes a member from the Quick Recipient list.
Empty Trash		Deletes all messages that have been transferred to the Trash mailbox.
Compact Mailboxes		Smooshes mailbox files, eliminating any unused space. Helps save hard drive space.
Forget Password		Deletes POP account password from Eudora. You'll have to enter your password the next time Eudora checks for mail.
Change Password		Allows you to change your saved POP account password.

Table 7-18: The Special menu options.

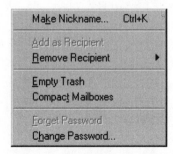

Figure 7-24: The Special menu in Eudora.

The Tools Menu

The Tools menu provides access to your mailboxes, the nickname window, the Ph server window (for those of you on a network that uses a Ph directory), your signature file, and the all-important Options dialogs. See Table 7-19 and Figure 7-25.

Option	Keyboard Shortcut	Description
Mailboxes		Displays Mailboxes window, which allows you to move messages between your various mailboxes.
Nicknames	Ctrl+L	Opens Nicknames window.
Ph	Ctrl+U	Opens Ph server window.
Signature		Displays the Signature file window.
Options		Displays the multiscreen Options (or Preferences) dialog boxes.

Table 7-19: The Tools menu options.

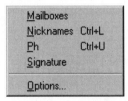

Figure 7-25: The Tools menu in Eudora.

The Window Menu

As in most Windows programs, this menu lets you switch between different window arrangements and between different open windows. See Table 7-20 and Figure 7-26.

Option	Description
Standard series of Windows management arrangements in Eudora.	For customizing the window options (Cascade, Tile, Arrange Icons, etc.)
<window names>	Lists the names of all the currently open windows.

Table 7-20: The Window menu options.

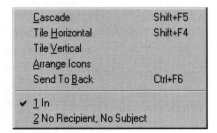

Figure 7-26: The Window menu in Eudora.

Pegasus Mail

Pegasus Mail is a feature-packed e-mail program, and perhaps its best feature is that it's free. Really. Author David Harris says he wrote and supports Pegasus for free because of "the intense satisfaction I get from knowing that people like using it."

Pegasus works with Novell NetWare LANs and on individual machines using Winsock. It works on Windows 95, Windows 3.*x*, Macintosh, DOS, and OS/2 machines.

Getting Pegasus

You can get Pegasus via FTP from risc.ua.edu as winpm210.zip or at http://www.cuslm.ca/pegasus/. After downloading the file and unzipping it, read wguide. Although it's in quaint DOS format, it's full of important information you must know about setting up Pegasus. We know that nobody ever reads documentation, but this is one case in which it really does pay off. It's clear, concise, and when Harris says something is *important*, it is.

Installing Pegasus

Before you install Pegasus, fire up your TCP/IP connection. Pegasus will look for it and will not display the configuration entries on the File menu until it finds an active Winsock.

First go to the File menu, and select Network Configuration to tell Pegasus where to get your mail. Once that is working, be sure to go farther down the File menu to Preferences so that you can tailor Pegasus to your liking.

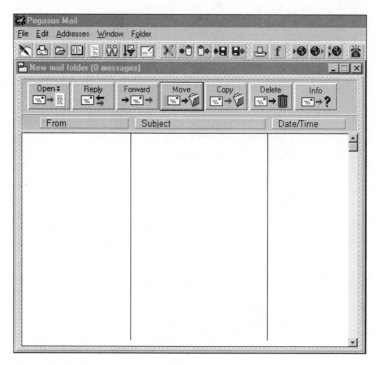

Figure 7-27: The main window in Pegasus Mail.

Windows 95 Users

A bug in Windows 95's NetWare emulation causes it to report a server connection as present when none is available. This will almost always cause the dreaded GPF. (Thought you left those behind when you left Windows 3.*x*, didn't you?) To correct this, force Pegasus to start in stand-alone mode. The easiest way to do so is to create a shortcut, then right-click on the shortcut to select Properties. Click on the Shortcut tab. In the Target field, add **-A** to the end of the command line.

Harris is still deciding if he will produce a true 32-bit version of Pegasus. He believes it won't enhance performance and that the time involved to write it won't be worth the effort. While he's mulling this over, rest assured that the 16-bit version is swift and pleasant to use.

A Quick Tour

Pegasus has a well-planned desktop. Many of the functions under the various menus are represented by icons on the toolbar. Sending and receiving mail is easily accomplished from the File menu. In fact, almost everything you do on a routine basis is under that menu.

When you compose your first message, you'll find that Pegasus has a rather funky editor that has charming quirks or frustrating kludges, depending on your frame of mind and level of coffee intake. Note that you cannot copy part of a line of text. Text must be copied a whole line, or series of lines, at a time. This is part of the heavy use of drag and drop in Pegasus, which is a welcome feature elsewhere. The editor also has a problem with the tab key that a workaround is described for in wguide.

To make up for these annoyances, go to the help file, and search for the Joke Page. It's worth it.

Pegasus also has:

❐ A spell checker (thank goodness).

❐ The ability to indicate which programs you wish to use to view different types of mail attachments.

❐ An open encryptor interface for encryption and digital signing modules.

❐ Background polling, which lets Pegasus send and receive mail while another program is in the active window.

❐ Glossary entries that enable you to store abbreviations for commonly used text strings, which you can expand at any time with a single key stroke.

❐ An offline mode so that mail can be composed and queued before being sent.

❐ Extension modules for French, German, Swedish, and Danish versions.

Managing Your Mail With Pegasus

When it comes to organizing mail, Pegasus really shines.

Mail Filters

Pegasus has powerful mail-filtering capabilities (see Figure 7-28). If you subscribe to a number of mailing lists or need to keep mail sorted according to sender, the filters make it easy. Go to the Mail Filtering section of the File menu. Click Add, and just fill in the blanks. Be sure to think through your keywords for the filter. Use keywords that are specific to the sort of mail you will receive, such as a mailing list name, a person's name, or the domain where lots of annoying people live. You can create mail folders as you go, and choose to copy, move, delete, forward, and a lot more, based on the filter. If you're getting e-mail from Mr. Clueless, put "Clueless" in a filter, and mark it for deletion. It will automatically be moved to the Delete folder and sent into oblivion when you exit Pegasus (or you can opt to have it destroyed right away).

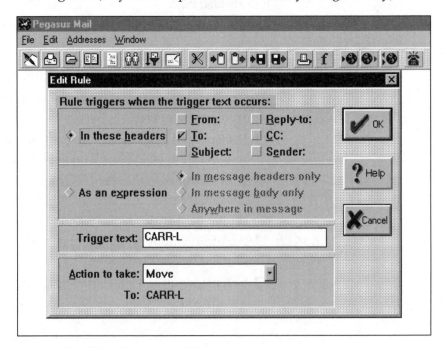

Figure 7-28: Editing Pegasus mail filters.

Address Books & Distribution Lists

Pegasus lets you create separate address books for local users or logged-in users. Pegasus can accept up to 180 characters in any address line. If you need to send a message to more addresses than will fit in this space or you have lists of users to whom you mail regularly, you can create distribution lists.

Advanced Features

Pegasus overflows with features to explore once you're beyond the basics. A couple of these capacities are notable, and one is downright nifty.

Noticeboards

Pegasus has a lot of support for use on a LAN. One aspect of that support is shared mail folders called Noticeboards. They can be set by the LAN administrator for read-only or with posting privileges. These Noticeboards work sort of like a local network bulletin board system. You can create hierarchies of folders based on different subjects and have others on your network read the messages and post responses.

Extensions

Extensions are like the Helper apps in Web browsers. An extension is a program used by Pegasus to add or enhance functionality. The foreign language versions of Pegasus are made available with extensions. Other extensions convert various mail folders from other programs into Pegasus format and provide additional LAN functions. Information for those who want to write extensions is readily available. (See the Pegasus Web page address.)

Using Pegasus for a Mailing List

Do you need a small mailing list? Would you like to avoid the hassle of setting up a listserv or majordomo mailing list with your ISP? Pegasus can be used to create and manage small mailing lists.

■ ■

TIP

If you wait and wait for your mail and then get a message saying that the connection has timed out, it's because Pegasus will try to make that connection only for so long. On a slow SLIP connection or a busy PPP, try setting the timeout for at least 90 seconds. You can do so from the Network Configuration dialog box, using the TCP/IP Socket Timeout field.

■ ■

Where to Go for More Help & Information

Considering that Pegasus is distributed and supported for free, an amazing amount of support is available. Your first stop would be the official Pegasus Web page at http://www.cuslm.ca/pegasus/. From there, you can gather numerous FAQs on installation, using Pegasus on various platforms, and just about any other subject relating to the program. Or send mail to support@pmail.gen.nz. This mail will retrieve an automatic reply listing all the available sources of help, including the latest FAQs, addresses for support mailing lists, and direct mail addresses for the program's author.

Even better are the mailing lists for Pegasus users (check the Pegasus Web page for details). There are separate lists for each platform, and one for announcements only. A bit of advice: Pegasus users seem to be a chatty bunch—the Windows mailing list can get upwards of 75 messages a day. Be sure to keep the subscription information so that you can unsubscribe if it becomes too much of a good thing.

Besides the wguide program, current versions of Pegasus come with internal help as well. In the Windows version, help is available by topic and keyword search.

E-Mail Connection

Here's another absolutely, positively free e-mail program. E-Mail Connection (Internet Edition) is straightforward to install, but it's quite insistent on your registering it first. The first e-mail you send will be to the developer, ConnectSoft. E-mail Connection works on a LAN or through a dial-up connection. Multiple users can share a single copy of the program.

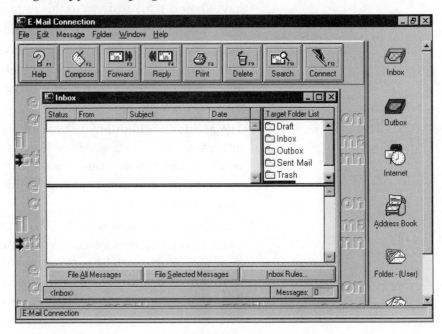

Figure 7-29: The main window in E-mail Connection.

Getting E-mail Connection

You can download a copy of E-mail Connection at http://www. connectsoft.com/products/free_emc25.shtml. You'll find a good bit of extra help there, including FAQs and a Knowledge Base of frequently asked technical questions. The program has a pretty good internal help system but is sometimes vague on certain issues (like what's functional in the freeware Internet Edition and what isn't).

A *Really* Quick Tour

E-mail Connection has many things going for it:

❏ A global address book that can be set to automatically capture all e-mail addresses from senders. If you accidentally deleted the one piece of e-mail you had from Ed and Dick announcing you as the $10,000,000 winner, you'll still have their e-mail address in this log.

❏ Mail filters using hierarchical folders to organize incoming mail. The hierarchical folder system helps to organize your mail, and the drag and drop feature is handy for accomplishing this. (However, a huge drawback is mentioned below.)

❏ The ability to schedule your e-mail sessions. Set connection preferences by frequency, time of day, and day of week. If connection time is metered by your ISP depending on prime and non-prime time, this feature could you save some bucks.

❏ Excellent search functions to find that elusive piece of e-mail from three months ago that mentioned something about a yak and rutabaga. Wait, the message had something about a yak in it, the attachment was a picture of rutabaga, or was it the other way around? No matter, you can search by sender or recipient name, message service of origin, subject header content, message body content, file attachment content, priority, or folder name.

❏ Dual-mode interface, which can be set to Easy for basic functions and Advanced (power user mode).

❏ A spell checker that can be set to automatically check spelling before you queue a message to send. Finally, a feature that will save us from ourselves.

But there are a few drawbacks. Actually, the more you dig into the free version, the more drawbacks you find. E-mail Connection lures you in with a pretty interface and a promise of heavy duty functionality. On many fronts, though, you'll find this free version doesn't support those functions, even though the screens and dialog boxes are right there for them. It's not nice to tease a power user. Among the disappointments:

- ❏ Remember those mail filters? This is most often used for sorting and managing any mailing lists you subscribe to, but E-mail Connection can't do that for mailing lists. Instead, it advises you to switch to the digest version of the list. This is really unacceptable if you have lists that don't support a digest version, and it's just plain annoying, like your mother telling you to make modeling clay out of flour and food coloring instead of buying you a can of Play-Doh.

- ❏ If several people are using a single copy of the program, they all share the same signature file. This can get dicey if your signature has pithy quotes that are not another user's cup of tea. If you and several other people are using a single copy of the program, it's best not to use the signature facility.

- ❏ Distribution lists are reduced to a simple "personal list" in this free version.

- ❏ Blind copies and return receipts are not supported.

Despite these limitations, E-Mail Connection is definitely worth a look, especially if a handsome interface, spell-checking, and searching capabilities are important to you. If you find you really like the freeware version, you might consider buying the commercial package. The main features it adds are the ability to download mail from commercial online services, such as AOL and Prodigy, and the ability to send postal mail (via MCImail) and FAXes from within the program.

E-MAIL POWER UTILITIES

The programs we've covered so far offer full e-mail services. You can also use a number of small utility applications to check your mail without having to launch your e-mail program or even to set up a mail server daemon on your PC. In this section, we'll look at two programs that offer these functions.

Mail Check

Some people can get through the day just fine only firing up Eudora once or twice to check their mail. For those of us who spend most of our day online and who conduct business in Cyberspace, there's always this nagging feeling that something really interesting or pressing has just popped into our mailbox. The answer to this anxiety is a mail-checking utility. Mail Check is a simple program that lets you keep constant vigil over your e-mail. Every so often, at an interval that you specify, Mail Check will log onto your POP account, check for new mail, and notify you if new mail has arrived. Simple, handy, quick, and small—perfect attributes for a power user's tool.

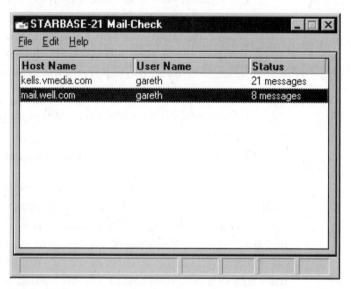

Figure 7-30: The main Mail Check window.

Getting & Configuring Mail Check

Mail Check is widely available on Net sites (such as Consummate Winsock) offering shareware and freeware programs for download. It is also available on the CD-ROM in the back of this book.

All you have to do to install Mail Check is run the setup program and tell it where you want Mail Check to go on your hard drive. Once inside the program, choose Preferences from the File menu to enter how often you want the program the check your mail. Also, enter your POP server information (server name, login, password) under Add Mailbox in the Edit menu. You can enter in multiple mailboxes if you like.

Checking Your Mail

To manually check your mail with Mail Check, choose the Check for Mail item from the File menu. The program will access your e-mail account(s) and alert you if you have messages and how many messages are in each mailbox. You can't read your mail from here; you'll have to launch your regular mail client for that.

Mail Check will automatically check your mailbox after the interval you've specified in Preferences. If the Mail Check window is up when it accesses your mailbox, you'll see the notification dialog box and your mail boxes message status. If you have the program minimized on your desktop, the notification box will pop up to alert you to new messages. You can then either launch the program to see your message status, or just launch your e-mail client to retrieve your messages.

TIP

A number of other mail check programs are available on the E-mail Clients page at the Consummate Winsock Apps site (http://cws. wilmington.net/). Some mail utilities, such as e-Mail Notify, can actually retrieve the headers of your mail messages so you can check to see not only if you have mail, but from whom and on what subjects.

Serve Yourself! Using the QVT/Net SMTPD Server

We're going to end our journey though the wonderful world of Windows TCP/IP e-mail tools with something that's not even an e-mail program. Instead, we're going to take a look at a basic e-mail server that you can install on your PC.

Why Set Up Your Own Mail Server?

We thought you might ask that! If you have a 24-hour Net connection, setting up an SMTP server on your PC will allow you to be able to have as many different e-mail accounts as you want. Assign ones for various mailing lists, ones for friends, and ones for various business functions (sales, tech, info, etc.). You can even give your cat an e-mail account! QVT/Net SMTPD handles only incoming mail, but its companion application QVT/Net Mail (which comes in the same shareware bundle of applications) offers outgoing mail, including good aliasing features and mailbox management. Together, the two programs can be used to create a super-cheap mailing list system.

Getting & Configuring QVT/Net SMTPD

QVT/Net SMTPD is part of a suite of TCP/IP applications (which includes mail, FTP, Gopher, news, a terminal program, and an FTP server). The package is shareware with a $40 registration fee. You can download it from http://cws.wilmington.net/suite.html #win-qvt.

Configuring the mail server is very straightforward. You simply fill out several Setup dialog boxes that pop up when you first launch the program. It basically wants to know the directory where the mailboxes will go and the type of server activity you want. And that's all there is to it.

Receiving E-Mail With QVT/Net SMTPD

If you have a 24-hour Net connection, the mail will be delivered continuously to your machine and routed into the mailboxes that you've set up. SMTP will look in front of the at sign (@) on all incoming messages and try to find mailboxes that match those names. It also uses the username and mailbox information set up in QVT/Net Mail. If it fails to resolve an address, it will put the mail in a box labeled Unknown. Cool, your own dead letter office!

Since you can use this SMTP program (or *daemon*) only for incoming mail, you'll still need to maintain an account on an ISP for outgoing mail. And don't forget to change the SMTP mail information in your e-mail program to reflect your new return address.

MOVING ON

Now that we're finished with our little workshop on one-to-one communications power tools, it's time we turned our sights to the one-to-many communications offered on Usenet newsgroups. Jumping into newsgroups can be a pretty hairy experience if you don't know what you're doing or what tools are available to you. That's where we, your humble authors, come in.

In the next chapter we'll survey some of the best Windows newsreader programs and tools for filtering, creating kill files, and managing your newsgroups. We'll explain how you can organize the 17,000 plus newsgroups available today, as well as ways to avoid the hazards of the highway. When we're finished, *spam*, *velveeta*, and *flames* will move effortlessly from your path as you cruise the Net in high gear. So get ready for a lost highway trek into the wilds of the global idea and information frontier known as Usenet newsgroups.

## Chapter 8

Windows Usenet Power Tools

Nothing epitomizes the global anarchy of the Internet more than the free-wheelin' ideas and information found in Usenet newsgroups. And while Net purists will argue that Usenet isn't *really* part of the Internet, as far as most people are concerned, the point is moot. Reading newsgroups is as much a part net.life as surfing the Web or using e-mail, even if Usenet groups aren't actually transported over TCP/IP networks.

To join in on Usenet's global discussions, you need a newsreader. And with the current number of newsgroups topping 17,000, a *good* newsreader is a necessity. An enormous amount of information is posted every day—over 150 megabytes—so being able to find the articles that you want can be like looking for a needle in a haystack.

A good newsreader should help you sort through the info glut, allowing you to use kill files, autoselecting options, and "bozo.filters." And, since some of the postings to Usenet are executable programs, pictures, movies, and other binary data, a good newsreader should allow you to easily encode and decode binary files for participating in these binary newsgroups.

By now, you probably won't be surprised when we tell you that we've found some newsreaders that fit the bill. These are our top contenders for the best Windows newsreaders—useful, powerful programs that give you a full suite of tools for accessing, managing, and participating in Usenet news. For a quickie look at our picks, check out Table 8-1. We'll look at each newsreader in detail in the sections that follow.

	News Xpress	WinVN	Free Agent	Comments
Kill Files	Yes	Limited	Yes	Ignores articles based on matched patterns.
Filtering	Yes	Limited	Yes	Filters articles based on matched patterns.
Binary Encoding/Decoding	Yes (both)	Yes (decode only)	Yes (both)	Includes built-in capabilities for creating (and/or decoding) binary articles.
Auto-pack Multipart Articles	Yes	Yes	Yes	Automatically combines multipart binary articles.
Helper Apps	Yes	Yes (limited)	Yes	Includes external viewers (GIF, JPEG, MIME, etc.).
Built-in Outgoing Mail	Yes	Yes	Yes	Sends/receives e-mail from within program.
Offline Reader	Yes	No	Yes	Allows you to read new news articles offline.
Special Features	Both easy and powerful	Helpful community of users	Excellent help files, internal multitasking	See sections below on each program for more info on special features.
Mac Version	No	No	No	Good for two-party families & businesses.
Ease of Use	Easy	Moderate	Easy	Easy as applied to an experienced user.
Cost	Freeware	Freeware	Freeware	Can't beat the price.
Comments	Inadequate help files	Dedicated mailing list of developers and users	Commercial version available	

Table 8-1: Windows TCP/IP newsreaders.

NEWS XPRESS

The new kid on the virtual block of newsreaders is a nifty little program called News Xpress. Available for both Windows 3.x and Windows 95, News Xpress is a powerful, handsome, easy-to-use, and small (413KB as opposed to Free Agent's 1.36 MB) newsreader created by Ken Ng of City University of Hong Kong. News Xpress was originally written as part of Ken's graduate studies and was not intended for public release. His project advisor was so impressed with it that he encouraged Ng to release it as freeware to the Internet community. It has quickly become a favorite of Windows users and is now running neck and neck with Free Agent in popularity.

TIP

To find the latest version of News Xpress, check out the numerous Winsock application sites or look on the FTP server at Ng's home site at ftp://ftp.hk.super.net/pub/ windows95/ wksutil/nx20b0.zip.

Installing & Configuring News Xpress

Installation of News Xpress is very straightforward. Make sure that you copy the ctl3dv2.dll file into your \windows\system directory and that you have only one copy of this file there. This is a file that handles the 3D look of the buttons in News Xpress.

When you launch the program for the first time, you will be presented with the setup dialog boxes for entering crucial information about your news and mail servers. You'll also be prompted to add the path and name of your sig file and the home directory for News Xpress' internal files. Don't fill out the News Server Authorization information unless your news server requires it. If you have questions about this, contact your ISP or system administrator.

TIP

Most newsreaders have a personal information section in their Preferences or Options menus in which you enter your real name, return e-mail address, and organization (if any). This information, including the organization, appears in the headers of your Usenet postings. Since this section can contain anything, if you're not online for business, you can have fun making up silly company names or putting other text in this section. There's a lot of wit and good humor on the Internet, but sometimes it gets intense and petty. It's fun to periodically add some levity . . . or a left curve.

Once you're inside the program, before you download your new newsrcfile (your local list of all Usenet newsgroups), you'll want to take care of a few important options in the dialog boxes located in Options under the File menu (see Figure 8-1).

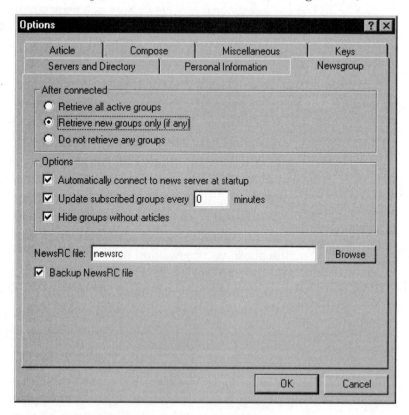

Figure 8-1: The Options dialog box in News Xpress.

We won't go into all of the options (there are a lot of them), but Table 8-2 covers some of more important configurations for new users.

Tab	Option	What it does
Servers and Directories	News (NNTP) server	The name of your news server—this should already be filled in from setup.
	News server authorization	This name/password box should be left blank unless your server requires it.
	Mail (SMTP) server	The name of your mail server. This should already be filled in from setup.
	Home directory	The directory where News Xpress support files are stored.
Personal Information	Full name, e-mail address, organization, default signature file	This information should have been entered on setup. The sig file is the path to the text document you want to sign your Usenet postings with.
Newsgroup	Retrieve all active groups	NX will update the list of all active newsgroups from your news server upon connecting.
	Retrieve new groups only (if any)	Will get the groups that have been added since your last connection.
	Do not retrieve any groups	Will not update your list of newsgroups.
	Automatically connect server at startup	Will connect to news server and perform the action chosen above when you launch NX.
	Update subscribed groups every....seconds	A time interval for how often you want News Xpress to update your newsgroup list while you're connected. 0 = no updates.

➡

Tab	Option	What it does
Newsgroup	Hide groups without articles	Will automatically filter any subscribed groups with no new, unread articles.
	newsrc file	The path/name of the newsrc file you are using.
	Backup newsrc file	If checked, a back-up copy will always be made of your newsrc file. This is especially useful if you like to sort, and otherwise monkey with, your newsrc file.

Table 8-2: Options in News Xpress.

The next step in getting to know News Xpress is understanding how the windows and toolbars work. Figure 8-2 shows the main window toolbar in News Xpress and what each tool does.

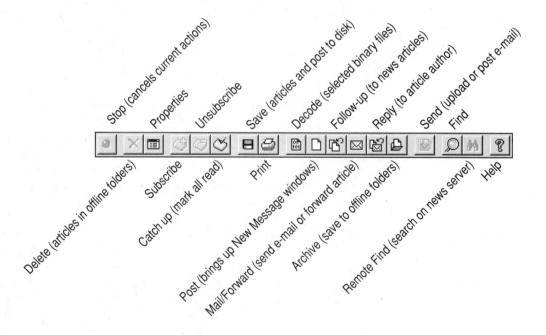

Figure 8-2: The main window toolbar in News Xpress.

The main window itself is divided into several subwindows accessed by tabs at the bottom of the window (see Figure 8-3). Table 8-3 describes what each window contains.

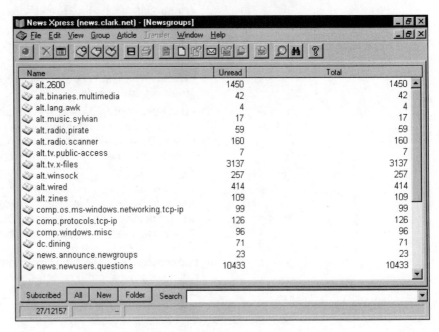

Figure 8-3: The main window in News Xpress.

Tab	What it contains
Subscribed	Selecting this tab takes you to a window displaying all of the groups you are currently subscribed to. News Xpress will take you to this window upon startup, since you are, by default, subscribed to three groups: news.announce.newgroups, news.announce.newusers and news.newusers.questions. The number of unread articles and the number of total articles is displayed.
All	Displays the entire list of newsgroups, both subscribed (marked with a newspaper icon) and unsubscribed (marked with a bullet). Only subscribed groups will show unread and total article counts.
New	Here's where you'll find a list of any new newsgroups that have been added to your news service since your last connection (unless you have Do Not Retrieve Any Groups selected in Options).

265

Tab	What it contains
Folder	This area is the heart of the offline reading and archiving. It contains the following folders:
	• **Copy-Self**—Places a copy of your posts into this folder.
	• **Outbox**—Messages composed and saved offline will be stored here until the next time you're connected and ready to send them.
	• **Trash**—The last rest stop for deleted offline articles on their way to oblivion.
	• **User-created folders**—You can create folders (say, ones for your main newsgroups) and use the Transfer menu to save selected articles in the respective folders. You can then read them offline.
Search (This is actually a box, not a tab)	You can use the search function in the Subscribed, All, and New windows. You can type any part of a newsgroup name (for example, "veterans") to see a list of all newsgroups dealing with that subject. Click on the Down arrow to view the main newsgroup categories (alt, bit, comp, sci, etc.). **Important:** The search box must be blank to display all of the newsgroups in the selected window (Subscribed, All, or New).

Table 8-3: Newsgroup Windows in News Xpress

Just below the tabs on the bottom of the main window is a series of status message boxes (see Figure 8-4). The box to the far left shows you the number of subscribed groups and the number of groups in newsrc file. The second box shows you the number of unread articles and the number of articles available. The third box displays status messages as News Xpress downloads files, retrieves articles, decodes images, and performs other actions.

27/12157	0/514	Reading headers 113505-116641 in alt.tv.x-files...

Figure 8-4: The status message boxes in News Xpress.

TIP

The first time News Xpress is snarfing the newsgroup list off of your server, it might be a good time to grab a cup o' java (the drinkable kind—we'll get to the programming kind in Chapter 24, "WWW Multimedia Power Tools"). With up to 17,000 newsgroups carried on some news servers, downloading the list can take a while. Relax. Read another part of this book . . . there's plenty of it to browse!

Subscribing To & Reading News

Once you've completed the basic setup, it's time to log on. If your Winsock connection is up and running, choose Connect from the File menu. News Xpress will look for a newsrc file. If it doesn't find one, it will create one and begin downloading the newsgroup list from your news provider. Once you have your list of newsgroups, you can begin going through the list and clicking on the groups that you want to add to your subscription list. A newspaper icon will appear to the left of each subscribed group. If you want, you can double-click on any group to go directly to it. It will also be added to your subscription list. Don't forget, you can use the Search feature to search through the All window for the groups you're looking for. Even if you don't know the name of a group, you can try guessing until you find the group you want. I found the group news.software.readers using this method.

TIP

If you are upgrading from another newsreader program to News Xpress, you don't have to download a new newsrc file. Just move your old newsrc file into the same folder as nx.exe before you launch News Xpress for the first time.

When it comes to using Usenet, you'll probably do one of three things: read articles, post new articles, reply to articles. Let's do some online reading first:

1. First you'll want to click on the Subscribed tab to view your selected list of groups. When the list appears, double-click on the group you want to read. A window containing the headers for the selected group will appear (see Figure 8-5). The left column of the header window contains a series of icons. Table 8-4 describes what each icon means.

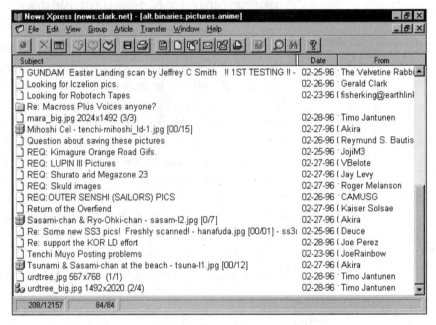

Figure 8-5: A newsgroup header window in News Xpress.

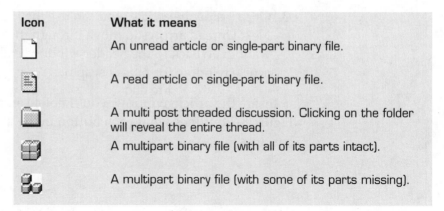

Icon	What it means
	An unread article or single-part binary file.
	A read article or single-part binary file.
	A multi post threaded discussion. Clicking on the folder will reveal the entire thread.
	A multipart binary file (with all of its parts intact).
	A multipart binary file (with some of its parts missing).

Table 8-4: The header window icons in News Xpress.

2. To read an article of interest, simply double-click on it. The article window will appear (see Figure 8-6).

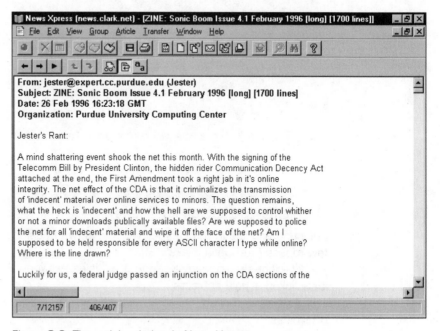

Figure 8-6: The article window in News Xpress.

3. Once inside the article, you can use the Previous, Next, and Next Unread arrows to move through the newsgroup. If you want to go back to the header window, collapse the current article window (or press Escape).

Inside the article window, you'll notice an additional toolbar. Figure 8-7 outlines what each button in the article window toolbar does.

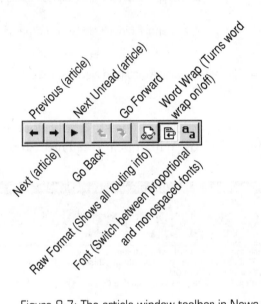

Figure 8-7: The article window toolbar in News Xpress.

Article-Selecting Tips

Selecting articles in the Header window is even easier if you know a few mouse/keyboard tricks:

Shift+right-click selects a range of articles between the first and last-clicked article subjects.

Right-click and drag (called a "swipe") lets you quickly select a range of articles.

Right-click allows you to select noncontiguous articles. Selects each article clicked but not those in between.

Ctrl+A will select all the articles in the current header window, which is useful if you want to quickly mark all the articles as read.

If you have selected all the articles by mistake, simply click somewhere in the list to deselect.

If you need to cancel an operation, such as opening an article, press the red Stop button.

That's basically all you need to know to be able to subscribe, unsubscribe, and read Usenet news articles online.

Offline Reading

If you end up with a large queue of subscribed newsgroups, you can spend a lot of time reading and posting online, which can get expensive. To address this problem, News Xpress has an offline reading feature. The offline reader allows you to access your news server, select the articles that you want to read, and then transfer them to News Xpress folders for viewing offline. The steps to using offline reading are easy.

The following procedure assumes you have an offline folder already created:

1. Within a newsgroup, select the articles you want to read using one of the selection methods outlined in the "Article-Selecting Tips" sidebar.

2. With the article headers highlighted, choose the newsgroup's folder from the list in the Transfer menu.

3. Your selected articles will be transferred and available under the Folder tab for reading and responding to after you disconnect News Xpress.

To use the offline reading feature and create an off-line folder and name it after the newsgroup, follow these steps:

1. Within the newsgroup, select the articles you want to read offline using one of the selection methods outlined in the "Article-Selecting Tips" sidebar.

2. Click on the Archive button (the open folder) on the main News Xpress toolbar. A new folder will automatically be created with the name of the newsgroup. For example: if you're selecting 25 articles from the alt.alien.research group (and who isn't?), after you press the archive button, a folder called alt.alien.research will appear in the folder window (available via the Folder tab).

3. Your selected articles will be transferred and available under the Folder tab for reading and responding to after you disconnect News Xpress.

If an offline folder doesn't already exist (and you *don't* want it named after the newsgroup), follow these steps:

1. Within a newsgroup, select the articles you want to read off-line using one of the selection methods outlined in the Article Selecting Tips sidebar.

2. Choose New from the Transfer menu. A dialog box appears asking you to name the folder. Enter any name you want, and press OK.

Your selected articles will be transferred and available under the Folder tab for reading and responding to after you disconnect News Xpress.

Figure 8-8 shows the Folder window, the place where all the offline reading and composing takes place.

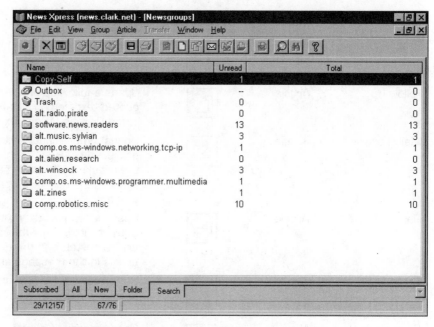

Figure 8-8: The Folder window in News Xpress.

Articles can be responded to using any of the methods described in Table 8-5 and then posted to the Internet upon re-connection. Outgoing mail is saved to the Out box in the Folder window. Articles that you read and do not want to keep can be deleted by pressing the Delete button (the red X). If you want to empty your trash, make sure to check Empty the Trash folders upon exiting under the Misc tab in Options. Otherwise, all the deleted articles will remain in the Trash folder.

Posting News & Sending Mail

Unless you're a total lurker (someone who reads but does not post), eventually you'll want to post an article or two to some of the newsgroups you read. With News Xpress, you have a number of options for how you can respond to an article or post an original. Table 8-5 outlines them.

Option	Menu	Button	What it does
Post	Article		Opens a new article window.
Follow-Up	Article		Opens a follow-up article window. Includes quoted text from original article, as specified in the Options dialog box (under Compose).
Mail/Forward	Article		Opens a mail window with the article title, preceded by (Fwd), in the Subject: field and the article itself in the message area. If no articles are selected, opens a blank mail window.
Reply	Article		Opens a reply window with article name in Subject: field, the e-mail address of the article poster, and the quoted text of the article in the message area.
CC by Mail	None		Sends copy of reply to author of original article. (On Edit toolbar.)
Copyself	None		Sends a copy of outgoing message to Copy-Self folder. (On Edit toolbar.)
Archive	Article		If Archive is chosen while an article is selected, it is moved to a newsgroup folder within News Xpress. The first time you archive something from a group, a new folder will be created.
Save	File		Saves the selected articles to disk.
Send	File		Sends your post, response, followup, or e-mail.
Cancel Post	Article	None	Allows you to cancel articles that you've already posted. Select article, and choose Cancel Post.

Table 8-5: Post and response options in News Xpress.

When you select any of the post/response options, a new article window pops up (see Figure 8-9). You can now compose your post, response, or e-mail, save it to the Outbox for later mailing, or send it immediately (by pressing the Send button in the main toolbar).

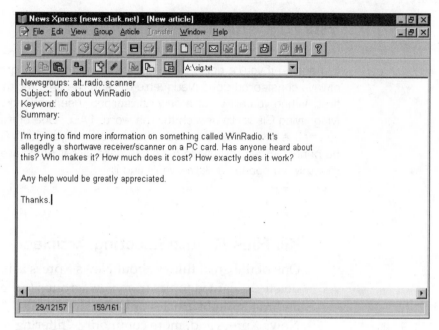

Figure 8-9: The new article window in News Xpress.

The Article Window has its own editing toolbar that appears at the top of the window. Figure 8-10 provides a diagram.

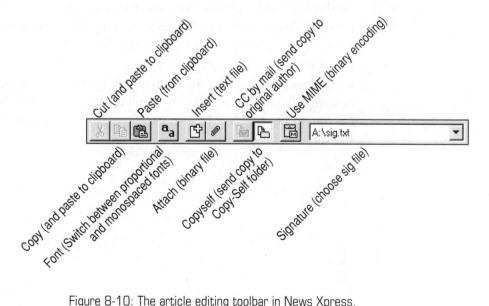

Figure 8-10: The article editing toolbar in News Xpress.

TIP

You've probably heard this a zillion times before, but we're gonna tell you again—if you're going to post a message to a newsgroup, it's always considered good Netiquette to read the FAQ for that group first. When you arrive at a new newsgroup, use the Find button (the Magnifying Glass) to search for the word "FAQ." One of the headers you nab is likely to be the FAQ for the group. If you can't find the FAQ, be patient. Scan the group for a few days. Most FAQs are posted monthly, so sooner or later, you'll find it.

Kill Files & AutoSelecting Articles

One of the great things about News Xpress is its ability to easily delete unwanted topics from newsgroups (called "killing" files) and to highlight articles of key interest (called "AutoSelecting" in News Xpress and, more commonly, "filtering"). The Add Killfile item under the Article menu is where you add items to both your kill file and autoselect lists. You can apply kill file and autoselect statements (called "patterns") for each newsgroup and to newsgroups as a whole ("global"). You can enter character strings, e-mail addresses, and numbers into the Subject: and/or the From: pattern boxes. These fields also accept regular expressions (see the next paragraph). At the bottom of the Add Killfile box, you can select whether you want your patterns to be applied to the kill file, the autoselect file, or as an exclusive kill. The items in your autoselect/kill file can also be viewed by pressing the Properties button on the toolbar. Table 8-6 describes the difference between the three kill file types.

Selection	Action
Kill	Automatically removes news articles matching the pattern string you specify in the Subject: and/or From: boxes. In the Properties box, kill patterns are preceded by no marking.
Exclusive kill	Removes everything from a newsgroup *except* strings matching the pattern(s) in the Subject: and/or From: boxes. Only one exclusive kill per newsgroup (and one global exclusive kill). In the Properties box, exclusive kill patterns are preceded by a <!>.
Autoselect	Automatically selects news articles matching the pattern string you specify in the Subject: and/or From: boxes. In the Properties box, autoselected patterns are preceded by a <+>. When you come to a group, the autoselected headers will be highlighted. You can begin reading the selected items by pressing the N key.

Table 8-6: The Add Killfile actions in News Xpress.

News Xpress can use regular expressions to construct very sophisticated text patterns to match. Regular expressions (or "regexp") are text pattern-matching sequences used in UNIX. They are sequences of statements, comprised of items, which are combinations of operators and characters. Table 8-7 shows the different operators used in News Xpress' regexp and what each of them does. After that, we'll discuss some ground rules, and look at a few examples, and hopefully things will become clearer.

Operator	What it does
?	Tags the preceding item as optional.
*	Tags the preceding item as appearing zero or more times.
.	Matches any character.
+	Tags the preceding item as appearing one or more times.
^	Matches item at the beginning of a line.
$	Matches item at the end of a line.

➡

Operator	What it does
[chars]	Matches the characters contained within brackets. Ranges of characters are separated by a dash (e.g., [a-r], [R-Z], [5-9], etc.).
[^chars]	Matches any characters not in the given list of characters.
		Used to separate statements. Can be used as an OR operator.
!	If preceding a statement, indicates an exclusive kill statement. Part of News Xpress, not really a regexp.
+	If preceding a statement, indicates an autoselect statement. Part of News Xpress, not really a regexp.

Table 8-7: Regular expressions used in the Kill and AutoSelect Files.

Rules

❐ A regular expression consists of one or more statements separated by a vertical bar character (|).

❐ A statement consists of one or more items.

❐ Items consist of zero or more operators and one or more characters.

❐ Characters that are used as part of an operator must be preceded by a backslash (\).

Anyone who spends time on Usenet will eventually bump into the "Make Money Fast" chain letter that has been floating around newsgroups for years. To filter these annoying posts out of your newsgroups, you create a global kill file (by choosing Add killfile from the Article menu) with the following regexp:

```
make (\$*|money)
```

This will weed out all articles with the strings "make $," "make $$" (or any number of additional dollar signs), or "make money."

Now, let's say you want to kill all instances of O.J. Simpson discussions from your newsgroups. You'd want to make sure to target:

"O.J. Simpson" (and "o.j. simpson")

"OJ Simpson" (and "oj simpson")

"Orenthal James Simpson"

"Orange Juice Simpson"

"The O.J. Simpson Fan Club"

and so on.

The regexp statement would be:

```
.*o.*j.*simpson.*
```

Since the regexp statements used in News Xpress are not case-sensitive, you don't have to do [Oo], [Jj] to match either uppercase and lowercase as you would in UNIX. The <.*> translates to repeat any character any number of times.

Kill files can come in handy in filtering out obnoxious posters in newsgroups (in this use, a killfile is often called a "twit filter" or a "bozo.filter"), racist postings, multi-newsgroup advertising (called "spamming"), and "test" messages inappropriately posted to non-test newsgroups.

- -

TIP

When you start fiddling around with autoselect and kill files, you'll want to test the results. Posting test messages to regular newsgroups is considered a big No No. A number of groups are specifically designed for test postings. Use the search box in the main News Xpress newsgroup window to find a test group. Don't forget to include the words "Ignore" or "No Reply" in your test posts' Subject: field. If you don't, your return e-mail box could get filled with "automatic echo" responses from other servers.

- -

You can also use regexp for autoselecting articles based on words and patterns. Let's say you wanted to search through the news.readers.software newsgroup to highlight information about News Xpress, WinVN, and Free Agent. The solution would be to put the following in the kill file/autoselect Subject: field and click on the Autoselect radio button:

```
nx|winvn|free agent
```

When you launch the article window for the news.readers. software group, all headers containing any of these character strings will be highlighted. Press the N key to begin moving through the new articles on your subject (and then you can use the forward and back arrows to move through them). If you want to see the headers for articles about News Xpress, WinVN, and Free Agent exclusively, press the Exclusive Kill button.

Binary Files: Posting & Decoding

During your travels on Usenet, you may have noticed a whole lot of newsgroups with the word "binaries" in the title. These are groups for people who want to post computer files other than messages: programs, movies, sounds, or (ahem!) pictures. Because Usenet was designed for transmitting text messages, posting messages made of computer code has required a few kludges. First, most must be uuencoded (specially processed to transform them into text files) before they are uploaded. Also, because some newsreaders accept messages only under a certain size, larger uuencoded files must then be broken up into several messages before being posted (called a "multipart binary"). All in all, it can get pretty tricky for uploaders and downloaders both.

Luckily, News Xpress makes handling binary files a snap. Decoding them is as simple as selecting them, in order, with a right mouse click or swipe and then pressing the Decode button. See Figure 8-11.

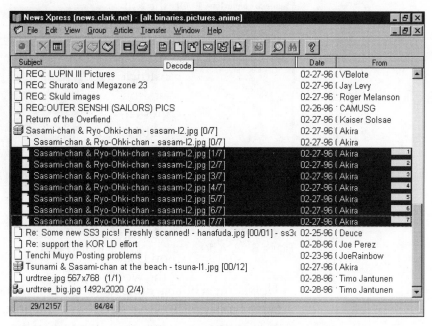

Figure 8-11: Selecting parts of a binary file to download.

When the download is complete, News Xpress will automatically load your PC's default media viewers (such as Picture Viewer for JPEGs and Media Player for MPG and AVI videos) and display the file. You can specify in the News Xpress Options the directory where you want your decoded files to be stored.

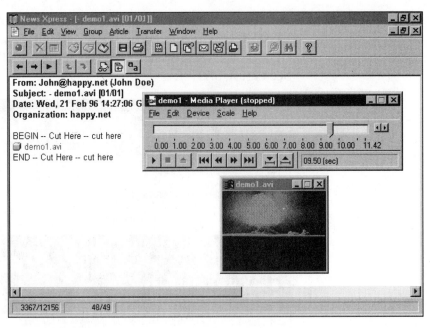

Figure 8-12: A decoded binary file in Media Player.

Uploading a binary file is almost as easy. When you want to attach a binary file to the message you are posting, just hit the Attach button (the paper clip) at the top of the New article window. An Attachment dialog box will appear (see Figure 8-13) allowing you to search your hard drive for the file you want to upload.

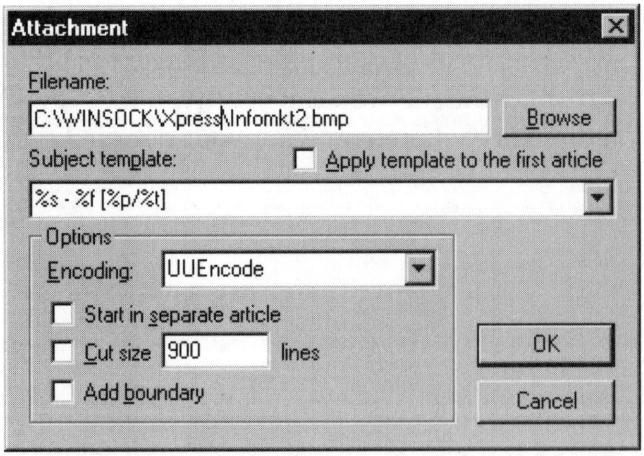

Figure 8-13: The Attachment dialog box in News Xpress.

Here's where you can also select the form you want the attachment to take: None, UUEncode, or Base64 (see Table 8-8).

Attachment Type	Effect	How Used?
None	Sends attached file in native format (no encoding).	To send ASCII-based messages that do not need encoding.
UUEncode	Sends attached file as a uuencoded binary.	The standard encoding method for attached binary files on newsgroups.
Base64	Sends attached files in Base64 encoded format.	Sending MIME-compliant messages. Enable by clicking the Use MIME button on the editing toolbar. Not recommended for binary newsgroups.

Table 8-8: Attachment types.

Once you press OK in the Attachment dialog box, the encoding and uploading will begin. You'll see the New Message window again with the binary attached. Choose the Send button to upload your file. When your article appears on the newsgroup, it will have amended the filename with the name of the attached file and [xx/yy], where xx is the number of the article and yy is the total number of articles (if it's a multipart binary file). So, for instance, if your binary upload was a single-part upload called beavis.jpg, the filename/number would be whatever you put in the Subject: field plus beavis.jpg [01/01]. If the name of the attachment is all you want in the header, leave the Subject: field blank.

Help!

One big drawback of News Xpress is that its help files are very spare and cryptic in spots. Luckily, a number of excellent FAQs and frequent discussions of News Xpress are on news.readers. software. To check out the FAQs, point your Web browser to http://www.duke.edu/~dl1/nx95.html and to http://www. duke.edu/~dl1/nx.html. The latter is a more complete manual for the 16-bit version, but much of it is applicable to the 32-bit Windows 95-compatible version. These documents can be very helpful in illuminating some of News Xpress' dark corners. For ongoing discussions, news.readers.software is the place to be.

WINVN

WinVN (or Windows Visual Newsreader) is a Windows-based newsreader that's a favorite among many Net oldtimers. When it was first released by Mark Riordan of Michigan State University in the late '80s, it was quite the thing. Now it has been eclipsed, in terms of power and ease of use, by other readers such as News Xpress and Free Agent. Its current developers (especially Sam Rushing and Jim Dumoulin of NASA) have made numerous changes to the program over the years in an attempt to keep WinVN viable.

One of the major drawbacks of WinVN is that it is "old code." It was first created in 1986 and has been continuously fiddled with and built on since then. A community of programmers and users has become involved in upgrading it, and the spirit of the early hackerdom still imbues this community. This is a double-edged sword. On the plus side, it means that lots of brilliant people are constantly trying to improve the program, and new versions are frequently released. You can imagine the downsides. All this "bit diddling" inevitably creates bugs and problems for less-than-expert users. The age of the core program means that some newsreader innovations found in other readers will probably never make their ways into WinVN. And, since it's freeware and somewhat of a hobby project for its creators/users, it's unlikely that WinVN will ever be rebuilt from the ground up.

The good news is that the current version (0.99-7, as we write this) is a very fine program with the features most newsgroup readers (that's you!) are after. If you like the look and feel of WinVN more than the other programs covered here, don't hesitate to give it a try.

Getting & Configuring WinVN

The latest version of WinVN can be found at its NASA home site, ftp.ksc.nasa. gov/pub/winvn, and at most WWW and FTP sites catering to Windows TCP/IP applications.

Configuration of WinVN will be obvious if you've ever configured a Windows newsreader. The first time you start the program, you will be asked to identify or create winvn.ini and newsrc files. You'll need to tell the program to create a new winvn.ini. If you don't already have a NEWSRC file, tell it to create that as well. Otherwise, just point it at the existing file. Next, you'll be prompted to enter your NNTP address, authorization info (if required from the news server), and your SMTP server information. Don't forget, if you're using Microsoft Mail, click on the MAPI radio button. Otherwise, choose SMTP. Next you'll be asked to fill in the Personal Info box (your name in the real world, return e-mail address, etc.). That's the basic setup.

WinVN comes with a DLL file called gwinsock.dll, which is the program's interface to your winsock.dll. If you're using Trumpet Winsock, you may have trouble with the gwinsock.dll. If so, use the alternate genasync.dll interface. To install this, change "Gensockdll=gwinsock.dll" in the [Communications] section of the winvn.ini file to "GenSockDLL=genasync.dll".

Subscribing To & Reading News

WinVN opens up to a main Newsgroup window and toolbar (see Figure 8-14). The first time you connect to your news server, you'll be asked if you want to download a new newsrc file. If you don't already have a newsrc file (which you should have already copied into the WinVN folder or pointed WinVN at during setup), choose Yes. Once you have it, you can search through the full newsgroup listing (using the Find and Find Next buttons on the toolbar) for the groups you want to subscribe to. To subscribe to a group, highlight it with a click, and then choose Subscribe Group from the Group menu. It will change color to the subscribed group color (defaulted to black), and move to the top of the newsgroup queue where all of your subscribed groups reside.

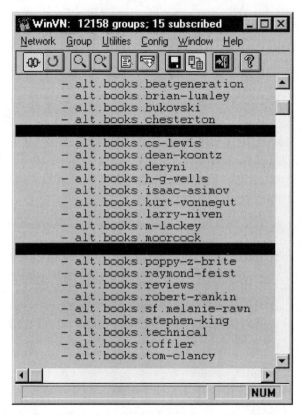

Figure 8-14: The main newsgroup window in WinVN.

To read a group, simply double-click on its name, and you'll be taken to the group's Header window (see Figure 8-15). In the left column of the Header window is a series of marks that indicate the status of each article. These marks are described in Table 8-9.

Figure 8-15: The Header window in WinVN.

Mark	What it means
<Space>	Indicates either that WinVN has no status info on this article or that it appeared unread in a previous news session.
>	This article has been selected with the Find command.
s	You have already seen this article.
n	This article is new.

Table 8-9: Article status information indicators.

Once you find an article you're interested in, double-click on it to bring up the Article window (see Figure 8-16). From here, you can read, reply, send e-mail, decode binary messages, print, or save the article to disk. The functionality of WinVN's reading, posting, and decoding files is very similar to News Xpress. Unfortunately, WinVN does not have built-in binary encoding.

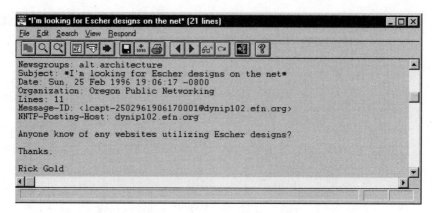

Figure 8-16: An article window in WinVN.

Kill Files & Filters in WinVN

WinVN does not fully support filtering and kill files (yet), but it does allow you to build what it calls GroupFilters. You have to enter your GroupFilter statements directly into the winvn.ini file. Table 8-10 shows what expressions are allowed.

Operator	What it does
*	Matches any string of characters.
!	Indicates a kill (as opposed to an autoselect). Kills should appear in the GroupFilter statement before autoselections.
|	Separates multiple expressions.

Table 8-10: Filter expressions in WinVN.

Rules

1. The GroupFilter expressions go in the [Group List] section of the winvn.ini file. The EnableGroup Filter line must be set to =1 (or On), and the expressions must be entered after GroupFilter=. It should look like this:

```
[Group List]
EnableGroup Filter=1
GroupFilter=expression|expression|expression
```

2. Expressions are matched left-to-right. Specific expressions are placed before general expressions.

3. Only groups that match your GroupFilter list will be displayed in your main newsgroup window, so if you use the GroupFilter, make sure to add an <*> at the end of your filter list if you want newsgroups to be displayed other than those in your select statement (see the third example below). This is very important.

4. If the GroupFilter statement in the INI file is:

```
GroupFilter=0
```

or

```
GroupFilter=*
```

all newsgroups will be displayed in the main newsgroups window.

Let's say you wanted to create a GroupFilter that would grab all of the newsgroups in the comp.os.ms-windows and comp.sys.ibm.pc hierarchies. You would create the following filter:

```
GroupFilter= comp.os.ms-windows.*|comp.sys.ibm.pc.*
```

You would receive only these newsgroups when WinVN connected to your server.

If you wanted to create a filter that removed all of the alt.lang and alt.irc newsgroups but kept all of the other groups in the alt. hierarchy, the filter would look like this:

```
GroupFilter=!alt.lang.*|!alt.irc.*|alt.*
```

To remove all binary newsgroups from your newsgroup list while retaining all other newsgroups, you would add this filter:

```
GroupFilter=!*binaries*|*
```

The <*> after the <|> tags all groups other than binaries as retrievable. If you are a parent, this is an easy way to shield your children from the pornographic binary groups. They'd probably never think to look in the INI file for the key to access these groups.

TIP

Future editions of WinVN promise full kill file and filtering options that will be available from within the program. You'll be able to filter and kill by subject, number of lines in message, e-mail address, author's name, message ID, and references. The kill file feature already exists but has yet to be implemented in the released version. If you're a real hacker dude (or dudette), you can get the source code from the NASA developers and do it yourself! If you have the latest MSVC compiler (16- or 32-bit), you can compile the source and enable it by defining "USE_KILLFILE".

Keeping Up With WinVN

Since WinVN changes so frequently, it's a good idea to get on the WinVN mailing list. Here you'll find announcements of the latest releases, bugs, bug fixes, and tricks, and you can also read exchanges among members of a devoted community of users. To subscribe to the list, send <subscribe winvn> in the body of an e-mail message to majordomo@news. ksc.nasa.gov. You might also want to check out the Web page at http://ksc.nasa.gov/software/winvn/winvn.html.

TIP

Using the <subscribe *listname*> command for a majordomo mailing list subscribes you to the list using your e-mail address from the header of your message. When you receive a return notice verifying your subscription, you'll notice that it will echo the subscribe command back as, in this case:

```
subscribe winvn your_email_address@site.domain
```

If you want to subscribe to the list from one e-mail address, but have the list mailed to a different address, you can use the following in the body of your message:

```
subscribe winvn other_email_address@site.domain
```

(For more information on mailing lists and mailing list commands, see Chapter 20, "Inside E-Mail.")

FREE AGENT

No discussion of Windows newsreaders would be complete without mentioning Forte's Free Agent. It too has many of the features of News Xpress and WinVN with a few additional nifty ones like internal multitasking, allowing you (for instance) to read news in one group while downloading images in another. Some people would argue that Free Agent is the best of the freeware newsreaders, but we liked the look and feel of News Xpress much better. Free Agent makes heavy use of multiple panes and icons (see Figure 8-17), which we found cluttered and more annoying than helpful. We also had trouble getting it to work on our machine. Your mileage may vary.

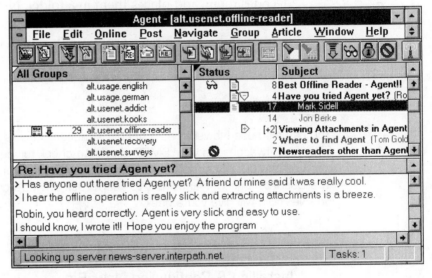

Figure 8-17: The main window in Free Agent.

If you'd like to investigate Free Agent for yourself, you can download it from Forte's Web site at http://www. forteinc.com/ forte/agent/freagent.htm.

NEWS POWER UTILITIES

There are a number of nifty applications you can use to make your news and information gathering on the Net more efficient. Here's a couple of pieces of software that you might want to consider adding to the ol' virtual tool chest.

NewsBin32: The News Robot

NewsBin32 is a shareware program billed as an automated NNTP downloader and decoder. It allows you to choose a series of binary newsgroups and automatically download them in bulk. It accesses the groups, downloads the specified number of files, decodes them, and places them in a folder. NewsBin32 is especially useful if you want to download all of the pictures, software, or media files on a binary group while you're doing something else.

TIP

You can also use NewsBin as a header grabber. Just as programs like E-mail Notify accesses your SMTP server to check for new mail, you can use NewsBin to check headers in newsgroups. If you're embroiled in a Usenet flame war and want to keep track of who's currently piling on, NewsBin will give you a peek.

Installing & Configuring NewsBin

NewsBin32 is $10 shareware. It can also be found in the News Client section of the major Winsock Web and FTP sites.

With your Winsock connected, launch NewsBin32. Using the Setup menu specify the news servers you'll be using and the newsgroups you'll want to download. The Setup menu is where you can also select the access mode (autostart, manual, download newsgroup list, etc.). The Download Group item should not be checked because NewsBin32 will try to download the complete list of newsgroups, which can take a long time on a slow dial-up connection.

TIP

NewsBin can access your newsreader's newsrc file. Just make a copy of it, and place it in the NewsBin folder.

Bulk Downloading Binaries

Using NewsBin32 couldn't be simpler. When you first launch it, you'll be asked how many articles you want NewsBin32 to search through (see Figure 8-18). The choices are 100, 250, 500, or All.

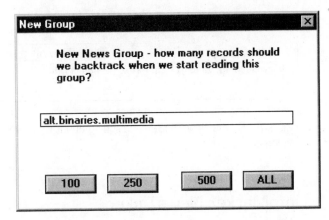

Figure 8-18: Select the number of files you'd like searched for downloading.

When you've made your selection, you're ready to press the Start menu, which will begin NewsBin32's search. If you've selected the auto mode, NewsBin32 will begin downloading and decoding all the binary files up to the number you've specified (see Figure 8-19). If you're in manual mode, you'll be prompted for each download. When downloading is complete, your news server connection will be terminated.

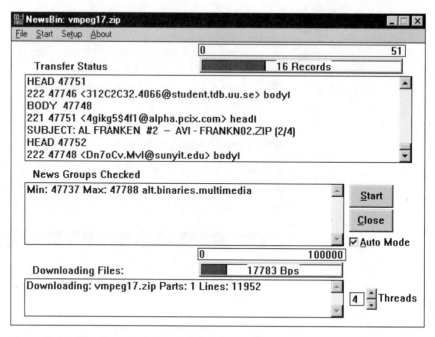

Figure 8-19: The NewsBin32 robot going about its downloading and decoding business.

infoMarket NewsTicker

New users of Usenet news are often confused by the terms *newsgroup* and *subscribing* and *unsubscribing*. The users are thinking in conventional terms of TV and print news and are shocked to discover that there's no news on them-there newsgroups! Sean says his dad is still steamed about this misleading terminology.

But when you think about it, there's plenty of news and information in newsgroups . . . it's just all mixed in with the rumors, shouting, chatting, and brainstorming. This is a new realm of socially constructed news that takes some getting used to. I hardly read the paper anymore or watch network news, but I feel no less informed. Most of my daily feed comes from Usenet, BBS conferencing (The Well), and Web publications.

For those who still hanker for more conventional headline news, there's a way you can be surfing the Net and scanning late-breaking news, business info, and sports scores at the same time.

InfoMarket NewsTicker is a freeware app from IBM that lives on your desktop as a scrolling banner. The banner displays the time and date, three control buttons, the news banner, and an ad window (see Figure 8-20).

Figure 8-20: The banner displayed by infoMarket NewsTicker.

NewsTicker is available from the IBM infoMarket Web site (http://www.infomkt.ibm.com/). Right now it's freeware, but there are hints on the Web site that IBM might start charging for it.

Once you have NewsTicker loaded onto your hard drive and your Winsock connection established, the NewsTicker banner will appear and begin to load the current news feed. You can click on the Setup icon (the hammer and screw driver) to access a dialog box of configuration options (see Figure 8-21). Here you can choose the news and sports feeds you want to see and the frequency with which the program refreshes the headlines.

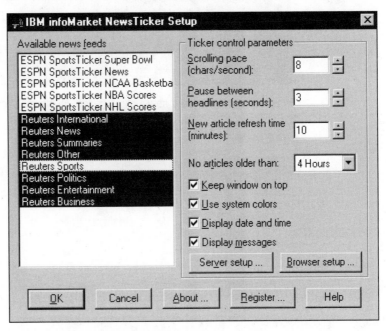

Figure 8-21: The Setup dialog box in NewsTicker.

As the Reuters and ESPN stories scan by, you can click on the ones that interest you. Your Web browser will be launched (if it's not open already), and you'll be presented with that story page accessed through the infoMartket Web site. You can also click on the News button to see a list of the latest news headlines. Double-clicking on any of these will also take you to that article on the Web.

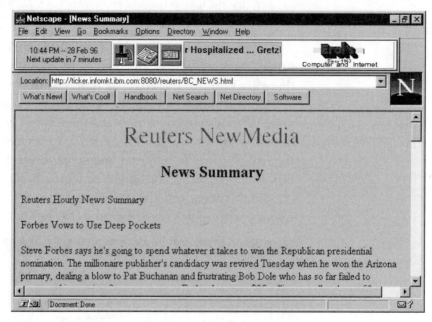

Figure 8-22: A Reuters news story loaded via NewsTicker.

MOVING ON

No matter which way you get your news, there's one thing that's always true—if there's one place where you can find tons o' facts (and FAQs!), stimulating conversation, wild behavior, and high weirdness, it's on Usenet. We hope you found some useful ideas in this chapter for navigating the anarchistic territory of Usenet news.

In the next chapter, we'll be leaving behind the world of text-based person-to-person communication via e-mail and Usenet and moving out into the multimedia wonders of the World Wide Web. We'll look at the browser clients you can use to access this rapidly expanding dimension of Cyberspace.

Probably no single technological development since the television has changed the way the world experiences media like the Web. It provides a place where almost anyone in the world (er...those with Net access, anyway) can become an amateur or professional publisher of text, pictures, sound, video, animation: you name it, and someone's probably putting it on the Web as we speak. The Web is the hot and hyped place to be at the moment. It's a place where fortunes are being made (and lost), celebrities are rising (and falling), and new ideas in media delivery (the good, bad, and ugly) are being brainstormed and experimented with. It's arguably the most incredible orgy of free expression and burgeoning free enterprise the world has ever seen. And this incredible universe can be yours for the cruising—if you have the right tools. Lucky for you, they're just a page turn away.

## Chapter 9

Windows Web Power Tools

Ahhh . . . yes, the World Wide Web! It's hard to look anywhere these days without running into a reference to it. URLs in advertisements are getting as common as fax numbers. Having your own home page has become a newbie rite of passage. Just about every time you turn on the TV, listen to the radio, or open up a newspaper, there's a story about an organization's new Web presence. Like it or not, the World Wide Web is fast becoming the world's new media appendage.

Even the rankest newcomer now considers himself or herself an ace Web surfer. In fact, the Web has become so ubiquitous that many new users think the Web is the Net. Of course, advanced users know that there's more to the Internet than just browsing pretty pictures on the Web. But still, it's getting tougher and tougher not to spend most of your online time in Webspace.

Browsers are your gateway to the World Wide Web. And while all Web browsers basically do the same thing—render HTML into pictures and text—the way they do it and the special functionality of each browser gives them each their own unique strengths and weaknesses.

In this chapter, we'll explore the three most popular World Wide Web browser programs for Windows. First, we'll take an in-depth look at Netscape Navigator, the browser that took the world by storm when it was first introduced just two short years ago. It has quickly become the standard for Web walkers worldwide (say *that* 20 times!). Next, we'll look at the two other contestants in the browser race: Microsoft's Internet Explorer and the venerable NCSA Mosaic. Table 9-1 gives you a brief comparison of how the different browsers stack up.

	Netscape Navigator	Microsoft Internet Explorer*	NCSA Mosaic	Comments
Tables	Yes	Yes	Yes	HTML 2.0 table-layout compatible
Frames	Yes	No	No	Able to support multiple windowing frames
Backgrounds	Yes	Yes	Yes	Allows loading of GIF background patterns
Java Support	Yes, Java applets and JavaScript	No–plans for future support	No	Supports Sun's Java programs (applets) and JavaScript
USENET Newsreader	Yes, separate news reading and posting features	Yes, reading and posting	Allows reading of Usenet news inline	Can read Usenet newsgroups
E-mail	Yes, incoming and outgoing with a full-featured e-mail program	No, accesses an external mail program	Yes, outgoing only with mailto: URL	Can send/receive e-mail from within program
Plug-ins	Yes, full range of plug-ins for inline viewing of proprietary file formations, animation, VRML, sound, and video	Yes, VRML plug-in	No	Supports extensions through plug-in technology
Special Features	GIF animation, pop-up navigation menus, drag-and-drop graphics and text, drag-and-drop FTP uploading	Scrolling marquee text, inline AVI video, new font HTML tag	Collaborate mode, Kodak PhotoCD viewing, AutoSurf feature	Features unique to this browser
Macintosh Version	Yes	Yes	Yes	Good for multiplatform families and businesses
Windows Versions	Windows 3.1, Windows NT, & Windows 95	Windows 3.1, Windows NT, & Windows 95	Windows 3.1, Windows NT, & Windows 95	Choose an OS, any OS

➡

	Netscape Navigator	Microsoft Internet Explorer*	NCSA Mosaic	Comments
Ease of Use	Easy	Easy, interface not as intuitive as Navigator	Easy	Level of ease for experienced users.
Cost	Free evaluation version, $49 for licensed copy, Navigator Gold will sell for $79	Freeware	Freeware	Can't beat the price
Comments	Netscape has become the de facto online standard.	Good solid performance, Inline images seem to load faster than they do in Navigator	Clean, bare-bones browser for people on the go, several out-standing features	

* This chart is based on Internet Explorer 2.0. As we were going to press, the alpha version of 3.0 was released. It contains many of the features missing from 2.0. See sidebar later in this chapter for more info.

Table 9-1: Web browser comparison chart.

As you probably know, one of the major innovations in Web browsers is the ability to use external programs, called *helper applications*, in viewing data formats that the browser doesn't natively support. Helper apps let you view video, listen to real-time audio, and cruise 3D virtual worlds, all without having to leave your browser. The latest advance in helper apps are plug-ins, programs that can be added on to the browser and work from within it. While these helper and plug-in programs are an integral part of getting the most out of the Web, we're not going to give them the in-depth treatment here (mainly in the interest of keeping things focused). For more information on helper apps and plug-ins, check out Part VII of this book, "The Power User's Guide to the Web."

NETSCAPE NAVIGATOR

Netscape Communication's Navigator program is the Cadillac of World Wide Web browsers. It supports just about every innovation that people are bringing to the World Wide Web, including extensions to the HTML language that no other program supports. And while Netscape's fast and loose interpretation of HTML has irritated some Net purists, everyone else is scrambling to keep up with its innovative features. And, what exactly are these features, you ask? Check out Table 9-2 for a current list.

Feature	Description
Java	Supports Sun's Java language.
JavaScript	Supports JavaScript, an API for scripting browser behavior.
Frames	Displays multiple subwindows within the main Navigator document window.
Tables	Provides extensive support for tabular formatting elements.
Background patterns	Supports GIF files as repeating background patterns in WWW pages.
Plug-ins	Supports third-party plug-in modules, allowing Navigator to display inline sounds, video, and other forms of media.
Mail client	Includes a full-featured e-mail client for sending and receiving mail.
News reader	Includes a full-featured Usenet newsreader for reading and posting articles to Usenet newsgroups.
Client-side image maps	Implements standard for imbedding image-map information within HTML code.
Progressive JPEG	Supports progressive JPEG image file format. (progressive JPEGs load one "layer" at a time—they look blurry at first, and then come into focus).
Special HTML features	Includes font colors, background colors, text alignment tags, word wrapping/unwrapping, META tags for MIME support, configurable horizontal rules (HR tags), multiple font sizes, centering, more control over image alignments through IMG tag extensions.
Automatic proxy configuration	Allows flexible proxy configurations for firewalls.
HTML uploading	Can be configured to allow file uploads through HTML forms.
FTP uploading	You can upload files to FTP sites using drag and drop.
Targeted windows	Automatically opens a new window if window targeting is used to refer to a new page.

Feature	Description
Improved security	Uses 300 bits of secure information when sending secure information.
Built-In HTML editor (Navigator Gold only)	Includes a basic HTML editor for easily creating your own Web pages with links, inline images, background textures, etc.

Table 9-2: Special features in Netscape Navigator.

Who's This "Mozilla" I Keep Hearin' About?

If you've spent any time hanging out on the Web with Navigator, you've probably bumped into the word *Mozilla*. When you mail a message from Netscape Mail, for instance, the X-mailer reference in the mail header reads: "X-Mailer: Mozilla 2.0 (Win95)." Seasoned Netheads often refer to Navigator itself as Mozilla.

So who or what is Mozilla? It was the nickname for the browser project that eventually became known as Navigator—it came from "Mosaic meets Godzilla," a reference to the leap in technology between Mosaic and Navigator. The company bigwigs obviously didn't want such a beastly and inelegant name for their revolutionary app, but Mozilla had already taken on a life of its own. Lots of people still refer to Navigator as Mozilla, and the little green dragon who haunts Netscape's Web site—and much of their promotional material—is named Mozilla.

Getting & Installing Netscape Navigator

With the entire online world trying to grab the latest copy of Navigator, getting your own copy requires a little effort. According to Netscape's reports, their servers log over 45 million hits a day—that's over one *billion* a month! That's enough to clog even the biggest data pipe. Luckily, Netscape Communications has installed over 30 FTP servers to handle the load. So, while you may have to wait your turn in line, you won't have to wait forever. And, unlike waiting in line at the DMV, you can do other stuff while you're waiting to make your connection.

TIP

To avoid the crowds, don't try to grab a new version of Navigator the day it's released. You've lived without it up to this point—you can probably wait a few more days. Once the smoke's cleared, try logging on to the site during off-peak hours.

To download Netscape Navigator, go to http://home. netscape.com, and follow the links to the latest versions. At the time this book was being written, two releases for Windows 95 were available: Navigator for Windows 2.0 and 2.0Goldb1. By the time you read this, Navigator should be at least at version 2.1. The version numbered 2.0Goldb1 is a beta release of Netscape Navigator Gold. This program has all of the features of Navigator 2.0.1 with the addition of a built-in HTML editor for creating your own click and drag HTML documents. When Gold goes into full release, it will be available for sale only at $79. Navigator 2.0.1 is available free for personal evaluation. Commercial copies (and manuals) can also be purchased at the Netscape home site.

Figure 9-1: The Gold beta version of Netscape Navigator.

Good Eatin' for Netscape Connoisseurs

If this brief taste of Netscape leaves you hankerin' for more, you should check out *The Official Netscape Navigator 2.0 Book* by Phil James (Netscape Press, 1996). A five-hundred (plus!) page smorgasbord of Netscape facts, it'll be sure to satisfy even the most gluttonous of Netscape gourmands. But it won't help you recover from overdone metaphors.

Configuring Netscape Navigator

Configuring Navigator correctly can mean the difference between just browsing the Net and really surfing. What do we mean by that? Well, Navigator allows you to do a lot more than just read Web pages. You can read and post Usenet news, send and receive e-mail, and view a wide variety of multimedia files—all without leaving your browser. However, to take advantage of these features, you'll have to make sure everything is set up correctly.

All of the configuration you have to do in Navigator (with the exception of installing plug-ins) is done from the Options menu. From this menu, you can configure:

❏ General Preferences

❏ Editor Preferences (Navigator Gold only)

❏ Mail and News Preferences

❏ Network Preferences

❏ Security Preferences

General Preferences

When you pull down the Options menu and select General Preferences, you'll see a configuration dialog box like the one shown in Figure 9-2.

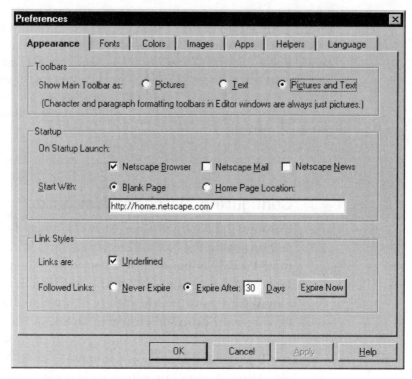

Figure 9-2: The Preferences dialog box in Navigator.

Most of the configuration options available from the Preferences menu deal with Navigator's user interface. With the exception of the Helpers and Apps tabs, these options configure the look and feel, not the actual operation, of the program. Table 9-3 describes what each option allows you to configure.

Tab	Configuration Options
Appearance	Controls the appearance of the toolbar and styles of links. Allows you to specify Navigator startup options. (See the tip that follows this table.)
Fonts	Allows you to choose the fonts you want Navigator to use when displaying fixed and proportional fonts. Also allows selection of character encoding language (see the description for the Language tab later in this table).

Tab	Configuration Options
Colors	Configures colors for text, backgrounds, links, and followed links.
Images	Toggles between displaying images while loading or after loading. Allows you to choose between automatic, dithered, and substitute colors for images.
Apps	Options for choosing applications to assist with Telnet, TN3270, and source viewing. Also allows you to select the default temporary folder.
Helpers	Configures helper applications to display various forms of media within and outside of Navigator.
Language	Allows you to specify the language you want to use as your default. Servers having the capability to serve pages with different languages use this option to decide which language to send.

Table 9-3: Preferences configuration options.

TIP

If you want Navigator to start with a local home page but you don't know the correct path to it, here's what you do. Start Navigator, and choose Open File in Browser from the File menu. Find your home page file on your hard drive, and open it. Copy your home page's URL from the Location box at the top of the browser window. Open the Preferences dialog box, and choose the Appearance tab. Paste the URL into the Start With Home Page Location text box, and click on the appropriate radio button. Whenever you relaunch Navigator, it will load this page.

Editor Preferences (Navigator Gold only)

If you plan on using Navigator Gold's HTML editor, you'll want to consider a few configurations, which are listed in Table 9-4.

Section	Configuration Options
General	Filling in the Author box will place your name in the HEAD tag of all the HTML documents you create. Reference Management is where you define whether images are kept with parent documents, and link integrity, whether local links are relative or absolute.
Default Colors/ Background	Configures color choices for text, link text, active link text, and followed links. You can also assign a default background color or texture to all of your HTML documents.

Table 9-4: Editor Preferences in the Gold version of Navigator.

Mail & News Preferences

This option dialog box is where you configure your e-mail and Usenet news settings. By now, most of these settings are probably familiar to you. Table 9-5 describes Navigator's mail and news configuration options.

Section	Configuration Options
Appearance	Changes the characteristics of fonts (fixed width, variable width, plain, bold, italic, etc.) used for displaying e-mail messages and Usenet articles. Also allows you to choose whether you want Netscape Mail or Microsoft Exchange to be used for sending/receiving mail.
Composition	Controls MIME compliance in messages, how messages are saved and copied, and the quoting behavior in replies.
Servers	Allows you to define which NNTP, SMTP, and POP servers to use for Usenet news and e-mail. Also configures maximum sizes for messages and automated e-mail-checking behavior.
Identity	Here's where you specify your name, e-mail address, reply to address, and organization. You can also define the path to your sig file (if any).
Organization	Configures behavior for passwords, message threading, and message sorting for both e-mail and news.

Table 9-5: Mail and news preferences in Navigator.

Network Preferences

This section allows you to configure how you want Navigator to act while you're on the Internet. From here, you can configure the cache options, the number of connections, and any proxy servers you might need. Table 9-6 explains.

Section	Configuration Option
Cache	Configures the directory to use when caching documents, the maximum size of the cache, and how often cached documents should be verified against their source. The more memory you can assign to caching documents, the better performance you'll get (because previously viewed documents won't have to be retrieved again).
Connections	Controls the number of simultaneous connections and the size of the connection buffer. (See the Tip that follows this table.)
Proxies	Allows you choose to use no proxies, manually configured proxy servers, or an automatic proxy configuration.

Table 9-6: Network preferences in Navigator.

TIP

The number of simultaneous connections you can handle refers to both HTTP as well as FTP connections. If you're using a modem to connect to the Net, you shouldn't use any more than four simultaneous connections. Increase the number of connections as your connection speed increases.

Security Preferences

As online commerce becomes more popular, how your browser works to secure your personal information becomes more important. These options allow you to configure how Navigator handles the security of your personal information and how it handles the use of security certificates (documents that identify a secure commercial entity so that you can feel safe sending credit card numbers or other sensitive information). Table 9-7 sketches out Navigator's security options.

Section	Configuration Option
General	In a Java-enabled browser, this section allows you to turn off Java. This section also controls how and when Navigator notifies you of any potential security risks.
Site Certificates	This section maintains the list of valid site certificates. Site certificates are used for insuring that the site you've connected to is who it says it is. This helps to prevent anyone from trying to spoof, or impersonate, a site. You can edit and delete site certificates as desired.

Table 9-7: Security preferences in Navigator.

Are There Security Holes in Navigator 2.0?

Rumors started to fly fast and furiously on the Net in late February '96 when Leonard Stein's World Wide Web Security FAQ (version 1.2.0, February 28, 1996) reported that there were some serious security holes in Navigator 2.0. According to Stein, the JavaScript feature of 2.0 could be used to gain access to a user's private information (e-mail address, URL history, and directory of user's hard drive) and to send that info to another remote machine without the user's knowledge. This process is called *softlifting*. Within a matter of hours, Netscape was fending off multiple phone calls from journalists and others wanting to know what Netscape was going to do about this problem.

It turns out that part of the FAQ information was inaccurate. These vulnerabilities were found in beta versions of Navigator 2.0. Most of them were fixed in the full release of 2.0. Several other holes are in the process of being fixed, and their fixes should be implemented in the versions of 2.x available by the time you read this. Even after this clarification, however, the Security FAQ was still concerned about the potential vulnerabilities in JavaScript and was recommending that Netscape build in some mechanism for turning JavaScript off. Netscape is considering the idea.

For more information on the current status of this issue, check out the World Wide Web Security FAQ at http://www-genome.wi.mit.edu/WWW/faqs/www-security-faq.html.

Browsing: Walkin' the Web With Style

If you've spent any amount of time wandering around the Web with one browser or another, you've probably learned that it ain't rocket science. Basically, it's pointing and clicking and oohing and aahing at all the cool sights and sounds. At its most mindless, it's not unlike channel surfing your television. *Mouse potato* is the slang for this Net equivalent of the couch spud.

We'll provide a few cool browsing tips and tricks that go beyond slavishly pressing the Forward and Back buttons and clicking on hyperlinks. In this section, we'll let you in on a few features that might help make your time online more productive.

Getting There & Back Again

Entering URLs is obviously at the heart of Web browsing. Navigator offers a number of options for doing this, depending on where your hands are when you need to get a URL box up and at 'em. You can choose Open Location from the File menu, press Ctrl+L, or enter a URL in the Location text box at the top of the Navigator window. The Location text box functions just like any other text area, so you can use the cut and paste options on any URLs you might come across in your online travels.

Navigator really shows its intelligence by providing a few handy shortcuts for entering URLs. You don't have to type the ubiquitous "http://" before the URL you're entering. If you don't, Navigator assumes that you're trying to go to a location on the Web and inserts the prefix itself. But that's not all! If the address that you're trying to reach is a commercial one (a www.*somename*.com address), all you have to do is type the *somename* part, and Navigator puts an "http://www." at the beginning and a ".com" at the end. For example, if you want to go to the always bustling Yahoo index (http://www.yahoo.com), all you have to do is type **yahoo**, and Navigator will do the rest! If you're accessing an FTP server that has "ftp" in the address (say ftp.netscape.com), you don't have to enter the "ftp:// prefix," but you do have to add the ".com" on the end.

Http:// In Other Words

Giving people URLs over the phone can be a big pain. Having to say "http colon forward slash forward slash" and "www" over and over again seems silly. Netscape has helped the situation with their URL shortcuts, but since not everyone's using Navigator or savvy enough to know that you mean http:// for any Web site, it's still a problem. "Triple-dub" is a word that some Net surfers at HotWired came up with for shortening "www." It still would be great if someone came up with a simple, elegant, one-word term for "http://www." If you think of a good one, send us e-mail—we'd love to hear it.

Besides manually entering URLs, you can use the Back and Forward buttons to move through your history list of visited sites. Or, you can go directly to the Go menu and pick an item from the history list. But that's the old way. Navigator offers pop-up navigation menus that appear with the click of the mouse. Here's how they work. Right-click the mouse in a blank spot on the Web page you're visiting (not on a link and not a picture) to access a pop-up menu similar to that shown in Figure 9-3.

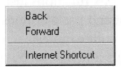

Figure 9-3: The navigation pop-up menu in Navigator.

Pretty handy, eh? Rather than going all the way to the toolbar to move between pages, you can move back or forward using the mouse.

Even more interesting things happen if you right-click the mouse on a link. Try it and see. What you'll get is a menu like the one shown in Figure 9-4.

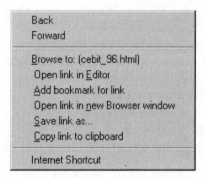

Figure 9-4: The link pop-up menu in Navigator.

In addition to being able to jump back and forth between Web pages, you can:

❏ Browse to <name of link>: Accomplishes the same function as clicking on the link.

❏ Open link in Editor: Opens the link document in Navigator's Editor window (Navigator Gold only).

❏ Add Bookmark for Link: Adds the URL specified in the link to your bookmark list. See "Bookmarks," later in this chapter, for more on bookmarks.

❏ New Window with this Link: If you want to check out a specific hyperlink, but don't want to lose track of where you are, use this function. The new page will appear in its own browser window. Browse around, and when you're finished, close the window to go back to where you were.

❏ Save this Link as: This function is particularly useful if you know a link refers to an article that you wanted to save. If you choose this option, you can save that article as a text file for later perusing. Or, if you want to take a gander at someone's HTML code, this function lets you save the HTML without having to visit the page.

TIP

Being able to save a link directly to a local file can be a handy way to save binary encoded files that your browser wants to load to the screen. Just right-click the button, save the file as text, and run it through your uudecoding program later.

❑ Copy this Link Location: Using this function, you can copy a link's URL directly to your clipboard for pasting it into another program. When writing this book, we used this method to copy links. You didn't actually think we typed all these URLs by hand, did you?

If you right-click the mouse button on an image, you'll get a few more choices in addition to the ones above:

❑ View this Image <name of image>: Navigator will display the image by itself in whatever helper application you've configured as your viewer for the picture type you're selecting. If you've set Navigator as the viewer of choice, the picture will appear in a new window by itself.

❑ Save this Image as: Allows you to save the image to disk. Since Navigator uses drag and drop functions, you can accomplish the same feat just by clicking the right mouse button on the image and dragging it to where you want to save it.

❑ Copy this Image Location: This choice copies the image URL to the clipboard.

❑ Load this Image: If you have problems loading an image, click on the broken image (or missing image) icon, right-click the mouse, and select this item. Navigator will attempt to load the image again. See Figure 9-5.

Figure 9-5: The two image icons—broken (error) and not loaded.

Frames & Navigation

One of the major innovations in Navigator 2.0 is the ability for Web page designers to separate their pages into "frames" or separate windows. This allows them to keep one part of the page (such as a navigation icon bar) visible at all times while other parts of the page change. Check out the Netscape home page (http://home.netscape.com) for an example of frames implementation (if you don't see the frames right away, scroll to the bottom of the page and click the Show Frames button).

Even if you thought frames were the coolest thing since sliced silicon wafers, you may have been frustrated when you tried to go to a previous frame by hitting the Back button. Instead of going to a previous frame, you probably found yourself back at the page you visited before the one with frames! What's going on?

With frames, one page can actually contain many HTML documents, each with its own unique URL. The trouble is that Navigator doesn't make any assumptions about which frame you're currently viewing when you press the Back button. If this drives you crazy, despair not! Just right-click the mouse button inside of the frame you want to back up in, and Navigator will present you with a special frames navigator. See Figure 9-6.

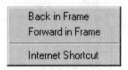

Figure 9-6: The frames navigator in Navigator.

Bookmarks

The Web has become unimaginably huge with over 26,000 commercial sites alone and probably millions of personal home pages. Finding your way back to an interesting site can be difficult if you didn't take the time to write down the URL, or if you didn't save it to your bookmark list.

Navigator's bookmark function allows you to keep your own personal hotlist of sites you've visited and want to return to. When you get to a site you want to bookmark, all it takes is a quick Ctrl+D (or a visit to the Add Bookmarks option in the Bookmarks menu) to save it for later browsing. When you want to return to that site, just click it on the bookmark list.

However, given all the interesting stuff that's floating through Cyberspace these days, it doesn't take very long for a bookmark list to get massive and unwieldy. Fortunately, Navigator provides a set of tools for customizing and organizing your ever-growing list of bookmarks.

You can access the bookmark functions by selecting the Bookmarks option from the Window menu (or pressing Ctrl+B). Navigator will display a window containing all of your bookmarks. You'll also notice the bookmark window has its own menu bar. In addition to some of the Navigator functions found on the main menu bar, this Bookmarks menu contains some new options, as outlined in Table 9-8.

Menu	New Option	Description
File	Open	Allows you to select a bookmark file as your active file.
	Import	Imports a saved bookmark file and appends it to the end of your existing file. Useful for sharing bookmarks with friends.
	Save As	Exports a bookmark file as an HTML document.
	What's New?	Checks modification dates on all or selected bookmarks. Tells you which locations have changed since the last time you visited.
Edit	Delete	Deletes a selected bookmark. If a folder is selected, the contents of the folder are deleted.
Item	Properties	Opens a Windows Properties dialog box that includes the name of the bookmarked site, the URL, a place for notes, and the Last Visited and Added On (to your bookmark list) dates.

➡

Menu	New Option	Description
Item	Go to Bookmark	Go to Web location specified in book-mark.
	Sort Bookmarks	Sorts selected bookmarks alphabetically.
	Insert Bookmark	Creates a new bookmark from scratch.
	Insert Folder	Creates and inserts a new bookmark folder.
	Insert Separator	Inserts a separator line into the bookmark list.
	Make Alias	Makes an alias of a bookmark to store the reference in another part of your list.
	Set to New Bookmarks Folder	Sets currently selected folder as the default folder all new bookmarks are to be added to.
	Set to Bookmark Menu Folder	Chooses folder to be displayed in Bookmarks menu.

Table 9-8: Bookmarks menu changes in Navigator.

Out of all of these options, the one that bears special mention is What's New? Think of this as your own personal Web robot, skipping nimbly across the Net, gathering information on all your favorite sites. All you have to do is select the bookmarks you want to check, select What's New? from the File menu, and let Navigator do the work. When it's finished, the little bookmark icons next to the bookmark entries will change to indicate their changed status. If your bookmarked pages have been changed since you last visited them, their bookmark icons will have a little glow around them. When you select the What's New? option, you are asked which items you would like checked (All or Selected Items). Once the check is complete, Navigator tells you how many pages were reached and how many have changed. You can then view your bookmark list to see which pages have new material. See Figure 9-7.

 No change since last visit.

 Changed since last visit.

 Unable to determine if changed.

Figure 9-7: The What's New? icons in Navigator.

Why such a useful function languishes in relative obscurity in the Bookmarks menus, we'll never know. Don't make the mistake of overlooking this very useful feature. It's a great way to save time by not returning to pages that haven't changed.

Mail & News

Since the release of Navigator 2.0, with its enhanced e-mail, Usenet news, plug-ins, and Java features, the folks at Netscape corporate HQ have made a big stink about not referring to their product as simply a "browser" anymore. Navigator is now being hyped as a full-featured Internet "platform." With all of these additions and innovations, it really does offer quite an impressive suite of tools. Although most power users will probably prefer the flexibility and added functionality of mail clients like Eudora and newsreaders like News Xpress, it is sometimes handy to have these options available (especially mail), without having to leave Navigator or launch another program. So . . . an actual platform? We say no. The biggest plank on the platform? OK, Netscape you've impressed even these two cynical bohemians.

Sending & Receiving E-Mail

Just one look at the e-mail client in Navigator (accessible from the Window menu), and you know that it's been elevated from a side feature to a serious e-mail tool. See Figure 9-8.

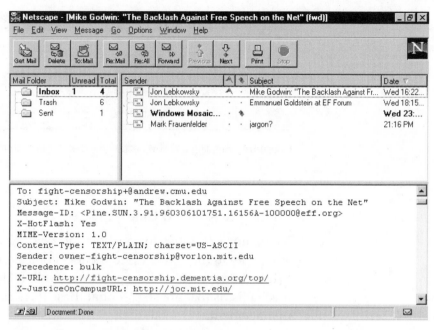

Figure 9-8: The e-mail window in Navigator.

Netscape's mail not only provides most of the features you'd find in a stand-alone mail reader (with the unfortunate exception of filtering), but it also allows you to send multimedia messages with sound, graphics, styled text, and hyperlinks.

If you want to read your e-mail, you'll have to go to the Netscape Mail window. However, if you're browsing the Web and want to tell someone (or show someone) a site you've come across, all you have to do is select Mail Document from Netscape's File menu. Netscape Mail will pop up a window where you can type your message and will even include the page you're currently viewing as an attachment (if you click on the Attachment button). See Figure 9-9. If the recipient views it with Navigator, he or she will see the page embedded in your e-mail message. A hyperlink to allow the recipient to go directly to the site is also included with the attached page.

Figure 9-9: Sending an HTML attachment with Navigator.

Posting & Reading Usenet News

Navigator's facilities for posting and reading Usenet news are adequate but not quite up to the level of a stand-alone news client. While it does most of the basic tasks well, it lacks the filtering mechanisms that are so essential these days for sane newsgroup management.

Accessible from the Window menu, the Netscape newsreader gives you the ability to read and post news, view articles by threads, and even download binary attachments. In fact, one feature that makes Netscape News very useful is its ability to display uuencoded pictures inline as they download—you don't have to wait for the whole file to download to see what you're getting. All in all, we can't recommend Netscape News to the power user, but for newbies and those in a pinch, it will let you read newsgroups and post articles.

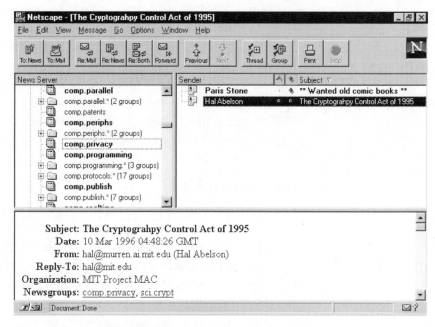

Figure 9-10: The Netscape News reader.

One major criticism of Navigator's e-mail and newsreading capabilities is that they suffer from a cluttered and cramped interface. Even though you can change the width and order of the column heads by clicking and dragging them, unless you have a 21-inch monitor (or larger!), you'll have trouble seeing all the information in the columns. This problem is not encountered with most stand-alone mail and news clients that have multi-window interfaces. We'll have to wait and see if Netscape does any interface tweaking in future releases. They'll have to if they want to bolster that platform claim.

File Transfer

Now that Navigator can upload and download files using FTP, is it time to throw out your dedicated FTP program? Well . . . maybe not yet. While Navigator does include some pretty nice FTP file-handling features, it still lacks the flexibility that a stand-alone FTP program like CuteFTP offers. However, for casual download-ing, it's hard to beat its convenience and drag-and-drop ease.

Downloading Files

Downloading files with Navigator is as easy as entering the URL of the FTP site and clicking on the files you want to download. Navigator takes over, downloads the files to your computer, automatically launches the appropriate uncompressing program (specified in the Helpers part of the Preferences dialog box), and hands you the file.

One of the better features of Netscape FTP is that you can just point and click to change directories and select files to download. Netscape will open a window with a progress indicator showing you how long your download will take. Check the time, go grab a cup a' joe (can you tell we drink a lot of coffee?), and when the time's up, your file will be downloaded and uncompressed.

Since Navigator 2.0 introduced floating download windows for file transfer, it also enabled a really useful new feature: simulta-neous downloads. Depending on the speed of your line and the number of simultaneous connections you configured in the Con-nections section of the Network Preferences Options dialog box, you can download a number of files at once. And even though each simultaneous connection slows down the speed of the other connections, you can usually eke every last bit of bandwidth out of your downloads by doing them all at once. Figure 9-11 shows a session with three simultaneous downloads.

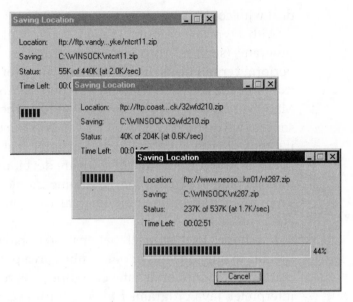

Figure 9-11: Simultaneously FTPing three files with Navigator.

Uploading Files

Navigator 2.x will even let you upload files to FTP sites that accept incoming files. Better yet, all you have to do is drag the file off the desktop, drop it into the Navigator window, and it's headed on its merry data way. Figure 9-12 shows a file being uploaded.

Java & JavaScript

If you keep up with the computer industry at all, you've probably heard a lot of buzz about a new thing called Java. Even though hackers (and writers!) love to guzzle coffee while sitting at their computers, all this talk about Java has little to do with caffeine and everything to do with a new computer language and virtual operating system that could have a serious impact on the way we deal with computers.

With a typical computer system, you buy platform-specific programs (such as Word for Windows and Excel, etc.), which perform certain tasks. If you're using Word for Windows, for example, the software will only run under Windows, not on the MacOS or on a UNIX platform. If you have the same word processor that we do (and we haven't given you *any* hints), you know it's choked with memory-hungry features that no one ever uses. All in all, the current state of software development makes for difficult (and expensive) programming problems for developers. Programs are becoming monumental, each one trying to be a . . . ah . . . platform.

Java hopes to change all that. Instead of having to write code specific to only one flavor of machine, Java programs are cross-platform; they run on whatever computer is running the Java interpreter. Java programs run on a "virtual computer" created inside your machine and one Java program written for one type of computer will pretty much run on any other.

Java is an object-oriented development system, allowing programmers to write small programs called *applets* that can be executed on the client's system. Because these programs are so small, the developers of Java are now offering a vision of a world in which instead of buying software, you lease it, grabbing applets off the Net as you need them for specific tasks. Feelings about whether this is a good idea or not are mixed. Only time will tell exactly how Java should best be used.

Navigator 2.0 is a Java-capable browser. Not only does it run the code, but it can run the applets inline with Web pages, allowing Web designers to insert animation, scrolling text, games, interactive forms, and live data in their Web pages.

TIP

We'll discuss Java in greater depth in Chapter 24, "WWW Multimedia Power Tools."

Web builders can use JavaScript inside of HTML documents. JavaScript shares a lot of the same syntax as Java, but it's not a stand-alone language. Instead, it's a way to allow Web site developers to script the behavior of Navigator itself, opening windows, showing the time, and even providing floating navigation windows that stay onscreen even after you've left a site. Like many scripting languages, JavaScript was designed so that someone who isn't a programmer can write basic scripts. Here is an example of what a JavaScript looks like:

```
<HTML>
<HEAD>
<SCRIPT LANGUAGE="JavaScript">
document.write("Hello net.")
</SCRIPT>
</HEAD>
<BODY>
That's all, folks.
</BODY>
</HTML>
```

For a basic tutorial and link list on JavaScript, check out the resource page at http://www.netscape.com/ comprod/products/ navigator/version_2.0/script/script_info/index.html. If you want to see what people are doing with Java and JavaScript, hop on over to http://www.gamelan.com, and check out some of the examples. (In Figure 9-12 the logo in the upper left frame is a spinning Java animation.)

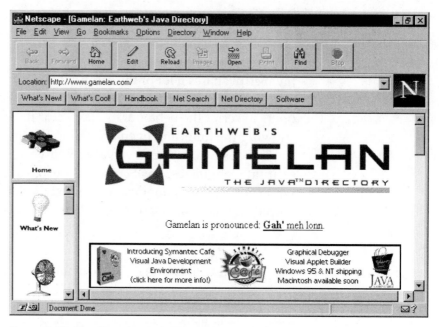

Figure 9-12: The Gamelan Java Directory.

Expanding Your Horizons With Plug-ins

These days, the boundaries of what can be done with multimedia on the Web are constantly being pushed. Many moons ago in net.time (about two human years), just having a downloadable QuickTime movie on your Web page was a big deal. Netsurfers today are able to experience 3D virtual worlds (with VRML), sound and animation extravaganzas and interactive games (using Shockwave), beautiful page layouts (with Amber), animation (with Emblaze), music (with different MIDI and WAV players), speech (with one of several text-to-speech programs), and even live audio and video broadcasts (with Streamworks, RealAudio, and TrueSpeech). Navigator's plug-in architecture has made all of this possible.

In the past, if you wanted to view a multimedia file, you had to make sure that a helper app was configured to view it. You didn't view the file from within your browser—you saw the display in a separate program. With the release of Netscape Navigator 2.0, the browser itself is now capable of accepting plug-in modules that can access whatever form of media is an inline part of a Web page.

Table 9-9 lists just some of the plug-ins available for Netscape for Windows, as of March 1996. By the time you read this, there will undoubtedly be others. For more details on what each plug-in does, turn to Chapter 24, "WWW Multimedia Power Tools."

Plug-in	What It Does	Platforms Supported Win3.1/Win95	Where to Get It
Acrobat	Allows you to view and print PDF documents from within Navigator.	No/Yes	Available on the Companion CD-ROM.
Envoy	Allows you to view and print Envoy documents from within Navigator.	Yes/Yes	Available on the Companion CD-ROM.
Internet Wave	Plays "streaming" audio.	Yes/Yes	Available on the Companion CD-ROM.
Lightning Strike	Provides inline support for Lightning Strike images.	Yes/Yes	Available on the Companion CD-ROM.
NCompass	Allows OLE controls to work inside of Navigator.	No/Yes	Available on the Companion CD-ROM.
PreVU	Allows you to view MPG videos while they're downloading.	No/Yes	http://www.intervu.com/
RealAudio	Plays streaming audio files.	No/Yes	http://www.realaudio.com/products/player2.0.html
SCREAM	Plays inline multimedia files.	No/Yes	http://www.savedbytech.com/
Shockwave	Allows you to view Director files within Navigator.	Yes/Yes	Available on the Companion CD-ROM.
TrueSpeech	Plays audio and video files in real-time.	Yes/Yes	Available on the Companion CD-ROM.
VDOLive	Plays audio and video files in real-time.	Yes/Yes	Available on the Companion CD-ROM.

Plug-in	What It Does	Platforms Supported Win3.1/Win95	Where to Get It
VRealm	Allows you to view 3D VRML files.	No/Yes	http://www.ids-net.com/
VR Scout	Allows you to view 3D VRML files.	No/Yes	http://www.chaco.com/
WebFX	Allows you to view 3D VRML files.	No/Yes	http://www.paperinc.com/webfxns.html
Wirl Lite	Allows you to view 3D VRML files.	No/Yes	Available on the Companion CD-ROM.
Word Viewer	Allows you to view Microsoft Word 6.0/7.0 documents inline.	Yes/Yes	http://www.inso.com/

Table 9-9: Plug-ins for Netscape Navigator.

Getting Outside Help: Helper Apps

Plug-ins are taking the browser world by storm, but many media types still don't have a plug-in written for them. What do you do? Use those friendly ol' helper applications!

Helper apps are external programs that you can evoke from within your browser. Once a helper app is configured correctly, Navigator will download the file and launch the helper application for you. You can then view (or listen or play with) the file from within the helper application.

Configuring helper apps is easy, as long as you follow a few simple strictures. Unless the application comes with an installer that configures Navigator (like RealAudio), you'll have to do a little tweaking in the Helpers section of the Preferences dialog box. Specifically, you'll have to enter the MIME type and subtype for your new file (see Chapter 20, "Inside E-Mail," for more info on MIME) as well as its extensions. Then, you'll have to pick a helper app from your computer using the Browse button. Once you're finished, just click OK, and you're ready to go!

You'll notice that most of the locations for the helper apps listed in the Where To Get It column in Table 9-10 do not include the actual filename. We omitted them because things change so quickly, by the time you go looking for these files a newer version may be available or the files may have different names. It's best to go to the site and poke around (or run a search) to find the latest version of the helper.

Media	Helper Application	Specific Formats Handled	Where To Get It
Graphics (2D)	Paint Shop Pro	Over 30 image formats	http://www.jasc.com/psp.html
	ThumbsPlus 3.0	Handles over 35 file types, including bitmap and vector graphics and video files.	http://www.cerious.com
	Lview Pro	GIF, JPG, TIF	http://world.std.com/~mmedia/lviewp.html
Graphics (3D)	WebSpace	VRML	http://www.sd.tgs.com/~template/WebSpace/
	QuickTime VR for Windows	QuickTimeVR/ QuickTime	http://qtvr3.quicktime.apple.com/ InWin.html/
Video	Net Toob	MPEG video, AVI, QuickTime	ftp://duplexx.com/pub/duplexx/
	VMPEG	MPEG	ftp://papa.indstate.edu/winsock-l/Windows95/Graphics/
	Streamworks	Streaming real-time MPEG video and audio	http://www.xingtech.com/
Audio	WHAM	WAV	ftp:// wuarchive.wustl.edu/systesm/ibmpc/win3/sounds/
	Wplany ("W-play-any")	Plays common audio file formats	ftp://ftp.ncsa.uiuc.edu/ PC/Windows/Mosaic/viewers/
	RealAudio	.RA streaming audio	http://www.realaudio.com/
	TrueSpeech	TrueSpeech streaming audio files	http://www.dspg.com/
Misc.	WinZip	Decompresses ZIP, TAR, GZIP, and other UNIX file compression formats	http://www.winzip.com/
	WinPack Deluxe	Decompresses ZIP, TAR, GZIP, Lharc, uuencode, BinHex, ARZ, and ZOO	ftp://ftp.winsite.com/pub/pc/win95/miscutil/

➡

Media	Helper Application	Specific Formats Handled	Where To Get It
Misc.	CU-SeeMe	CU-SeeMe video conferencing	ftp://comet.cit.cornell.edu/pub/CU-SeeMe/
	Acrobat	Adobe Acrobat	http://www.adobe.com/
	Microsoft Word Viewer	MS Word	http://www.microsoft.com/msword/Internet/Viewers/
	Panorama	SGML	ftp://ftp.ncsa.uiuc.edu/Mosaic/Windows/viewers/
	Ghostscript/GSView	PostScript	http://www.cs.wisc.edu/~ghost/index.html

Table 9-10: Helper applications useful with Navigator (and other browsers).

TIP

After you've configured all of the helper applications for your browser, you'll want to give them a try. The one stop shop for this is the WWW Viewer Test Page at http://www-dsed.llnl.gov/documents/WWWtest.html. Here you can quickly test external applications for text, images, audio, video, specific document formats, models, and objects.

MICROSOFT INTERNET EXPLORER

Microsoft's entry into the browser market—and one of the opening salvos in its nefarious plans for taking over Cyberspace—is called Internet Explorer (or MSIE). It is a solid, speedy (as far as browsers go, anyway), and small (738K) piece of freeware built upon NCSA Mosaic. It has a number of advanced features, including built-in support for AVI videos, scrolling marquees, client-side image mapping, and other extended HTML tags. (If you don't know what all this geekspeak is about, see "Advanced Features in Explorer" later in this chapter.)

So, what features is MSIE missing? It still lags behind Navigator in terms of Java support, JavaScripting, Frames, and news and mail features. The MSIE newsreader is awful and not something even an introductory user is likely to tolerate for very long. MSIE has no internal mail support (but works in an integrated fashion with Microsoft Exchange). You can rest assured that Mr. Bill will not stop 'til Internet Explorer is giving Netscape a true run for its money. So, keep your eye on Microsoft's Web site for late-breaking new releases (2.0 is the current version at press time).

Who Can Keep Up?

Just to give you an idea of how fast things move in Cyberspace: we finished this section on Explorer 2.0 only to find that Explorer 3.0alpha had been released while we were writing it. Version 3.0 promises to heat up the battle in the great browser wars. The list of new features announced for 3.0 include:

- ❏ Frames support.
- ❏ Enhanced tables.
- ❏ Multiple simultaneous downloading.
- ❏ Speed increases through multiple connections, progressively-rendered graphics (text loads first), greater cache control.
- ❏ Support for BMP graphics, animated GIFs, and viewing of documents in the DOC format.
- ❏ Enables user-programmabilty with embedded OLE controls ("Active-X") and Visual Basic scripts.
- ❏ Keyboard shortcuts for all browser functions.
- ❏ Enhanced security.

Check the Internet Explorer Home Page at http://www.msn.com/ie/ie.htm for more details about 3.0 and its availability.

Configuring Explorer

Configuring Internet Explorer is simple when you use the Setup wizard that comes with it. Once you launch the program, you'll find additional configuration options in the Options item under the View menu. See Figure 9-13.

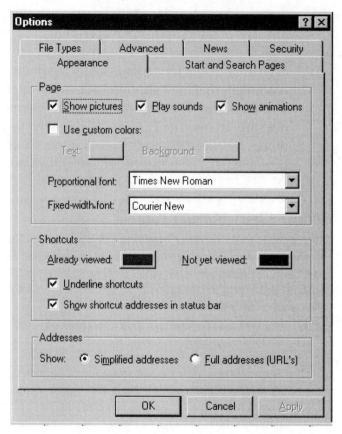

Figure 9-13: The Options dialog box in Internet Explorer.

While most of these configurations are straightforward, a few bear special attention. Under the Advanced tab are two sections: History and Cache (see Figure 9-14). The History option allows you to specify the number of URLs Explorer will store in the History folder (or some other folder that you specify). The default is set to 300. If you'd like to keep a complete log of your Net travels, leaving this number high will save all of your visited URLs. And, since the URL shortcut files are small, the log won't take up a lot of disk space.

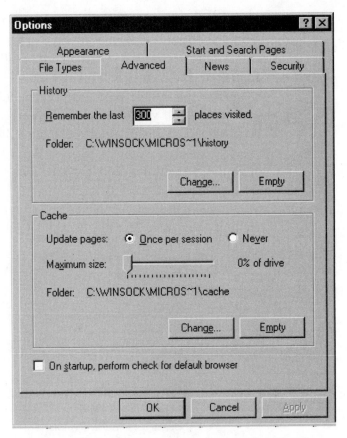

Figure 9-14: The Advanced dialog box in Internet Explorer.

The same cannot be said for the disk cache, a feature that allows you to save parts of Web pages (HTMLs, graphics, video, etc.) so that they don't have to be re-downloaded from the Web. If you have a very large hard drive, this feature can save accessing time at sites you frequent. You can use the slider bar in the Cache section under the Advanced tab of the Options dialog box to assign the percentage of your hard drive you'd like to devote to the Explorer cache. If you don't want Explorer to save any Web documents, move the slider all the way to 0%. You can use the Update pages (Once per session or Never) option to choose how often the cache is checked against the pages you are accessing to confirm that it contains the most recent version of the document. If the page on the Web has changed, Explorer will download a new copy and replace the one in the cache. Of course, if you have the cache set to 0%, it doesn't matter which button is selected. If you want to clear out the cache, press the Empty button. The Change button allows you to select new folders for the cached and history files.

You can use the URLs saved in the cache folder as shortcuts to pages on the Web. If you double-click on any of the URLs, MSIE will be launched (if it isn't already), and you'll access the Web page you've selected. You can also use Windows drag and drop. Just open the History window, grab the icon for the URL you want to access, and drop it into Explorer.

Explorer can handle a number of media types internally (without needing external helper applications). Table 9-11 is a list of the main media types Explorer supports.

Type	Description
AIF/AIFF/AIFC	Sound file format
AU/SND	Sound file format
WAV	Sound file format
MID	Sound file format
JPG	Graphic file format
GIF	Graphic file format
XBM	Graphic file format
VRML	3D virtual reality file format
AVI	Microsoft's video standard
Marquees	Horizontally scrolling text messages

Table 9-11: Media types supported by Internet Explorer.

Internet Explorer looks on your hard drive for registered media players and file types when attempting to load a media file it doesn't handle internally. If you have an external application that Explorer can use (let's say the QuickTime for Windows player), Explorer will launch it automatically and display the desired file. By selecting the File Types tab under Options (available from the View menu), you can change helper applications (using the Edit button), remove applications, or create new MIME file types and map applications to them. You can configure all the helper apps in Table 9-10 for use with Internet Explorer.

Advanced Features in Explorer

While Internet Explorer does not have all of the high-end features of Navigator, it does sport some nifty innovations of its own. Let's take a look at them:

Inline AVI Files

Embedding videos in Web pages seems to be all the rage these days. By using HTML tags, you can define where an AVI video should appear on a Web page. Several plug-ins, such as PreVU, are available for Navigator that embed videos. Microsoft has built the capability into Internet Explorer to display AVI (Audio Video Interactive) clips into HTML pages. The main attribute for this is DYNSRC=*URL* added to the existing IMG tag. See Figure 9-15 for an example of an embedded AVI and the HTML code that was used to create it. (The earth.gif is included in the HTML to accommodate browsers that do not support embedded AVI files.)

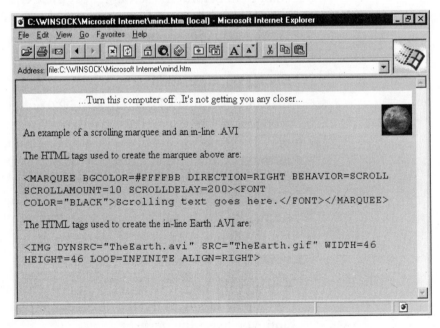

Figure 9-15: An inline AVI video (the earth) and a scrolling marquee.

Scrolling Marquees

Internet Explorer contains an HTML extension for creating scrolling marquees within HTML documents. The MARQUEE tag includes a number of attributes to control its appearance and behavior. You can define the direction it scrolls (DIRECTION= LEFT or RIGHT), the number of times it scrolls (LOOP=n), and the color field behind the scrolling text (BGCOLOR=#rrggbb or nameofcolor). Figure 9-15 shows an example of a marquee and the HTML code used to create it.

Background Sounds

Just a few short weeks before MSIE 2.0 was released we were wondering when someone was going to create a way to effectively play background sounds on Web pages. Internet Explorer 2.0 introduces that option. Using the BGSOUND tag, you can add sounds to your pages. Sounds can be in AU, WAV, or MID format. The attributes for the tag are SRC=URL for the location of the sound file and LOOP=n for defining the number of repetitions. For example:

```
<BGSOUND SRC="kata.wav" LOOP=1>
```

will play the kata.wav sound file once when the page is accessed. Setting the LOOP to INFINITE or -1 will play the file continuously until you leave the page.

Extended Font Tags

Microsoft's addition of a FONT tag allows Web page designers to assign one or more font preferences to text in an HTML document. If the selected fonts do not exist on the client side, the receiving system's default font is used. The tag with attributes would read <FONT FACE="font,font,font">. For example:

```
<FONT FACE="Optima,Futura,Helvetica">Text goes here.</FONT>
```

You can also add color to the fonts by using the COLOR attribute. The form for this is:

```
<FONT COLOR=#rrggbb or nameofcolor>Text goes here.</FONT>
```

TIP

If you have no idea what we're talking about with all this tag and attribute gibberish, we highly recommend Laura Lemay's two volume series *Teach Yourself Web Publishing with HTML in a Week* and *More Teach Yourself Web Publishing with HTML in a Week* (Sams Publishing 1995). These books cover HTML, from the basics to advanced techniques such as forms and Netscape extensions. Laura's books do not cover the new Microsoft HTML extensions covered here. For that, you can check out the "Complete List of HMTL Tags" (recently updated to include the IE 3.0 extensions) at the Microsoft home site. Point your browser to http://www.microsoft.com/ie/author/html30/ie30html.htm

VRML Add-In

VRML stands for Virtual Reality Modeling Language, a new standard for creating and delivering 3D virtual environments on the World Wide Web. MSIE 2.0's first plug-in (called an "add-in" by Microsoft) is a VRML viewer. You can download the viewer from http://www.microsoft.com/windows/ie/ie.htm. The viewer is automatically installed after downloading. To try it out, open up one of the VRML files that comes with the add-in (named Sphere0, Sphere1, and so on). See Figure 9-16.

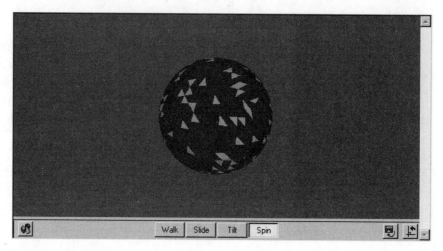

Figure 9-16: A 3D object in the VRML add-in module.

Microsoft's VRML viewer works with the mouse, a joystick, or the arrow keys. The toolbar along the bottom of the VRML window allows you to configure the viewer and provides controls for interacting in the 3D environment. Figure 9-17 gives an overview of the VRML toolbar.

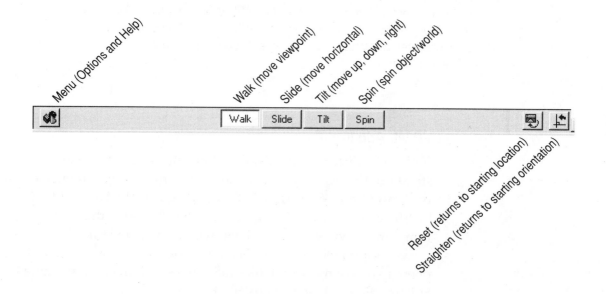

Figure 9-17: The VRML toolbar.

Once you have the VRML add-in up and running and you want to play with it, check out the VRML objects and worlds linked to http://www.microsoft.com/windows/ie/sites.htm. See Chapter 24, "WWW Multimedia Power Tools," for more information about VRML.

RealAudio

Internet Explorer also comes with RealAudio, an external application that plays audio files in real time. This application allows you to listen to audio programming over the Internet without having to download the entire sound file first. RealAudio accesses files in the RealAudio (or RA or RAM) format only. To use RealAudio with Internet Explorer, all you need to do is double-click on an RA file. The RealAudio player will pop up and begin playing the selected file. You can quit the player any time you wish and save the audio file to disk when it's done loading. For links to a number of sites supporting RealAudio "netcasts," check out the RealAudio home page at http://www.realaudio.com/. You cannot play WAV or AU files through the RealAudio player, but you can convert sound files of these types to RA using the converter available for downloading at the RealAudio site.

To check out some of Explorer's built-in media features (such as continuously looping background sound files and inline video), check out Microsoft's demonstration page at http://www.microsoft.com/ ie/showcase/howto/iedemo.htm (see Figure 9-18).

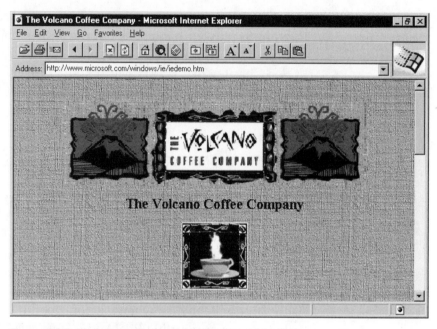

Figure 9-18: Microsoft's Explorer Showcase, which displays an AVI of a spinning cup of the noble bean while playing some big-band drumming as a background sound.

TIP

Did you know that you can turn any Web graphic into Windows 95 wallpaper? All you need to do is locate the inline image you want using your browser. Right-click on it, and choose Set As Wallpaper from the pop-up menu. You can do the same thing with Web background textures, too.

MOSAIC

Mosaic is where all of this browser business began. Spawned in 1993 at the National Center for Supercomputing Applications (NCSA) in Urbana-Champaign, Illinois, Mosaic spread over the Net and the burgeoning World Wide Web like a bread mold. Before Mosaic, Web browsers only offered hypertext, text documents with links that could span the Internet. Mosaic opened up a whole new media universe by allowing graphics, sounds, and videos to be transferred using Web server software. In a brilliant design move, Mosaic called external helper applications to process linked hypermedia. Instead of requiring that graphics, sound, and video capabilities be built into Mosaic itself, it allowed the user to assign media applications already on the user's hard drive to use with Mosaic.

The excitement over Mosaic created a California gold rush in World Wide Web development. In what seemed like a few short months, it went from nobody having a clue what the WWW was to the unavoidable subject of conversation. Your humble authors (never ones to miss a party) were caught up in the maelstrom as well. We wrote *Mosaic Quick Tour* (Ventana, 1994), the first book on Mosaic and the World Wide Web. For a while we gloated over the fact that we "wrote the book on the subject." And then, along came Navigator. As quickly as Mosaic rose, its popularity plummeted (along with our book sales!).

TIP

We thought we'd take this opportunity to remind you that we, Gareth Branwyn and Sean Carton, wrote the book on Mosaic and the World Wide Web! Why not consider buying a copy of this rare piece of Net history? You'll be able to tell your grandchildren: "I bought the very first book on Mosaic and the World Wide Web! Why those were the good ol' days . . . when we had to hand crank our Internet connections . . . ." *Mosaic Quick Tour* is a thoughtful gift for all of the Internet historians on your holiday shopping list.

Getting & Configuring NCSA Mosaic

The latest full release of NCSA Mosaic for Windows 95 is version 2.1.1. It can be accessed via the Mosaic for Microsoft Windows home page at http://www.ncsa.uiuc.edu/SDG/Software/ WinMosaic/ (see Figure 9-19). By way of improvement over the 2.0 version, it offers the addition of client-side image mapping (allowing image maps to be embedded in HTML documents) and integration of Kodak's PhotoCD viewing technology (see below). The latest version of the beta release is available from ftp.ncsa. uiuc.edu/Mosaic/Windows/ Win95/.

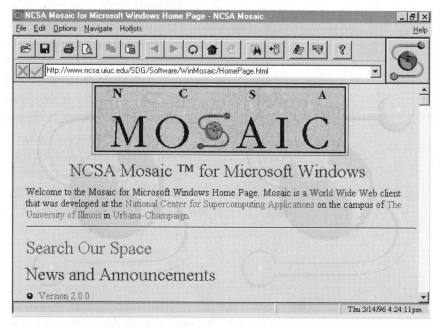

Figure 9-19: The Mosaic For Microsoft Windows home page.

One you have Mosaic downloaded and uncompressed, no other special configuring is required. You'll want to use the Preferences dialog box (accessed from the Options menu) to enter the usual information about yourself, your Internet services, directories for storing various files, and so on. Look over the setting under the Cache tab, and decide how you want Mosaic to handle cached documents.

Mosaic Today

With all the publicity and hoopla surrounding Netscape Navigator and Internet Explorer, it's easy to forget about Mosaic, the grand dame of Web browsers. Let's not completely write off this groundbreaking software yet. In fact, Microsoft's Internet Explorer is actually a license re-working of Mosaic. Numerous other companies, including Ventana, Spry, and Quarterdeck, have licensed versions of Mosaic. The first CompuServe Web browser was built on Mosaic as well (they have since switched to a licensed version of Netscape Navigator). Heck, even Navigator is a sibling of Mosaic! So, even if your browser doesn't look like Mosaic, it may have some Mosaic under the hood. The latest version of NCSA Mosaic (version 2.0.1b as we write this) has all of the basic features found in Navigator and Explorer with a few unique capabilities that bear looking into.

TIP

Mosaic has addressed the hassle of having to constantly enter http://, mailto:, ftp://, etc. with a series of keystrokes that automatically enters the appropriate URL prefix:

Ctrl+h = http://

Ctrl+f = ftp://

Ctrl+g = gopher://

Ctrl+n = news

Ctrl+m = mailto:

Collaborative Sessions

One of the coolest features of Mosaic 2.x is the ability to interact with other Mosaic users while you're online. The Collaborate option, accessed from the File menu, lets you initiate a chat session with one or more people. You can take session participants on guided tours of Web sites, exchange files through Windows' drag and drop feature, or just use it for chat sessions. This feature has great potential for teachers, business people, and others who want to point out Internet features to others over an Internet connection. There may even be a job for "official" Internet tour guides in this.

To set up a collaborative session, enter the name of the host computer sponsoring the session and the port number. One person must be the host and all of the others sign on as session participants (see Figure 9-20).

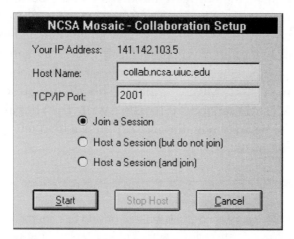

Figure 9-20: The setup box for Mosaic's Collaborate option.

To host on a PPP or SLIP connection, enter your IP address and any port number (say 1), choose the Host a Session (and join) radio button, and press Start. Session participants enter *your* IP address as the host, select the Join a Session button, and then click Start. As the participants connect, you'll see each other's chat aliases (as defined under the Services tab in Mosaic's Preferences area) and any messages being sent. See Figure 9-21.

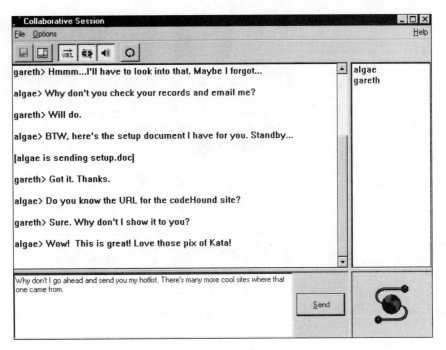

Figure 9-21: A Collaborate session window in Mosaic.

Advanced Hotlist Manager

Mosaic 2.*x* has a high-powered hotlist manager that rivals
Navigator's bookmarks. You can store Web sites in hierarchical
lists and folders and easily change and arrange their contents. The
hotlist manager has a What's New feature that can check the URLs
in your hotlist (or a subsection of it) to see if their corresponding
Web pages have been updated. If Mosaic finds that the date on the
Web page is newer than the date stored on the hotlist, it will mark
that item as New. If it finds the page, but can't log on to it, Mosaic
tags it with a question mark. If it detects that a page has moved or
been taken off of the server, Mosaic marks it with an X. Selecting
Remove Items that Don't Exist (how's that for an existential
choice?) from the Hotlist Manager's Options menu deletes all of
the dead sites from your hotlists. See Figure 9-22.

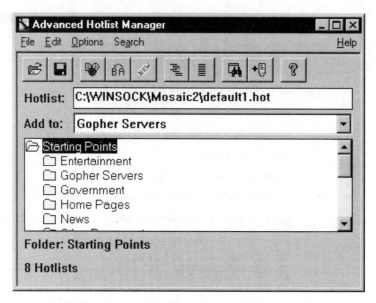

Figure 9-22: The Advanced Hotlist Manager in Mosaic.

AutoSurf

AutoSurf is Mosaic's answer to the offline newsreader. Using AutoSurf (see Figure 9-23), you can automatically access and download (with inline images or without) a series of Web pages to your Mosaic cache for later offline reading. You can define how many links and sublinks you want Mosaic to follow, whether you want the surfing to be constrained to the server you're accessing, and the maximum number of documents to download. An output log gives you detailed information about the surf in text or HTML format. Mosaic 2.x also has an Advanced Disk Cache Manager that allows you to decide which cached documents to purge and which to mark as Never Purge. You can also select specific types of documents (HTML, GIF, MSVIDEO, etc.) to cache. The Advanced Disk Cache Manager is located under the Cache tab in Preferences (accessed from the Options menu).

Figure 9-23: Page surfing the Web with AutoSurf in Mosaic.

TIP

Here's a great way to use Mosaic's AutoSurf. Set it to surf any of the What's New pages (such as NCSA page at [http://www.ncsa.uiuc.edu/SDG/Software/ Mosaic/Docs/whats-new.html]) at a level 1 depth. This will download the home page of each new site announced on What's New (changed daily). Once downloaded, you can browse through the pages and follow up in real-time on the sites that interest you. Make sure that you have plenty of disk space on your hard drive and that you select an appropriate maximum number to download in the AutoSurf dialog box.

Kodak PhotoCD

As of version 2.01b, Mosaic comes with Kodak PhotoCD viewing capability built into it. This feature allows you to view pictures on Web pages in the PhotoCD format using a series of tools for manipulating the image. You can crop, zoom in/out, enlarge/reduce, rotate, and pan. We're not really sure how useful this feature is, but it's fun to play with. To try it out for yourself, check out the Kodak PhotoCD demo page at: http://www.kodak.com/digitalImaging/cyberScene/demo/demo.shtml. The PhotoCD menu (accessible with a right mouse click) is pictured in Figure 9-24.

Figure 9-24: Kodak PhotoCD viewing in Mosaic.

Presentation Mode

If you want to use Mosaic as an information kiosk or for a presentation, you can remove all menu items, tool bars, and message boxes so that only the document window fills the screen. You can do this by selecting Presentation Mode from the Options menu. Alt+P toggles presentation mode on and off. This feature can come in handy in educational and business settings.

Audio Events

While Mosaic does not support Internet Explorer's tag for embedding background sounds in HTML pages, it does allow you to assign WAV audio files to events (Navigate Forward, Navigate Back, Document Loaded, Startup, etc.). This feature can be helpful in situations in which you'd like audio cues to tell you what Mosaic is up to. For instance, you can assign a sound to Document Loaded to give you an idea how many pages are being loaded during AutoSurf if you're not at your computer screen. Audio events are also useful if you're using Mosaic as an information kiosk.

Mosaic's Future

While it's hard to imagine Mosaic ever retaking the high ground in the browser wars, it is clear from the latest release that they are not out of the game yet. Growing out of the university setting, Mosaic started out with education and science in mind. It was intended as a learning and idea communication tool. Now that the rest of the world has caught up and the Web and browser business has gone mega-commercial, NCSA has returned to its roots, making useful tools for education and research. The Collaborate mode is a recent example of such tools and a precursor to NCSA Montage, a program being developed for distant team collaboration. Given the meteoric rise of Netscape Navigator and the recent introduction of Microsoft into the browser business, rumors have been circulating that maybe NCSA would not produce future versions of Mosaic. They've been assuring people that this is far from the case. They're excited about the additions and changes they've made to current versions, and they say they have big plans for the future. Given their groundbreaking efforts in the past, we can't wait to see what they come up with.

TIP

To keep up with the latest on Web browsers and plug-ins, there's one place to be: David Garaffa's BrowserWatch site. Here you'll find a comprehensive list of browsers and plug-ins, with descriptions, platform information, and links to company home pages and FTP sites where you can download applications. There's also an up-to-the-minute news page contributed to by many helpful (and informed) netizens. We don't have to tell you that things in Cyberspace move fast. BrowserWatch is a great way to stay current with all new browser technologies. BrowserWatch is located at http://www.browserwatch.com/.

MOVING ON

Now that we've finished showing you how to browse the Web with three of the best Web tools for Windows, it's time to dig deeper into our toolbox to look at those specialty tools that you might not use every day but are darn handy to have at the ready when you need 'em. While we won't have the time (or space) to really get into the finer points of each one, we will tell you where to find it, when's a good time to drag it out of the toolbox, and some timesaving tricks that you might have missed in the owner's manual. Bob Villa, eat your heart out.

## Chapter 10

Windows Net Tools Gallery

Let's see . . . you got your e-mail client, your newsreader, and your Web browser. You think you're ready to go, don't ya? Well hold on there a minute! We're not done just yet. We're dyin' to show you a few cool miscellaneous tools.

In this chapter, we'll look at a number of tools that you can probably live without but are very handy to have around. For starters, we'll look at tools for transferring files both from the Net to your computer and out of your computer to other wired folks. We'll then talk about Telnet clients that you can use to connect to remote UNIX machines (see Part IV for more on UNIX). Wrapping that up, we'll mosey on over to tools you can use for tracking data on the Net and some interesting Net utilities.

TIP

All programs we're going to discuss in this chapter can be found at the Consummate Winsocks Apps list or TUCOWS. If you're interested in keeping up with the latest Windows tools, CWS is the place to be. It's organized into sections (Mail clients, Web browsers, Servers) and includes a searchable index. To see for yourself, go to http://cws.wilmington.net/. The site also has thoughtful, and usually right-on, reviews of most of the software available. Another similar site is TUCOWS at http://www.tucows.com/. Check out the nifty bovine decor!

FILE TRANSFER TOOLS

Though it sounds like an obvious (and strange) thing to point out, the Internet is a network. That means once you connect your computer to the Net via a TCP/IP connection, your computer becomes a member of the network, not only able to receive information and files, but to send information as well. It's not just a place to send messages to friends, read and post Usenet articles, or browse the Web—it's a way of connecting your computer to the online world.

File transfer tools let you take advantage of the fact that once you're on the Net, you're *on* the Net. And while this means you can snag files directly to your computer, it also means you can transfer files from your hard drive directly to another online computer. With the right tools, you can even set up your computer so that others can transfer files directly to you from anywhere in the world via the Internet.

fpArchie

Now why didn't someone think of this before? Typically, when you look for a particular file on the Net, you have to type your search into an Archie server, write down the information it gives you, fire up your FTP client, re-enter the information, and download the file. Isn't all that searching, writing, and data entry the type of stuff that computers are supposed to free us from? Peter Tanis thought so—that's why he wrote fpArchie, a combination of Archie and FTP clients. See Chapter 26 for more information on using Archie.

All you have to do is select an Archie server near you from the Servers tab, enter the name of the file you're looking for, select the appropriate search criteria, and press the Find Now button (see Figure 10-1).

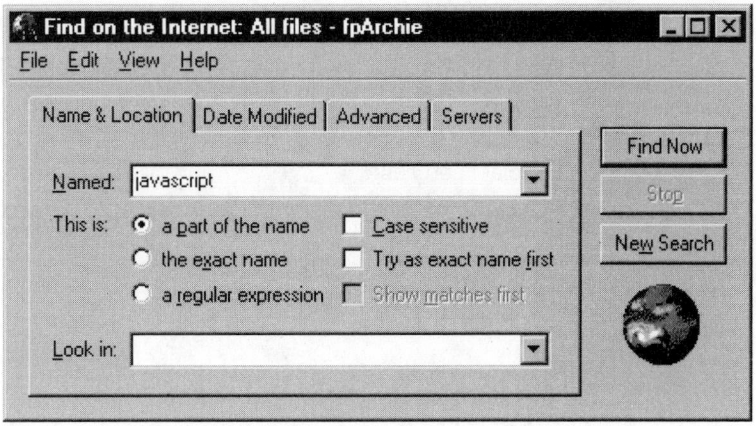

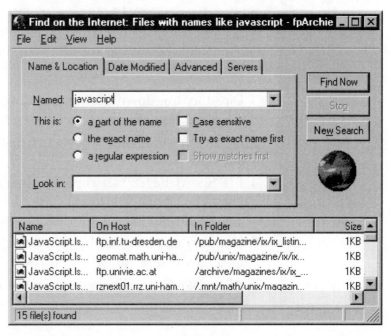

Figure 10-1: Searching for files with fpArchie.

When the Archie server sends back its list of found files, fpArchie transforms that list into a standard Windows view—for example, by list or icon (see Figure 10-2). Then, all you have to do to get the file is right-click on the mouse and select Retrieve. FpArchie slips into FTP mode and nabs the file for you.

Figure 10-2: A list of found files in fpArchie.

Program Name:	fpArchie
Type:	Combination FTP/Archie client
System:	Windows 95 (coming for Windows NT)
Special Features:	Allows regular expression searches.
Where to get the latest version:	http://www.euronet.nl/~petert/fpware

Table 10-1: A brief review of fpArchie.

CuteFTP

FpArchie sports a simple interface and a basic FTP feature, but sometimes you need a more serious FTP tool. One of the best is CuteFTP (which isn't really that cute).

CuteFTP is a shareware ($30) program designed to provide all of the sophisticated features of File Transfer Protocol in a totally windows-savvy interface. Although CuteFTP is fairly new, it has already generated a bit of a buzz. Because CuteFTP supports many file- and directory-hacking features, it's a very useful tool for anyone who has to maintain files on remote machines—especially people who have to support Web sites. It has a nice laundry list of features, such as:

❏ Directory tree downloading: Can download entire directories *and* subdirectories.

❏ Quick stop command: Allows you to quickly terminate any operation.

❏ FTP Site Manager: Netscape Bookmarks-like folder/file hierarchy that allows you to store FTP sites in folders along with all kinds of information about the site.

❏ Directory and index caching: You don't have to re-download remote directories/indexes every time.

❏ Allows command-line options and scripting.

❏ Tons of user-configurable options: Including audio events, mouse events, fully configurable windows, and styles.

❏ Firewalls: Supports network security features.

❏ Text-file display: Can display text files found on FTP sites.

❏ Custom FTP commands: Allows you to built your own file of custom FTP commands.

❏ AutoRename: Can automatically rename files being uploaded (e.g., .htm —> .html).

❏ Can create masks for filtering out unwanted file types using UNIX regular expressions.

❏ Drag-and-drop: Files can be uploaded and downloaded by dragging and dropping.

❏ Supports multiple simultaneous logins.

As you can probably tell from the list of features, CuteFTP offers lots of control over FTP file management. It's a nice combination of Windows ease of use and UNIX flexibility. (See Figure 10-3).

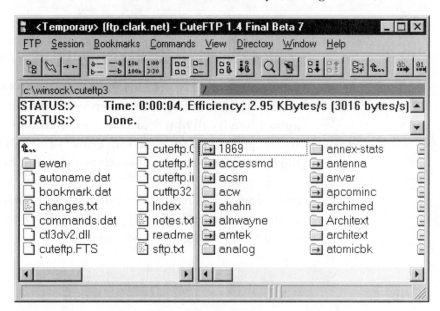

Figure 10-3: The main window in CuteFTP.

For day-to-day use, CuteFTP is pretty handy. You can just drag and drop files in and out of the directory windows so, for instance, you can drag files from your hard disk into the directory on a remote server where you have your Web pages. Or, to download something from a remote site, all you have to do is drag the desired item from the directory on the remote server to a directory on your machine.

Program Name:	CuteFTP
Type:	FTP client
System:	Windows 95, Windows 3.1
Special Features:	Drag-and-drop file uploading and downloading. Allows you to save bookmarks for frequently accessed sites. Other features include index/directory caching and filtering.
Where to get the latest version:	ftp://enterprise.net/pub/mirror/winsock-l/ftp/CuteFTP.Betas/

Table 10-2: A brief review of CuteFTP.

WFTPD (Windows FTP Daemon)

Say you're sitting at your computer writing a book. You get to a certain point in the chapter when you remember that your co-author (we'll call him Sean) has a file that you need. Now, you could call him up (or send him e-mail) and ask him to attach the file to a mail message and send it to you. But he's usually down for his beauty rest by 9:00 PM. If he's running an FTP server on his computer, you can just fire up fpArchie or CuteFTP, connect to his computer, and grab the file yourself—all without having to wake him up (he's real grumpy if you do).

WFTD is a shareware program ($20) that turns your PC into an FTP server so that people can log in (using any FTP client, including Mac and UNIX programs) to your computer to send and receive files. Just run it in the background, set a few permissions, designate which directories you want to give the world access to, and poof! Your humble PC is now in the same league as any of those fancy schmancy UNIX boxes that call themselves FTP servers.

Server Security

Just a note on security before we go any further. Ordinarily, when you're online with a PPP or SLIP account, your PC is pretty much impervious to wily crackers. That all changes when you set yourself up as an FTP (or other) server.

Once you set up your workstation as a server, you're inviting people into your machine. To make sure that they behave themselves, you should take a few precautions. First, don't allow unlimited access to your hard drive to anonymous users. Designate a special folder for Internet access, and make sure you restrict anonymous user access to only that directory. If you must give someone access to your entire drive, make sure that you trust that person and protect their access with a hard-to-hack password.

Second, unless you know the identity of every person who uploads a file to your computer, check each file for viruses before you open it. You never know what might be hidden inside. FTP daemons like WFTPD come with log capabilities. Make sure you keep the log running as long as the server is online.

Finally, don't tell the world about your server unless you're prepared to deal with the hassles that come with running a publicly accessible site. Security-through-obscurity is sometimes the best security of all.

The greatest feature of WFTPD is that it's incredibly easy to set up and use. With a few clicks of the mouse (see Figure 10-4), you can start serving the world (or at least your own little circle of it). WFTPD can also be used as a poor person's Web server by placing HTM documents in a directory and pointing anonymous users there. Voila. Instant Web server.

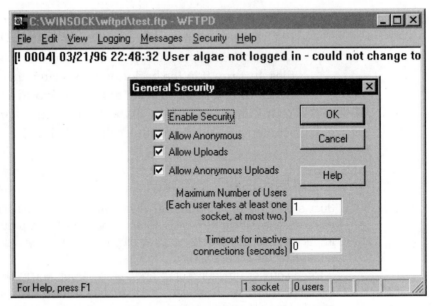

Figure 10-4: Pretend you're a big shot Internet server with WFTPD.

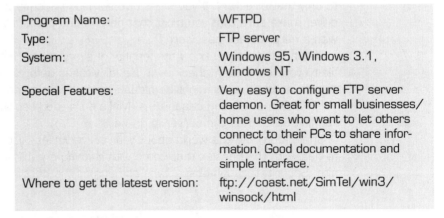

Program Name:	WFTPD
Type:	FTP server
System:	Windows 95, Windows 3.1, Windows NT
Special Features:	Very easy to configure FTP server daemon. Great for small businesses/home users who want to let others connect to their PCs to share information. Good documentation and simple interface.
Where to get the latest version:	ftp://coast.net/SimTel/win3/winsock/html

Table 10-3: A brief review of WFTPD.

TELNET TOOLS

Even though you can do just about everything you need to do on the Net with Windows, there are still times when you need to access a remote UNIX machine. If you develop Web sites and just want to get in to do some simple editing, having the ability to Telnet in, edit your file online, and save it can make life a lot easier. Why should you have to download the file, edit it on your PC, and upload it again? You don't.

Besides giving you the ability to edit files in place, Telnet also allows you to use a remote machine's resources. If you have to do any CGI programming for a Web site you're working on, play on a MUD or MOO, or even just need a quick and dirty way to check your e-mail, Telnet can be a useful tool.

NetTerm

NetTerm is a popular shareware ($20) client for Telnet. It has all the features you might be looking for in a Telnet program. On top of that, it provides a simple FTP client so that you can easily work on a file on a remote machine and then transfer it back to your PC—all within the same program. Add to this the ability to emulate several popular terminal types and save connection aliases for quick point-and-click connections to Telnet sites, and you've got yourself a nice tool. Here's a complete list of NetTerm's features:

- ❏ Multiple terminal emulations: VT102, VT220, FTTERM, ANSI
- ❏ Kermit and Zmodem send and receive
- ❏ FTP client and server, remote file editing
- ❏ Multiple simultaneous connections
- ❏ Scrollback buffer with print and copy, logging
- ❏ Macros for automating repetitive keystrokes
- ❏ Configurable fonts, colors, font size, number of lines
- ❏ Ability to capture Screens
- ❏ Socks and TIS firewall support

As you can probably tell from the list of features, NetTerm excels when it comes to editing remote files. Features that allow you to set file permissions and issue custom FTP commands make life a lot easier when you're putting files onto a UNIX machine and don't want to have to Telnet in.

Figure 10-5: Connecting with NetTerm.

Program Name:	NetTerm
Type:	Full-featured Telnet client, includes FTP client/server.
System:	Windows 95, Windows 3.1
Special Features:	Graphical, easy to use. Uses companion FTP client and server for easy file transfer. Can save connection files as aliases for easy connection straight from the Finder.
Where to get the latest version:	http://cws.wilmington.net/

Table 10-4: A brief review of NetTerm.

DATA-FINDING TOOLS

These days, you can find just about anything you want on the Web. Between all the Web-walking search engines, comprehensive indexes, and file repositories, the Web has become our front door to the information storehouse. Add to that the ability of Web browsers to access other data sources, such as Gopher and FTP, and you may wonder why you'd ever need another data access tool.

The truth is, you really don't . . . if you're content to use your Web browser for everything. For the same reasons that you probably don't want to always use Netscape Navigator or Microsoft Internet Explorer for reading your mail and Usenet news, you might sometimes want the flexibility of a stand-alone search client.

Using a dedicated search client has several advantages. First, because the tools are designed to perform only one task, they usually take up less memory and perform their functions faster without the extra overhead of a browser. Secondly, because Web clients can't be all things to all people, their abilities are often limited when it comes to browsing non-Web sources of information. A dedicated client can do many things that a browser can't, allowing you access to many special features and streamlining your searches.

- -

TIP

For more information on Internet search tools, techniques, and search site addresses, see Chapter 26, "Data Tracking."

- -

QVT/Gopher

Gopherspace is a section of the Internet accessible through Gopher clients and linked together through hierarchical Gopher menus. Users can browse menus of information, select documents that they want to view, and then either download them or view them through the Gopher client. Gopher's not as popular as it used to be, but there's still lots of goodies available for the burrowing. (No discussion of Gopher is complete without at least one goofy gopher analogy.) For more information on Gopher and how to use it, see Chapter 26.

One main difference between Gopherspace and the Web is that Gophers don't use hypermedia links. On the Web, you can link to other documents from within a document, setting up contextual links to source materials, pictures, sounds, and other data. In Gopherspace, the linking takes place on a document level. Once you're inside a document, you have to return to the menu to get to another document. However, as a precursor to the Web, Gophers did allow you to view and/or save multimedia data, search for documents, and get information from the far reaches of Cyberspace. Sadly, Gopher seems to be a search technology verging on extinction. Most of the Gopher clients available for Windows 3.1 are not being upgraded to Windows 95.

QVT/Gopher (see Figure 10-6) is a Gopher client that comes with QVT/Net, a suite of shareware ($40) Internet tools. QVT/Gopher is a fast way to browse Gopherspace using a simple no-nonsense interface. Since Web browsers allow you to browse Gopher servers, there really aren't many reasons to use a standalone client, but QVT/Gopher offers a few advantages over a browser, namely speed and size. QVT/Gopher is fast—most operations appear to take place almost instantly, even over a 28.8Kbps modem. QVT/Gopher is only 44KB in size. It also has very low overhead, which makes it useful if you've got lots of other programs open or are using a senile ol' PC with limited memory.

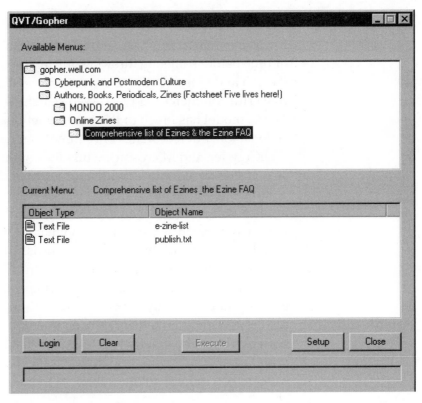

Figure 10-6: QVT/Gopher in action.

Program Name:	QVT/Gopher
Type:	Gopher client
System:	Windows 95, Windows 3.x
Special Features:	Bare-bones Gopher client. Presents a simple graphical interface. Uses helper apps to view multimedia data and e-mail.
Where to get the latest version:	http://cws.wilmington.net/

Table 10-5: A brief review of QVT/Gopher.

SqURL, Jr. (& SqURL)

It was inevitable. You have your Gophers, so it was just a matter of time before someone threw a squirrel into the mix. SqURL, Jr. (Search and Query URLs) is a freeware version of SqURL, a powerful commercial ($49.95) Web-searching and indexing tool. The Jr. model has much of the same functionality as the commercial version, but it searches only three search sites (Yahoo, WebCrawler, and Microsoft), while the commercial version has 15 search sites wired into it (with another 13 in the works).

How SqURL, Jr. (and SqURL) works is simple. You launch the application, enter a filename for your search (whatever you want to save the search as), specify both what folder you want your search saved in and the search key words. Your little search rodent takes off across the Web, checking in with each search engine to find what it has on your keywords. When complete, SqURL, Jr. allows you to launch your Web browser and displays the search results as a hyperlinked HTML document. If you run the same search over again, SqURL will tell you what has been added since your last search. SqURL also does parallel searches, allowing you to search on more than one subject at a time. See Figure 10-7.

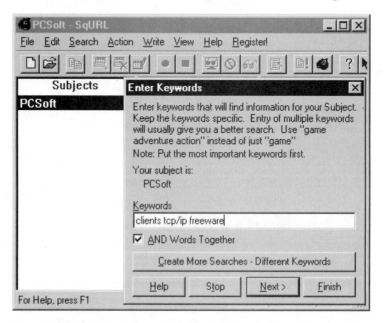

Figure 10-7: SqURL, Jr.'s little NUT house.

Program Name:	SqURL, Jr.
Type:	Multi-Web search engine lookup and storage of search findings.
System:	Windows 95, Windows NT, Windows 3.x
Special Features:	All of SqURL's special features are reserved for the commercial version. Saves searches as (groan) NUT documents.
Where to get the latest version:	http://bluesquirrel.com/index/html

Table 10-6: A brief review of SqURL, Jr.

iSeek

InfoSeek, one of the most popular search engines, offers a freeware utility that puts its search facilities on your desktop. By keeping the iSeek Query Bar (see Figure 10-8) on your desktop, you can search for something on InfoSeek by entering the search word or phrase into the search text box. Your query will be sent to InfoSeek, and when it has completed its search, it will launch your browser and present you with the results.

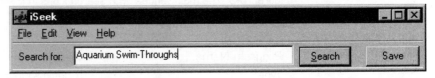

Figure 10-8: The Query Bar in iSeek.

ISeek also allows you to keep search locations in the iSeek window and manage them in much the same way that you manage files in Windows (see Figure 10-9). You can even assign different icons (such as education, news, sports, politics) for your saved searched pages. ISeek comes pre-wired with a number of generic search URLs (for topics such as sports, stocks, politics, and headline news). Because the material on InfoSeek is always changing, clicking on one of these generic icons will offer you the latest info on that subject. You can create your own generic icons for subjects that you want to keep abreast of and simply double-click on that icon every day (or whenever) and you're off! ISeek's icons are OLE objects, so you can even imbed them.

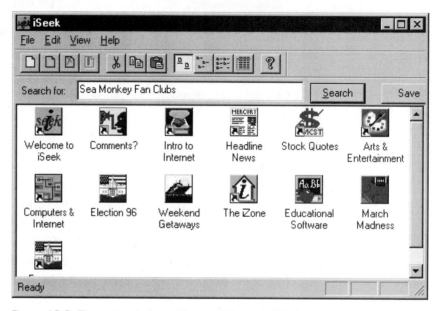

Figure 10-9: The main window with search icons in iSeek.

Program Name:	iSeek
Type:	A desktop interface to InfoSeek, the popular search engine.
System:	Windows 95
Special Features:	Allows you to save search icons. Drag-and-drop capability. Can imbed search icons in other documents.
Where to get the latest version:	http://guide.infoseek.com/

Table 10-7: A brief review of iSeek.

MISCELLANEOUS NET UTILITIES

Sometimes you just need to grab a quick bit of information about someone, have a brief chat, or let other people know what you're doing while you're online. These utilities address these needs.

Here32

If you want to run a server daemon on a temporary Net connection, how do you let others, your friends and co-workers, know that you're online and ready for access? You can call them, but that's intrusive if they don't have a need to access your server at the time. You can e-mail them, but they may not get the message before you disconnect your PPP/SLIP connection. The answer is Here, a shareware utility program ($10) that lets you upload your current server-assigned IP address to the .plan or .project file of a UNIX host. This allows users on the Internet to finger your UNIX shell account, find out what your currently assigned IP address is, and then log in to your machine. This way, you can run various daemons on your PC for FTP, talk, HTTP, and other services while you're online. Here includes a finger client so that you can finger other people's machines to see if they're currently online and what their IP addresses are. See Figure 10-10.

Here is a total no-brainer to use. You simply launch it, enter the host, username, and password in the Login box (under Settings), turn it on (under Post), and you're all set. Then, when prospective users of your PC servers finger your UNIX account, they'll see something like this:

```
HERE ON [Name of host] [Your IP address] [Time/Date]
```

If you have Auto-Post turned on (in the Settings menu), it will send a HERE OFF message to your UNIX account's .plan or .project file (whichever you've selected for Here to post to) when you exit Here.

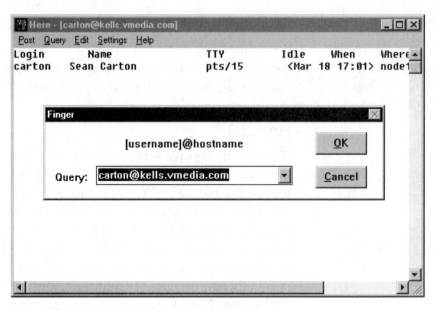

Figure 10-10: The no-nonsense Here interface.

Program Name:	Here32
Type:	IP address poster and Finger client
System:	Windows 95, Windows 3.x
Special Features:	Here saves the last 25 fingerings, so that the accounts that you usually finger are at . . . well . . . your fingertips.
Where to get the latest version:	http://www.cris.com/~beers/here/

Table 10-8: A brief review of Here32.

WinTalk

Sometimes you just gotta chat with someone. While Internet Relay Chat (IRC) is the place to go for real-time chat with hundreds of people, to chat one-on-one with someone you know is online, you can use the program WinTalk.

WinTalk is a client that lets you hook up with a talk daemon on a UNIX machine, providing you with a nifty split-screen on which to type simple text conversations over the Net. And, with the talk daemon (provided with WinTalk), people can "call" you while you're using your computer if they need to chat.

In this day of Internet phones, IRC, and powerful multiuser chat software, why use WinTalk? Several reasons. First, if you only have one phone line, it provides a way for your wired friends to reach you while you're online. Second, if you ever need to reach someone who's logged in at the school or company computer lab, he or she probably doesn't have a phone nearby. You can talk to this person in real-time as long as his or her computer has talk capability.

To use WinTalk, the first thing you'll have to do when you launch it is enter your local username. Once that is entered, WinTalk will finish launching and minimize to the taskbar. To initiate a session, all you do is right-click on the WinTalk icon on the taskbar, and choose Talk. Enter the user@host.domain and WinTalk will launch the talk window and attempt to reach the user. If the user "answers," a ding.ding will sound (or any other WAV file you assign). Everything that you type appears in the top of the screen, and everything that the person you're talking to types appears at the bottom. Figure 10-11 shows a conversation in progress with WinTalk.

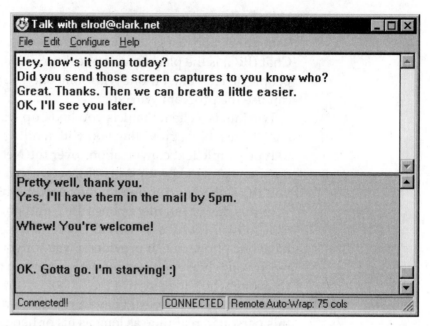

Figure 10-11: Gareth chatting with his friend Sean using Talk.

Program Name:	WinTalk
Type:	Windows version of UNIX talk client and daemon
System:	Windows 95 and Windows 3.1 (both are zipped together)
Special Features:	Allows you to keep a phone book of frequently called users. Can be used as a talk helper app (if the HTTP server you are connecting to is set up properly and you've mapped WinTalk as an application/x-wintalk MIME type).
Where to get the latest version:	http://www.elf.com/elf/wintalk.html

Table 10-9: A brief review of WinTalk.

SocketWatch

SocketWatch is a network time keeper that updates your PC clock with a global time-keeping service. SocketWatch sleeps in the background on your PC until you launch your Internet connection. Once connected, at an interval you specify, SocketWatch gets the correct time. You can also configure SocketWatch to make a Net connection, check the time, and then log out. Users of the Timex Datalink watch can set their watches automatically with SocketWatch.

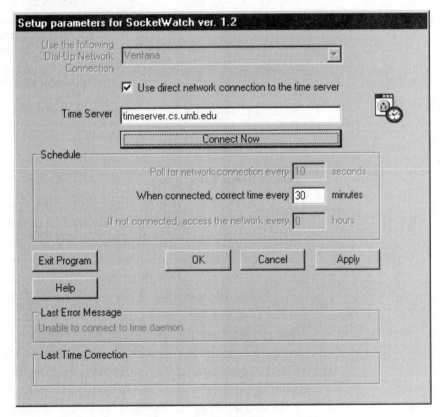

Figure 10-12: The setup screen in SocketWatch.

TIP

SocketWatch does not come preconfigured with a time server. You need to access the Help file and choose a time server near you.

Program Name:	SocketWatch ("Swatch")
Type:	NTP (Network Time Protocol) daemon.
System:	Windows 95
Special Features:	Can automatically make a connection to check the time. Can be used with the Timex Datalink watch.
Where to get the latest version:	http://vanbc.wimsey.com/~atekant/swatch.htm

Table 10-10: A brief review of SocketWatch ("Swatch").

MOVING ON

Well, your toolbox is now chock full of Internet power tools. "The right tool for the job," as they say. We've covered a variety of tools because users have different needs. Some want lean, mean, and small tools that specialize in one thing. Others won't be happy 'til someone develops the ultimate Net tool that does everything with equal élan. It's a matter of personal choice. Whatever you choose, make sure that you're using tools you're comfortable with and that perform well. Experiment. Don't be afraid to try new features of the programs you're already using and to try new programs as they become available. As the Net expands, new and better stuff is coming out every day. The tools we covered in this section will help you learn about the tools that will replace them.

So what's ahead at this point? The wonderful world of UNIX! Now, don't get scared, and run off to Chapter 20. Why not geek out with us as we dissect UNIX and learn how you can use its powerful features to access the Net? We'll cover everything from logging in to reading e-mail to browsing the Web from your shell account.

If you just don't have the stomach for it (the few, the proud, the UNIX savvy), skip ahead to Part V, and learn more about using e-mail more effectively. We'll tell you, among other things, what all that gibberish is in your e-mail headers and how to keep your e-mail private and secure.

## Part III

Macintosh Power User's Tools

## Chapter 11

Inside MacTCP Connections

Chances are, since you're reading this book, you're already on the Internet using MacTCP and some sort of MacTCP dial-up with the SLIP or PPP protocol. If you're like most people, you probably got your connection going either by following step-by-step directions from your service provider or by using a connection script someone gave you. Those directions or that script may have gotten you connected, but you're probably still in the dark about how all of this stuff works.

In this chapter we're going to shed some light on the sometimes dark subject of Macintosh TCP/IP connectivity. There's a lot more to that little MacTCP control panel than meets the eye, and knowing what everything is and how to use it is crucial if you want to get the most out of your connection. The same thing goes for whatever SLIP or PPP dialer you're using—they can be cantankerous beasts if you don't know how they work.

TIP

We're not trying to run your life, but if you haven't done so already, you may want to go back to Chapter 3, "TCP/IP Primer," and bone up on the basics of TCP/IP before you go any further. We're going to cover a lot of stuff in this chapter, stuff that'll probably sound like gobbledygook if you aren't prepared. So go back if you need to, bone up, and come back. We'll wait.

First, we'll dig deep into the MacTCP control panel—what it is, why you need it, where to get it, and how to configure it so your connection performs at peak efficiency. If you're already running MacTCP, you may want to look over the "What Is It?" section to get a brief overview and then move on. Then we'll take a look at the different TCP/IP dialer programs, how to configure them, and what to do when something goes wrong. Of course, getting connected isn't everything—staying connected is just as important. We'll show you how to keep your connection running by going over some of the best Mac TCP/IP connection monitoring tools. Finally, because technology marches on, we'll take a brief look at some of the new MacTCP technologies coming our way so that you'll be prepared when they show up on your desktop.

TIP

In this chapter, we're going to focus on dial-up TCP/IP connections, mainly because that's what most of us have. If you're connecting with MacTCP over a LAN, read over the section of MacTCP, skip the SLIP and PPP stuff, and then jump ahead to "Monitoring Your Mac TCP/IP Connection." You may also want to go back to Chapter 4, "Above & Beyond 28.8 Kbps," and review some of the information about connecting to the Net through a LAN.

Just like everything else with computers, getting a MacTCP connection up and running doesn't involve magic, unattainable skills, or secret knowledge—just a basic understanding of how things work. Oh yeah . . . and did we mention a lot of knuckle biting, hair pulling, and colorful use of language? Welcome to the magic of TCP/IP!

MACTCP BASICS

If you remember even a little of what you learned in Chapter 3, "TC/IP Primer," you'll recall that for a computer to be connected to the Internet, it has to be able to speak the TCP/IP protocol. MacTCP allows your computer to do just that. As we told you in Chapter 3, a TCP/IP communications protocol stack is composed of four layers:

❐ Application Layer
❐ Host-to-Host Transport Layer
❐ Internet Layer
❐ Network Access Layer

Each of these layers is responsible for a different function: the Application Layer takes care of the user interface and the different programs used on the Internet, the Transport Layer delivers the information generated by the Application Layer, the Internet Layer makes sure the data gets to where it's supposed to go by handling the addressing of the data, and the Network Access Layer provides the medium for the information to travel.

MacTCP is a combination control panel/system extension that provides the Transport and Internet Layers functions for your Macintosh with the following network protocols:

❐ Internet Protocol (IP)
❐ Internet Control Message Protocol (ICMP)
❐ User Datagram Protocol (UDP)
❐ Address Resolution Protocol (ARP)
❐ Reverse Address Resolution Protocol (RARP)
❐ Routing Information Protocol (RIP)
❐ Bootstrap Protocol (BootP)
❐ Transmission Control Protocol (TCP)

In addition, the MacTCP control panel gives you an easy interface for configuring all the settings you need to get a TCP/IP connection running (See Figure 11-1).

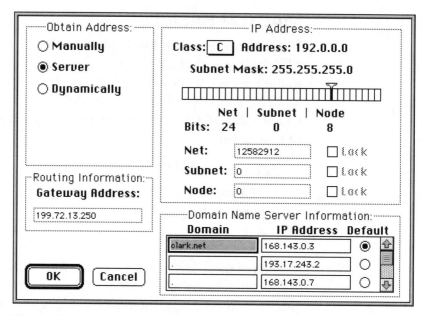

Figure 11-1: MacTCP networking settings.

Getting MacTCP

Here's the rub—even though most of the software you'll ever need to connect your Mac to the Net is completely free, MacTCP isn't. You have to pay for it unless you're running System 7.5.x which includes MacTCP. And unlike Windows users who have several different shareware sources for TCP/IP communications stacks, MacTCP is pretty much the only game in town if you want TCP connectivity on your Mac. So, where can you find it?

If you are running System 7.5, you've already got it with your system software. If you aren't already on the Net with a TCP/IP connection, you may want to poke around in your Control Panels folder and see if it's installed. If you have System 7.5 and you can't find MacTCP in your Control Panels folder, you'll have to install it from your original system software disks.

Before we move on to how to configure MacTCP properly for your machine, we want to offer a little advice. MacTCP is one darn persnickety control panel. If you've gotten a copy from a friend, throw it out! You should always use a fresh (not previously installed) copy of MacTCP when you set up a connection with your Mac. Strange things can happen if you don't. Trust us on this one.

Installing MacTCP

Installing MacTCP is easy. You have two choices. First, if you have System 7.5, you can install it off of the System 7.5 CD-ROM (or floppies).

Installing MacTCP from the System 7.5 Disk

If you bought a Mac with a CD-ROM drive, then you probably received a CD labeled "Apple Macintosh CD" containing your system software. If you purchased System 7.5 separately, you have either a bunch of floppies or a System 7.5 CD-ROM. If you bought a PowerBook, you may not have received any floppies at all — you probably had to make them yourself. (You did make backup copies of your system software, didn't you?)

Whatever way you got it, the procedure for installing MacTCP is pretty much the same:

1. Insert the first system software disk (or CD-ROM) into your computer, and turn it on.

2. Next, double-click on the System 7.5 Installer icon (shown in Figure 11-2). If your system software is on a CD-ROM, you may have to open a folder called System Software Install or Installation to find the Installer. The Installer will start, and you'll get a friendly welcome screen.

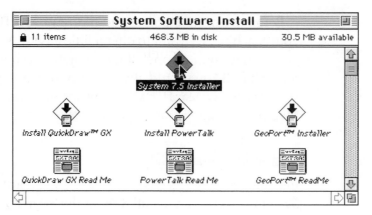

Figure 11-2: The System 7.5 Installer.

3. Press the Continue button, and you'll be greeted with the main install screen (shown in Figure 11-3).

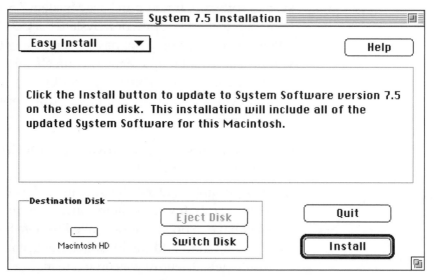

Figure 11-3: System 7.5 installer main screen.

4. Since you just want to install MacTCP at this point and not all the system software, pull down the Easy Install menu in the upper-left corner of the screen, and select Custom Install. The area in the middle of the screen will list of all the different system software components you can install. (See Figure 11-4.)

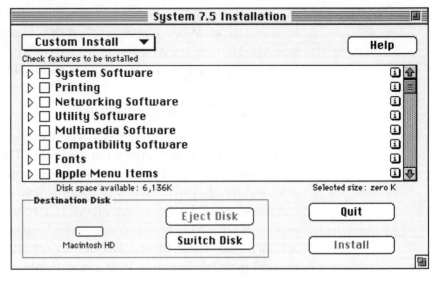

Figure 11-4: The menu of custom installation options in System 7.5.

5. MacTCP is a networking protocol and can be found in the list by single-clicking the arrow next to the (surprise!) Networking Software item. When you click the arrow, a list of various networking extensions will appear, each with a little check box next to it. Click once in the box next to MacTCP to select it for installation.

6. Next, click the Install button, and the installer program will begin its work. If you're installing from floppies, you'll probably be prompted to insert them as needed. When you're finished, press the Restart button to reboot your Mac with your newly installed MacTCP.

CONFIGURING MACTCP

If you're moving up to the wonderful world of TCP connections with your Mac, in this section you'll learn the hows and whys of configuring MacTCP. If you've already installed MacTCP and have it up and running, you're about to learn what everything is as well as a few ways to tweak your settings to get the optimum performance out of your connection. Plus, we'll cover troubleshooting, tips, and tricks. When you're finished (if you pay attention!), you'll be a MacTCP expert. At the very least, you'll be able to throw out a lot of network jargon so you can sound like a big shot.

The MacTCP Control Panel

When you first installed MacTCP, you installed the MacTCP control panel in your Control Panels folder. The MacTCP control panel is actually a hybrid of a control panel and a system extension. It not only provides a way to control your TCP connection, but it also provides the system-level TCP (and others) networking protocols your Mac needs to access the Internet. You'll never actually "see" these protocols, but they function in the background maintaining your TCP connection.

Let's take a closer look. Go to your Control Panels folder, and double-click on MacTCP. Figure 11-5 shows what you should see.

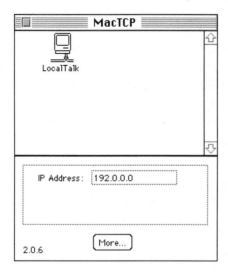

Figure 11-5: The initial controls for MacTCP.

Doesn't look very complicated does it? All you have is a couple of icons, a field labeled IP Address, and a modest little button labeled More. The Rosetta Stone of Mac connectivity is hidden behind that button.

Controlling Your Physical Network Connection

You'll recall that a TCP/IP protocol stack contains a Physical Layer, the hardware required to actually transmit the networking protocols. The field at the top of the MacTCP control panel controls your access to the Physical Layer of your TCP stack. Each icon represents a different physical networking type that MacTCP can use to transmit the IP datagrams. Depending on which one you highlight, you can tell MacTCP what type of network you're using for your IP connection.

One of the really nifty things about MacTCP is that it can transmit IP packets over whatever kind of network you have installed on your Mac. If you're on an AppleTalk network that uses a DDP-IP gateway as a connection to the Internet, you can use AppleTalk to do your Netsurfing. Or, if you're on an Ethernet (a common setup if you're using a Mac in a university or other school computer lab), you'll make your connection to the Net using the Ethernet (or EtherTalk) physical network layer.

But, chances are, if you're at home using a modem to dial in to the Internet, you're using a PPP or SLIP connection as your physical networking layer. If so, the icon for PPP or SLIP will show up in the physical network connection box at the top of your MacTCP control panel.

TIP

This might seem obvious, but it bears pointing out. If you haven't installed SLIP or PPP software on your Macintosh, you won't see their icons in the MacTCP control panel.

By selecting an icon in the physical network connection box at the top of the MacTCP control panel, you can control which way the IP datagrams leave your machine. If you have several different types of networking installed, selecting the appropriate icon allows you to switch your IP connection between the different connections available.

TIP

If you're using several different physical layers in your Mac, you'll have to reboot your computer when you switch between the various connection types.

Your IP Address

Right below the physical connection box, smack-dab in the middle of the control panel, you'll find a field labeled IP Address. Depending on how you have MacTCP configured, this field may be grayed-out (Figure 11-6) so that you can't enter any information into it, or it may be highlighted in black, allowing you to change its contents (Figure 11-7). Don't worry about this right now—we'll get to how to change this number in a bit.

Figure 11-6: You can't change this IP number . . .

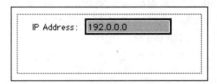

Figure 11-7: . . . but you can change this one.

The IP Address field contains the actual Internet IP address of your machine. In most cases, your Mac is assigned an IP number in one of three ways. First, you may be assigned a specific IP address by your service provider or network administrator. This number is yours and yours alone and shouldn't be changed if you want to stay connected.

Second, you may be automatically assigned an IP address by your network. In some cases, you'll always get the same IP number each time you connect. In other cases, you may end up with a different number depending on what IP numbers your server has available.

If you're on the Net, it's important that you know the IP address of your machine if you want to do point-to-point exchanges of information with other people online. For example, if you want to use the popular videoconferencing software CU-See Me to hold a video-chat with your friend in Malaysia (more on how to do that in Chapter 28, "Audio/Video Power Tools"), you'll need to know your Mac's IP number (as well as your friend's IP number) in order for your two computers to connect to each other across the Net.

TIP

In some instances, you can use your machine's name to connect. How do you know the name of your computer? See "MacTCP Watcher," later in this chapter.

The Administrator Dialog Box

Now let's press the magic More button. A dialog box like the one in Figure 11-8 will appear. Looks like a lot of stuff, huh? Well, it is. The Administrator dialog box is the heart and soul of MacTCP. Here's where you can configure all the important aspects of your TCP/IP connection.

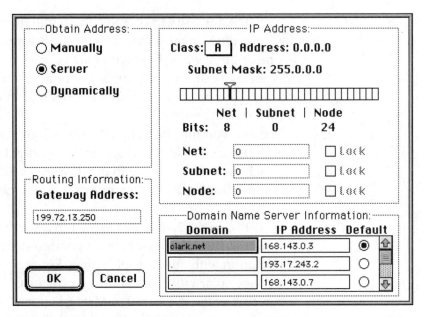

Figure 11-8: The Administrator dialog box in MacTCP.

TIP

What's that you say? Nothing happens when you press the More button? In fact, it's grayed out. Well, if you're on a LAN it's because your sysadmin has already configured everything for you and has locked you out so that you don't muck things up. If you're a card-carrying computer geek and are dying to know what's behind that button (so you can follow along in our little power user hymnal), you can beg said administrator to give you access. But, you know how network administrators are—good luck!

Configuring Your IP Address

We briefly touched on this before when we discussed the IP Address field, but your Macintosh can obtain your Internet IP address in one of three ways: manually, by the server, or dynamically. The three buttons in the Obtain Address area of the Administrator dialog box control how you get an IP address when you hook up to a TCP/IP network. Let's take a closer look at these three types of IP address assignment schemes:

❑ **Manually:** In a manual IP address setup, your machine's IP address is assigned by your system administrator (or your ISP) and never changes. If you're using a manual IP configuration with MacTCP, you must enter the IP address and gateway yourself the first time you configure MacTCP. If you're using a Mac on a preconfigured network, these numbers already may have been set for you.

❑ **Server:** If your Mac's IP address is set by the server, the IP address assigned to your computer is automatically set by the network every time you make a MacTCP connection (or every time you boot the computer if you're on a hardwired net). MacTCP uses the BootP protocol to talk to the main network computer, which then assigns an IP address based on which addresses are available or which address has been preset for your Mac. If you're connecting to the Internet via a PPP account, you'll probably use this setting because the PPP protocol allows for automatic assignment of IP addresses when you connect to your ISP. This is by far the easiest way to get your connection up and running.

❑ **Dynamically:** Much like server-assigned addressing, dynamic IP addressing allows the network to decide what your IP address should be. However, when an address is assigned dynamically, the whole address isn't assigned— just the node (the last part of the address). You must set the Net and Subnet portions of the address in the IP Address box on the right side of the Administrator dialog box (more on how to do that in a moment).

TIP

There's a big difference between Server and Dynamic addressing, as far as MacTCP is concerned. When you ask your systems administrator or Internet Service Provider what type of addressing you should use, check to make sure that they know the difference. The Server setting allows the whole address to be set for you using the BootP or RARP protocols. The dynamic setting allows only the node part of the address to be assigned.

If you're using Server addressing, just click the Server button, and your address is assigned for you when you connect. The server you're connecting to does all the work, configuring your IP address, gateway numbers, and subnet masks. However, not everyone is so lucky. If you're using the Manual or Dynamically settings, things get a little hairier. In the following sections, we'll look at how to configure an IP address for systems using manual and dynamic addressing.

Manual Addressing

If you're on a system with manual addressing, click the Manually button, and go back to the first part of the MacTCP control panel by clicking the OK button. In the IP Address box, enter the IP address you've been assigned, and then click the More button to go back to the Administrator dialog box.

In the IP Address section of the dialog box, you should now see that the Class has been set for you. MacTCP is no dummy, and it knows how to set the class of the connection based on the IP address you've entered, as shown in Table 11-1.

First Octet Value	Class
1—127	A
128—191	B
192—254	C

Table 11-1: MacTCP IP address class assignments.

If you need help remembering what IP address classes are, go back to Chapter 3 and brush up on your TCP/IP concepts. However, you probably don't have to worry about it—just take MacTCP's word for it.

Next, you have to set the subnet mask, providing that your network uses subnetting. If your network doesn't use subnet masks, move the Subnet Mask slider all the way to the left by dragging the little arrow-shaped slider on the Subnet Mask bar (shown in Figure 11-9).

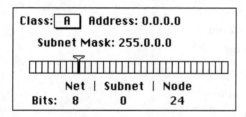

Figure 11-9: No subnet mask needed? Move the slider to the left.

If you do need a subnet mask for your network, move the slider until the correct subnet mask value appears in the Subnet Mask field above the slider. You should get the correct subnet mask value from your service provider or sysadmin—don't try to guess!

TIP

If you can't connect to anything after you've gotten your system configured, check your subnet mask. A computer with an incorrectly set mask will show that it's on the network and has its own IP number, but that's it.

If you count the number of squares on the subnet mask slider bar, you'll notice that there are 32 of them. Remember our discussion on IP addresses and subnet masks in Chapter 3? Each box represents a subnet mask bit. Moving the slider along the bar indicates how many bits are used on your network to indicate the network part of the address. That's why as you move the slider, the value of the Subnet Mask field changes—it's indicating the value of the mask.

If you're feeling really bold, you can enter the decimal representation of the subnet mask information in the Net, Subnet, and Node boxes below the slider, though you don't have to.

Dynamic Addressing

If your IP address node is assigned dynamically by your server, click the Dynamically button in the Obtain Address field. Two boxes will appear below the Dynamically button (shown in Figure 11-10). Ignore them for now.

Figure 11-10: Obtaining your IP address dynamically.

MacTCP provides you with a range of IP address node numbers based on the settings in the IP Address section of the MacTCP Administrator dialog box. You'll need to make these settings first. set the Class and Subnet Mask settings to those provided by your systems administrator or ISP. You can set the Class via the pop-up Class menu and the Subnet Mask using the Subnet Mask slider.

Once you've set the IP address information, the numbers that appear in the two Node Range boxes will indicate the nodes available to you based on your IP address settings. Unless someone tells you otherwise, leave these numbers alone—they indicate the different possible nodes you can use on your network. However, in some cases you may need to change them if you have machines on your network with preset IP addresses that can't (and shouldn't) be changed. Again, knock on the ol' sysadmin's door, and make sure of the settings you should use before you put any numbers in the From and To boxes. It also never hurts to bring gifts of coffee, Jolt Cola, or Cheetos if you must disturb the local network guru.

Dynamic Addressing on a LAN: Recipe for Disaster?

Some people have reported problems when using MacTCP on an Ethernet LAN with dynamic addressing. It seems that when MacTCP sends out a packet to the LAN requesting an IP number, that packet contains both the sender's IP address and the Ethernet address of the Mac sending the request. Ordinarily, this is standard procedure. However, MacTCP uses the address it's testing as the sender's IP address. When the request goes out, it's received by every single Mac on the LAN. All the computers on the network then automatically update their information tables using the requested IP address as the new IP address for the Mac trying to get on the network. When that happens, any data destined for the new Mac will be directed to the IP address the new machine originally requested, regardless of whether or not that's the IP it was actually assigned. Result? Kablooey! No information can go anywhere because the addressing tables for the whole network are scrambled.

Here's the solution: if you're an administrator setting up an Ethernet LAN using TCP/IP with MacTCP, either assign the addresses manually or install a BootP or RARP server so that MacTCP can find its address from the server at boot time. The problem's not really a bug in MacTCP. MacTCP tries to use the ARP in dynamic addressing for something it was never designed to do. Beware.

Gateway Address

The Gateway Address setting in the Administrator dialog box is easy. In most cases, MacTCP is able to use the Routing Address Protocol (RAP) to find the default gateway machine on your TCP/IP network. The RAP checks the machines on your network to determine which one is the gateway to the Internet. However, if you're using the Manual address settings and you're absolutely sure that your network doesn't use RAP, you can enter the gateway IP number here. Don't experiment—ask someone if you don't know.

Domain Name Server Information

Here's where the fun begins! The Domain Name Services settings in MacTCP are probably the most misunderstood part of getting a MacTCP connection up and running correctly. With the right DNS settings (which you can get from your ISP or systems administrator), you'll be rewarded with a smooth, consistent TCP/IP connection. Set them incorrectly, and you'll be tearing your hair out because you can't connect to anything. But don't worry! If you follow a few simple rules, you'll be a DNS maven in no time.

MacTCP uses the Domain Name Services you specify in the Domain Name Server Information section of the Administrator dialog box. See Figure 11-11.

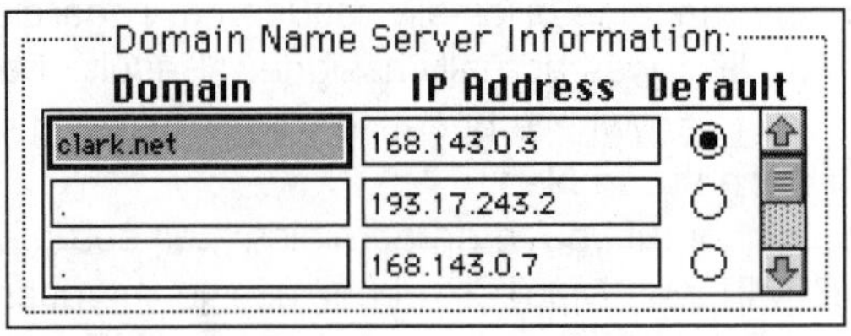

Domain Name Server Information:		
Domain	**IP Address**	**Default**
clark.net	168.143.0.3	●
.	193.17.243.2	○
.	168.143.0.7	○

Figure 11-11: Domain Name Services Information section of the Administrator dialog box in MacTCP.

At first glance, it looks pretty simple—just enter the domain name of your DNS in the Domain box, and enter the DNS's IP address in the IP Address box, right? Well, kinda. What complicates things is that MacTCP uses a complex set of rules to choose which DNS to use in order to resolve names sent to that DNS.

❐ Rule 1: If a domain name contains a period (seansa.slacker.com) MacTCP figures it's a fully qualified domain name and sends it off to the domain name server for that domain. For example, if we had a DNS entry for slacker.com, MacTCP would send the name seansa.slacker.com to the DNS entry for slacker.com.

❐ Rule 2: If a domain name doesn't contain a period, MacTCP appends the name to the domain specified as the default DNS. Taking an example from Rule 1, if our default DNS was slacker.com, and we tried to FTP to seansa, MacTCP would expand seansa to seansa.slacker.com and then send the name to the slacker.com DNS.

❐ Rule 3: If the expanded domain name from Rule 2 exactly matches an entry in the MacTCP Hosts file, the name is resolved from the IP address indicated in the Hosts file. For example, if seansa.slacker.com was assigned an IP address of 143.43.22.1 in the Hosts file, seansa.slacker.com would immediately be resolved into 143.43.22.1 without ever having to pass through a DNS. Any periods at the end of the domain name are ignored. (More about the Hosts file in a minute.)

❐ Rule 4: If a domain name still hasn't been found, MacTCP goes through the list of all the name servers in the Domain Name Server Information list and makes a list of all the DNSes that match the domain of the name it's trying to look up. If MacTCP finds a domain indicated by a period in the Domain box, it consults that DNS. MacTCP will always use the default DNS, even if it doesn't contain the same domain as the name being looked up.

❐ Rule 5: Once a list is built, MacTCP tries to resolve the name from each name server until a match is found. If a match is not found, MacTCP issues an error indicating that the name cannot be resolved.

Simple. (Yeah right!) Even though it seems like a lot to go through just to find a name, in practice setting up your DNS entries isn't that difficult. In most cases, you should enter the DNS information for the main name server in your domain in the first level of boxes and then check the Default button. This will make sure that you at least have one name server. Unless you want to use only numerical IP addresses, this is a must.

Next, enter the same information in the second level of boxes, but instead of entering a domain name in the Domain box, enter a period. This will make sure that your main name server will be used to look up both names within your domain as well as names outside of your domain. See Figure 11-12.

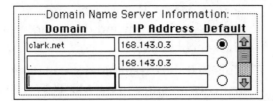

Figure 11-12: The bare minimum DNS entries for MacTCP.

At this point, if you're sure that your DNS will never go down, you can stop. However, it's always good to have a backup server or two specified in your DNS table. Most systems and service providers will provide you with a list of two or more alternate DNSes to use. Just enter the alternate DNS information in the appropriate boxes, using a period for the name of the server (Figure 11-13).

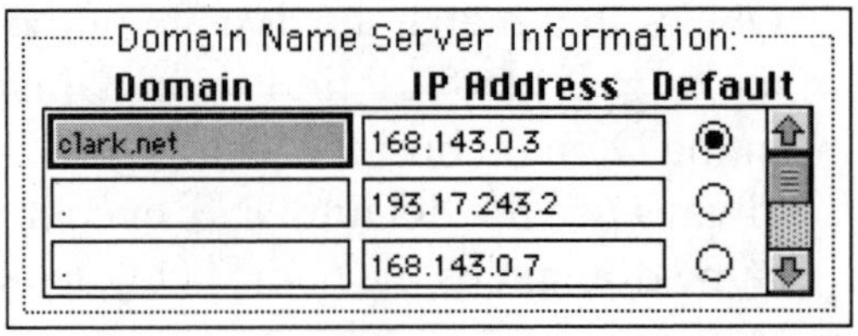

Figure 11-13: MacTCP with several Domain Name Servers specified.

TIP

Once you have the correct DNS settings in MacTCP, you'll type less! For example, if your service provider (or LAN) used the slacker.com domain, you could contact the FTP server (ftp.slacker.com) by just referring to ftp rather than the entire name. MacTCP will automatically attach to slacker.com!

The Hosts File

If you want to bypass the DNS all together (or if you have an unreliable DNS) and you know the IP addresses of the computers you frequently need to communicate with, you can do what those

UNIX guys and gals do — use a hosts table. You will need to specify at least one Domain Name Server, but MacTCP won't use it unless it can't find the address in the table.

When you install MacTCP, it creates a file in your system folder called Hosts. If you have MacTCP installed right now, go look for it. It should look something like this:

```
; Hosts
; This file is parsed by the MacTCP domain name resolver and
; the resource records are loaded into the resolver's cache.
;
; The Hosts file follows a SUBSET of the Master File Format
; (see rfc1035 pg 33).
; Each line in this file has the form:
;    <domain-name> <rr> [<comment>]
; <domain-name> is an absolute domain name
; (see rfc1034 pg 11).
; <rr> = [<ttl>] [<class>] <type> <rdata> OR [<class>]
; [<ttl>] <type> <rdata>
; A comment starts with ";" or by a line beginning with a " ".
;
; NOTES:
;    $INCLUDE is not implemented
;    Class is always IN, ttl is in seconds, type can be A,
;    CNAME or NS.

; Examples

;knowAll.apple.com.  A     128.8.1.1
;address of host knowAll.apple.com.
;
;apple.com.          NS    knowAll.apple.com.
; apple.com name server
;.                   NS    knowAll.apple.com.
; root name server
;
;myHost.apple.com.   IN    604800   A    128.8.1.2
; ttl of 1 week
;JohnS.apple.com.    A     128.8.1.3
;Sculley.apple.com.  CNAME      JohnS.apple.com.
; canonical name for alias Sculley.apple.com
```

Just like the hosts file on your main server, the MacTCP Hosts file allows you to directly map names to IP addresses. Then, if your name server goes down, MacTCP will look directly into the Hosts file to find the IP address for the machine you're trying to reach.

The Hosts file uses the following syntax to map IP addresses and domain names:

```
name    type    data    ;comment
```

Table 11-2 shows the three different types of data you can use in the type field,

type Value	Description
A	The data field is an IP address.
NS	The data field holds the name of the DNS, which should be used for the domain name in the name field.
CNAME	The data field contains the "canonical" or official name of the domain name in the name field.

Table 11-2: MacTCP Host table types.

For example, say you frequently used the following hosts (listed with their corresponding IP addresses. (These are for example only. Any similarity to real domains and IP addresses is purely coincidental.)

```
garethsa.slacker.com    122.22.45.21
nigel.linux.com         132.32.33.1
boingboing.com          144.22.21.128
natty.boh.com           128.45.222.123
```

You could enter them in to your Hosts file like so:

```
garethsa.slacker.com    A    122.22.45.21     ;Gareth
nigel.linux.com         A    132.32.33.1      ;Nigel
boingboing.com          A    144.22.21.128    ;braincandy
natty.boh.com           A    128.45.222.123   ;recreation
```

If you wanted to specify a specific DNS for a domain, you can do it in the Hosts file for quicker domain name resolution. The following line would indicate that overlord.neowobbly.com is the Domain Name Server for the neowobbly.com domain:

```
neowobbly.com    NS    overlord.neowobbly.com
```

Finally, if you want to use an alias for a certain domain name, you can do it in the Hosts file. The following entry would allow kata.neowobbly.com to stand in for server1.neowobbly.com when you wanted to access that particular host:

```
kata.neowobbly.com  CNAME      server1.neowobbly.com
```

INSIDE MAC TCP/IP DIAL-UP CONNECTIONS: INTERSLIP & MACPPP

If your Mac is directly connected to a LAN, you can skip this part and go on to "Monitoring Your TCP/IP Connection," later in this chapter. But if you are making the TCP/IP connection via a modem (and this includes you lucky ISDN users, too), then read on.

Just like we pointed out with the MacTCP control panel, even if you're currently on the Net with a TCP/IP connection, chances are that you got there in one of five ways: 1) sheer luck, 2) divine grace, 3) alien intervention, 4) a helpful friend, or 5) by following a step-by-step set of directions given to you by your service provider. Whatever the case, you probably have little or no idea what the settings in your SLIP or PPP connection do. Here are some clues.

MacPPP

We'll take care of the light work first. If you have the opportunity to use PPP with your ISP, do so. It's very easy to set up, takes care of most of the dirty work, and can be used in manual login mode (also known as *terminal mode*) if you need help debugging your initial login script. Very handy to the power user.

Consisting of two separate files (the ConfigPPP control panel and PPP extension—see Figure 11-14), MacPPP is the most common implementation of the PPP LAP (Link Access Protocol) for the Mac. Other vendors (InterCon in particular) make other Mac implementations of PPP, but MacPPP rules MacLand mainly because it's stable, easy to set up, and (above all) free!

Config PPP   PPP

Figure 11-14: Config PPP control panel and PPP extension.

The only thing that's confusing about using MacPPP is that there are four or five different implementations of it are floating around the Net. Each has something to recommend it, but for simplicity's sake, until you really know what you're doing, stick with the original—MacPPP 2.0.1. You can snag it from http://hyperarchive.lcs.mit.edu/HyperArchive/Archive/comm/tcp/conn/mac-ppp-201.hqx. If you're using MacPPP right now, check the version number. If you don't have 2.0.1, get it.

The Main Config PPP Control Panel: A Tour

We'll ignore the PPP extension. All you need to do is drop it in your Extensions folder. The real action takes place in the ConfigPPP control panel. Go to your Control Panels folder, and double-click on the ConfigPPP icon. If you're using version 2.0.1 (like we told you!), you should see something like Figure 11-15.

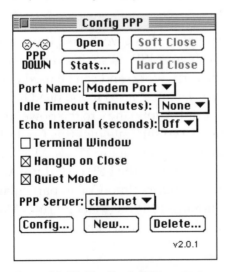

Figure 11-15: The ConfigPPP control panel.

Here's a brief rundown of the functions of the MacPPP control panel.

The Connection Indicator

See those frowny faces? They get real happy when your PPP connection is established. (And so do you!) You can also tell if you're connection's up when PPP Down changes to read PPP Up.

Open Button

Click this button to bring up your connection. If this button is grayed out, it could mean one of two things. First, when you make a successful connection, Open becomes dimmed. If you haven't made a connection yet and Open is dimmed, you've got problems. First, check to make sure that the PPP extension has been installed in the Extensions folder. If it is, go to your MacTCP control panel, and make sure that the PPP icon has been selected. If it hasn't, select it. If it's selected and the Open button is still dimmed in ConfigPPP, try reinstalling MacPPP.

TIP

If you use a lot of system extensions and control panels, you may have problems with MacPPP. If a dialog box pops up saying that there's insufficient memory to initialize PPP when you start your computer, and the Open button is dimmed, you'll need to reduce the number of extensions before you can get MacPPP to work.

Hard Close & Soft Close

Both of these buttons do the same thing—close your connection and disconnect your modem from your ISP. However, it's not what they do when you press them but what they do *after* you press them that often causes confusion. If you press Hard Close, Config PPP will disconnect you from your PPP connection and then refuse to honor any additional TCP/IP requests from your software. Soft Close is a different story. While Soft Close will disconnect you from your account, if any programs you are running request a TCP/IP connection, a Soft Closed MacPPP will automatically dial and make the connection to establish a TCP/IP link.

Stats

Now here's where things could get confusing if you didn't have our expert (and humble) assistance to guide you. If you're connected with MacPPP and you push the Stats button, you should see a display similar to that shown in Figure 11-16.

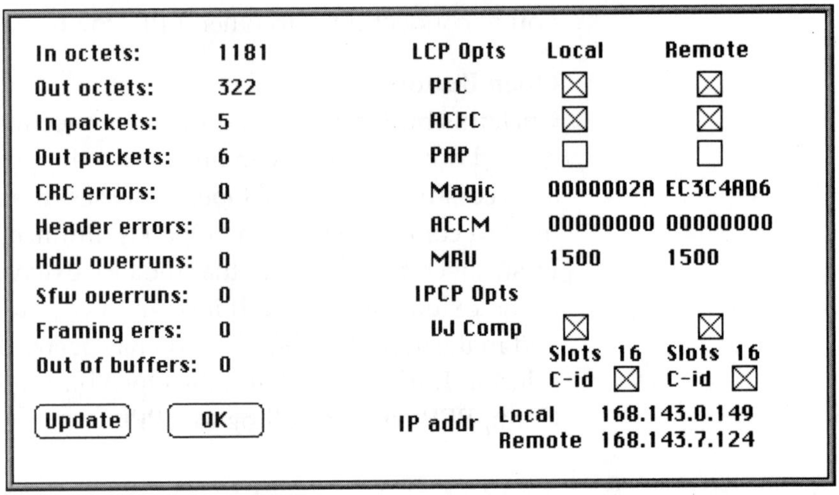

In octets:	1181	LCP Opts	Local	Remote
Out octets:	322	PFC	☒	☒
In packets:	5	ACFC	☒	☒
Out packets:	6	PAP	☐	☐
CRC errors:	0	Magic	0000002A	EC3C4AD6
Header errors:	0	ACCM	00000000	00000000
Hdw overruns:	0	MRU	1500	1500
Sfw overruns:	0	IPCP Opts		
Framing errs:	0	VJ Comp	☒	☒
Out of buffers:	0		Slots 16	Slots 16
			C-id ☒	C-id ☒

[Update]   [OK]   IP addr   Local   168.143.0.149
                                       Remote 168.143.7.124

Figure 11-16: The Stats window in MacPPP.

The readouts on the left side of the window are counters that indicate the status of your connection. If you're not connected with MacPPP when you view this window, all the indicators should read 0. If you are connected, these indicators will give you helpful information about how good a connection you have. It's not imperative that you know what each indicator means, but it is important to know which ones indicate a good connection.

The In octets, Out octets, In packets, and Out packets indicators show the amount of data (packets and PPP datagrams) flowing in to and out of your computer. If you are trying to make a connection to a remote host and the Out indicators read greater than 0 but the In indicators remain at 0, you probably aren't properly connected. Close the connection, and try again.

The five errors indicators and the overrun indicators are helpful when trying to troubleshoot your connection. If you have connected with MacPPP and see no errors but still can't connect to any remote hosts with your TCP/IP software, you are probably encountering TCP/IP errors or a badly configured MacTCP control panel. However, if your connection seems sporadic or nonexistent and these fields indicate a lot of errors, your problems are almost certainly with your modem. See Chapters 1 and 2 if you need help properly configuring your modem.

The right side of the Stats window deals entirely with elements of the PPP protocol.

So what's all this mean? Starting from the top, the first three rows show whether Protocol Field Compression (PFC), Address and Control Field Compression (ACFC), and PPP Authentication Protocol (PAP) are being used during the connection, either on your machine or on the remote host. Since PPP negotiates all these attributes when the connection is made, you don't have to worry about setting these.

The Magic line indicates the values for PPP's magic number. In a great moment of inspiration, the creators of the PPP protocol developed the magic number system to be able to find out whether a connection is looped back or bouncing information from your computer to the host and back again. To determine if the connection is looped-back, MacPPP generates a random magic number, which it then transmits to the remote host. The remote host is supposed to generate its own magic number. Because the two magic numbers are randomly generated, they should never match. If they do, PPP knows that the connection has looped back.

ACCM indicates the value of the Asynchronous Control Character Map, a number that PPP uses to remap control characters that must go through the connection. When a control character has to be transmitted through the connection, it is remapped to a new value. This keeps characters that might be interpreted as modem commands from interrupting the connection.

The MRU (Maximum Receive Unit) number on the next line shows you the codes PPP is using to determine how long a frame or block of information it should send or receive. This value goes up when you have a good, clean connection because more data can be sent without error. However, with a poor-quality connection, this value will go down in order to minimize errors in the information sent and received.

VJ Comp indicates whether Van Jacobson TCP/IP compression is being used. This type of compression can be used to minimize the amount of TCP/IP header information being sent back and forth between your machine and the remote host. Generally, connections using Van Jacobson compression will operate faster than uncompressed TCP/IP connections.

Finally, the last two lines next to IP addr indicate the IP addresses of your machine and the local host.

Port Name
This pop-up menu should be no surprise to you at this point—especially if you were a good soldier and read Chapters 1 and 2. Pulling down this menu allows you to select which communications port you want MacPPP to use to make a connection. For most of you, this will be the Modem Port.

Idle Timeout (minutes)
From this menu, you can control how long MacPPP has to wait before it decides you fell asleep in your overstuffed executive chair and disconnects you from the remote host. If you pay for your connection by the minute, this menu can save you a lot of money by automatically disconnecting you if you forget to break the connection yourself. If you have a full-time connection, you can set this value to None so that MacPPP will always stay connected. See Figure 11-17 to see how to select an Idle Timeout value in MacPPP.

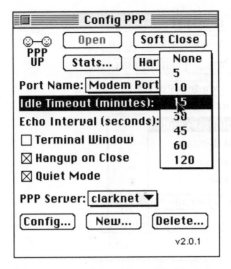

Figure 11-17: Selecting an Idle Timeout value.

Echo Interval (seconds)

If you choose a value other than Off from this menu, MacPPP will send out an LCP (Line Control Protocol) packet at the interval you select. This allows MacPPP to determine whether the connection is still active. If MacPPP doesn't receive a response after three LCP packets, it will assume that the link has gone dead and will disconnect. The only problem with using this setting is that MacPPP may disconnect you if you have a slow connection. However, the benefit of being able to have MacPPP automatically check the connection for you usually outweighs the drawbacks. See Figure 11-18 for an example of how to set the Echo Interval.

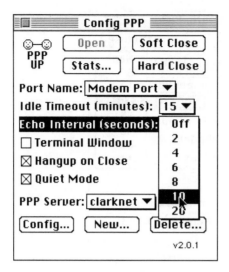

Figure 11-18: Selecting an Echo Interval.

Terminal Window

If you check this box, MacPPP will pop up a simple terminal window (shown in Figure 11-19) when you click the Open button. You can then manually log in to your PPP account, without having to worry about building a connect script. This can be pretty handy when you are first trying to get a connection to work because it allows you to see exactly what's going on with the connection.

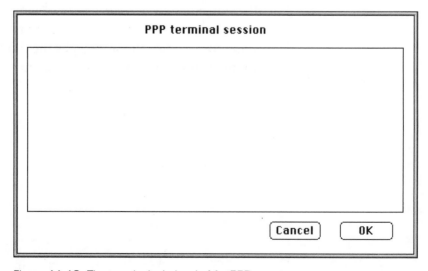

Figure 11-19: The terminal window in MacPPP.

Hangup on Close

Selecting this box will make sure that MacPPP hangs up the modem whenever your PPP connection is closed. It's probably a good idea to keep this checked.

Quiet Mode

Checking the Quiet Mode button will keep MacPPP from informing you about problems and asking you if you want to disconnect when the link goes dead. It's probably a good idea to keep this option off until you get your connection up. After that, it's up to you if you want to be bothered.

PPP Server

This pull-down menu lets you select which server you want to connect to. MacPPP can store information about several different PPP server connections. However, choosing a server from this pull-down menu doesn't affect any MacTCP settings. If each server you want to use utilizes different TCP/IP and DNS settings, you'll also have to get a utility such as MacTCP Switcher (available at ftp://ftp.acns.nwu.edu/pub/jlnstuff/mactcp-switcher/) to switch between them.

Config

Pressing this button will bring up the MacPPP Configuration window. Here you can configure your MacPPP server information. More about this in the "MacPPP Server Configuration" section on the next page.

New

Press this button to create a new PPP server configuration. See the "MacPPP Server Configuration" section for more information about PPP server configurations.

Delete

If you need to delete a server configuration, press the Delete button. See, we told you this wasn't rocket science!

MacPPP Server Configuration

While the MacPPP Configuration dialog box isn't a complicated beast (see Figure 11-20), it does allow you to control several fairly sophisticated aspects of your PPP connection.

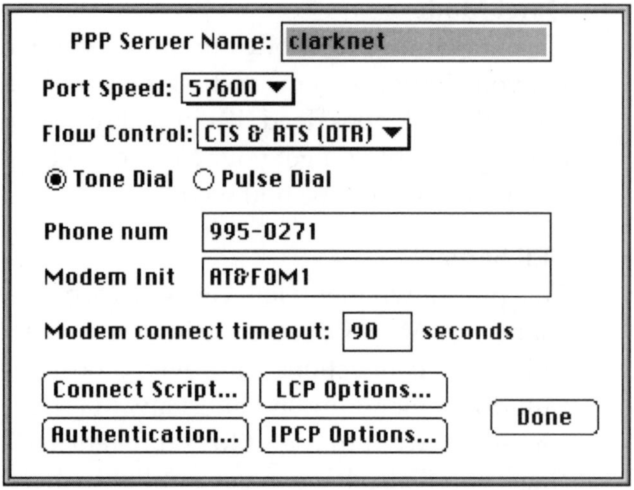

Figure 11-20: The Configuration dialog box in MacPPP.

The first screen of the Configuration dialog box (available by hitting the Config button on the Config PPP control panel) is where you set all the options that control your modem's role in your MacPPP connection. None of these options should be new to you—Port Speed, Flow Control, Tone or Pulse Dial, Phone Num, Modem Init string. The only option that needs clarification is Flow Control. Even though MacPPP allows you several different options for modem flow control, you should always pick CTS & RTS (DTR) unless explicitly told otherwise. This choice allows full hardware flow control for greater connect speeds.

Connect Script

One really nice thing about MacPPP is how easy it is to script your connection. Unlike InterSLIP (and a few other PPP or SLIP programs), MacPPP doesn't force you to learn a complicated scripting language. Instead, you just need to fill out a simple form, push a few buttons, and you're finished! Of course, you can bypass the whole operation by using the terminal window, but that's not the most elegant solution.

Push the Connect Script button to access the Connect Script dialog box.

Wait timeout: 40 seconds		<CR>
⦿ Out ○ Wait		☐
⦿ Out ○ Wait		☐
⦿ Out ○ Wait		☐
⦿ Out ○ Wait		☐
⦿ Out ○ Wait		☐
⦿ Out ○ Wait		☐
⦿ Out ○ Wait		☐
⦿ Out ○ Wait		☐
	Cancel OK	

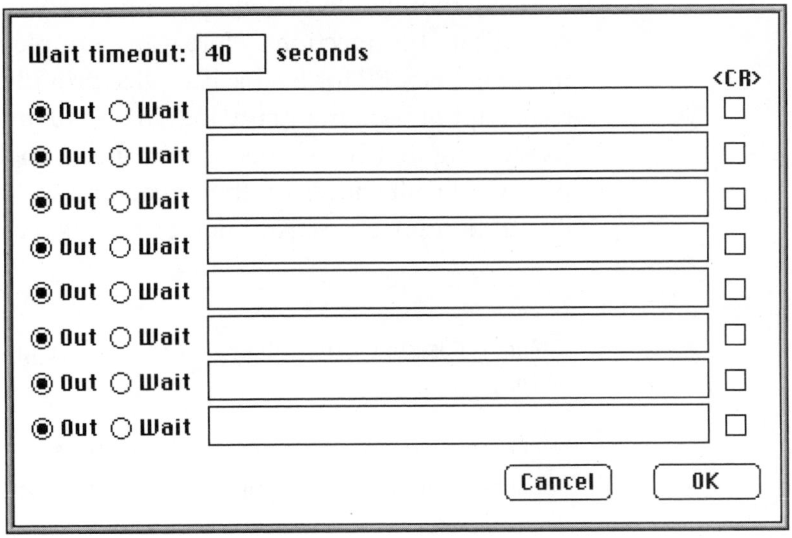

Figure 11-21: The Connect Script dialog box in MacPPP.

MacPPP connect scripts are simple because they acknowledge only two states—either MacPPP is waiting for information from the server or it's sending information to the server. You tell MacPPP to wait for information from the server by selecting the Wait radio button, and you tell MacPPP to send information to the server by selecting the Out button. If you select Wait, MacPPP will wait for the text in the box to the right of the button to be sent from your server. The string in the box has to be an exact match (including case) for what the server sends, but it doesn't have to include the whole string. For example, if your system uses the string "Account Username:" to prompt for your username, telling your connect script to wait for the string "name:" will work fine.

To send information to the server, just click the Out button, and enter a character string to output in the box. If the information you're sending requires you to press Enter after you've typed it (such as username and password information), just put a check in the <CR> box to the far right.

Using this simple system, you can easily script some pretty complicated connections. Here's an example of how Sean configured his MacPPP for his local service provider. The first script is a transcript of Sean manually logging on to his service provider. Everything that Sean typed is indicated in boldface. Ordinarily the password isn't shown on the screen, but we've included it here for illustration purposes. And no, it's not his real password:

```
CONNECT 57600 Clark.net

Annex Command Line Interpreter   *   Copyright 1991 Xylogics,
Inc.

Checking authorization, Please wait...
Connecting to port 33 on annex7.clark.net.

   Welcome to ClarkNet!

Log in as "guest" for ClarkNet info and registration.

ClarkNet Username: elrod
ClarkNet Password: hackOmat1c

Permission granted


            ClarkNet's Menu


    1)  Enter clarknet host      (UUCP users only)
    2)  Enter explorer host      (All users and guest)
    3)  SLIP                     (SLIP users only)
    4)  PPP                      (PPP users only)
    5)  Hosts?                   (All users)
```

```
  6)  Who?                        (All users)
  7)  Telnet                      (IP users only)
  8)  Exit                        (All users)

Enter Number (1-8): 4

Switching to PPP.
~}#¿!}!}!} }4}"}&} } } } }%}& P¿?}'}"}(}" ≥~~}#¿!}!}"}
}4}"}&} } } }
```

Now, how would that translate to a connect script? Figure 11-22 shows the connect script information that works for this connection and MacPPP.

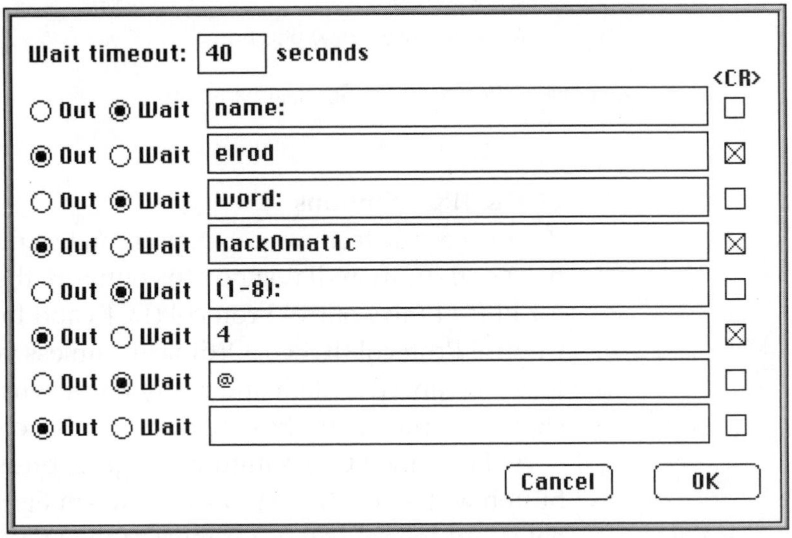

Figure 11-22: Sean's MacPPP connect script.

Notice that he doesn't use the full string "ClarkNet Username:" or "ClarkNet Password:." Using just the tail-end of the string makes sure that the script will keep working if Clark Net changes the login prompt to Username: or Enter Your User name:. You'll also notice that the script ends with an at sign (@). This character is generated by the PPP handshaking information coming from the ISP. You may need something different. Check with your ISP.

Occasionally, you may have to insert special information into your connect scripts or force your script to wait a specific amount of time. Luckily, the creators of MacPPP thought of this and have included several symbols you can use to add special controls to your scripts. See Table 11-3.

Character	Stands for	Used in Out string?	Used in In string?
\r	carriage return	yes	yes
\^	caret	yes	yes
\\	backslash	yes	yes
\number	number=8-bit octal value	yes	yes
\b	send a 100 millisecond break	yes	no
\d	wait one second	yes	no
\t	make terminal window pop up	yes	no

Table 11-3: MacPPP Control Script Special Characters.

LCP & IPCP Options

If you're a true technoweenie, you can use these two buttons in the Configuration dialog box to configure the low-level options for PPP's Link Control Protocol (LCP) and Internet Protocol Control Protocol (ICPC). Ordinarily, unless you're setting up a fairly advanced system and really know what you're doing, you shouldn't mess with these options...with a couple of exceptions.

As far as the LCP configuration goes, pressing the LCP Options button will access the window shown in Figure 11-23. You can enter any special values for most of the LCP information we spoke about in the Stats dialog box. Usually, you won't have to touch these settings.

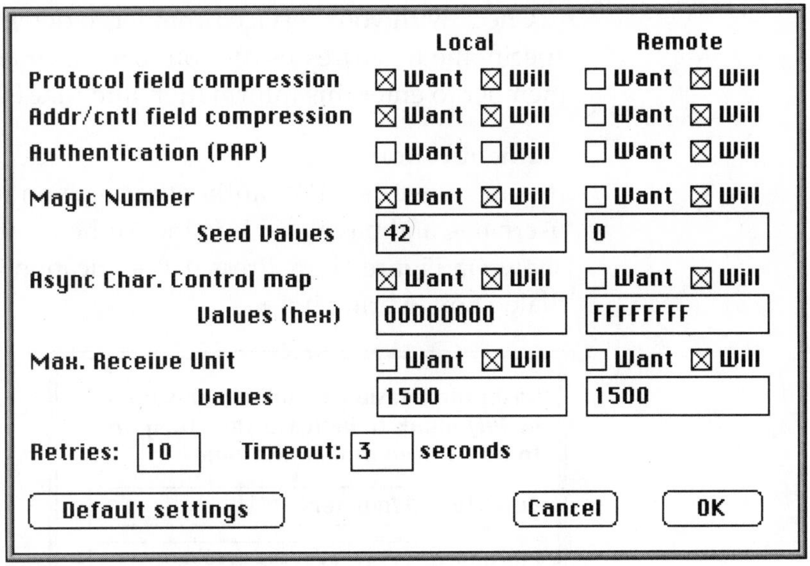

	Local	Remote
Protocol field compression	☒ Want ☒ Will	☐ Want ☒ Will
Addr/cntl field compression	☒ Want ☒ Will	☐ Want ☒ Will
Authentication (PAP)	☐ Want ☐ Will	☐ Want ☒ Will
Magic Number	☒ Want ☒ Will	☐ Want ☒ Will
Seed Values	42	0
Async Char. Control map	☒ Want ☒ Will	☐ Want ☒ Will
Values (hex)	00000000	FFFFFFFF
Max. Receive Unit	☐ Want ☒ Will	☐ Want ☒ Will
Values	1500	1500

Retries: 10   Timeout: 3   seconds

[Default settings]   [Cancel]   [OK]

Figure 11-23: The LCP Options dialog box.

If your PPP connection server doesn't negotiate a dynamic IP address when you log on, you may have to enter it in the IPCP window. Press the IPCP Options button to access the Internet Protocol Control Protocol dialog box, shown in Figure 11-24.

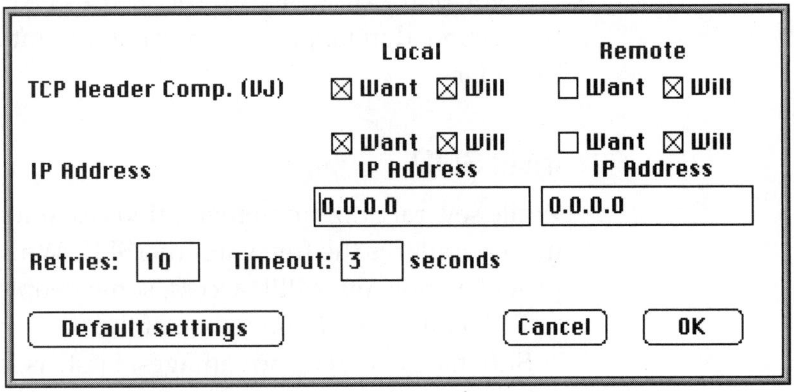

	Local	Remote
TCP Header Comp. (VJ)	☒ Want ☒ Will	☐ Want ☒ Will
IP Address	☒ Want ☒ Will	☐ Want ☒ Will
	IP Address	IP Address
	0.0.0.0	0.0.0.0

Retries: 10   Timeout: 3   seconds

[Default settings]   [Cancel]   [OK]

Figure 11-24: The IPCP Options dialog box.

Check with your service provider to determine if you need to specify the IP addresses for your computer and the server. Remember to enter this information into MacTCP also.

Authentication

If your server uses PAP authentication, you need to enter your username and password into the Authentication dialog box shown in Figure 11-25. Press Authentication in the Configuration dialog box to bring it up.

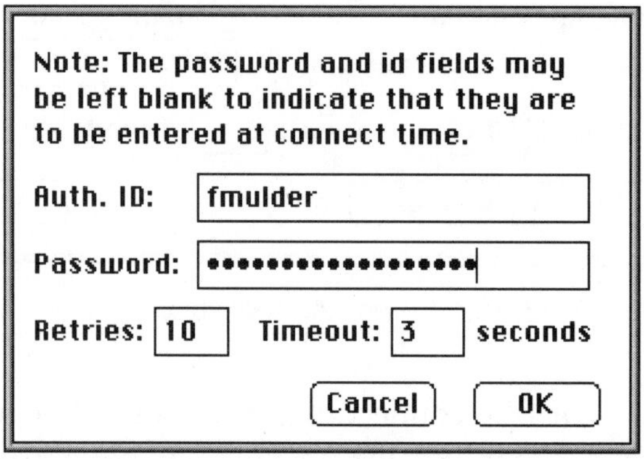

Figure 11-25: The Authentication dialog box in MacPPP.

If you don't know if your server uses PAP to negotiate the connection, don't enter any information until you check with your provider.

InterSLIP

While several SLIP implementations exist for the Macintosh, the most popular is the freeware InterSLIP. While many service providers now offer PPP access, some people still have to use SLIP. You'll know if you're one of them.

SLIP has several disadvantages. First, as far as the official Internet standards community is concerned, it's not a standard. This doesn't mean that SLIP implementations won't work; it just means that as far as protocols go, SLIP's days are numbered. Second, because SLIP is an extremely lean protocol, it doesn't do much for you. Unlike PPP, which negotiates many aspects of the connection, SLIP requires that you and your service provider use exactly the same settings. If you don't, your connection won't work. Period. Finally, unlike MacPPP, InterSLIP doesn't allow you to manually log in to your connection. Instead, you have to write a write a connection script before you can log in.

We're not saying that SLIP is all bad. Because it's a lean protocol that requires you to manually set most of the options, a SLIP connection requires very little overhead. This often means faster transfers. Also, because InterSLIP uses Connection Control Language (CCC) for scripts, you can do some pretty fancy stuff if you have to script a complicated login procedure.

Setting Up & Using InterSLIP

If you have installed InterSLIP, you installed three different files—the InterSLIP extension, InterSLIP Control control panel, and InterSLIP Setup application, which appeared under the Apple menu if you're using System 7.*x*.

Up to this point, if you've been using InterSLIP to successfully connect to your service provider you:

❏ Got a connect script from your ISP.

❏ Wrote your own connect script (in which case you can probably skip this section).

❏ Got connected with a pre-rolled connect script.

There's not a heck of a lot to worry about when configuring InterSLIP. As we mentioned before, the Serial Line Internet Protocol (SLIP) is pretty simple, with very few configuration options (see the InterSLIP configuration dialog box shown in Figure 11-26). No weird LCP parameters as with PPP, no obscure authentication settings—just a few common modem settings, your IP address, and a DNS address.

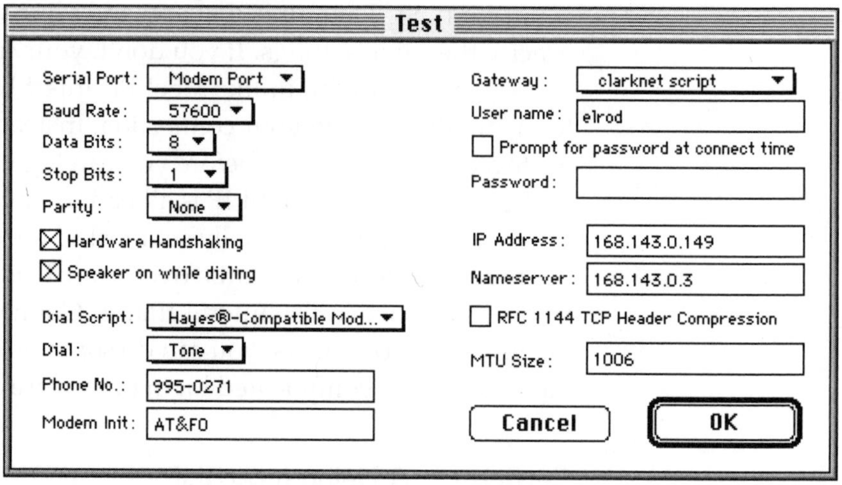

Figure 11-26: The InterSLIP configuration dialog box.

The tricky part comes when you have to tell InterSLIP how to make a connection to your host computer. Unlike MacPPP, there's no terminal window for manual logins and no built-in facility for scripting. Instead, InterSLIP uses two types of scripts, modem scripts and gateway scripts, to initiate and negotiate logins.

In Figure 11-26, you'll notice two pull-down menus: Dial Script and Gateway. If you pull down the Dial Script menu in a freshly installed version of InterSLIP, you'll see two choices: Direct Connection and Hayes Compatible Modem. If you're dialing in from home with a name-brand modem, you should choose Hayes Compatible Modem. The other choice is for dedicated SLIP networking lines, which you're probably not using if you're connecting from home.

Dial Scripts

InterSLIP uses the same modem dialing scripts used by AppleTalk Remote Access, and scripts exist for nearly every modem in existence. Most of the time, you should be perfectly fine with the standard Hayes script, but if you want to use a script specifically designed for your modem you should check out the HyperMac Archives at http://hyperarchive.lcs.mit.edu/HyperArchive/. This nicely HTML-ized version of the famous InfoMac archives has a zillion different modem scripts for nearly every modem. Just use the search form to find a script for your modem. Once you download it, place it in the Dial Scripts folder, which can be found in the InterSLIP folder located in your System folder's Preferences folder. Once you go back to the InterSLIP configuration dialog box, your script should show up in the Dial Script menu.

Gateway Scripts

Like modem Dial scripts, InterSLIP's Gateway scripts are written in CCL , the Connection Control Language developed for AppleTalk Remote Access. However, unlike a modem Dial script, a Gateway script must be customized for the specific way your service provider allows you to initiate your SLIP connection. CCL is a tricky scripting language to learn, especially for users not used to programming. Luckily for most of us, ISPs who allow SLIP access usually have InterSLIP scripts (both Gateway and Dialing if necessary) available for you to use in your Mac. If your ISP provides you with an InterSLIP Gateway script, place it in the Gateway scripts folder located in the InterSLIP folder in the Preferences folder. Then, when you go back to the Configuration dialog box, select it by pulling down the Gateway menu. If your ISP doesn't provide you with a script, ask for one. If you can't get one from them, you can always do it yourself (or DIY, as the kids say).

DIY CCL Scripts

Probably the best way to write your own CCL script is to use that time-honored tradition of programmers around the world—borrow someone else's code and modify it. After all, why reinvent the wheel? You just need something that works. If you look on the HyperArchive (http://hyperarchive.lcs.mit.edu/ HyperArchive/), you'll discover a bunch of scripts just begging to be hacked!

Just like we did in the PPP section, we're going to use Sean as the example for our journey into scripting. To begin with, you'll need to know what steps you'll have to go through to log in to your account and initiate SLIP. A good way of finding this out (and saving a record so you have something to work off of) is to dial in to your account with a terminal program and then save the session to a text file (often called *Capturing* or logging *the session*). Later, you can print out the record of your session so that you have something to work off of. Here's what happened when we dialed up Sean's ISP and logged in to the connection:

```
CONNECT 57600 Clark.net

Annex Command Line Interpreter   *   Copyright 1991 Xylogics,
Inc.

Checking authorization, Please wait...
Connecting to port 27 on annex7.clark.net.

   Welcome to ClarkNet!

Log in as "guest" for ClarkNet info and registration.

ClarkNet Username: elrod
ClarkNet Password: DntUW1sh


Permission granted


                ClarkNet's Menu

        1)  Enter clarknet host        (UUCP users only)
        2)  Enter explorer host        (All users and guest)
        3)  SLIP                       (SLIP users only)
        4)  PPP                        (PPP users only)
        5)  Hosts?                     (All users)
        6)  Who?                       (All users)
        7)  Telnet                     (IP users only)
        8)  Exit                       (All users)

Enter Number (1-8): 3

Switching to SLIP.
Annex address is 168.143.7.124.  Your address is
168.143.0.149.
```

Everything that Sean needed to type is in boldface. (Again, that isn't really his password, so don't get any ideas.) So what has to happen for a SLIP connection in this case? We can break it down to a few simple steps:

1. Wait for prompt ClarkNet Username:.
2. Send string "elrod", and press Enter.
3. Wait for prompt ClarkNet Password:.
4. Send string "DntUW1sh", and press Enter.
5. Wait for prompt Enter Number (1-8):.
6. Send string "3", and press Enter.
7. Wait for string "Switching to SLIP.

   ```
   Annex address is 168.143.7.124.  Your address is
   168.143.0.149."
   ```

8. Initiate SLIP connection.

Let's take a look at a sample script. The original script was written by Steve Michel to allow InterSLIP to connect using TIA (The Internet Adapter—a SLIP-type connection that works through regular dial-up accounts). Even though we modified it, it's worked for us and should work for you. One caveat—because this script doesn't negotiate an IP address, you'll need to specify one in the Configuration dialog box.

Okay. Let's take this step by step. We'll follow the same procedures that we identified before and show you how to write that step in CCL. Note that for the sake of clarity, some "steps" have been combined.

Step 1. Wait for prompt ClarkNet Username:.

```
@originate
note "Waiting for prompt"
matchclr
matchstr 1 2 "ClarkNet Username:"
matchread 100
note "No username prompt"
jump 99
```

Huh? First, the line @originate tells InterSLIP that we're beginning a connection. Most of the time your scripts should begin with this line.

Next, note "Waiting for prompt" puts the message Waiting for Prompt on the screen so that the user knows what's going on.

The following line matchclr clears InterSLIP's pattern buffers—the place in memory it holds strings it's comparing. You should always use matchclr before doing any comparisons.

At this point, we make our first check. matchstr 1 2 "ClarkNet Username:" tells InterSLIP to use pattern-buffer number 1 to store the incoming text and then check to see if it matches the string "ClarkNet Username:." If it does, the script jumps to the next step—step number 2.

Since data doesn't appear instantly, the following line, matchread 100, tells InterSLIP to wait 6 tenths of a second before moving on. (Matchread takes a value that indicates a number of ticks or 60ths of a second. A hundred ticks is .6 seconds.) If no match is made in that time, the final line tells InterSLIP to go to step 99, a general error handler that will notify the user of a problem and then quit:

```
@label 99
pause 1
sound
pause 60
exit -1
```

Whew. We got through that. Let's go to the next two steps.

Step 2. Send string "elrod", and press Enter. Step 3. Wait for prompt ClarkNet Password:.

```
@label 2
note "Sending user name"
write "^5\13"
matchclr
matchstr 1 3 "ClarkNet Password:"
matchread 50
note "No password prompt"
jump 99
```

Hey! Some of this is starting to look familiar. The first line, @label 2, is a label indicating a part of the larger script, and the next line tells the user that the script is sending the username to the server. Then things get a little strange.

The third line, write "^5\13", is a CCL command that says "send the user name entered into the Configuration dialog box to the server and press Enter." It's pretty easy to figure out where the write command comes from, but what's "^5/13" mean?

In order to remain flexible, CCL scripts don't store the username and password in the script itself. Otherwise, every time you changed your password you'd have to change the script. Instead, CCL has defined a set of ten configuration parameters that can be used as codes within a script to indicate a value entered in the configuration information in the program. Table 11-4 lists the ten configuration parameter codes.

Code	Value
^0	The text from the input stream that triggered the most recent match.
^1	Telephone number to dial.
^2	Modem speaker toggle–0 if speaker should be off, 1 if the speaker should be on.
^3	Tone or pulse dialing.
^4	Modem initialization string.
^5	Username.
^6	Password.
^7	IP address.
^8	Van Jacobson SLIP compression indicator.
^9	MTU value.

Table 11-4: CCL configuration parameter codes.

By placing a "^5" in the script, we're saying "put the username here." The "\13" at the end indicates that ASCII code 13 (a return) should be entered after the username.

The next few lines are much like what we saw in the first step. We clear the pattern buffers, wait for a new string "ClarkNet Password:", and then jump to a new step if we get it (step 4). If not, we wait a bit and then exit with an error by going to step 99.

Step 4. Send string "DntUW1sh", and press Enter. Step 5. Wait for prompt Enter Number (1-8):.

```
@label 3
note "Sending password"
write "^6\13"
matchclr
matchstr 1 4 "Enter Number (1-8):"
matchread 120
jump 99
```

No surprises here. Send the password (code ^6) and enter, then wait for the menu prompt so that we can enter a 3 to initiate a SLIP connection. When we get a prompt, jump to step 5. Wait 1.2 seconds (120 ticks). If we still don't get a prompt, jump to step 99, display an error, and quit.

Step 6. Send string "3", and press Enter. Step 7. Wait for string "Switching to SLIP...".

```
@label 4
note "Starting Connection"
write "3\13"
matchclr
matchstr 1 5 "Your address is 168.143.0.149."
matchread 120
note "SLIP didn't start."
jump 99
```

Note here that the third line outputs a 3 and a carriage return, not a configuration code 3. Configuration codes all have carets (^) in front of them. The only other thing that's different is that we didn't try to match the whole string "Switching to SLIP. Annex address is 168.143.7.124. Your address is 168.143.0.149."—it's too long. Instead, we just try to match the end of the line.

This example is for illustration only. There's no real standardization for how SLIP connections operate, so you'll probably have to do some experimentation to determine just what your server sends when a connection has been made. For example, if your server assigns an address, you may not be able to match for an exact address, but you may be able to match part of the string. Sorry folks, but you're going to have to rough it here and do some hacking.

Step 8. Initiate SLIP connection.

```
@label 5
exit 0
```

That's it! Since we can only reach the final step by successfully completing all the other steps, we know that the connection is ready to go. The last line, exit 0, tells the script to stop and begin the connection.

The Finished Script

Here's the finished script. Lines beginning with an exclamation point (!) are comments and don't affect the script's function:

```
! Simple CCL script
! Modified from Steve Michel's Netcom TIA connection script
! by Sean Carton
! For the Internet Power Toolkit
!
!STEP 1
!Begin. Wait for username prompt.
!
@originate
note "Waiting for prompt"
matchclr
!  You'll have to change this line for your own system.
matchstr 1 2 "ClarkNet Username:"
matchread 100
! No prompt? End with an error.
note "No username prompt"
jump 99
!
!STEP 2
!Send the username and wait for password prompt
!
```

```
@label 2
note "Sending user name"
write "^5\13"
matchclr
!  You'll have to change this line for your system.
matchstr 1 3 "ClarkNet Password:"
matchread 50
! No prompt? Tell the user and exit.
note "No password prompt"
jump 99
!
! STEP 3
! Send the password and then wait for the menu prompt
!
@label 3
note "Sending password"
write "^6\13"
matchclr
matchstr 1 4 "Enter Number (1-8):"
! No prompt? Then exit.
matchread 120
jump 99
!
!STEP 4
!Send choice to begin SLIP and wait for indication that it
!worked.
!
@label 4
note "Starting Connection"
write "3\13"
matchclr
! This is tia's message.
matchstr 1 5 "Your address is 168.143.0.149."
matchread 120
!Didn't get SLIP started? Then quit.
note "SLIP didn't start."
jump 99
!
!STEP 5
!Initiate SLIP connection
```

```
!
@label 7
exit 0
!
! Error handler
!
@label 99
pause 1
sound
pause 60
exit -1
```

TIP

If you want more information about CCL, our best advice to you is to look at other scripts. That's how programmers learn to program, and it's the best way to find out how other people are writing scripts. If you need a quick reference to CCL, look at the section called "Scripting" in the "InterSLIP Docs" that come with InterSLIP.

MONITORING YOUR MAC TCP/IP CONNECTION

One problem with TCP/IP networking on the Mac is that it's tough to tell what's going on. The lazy way of checking your connection is launching a TCP/IP client and trying to connect to a server someplace. If it connects, it's working. But what if it doesn't? Or what if things are running amazingly slow. Is everything working properly? Is it a traffic jam on the Information Highway, or do you have water in your gas tank? Wouldn't you like to know just what the heck is going on behind the interface? Let's take a look a few tools that can help.

MacTCP Watcher

If you're going to use a TCP/IP connection with your Mac, you have to install this program. MacTCP Watcher provides you with a simple one-window display of all the TCP/IP activity and lets you know at a glance such important information as the amount of information going back and forth, your current IP address and hostname, any errors that have occurred, and how many packets have had to be retransmitted due to a bad connection.

Installing MacTCP Watcher

Installing MacTCP Watcher is easy. Just follow the simple instructions on the Companion CD-ROM. Then, double-click on the folder to open it, and you should see the MacTCP Watcher folder shown in Figure 11-27.

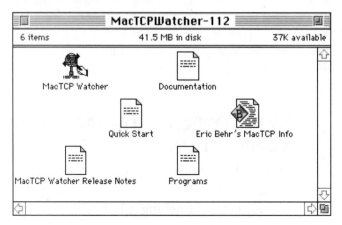

Figure 11-27: The contents of the MacTCP Watcher folder.

Using MacTCP Watcher

First, your TCP/IP connection must be running. Then, double-click on the MacTCP Watcher icon to access the window shown in Figure 11-27. As you can see, MacTCP Watcher gives you lots of useful information. See Table 11-5 for an explanation of the different values.

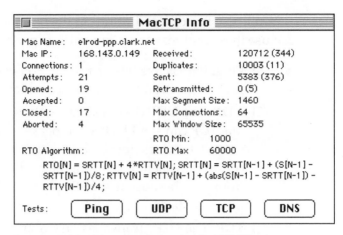

Figure 11-28: The main window in MacTCP Watcher.

Information	Description
Mac Name	The domain name assigned to your computer
Mac IP	Your Mac's IP address
Connections	The number of TCP/IP connections
Attempts	The number of connection attempts since MacTCP Watcher was started
Opened	Number of connections actually opened
Accepted	Number of connections accepted from your machine
Closed	Number of connections successfully closed
Aborted	Number of connections canceled or abruptly closed
Received	Number of bytes (and packets) received
Duplicates	Number of duplicate bytes (and packets) received
Sent	Number of bytes (and packets) sent
Retransmitted	Bytes (and packets) retransmitted due to errors
Max Segment Size	Maximum TCP data segment size
Max Connections	Maximum allowable simultaneous TCP connections
Max Window Size	Maximum size of TCP data window
RTO Max	Maximum amount of time for Retransmission TimeOut
RTO Min	Minimum time before Retransmission TimeOut

Table 11-5: MacTCP Watcher information.

You'll also notice four buttons at the bottom of the window. You can use these buttons for testing various parts of your connection:

- ❏ **Ping:** Ping is like Internet sonar. You use it to bounce a data packet from your computer to a remote host and back.
- ❏ **UDP:** The UDP (User Datagram Protocol) checks to see if MacTCP can send UDP echo packets out and receive them. UDP does not provide end-to-end tests for reliable connections before sending the packets. This is different from ping because it specifically tests the UDP part of the protocol stack.
- ❏ **TCP:** The TCP (Transmission Control Protocol) tests the ability of MacTCP's Transport Layer to send and receive TCP packets. TCP does perform reliability tests (tests to determine how good the connection is) before sending packets.
- ❏ **DNS:** Tests to see if the Domain Name Services that you've set up in MacTCP can resolve domain names into IP addresses. A failed DNS look-up is the surest sign that your connection has gone haywire.

TIP

MacTCP Watcher is particularly useful if you're trying to get a SLIP connection working. Unlike MacPPP, which has its own statistics readout that tells you what's going on, InterSLIP has no facilities for actually telling you if your TCP/IP connection works.

MacTCP Monitor

If you feel that MacTCP Watcher is a bit too technical, you may want to keep track of your TCP/IP connection with MacTCP Monitor. Instead of using confusing technical data, MacTCP Monitor uses two colored graphs to show the status of your connection. At a glance, you can see a real-time graph of your

TCP/IP connection throughput and a nifty indicator that shows the active TCP/IP connections and if they're receiving or transmitting data.

Installing MacTCP Monitor

Mac TCP Monitor can be downloaded from http:// hyperarchive.lcs.mit.edu/HyperArchive/Archive/comm/inet/ mactcp-monitor-10d30.hqx. Download, decompress, and run. Note: You must have System 7 or greater to run MacTCP Watcher (systems prior to 7.5 also require certain extensions—see the documentation for more information).

Using MacTCP Monitor

Using MacTCP Monitor is easy. Double-click on the MacTCP Monitor icon to access the two windows shown in Figure 11-29.

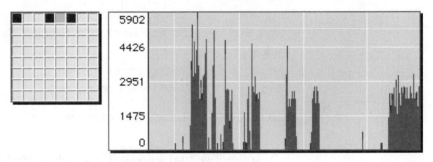

Figure 11-29: MacTCP Monitor windows.

The longer window is a graph representing the number of bytes being sent and received over your TCP/IP connection every second. The graph sits idle if you aren't sending or receiving any data. Once your connection becomes active, the graph will begin moving to the left. Each line in the graph represents one second of activity. Each color in the graph represents a different TCP/IP state: red showing that data is being transmitted, and green indicating that data is being received. If you want, you can change these colors from the MacTCP Watcher Preferences menu (accessed from the File menu).

The smaller, square window is the TCP Connection States window. It's an 8x8 grid, and each element in the grid represents a different TCP/IP connection. When you have one or more connections going, the individual cells light up in different ways to indicate the status of that particular connection. As with the Data Transfer Graph, the colors in the Connection States window have different meanings:

Color	Indicates status as:
Gray	Connection closed
Dark Blue	Listen for connection
Dark Blue	Synchronize Sequence Numbers (SYN) bit received
Dark Blue	SYN bit sent
Dark Blue	Connection established
Light Blue	Wait state 1
Light Blue	Wait state 2
Light Blue	Close wait indicator
Light Blue	Connection closing
Light Blue	Last Acknowledgment Segment (ACK) sent
Yellow	Waiting
Green	Reading (receiving) data
Red	Writing (transmitting) data

Table 11-6: TCP Connection State indicators.

You'll notice that some of these colors are the same. The creator of MacTCP Monitor didn't want to confuse you with a rainbow of flashing colors since you don't need to keep track of every stage of your connection. However, if you want to carefully monitor your connection, go to the Preferences menu (under the File menu), and open the Connection State Colors dialog box. There you can assign new colors to monitor the different states.

CUTTING EDGE MAC CONNECTIONS: OPEN TRANSPORT

When Apple first introduced the PowerMac 9500 in early 1995, they also released what will eventually be the future of Macintosh TCP/IP connectivity — Open Transport. Open Transport is a new set of networking and communications subsystems for the Macintosh that are designed to do away with users having to worry about "transport dependence"—that is, having to worry about what type of network they're connected to at any one time.

As more and more people connect their computers to more and different types of networks, things can get very confusing. If you're on an EtherTalk LAN that's not connected to the Internet, you may need to use a PPP connection through your modem to get on the Internet. Making this change may require you to change all sorts of communications settings—quite a pain if you have to do it several times a day.

Worse yet, the days of people having only one TCP/IP connection are coming to a close. These days, it's not uncommon to have two different dial-up TCP/IP connections—a personal service provider connection for play and a connection to your company network for business. If you're using MacTCP, switching between the two configurations requires you to enter all new information into MacTCP and then restart your computer. You can use MacTCP Switcher (available from ftp://ftp.acns.nwu.edu/pub/jlnstuff/mactcp-switcher/) to change configurations, but you still have to restart your Mac once you've made the switch.

The goal of Open Transport is to solve these problems and more, resulting in more flexibility to the user, greater control for the network manager, and overall better ease of use. Unfortunately, at this time, the reality is far from the dream.

Open Transport System Requirements

Thanks to Apple's latest round of bug fixes, System 7.5 Update 2.0, Open Transport, is now viable on all desktop and portable MacOS machines running a Motorola 68030 or 040 processor, or a PowerPC 601, 603(e) or 604 processor. Apple also recommends you run System 7.5.3. (although they maintain that 7.1, 7.1.1, and 7.1.2 will also work). On 680x0 machines, Open Transport requires 5MB of RAM, and System 7.5.3 requires 4MB (minimum). On PowerPC boxes, the minimums jump to 8MB for Open Transport and 8MB for System 7.5.3. Open Transport is designed to completely replace MacTCP, so if you have one of these Macintoshes, you probably don't have MacTCP installed on your computer.

Open Transport Problems

One of the major problems that people have been experiencing with Open Transport is that it's often incompatible with many of their existing TCP/IP programs. If you want to use Open Transport for a TCP/IP connection from home, for instance, you can only use the following LAPs:

- ❒ InterSLIP version 1.0.1 or newer
- ❒ InterPPP II version 1.1 or newer
- ❒ MacSLIP version 3.0.2or newer
- ❒ MacPPP version 2.1.4SD or newer (but not 2.2.0)
- ❒ FreePPP 1.0.5 or newer
- ❒ SonicPPP version 1.0.2 or newer
- ❒ VersaTerm SLIP 1.1.4 or newer

Technically you can use any of the LAPs listed above, but most people have reported the best luck with FreePPP, a MacPPP variation available at http://hyperarchive.lcs.mit.edu/HyperArchive/Archive/comm/tcp/conn/free-ppp-105.hqx.

Open Transport Recommendations

At the time we wrote this chapter, Open Transport was in a state of flux. While it promises to make connections easier and more reliable, Open Transport has yet to deliver on that promise. Many people report crashes and system hangs with many TCP/IP programs, and others find that they can't connect at all. We're sure that there are some people out there running Open Transport without problems, but they're pretty hard to find. While many people have installed Open Transport along with their System 7.5.3 updates, many have switched back to MacTCP.

Our recommendation? At this point, stick with MacTCP. It's been time-tested, lots of help is available, and every existing Mac TCP/IP program was designed to use it correctly. If you have Open Transport installed in your machine and you find that everything runs Okay, leave it alone. However, if you are experiencing problems, you may want to install MacTCP. If you decide to switch to MacTCP, you'll have to remove the following files from your Mac:

Remove the following files from the Extensions folder:

Open Tpt Internet Library

OpenTptInternetLib

Remove the following files from the Control Panels folder:

TCP/IP

You should leave all the other Open Transport files alone. Note that Apple doesn't recommend that you do this, but reports from all over the Net say that people have gotten good results with MacTCP on PCI Macs. Remember, though — as with most things that have to do with computers, the situation with Open Transport can change rapidly. Check the Online Companion for updates before you decide to remove Open Transport from your computer.

MOVING ON

Now that you've gotten your TCP/IP connection running smoothly (we hope!) it's time to move on to actually using it. We'll examine some of the most popular Macintosh TCP/IP power tools and how to get the most out of them in the next four chapters. These chapters won't be primers on how to set up your e-mail account, news reading software, or Web browsers because we're assuming you already know how to do that. Instead, you'll learn tips and tricks, get handy quick-reference guides to all of the features, and concise explanations of features that may have been glossed over in the documentation. And, while we're at it, we'll throw in some information on cutting-edge ways to extend your programs and make the most out of your connections with the coolest power tools available.

We're going to start with the one function of your online life you probably use the most—e-mail. In the next chapter, we'll take a look at several of the most popular and useful Macintosh TCP/IP e-mail tools.

## Chapter 12

Mac E-Mail Power Tools

Undoubtedly, e-mail is the most commonly used and arguably the most useful service on the Internet. It enables us to keep in touch with far-flung friends and to get tons of publications and lively discussions delivered to our e-mail boxes. It's also had a tremendous impact on global business communications.

E-mail provides an entirely new wrinkle on communicating in a quick, casual, and often, spontaneous way. Just think of all the people you talk to via e-mail (many whom you've met online) with whom you wouldn't stay in such close contact by snail mail or telephone.

Unlike the phone, e-mail doesn't interrupt and demand our immediate attention. It waits patiently for us to answer. Unlike Usenet newsgroups, e-mail is private, allowing conversations free of the self-editing that comes with posting messages that will be read by the public. E-mail is point-to-point communications, offering relative privacy in an increasingly public world.

Macintosh users with TCP/IP connections are blessed with some excellent e-mail packages. (Some of them are even free!) Pick any of the programs discussed in this chapter, and you'll find them easy to use and full of useful features. All of them are available online and can be used (at least for a trial period) without charge. We'll also look at several e-mail power tools. These aren't mail readers but e-mail extensions that allow you to filter your mail, separate it, check it without having to fire up your e-mail program, and even send sound and video files!

We're assuming that you already know the basics of reading and sending e-mail. However, you may not know how to get the most out of the programs you use. What we're going to do in this chapter is provide you with some handy tools and tricks that can expand your e-mail options and improve the management of your e-mail.

SENDING & RECEIVING E-MAIL

Since you spend so much time using e-mail, it's important that you're comfortable with your e-mail program and knowledgeable about what it does. A good e-mailer, properly configured, can make information glut easier to deal with. A bad e-mail program can make your life miserable.

Each of the programs discussed in this chapter has its own strengths and weaknesses, and you'll have to decide for yourself what you like based on your specific needs. If you're in a hurry, take a glance at Table 12-1 for a comparison of the three e-mail programs we'll cover, Eudora Light, Claris Emailer, and PowerTalk. In the sections that follow, we'll look at each program in greater detail.

	Eudora Light	Claris Emailer	PowerTalk	Comments
Filtering	No	Yes	No	Auto-sorting e-mail.
Address Book	Yes w/aliasing	Yes	Yes, w/ extensive filing features.	Place to keep e-mail addresses and names. Aliasing allows you to create mailing lists.
Spell Checker	No	No	Depends on the application used to create the message.	A Dan Quayle must-have!
Helper Apps	No	Yes—opens enclosures with correct application.	Works from within PowerTalk-compatible applications.	The program can use external viewers (GIF, JPG, MIME, etc.).
Customizable	Yes, AppleScript	Yes, AppleScript	Yes, plug-in modules for many types of messaging.	The functionality can be expanded beyond the "stock" model.
Special Features	Ph & finger server access	Retrieves mail from commercial services.	Works as system extension. Allows sending mail from within applications.	See sections below on each program for more info on special features.
Windows Version	Yes	No	No	Good for multiplatform families and business.
Ease of Use	Easy to moderate	Easy	Moderate	Easy (for an experienced user).
Cost	Freeware	Commercial ($49). Demo available.	Built in to System 7.5.	Can't beat the price.
Comments	The standard for Mac TCP/IP mail programs. Some parts of the interface are clunky.	Incredibly well designed. If you have several e-mail accounts, get this program.	Can be difficult to use until you understand its document-centric concept.	

Table 12-1: Comparison of Mac e-mail programs.

Eudora Light

Originally a shareware program written by Steve Dorner, Eudora is now a full-fledged, powerful e-mail program published by Qualcomm as Eudora Pro. Luckily for us budget-conscious Netheads, Qualcomm distributes a freeware version called Eudora Light. Even though Light doesn't have all of the power features of Pro (such as automatic mail filtering), it's still a great program that will meet most people's e-mail needs.

Since you may already have this program (and if you don't, it's fairly easy to install), we won't go into the basic setup procedure here. What we will do is cover the many options available within Eudora.

Getting Eudora

If you don't already have Eudora Light, you have two choices—first, you can install it from the Internet Power Toolkit CD-ROM. Full instructions are available on the disk. Or, if you want to make sure you have the absolute latest version, it is available from Qualcomm's Web site at http://www.qualcomm.com/ or direct at http://www.qualcomm.com/ProdTech/quest/light.html. Just follow the directions on the screen to download it. Once you've downloaded and decompressed it, double-click on the Eudora icon. The multiscreened Settings dialog box will appear. This is the same dialog box that's available as the Settings item in Eudora's Special menu. If you have any questions about the basic setup, check the Eudora help file. Qualcomm also has a free 136-page manual that you can download at the light.html Web page.

Once you've downloaded and decompressed Eudora, Eudora Light will appear as an icon. That's it! Nothing more to install—you're ready to go.

Eudora Light Settings

Now that you've got Eudora Light all uncompressed and ready to go, it's time to get it set up correctly. In this section, we'll walk you through all the settings you need to set in order to get Eudora Light to run without a hitch.

Getting Started

Here's where you enter the basic information you need to be able to get your e-mail with Eudora. If all you want to do is basic mailing, you can get away with just filling out the information in the Getting Started dialog box.

Under the Getting Started icon, the POP Account text box refers to your e-mail address (e.g., binky@lifeinhell.com). Eudora uses this information to get both your username (everything that comes before the @) and the name of your system's POP mail server (everything after the @).

Acronym Alert! POP & SMTP

Uh oh, dreaded acronyms again! POP and SMTP are the two protocols that your computer uses to receive and send mail.

POP (first proposed in RFC #918) stands for Post Office Protocol. No, it doesn't describe how to keep from annoying disgruntled employees at the U.S. postal service. POP describes how workstations (i.e., your computer) can receive mail from a host computer. The exact details aren't terribly important, but you should know that POP servers are designed to be secure, only allowing users with valid passwords to get their private mail. When mail comes in from across the Net to the host where the POP server is located, it's stored until you dial in and give the right password. Then the mail is forwarded to your machine. On the other hand, SMTP (Simple Mail Transport Protocol) was designed to pass mail back and forth between UNIX hosts, as well as a way for you to pass mail between your computer and the host computer. When you send a message out to the Net from your machine via Eudora (or another e-mail program) it goes to the SMTP server, which packages it and sends it to its destination.

If you don't want to enter your real name into the Real Name text box, you don't have to. If you leave it blank, no name will appear in the From: mail header.

Finally, make sure that the MacTCP radio button is checked if you're using TCP/IP (see Figure 12-1). Select the Communications Toolbox if you're making a connection directly from your machine to a host's POP mail server (see the "Skinny on Eudora's Dial-up Capabilities" sidebar later in this chapter). Checking the offline radio button (no connections) allows you to open Eudora without it trying to launch your PPP or SLIP connection. Unfortunately, you have to select this before you exit a session to have it work for the next session.

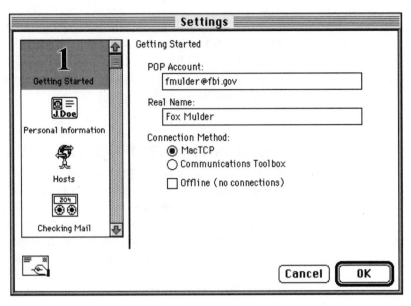

Figure 12-1: The Getting Started dialog box in Eudora.

Personal Information

Here's where you enter optional information about your account. You'll notice that your POP account and name have transferred over from the Getting Started dialog box and that there are two empty text boxes—Return Address and Dial up username. If you use a different address for returned mail, enter it in the Return Address text box. See Figure 12-2.

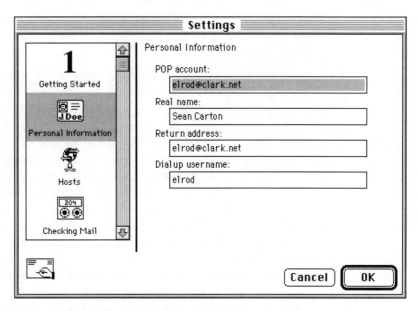

Figure 12-2: The Personal Information dialog box in Eudora.

TIP

Take care when entering a return address. If you make a mistake typing your address no one will be able to reply to your messages. Not a good thing.

If your username is different than your e-mail name and you're using the Communications Toolbox to connect with Eudora, enter the system username in the Dial up username text box.

The Skinny on Eudora's Dial-up Capabilities

While you are poking around Eudora, you may notice a Communications option under the Special menu. You may also notice that it's grayed out, and nothing you seem to do makes it available. Here's why.

Eudora was developed years before SLIP/PPP accounts became commonplace. So in order to provide a way for the TCP-impaired to get their mail, the author devised a way for Eudora to use a regular UNIX shell account to send and receive mail. That's what the Communications option is for. If you select Communications Toolbox in the Getting Started dialog box in Eudora's Settings, the Communications option will be enabled. Selecting it brings up a Communications Toolbox dialog box that you can use to dial in to your shell account. At least that's the theory.

In practice, to get the dial-up option to work, you have to hack a settings file with ResEdit, compile a program on your UNIX account, and deal with some complicated scripting. Frankly, we could never get this option to work—even after days of trying and sending several help messages to appropriate newsgroups.

So what should you do if you want to use Eudora and you don't have a SLIP/PPP account or can't get connected with MacTCP? In short, don't bother. Use one of the excellent UNIX mail readers (such as Pine or elm—see Chapter 17) from your shell, or establish a pseudo-TCP/IP connection with a utility like TIA or SLiRP (utilities that allow you to use your shell account like a SLIP/PPP account). You'll be a lot less frustrated and save the time you would have spent trying to get Eudora's Byzantine dial-up connection working.

Hosts

The Hosts dialog box is where you tell Eudora about all the different host computers you'll be using for your various online tasks. Table 12-2 describes these options. Figure 12-3 provides an example of what you should see.

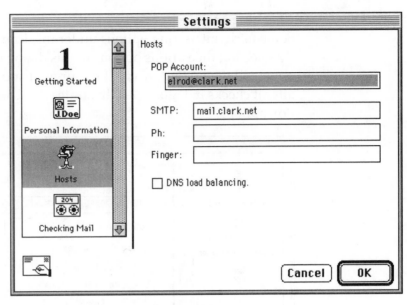

Figure 12-3: The Hosts dialog box in Eudora.

Option	Description
POP Account	Specifies the name of the POP server you use to get your mail. This should already contain the information provided in the Getting Started screen.
SMTP	Specifies the address of the SMTP server used to send mail. If this field is left blank, Eudora will use the same address in the POP Account text box.
Ph	Specifies the address of the campuswide Ph phone book server. If you're using a commercial ISP, you probably won't need this option.
finger	Specifies the address for your finger server. If this field is left blank, Eudora uses the address in your SMTP text box.
DNS load balancing	If you're on a LAN or a system with multiple machines running your network services (POP, SMTP, Ph, finger), checking this box allows Eudora to use a random computer on the LAN when accessing these services instead of using the first IP address returned by the DNS.

Table 12-2: Hosts dialog box options.

Checking Mail

Some fairly interesting options under this icon bear looking into. By selecting the various options in this dialog box, you can control how (and when) Eudora checks your mail and what it does with it after it checks it. Figure 12-4 illustrates the Checking Mail Dialog Box options.

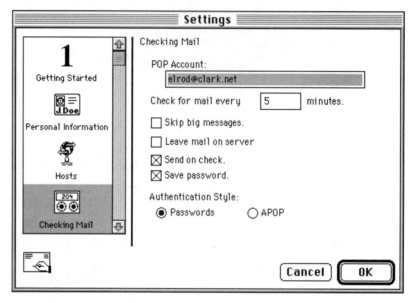

Figure 12-4: The Checking Mail dialog box in Eudora.

Option	Description
POP Account	Specifies the address of the POP server used for getting mail.
Check for mail every...minutes	Specifies the interval at which Eudora logs on to the POP server and checks for new mail.
Skip big messages	Leaves messages over 40K on the server and only downloads the first few lines.
Leave mail on server	Does not delete mail from POP server after checking.

Option	Description
Send on check	Sends mail queued in Out mailbox after logging on to check for new mail.
Save Password	Saves password for POP server so it doesn't have to be entered every time Eudora checks the mail.
Authentication Style: Passwords	Uses plain-text password for user authentication on POP server.
Authentication Style: APOP	Uses APOP protocol (encrypted secret password & timestamp) for authentication when logging on to server. See RFC1 #460.

Table 12-3: Eudora Checking Mail dialog box options.

Sending Mail

Eudora offers a slew of options for sending mail. In general, Eudora should work fine if you use the default options, but if you have any special cases or preferences, you may want to fiddle with these settings a bit (Figure 12-5). Note that Return Address and SMTP Server should already be set from the information you entered in the Personal Information and Hosts dialog boxes.

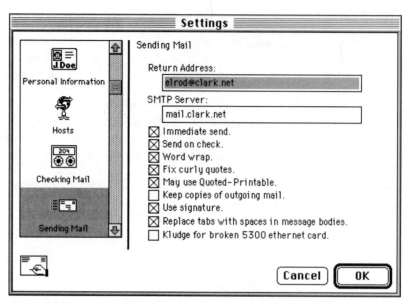

Figure 12-5: Sending Mail dialog box in Eudora.

Option	Description
Return Address	Specifies the address that message replies go to. This must be a valid e-mail address, or you won't get any replies to your messages.
SMTP Server	Specifies the SMTP server address used for outgoing mail.
Immediate send	Sends mail as soon as you click the Send button in the mail composition window.
Send on check	Sends mail to server after checking POP server for new mail.
Word wrap	Toggles outgoing text word wrap, usually at 76 characters.
Fix curly quotes	Changes curly quotes into straight quotes for compatibility with 7-bit e-mail systems.
May use Quoted-Printable	Allows the use of 8-bit (foreign and special characters) in e-mail messages. Useful for corresponding with people not using the Latin alphabet.

Option	Description
Keep copies of outgoing mail	Places a copy of each outbound e-mail message in the Out mailbox. Useful if you tend to drink while e-mailing and can't remember the next morning what you wrote the night before.
Use signature	Appends signature file (defined with Signature option in Windows menu) to outgoing mail messages. See Chapter 17, UNIX E-Mail Tools," for more information on signature files.
Replace tabs with spaces in message bodies	Replaces tab characters with space characters in message bodies. Useful for compatibility with mail readers not able to display tabs. If this option is left un-checked, pressing the Tab key will move the cursor to the To: field.
Kludge for broken 5300 ethernet card	If you have a Powerbook 5300 with a Global Village Ethernet card, check this — it'll make sure Eudora works correctly with this configuration.

Table 12-4: Sending Mail dialog box options.

Attachments

Eudora allows you several options for sending, or attaching, files with your e-mail. Unfortunately, there's no hard-and-fast standard (though MIME is getting there) for sending and receiving files via e-mail, so you'll have to know what type of computer and mailer the recipients of your files have before you decide how to send e-mail to them. The options in the Attachments dialog box allow you to tailor your attachments so that the people getting them receive them in one piece. This dialog box (Figure 12-6) also allows you to specify the destination folder for any incoming attachments as well as the file creator for any e-mail you save. See Table 12-5 for a description of the features in this dialog box.

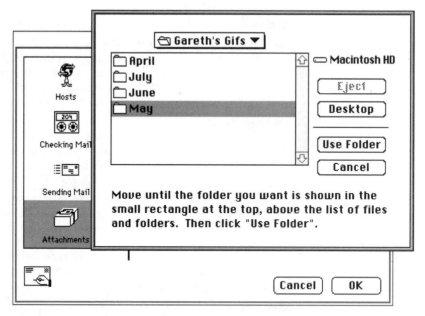

Figure 12-6: Selecting an attachments folder in Eudora.

Option	Description
Encoding Method: AppleDouble	Preserves Macintosh resource and data forks via MIME when sending files. Useful for any recipient using a MIME-compatible e-mail program.
Encoding Method: AppleSingle	Uses MIME, but usually files arrive with resource and data forks intact only if the recipient is using a Macintosh.
Encoding Method: BinHex	Encodes attachments into BinHex for compatibility with older versions of Eudora and non-MIME e-mail systems.
Always include Macintosh information	Includes Macintosh resources in MIME attachments.
Attachment Folder	Pressing this button presents you with a dialog box you can use to specify where incoming attachments should be saved. See Figure 12-6.
TEXT files belong to	Clicking this button allows you to pick an application to use as the default application for reading any messages saved from Eudora.

Table 12-5: Attachments dialog box options.

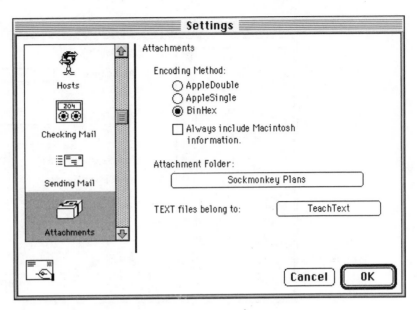

Figure 12-7: The Attachments dialog box in Eudora.

Fonts & Display

You can customize the look and feel of Eudora in the Fonts & Display dialog box (Figure 12-8). Choose the font you want to use to view your messages and the one to use when printing mail. Here are some of the other options. You'll probably be better off leaving these as they are. However, if you want your text displayed in some sort of weird font, go ahead. Just make sure that you use the more standard font sizes—9, 12, or 14. Anything else may result in pixelated or rough characters. Oh, and if you're wondering where the Mishawaka font came from, don't worry—you haven't been infected with some weird virus. It's the standard font built in to Eudora. It doesn't look bad. You may want to use it. Table 12-6 describes the options in this dialog box.

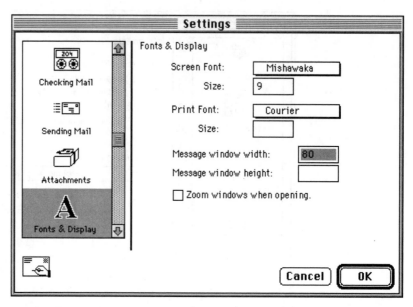

Figure 12-8: The Fonts & Display dialog box in Eudora.

Option	Description
Screen Font	Font used to display onscreen text.
Size	Size of font used to display onscreen text.
Print Font	Font used when printing from Eudora.
Size	Size of font used when printing from Eudora.
Message window width	Width (in characters) of message window.
Message window height	Height (in characters) of message window.
Zoom windows when opening	Show zooming effect when opening a window. Turning this option off usually speeds up Eudora Light a little bit.

Table 12-6: Fonts & Display dialog box options.

Getting Attention

In case you fall asleep at your keyboard (we don't know about you, but we do that a lot) or tend to forget that you left Eudora running in the background, you can use this dialog box (Figure

12-9) to specify how you want Eudora to wake you up and tell you about your new mail (Figure 12-10). Table 12-7 describes the options you can set in this dialog.

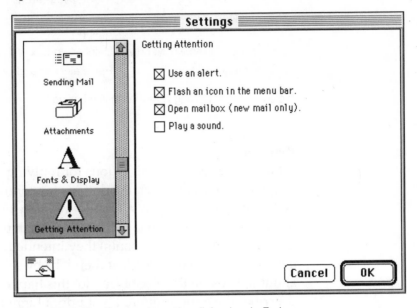

Figure 12-9: The Getting Attention dialog box in Eudora.

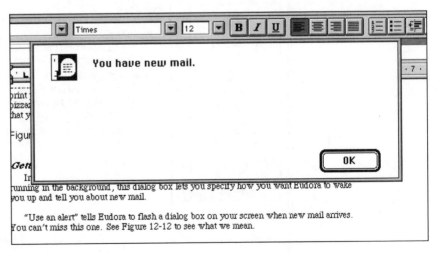

Figure 12-10: Mail call in Eudora.

Option	Description
Use an alert	Displays a dialog box (shown in Figure 12-10) when mail arrives.
Flash an icon in the menu bar	Displays icon on application menu when mail arrives.
Open mail box (new mail only)	Displays In box with new message list.
Play a sound	Plays alert sound.

Table 12-7: The Getting Attention dialog box options.

Replying

Eudora gives you several options for replying to mail (Figure 12-11), not the least of which are options for controlling who on a list your reply goes to. Many a friendly relationship has been nipped in the bud when someone on a mailing list replied to the whole list instead of just the person(s) they intended. Some unfortunate e-mail newbies have even lost their jobs by sending whiny letters about the boss *to* the boss! Don't let this happen to you! Table 12-8 describes the options offered by Eudora Light for replying to mail.

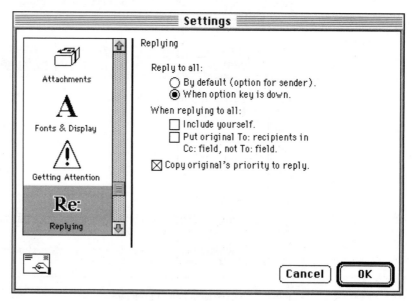

Figure 12-11: Replying dialog box in Eudora.

Option	Description
Reply to all: By default (option for sender)	Replies to all the recipients of a message. To reply to the sender only, you must hold down the option key while selecting Reply from the Message menu.
Reply to all: When option key is down.	Replies to all the recipients when you hold down the option key while selecting Reply from the Message menu.
When replying to all: Include yourself	Replies to all recipients including yourself.
When replying to all: Put original To: recipients in Cc: field, not To: field	Puts the original recipients in the Cc: field, and only the original sender is placed in the To: field.
Copy original's priority to reply	Applies original message's priority status to reply.

Table 12-8: The Replying dialog box options.

Miscellaneous

True to its name, the Miscellaneous dialog box (Figure 12-12) contains all the settings that just wouldn't fit into any of the other categories. Table 12-9 lists the Miscellaneous options.

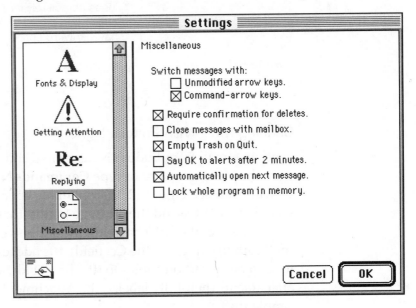

Figure 12-12: The Miscellaneous dialog box in Eudora.

Option	Description
Switch messages with: Unmodified arrow keys	Allows you to move from message to message by using the arrow keys. Pressing the Up or Left arrow key opens the previous message while pressing the Down or Right arrow key opens the next message.
Switch messages with: Command-arrow keys	Switches messages using the arrow keys and simultaneously holding down the Command key.
Require confirmation for deletes	Asks for confirmation before deleting messages.
Close messages with mailbox	Closes all currently open messages from a mailbox when the mailbox itself is closed.
Empty Trash on Quit	Toggles emptying Trash folder when you quit Eudora.
Say OK to alerts after 2 minutes	Automatically presses the OK button if an alert on the screen is not responded to after two minutes.
Automatically open next message	Automatically opens the next message in line after you have deleted or transferred the current message.
Lock whole program in memory	If you don't have a PowerMac, checking this box will make sure that Eudora Light loads completely into RAM. Checking this option can speed up Eudora Light if you have RAM to spare.

Table 12-9: Miscellaneous dialog box options.

Sending Mail With Eudora Light

Sending e-mail from Eudora is easy. First, choose New Message from the Message menu or type **Command+N**. A window will then appear (see Figure 12-13) containing spaces for the address of who you want to send the message to (the To: field), the subject of your message (the Subject: field), the address of who you want to send carbon copies to (the Cc: field), the address of who you want to send blind carbon copies to (the Bcc: field), and a list of your attachments (helpfully labeled the Attachments: field). Pretty simple stuff.

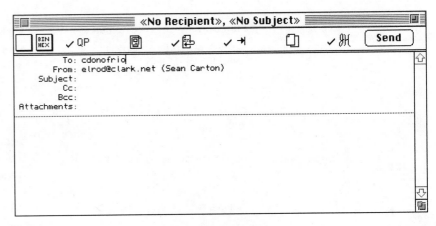

Figure 12-13: Creating a new message in Eudora.

The message bar icons that appear just below the title bar are a bit on the cryptic side. We hope Table 12-10 will straighten things out.

Icon	Type	Function	Choices	Description
	Pop-up menu	Sets priority level	>>Highest, >High, Normal, <Low, <<Lowest	Assigns a priority level (Highest, High, Normal, Low, or Lowest) to a message so the recipient knows the importance you attach to a message.
BIN HEX	Pop-up menu	Applies encoding	AppleDouble	Encodes attachment into AppleDouble format, which uses MIME types for resource encoding. Use this setting for most recipients.
			AppleSingle	Encodes attachment into AppleSingle format for Macintosh recipients.
			BinHex	Encodes attachment in BinHex format. Useful for compatibility with older versions of Eudora and most mailers.

➡

Icon	Type	Function	Choices	Description
QP	Toggle icon	Applies quoted-printable encoding	On/Off	Enables/disables MIME quoted-printable encoding for 8-bit message compatibility.
	Toggle icon	Applies Macintosh encoding	On/Off	Encodes Macintosh resources into MIME attachments.
	Toggle icon	Applies word wrap	On/Off	Wraps words at approximately 76 characters per line.
	Toggle icon	Inserts tabs in body	On/Off	When On, inserts eight space characters for every tab. When Off, returns cursor to To: field.
	Toggle icon	Keeps copies	On/Off	Keeps a copy of each outgoing message in Out mailbox.
	Toggle icon	Appends signature	On/Off	Appends signature defined in Signature menu (under Windows menu) to outgoing message.
Send	Button	Sends message	Send	Sends message to SMTP server.
Queue	Button	Queues message	Queue	Adds message to mail queue in Out mailbox.

Table 12-10: The New Message icons.

Remember, the default values for these message bar options are set when you configured Eudora in the Settings dialog box. Use these buttons only when you need to occasionally change a default value.

Once you've completed your message, all you have to do to send it is press the Send button. If you chose Send on check in the Sending Mail section of the Settings dialog box, the Send button will read Queue instead. Pressing it sends your message to the Out mailbox where it'll wait to be sent until Eudora checks for new mail. Note: there appears to be a bug in version 1.5.4 which causes Eudora Light to not change the Send button to a Queue button. We don't know if this will be fixed in future versions.

If you want to attach a document to your message, select Attachment Document from the Message menu. Eudora will provide you with a file dialog box where you can select the file you wish to attach to your message. If you want to learn about attaching files, we'll cover more (much more!) in Chapter 20, "Inside E-Mail."

What the Heck is Eudora?

Almost everyone, when first exposed to Eudora, asks "Why Eudora?" Creator Steve Dorner says he couldn't help thinking about Eudora Welty's short story "Why I Live at the Post Office" while he was working on this Post Office Protocol program. Thing is, when you respond to a new user's question with "He named it after Eudora Welty," you've still got some explainin' to do. If you want to read the story that inspired the software, it's in a collection called *A Curtain of Green & Other Stories*.

Receiving Mail With Eudora Light

To check if you have any new mail messages, select Check Mail from the File menu (or press **Command-M**). A dialog box will prompt you for your password. Then Eudora will make the connection to your POP account and then download your new messages. To let you know what's going on, a handy status bar appears as Eudora downloads your new mail. If you don't have any new mail, a dialog box will pop up informing you that you have no new mail. After your new mail is downloaded, it's listed in the In window. See Figure 12-14.

TIP

If you want Eudora to check your mail automatically when you first start 'er up or you want to leave Eudora open to periodically check for new messages as you work, select the Save Password option in the Checking Mail section of the Settings dialog box.

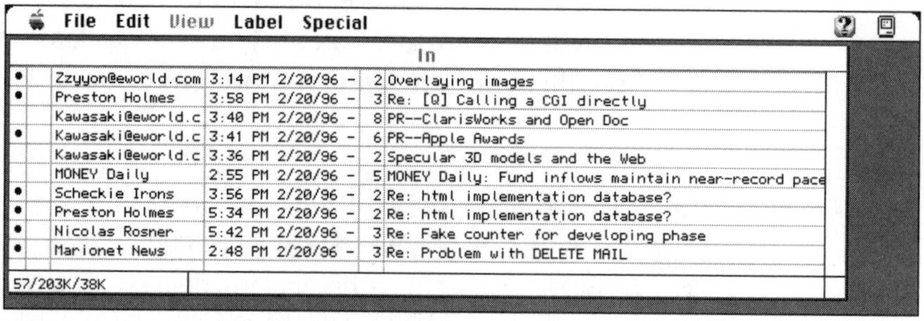

```
  File   Edit   View   Label   Special                              ?   ▯
                                     In
 ● │ Zzyyon@eworld.com │3:14 PM 2/20/96 - │ 2│Overlaying images
 ● │ Preston Holmes    │3:58 PM 2/20/96 - │ 3│Re: [Q] Calling a CGI directly
   │ Kawasaki@eworld.c  │3:40 PM 2/20/96 - │ 8│PR--ClarisWorks and Open Doc
 ● │ Kawasaki@eworld.c  │3:41 PM 2/20/96 - │ 6│PR--Apple Awards
   │ Kawasaki@eworld.c  │3:36 PM 2/20/96 - │ 2│Specular 3D models and the Web
   │ MONEY Daily        │2:55 PM 2/20/96 - │ 5│MONEY Daily: Fund inflows maintain near-record pace
 ● │ Scheckie Irons     │3:56 PM 2/20/96 - │ 2│Re: html implementation database?
 ● │ Preston Holmes     │5:34 PM 2/20/96 - │ 2│Re: html implementation database?
 ● │ Nicolas Rosner     │5:42 PM 2/20/96 - │ 3│Re: Fake counter for developing phase
 ● │ Marionet News      │2:48 PM 2/20/96 - │ 3│Re: Problem with DELETE MAIL
 57/203K/38K
```

Figure 12-14: The In mailbox in Eudora.

As you can see, the In mailbox window is divided into six sections as described in Table 12-11.

Field	Value	Description
Status	ï	Unread message.
	<nothing>	Read message.
	D	Message has been redirected.
	F	Message has been forwarded.
	R	Message has been replied to.
Priority	Double up caret	Sender has assigned Highest priority to message.
	Single up caret	Sender has assigned high priority to message.
	<nothing>	Sender has assigned Normal priority to message
	Single down caret)	Sender has assigned Low priority to message.
	Double down caret	Sender has assigned Lowest priority to message.

Field	Value	Description
Sender	Name or e-mail address	Name appearing in the From: field of incoming message header.
Date	Date & time	Date and time message was sent.
Size (K)	Integer	Size in kilobytes of incoming message text. This does not include size of attachment.
Subject	String	String appearing in the Subject: field of incoming message header.

Table 12-11: The In Mailbox fields.

To read a message, double-click on the line in the In mailbox that lists the message you want to read. A message window will open (Figure 12-15), containing the message.

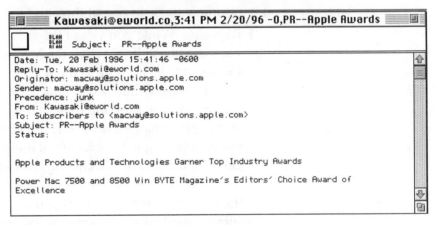

```
Kawasaki@eworld.co,3:41 PM 2/20/96 -0,PR--Apple Awards

        BLAH
        BLAH    Subject:  PR--Apple Awards
        BLAH

Date: Tue, 20 Feb 1996 15:41:46 -0600
Reply-To: Kawasaki@eworld.com
Originator: macway@solutions.apple.com
Sender: macway@solutions.apple.com
Precedence: junk
From: Kawasaki@eworld.com
To: Subscribers to <macway@solutions.apple.com>
Subject: PR--Apple Awards
Status:


Apple Products and Technologies Garner Top Industry Awards

Power Mac 7500 and 8500 Win BYTE Magazine's Editors' Choice Award of
Excellence
```

Figure 12-15: The message window in Eudora.

You'll notice two icons at the top of the message window. The blank icon is the priority-setting pop-up menu. Just as with outgoing messages, you can set the priority of the message from this menu. For messages you receive, this can be useful to re-mind yourself which incoming messages are important and which ones aren't.

The other icon (the one labeled "blah blah blah") is a toggle icon. Clicking once on this icon displays all the message headers contained in the incoming message (for help decoding message headers, turn to Chapter 20, "Inside E-Mail"). Clicking this icon again hides the message headers.

Receiving Attachments

If the message you received includes an attachment, you'll see a line at the end of the message indicating the name of the attachment. You don't have to do anything more to get the attachment—it's already in the folder you specified for attachments in the Settings dialog box.

Replying To, Forwarding & Redirecting Incoming Mail

Besides reading a message and then just discarding it, you can send it to someone else in one of three different ways:

- ❏ **Replying**: While you've got the message window open, you can choose Reply from the Message menu (or press **Command+R**) to reply to the sender of the message. A new message window will open containing the text of the message you're replying to (each line of which preceded by a greater than symbol—>). You can delete the text you're replying to by selecting it and pressing the Delete key, edit the text by clicking on it, or just add your own words to the message and send it as is. You can edit any of the header information, so if you want to change the subject, send copies to some people, or add attachments, go ahead.

- ❏ **Forwarding**: If you want to forward a message you're reading to someone else, select Forward from the Message menu. Eudora will open a new message window containing the original message and the header information from the original message. Your name will be in the From: field in the header of the message, and the cursor will be in the To: field so that you can indicate who you wish to send the message to.

❑ **Redirecting**: Redirecting is almost like forwarding. When you redirect a message, the original message is copied directly into the new message window (without the header information) and the address in the From: field stays the same, with the addition of information that indicates that the message comes "by way of" you.

Managing Your Mail With Eudora Light

The biggest difference between Eudora Light and Eudora Pro (the commercial version of Eudora) is the mail-handling features. Eudora Pro contains a slew of features for automatically filtering and organizing your e-mail. With Eudora Light, you'll have to do most of the work yourself.

Filing E-Mail

If you get a lot of e-mail, the best way to keep track of it is to organize it into different folders or mailboxes. Eudora Light comes with two preconfigured mailboxes: In and Trash. You're already familiar with the In mailbox—it's the directory that mail is delivered to when it arrives on your machine. The Trash mailbox contains all the messages you want to delete. If you have selected Empty Trash on Quit in the Miscellaneous section of the Settings dialog box, Eudora will delete all the messages in the Trash when you quit the program. Otherwise, you'll have to remove them yourself by selecting Empty Trash from the Special menu.

If you want to organize your e-mail into folders, begin by selecting a message you want to file by clicking on it once in the In mailbox so that it's highlighted. Then go to the Transfer menu, and select New. Eudora will then present you with the dialog box shown in Figure 12-16.

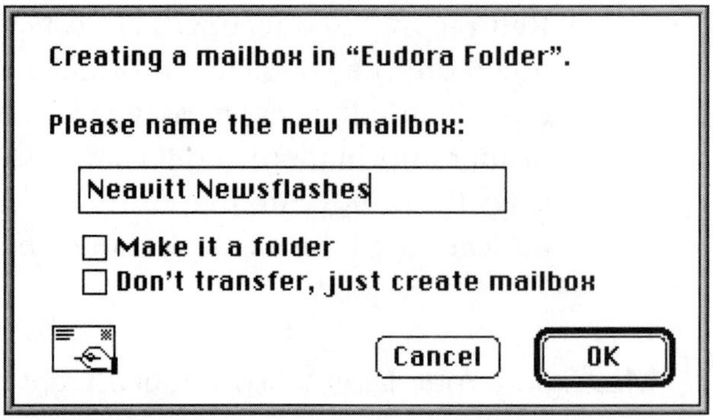

```
Creating a mailbox in "Eudora Folder".

Please name the new mailbox:

Neavitt Newsflashes

☐ Make it a folder
☐ Don't transfer, just create mailbox

                        ( Cancel )   ( OK )
```

Figure 12-16: The new mailbox dialog box in Eudora.

First, enter the name of the folder that you want to create in the text box at the top of the dialog box. Give the new mailbox a name that pertains to the messages you're putting in it.

Next, you have three choices: Make it a folder, Don't transfer, just create mailbox, or nothing at all. If you don't select any of the choices, but you've typed a name in the Please name the new mailbox text box, Eudora will create a new mailbox with the name you specified and place the message you've selected into that mailbox. The name of the mailbox will appear on the Transfer menu. When you want to send another message to that mailbox, just select the message in the In window, and then select the destination mailbox from the Transfer menu.

If you just want to create a new mailbox but not put any messages into it, type the name of the new mailbox in the text box, and check Don't transfer, just create mailbox. A new mailbox name will show up under the Transfer menu.

You can also organize your mailboxes into folders. While you'll never see any folder icons, you'll get a hierarchical menu on the Transfer menu labeled with the name of the folder you've created. You can then create mailboxes within that folder and transfer messages to the mailboxes you created.

Using Nicknames

Once you start using your e-mail frequently, you'll probably assemble a pretty hefty list of e-mail addresses. Keeping track of them isn't easy, unless you use Eudora's Nickname feature. Nicknames allow you to assign a single-word name to an e-mail address. For example, if you were sending mail to Fox Mulder all the time, you could give his e-mail address the nickname "spooky" to avoid having to type the whole thing in.

To start your nickname file, select Nicknames from the Window menu. The Nicknames window (shown in Figure 12-17) will then appear. You can store and annotate your Nickname list in this window.

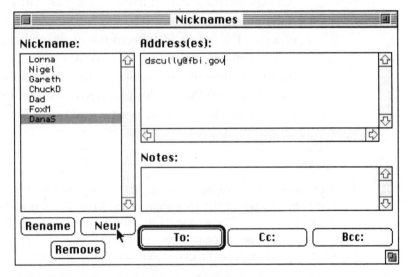

Figure 12-17: Creating a nickname in Eudora.

To add a new nickname, click the New button. Enter the word you want to use as the nickname for the person's e-mail address. Click OK, and you'll be placed back in the Nicknames window, with the cursor in the Address(es) list box. Type the e-mail address of the person into this box.

TIP

The Nicknames window can also be used to create mailing lists. You can enter as many addresses as you wish in the Address(es) list box, as long as you separate each address with a comma. Whenever you send mail to the nickname you've specified (say, "IPTK Mailing List"), the message will go out to all the addresses that belong to that nickname.

If you need a reminder of who a person in your list is, enter your notes in the Notes text box. These notes are never sent with a message, so feel free to fire at will! Nicknames can be cross-referenced into mailing lists. As long as you've already defined a nickname, you can use it in the Address(es) list box instead of entering the entire address in the message header.

You can use nicknames in several ways. If you press the To button while a nickname is selected, that address will be placed in the To: field in the header of a new message. Likewise, pressing Cc or Bcc will place that nickname into the appropriate field.

TIP

If you want to create an "instant nickname" from a message you're reading, just select the message in the In mailbox, and then select Make Nickname (Command-K) from the Special menu. Eudora will ask you for a nickname for the person in the From: field and then place that new address and nickname in the Nickname file.

Quick Recipients

If you frequently correspond with certain people (or lists of people that you've set up with nicknames), you may want to add them to the Quick Recipient list. If a nickname has been selected as a Quick Recipient, you can send, reply, forward, or redirect a message to that nickname by selecting it from the hierarchical menus, (New Message To, Reply To, Forward To, and Redirect To) under the Message menu.

When you select one of these menu items, another submenu will appear to the right of the menu selection, allowing you to select a nickname you wish to send a message to. Selecting a nickname will cause a new message window to appear, addressed and ready to go.

To add a nickname to your Quick Recipient list, open the Nickname window, select the nickname (or names, by shift-clicking) you wish to add, and then click once to the left of the first letter of the nickname (you can tell when the cursor is in the right place . . . it changes to a small menu). A bullet next to the nickname indicates that the nickname has been added to the Quick Recipient list. See Figure 12-18.

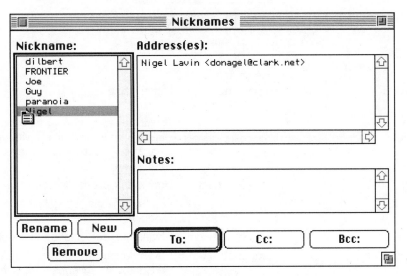

Figure 12-18: Adding a nickname to the Quick Recipient list.

Eudora Light Quick Reference

Eudora Light has many features, and keeping them straight is important if you want to get the most out of the program. Here's a handy quick reference to ease you through your e-mail travels.

Figure 12-19: The File menu in Eudora.

Option	Keyboard Shortcut	Description
Indent Line		
New Text Document		Opens a new text-editing window. This window is not where you create a new message. —It's just a place to edit text.
Open	Command+O	Opens a previously saved mail file.
Open Selection		Displays message highlighted in the message list window.
Close	Command+W	Closes current message window.
Save	Command+S	Saves current message to a text file. If Guess Paragraphs is checked, Eudora saves the file and deletes any extra carriage returns. If Include Headers is checked, Eudora includes all Internet mail header information in saved message.
Save As...		Saves a message with a new filename.
Send Queued Messages	Command+T	Sends all messages in Out mailbox.
Check Mail Check Mail <TIME>	Command+M	Checks POP server for mail. If you have instructed Eudora to check for new mail at regular intervals, the time of the next mail check will appear.
Page Setup		Opens standard Mac Page Setup dialog box.

➡

Option	Keyboard Shortcut	Description
Print	Command+P	Prints current message to the printer specified in the Chooser.
Print Selection		Prints only the part of the message highlighted in the message box.
Quit	Command+Q	Um . . . you can probably figure this one out yourself.

Table 12-12: The File menu options.

Figure 12-20: The Edit menu in Eudora.

Option	Keyboard Shortcut	Description
Undo	Command+Z	Reverses most recently completed action.
Cut	Command+X	Cuts selected text and places it in the system clipboard.
Copy	Command+V	Copies selected text to clipboard.
Paste	Command+W	Pastes text from the clipboard to the current message window.

Option	Keyboard Shortcut	Description
Clear		Deletes selected text.
Paste as Quotation	Command+i	Pastes text currently in clipboard into the current message, placing a greater than symbol (>) at the beginning of each line.
Select All	Command+A	Selects all the text (including headers) contained in the current message window.
Wrap selection		Initiates word wrap, breaking each selected line with a carriage return.
Finish Nickname	Command+,	No, this has nothing to do with Laplander terms of endearment. Instead, choosing this option instructs Eudora to complete any partial nicknames you have entered in the To:, Cc:, or Bcc: fields in the header of a new message.
Insert Recipient		Allows you to insert another nickname into a new message header.
Find		Allows you to find a string in the current message or any other messages.
Sort		Sorts e-mail messages in current In mailbox by Status, Priority, Date, Sender, or Subject.

Table 12-13: The Edit menu options.

Figure 12-21: The Mailbox menu in Eudora.

Option	Keyboard Shortcut	Description
In	Command+I	Opens In mailbox.
Out		Opens Out mailbox.
Trash		Opens list of items to be discarded.

Table 12-14: The Mailbox menu options.

Figure 12-22: The Message menu in Eudora.

Option	Keyboard Shortcut	Description
New Message	Command+N	Opens a new message window in which you can address and enter your new outgoing e-mail messages.
Reply	Command+R	Replies to currently selected message. Appends "Re:" to original subject before placing it in the Subject: field, and places the e-mail address of the original sender in the To: field. If the original message had more than one recipient, holding down the Option key while selecting Reply sends your reply to everyone who originally received the message (depending on how you adjusted your Reply Settings).
Forward		Transfers current message to a new e-mail address. Original message is quoted in the new message.
Redirect		Sends current message to another e-mail address. The original sender remains in the From: field of the header, and the original message is not quoted.
Send Again		Resends message returned from mail transport server. Reformats and removes the error headers from the returned message.

Option	Keyboard Shortcut	Description
New Message To		Same as New Message but allows you to choose recipient from Quick Recipient list.
Reply To		Replies to current message, allows you to pick recipient of reply from Quick Recipient submenu.
Forward To		Forwards message to user(s) specified in the Quick Recipient list.
Redirect To		Redirects message to user(s) named in Quick Recipient list.
Send Message Now	Command+E	Sends mail directly to SMTP server.
Attach Document	Command+H	Accesses a standard file dialog box so you can choose what file you wish to attach to your message.
Change		Hierarchical menu that allows you to change the outgoing message priority as well as how the message should be sent from the queue to the SMTP server.
Delete	Command+D	Deletes current message.

Table 12-15: The Message menu options.

Figure 12-23: The Transfer menu in Eudora.

Option	Keyboard Shortcut	Description
In		Transfers message to In mailbox.
Trash		Transfers message to the Trash.
New...		Creates a new mailbox, and saves current message to it, depending on user options.
<user defined mailboxes>		You can select a user-defined mailbox from this menu.

Table 12-16: The Transfer menu options.

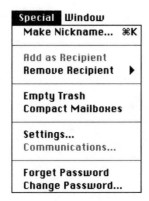

Figure 12-24: The Special menu in Eudora.

Option	Keyboard Shortcut	Description
Make Nickname	Command+K	Places currently selected e-mail address into the Nickname list. Eudora will prompt you for a name for the new nickname, and you can choose an option to add it to the Quick Recipient list. If you check Put it on the recipients list, Eudora adds the address to the Quick Recipient list.
Add as recipient		Adds currently selected e-mail address to the Quick Recipient list.
Remove Recipient		Removes a member from the Quick Recipient list.
Empty Trash		Deletes all messages that have been transferred to the Trash mailbox.
Compact Mailboxes		Compresses mailbox files, eliminating any unused space. Helps save hard drive space.
Settings		Accesses Settings dialog box.
Communications		Used for configuring Apple Communications Toolbox for dial-up access to POP account. This option is available only if Communications Toolbox is selected under the Getting Started icon of the Settings dialog box.
Forget Password		Deletes POP account password from Eudora. You'll have to enter your password the next time Eudora checks for mail.
Change Password		Allows you to change your saved POP account password.

Table 12-17: The Special menu options.

Figure 12-25: The Window menu in Eudora.

Option	Keyboard Shortcut	Description
Mailboxes		Displays the Mailboxes window, which allows you to move messages between your various mailboxes.
Nicknames	Command+L	Opens Nicknames window for configuring Nicknames.
Ph	Command+U	Opens Ph server window.
Signature		Displays blank text area to enter Signature information.
Send to Back	Command+B	Sends the upper window to the back of the windows on the screen.
<window names>		Displays the names of all the open windows under the divider bar in the Window menu.

Table 12-18: The Window menu options.

Claris Emailer

Unlike almost all of the software described in this book, which is freeware or shareware, Claris Emailer will set you back about fifty to ninety bucks (the MSRP is $89, but the street price varies). So why are we including it? One reason—if you're a power user with several e-mail accounts, no other Mac e-mail program available can make your life easier and more productive. It doesn't hurt either that Claris Emailer is one of the most intuitive, user-friendly products you can buy.

The best part about Claris Emailer is its ability to gather all your e-mail messages into one mailbox. Using some truly impressive techno-wizardry, one click of the mouse sends Emailer scurrying out on the Net, where it logs on to all your e-mail accounts, gets your new messages, and downloads them to your Mac. Emailer can even handle accounts on commercial services, such as America Online and CompuServe. And on top of one-stop e-mail, Claris Emailer adds powerful filtering and auto-responding features that organize all your correspondence.

Getting & Installing Claris Emailer

To nab a 30-day trial copy of Claris Emailer, hop on over to ftp://ftp.fogcity.com/pub/Emailer/Trials/ to download a copy. At the time this book was written, the filename of the current version was 10v3Trial.hqx. By the time you read this, the name may have changed. Fog City Software (the creators of Emailer) keep only the current version here, so download the big file you'll find in this directory.

Configuring Claris Emailer

When you start Claris Emailer for the first time, you'll be taken step-by-step through an easy setup procedure that allows you to configure Emailer to work with all of your accounts. (See the Easy Setup window in Figure 12-26.)

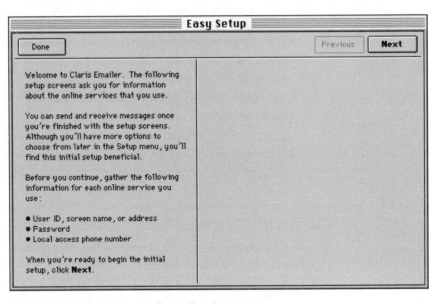

Figure 12-26: Easy Setup in Claris Emailer.

TIP

If you use America Online, an Internet POP/SMTP account, and/or eWorld, you'll be able to get all your mail through your TCP/IP connection. However, if you have CompuServe, you'll have to enter your local dial-up number and dialing information when you configure Claris Emailer.

One feature of the Claris Emailer setup bears a closer look. In the Schedule dialog box (shown in Figure 12-27), you'll be able to program Claris Emailer to automatically check and download your e-mail at specified intervals. If you have a direct Net connection or spend a lot of time online, this can be a great feature—just leave Emailer running in the background (maybe put an alias in your Startup Items folder), and get your mail automatically! Or, leave your computer on overnight, and wake up to your e-mail, ready to be read with your morning cup o' joe!

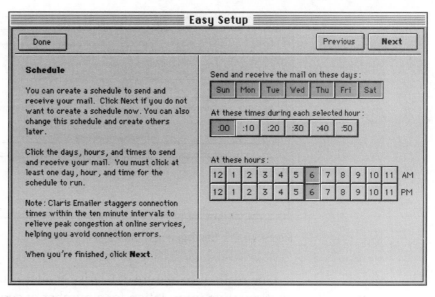

Figure 12-27: The scheduling screen in Claris Emailer.

TIP

If you have a direct Net connection at your job and you leave Claris Emailer running all of the time, make sure that you don't set Schedule to check your e-mail when you're not coming in to work. When Emailer gets your mail, it deletes it from the server. If you have Emailer snatch your mail over the weekend (or while you're away), you won't be able to get it at home or on the road!

Sending Mail With Claris Emailer

To send a message, select New from the Mail menu (or press **Command+N**) to access a window entitled Out Box Item (shown in Figure 12-28).

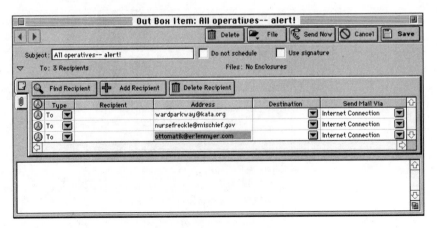

Figure 12-28: Sending a new message in Emailer.

One really nice feature of Claris Emailer is that it contains configuration information for a number of commercial service providers. If you want to send mail to people on those services, you don't even have to remember any sort of special "Internet-to-service" address stuff. Just use the address they use on their service, select the service from the Destination menu, and the message is off! Table 12-19 lists the services that Claris Emailer recognizes.

Service Name	Service Name
America Online	MCI Mail
Apple Computer	Microsoft
Applelink	Netcom
AT&T Mail	NiftyServe
BIX	Prodigy
BMUG	PSI
Claris	RadioMail
CompuServe	SprintMail
Delphi	UUCP
EasyLink	
eWorld	
FidoNet	
Genie	
Internet	

Table 12-19: Commercial services recognized by Claris Emailer.

NOTE: If you choose Internet from the list in Table 12-19, you'll have to enter the entire e-mail address for the recipient.

Enclosures

Claris Emailer really simplifies the process of attaching files to mail messages, even those you send between the Internet and commercial services. Adding an attachment (or *enclosure*, in Emailer lingo) takes just a click of a button (see Figure 12-29), and making sure it arrives intact mainly just involves choosing the Service Default option. As long as you've set the Destination correctly, you can't go wrong.

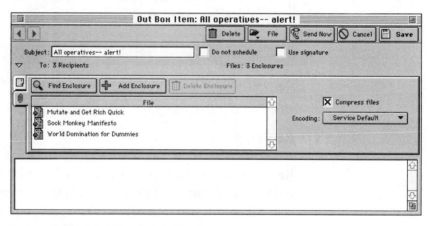

Figure 12-29: Attaching files in Emailer.

Receiving Mail With Claris Emailer

Most of the action in Claris Emailer takes place in the Browser window. Here you'll find all your unread messages, system information, and filtering summaries (see Figure 12-30). Reading your new messages is as easy as clicking on the line that contains the message you want to read. You can also file and delete your messages directly from this window.

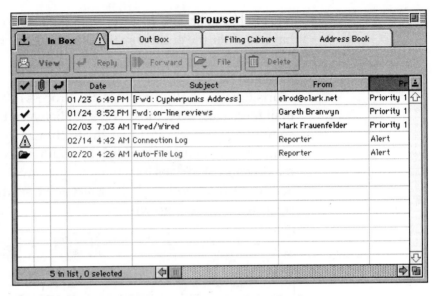

Figure 12-30: The In Box Browser window in Claris Emailer.

Replying

If you want to reply to the message you're reading, press the Reply button at the top of the screen. If you want to quote part of the message, click and drag on the text in the message window to select it before you press Reply. The text you've selected will be quoted in your reply message. See Figure 12-31.

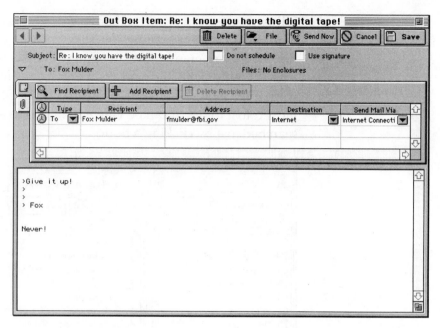

Figure 12-31: Using the quoting feature while replying to a message in Claris Emailer.

Forwarding

Forwarding a message is even easier. Just press the Forward button. The full text of the message will be placed in the body of your new message where you can edit or add to it.

Managing Your Mail With Claris Emailer

While many other e-mail programs seem to go out of their way to make the whole process as difficult as possible, Claris Emailer makes it simpler and more intuitive than any other product we've seen.

Managing your e-mail is where Emailer really shines. Not only does it gather all your messages in one place, but it also helps you organize them with filters and filing. Additionally, managing attached files (often a very confusing part of any e-mail program) becomes as easy as dragging and clicking on enclosure icons.

Filing

If you're on a lot of mailing lists (like we are), the ability to organize mail from many different sources is essential. Claris Emailer allows you to define as many new mailboxes (called *folders*) as you want in its Filing Cabinet (see Figure 12-32). Once mail has been moved to a folder, it can be viewed, moved to another folder, and searched just by clicking a button.

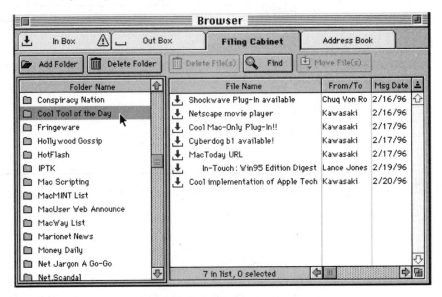

Figure 12-32: Sean's (very full!) Filing Cabinet in Claris Emailer.

Automatic Mail Handling

Once you've set up folders for your mail, you're one step closer to total e-mail automation! Claris Emailer allows you to define a set of rules for incoming mail called Mail Actions, which can automatically file, delete, or even respond to incoming e-mail.

Defining a Mail Action is easy and involves nothing more than picking a field (or two) to use (you can sort on From:, To:, Cc:, Reply to, any recipient, Subject:, Message, Mail account, or All mail), a decision criteria (is, contains, is not, etc.), and a string to search for. Once you've made your selections, just pick an action for the mail—file, delete, respond—and you're finished! See Figure 12-33.

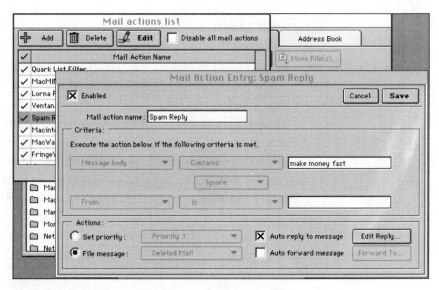

Figure 12-33: The Mail Actions dialog box in Claris Emailer.

Dealing With Enclosures

If you receive a message with an attached document, Claris Emailer will do its best to decode it and save it in a format you can open with your Mac. Using Apple Events, Emailer will even allow you to open an enclosure with the program that created it — just by clicking on it in the Enclosures window (shown in Figure 12-34). Also, if you're using System 7.5 and have the Drag Manager extension, you can save an enclosure to a folder on your hard drive just by dragging its icon out of the Enclosures window.

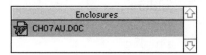

Figure 12-34: An enclosure has arrived in Claris Emailer!

PowerTalk

PowerTalk is one of those enigmas of Macintosh software. Everyone (who has System 7.5 or later) has it, yet almost no one uses it. In fact, it'd probably be safe to say that many people don't even know it exists. So what is it?

PowerTalk is a revolutionary way of looking at communications. Rather than regarding messages as entities to be viewed with an e-mail program, PowerTalk treats messages as documents, allowing you to create and view messages with the program that created them. The theory is that you could write a note in Microsoft Word, select Mail from the File menu, and send off your document. See Figure 12-35 to see how easy it is.

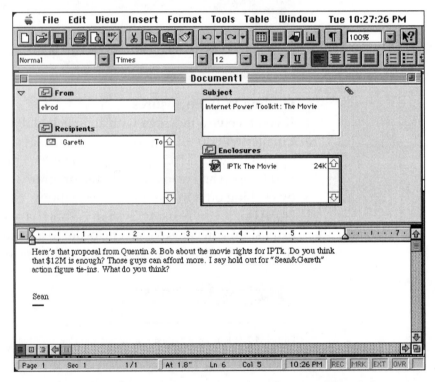

Figure 12-35: Sending a PowerTalk message from Microsoft Word 6.0.

On the other end of the line, the recipient (presumably also using PowerTalk) would find that your document had arrived in the In box on his or her desktop. The In box is another innovation in PowerTalk—not only does it get your mail, but it also holds new faxes, voice mail messages, and other communications. It's a universal mailbox. (See Figure 12-36.)

Figure 12-36: The In box in PowerTalk.

When your intended recipient opened his or her mailbox, it would contain a copy of the document you just sent. With a click of the mouse the recipient can open the document, read it, edit it, and send it back to you—all without ever opening an e-mail program. At least that's the theory.

So why aren't more people using it? Several reasons. First, the e-mail functions only work best when you're connected to a LAN. Sure, you can get Personal Mail Service Access Modules such as the excellent shareware MailConnect (available from http:// hyperarchive.lcs.mit.edu/HyperArchive/Abstracts/comm/tcp/ mail/mail-connect-12-psam.hqx.abs), but there are often problems with getting it to work reliably with a dial-up TCP/IP connection.

Second, as a system-level resource, PowerTalk takes some getting used to. Most people are set in their application-centric ways. "Want e-mail? Start up an e-mail program!" seems to be what immediately comes to mind when we think of e-mail communications. PowerTalk is a radically different concept in which applications cease to matter (except as creators of documents) and documents themselves are king.

Third, PowerTalk's resources are big and bulky, and they eat RAM for lunch. With so many vital applications fighting tooth and nail for any available RAM, most people aren't too inclined to devote the required resources to PowerTalk.

Finally, PowerTalk suffers from the fate of so much Apple stuff—it's a really cool product that hasn't been promoted. No one knows what it is, much less how to use it. In fact, you'd be hard-pressed to find any good documentation on using it.

To get a better understanding of PowerTalk and how you can use it, you need to know a little bit about the major parts. Much like Macintosh networking, setting up and using PowerTalk involves stops at several major locations. Knowing what does what is crucial to getting everything in working order.

Key Chain

The PowerTalk Key Chain (shown in Figure 12-37) is the heart of PowerTalk. The Key Chain allows you to keep all your passwords and access codes for all the services you're using in one place, accessible with a single Key Chain password that you assign. In addition, the Key Chain allows you to add and remove services as easily as choosing them from a menu.

Key Chain

Figure 12-37: The Key Chain in PowerTalk.

In Tray

The In Tray (shown in Figure 12-38) is where all your incoming information arrives. If you have PowerTalk services installed for office e-mail, Internet e-mail, faxes, and voicemail, all the documents from those services will arrive in the In Tray. Just double-click to view the document.

✓	Subject	Sender	Date Sent	Location	Priority
	<No Subject>	Michael B McNe...	2/17/96, 6:57 PM	local	normal
	Books and chilli	rdeckard@geko...	2/4/96, 7:53 AM	local	normal
	Hot sauce books	Jim Mehl	2/4/96, 7:49 AM	local	normal
	KEVIN AND THALIA on GMA ...	TERRY KNAB	2/4/96, 8:01 AM	local	normal
	Re: CHILE-HEADS Digest V2 ...	bachris@telera...	2/4/96, 9:10 AM	local	normal
	SUBSCRIBE APPLE-INTERNE...	listproc@soluti...	2/4/96, 7:31 AM	local	normal
	SUBSCRIBE APPLE-INTERNE...	listproc@soluti...	2/4/96, 7:31 AM	local	normal

In Tray for elrod — 7 items

Figure 12-38: Sean's In Tray in PowerTalk.

Business Cards & Catalogs

PowerTalk also provides a quick and easy way to store all the information about the people you communicate with in one place—a personal catalog. The catalog stores all your PowerTalk Business Cards—data containers that hold all the personal information (including pictures!) about your contacts. To send a message, you can just address it by dragging a Business Card out of a Catalog and into your message. Figure 12-39 shows Sean's PowerTalk Business Card.

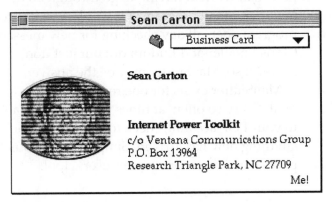

Sean Carton

Business Card

Sean Carton

Internet Power Toolkit
c/o Ventana Communications Group
P.O. Box 13964
Research Triangle Park, NC 27709

Me!

Figure 12-39: Sean's Business Card in PowerTalk.

Locations

PowerTalk is meant to be used by people on the go, so it has provisions for different configurations depending on where you are. Each configuration can hold a different list of services—an office configuration might hold fax, voicemail, LAN mail, and Internet mail while a home configuration might hold only Internet mail.

E-MAIL POWER UTILITIES

The e-mail programs we've covered so far cover a wide range of services. In fact, many people get through life just fine without ever doing anything with their e-mail beyond firing up Eudora once or twice a day. They receive mail, read it, send some mail, and go about their lives. Efficient, yes—but boring. For the power user, there's more to e-mail than just reading it. In this section, we'll examine several utilities for improving the ways you deal with your e-mail.

MailSniffer

Have you ever been online and wished that you could check for new mail without having to go through all the rigmarole of opening your e-mail program? Or would you like to leave your e-mail program open all day checking for new messages at intervals (like Claris Emailer and Eudora do) but just don't have the RAM to spare? If so, MailSniffer may be the answer.

MailSniffer exists for one reason only—to tell you if you have e-mail. Every so often, at times you specify, MailSniffer will log on to your POP account, check for new mail, and then notify you if anything new has arrived. Simple, handy, quick, and small—perfect attributes for a power user's tool.

Installing & Configuring MailSniffer

To install MailSniffer, just pop the Companion CD-ROM into your drive, start it up, and follow the simple instructions you'll find. Couldn't be easier.

After you've installed MailSniffer, configuring it will take only a second. Select New from the File menu to start a new sniffer, and then choose Setup from the Sniffer menu. Enter your e-mail account username and password, and tell MailSniffer how often you want it to sniff for mail. Close the window, save your configuration, and you're finished.

Checking Mail With MailSniffer

Leave MailSniffer running in the background while you work. It takes a measly 512K, so unless you've got a seriously low-memory configuration, you shouldn't have a problem. When mail arrives in your POP account, MailSniffer will notify you via the method you chose in the Setup dialog box and then will list your new mail onscreen in its window (see Figure 12-40). Read over the subjects, then decide if you want to use your e-mail program to retrieve anything that looks interesting. ("Wow . . . Gillian Anderson answered my fan mail!")

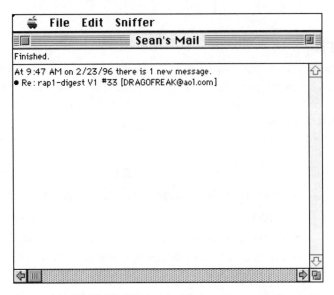

Figure 12-40: MailSniffer just sniffed some new mail.

VideoMail Pro

If you really want to wow your wired friends with your techno-wizardry, there's few ways better than to surprise them with a video mail message. How do you send a video message? With VideoMail Pro and a video input source, of course! With VideoMail and a digital video camera (like the Connectix QuickCam) you can record a movie of yourself, type a description, and mail it off to your friends—all from the same program.

Installing & Configuring VideoMail Pro

To install VideoMail Pro on your Macintosh, just follow the simple instructions on the Companion CD-ROM.

You can't escape configuring VideoMail Pro, at least until you register the program (for $35). When you start VideoMail Pro, you'll have to enter your SMTP server address and username before you can continue. Once you've entered that information, you're ready to create a message.

TIP

Remember—video files are bandwidth hogs. A short, five-second video can be as large as 800K and take over five minutes to download with a 28.8 kbps modem. Make sure your friends can handle the load before you send them a video message.

Creating a Message With VideoMail Pro

VideoMail Pro will allow you to create audio-only, video-only, or audio/video files to send along with your mail messages. If you want to create an audio-only message, all you'll need is a Mac that can record sound (any Mac newer than the LC) and the

QuickTime system extensions. If you want to use video, you'll need a video source. You can use either a camera like the $99 Connectix QuickCam or a video input-capable Macintosh with a VCR attached.

Creating a message merely involves starting a new message (from the Message menu) and then pressing a button at the top of the message window indicating which type of media you want to attach to your message.

Figure 12-41: The Audio, Video, Send Message, and Discard Message buttons in VideoMail Pro.

Once you've finished recording your message, the screen will change to show you your newly recorded message (Figure 12-42). If you're just sending audio, a picture ad for VideoMail Pro will accompany your soundtrack. If you recorded video, you'll see the first frame. To preview it before you send it, just use the QuickTime controls. Once you're satisfied, hit the Send button.

Figure 12-42: A recorded message ready to be sent.

Reading VideoMail With Other E-Mail Programs

VideoMail Pro is just a program that sends e-mail. If you want to receive multimedia messages, you'll need a MIME-compliant e-mail program to download the attachments. When the message arrives at your friend's computer (via MIME e-mail) they'll be able to use any QuickTime-compatible video viewing program to watch it.

TIP

Claris Emailer makes a terrific complement to VideoMail Pro. Because Emailer allows you to open attachments by double-clicking on the attachment's icon in the Attachments box, all you need to do when you receive a VideoMail message from a friend is click!

Serve Yourself! Using the Apple Internet Mail Server

We're going to end our journey though the wonderful world of Macintosh TCP/IP e-mail power tools with something that's not even an e-mail program. Instead, it's an e-mail server that you can install on your Mac.

Why Set up Your Own Mail Server?

We thought you might ask that! Several reasons. First, if you have a full-time Net connection, it's a way of getting as many e-mail accounts as you want. Use one for various mailing lists, one for friends, one for business. You can even give your dog an account! Second, many people have found that using the Apple Internet Mail Server as their outgoing SMTP server allows them to send large files more quickly and easily than through their service providers. When you run your own mail server, the messages go out to the Net right away instead of being stored and forwarded by an ISP. Finally, as more (and more) people come online, they're discovering that mailing lists are a great way to stay in touch with friends and business associates. However, if you pay an ISP to set up a mailing list for you, you can end up spending as much as 10 to 25 cents *per name* on your list. It's not hard to see how the costs could get out of control pretty fast. With your own e-mail server, you can run a shareware mailing list program called Macjordomo for a fraction of the cost of using a commercial ISP's mailing list services.

Installing & Configuring Apple Internet Mail Server (AIMS)

To install the Apple Internet Mail Server, just follow the simple instructions you'll find when you download and decompress the file.

To configure the mail server, you'll first have to decide how you're going to use it. If you're just going to use it as a way to send large messages, go to the Account Information section (under the Server menu), and create an account for yourself. If you're going to be using AIMS for incoming mail, you can set up other accounts, too.

Unless you're going to be running AIMS on a standalone machine, you should then go to the Preferences dialog box (also accessible from the Server menu), and set the maximum number of connections to two. This will reduce the load on your machine.

Configuring Your E-Mail Programs to Work With Apple Internet Mail Server

If you have a 24-hour Net connection and you're going to be using AIMS for both incoming and outgoing mail, you need to change the SMTP and POP server information in your e-mail programs to reflect your new address. If you set your account information correctly, your e-mail address should now be account name @Your.Machine.Name. The SMTP and POP server addresses should be set to the address of your Mac.

If you're only going to be using AIMS for outgoing mail, you'll need to remember a few things. First, if the mail server isn't going to be up all the time, you should only change the settings for outgoing mail in your e-mail programs. Likewise, you should point the return address information toward your ISP e-mail account. That way you can make sure that e-mail coming from your own Mac mail server has somewhere to go if your Mac is offline.

Macjordomo: Roll Your Own E-Mail Lists

If you want to start your own mailing list and you're running the Apple Internet Mail Server, all you need is Macjordomo.

If you're on a mailing list, you're probably familiar with the popular UNIX-based mail server called Majordomo. Macjordomo is not a port of Majordomo, but it does function in much the same way. You set up a mailing list, tell Macjordomo a few rules about how to handle the mail coming in, and let it rip! People can add themselves to your mailing list using familiar commands such as:

        SUBSCRIBE List_Name   Your_FirstName   Your_LastName

to add themselves and:

        UNSUBSCRIBE List_Name

to take themselves off your list. Macjordomo even contains commands that allow users to receive digested instead of real-time e-mail!

So if you want to try it out, go ahead. Download a copy for yourself. Installation is a snap—just decompress the file after you've downloaded it. It comes with a very complete help file that should get you started right away.

MOVING ON

Now that we're finished with our little workshop on one-to-one communications power tools, it's time we turned our sights to the one-to-many communications offered on Usenet newsgroups. Jumping into newsgroups can be a pretty hairy experience if you don't know what you're doing or what tools are available to you. That's where we, your humble authors, come in.

In the next chapter, we'll survey some of the best Mac newsreader programs and tools for filtering, creating kill files, and managing your newsgroups. We'll explain how you can organize the 16,000 plus newsgroups available today, as well as ways to avoid the hazards of the highway. When we're finished, *spam*, *velveeta*, and *flames* will move effortlessly from your path as you cruise the Net in high gear. So get ready for a lost highway trek into the wilds of the global idea and information frontier known as Usenet newsgroups.

## Chapter 13

Mac Usenet Power Tools

Nothing epitomizes the global anarchy of the Internet more than the free-wheelin' ideas and information found on Usenet news-groups. While Net purists will argue that Usenet isn't *really* part of the Internet, as far as most people are concerned, the point is moot. Reading newsgroups is as much a part of Net life as surfing the Web or using e-mail, even if Usenet groups aren't actually transported over TCP/IP networks.

To join in on Usenet's global discussions, you need a newsreader. And with the current number of newsgroups topping 16,000, a *good* newsreader is a necessity. There's an enormous amount of information posted every day—over 150 megabytes—so finding the articles that you want can be like looking for a needle in a haystack.

A good newsreader should help you sort through the info-glut, allowing you to use kill files, autoselecting options, and bozo filters. And, since some of the postings to Usenet are executable programs, pictures, movies, and other binary data, a good newsreader should allow you to easily encode and decode binary files so you can participate in these binary newsgroups.

By now, you probably won't be surprised to learn that we've found some newsreaders that fit the bill. These are our top contenders for the best Mac newsreaders—useful, powerful programs that give you a full suite of tools for accessing, managing, and participating in Usenet news. For a quick look at our picks, check out Table 13-1.

	Yet Another NewsWatcher	Nuntius	NewsHopper	Comments
Kill files	Yes	No	Yes	Ignores articles based on matched patterns.
Filtering	Yes	No	Yes	Filters articles based on matched patterns.
Binary Encoding/Decoding	Yes (both)—using helper applications.	Yes. Decoding built-in.	Yes. Decoding with helper apps.	Includes built-in capabilities for creating (and/or decoding) binary articles.
Auto-unpack multi-part articles	Yes	Yes	Yes	Automatically combines multi-part binary articles.
Helper Apps	Yes. HTTP, uudecode, FTP, Gopher, finger, Ph.	Yes, uses external editor. Includes own uudecoding routines.	Yes, for all features: text editor, e-mail, uudecoding, and ftp.	Includes external viewers (GIF, JPG, MIME, etc.).
Built-in mail	Yes (outgoing only).	Yes. Using helper apps & scripting.	No, uses user-defined helper app.	Sends/receives e-mail from within program.
Off-line reader	No	No	Yes. No online reading features.	Allows you to read new news articles offline.
Special Features	Powerful and easy to set up. Anonymous remailer support. Automatically gets FAQs for newsgroups. The Mac standard.	Multi-threaded. Extensive balloon help. Uses user-defined text editor for outgoing messages.	Offline news reader. Only retrieves articles based on pre-defined filters.	See sections below on each program for more info on special features.
Windows Version	No	No	No	Good for two-party families and businesses.
Ease of Use	Easy	Easy, but some people find interface confusing.	Moderately difficult to configure.	"Ease" as applied to an experienced user.
Cost	Freeware	Freeware	Demo limited to 5 newsgroups before registration ($59).	
Comments	Excellent documentation.	Simple. No-frills.	Can be a powerful tool for people who have to read the same newsgroups frequently.	Downloading can take a long time.

Table 13-1: Newsreader comparison chart.

As you can see, there's a variety of special features to choose from, but all of the programs we've selected as Usenet power tools will get the job done. In the sections that follow, we'll look at each newsreader in detail. Later, we'll take a look at a few tools that aren't newsreaders per se, but are useful tools for managing your Usenet news.

YET ANOTHER NEWSWATCHER

Yet Another NewsWatcher is, as its name implies, yet another version of John Norstad's NewsWatcher program, one of the first (and best) newsreaders for the Mac. NewsWatcher is a great program—it operates the way a Mac newsreader should, allowing you to post (send), read (receive), and download binaries from Usenet newsgroups with a click of the mouse. It provides an easy click-and-drag interface for subscribing to groups, and it even works with a variety of helper applications so that you can jump to HTTP, FTP, Gopher, finger, Ph, and other links directly, without having to open the helper applications yourself. Just hold down the command key, click on the URL, and NewsWatcher does the rest. Nifty!

So why aren't we going to be covering NewsWatcher itself? Three reasons. First, NewsWatcher doesn't allow you to use kill files or filters to sift through Usenet's data-tsunami. Second, while NewsWatcher allows you to easily download and decode multi-part binary files, it doesn't provide any features for posting your own binary files. Finally, as government regulation and corporate direct e-mail become more prevalent, it's more important than ever that you be able to post anonymous articles to Usenet. NewsWatcher doesn't give you that option.

That's where Yet Another NewsWatcher steps in. In fact, Yet Another NewsWatcher not only fills these voids, but it also offers some nice interface features of its own. Yet Another NewsWatcher is a great example of the true spirit of the Internet; John Norstad released the source code for NewsWatcher, others saw gaps that needed to be filled and took it upon themselves to fill these gaps. It's a great example of what can happen when people decide to do something just for the joy of doing it.

Installing & Configuring Yet Another NewsWatcher

To install Yet Another NewsWatcher, just decompress the file that you download. Yet Another NewsWatcher should be ready to go.

Yet Another NewsWatcher (YAN) uses the same preferences file as NewsWatcher. If you already use NewsWatcher, the first time that you fire up YAN, you'll go straight to the list of newsgroups. However, if you've never used NewsWatcher or YAN, you'll have to answer a few questions before you can start reading news.

TIP

If you've ever used NewsWatcher or YAN before and you want to start fresh, you'll need to delete the old preferences file. Go to the Preferences folder (in the System folder), and delete all the files that begin with NewsWatcher. Under most conditions, you'll have to at least delete the NewsWatcher Prefs file.

You'll need to tell YAN about your current computer setup. You have three choices (as shown in Figure 13-1):

- ❒ **Lab:** If you're using YAN in a computer lab or in an environment where you can't save your settings to a local disk, chose the Lab button. YAN will prompt you to insert a disk on which to save your settings. When you want to use YAN next time, just insert your disk, and double-click on the NewsWatcher Prefs file to start YAN with your own settings.

- ❒ **Shared:** If you're not going to be the only one using YAN on the computer you're using, choose the Shared button. You'll then be able to create your own settings folder to store your personal information on the hard drive. Later, when you go back to use YAN, you can start it with your settings by double-clicking on the NewsWatcher Prefs file in your own folder.

❐ **Private:** If you're the only one using your computer, choose the Private button. YAN will save your settings in the Preferences folder in the System folder on your hard drive.

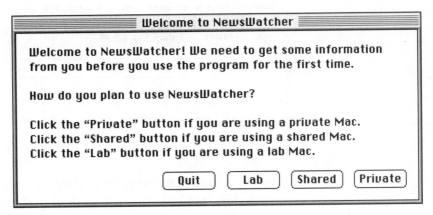

Figure 13-1: Starting Yet Another NewsWatcher for the first time.

TIP

YAN's ability to save different configuration files via the Lab or Shared settings can be useful even if you don't intend to share your computer with anyone else. By allowing you to create separate preferences files, you'll be able to use YAN with more than one news server—a helpful feature if you happen to have a limited local server that doesn't give you access to some newsgroups. If this is the case, you can use a publicly accessible news server. See http://www.geocities.com/Athens/2694/freenews.html for a list of servers you can use.

Once you choose your setup, you'll go through several screens to configure YAN. First, you'll enter the address of your local news server as well as the address of your mail server (see Figure 13-2). (For more info on mail server settings, check out Chapter 12, "Mac E-Mail Power Tools.")

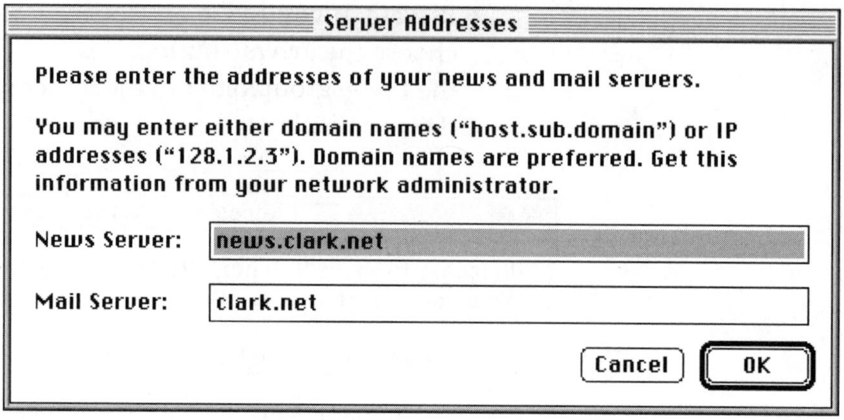

Server Addresses

Please enter the addresses of your news and mail servers.

You may enter either domain names ("host.sub.domain") or IP addresses ("128.1.2.3"). Domain names are preferred. Get this information from your network administrator.

News Server: `news.clark.net`

Mail Server: `clark.net`

[Cancel] [OK]

Figure 13-2: Entering your server information.

You'll be prompted to enter personal information about yourself (see Figure 13-3). As we discussed in the last chapter, the information you enter for your Full Name and Organization aren't important (as far as the computer is concerned). However, if you want people to respond to your posts via e-mail, enter your correct e-mail address in the Email Address text box.

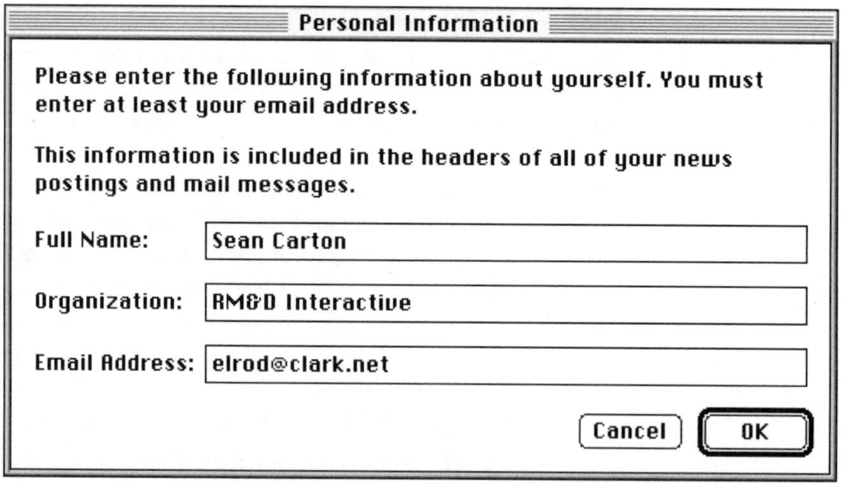

Personal Information

Please enter the following information about yourself. You must enter at least your email address.

This information is included in the headers of all of your news postings and mail messages.

Full Name: `Sean Carton`

Organization: `RM&D Interactive`

Email Address: `elrod@clark.net`

[Cancel] [OK]

Figure 13-3: Entering your personal information.

Once you've entered your personal info, you're finished! YAN will log on to your news server (see Figure 13-4), grab the full list of available newsgroups (see Figure 13-5), sort them (see Figure 13-6), and then display the list on your screen.

Figure 13-4: YAN logging on to your news server.

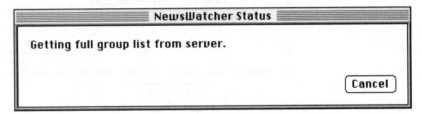

Figure 13-5: YAN grabbing the list of available newsgroups.

Figure 13-6: YAN sorting newsgroups.

TIP

While YAN is snarfing the newsgroups from your server, it might be a good idea to grab a cup o' java (the drinkable kind—we'll get to the programming kind in Chapter 28, "Audio/Video Power Tools"). With over 17,000 newsgroups carried on some news servers, downloading the list can take a while. Relax. Read another part of this book...there's plenty of it to browse!

Once YAN finishes downloading the list of all the available newsgroups, it will display them on your screen in the Full Group List window (see Figure 13-7). However, if this is the first time you've used Yet Another NewsWatcher, a dialog box will appear asking you about creating a new set of filters. For now, just click Use Default. We'll cover filters later. For now, get ready to dive head first into Usenet.

Figure 13-7: The newsgroups!

Reading & Subscribing

When it comes to using Usenet, you'll always be doing one of two things—reading articles or posting articles of your own. In this section, we'll examine what you need to know in order to read Usenet articles with YAN.

When you begin using YAN, you'll have two windows open on your screen—the Full Group List window and another, smaller window labeled Untitled. The Full Group List window contains the names of all the Usenet newsgroups available from your server. Opening a newsgroup and reading the articles there is easy—just scroll down to a newsgroup that looks interesting, and double-click on its name. YAN will grab a list of articles in that newsgroup and open a window containing the articles, sorted by subject (see Figure 13-8).

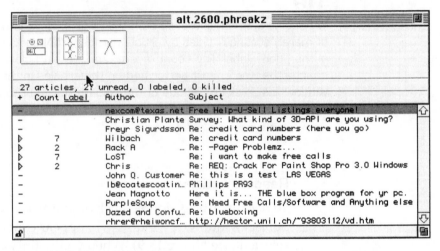

Figure 13-8: The Subject window.

Let's take a closer look at what you see in the Subject window. First, you'll notice three buttons at the top of the window. The two buttons on the right are used for editing and creating filters for the newsgroup. (We'll cover filtering later on.) The button on the left is for a feature that's not been implemented yet.

Below the buttons, YAN shows the number of articles in the newsgroup, how many of those you've read, how many are labeled, and how many have been killed or blocked out. If you're starting YAN for the first time, you shouldn't have any labeled or killed articles.

Finally, the Subject window lists all the different threads (groups of articles with the same subject) available in that newsgroup. YAN collapses threads for easier reading, displaying the subject for the article in the thread that arrived most recently. If you want to see the other subjects in a thread, click the right-pointing triangle next to a thread, and YAN will display the thread's other articles.

TIP

YAN sorts articles differently than the original NewsWatcher. Instead of merely sorting articles by article number, YAN sorts by subject, author, date, label, line count, score, and, yes, article number. To change the type of sort performed on the articles in the Subject window, just click on the title of the column you want to use as the main sort criterion.

Reading Articles

To read an article, double-click on the article's subject in the Subject window. A window will appear containing the article you selected (see Figure 13-9). When you're finished reading the article, just close the window.

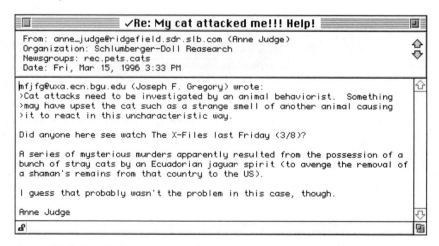

Figure 13-9: Reading an article in YAN.

Article-Selecting Tips

Selecting articles in the Subject window is even easier if you know a few keyboard tricks:

❏ Shift-click selects an article or range of articles in between the first- and last-clicked article subjects.

❏ Command-click allows you to select articles noncontiguously. Selects each command-clicked article but not those in between.

❏ Command+A selects all the articles in the current Subject window, which is useful if you want to quickly mark all the articles as read.

❏ If you have selected all the articles by mistake, choose Deselect All from the File menu. Don't try to click on the articles! If you do, YAN will open every single one of them!

❏ If you need to cancel an operation such as opening an article, press Command+period.

If all you want to know are the bare basics of reading Usenet articles, that's it! You now know everything. But we're interested in power tools, right? And in the power tool department, YAN doesn't disappoint. A host of power options are available to an avid news reader such as yourself to make your news reading more efficient and enjoyable. Tables 13-2, 13-3, and 13-4 list the options and how to use them.

Option	Menu	Window used from: Message?	Subject?	Description
Next Article	News	Yes	Yes	Moves to next article in thread. If you're at the last article in a thread, YAN reads the next article in the Subject window.
Next Thread	News	Yes	Yes	Moves to next thread in Subject window.
Next Group	News	Yes	Yes	Moves to next newsgroup. YAN will mark all the articles in the current group as read, close the current group window, and open a new group window.

Option	Menu	Window used from: Message?	Subject?	Description
Mark Read	News	Yes	Yes	Can be applied to multiple articles. Marks current article as read in Message window. Marks selected articles as read in Subject window.
Mark Unread	News	Yes	Yes	Can be applied to multiple articles. Marks current message unread in Message window. Marks selected articles as unread in Subject window.
Mark Others Read	News	No	Yes	Can be applied to multiple articles. Marks all articles not selected as read.
New Message	News	Yes	Yes	Enables you to create and post a new article to the current newsgroup. See "Posting an Article," later in this chapter.
Reply	News	Yes	Yes	Can be applied to multiple articles. Enables you to reply to the current article. YAN will include a copy of the currently selected article in the reply. If multiple articles are selected, YAN will open a new window for each one. See "Posting an Article" later in this chapter for more information on posting replies.
Forward	News	Yes	Yes	Can be applied to multiple articles. Forwards the currently selected message via e-mail. If multiple articles are selected, YAN will open a new window for each article. See "Posting an Article" later in this chapter for more information on forwarding articles.
Redirect	News	Yes	Yes	Can be applied to multiple articles. Redirects currently selected message via e-mail. If multiple articles are selected, YAN will open a new window for each article. See "Posting an Article" later in this chapter for more information on redirecting articles.

Table 13-2: Article reading options available from News menu.

Option	Menu	Window used from: Message?	Subject?	Description
Open All References	Special	Yes	No	Opens all news articles referred to by the current message. Notifies you if articles are not available.
Cancel Article	Special	Yes	Yes	Can be applied to multiple articles. Cancels currently selected articles by sending a cancel control message out to Usenet. You can cancel only articles that you authored.
Open URL	Special	Yes	No	Opens selected URL in article with Web browser specified in the Preferences dialog box. You can accomplish the same thing by Command-clicking the URL.

Table 13-3: Article reading options available from Special menu.

Option	Menu	Window used from: Message?	Subject?	Description
Find/Find Again	File	Yes	Yes	Searches for a string in current window. If the window currently open contains an article, YAN will search for the string in that article. If the current window is the Subject window, YAN will search for the string in the article listing.
Show Details	File	Yes	No	Shows Usenet headers.
Rot-13	File	Yes	No	Performs Rot-13 decryption on current article. Rot-13 is a simple encryption method used for hiding potentially objectionable material from accidental viewing. Not used much these days.

Table 13-4: Article reading options available from File menu.

Subscribing to Newsgroups

Of course, having to scroll through 17,000 plus newsgroups to find the one that you want to read can be a somewhat arduous task. Luckily, YAN gives you the option of creating a subscription list—a list of newsgroups that you read frequently. After opening YAN, you can open this list of subscribed newsgroups and go straight to the groups you want.

To subscribe to a newsgroup, select New Group Window from the File menu. You'll be asked about filtering again—just select Use Default for now. YAN will display a small window labeled Untitled (as shown in Figure 13-10). Next, find a newsgroup you want to subscribe to in the Full Group List window. Then, click on the name of the newsgroup, hold down the mouse button, and drag the selected newsgroup into your New Group window. After about a second, the group name will show up, along with a number indicating how many articles are available to read.

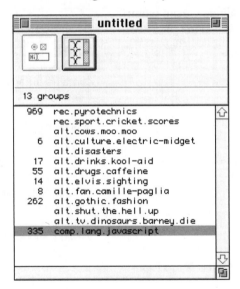

Figure 13-10: A New Group window in YAN.

After you have a list of newsgroups you're happy with, you can save your list by selecting Save from the File menu. Next time you start YAN, open your list by choosing Open from the File menu.

Posting an Article

Unless you're a complete lurker, you'll probably want to post an article or two to some of the newsgroups you've been reading. With YAN, you basically have two options if you want to send an article to USENET: either you can create an entirely new article or you can respond to someone else's.

TIP

You've probably heard this a zillion times before, but we're gonna tell you again—if you're posting a message to a newsgroup, it's considered good Netiquette to read the FAQ for the group first. The creator of YAN obviously agrees, because he provided you with a way of getting the FAQs that's so easy you have no excuse not to. If you want to read the FAQ for a newsgroup you've selected, go to the Special menu, and choose Get Newsgroup FAQ. YAN will launch your Web browser, which will go directly to the Ohio State FAQ archive section that contains the correct FAQ.

If you want to post an entirely new article, select New Message from the News menu. YAN will display a new message window (see Figure 13-11) in which you can type your article.

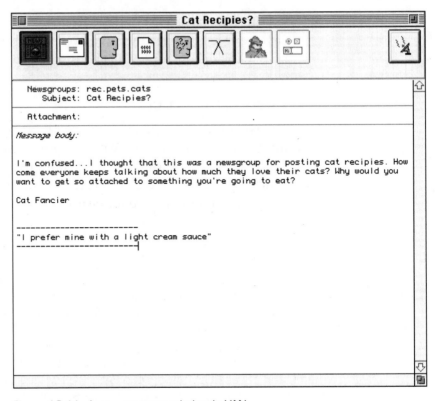

Figure 13-11: A new message window in YAN.

Pretty graphics, eh? One of the really nice features of YAN is that it goes out of its way to present a very handy interface, placing the features you need most in front of you at all times without requiring you to dig through several layers of menus to get to them. Those icons at the top of the screen allow you to toggle important article-sending options with just a click. In Table 13-5 you can see what's what.

Icon	Function	Description
	Posts as news	Posts article to newsgroup(s) listed in Newsgroup field.
	Posts as mail	Sends a copy of article to the e-mail address you've indicated.

Icon	Function	Description
	Sends to self	E-mails a copy of the posting to yourself.
	Attaches a file	Attaches a binary file for posting.
	Posts via anonymous remailer	Posts article using one or more anonymous remailers that have been specified in the preferences section.
	Creates a filter for replies	Creates a new filter using the subject of your article.
	Encrypts or signs using PGP	Not implemented yet.
	Edits settings	Not implemented yet.
	Posts article	Posts article to newsgroup and mails copy if Send to self or E-mail reply has been selected.

Table 13-5: New message window icons.

Binary Files: Posting & Decoding

During your travels on Usenet, you may notice a whole load of newsgroups with the word *binaries* in the title. These groups are for people who want to post computer files other than messages— such as programs, movies, sounds, or (ahem!) pictures. Because Usenet was designed for transmitting text messages, posting messages made of computer code has required a few kludges.

First, the files must be uuencoded (specially processed to transform them into text files) before they are uploaded. Mac files can be BinHexed, but they're a special case and should be posted to Mac-only newsgroups. Also, because some newsreaders accept messages only under a certain size, these large uuencoded files must then be broken into several smaller messages before being posted. All in all, it can get pretty tricky for both the uploaders and the downloaders.

Luckily YAN makes handling binary files a snap. Decoding them is as simple as selecting the various parts that make up the file by shift-clicking on them in the Subject window (see Figure 13-12). Once you've selected all the parts, just choose Extract Binaries from the Special menu, and let 'er rip!

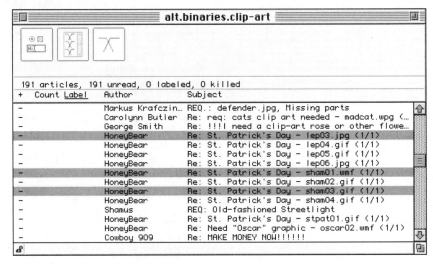

Figure 13-12: Selecting parts of a binary file to download.

It's important to note here that YAN doesn't actually do the decoding itself. Instead, it hands off the decoding to the appropriate helper application (specified in the Preferences dialog) to do the dirty work. Table 13-6 lists the recommended binary decoding helper apps and where to get them.

Program	Function	Where to get it
UUundo	Performs uudecoding	http://hyperarchive.lcs.mit.edu/HyperArchive/ Archive/cmp/uu-undo-10.hqx
Base64	Performs Yet Another Base64 decoding	http://hyperarchive.lcs.mit.edu/HyperArchive/ Archive/cmp/ya-base64-120.hqx
Stuffit Expander	Performs BinHex decoding	http://hyperarchive.lcs.mit.edu/HyperArchive/ Archive/cmp/stuffit-expander-352.hqx

Table 13-6: Binary decoding helper apps.

Uploading is just as easy. When you want to attach a binary file to the message you are posting, just press the Attach File button at the top of the new message window. YAN will display a file dialog box that you can use to find the file you wish to upload. YAN will break your article into chunks (the size of which you can specify in the Messages Files section of the Preferences dialog box) before uploading.

Posting Anonymously

One feature that sets YAN apart from the rest of the pack of newsreaders is that it allows you to post messages to Usenet through anonymous remailers. As government regulation of the Internet grows and the free speech that users on the Net have always enjoyed becomes more limited, being able to speak your mind is more important than ever. YAN can help you keep your voice in Cyberspace.

Setting up YAN for simple anonymous posting is easy—just enter the address of the anonymous remailer you want to use in the Anonymity Information section of the Preferences dialog box. See the sidebar "Free Speech Now: Anonymous Remailers" for more information if you don't know how to find an anonymous remailer. If you just want to try out an anonymous remailer, YAN comes preconfigured to use the remailer at replay.com, a site in Amsterdam run by Replay and Company Unlimited. Make a test post to alt.test to see what happens.

Free Speech Now: Anonymous Remailers

With the passage of the Communications Decency Act (CDA) in February 1996, the chance of getting into legal trouble for posting files that someone, somewhere in the U.S. might find indecent suddenly became a reality. Written by a few technologically challenged senators whose time spent online could probably be measured on an egg timer, this law was touted as a way to "protect our children" from "porn on the Internet." Instead it placed vague and broad restrictions on free speech that would never have been tolerated in the world of print media. These restrictions make it a crime to post anything containing anything from hard-core porn to the "seven dirty words" you can't say on TV and radio.

Luckily, if you have something controversial to say, you don't have to be silenced by the CDA. Anonymous remailers, programs that strip all identifying information out of a message and then forward it to its destination ("remail" it), allow you to post any message you want without having to worry about the Cybercops barging through your door.

While we'll cover anonymous remailers in greater depth in Chapter 24, "WWW Multimedia Power Tools," it's important that you know where to find a list of anonymous remailers. Now that you've got a newsreader working, check out the alt.anonymous and alt.privacy.anon-server newsgroups for periodic listings of anonymous remailer sites. Try several with YAN, and see which ones work best for you. For more information on how YAN works with anonymous remailers, read the document "YA-NewsWatcher and Anonymity," which you'll find in the Docs folder of the YA-NewsWatcher folder.

For more information on anonymous remailers, check out Francis Litterio's Anonymous Remailers page at http://world.std.com/~franl/crypto/remailers.html.

For more information about free speech on the Internet, see the Electronic Frontier's pages at http://www.eff.org/blueribbon.html.

Filters, Kill Files & Bozofilters

How much would you pay never to be bothered by those obnoxious "Make Money Fast" and "WinCash" posts? Well, with YAN you don't have to pay anything—the ability to filter annoying articles (and their authors!) is built in.

YAN gives you a wide range of filtering mechanisms that allow you (with a little tweaking) to read only the news you want and provide a sure-fire way to avoid much of the "spam" that's choking Usenet these days. Here's how it works.

YAN divides its filter types into three separate categories:

❐ The global filter: These filters apply to all the newsgroups and are applied before any newsgroup-specific filters. You should use global filters to alert you to any subjects that you always are looking for, regardless of which newsgroup you're in. For example, if you're the vain type, you might want to have a global filter that looks for your name. On the other hand, global filters are great for automatically killing articles that you'll never want to read. ("Make Money Fast" posts immediately come to mind.)

❐ The regional hierarchical filter: These filters are applied to a specific newsgroup hierarchy. You can apply the filters to any level of the hierarchy, and they are applied to newsgroups in order of the length of the newsgroup name. For example, if you were looking for pictures of fuzzy bunnies in the alt.binaries.pictures.animals newsgroup, and you thought other groups in that hierarchy might carry pictures of fuzzy bunnies, you could apply a filter that looked in the subject lines of all alt.binaries and alt.binaries.pictures newsgroups. The filter would be applied to the alt.binaries hierarchy before going on to the alt.binaries.pictures groups.

❐ The newsgroup filter AKA local filters: These filters apply only to a specific newsgroup. They are applied last in the list of filters so the local newsgroup filter can override any previous, more general filters. For example, if you killed articles with "Make Money Fast" in the subject with a higher level filter, you might want to have a filter in alt.scams, which "unkills" the subject so that you can read about "Make Money Fast" scams in the appropriate newsgroup.

You can create filters in two ways—by hand or automatically, based on a selected article. The automatic way is often easier, and you can tweak the settings. For general usage, you may want to create your filters automatically. Here's how.

When you're reading an article that represents a type of article you'd like to filter out, select New Filter from the Filters menu. YAN will display a filter configuration dialog box (as shown in Figure 13-13).

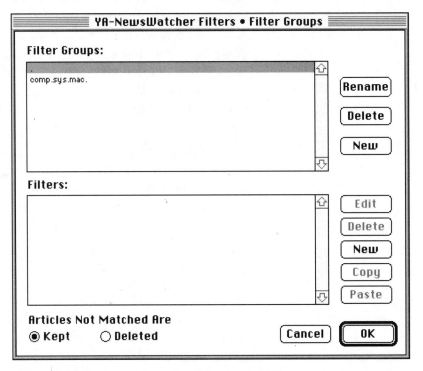

Figure 13-13: A filter configuration dialog box in YAN.

You'll notice that the name of the newsgroup you were reading appears in the top For box. This is where YAN looks to see which newsgroup a filter applies to. If you don't change anything, YAN will create a filter specifically for the newsgroup you're currently reading. However, if you want to create a more general filter, use the pop-up menu to the right of the box (it looks like a box with an arrow pointing down in it) to select the level in the newsgroup hierarchy you want to filter.

Right below the newsgroup box is a pop-up menu that you can use to choose the field you want the filter to consider when making its filtering decision. This choice defaults to the From: field, but you can choose from several more fields:

- ❐ Subject
- ❐ From
- ❐ Keywords
- ❐ Summary
- ❐ Date
- ❐ Organization
- ❐ References
- ❐ Distribution
- ❐ Lines
- ❐ Newsgroups
- ❐ Path
- ❐ NNTP-Posting host
- ❐ X-ref

Below the field selector menu is a menu labeled "Contains the string" that describes what type of match the filter should look for. Select the option that best applies to the string you're filtering:

- ❐ Word Begins With
- ❐ Contains The String
- ❐ Word Ends With
- ❐ Phrase Begins With
- ❐ Contains The Word
- ❐ Phrase Ends With
- ❐ Phrase Exactly Equals
- ❐ Contains The Regular Expression

Below these two pop-up menus is a box where you can enter the string that the filter will try to match. If you are letting YAN create a filter for you, the subject of the article you used as a model will be displayed here.

The Label: pop-up menu can be confusing. If you choose this menu, you'll see a list of 34 different color chips ranging from bright red to black. Use this menu to choose the color in which you want YAN to display an article filtered by the filter you're creating. If you allow the filter to display articles, the color you choose is not important— as long as you don't choose gray or black. Choosing gray means that your filter becomes a kill filter or a bozofilter, deleting any articles that match the criteria you set in the filter. Black, on the other hand, doesn't kill articles, but it does leave articles that match the criteria in the filter unlabeled in the Subject window.

YAN allows you to assign a weight to your filters to give you greater flexibility in applying them. When YAN displays your filtered messages, it displays them in order from highest- to lowest-weighted score. For example, if you had two filters for one newsgroup: a filter that looked for articles with "demo" in the subject (with a weight of 500) and a filter that looked for articles with "beta" in the subject (with a weight of 100)—an article with "beta demo" as the subject would score 600 weight points. When listing the articles, YAN would put the "beta demo" article above an article with just "demo" or "beta" in the subject line.

If you don't want your filters to last forever, enter in the Expire box, the number of days you want YAN to wait before expiring the filter.

To create a filter from scratch, the procedure is similar to the one you follow when creating a new filter based on an article. While you're reading a newsgroup that you've subscribed to, go to the Filters menu and select the New Filter option. Start your filter creation from the filter configuration dialog box. Just press the New button, and enter all the appropriate information for the filter by hand, starting with the Filter Group Name dialog box (shown in Figure 13-14).

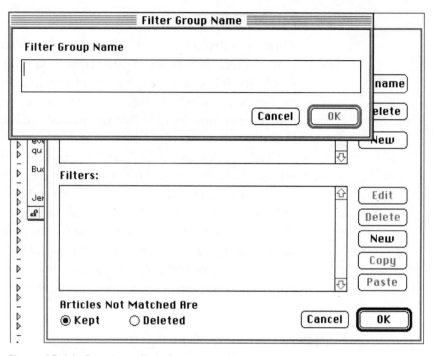

Figure 13-14: Creating a filter from scratch.

TIP

YAN's filtering capabilities can be very powerful. If you want more information on how to use YAN's filtering system, read the article called "YA-NewsWatcher and Filtering," which you'll find in the Docs folder with the YAN application. If you want more general assistance on filtering, check out Chapters 21 ("E-Mail Privacy & Security") and 26 ("Data Tracking") in this book.

NUNTIUS

Running a distant second behind the NewsWatcher family of newsreaders, Nuntius is a good bet if you value simplicity over flexibility. It sports a simple, Finder-like interface that displays newsgroups as lists in their own windows. Compared to YAN's complicated and feature-rich menu system, Nuntius seems almost Spartan.

Reading, posting, and decoding binaries can all be done with a mouse click or two, and even someone who's never used a newsreader before can probably figure out how everything works in a matter of minutes. If Nuntius has a motto, it's "less is more"— it doesn't even include a text editor for outgoing messages (you have to use your own). But regardless of whether you admire its bare-bones approach, Nuntius's reputation as a quick, fat-binary application has garnered it a loyal following over the years.

TIP

So what's a "nuntius" anyway? It's a Latin word meaning "messenger" or "emissary"—a fitting name for a program that brings you messages from all over the world!

Installing & Configuring Nuntius

To install Nuntius, first go to the author Peter Speck's FTP site, and snag the latest version. You'll find it at ftp://ftp.ruc.dk/pub/nuntius/. If you can't get on to this FTP site, you can grab Nuntius off the Web at http://hyperarchive.lcs.mit.edu/HyperArchive/Archive/comm/tcp/nuntius-204.hqx. Uncompress the file, and you're ready to go.

When you start Nuntius for the first time, you'll be prompted to enter the name of your news server (see Figure 13-15). Take care that you enter it correctly. If you mess up, you'll have to dig in the System folder and trash the Nuntius Preferences file (found in the Preferences folder) to reset Nuntius.

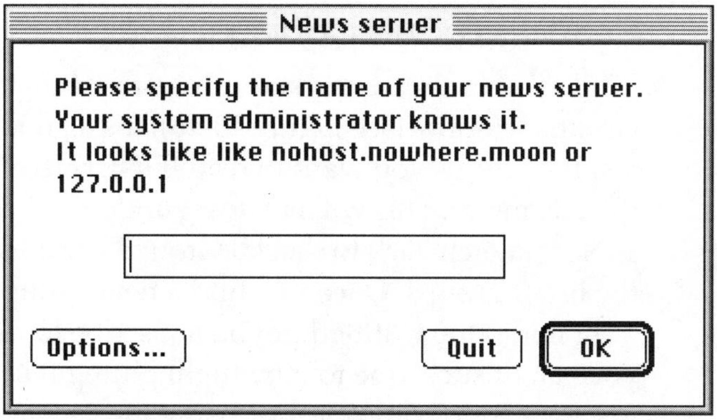

News server

Please specify the name of your news server.
Your system administrator knows it.
It looks like like nohost.nowhere.moon or
127.0.0.1

Options...   Quit   OK

Figure 13-15: Entering your news server information.

Once you've entered your server information, kick back and wait while Nuntius logs on to your news server and downloads the list and descriptions of all the newsgroups available to you (see Figure 13-16). Once the newsgroups are downloaded, select Show List of All Groups from the File menu, and you'll see a list that looks a lot like a kinda wacky Finder folder listing in an All Groups window. News hierarchies are represented by folders, and individual newsgroups are represented by document icons.

If you want to be able to post articles, Nuntius requires more information. Select Your Name from the Prefs menu. Enter the required information in the dialog box. You'll also have to specify an editor to use in writing your articles. Select Editing Articles from the Prefs menu, and choose a text editor. Once you do that, you're ready to go!

TIP

If you get stuck in your explorations of Nuntius, turn on the Balloon Help. Nuntius includes excellent online help, and just about every feature, option, or configuration doohickey has its own balloon to explain what it is.

Reading & Subscribing

While you can read newsgroups just by clicking on them in the All Groups window (see Figure 13-16), it's a good idea to subscribe to just the groups you want to read. First, select New GroupList from the File menu. This will create a window called Untitled group list 1. Now switch back to the All Groups window and scroll through the list of groups. Once you find a newsgroup you're interested in, drag it into the Untitled. If you subscribe to a group by mistake, you can unsubscribe to it by highlighting it in the subscribed groups window and then pressing the Delete key.

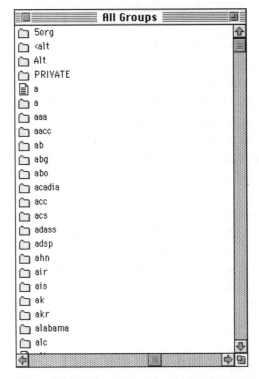

Figure 13-16: The All Groups window in Nuntius.

Once you've subscribed to a few lists, you can read the messages in a list by double-clicking on the name of the newsgroup. Nuntius will then display all the messages in the newsgroup in a scrollable list in a new window. Threads are grouped together and separated by rows of periods (as shown in Figure 13-17).

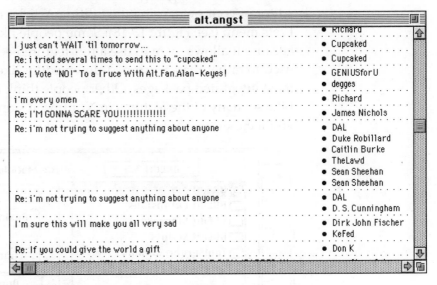

Figure 13-17: A list of threads in Nuntius.

TIP

If you want to open an entire hierarchy all at once, hold down the Option key while clicking on the triangle to the left of the folder. If you want to collapse an entire news hierarchy back into a folder, hold down the Option key while clicking on the down-pointing triangle to the left of the open folder in the listing.

Posting an Article

Nuntius's spare design and quirkiness are most apparent when posting an article to a newsgroup. Unlike every other Mac newsreader we tried, Nuntius doesn't include a text editor to create and edit outgoing messages. Instead, you must define a text editor of your own, using the Editing Articles option from the Prefs menu (see Figure 13-18). Some people like this feature because it allows them to use a full-featured editor that they're used to rather than a stripped-down editor like the ones found in most integrated packages. Other people think it's an annoyance. Like so many of the features in Nuntius, it's one of those that you'll either love or hate.

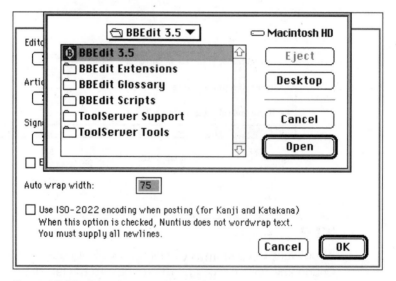

Figure 13-18: Choosing an editor in Nuntius.

Posting a new thread (an article unrelated to the article you're currently reading) is easy. Just select Post article in new thread from the Threads menu. The procedure for posting a follow-up to an article you're reading is more involved. You must first highlight the part of the post you want to quote in your follow-up, select Post follow-up article from the Article menu, switch to your text editor, add your response, save the file, and return to Nuntius. See Figure 13-19.

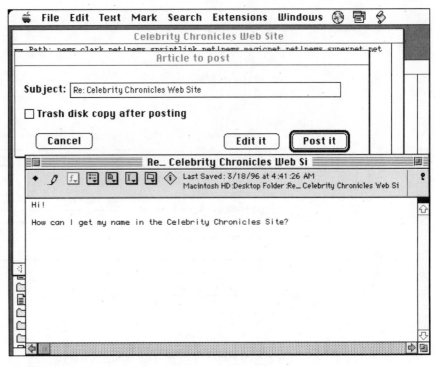

Figure 13-19: Posting a follow-up.

Binary Files: Posting & Decoding

Nuntius doesn't include any means to post binary files. If you want to post a binary file, you'll need to uuencode it yourself, and then read it into your text editor when you're sending a message. If you need to break the file into several different chunks, you'll have to do that yourself, too.

Downloading binary files is a different story. Nuntius has its own multithreaded uudecoder, which makes downloading binary files as easy as highlighting all the parts of the file in the article list and then selecting Extract Binaries from the File menu. As the binary file downloads, Nuntius displays a progress bar to show you how the download is progressing (see Figure 13-20). Also, because Nuntius utilizes multithreading in its design, you won't be paralyzed while the file downloads. Just click on the article list to go back to reading while you're downloading.

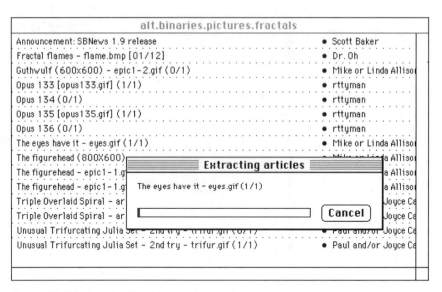

Figure 13-20: Downloading binaries in Nuntius.

Organizing Your Newsgroups

Using Nuntius's subscribe feature is the best way to organize your newsgroups. You can store different lists of newsgroups in different group lists by using the New GroupList, Open, and Save commands from the File menu. You can create newsgroup group lists for all the different types of newsgroups you read and open only the group lists containing the groups you want to read at the time. Figure 13-21 shows Nuntius being used with several different group lists open.

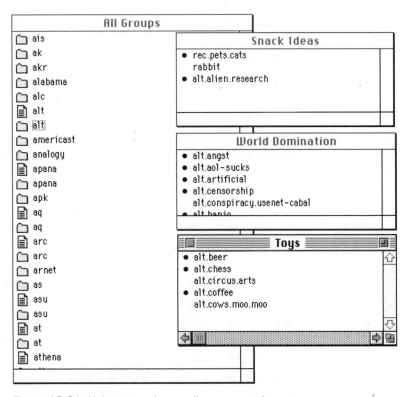

Figure 13-21: Using several group lists to organize your newsgroups.

NEWSHOPPER

Excuse us while we express our unbridled enthusiasm for this news tool. Wow! If you're a Net fiend, hopeless neophile, or just want to be able to get the news you want when you want it, then NewsHopper is the power tool for you.

Unlike most other Mac newsreaders, NewsHopper allows you to read articles offline. You start it up, tell it what newsgroups you want to read, assign filters for the types of articles you're looking for, press Connect, and sit back. NewsHopper jumps online, checks for the news you want, and then downloads only those

527

articles matching the filters you've defined. Of course, you get the subject, authors, and dates of all the other articles, too (you can download them later if you want), but you have to wait for downloading only when NewsHopper encounters an article matching your criteria.

Why would you want to use NewsHopper? Well, let's use Sean as an example. He's a software junkie, a tireless Netsurfer who spends his off hours scouring the Net for cool new Net tools to goof around with. Before he discovered NewsHopper, he would pour over newsgroup subject listings looking for words like "cool," "tool," "new," "beta," or "demo," downloading and reading articles that contained these words. Needless to say, it took some time.

With NewsHopper, all he has to do is define a list of newsgroups he wants to read, set up a few filters containing the words he's looking for, and press the Connect button. He can then go raid the refrigerator, walk his beagles, or read the latest issue of *Sock Puppet Monthly* while NewsHopper searches Usenet for the news and wares he wants. When he returns to his computer, NewsHopper has his news waiting. And, because he can read them offline, he doesn't have to wait for each article to download as he reads it. Sean's a happy camper.

By using a little utility called NewsHopper QuickKeys (available at http://hyperarchive.lcs.mit.edu/HyperArchive/Archive/comm/tcp/news-hopper-quickeys-11.hqx), you can even program your computer to get your news overnight. Wake up every morning to a fresh hard drive o' goodies!

Installing & Configuring NewsHopper

You can get the NewsHopper demo (limited to five newsgroups per news file) at ftp://ftp.demon.co.uk/pub/mac/newshopper/.

NewsHopper uses Internet Config to set your preferences, so you'll need to run Internet Config before starting NewsHopper. Go to the Misc folder (in the NewsHopper folder), open it, and run Internet Config. If you need help, Internet Config comes with an excellent help file called User Documentation. Read it. Internet Config is becoming a standard way to set the Internet preferences for all your Net tools, so you'll want to set it correctly before you start. If you're already using Internet Config, fire up NewsHopper.

Reading & Subscribing

Since NewsHopper is primarily an offline newsreader, configuring the newsgroups you want to read is the key to using it successfully. Using the New option from the File menu, you create a new group of newsgroups you want to read. NewsHopper then creates a folder for your new group. Next, using the Groups menu, you subscribe to the groups you want. Each newsgroup will appear in your News window (see Figure 13-22).

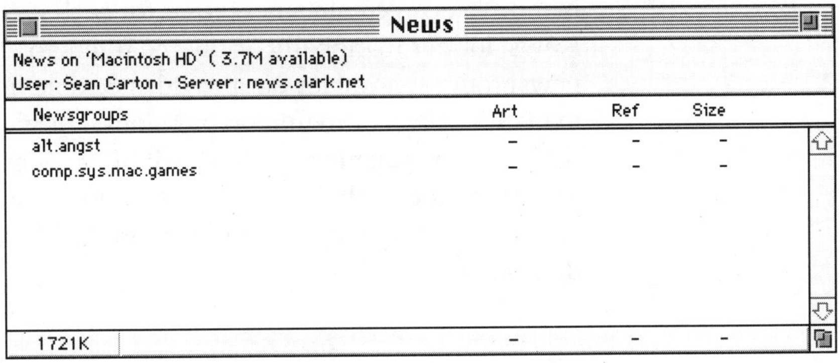

News on 'Macintosh HD' (3.7M available) User : Sean Carton – Server : news.clark.net			
Newsgroups	Art	Ref	Size
alt.angst	–	–	–
comp.sys.mac.games	–	–	–
1721K	–	–	–

Figure 13-22: The News window in NewsHopper.

As you subscribe to each group, you can specify whether you want NewsHopper to get all the articles, a set number of articles, or just the subjects and authors of each article (see Figure 13-23). Once you've established which articles you want NewsHopper to get, you're ready to set up your filters.

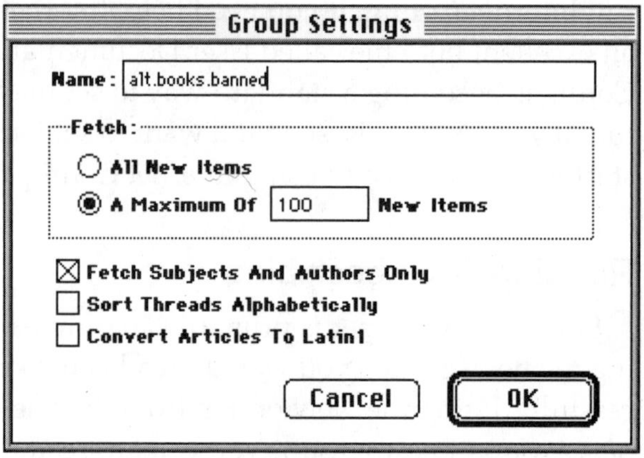

Figure 13-23: Subscribing options in NewsHopper.

You can set filters from the Edit Filters option of the Articles menu. You can create a new filter for each group, or you can set NewsHopper to globally apply the filters to all your subscribed newsgroups. NewsHopper provides flexible filtering, allowing you to match strings or regular expressions. For more information on how to use regular expression, visit http://ugrad-www.cs.colorado. edu/unix/regex.html in any combination of subject, author, header, or even text of the message. See Figure 13-24 for a view of the Filter dialog box.

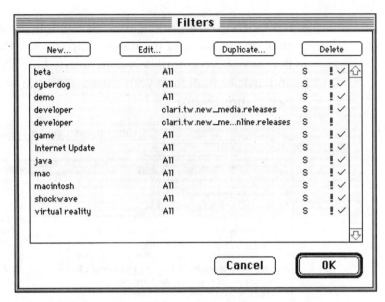

Figure 13-24: The Filter dialog box in NewsHopper.

Once you've set up your filters, select Connect from the File menu, and NewsHopper goes online, downloading the full text of the articles you've specified in the filters, and downloading only the subjects and authors of articles not matching your criteria. As NewsHopper downloads, it displays a handy progress bar to tell you how it's doing (see Figure 13-25).

Figure 13-25: Downloading new articles in NewsHopper.

Once NewsHopper is finished fetching articles, you can double-click on the name of the newsgroup to view the articles. Articles that have been completely downloaded are shown in boldface, and articles matching your filtering criteria will be highlighted (see Figure 13-26).

clari.tw.new_media		
Display: All ▽		
Computer industry friends and foes gather	Reuter / Therese Pol...	3/17/96
APEC finance ministers to set up computer links	Reuters	3/17/96
Infonautics Goes Public 03/15/96	NB / SFO	3/15/96
Japanese students surf net for jobs	UPI	3/15/96
Hongkong Telecom Internet Service Due 03/15/96	NB / HKG	3/15/96
SurfWatch AT&T WorldNet's Parental Control Software 03...	NB / MSP	3/15/96
First Floor Yahoo Exchange Technologies 03/15/96	NB / LAX	3/15/96
****Businesses Choose Intranet Over Internet - Study 03...	NB / SFO	3/15/96
****Java Much More Than A "Lightweight Brow... •	NB / BOS	3/15/96
Netscape pushes to beat Microsoft in Europe	Reuter / William Bos...	3/15/96
Singapore moves to check CD-ROM influence	Reuters	3/15/96
Sun to work with Taiwan on Java •	UPI	3/15/96
FEATURE - Asia tackles dark side of cyberspace	Reuter / Valerie Lee	3/14/96
	Reuter / Valerie Lee	3/15/96
Rival Internet search firms target IPO goldmine!	Reuter / Samuel Perry	3/15/96
Ziff-Davis shuffles business units	Reuters	3/14/96
AT&T receives 212,000 Internet orders	UPI	3/15/96
U.S. Trade Commission cracks down on nine online scams	Reuters	3/14/96
Heading Off HK Telecom, Asia Online Unveils Cybermall 03...	NB / HKG	3/14/96
Ziff A Partner In New Web Venture 03/14/96	NB / TOR	3/14/96
AT&T Internet Service Officially Available 03/14/96	NB / MSP	3/14/96
Chicago Tribune Debuts On Web 03/14/96	NB / MSP	3/14/96
Infoseek's Breakthrough Internet Searching 03/14/96	NB / SFO	3/14/96
Open Market's "3-Tier Architecture" For Web 03/14/96	NB / BOS	3/14/96
Taiwan scraps with China, but only on the Internet	Reuters	3/14/96
AOL on top for now but challenges ahead	Reuter / Therese Pol...	3/14/96
	Reuters	3/14/96

Figure 13-26: The article list in NewsHopper.

Posting an Article

Posting articles with NewsHopper is standard fare. You can select an article you want to follow up, post a new article, or forward an article via e-mail (using the E-mail Helper you've defined in

Internet Config). If you post an article, NewsHopper will open a window for you to type your message in, or you can configure the program to launch an external editor (using the General option from the Settings menu, which you'll find in the Edit menu). Figure 13-27 shows an article being posted using NewsHopper's internal editor.

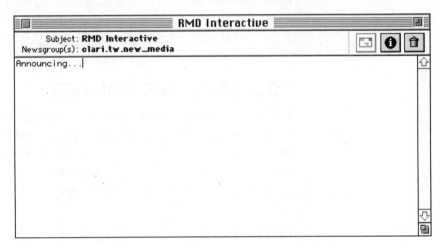

Figure 13-27: Posting an article in NewsHopper.

Binary Files: Posting & Decoding

NewsHopper doesn't provide any automatic binary file posting facilities. If you need to post a binary file, you'll have to uuencode it yourself and either paste it into a new message in NewsHopper or open and send it using an external editor.

If you want to download and decode a binary posting, NewsHopper uses the uudecoder you set up in Internet Config to decode your binary messages. In our tests, NewsHopper didn't do a very good job of decoding multi-part binaries. You may want to rely on Yet Another NewsWatcher for that.

TIP

If you're using NewsHopper to read a binaries newsgroup, make sure you have it set to download only subjects and headers of all the files in the newsgroup. If you set NewsHopper to download full articles, prepare to wait a long time while it downloads every part of every binary posted to the newsgroup. This could literally be megabytes of files, so take care.

USENET POWER UTILITIES

For most of you, even the power users, the newsreaders we've covered so far will fulfill all your news needs. However, there are special cases in which you may need some extra tools to get the most out of Usenet. Here are some of the best utilities to help you quickly download, filter, and manage Usenet news.

NNTP Sucker

If you have the overwhelming desire to download every newsgroup off the Net, or if you're a sysadmin for a LAN in which not everyone has access to the Net but would still like to be able to read Usenet news, NNTP Sucker may be the answer.

NNTP Sucker literally sucks newsgroups from NNTP servers (news servers) and deposits the downloaded newsgroups on your hard drive. Depending on the speed of your connection, your patience, and the size of your hard drive, NNTP Sucker can be used to get anything from one to thousands of newsgroups so that you can read them locally.

If you want to give NNTP Sucker a try, you can download it from the InfoMac HyperArchive at http://hyperarchive.lcs.mit. edu/HyperArchive/Archive/comm/tcp/nntp-sucker-15.hqx. It comes with a complete help file and is fairly easy to configure. Most of the information you'll need to enter is in one dialog box (see Figure 13-28). NNTP Sucker can be configured to run at selected time periods, so it's a great tool for anyone who wants to have his or her own personal Usenet news server.

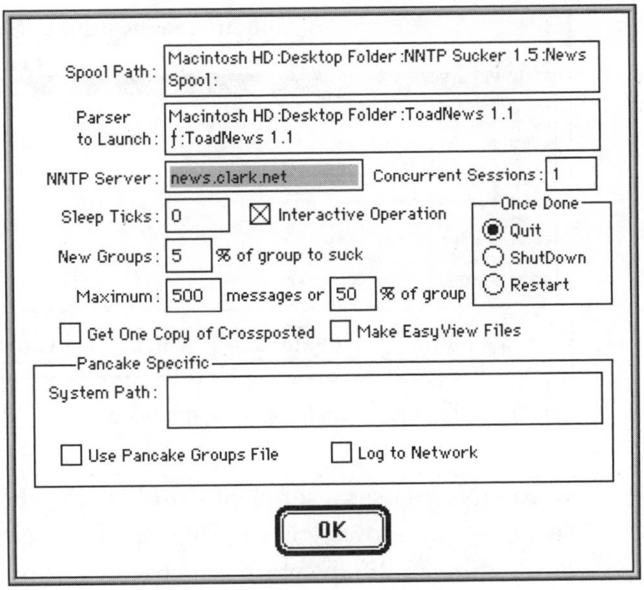

Figure 13-28: The configuration dialog box in NNTP Sucker.

There's only one catch. NNTP Sucker downloads raw news spool files. These files contain all the messages in the newsgroup that you've downloaded. To get at 'em, you'll need an unbatching program like ToadNews.

ToadNews

ToadNews (available at http://hyperarchive.lcs.mit.edu/HyperArchive/Archive/comm/uucp/toad-news-11.hqx) works with NNTP Sucker (or any other Mac UUCP or TCP/IP newsgroup batch downloader) to unbatch Usenet news batch files and make them available so they can be read by an offline newsreader. It can be configured to automatically unbatch any news files it finds in a preconfigured news spool directory. Used in conjunction with NNTP Sucker, ToadNews lets you run your own personal Usenet news service for your LAN, BBS, or just for yourself (if you happen to be really compulsive about these things!).

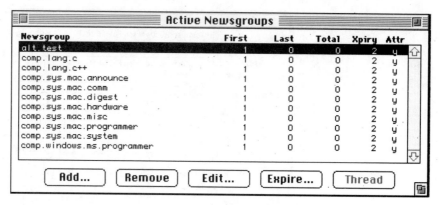

Figure 13-29: ToadNews Newsgroups window.

ToadNews uses a series of simple dialog boxes to configure its services and allows you to utilize a simple Newsgroups window (see Figure 13-29) to set up which newsgroups you want to uncompress. In addition, you can use the ToadNews Scheduler window (see Figure 13-30) to schedule automatic tasks such as threading, expiring, or unbatching.

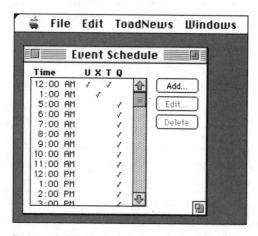

Figure 13-30: ToadNews Scheduler window.

ToadNews can run completely unattended, so if you've got an extra Mac with a large hard drive lying around, you can provide news services to anyone you'd like connecting to your server. With the combination of threading, posting, expiring, and unbatching, the NNTP Sucker/ToadNews combo offers a great solution for any small LAN or BBS operator who wants to provide news but doesn't want the hassles associated with setting up a complicated UNIX box.

rnMac

So you've got ToadNews and NNTP Sucker up and running. Your office is excited because they'll be able to waste tons of time . . . er . . . we mean *do serious research* using Usenet. There's only one problem. How do they read the files unpacked by ToadNews? rnMac is the answer!

rnMac (available from http://hyperarchive.lcs.mit.edu/ HyperArchive/Archive comm/uucp/rn-mac-13b9.hqx) is a Mac offline newsgroup reader that can function quite well on a LAN (assuming the user has access to a shared server) to read Net news processed by the combination of NNTP Sucker and ToadNews.

A port of the famous UNIX newsreader rn, rnMac isn't pretty (see Figure 13-31), but it gets the job done. While it doesn't sport the bells and whistles of Yet Another NewsWatcher or Nuntius, it does provide an adequate interface for anyone who just wants to dabble in Usenet.

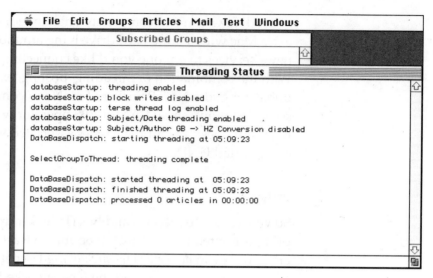

Figure 13-31: The rnMac interface.

MOVING ON

No matter which way you get your news, there's one thing that's always true—if there's one place where you can find tons o' facts (and FAQs!), stimulating conversation, wild behavior, and high weirdness, it's Usenet. We hope you found some useful ideas in this chapter for navigating the anarchistic territory of Usenet news.

In the next chapter, we'll be leaving the world of text-based, person-to-person communications via e-mail and Usenet and moving into the multimedia wonders of the World Wide Web. We'll look at the browser clients you can use to access this rapidly expanding dimension of Cyberspace.

Probably no single technological development since television has changed the way the world experiences media like the Web. It provides a place where almost anyone in the world (those with Net access, anyway) can become an amateur or professional publisher of text, pictures, sound, video, or animation: you name it, and someone's probably putting it on the Web as we speak. The

Web is the hot and hyped place to be at the moment. It's a place where fortunes are being made (and lost), celebrities are rising (and falling), and new ideas in media delivery (the good, bad, and ugly) are being brainstormed and experimented with. It's arguably the most incredible orgy of free expression and burgeoning free enterprise the world has ever seen. And this incredible universe can be yours for the cruising—if you have the right tools. Lucky for you, they're just a page turn away.

## Chapter 14

Mac Web Power Tools

Ahhh . . . yes, the World Wide Web! It's hard to look anywhere these days without running into a reference to it. URLs in advertisements are as common as fax numbers. Having your own home page has become a newbie rite of passage. Just about every time you turn on the TV, listen to the radio, or open a newspaper, there's a story about an organization's new Web presence. Like it or not, the World Wide Web is fast becoming the world's new media appendage.

In fact, the Web has become so ubiquitous that most new users think the Web is the Net. Of course, advanced users know that there's more to the Internet than just browsing pretty pictures on the Web. But still, it's getting tougher and tougher not to spend most of your online time in Webspace.

Browsers are your gateway to the World Wide Web. And while all Web browsers basically do the same thing—render HTML into pictures and text—the way they do it and the special functionality of each browser gives them their own unique strengths and weaknesses.

In this chapter we'll explore the three most popular World Wide Web browser programs for the Macintosh. First, we'll take an in-depth look at Netscape Navigator, the browser that took the world by storm when it was first introduced just two short years ago. It is quickly becoming the standard for Web walkers worldwide (say *that* 20 times!). Next, we'll take a quick look at the two runners-up in the browser race: Microsoft's Internet Explorer and the venerable NCSA Mosaic. Even if you're a certified Navigator evangelist, you should check these two programs out because they offer features you might find useful when you want a break from browsing with Navigator. Table 14-1 gives you a brief comparison of how the different browsers stack up.

As you probably know, one of the major innovations in Web browsers is the ability to use external programs, called *helper applications*, to view data formats that the browser doesn't natively support. Helper apps let you view video, listen to real-time audio, and cruise 3D virtual worlds, all automatically. The latest advance in helper apps are plug-ins, programs that can be added to the browser and work from within it. While these helper and plug-in programs are an integral part of getting the most out of the Web, we're not going to give them the in-depth treatment here (mainly in the interest of keeping things focused). For more information on helper apps and plug-ins, check out Part VII, "The Power User's Guide to the Web."

	Netscape Navigator	Microsoft Internet Explorer	NCSA Mosaic	Comments
Tables	Yes	Yes	Yes	Supports HTML 2.0 table-layout.
Frames	Yes	No	No	Supports multiple windowing frames.
Backgrounds	Yes	Yes	Yes	Supports GIF background patterns.
Java Support	Yes, Java applets and JavaScript.	No, plans for future support.	No	Supports Sun's Java programs (applets) and JavaScript.
USENET Newsreader	Yes, separate news reading and posting features.	Yes, reading and posting	Supports reading of Usenet news inline	Reads Usenet newsgroups.
Email	Yes, incoming and outgoing with a full-featured e-mail program.	Yes, outgoing only	Yes, outgoing only with mailto: URL	Sends/receives e-mail from within program.
Plug-ins	Yes, full range of plug-ins for inline viewing of proprietary file formations, animation, VRML, sound, and video.	Yes, uses Netscape plug-ins.	No	Supports extensions through plug-in technology.
Special Features	GIF Animation, pop-up navigation menus, drag-and-drop for graphics and text.	Marquee scrolling text, inline video for AVI and QuickTime, supports VRML and GIF animations, Supports background sounds.	None	Includes unique formatting features.
Power Macintosh Version	Yes	Yes	Yes	PowerMac native program.
Windows Version	Yes, Windows 3.1, Windows NT, and Windows95	Yes. Windows 3.1, Windows NT, and Windows95	Yes. Windows 3.1, Windows NT, and Windows95	Good for multiplatform families and businesses.
Ease of Use	Easy	Easy, interface not as intuitive as Navigator.	Easy	Easy for experienced users.
Cost	Free evaluation version, $49 for licensed copy	Freeware	Freeware	Can't beat the price.
Comments	Navigator has become the de facto online standard.	Good, solid performance; inline images seem to load faster than they do in Navigator, with the addition of VRML and plug-in support, could be a contender for Navigator's spot.	Clean, bare-bones browser for people on the go, Doesn't support fancy animations and plug-ins but is fine for general browsing.	

Table 14-1: Comparison of Web browsers.

NETSCAPE NAVIGATOR

Netscape Communications' Navigator program is the Cadillac of World Wide Web browsers. It supports just about every innovation that people are bringing to the World Wide Web, including extensions to the HTML language that no other program supports. And while Navigator's fast and loose interpretation of HTML has irritated some Net purists, everyone else is scrambling to keep up with its innovative features. What exactly are these features, you ask? Check out Table 14-2 for a current list.

Feature	Description
Java	Supports Sun's Java language.
JavaScript	Supports JavaScript, an API for scripting browser behavior.
Frames	Displays multiple windows of information in one screen.
Tables	Provides extensive support for tabular formatting elements.
Background patterns	Supports GIF files as repeating background patterns in WWW pages.
Plug-ins	Supports third-party plug in modules that allow Navigator to display inline sounds, video, and other forms of media.
Mail client	Includes a full-featured e-mail client for sending and receiving mail.
News reader	Includes a full-featured Usenet newsreader for reading and posting articles to Usenet newsgroups.
Client-side image maps	Implements standard for imbedding image-map information within HTML code.
Progressive JPEG	Supports progressive JPEG image file format.
Special HTML features	Includes font colors, background colors, DIV text alignment tags, word wrapping/unwrapping, META tags for MIME support, configurable horizontal rules (HR tags), multiple font sizes, centering, and more control over image alignments through IMG tag extensions.
Automatic proxy configuration	Allows flexible proxy configurations for firewalls.

Feature	Description
HTML uploading	Can be configured to allow file uploads through HTML forms.
FTP uploading	You can upload files can be uploaded to FTP sites using Macintosh drag and drop.
Targeted windows	Automatically opens a new window if window targeting is used to refer to a new page.
Improved security	Uses a 300 bits of secure information when sending secure information.

Table 14-2: Special features in Navigator.

Yow! That's a lot of features, and most are supported only by Navigator. It's easy to see why everyone's using it. You should be, too. Read on to find out how.

Who's This "Mozilla" I Keep Hearin' About?

If you've spent any time hanging out on the Web with Navigator, you've probably bumped into the word Mozilla. When you mail a message from Netscape Mail, for instance, the X-mailer reference in the mail header reads: X-Mailer: Mozilla 2.0. Seasoned Netheads often refer to Navigator itself as Mozilla.

So who or what is Mozilla? It was the nickname for the browser project that eventually became officially known as Navigator. The company bigwigs obviously didn't want such a beastly and inelegant name for their killer app, but Mozilla had already taken on a life of its own. Lots of people still refer to Navigator as Mozilla and the little green dragon who haunts Netscape's Web site is named Mozilla.

Getting & Installing Netscape Navigator 2.0

With the entire online world trying to grab the latest copy of Navigator, getting your own copy requires a little effort. According to Netscape's reports, their servers log over 45 million hits a day—over one *billion* a month! It's enough to clog the biggest data pipe. Luckily, Netscape Corporation has over 30 FTP servers to handle the load, so while you may have to wait your turn in line until you can get in, you won't wait long.

TIP

To avoid the crowds, don't try to grab the new version of Navigator the day it's released. You've lived without it up to this point—you can probably wait a few days. Once the smoke's cleared, try logging on to the Netscape site during off-peak hours.

To download Navigator, go to http://home.netscape.com, and follow the links. At the time this book was written, the current Navigator release was 2.01, with Java support fully integrated into the browser. Download the latest version, uncompress it, and use the Installer program to put it on your hard drive.

Good Eatin' for Netscape-Hungry Netsurfers

If this brief taste of Netscape leaves you hankerin' for more, you should check out *The Official Netscape Navigator 2.0 Book* by Phil James (Netscape Press, 1996). A five-hundred (plus!) page smorgasbord of Netscape facts, it'll be sure to satisfy even the most gluttonous of Navigator gourmands. But it won't help you recover from overdone metaphors. Sorry.

Configuring Netscape Navigator

Configuring Navigator correctly can mean the difference between just browsing and really surfing the Net. What do we mean by that? Well, Navigator allows you to do a lot more than just read Web pages. You can read and post Usenet news, send and receive e-mail, and view a wide variety of multimedia file types—all without leaving your browser. However, to take advantage of these features, you'll have to make sure everything is set up correctly.

All of the configuration you have to do within Navigator (with the exception of installing plug-ins) in done from the Options menu. From this menu you can configure the following components of Navigator:

❐ General Preferences

❐ Mail and News Preferences

❐ Network Preferences

❐ Security Preferences

General Preferences

When you pull down the Options menu and select General Preferences, you'll see a configuration dialog box like the one shown in Figure 14-1. From here, you can configure Navigator's user interface options—the stuff you see and how Navigator handles the data it encounters on the Web. You can move between each section by clicking on the tab at the top of the dialog box.

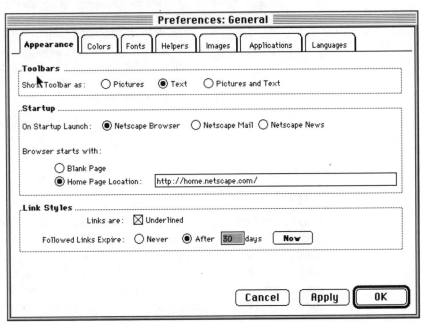

Figure 14-1: General Preferences dialog box in Navigator.

With the exception of the Helpers and Application tabs, these options configure the look-and-feel, not the actual operation, of Navigator. Table 14-3 describes what each option controls.

Section	Configuration Options
Appearance	Controls the appearance of the toolbar and styles of links. Allows you to specify Navigator startup options. (See the Tip that follows this table.)
Colors	Configures colors for text, backgrounds, links, visited links, and toolbar. Note: Unless you select the Always Use Mine button in the Colors section, pages using Navigator's HTML extensions can override the color choices you make.
Fonts	Allows you to choose the fonts you want Navigator to use when displaying fixed and proportional fonts. Also allows selection of character encoding language so that international characters are displayed correctly.
Helpers	Configures helper applications to display various forms of media within and outside of Navigator.
Images	Toggles between displaying images during loading or after loading.
Applications	Options for choosing applications to assist with Telnet, TN3270, and source viewing. Also allows you to select the default download folder.
Languages	Allows you to specify the language you want to use as your default. Servers having the capability to serve pages with different languages. Use this option to decide which language to send.

Table 14-3: The General Preferences dialog box configuration options.

TIP

If you want Netscape Navigator to start with a local home page, but don't know how to enter in the correct URL for a local file, just start Navigator, choose Open File from the File menu, find your local home page file, and open it. Copy (using Command+C) the URL for your local page from the Location area at the top of the browser window, open the General Options dialog box, and paste (using Command+V) the URL into the Home Page Location URL field.

Mail & News Preferences

Here's where you configure Navigator's e-mail and Usenet news options. By now, most of these settings should be familiar. Table 14-4 describes Navigator's mail and news configuration options.

Section	Configuration Options
Appearance	Changes the fonts used for displaying e-mail messages and Usenet articles. Also allows you to choose the type style and size used for displaying quoted text.
Composition	Controls MIME compliance in messages so that MIME attachments show up correctly, how messages are saved and copied, and the quoting behavior in replies.
Servers	Allows you to define which NNTP, SMTP, and POP servers to use for Usenet news and e-mail. Also configures maximum sizes for messages and automated e-mail–checking behavior.
Identity	Here's where you specify your name, e-mail address, reply-to address, and organization. You can also configure signature file behavior.
Organization	Configures behavior for passwords, message threading, and message sorting for both e-mail and news.

Table 14-4: Mail and news preferences in Navigator.

Network Preferences

This section allows you to configure how you want Navigator to act while you're on the Internet. From here, you can configure the cache options, the number of connections, and any proxy servers you might need. Table 14-5 explains:

Section	Configuration Options
Cache	Configures the directory to use when caching documents, the maximum size of the cache, and how often documents should be cached.
Connections	Controls the number of simultaneous connections and the size of the connection buffer.
Proxies	Allows you choose to use no proxies, manually configured proxy servers, or an automatic proxy configuration.

Table 14-5: Network preferences in Navigator.

TIP

The number of simultaneous connections you can handle refers to both HTTP as well as FTP connections. If you're using a modem to connect to the Net, you shouldn't use any more than four simultaneous connections. Increase the number of connections as your connection speed increases.

Security Preferences

As online commerce becomes more popular, how your browser secures your personal information becomes more important. These options allow you to configure how Netscape handles the security of your personal information and how it handles the use of security certificates (documents that identify a particular commercial entity as secure, so that you can feel safe using it when you send your credit card numbers or other information). Table 14-6 sketches out Navigator's security options.

Section	Configuration Options
General	This section allows you to turn off JavaScript if you want. This section also controls how and when Navigator notifies you of any potential security risks.
Site Certificates	This section maintains the list of valid site certificates. Site certificates are used for positively identifying sites to prevent anyone who may be trying to spoof, or impersonate, a site. You can edit and delete site certificates from this section.

Table 14-6: Security preferences in Navigator.

Are There Security Holes in Navigator 2.01?

Rumors started to fly fast and furiously on the Net in late February '96 when Leonard Stein's World Wide Web Security FAQ (version 1.2.0, February 28, 1996) reported that there were some serious security holes in Navigator 2.0. According to Stein, the JavaScript feature of 2.0 could be used to gain access to a user's private information (e-mail address, URL history, directory of user's hard drive, etc.) and to send that info to another remote machine without the user's knowledge. This process is called *softlifting*. Within a matter of hours, Netscape was fending off multiple phone calls from journalists and others wanting to know what Netscape was going to do about these security problems.

It turns out that part of the FAQ information was inaccurate. These vulnerabilities were found in versions of Netscape 2.*x*. Most of them were fixed in the full release of 2.0. Several other holes were fixed and implemented in 2.01. Even after this clarification, however, the Security FAQ was still concerned about the potential vulnerabilities in JavaScript and was recommending that Netscape build in some mechanism for turning JavaScript off. Netscape has done just this with the Disable Javascript option on the Security\General tab.

Browsing: Walkin' the Web With Style

If you've spent any amount of time wandering around the Web with one browser or another you've probably learned that it ain't rocket science. Basically, it's pointing and clicking and ooh-ing and ah-ing at all the cool sights and sounds. At its most mindless, it's not unlike channel surfing your television. "Mouse potato" is the slang for this Net equivalent of the couch spud.

But, there are a few cool browsing tips and tricks beyond slavishly pressing the Forward and Back buttons and clicking on hyperlinks. In this section, we'll let you in on a few features that might help make your time online more productive.

Getting There & Back Again

Entering URLs is obviously at the heart of Web browsing. Navigator offers a number of options for doing this, depending on where your hands are when you need to get a URL box up and at 'em. You can choose Open Location from the File menu (Figure 14-2), press Command+L, or enter a URL into the Location text box at the top of the Navigator window. The Location text box functions just like any other text area, so you can use the cut and paste options on any URLs you might come across in your online travels.

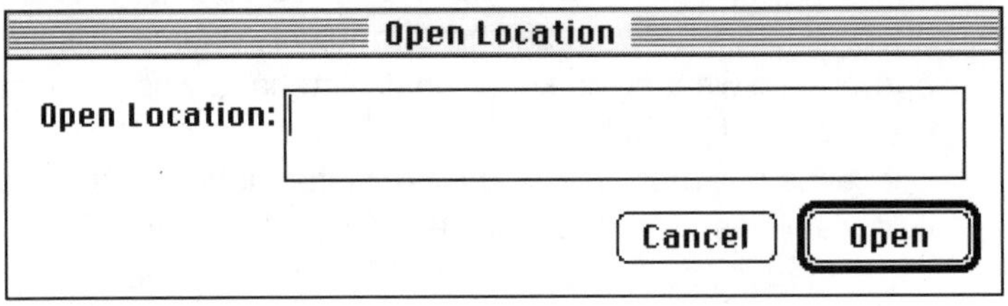

Figure 14-2: The Open Location dialog box in Navigator.

Navigator really shows its intelligence by providing a few handy shortcuts for entering URLs. You don't have to type the ubiquitous "http://" before the URL you're entering. If you don't type "http://", Netscape Navigator assumes that you're trying to go to a location on the Web and inserts the http prefix itself. But that's not all! If the address that you're trying to reach is a commercial one, a www.*somename*.com address, all you have to do is type the *somename* part, and Navigator puts an "http://www." at the beginning and a ".com" at the end. For example, if you wanted to go to the ever-present Yahoo index (http://www.yahoo.com), all you have to do is type **yahoo**, and Navigator does the rest! If you're accessing an FTP server that has ftp in the address (say ftp.netscape.com), you don't have to enter the "ftp://" prefix, but you do have to add the ".com" on the end.

Http:// in Other Words

Giving people URLs over the phone can be a big pain. Having to say "http colon forward slash forward slash" and "www" over and over again seems silly. Netscape has helped the situation with their URL shortcuts, but since not everyone's using Navigator or savvy enough to know about that you mean http:// for any Web site, it's still a problem. "Triple-dub" is a word that some net surfers at HotWired came up with for shortening "www." It still would be great if someone came up with a simple, elegant, one-word term for "http://www." If you think of a good one, send us e-mail—we'd love to hear it.

Besides manually entering URLs to move around, you can use the Back and Forward buttons to move back and forth through your history list of sites you've visited. Or, you can go directly to the Go menu and pick an item off the history list. But that's the old way. Navigator offers pop-up navigation menus that appear with the click of the mouse. Here's how they work. Hold down the mouse button in a blank spot on the Web page you're visiting (not on a link and not a picture) to access a pop-up menu similar to the one in Figure 14-3.

Figure 14-3: The navigation pop-up menu in Navigator.

Pretty handy, eh? Rather than going all the way to the toolbar to move between pages, you can just hold down the mouse button and select Back or Forward.

Even more interesting things happen if you click and hold the mouse on a link. Try it and see. You'll get a menu like the one shown in Figure 14-4.

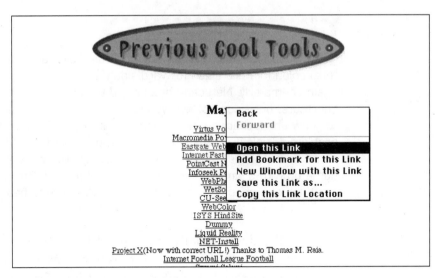

Figure 14-4: The link pop-up menu in Navigator.

In addition to being able to jump back and forth between Web pages, you can:

❐ Open this Link: Accomplishes the same as clicking on the link.

❐ Add Bookmark for this Link: Adds the URL specified in the link to your bookmark list.

❐ New window with this Link: Use this function when you want to check out a specific hyperlink but don't want to lose track of where you are. The new page will appear in its own separate window. Browse around, and when you're finished, close the window to go back to where you came from.

❐ Save this Link (as either a text or raw HTML file): This function is particularly useful if you know that a link refers to an article that you wanted to save. If you choose this option, you can save that article as a text file for later perusing. Or, if you want to take a gander at someone's HTML code, this function lets you save the HTML without having to visit the page.

❒ Copy this Link Location (to the Clipboard): Using this function, you can copy the URL for the link directly to the Clipboard so that you can paste it into another program. When writing this book, we used this method all the time to copy links. You didn't actually think we typed all this stuff, did you?

If you hold down the mouse button on an image, you'll get a few more choices:

❒ View this Image: Navigator will display the image by itself in whatever helper application you're configured as your viewer for the picture type you're clicking on. If you've set Navigator as the viewer of choice, the picture will appear in a new window by itself.

❒ Save this Image as: Allows you to save the image file to disk. If you have System 7.5 and the drag and drop extensions installed, you can accomplish the same feat just by clicking the mouse button on the image and quickly dragging it to where you want to save it.

❒ Copy this Image: This choice copies the image to the clipboard, ready to be pasted into whatever document you wish.

TIP

Using Copy this Image is a great way to build your collection of cool desktop patterns. If you find an image you want to grace your desktop, just hold down the mouse button, select Copy this image, go to the Control Panels folder, open the Desktop Patterns application, and press Paste. Poof! A new Desktop pattern!

❒ Copy this Image Location: Copies the URL for the image into the clipboard.

❐ Load this Image: If you have problems loading an image, click on the broken image (or missing image) icon, hold down the mouse button, and select this choice. Navigator will attempt to load the image again. See Figure 14-5.

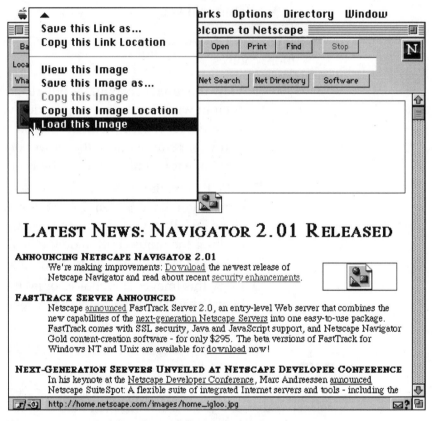

Figure 14-5: The two image icons—showing images not loaded.

Frames & Navigation

One of the major innovations in Navigator 2.0 is the ability for Web page designers to separate their pages into separate "frames," or sub-windows. This allows them to keep one part of the page (such as a navigation icon bar) visible all the time while the other parts of the page change. Check out the Navigator home page (http://home.netscape.com) for an example.

Even if you thought that frames were the coolest thing since sliced silicon wafers, you may have been frustrated when you tried to go to a previous frame by hitting the Back button. Instead of going to a previous frame, you probably found yourself back at the page you visited before the one with frames! What's going on?

With frames, one page can actually contain many HTML documents, each with its own unique URL. The trouble is that Navigator doesn't make any assumptions about which frame you're currently viewing when you press the Back button. If this drives you crazy, despair not! Just hold down the mouse button inside of the frame you want to back up in, and Navigator will present you with a special frames navigator. See Figure 14-6.

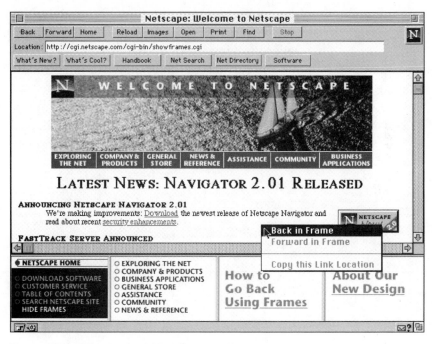

Figure 14-6: Going back within a frame in Navigator.

Bookmarks

The Web has become unimaginably huge with over 26,000 commercial sites alone and probably millions of personal home pages. Finding your way back to an interesting site can be difficult if you didn't take the time to write down the URL. Or, if you didn't save it to your Bookmark list.

Navigator's Bookmarks function allows you to keep your own personal "hotlist" of sites you've visited and want to come back to again. When you get to a site you want to visit regularly, all it takes is a quick Command+D (or a visit to the Add Bookmark option on the Bookmarks menu) to save it for later browsing. If you want to return to that site later, all you have to do is pick it from the Bookmarks menu.

However, with all the interesting sites out there, it doesn't take long for a bookmark list to get out of hand with all the bookmarks becoming jumbled together. Fortunately, Navigator provides a fairly complete set of tools for customizing and organizing your ever-growing list of bookmarks.

You can access the Bookmarks list directly by selecting the Bookmarks option from the Window menu. Navigator will display a narrow window containing all your bookmarks. You'll also notice that the top menu changes, too. In addition to some of the ordinary Navigator functions, you'll find new menu choices, which are described in Table 14-7.

Menu	New Option	Function
File	Import Bookmarks	Imports a saved Bookmarks file. Useful for sharing bookmarks with friends.
	What's New	Checks modification dates on all or selected bookmarks. Tells you which locations have changed since the last time you visited.
	Save Bookmark File As	Exports a Bookmarks file.
Edit	Delete Bookmark	Deletes a selected bookmark.
Item	Edit Bookmark	Opens editing dialog box for selected bookmark. Allows you to view and change the name of the bookmark, the URL, and the description. Also provides information on the date last visited, date the bookmark was added, and any information on aliases.
	Go to Bookmark	Goes to Web location specified in bookmark.
	Sort Bookmarks	Sorts selected bookmarks alphabetically.
	Insert Bookmark	Creates a new bookmark from scratch.
	Insert Folder	Creates and inserts a new Bookmark folder.
	Insert Separator	Inserts a separator line into the bookmark list.
	Make Alias	Makes an alias of a bookmark to store the reference in another part of the list.
	Set to New Bookmarks Folder	Sets currently selected folder as the default folder all new bookmarks are added to.
	Set to Bookmark Menu Folder	Chooses folder to be displayed in Bookmarks menu.

Table 14-7: Bookmarks menu options in Navigator.

Pay close attention to the What's New? function. Think of this function as your own personal Web robot, skipping nimbly across the Net, discovering new information. All you have to do is select the bookmarks you want to check, select What's New? from the File menu, and let Navigator do the work. When it's finished, the little bookmark icons next to the bookmark entries will change to indicate their changed status. See Figure 14-7.

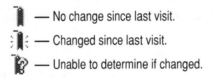

— No change since last visit.

— Changed since last visit.

— Unable to determine if changed.

Figure 14-7: The What's New? icons in Navigator.

Why such a useful function languishes in relative obscurity in the Bookmarks menus, we'll never know. Don't you make the same mistake. Make a note to use it often. It's a great way to keep up on your Web surfing!

Mail & News

After the release of Netscape Navigator 2.01 with its attendant e-mail, Usenet news, and Java features, the folks at Netscape corporate headquarters have made a big stink about not referring to their product as a "browser." No, Navigator is a "platform," a tool for finding your way through all aspects of online life. And with the mail and news features, it's easy to see why.

Besides being a killer browser, Navigator is now a full-featured e-mail client and newsreader. While old versions had the ability only to send e-mail and read Usenet news, the new 2.0 (or later) version includes a complete suite of tools for staying in touch, both reading mail and posting to newsgroups.

Sending & Receiving E-Mail

Just one look at the e-mail client in Navigator (accessible from the Windows menu) , and you know that it's a serious e-mail tool. With it, you can do just about everything you need to do to read mail except filtering messages. See Figure 14-8.

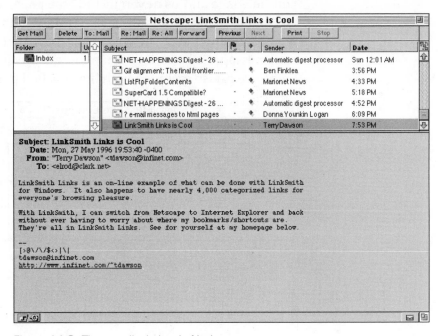

Figure 14-8: The e-mail window in Navigator.

Navigator's mail not only provides most of the features you'd find in a stand-alone mail reader like Eudora (except filtering), but it also allows you to send multimedia messages with sound, graphics, styled text, and hyperlinks.

If you want to read your e-mail, you'll have to go to the Netscape Mail window. However, if you're browsing the Web and want to tell someone (or show someone) a site you've come across, all you have to do is select Mail Document from the File menu. Netscape Mail will pop up a window where you can type your message and will even include the page you're currently viewing as an attachment. See Figure 14-9. If the recipient views it with Navigator, he or she will see the page embedded in your e-mail message. A hyperlink that allows the recipient to go directly to the site is also included with the attached page.

Figure 14-9: Sending an HTML attachment with Navigator.

Posting & Reading Usenet News

Navigator's facilities for posting and reading Usenet news are adequate but not nearly as complete as you'll find in a stand-alone news client. While it does most of the basic tasks well, it does lack the important filtering mechanisms that make YAN such a useful program.

Accessible from the Windows menu, the Netscape newsreader gives you the ability to read and post news, view articles by threads, and even download binary attachments. In fact, the one feature that makes Netscape News very useful is its ability to display uuencoded pictures in-line as they download—you don't have to wait for the whole file to download to see what you're getting. All in all, we can't recommend Netscape News to the power user, but for newbies, and those in a pinch, it will let you read newsgroups and post articles.

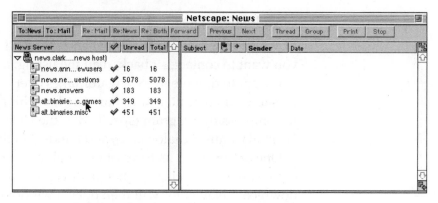

Figure 14-10: The Netscape News reader.

The major drawback for using these facilities as your only news and e-mail programs is that they suffer from a cluttered and confusing interface. Even though you can change the width and order of the column heading by clicking and dragging, unless you have a 21-inch monitor (or larger!), you'll probably have trouble seeing all the information in the columns. Moving to a multi-window interface (such as the ones Yet Another NewsWatcher and Eudora have) would clear this problem up. We'll have to wait and see if Netscape tweaks Navigator's interface in the future. We think they'll have to if they want to bolster that platform claim.

File Transfer

Now that Navigator can upload and download files using FTP, is it time to throw out your dedicated FTP program? Maybe in the future, but not just yet. While Netscape does include some pretty nice FTP file-handling features, it still lacks the flexibility that a stand-alone FTP program like Anarchie or Fetch offers. However, for casual downloading, it's hard to beat the ease of use that Navigator offers.

Downloading Files

Downloading files is a snap. Just enter the URL for the FTP site you want to contact, sit back, read the listing, and click on the files you want to download. Navigator takes over and downloads the files to your computer, automatically launching the appropriate uncompressing program (specified in the Helpers part of the General Controls dialog box), and hands you the file.

One of the better features of using Navigator FTP is that you can just point and click to change directories and select files to download. Navigator will then open a window with a progress indicator showing you how long your download will take. Check the time, go grab a cup o'joe (can you tell we drink a lot of cof-fee?), and when the time's up, your file will be downloaded and uncompressed.

Since Navigator 2.0 introduced floating download windows for file transfers, it also enabled a really useful new feature—simulta-neous downloads. Depending on the speed of your line and the number of simultaneous connections you configured in the Con-nections section of the Network Options dialog box, you can download a number of files at once. And even though each simultaneous connection slows the speed of the other connections, usually you can eke every last bit of bandwidth out of your downloads by doing them all at once. Figure 14-11 shows a session with three simultaneous downloads.

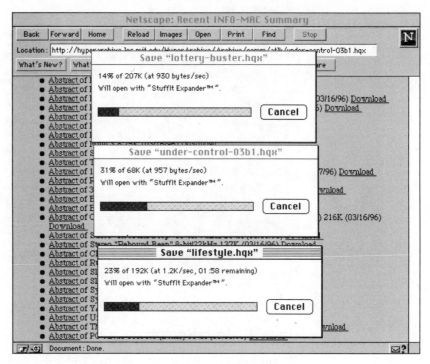

Figure 14-11: Simultaneously FTPing three files with Navigator.

Uploading Files

Navigator will even let you upload files to FTP sites that accept incoming files. Better yet, all you have to do is drag the file off the desktop, drop it in the Navigator window, and it's headed on its merry way. You must have the Drag Manager and Macintosh Drag and Drop installed for this to work, but if you've got System 7.5 (or later), you're good to go. Figure 14-12 shows a file about to be uploaded.

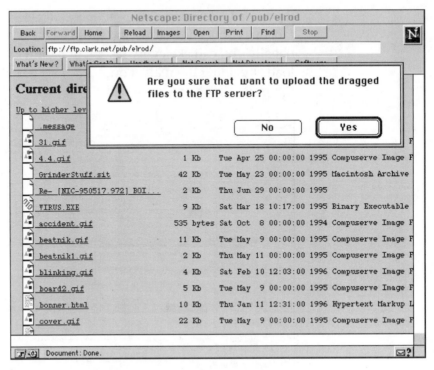

Figure 14-12: Uploading a file using Netscape FTP.

Java & JavaScript

If you keep up with the computer industry at all, you've probably heard a lot of buzz about a new thing called Java. Now, even though hackers (and writers!) like to guzzle coffee while sitting at their computers, the talk about Java has nothing to do with caffeine and everything to do with a new computer language and virtual operating system that could have a serious impact on the way we deal with computers.

No matter what kind of computer you have, you have to buy platform-specific programs that often do many tasks. If you're using a word processor, the copy that you use will probably run only on a Mac, not on a PC. Also, if your word processor is like ours (we won't tell you which one, but its initials are MSW), it probably is choked with memory-hungry features that no one ever uses. All in all, the current state of software development makes for difficult (and expensive) programming problems for developers.

Java hopes to change all that. Instead of having to write code specific to only one type of machine, Java programs are cross-platform; they run on whatever computer is running the Java interpreter. Java programs run on a "virtual computer" created inside your machine, and one Java program written for one type of computer will pretty much run on any other.

Also, Java is an object-oriented development system, allowing programmers to write small programs called *applets* that can be executed on the client's system. And because these programs are so small, the developers of Java are now offering the vision of a world in which instead of buying software, you lease it, grabbing applets off the Net as you need them for a specific task.

What's all this mean to Navigator? Navigator is the first browser available for the Mac that runs Java applets. Not only does it run the code, but it can run applets inline with Web pages, allowing Web designers to insert animation, scrolling text, games, interactive forms, and live data right in to a Web page.

TIP

Running Java applets can be pretty memory-intensive. For best results, increase the Preferred Size of the memory to at least 8000K by selecting Get Info in the Finder while the Navigator application is selected.

And what's JavaScript? Actually, although it shares a lot of the same syntax with Java, it's not a stand-alone language. Instead, it's a way of allowing Web site developers to script the behavior of Navigator itself, opening windows, showing the time, and even providing floating navigation windows that stay onscreen even after you've left a site. Like many scripting languages, JavaScript was designed so that someone who isn't a programmer can write basic scripts.

If you want to see what people are doing with Java and JavaScript, hop on over to http://www.gamelan.com, and check out some of the examples. If you haven't seen Java in action before, you'll probably be amazed (see Figure 14-13). For a basic tutorial and link list on JavaScript, check out the resource page at http://www.netscape.com/ comprod/products/navigator/ version_2.0/script/script_info/index.html. We'll discuss Java in greater depth in Chapter 28, "Audio/Video Power Tools."

Figure 14-13: The Gamelan Java directory.

TIP

Javascript may cause some security problems. If you're unsure about using Javascript on your Mac, turn off Javascript by going to the General section of Security preferences available from the Options menu.

Expanding Your Horizons With Plug-ins

These days, the boundaries of what can be done with multimedia on the Web are constantly being pushed. Many moons ago in net.time (about two human years), just having a downloadable QuickTime movie on your Web page was a big deal. Netsurfers today are able to experience such cool stuff as 3D virtual worlds (with VRML), sound-and-animation extravaganzas and interactive games (with Shockwave), beautiful text layouts (with Amber), animation (with Emblaze), music (with different MIDI players), speech (with one of several text-to-speech programs), and even live audio and video broadcasts (with StreamWorks, RealAudio, and TrueSpeech). Navigator's plug-in architecture made it all possible.

In the past, if you wanted to view a multimedia file, you had to make sure that you had a helper app configured to view it. You didn't view the file from within your browser—you saw the display in a separate program. With the release of Netscape Navigator 2.01, the browser itself is now capable of accepting plug-in modules that can access whatever form of media is an inline part of a Web page.

Table 14-8 lists many of the plug-ins available for Netscape for the Mac as of March 1996. By the time you read this there will surely be more. However, as you can see, there's a lot of them here already, so this should be a good place to start. To find out more details about what each plug-in does, turn to Chapters 24, "WWW Multimedia Power Tools," and 28 "Audio/Video Power Tools."

TIP

If you want to keep up on the latest in Netscape plug-ins, check out BrowserWatch (http://www.browserwatch.com). It's an incredible resource for the absolute latest in Netscape plug-ins and other Web-browser related news.

Name of Plug-in	What It does	Where to Get It
Amber	Displays Adobe Acrobat.	http://www.adobe.com/Amber documents in Web page.
Crescendo	Plays MIDI music.	http://www.liveupdate.com/crescendo.html
Emblaze	Displays animation.	http://www.Geo.Inter.net/technology/index.html
Envoy	Displays Novell Envoy documents	http://www.twcorp.com
ExpressVR	Allows you to view VRML worlds.	http://www.cis.upenn.edu/~brada
KM's Multimedia Plug	DisplaysQuickTime, MPEG, MIDI, WAV, AU, AIFF, and PICT files.	ftp://ftp.wco.com/users/mcmurtri/MySoftware/
Lightning Strike	Lightning Strike (Displays fractal compression) images.	http://www.infinop.com
MIDI Plugin	Plays MIDI sound files.	http://www.planete.net/~amasson
Movie Star	streaming QuickTime—watch QuickTime movies as they download.	http://130.91.39.113/product/mspi/mspi.htm
Real Audio	Plays streaming, real-time audio.	http://www.realaudio.com
Shockwave	Displays Macromedia Director interactive files.	http://www.macromedia.com
Shockhand	Displays Macromedia Freehand graphic files.	http://www.macromedia.com
Sizzler	Shows Animation.	http://www.totallyhip.com
Speech	Converts page text-to-speech.	http://www.albany.net/~wtudor
Talker	Converts page text-to-speech.	http://www.mvpsolutions.com
TrueSpeech	Allows you to listen to streaming, real-time audio.	http://www.dspg.com
ViewMovie	View inline QuickTime movies. download.html.	http://www.well.com/user/ivanski/
WhurlPlug	Displays 3DMF files (Apple's QuickDraw 3D format).	ftp://ftp.info.apple.com/Apple.Support.Area/QuickDraw3D/Test_Drive/Viewers

Table 14-8: Plug-ins and where to get 'em.

Getting Outside Help: Helper Apps

Plug-ins are taking the browser world by storm, but many types of data don't have a plug-in written to handle them. What do you do? Use a helper application!

Helper apps allow you to view any type of data that you download, provided the helper app can handle it. Once a helper app is configured correctly, Navigator will download the file and launch the helper app. You can then view (or listen or play with) the file from within the helper application.

Configuring helper apps is pretty easy, as long as you follow a few simple strictures. Unless the application comes with an installer that configures Navigator (like RealAudio does), you'll have to do a little tweaking in the Helpers section of the General Preferences dialog box. Specifically, you'll have to enter the MIME type and subtype for your new file as well as its extensions. Then, you'll have to pick a helper app from your computer using the Browse button. Once you're finished, just click OK, and you're ready to go!

You'll notice that most of the locations for the helper apps listed in the Where to Get It column in Table 14-9 do not include the actual filename. We omitted them because things change so quickly, by the time you go looking for these files, a newer version may be available or the files may have different names. It's best to go to the site and poke around (or run a search) to find the latest version of the helper.

Helper Application	What Does It Play/View?	Where to Get It
Acrobat Reader	Adobe Acrobat files	http://www.adobe.com/
AVI to QT	AVI (Microsoft) video (doesn't actually show the file, but converts it to QuickTime)	http://hyperarchive.lcs.mit.edu/ HyperArchive/Archive/gst/
Balthazar	WAV files	http://hyperarchive.lcs.mit.edu/ HyperArchive/Archive/gst/snd
CU-SeeMe	CU-SeeMe videoconferencing	http://www.cu-seeme.com
GhostScript	PostScript	http://hyperarchive.lcs.mit.edu/ HyperArchive/Archive/gst/grf/

Helper Application	What Does It Play/View?	Where to Get It
JPEGView	GIF, JPEG, TIFF files	http://hyperarchive.lcs.mit.edu/HyperArchive/Archive/gst/grf/
MacBinaryII+	.BIN (Mac binary files)	http://hyperarchive.lcs.mit.edu/HyperArchive/Archive/cmp/
MPEG Audio	MPEG sound files	http://hyperarchive.lcs.mit.edu/HyperArchive/Archive/ gst/snd/
QTVRPlayer	QuickTimeVR / QuickTime	http://qtvr.quicktime.apple.com/
RealAudio	.RA streaming audio	http://www.realaudio.com
SimpleText	PICT	comes with Macintosh
SoundMachine	AU, .SND, and AIFF sound files	http://hyperarchive.lcs.mit.edu/HyperArchive/Archive/gst/sound/
Sparkle	MPEG video	http://hyperarchive.lcs.mit.edu/HyperArchive/Archive/ gst/mov/
StreamWorks	Streaming real-time audio and video	http://www.xingtech.com/
StuffItExpander	Decompresses HQX, SIT, CPT, and ZIP files	http://www.aladdinsys.com
tar	TAR (UNIX compressed directories) files	http://hyperarchive.lcs.mit.edu/HyperArchive/Archive/cmp/
TrueSpeech	TrueSpeech streaming audio files	http://www.dspg.com/
Voyager	VRML	http://www.virtus.com/
VRML Equinox	VRML Files	http://www.ipsystems.com/nps/EquiInfo.html
Whurlwind	Plays 3DMF files	http://hyperarchive.lcs.mit.edu/HyperArchive/Archive/ gst/grf/

Table 14-9: Helper applications useful with Navigator (and other browsers).

After you've configured all of the helper applications for your browser, you'll want to give them a try. The one stop shop for this is the WWW Viewer Test Page at http://www-dsed.llnl.gov/documents/WWWtest.html. Here you can quickly test external applications for text, images, audio, video, specific document formats, models, and objects.

MICROSOFT INTERNET EXPLORER

My, my, my—how quickly things change. We finished the preceding part about Navigator on a Saturday night and got ready to write off Microsoft's Internet Explorer as a low-powered contender for Navigator the next day. However, Sunday dawned to an e-mail message announcing that the new version of MSIE released overnight supported almost all the features of Navigator! And, by the time you read this, Microsoft's Internet Explorer may support *all* of Navigator's features, making for some pretty stiff competition at the top of the browser heap. We do live in interesting times!

Before we go on, a little background. Microsoft first released its Web browser, called Internet Explorer, with Windows 95. In keeping with Microsoft's mission to take over the world, they included Internet support and something called the Microsoft Network with each copy of the new OS. When Windows 95 came out, the buzz was that the Microsoft Network, now just a mouse-click away for most Windows 95 users, would quickly overshadow the Internet as the worldwide network of choice. Needless to say, that didn't happen.

Not content with only owning 80 percent of the computer world, Microsoft, seeing its network fade but sensing a new opportunity, released a version of Internet Explorer for the Macintosh. However, no one in the Mac community paid much attention to it. It didn't do much of the stuff that Navigator did, it had a pretty lame interface, and, of course, it came from Microsoft. Three strikes and you're out as far as most Mac users were concerned.

However, with the new release of the upgraded Microsoft Internet Explorer for the Mac, all that may be changing. Only time will tell, but if Microsoft keeps improving this thing at the current rate, Netscape's lock on the world of browsers may be vulnerable. Why? Let's take a look at some of the features.

Special Features

Internet Explorer's real strength is in its multimedia support. And, now that it supports Navigator plug-ins, there's virtually no limit to the types of inline media it can support.

But the best thing about Internet Explorer is that it supports some cool stuff *without* resorting to third party plug-ins. Sound, video, virtual reality (VRML)—all are supported in an application almost half the size of Navigator. Table 14-10 lists the type of media supported by MSIE.

Type	Description
QuickTime	Apple's video standard
AVI	Microsoft's video standard
AIFF	Sound file format
AU	Sound file format
WAV	Sound file format
MIDI	Sound file format for background sounds
VRML	3D virtual reality file format
QuickDraw3D (3DMF)	Apple's 3D file format
JPEG	Graphic file format
GIF/GIF Animation	Graphic file format
"Marquee" text	Horizontally scrolling text messages

Table 14-10: Multimedia data types supported by Internet Explorer.

VRML, QuickTime, GIF, and JPEG images can all be displayed inline on a page and MIDI and WAV sound files can be played as continuously looping background sounds. Other formats, AVI, AIFF, AU, and WAV files, can all be displayed in separate windows. Figure 14-14 shows Microsoft's demonstration page, complete with AVI movie (the cup), marquee text, and background sounds. Go to http://www.microsoft.com/windows/ie/iedemo.htm to hear for yourself.

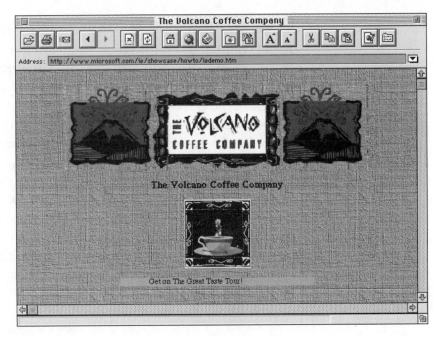

Figure 14-14: Microsoft's demonstration page.

What features are missing from MSIE? It still lags behind Navigator in regards to the stuff Netscape pioneered: Java, JavaScript, and frames. But it's coming, and by the time you read this, Internet Explorer may already support these formats. Keep watching.

TIP

If you want a more in-depth look at some of the new features of Internet Explorer, check out the Microsoft Internet Explorer section in Chapter 9, "Windows Web Power Tools."

Getting, Installing & Configuring Explorer

To get your hands on the latest version of Internet Explorer, bop on over to the Microsoft Network's site at http://www.msn.com/ie/ie.htm. From there, you can follow the links to download Internet Explorer. Once you've gotten it and decompressed it, just double-click, follow the instructions, and you're finished!

Configuring Internet Explorer is really simple, especially if you already use Internet Config. As of the 2.0beta3 version of Internet Explorer for the Mac, you have the option of setting your own preferences or accepting the preferences set with Internet Config. In most cases, you should probably accept the Internet Config option, available from Options option under the Edit menu (see sidebar "Internet Config—One Stop Setup" for more info on IC). Figure 14-15 shows some of the configuration options available in Internet Explorer.

■ ■

Internet Config—One Stop Setup

If you've ever screamed (or at least whimpered) in frustration because you can't seem to keep all the settings of your Net programs straight, Internet Config is the answer. A nifty little program written by the unstoppable Peter Lewis along with the mysterious Quinn "The Eskimo!" (really, that's all we know about him/her!), it provides one interface for setting all your Internet configuration options. Currently, Internet Config is supported by:

❐ NewsWatcher 2.0b21 and higher

❐ Register 1.1 and higher

❐ NotifyMail 2.5 and higher

❐ BlitzMail 2.0.2 and higher

❐ MacGzip 0.2.2 and higher

❐ FTPd 2.4.0 and higher

❐ ICeTEe

❐ Internet Config Access

❐ Mpack 1.5 and higher

❐ BBEdit 3.1.1 and higher

❐ NewsHopper 1.1 and higher

❐ Anarchie 1.5.0 and higher

❐ NCSA Telnet 2.6.1d7 and higher

❐ Black Night 0.1.4 and higher

❐ Microsoft Internet Explorer

And many Mac software developers have plans to include Internet Config support in future releases. With Internet Config, you enter your personal, e-mail, helper app, server, file transfer, and font information once, and any program using Internet Config gets your settings from there. Simple!

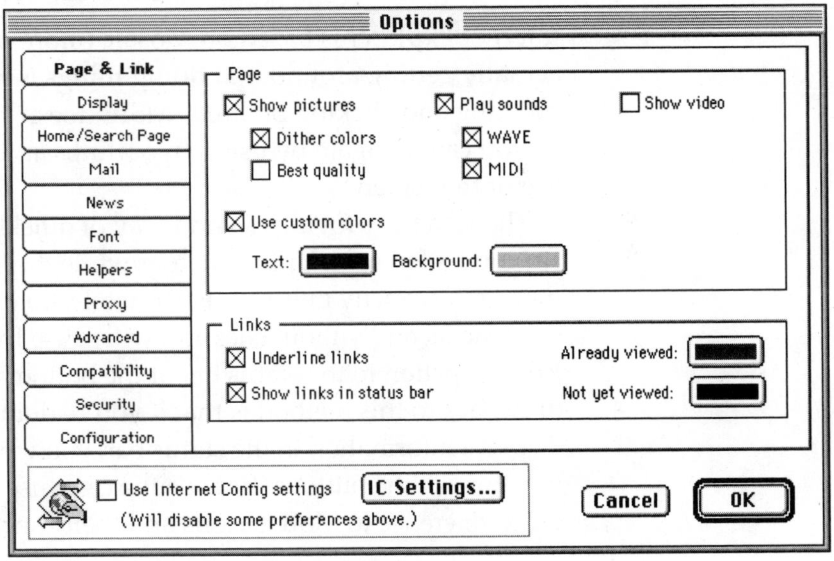

Figure 14-15: Configuring Microsoft Internet Explorer.

Netscape Navigator to Microsoft Internet Explorer—Moving Your Bookmarks

If you've been using Netscape Navigator and want to transfer your bookmarks to Internet Explorer, here's all you have to do:

1. Go to the File menu, and choose the Import Favorites option.

2. Using the File dialog box, go to the Preferences folder in your System folder and open the Netscape *f* folder. Then open the Bookmarks.html file.

3. MSIE will import all your Navigator bookmarks into your Favorites list; even keeping the folder structure (if any) you set up in Navigator.

Walking the Web With Bill's Browser

Internet Explorer is based on Mosaic (more on that later), so actually getting around and doing things is really as easy as pointing and clicking on links. MSIE doesn't support frames yet, so you can navigate by using hyperlinks and the icon bar at the top of the screen.

The icon bar provides a good way of quickly accessing many of Explorer's features. Unfortunately, while the icons are attractive, they aren't exactly intuitive. Fortunately, holding the mouse button over each icon (without clicking) will cause Explorer to display the icon's function in the status bar at the bottom of the page. The only drawback to this method is that if you're doing something that displays information in the status bar, you won't be able to see the functions of the buttons. If that's the case, use Table 14-11 for a quick reference to MSIE's icons and their functions.

Icon	Function
	Opens address or file
	Prints current page
	Sends new mail message
	Goes back
	Goes forward
	Stops transfer
	Reloads page
	Returns to home page (defined in Options)
	Opens search page at http://www.msn.com/access/ allinone.htm
	Opens newsreader
	Opens Favorites list
	Adds current page to Favorites list
	Increases font size
	Decreases font size
	Cuts selected text

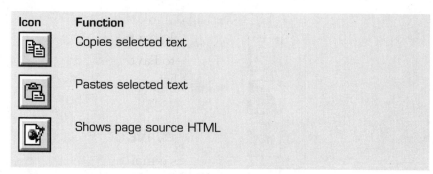

Icon	Function
	Copies selected text
	Pastes selected text
	Shows page source HTML

Table 14-11: The Navigation icons in Microsoft Internet Explorer.

Internet Explorer also makes your browsing easier by providing a pop-up menu, which is accessible by holding down the mouse button in the main browser window. With this handy navigation tool, you can:

- ❑ Clone Window: Open a new window containing a copy of the current page.
- ❑ Set Home Page: Set the current page as your home page.
- ❑ Set Search Page: Set the current page as your search page of choice.
- ❑ Add Page to Favorites: Add a bookmark for the current page to your Favorites list.
- ❑ Copy Image: Copy the selected image to the clipboard.
- ❑ Load Missing Image: Attempt to reload the selected, unloaded image.
- ❑ Open Image in New Window: Open the currently selected image in its own window.
- ❑ Download Image to Disk: Save a copy of the selected image to a file.
- ❑ Open Link: Go to a link.
- ❑ Open Link in New Window: Open the currently selected link into a new window.

❐ Download Link to Disk: Save the page referred to in the current link to a file.

❐ Add Link to Favorites: Add the selected link to your Favorites list.

E-mail & Usenet News

Internet Explorer's e-mail and news posting features are fairly limited, but with the release of 2.0b3, they've started to improve. At this point, no one outside of Microsoft knows if Explorer will ever rival Netscape Navigator's e-mail and Usenet news support, but MSIE is well on its way.

First, the mail. MSIE allows you to send e-mail messages but not receive them. You can send a new message that contains either a new message by itself or a new message containing the URL of the page you're currently viewing. See Figure 14-16.

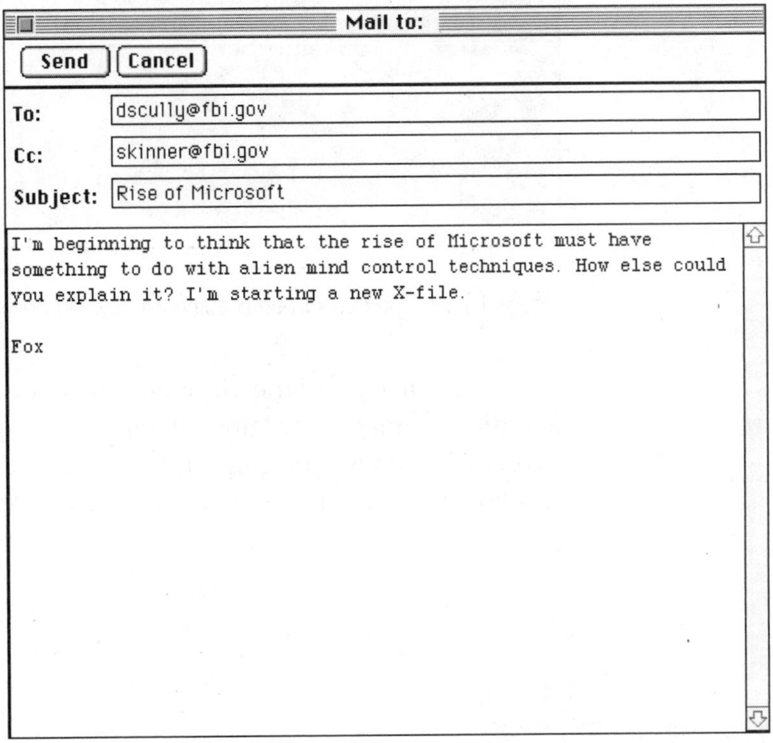

Figure 14-16: Sending an e-mail message with Internet Explorer.

The newsreading functions are a bit more robust. You can access the newsreader by pressing the News button on the icon bar or by typing **news:** in the location field at the top of the screen. MSIE will then download a list of all the newsgroups and display them in the main window (see Figure 14-17). Individual newsgroups are represented by their names, and newsgroup hierarchies are set off with an asterisk (*). To navigate, read, and post, just point and click.

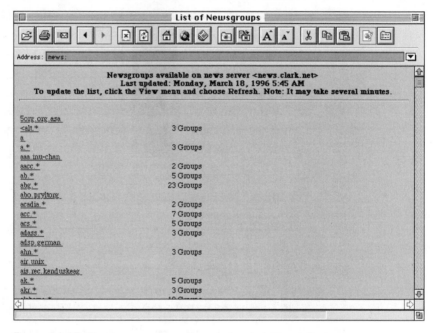

Figure 14-17: The newsgroup reading window in Internet Explorer.

One nice feature of the MSIE newsreader is that it will uudecode and display images contained in binary newsgroups. All you have to do is click on the message and wait. Internet Explorer will then display the image as it downloads. See Figure 14-18.

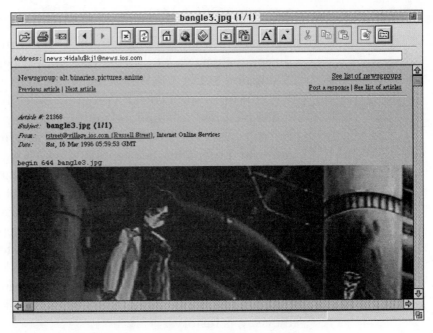

Figure 14-18: Viewing an image with the MSIE newsreader.

What's Ahead?

Good question! The answer is that no one knows. Judging from the fact that MSIE is rapidly gaining ground on Netscape Navigator, it may not be long until we're all thrust into the middle of a major browser war. Wait and watch. Until then, Microsoft has made rumblings about supporting Java and JavaScript in future releases, so by the time you read this, those upgrades may have already been made. Keep checking the Microsoft Network Web site (http://www.msn.com) and Browserwatch (http://www.browserwatch.com) for updates.

NCSA MOSAIC

Contrary to what you might think if you've just arrived online during the past year or so, the Web didn't begin with Netscape Navigator. In fact, the Web actually began as a text-only medium, with the browser of choice a program called lynx. There were no inline pictures, no sound, no multimedia zippiness (well, if you can call current speeds *zippy*)—just text and links within the text. For over a year after its inception, the Web was really just a way for researchers to exchange data over the Internet.

Mosaic changed all that. The brainchild of the folks at the National Center for Supercomputing Applications (NCSA), Mosaic was developed as a graphical front end to the embryonic World Wide Web. Originally only available for high-end UNIX machines, Mosaic was eventually ported to Mac and PC platforms. As the possibilities of the new medium of the Web began to dawn on people, things really began to take off. And the rest, they say, is history.

These days, Mac Mosaic lags a distant third behind Netscape Navigator and Microsoft Internet Explorer, both in functionality and usage, but is starting to catch up. In April, the NCSA released a new version of Mosaic which supports inline sounds as well as Netscape frames (something Microsoft's browser doesn't even do yet!). Clearly, there may be hope for Mosaic yet.

So Why Use It?

Mosaic doesn't support most of the new multimedia features sported by Navigator and Explorer. It doesn't support plug-ins, inline video, or sounds, and very little special formatting. Mosaic does support tables, frames, and background images, but other than that, it's bare-bones.

So why use it? First of all, if you're a Web developer, Mosaic makes a great platform for testing the compatibility of your Web pages. As a rule of thumb, if what you've done looks good in Mosaic, chances are it'll look great in any other browser. Developers shouldn't overlook this fact because, while many people may not use NCSA Mosaic these days, many folks still use a flavor of it (or something like Explorer, which is based on Mosaic). Many of the browsers bundled with Internet startup-type packages are customized versions of plain-vanilla Mosaic.

The one thing that Mosaic has going for it is that it's fast. Because it doesn't contain a lot of the programming overhead that Explorer and Navigator do, browsing the Web with Mosaic can get downright speedy. In addition, Mosaic supports a "kiosk" mode that allows you to hide all the navigation bars and menus, making it ideal for setting up unattended Web browsing stations in public areas.

Getting NCSA Mosaic

If you want to see what Mosaic can do for you, hop on over to the NCSA Web site (http://www.ncsa.uiuc.edu), and go to the section on Mosaic. You'll be able to download both PowerPC and 68K Mac versions, so you should be able to find one to suit your needs.

The Future of Mac Mosaic—Is There One?

Mosiac keeps plugging along, but probably will never match or pass the development of Netscape Navigator or Microsoft Internet Explorer. While the most recent release of Mosaic does include many new features, the NCSA isn't in the business of competing with Netscape and Microsoft. If you want a good way to test your pages, or just want to use a browser that's free, Mosaic may be the way to go.

MOVING ON

Now that we've finished showing you how to browse the Web with three of the best Mac Web tools, it's time to dig deeper into our toolbox to look at those specialty tools that you might not use every day but are darn handy to have at the ready when you need 'em. While we won't have the time (or space) to really get into the finer points of each one, we will tell you where to find it, when's a good time to drag it out of the toolbox, and some timesaving tricks that you might have missed in the owners manual. Bob Villa, eat your heart out.

## Chapter 15

Mac Net Tools Gallery

OK. Let's see . . . you got your e-mail client, your newsreader, and your Web browser. You think you're ready to go, don't ya? Well hold on there a minute! We're not finished yet. There are still a few cool tools that we're just dying to show you.

In this chapter, we'll look at a number of Net tools that don't fit neatly into any one category. These are all tools that you can probably live without, but they're very handy to have around. What kind of stuff are we talking about? Well, for starters we'll look at tools that transfer files (using FTP, File Transfer Protocol) both from the Net to your computer and from your computer to other wired folks. We'll then move on to how you can use some of the various Telnet clients to connect to remote UNIX machines. (See Part IV for more info on UNIX.) Wrapping that up, we'll mosey on over to some tools you can use for tracking down data on the Net and some interesting Net utilities.

TIP

Just about every program we're going to talk about in this chapter can be found at the Mother of All Macintosh Software Sites—the InfoMac HyperArchive at MIT. If you're interested in keeping up with the latest Mac tools, InfoMac is the place to be. Everything's organized into thematic directories viewable in alphabetical or date order. If you don't know what you want, there's a nice search function. To see for yourself, go to http://hyperarchive.lcs.mit.edu/HyperArchive/Archive/comm/tcp/

FILE TRANSFER TOOLS

Though it sounds like an obvious (and strange) thing to point out, the Internet is a network. That means once you connect your computer to the Net via a TCP/IP (Transmission Control Protocol/Internet Protocol) connection, your computer becomes a member of the network, able to not only receive information and files, but to send information as well. It's not just a place to send messages to friends, read and post Usenet articles, or browse the Web—it's a way of connecting your computer to the online world.

File transfer tools let you take advantage of the fact that once you're on the Net, you're *on* the Net. While this means you can now snag files directly to your computer, it also means that you can take files from your hard drive and transfer them directly to another online computer. With the right tools, you can even set up your computer so that others can transfer files directly to you from anywhere in the world via the Internet.

Anarchie

Now why didn't someone think of this before? Typically, when you go looking for a particular file on the Net, you have to type your search into an Archie server (a computer on the Net that lets you search for files on FTP sites), write down the information it gives you, fire up your FTP program, re-enter the information, and download the file. Seems pretty tedious, doesn't it? Isn't all that searching, writing, and data entry the type of stuff that computers are supposed to free us from? Peter Lewis thought so—that's why he wrote Anarchie, a brilliant combination of Archie and FTP clients.

Even though its title evokes images of a comic-book character gone bad, Anarchie is anything but anarchistic. Instead, using a simple, easy-to-use interface, Anarchie takes most of the anarchy out of having to find and download files.

All you have to do is select an Archie server near you from a pop-up menu of Archie servers available from the Archie option on the File menu, enter the name of the file you're looking for, hit the Find button, and you're off! Anarchie sends your query to the Archie server you've specified and even gives you an estimate of how long it'll take to get a list of files back (see Figure 15-1).

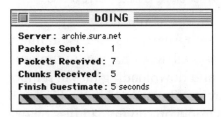

Figure 15-1: Searching for files with Anarchie.

When the Archie server sends back the list of files it has found, Anarchie transforms that list into a handy clickable window (see Figure 15-2). Then, all you have to do to get the file is double-click on it!

Name	Size	Date	Zone	Machine	Pa
Archie.XBoing.V1.5.Re.gz	2k	8/5/93	5	ftp.lth.se	
better_boing.au	3k	3/22/94	5	ftp.unicamp.br	
boing.au	1k	6/15/94	1	ftp.rutgers.edu	
boing.au	3k	1/1/4	1	ftp.rutgers.edu	
boing.au	22k	2/9/94	1	netlib.att.com	
boing.au	22k	11/17/94	1	netlib.att.com	
boing.au	3k	12/16/94	1	moose.cs.indiana.edu	
boing.au	3k	3/9/94	1	ftp.cs.umass.edu	
boing.au	3k	9/19/94	2	ftp.iro.umontreal.ca	
boing.au	3k	9/19/94	2	ftp.iro.umontreal.ca	
boing.au	3k	9/19/94	2	ftp.iro.umontreal.ca	
boing.au	3k	8/16/93	2	ftp.iro.umontreal.ca	
boing.au	3k	8/16/93	2	ftp.iro.umontreal.ca	
boing.au	3k	9/19/94	2	ftp.iro.umontreal.ca	
boing.au	3k	9/19/94	2	ftp.iro.umontreal.ca	
boing.au	3k	8/16/93	2	ftp.iro.umontreal.ca	
boing.au	3k	8/28/95	2	ftp.iro.umontreal.ca	
boing.au	3k	8/16/93	2	ftp.iro.umontreal.ca	
boing.au	3k	8/16/93	2	ftp.iro.umontreal.ca	
boing.au	22k	2/9/94	5	ftp.hea.ie	
boing.au	3k	6/28/94	5	ftp.deakin.edu.au	
boing.au	3k	12/21/93	5	ftp.deakin.edu.au	
boing.au	3k	3/8/94	5	ftp.sunet.se	
boing.au	22k	11/17/94	5	ftp.hea.ie	

Window title: **bOING from archie.sura.net**

Figure 15-2: A list of found files with Anarchie.

Even though Anarchie's forte is finding files, it's a full-featured FTP client as well. In fact, if you're running System 7.5 (or later), uploading and downloading files to remote sites can become as easy as moving files around in the Finder. If your Mac supports Drag and Drop, you can upload files by dragging them into the remote server window and download files from the remote server by dragging them out of the window onto your Desktop or hard drive.

Program Name:	Anarchie
Type:	FTP client/Archie client
System:	7.5 or later for all features
Special Features:	Drag-and-drop file uploading and downloading. Automatically sets file types. Allows saving of bookmarks for frequently accessed sites. Uses integrated Archie client.
Where to get the latest version:	ftp:// share.com/pub/peterlewis/

Table 15-1: A brief review of Anarchie.

Fetch

Anarchie sports a nice interface and some swanky automation, but sometimes you need a serious FTP tool. That tool is Fetch.

Fetch has been around for a long time (since 1989), and with each new release it keeps getting better. Because Fetch supports many file and directory-hacking features not found in Anarchie, it remains a popular tool for anyone who has to maintain files on remote machines—especially people who have to support Web sites. What kind of features are we talking about?

- ❏ Searching: Uses Site Index command to search indexes of files on site.

- ❏ File permissions: Sets read, write, and execute file permissions for selected files. Very useful if you're putting up a Web site on a UNIX box.

- ❏ Directory tree upload/download: Uploads and downloads entire directories and subdirectories.

- ❏ File conversion: Converts to and from AppleSingle, BinHex, and MacBinaryII file formats.

- ❏ Suffix mapping: Maps downloaded files to correct Mac applications so that they show up with correct icons.

- ❏ Firewalls: Supports network security features if you're using it behind a firewall.

- ❐ Text-file display: Displays text files found on FTP sites.
- ❐ Custom FTP commands: Allows you to enter custom FTP commands directly to the FTP server if you need to. Can be useful in sticky situations.
- ❐ URLs: Creates and reads files containing lists of FTP sites formated as URLs—for example ftp://ftp.cdrom.com/pub/win95.
- ❐ File post-processing: Automatically decompresses StuffIt, MacBinary, BinHex4 and AppleSingle files.
- ❐ Apple Events: Fully scriptable and recordable.
- ❐ Drag and drop: Files can be uploaded and downloaded by dragging and dropping from the Finder.
- ❐ Multiple, simultaneous connections: Supports and maintains multiple connections. Fetch can even reconnect with servers whose connections have terminated.

As you can probably tell from that feature list, Fetch excels when it comes to having control over the FTP server you're accessing. Features that allow you to set file permissions and issue custom FTP commands make life a lot easier when you're putting files into a UNIX machine and don't want to have to Telnet in to muck around (see Figure 15-3). It's almost like a nice combination of Macintosh ease of use with UNIX flexibility.

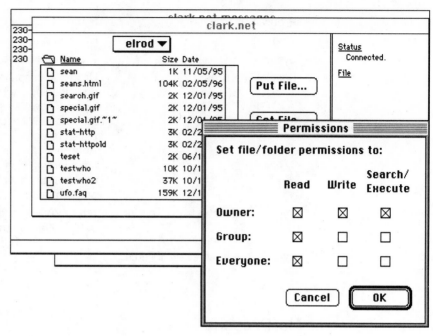

Figure 15-3: Setting file permissions with Fetch.

For day-to-day use, Fetch is pretty handy. You can just drag and drop files into and out of the main directory listing window, and Fetch will automatically set their types and map the correct suffixes onto them (see Figure 15-4).

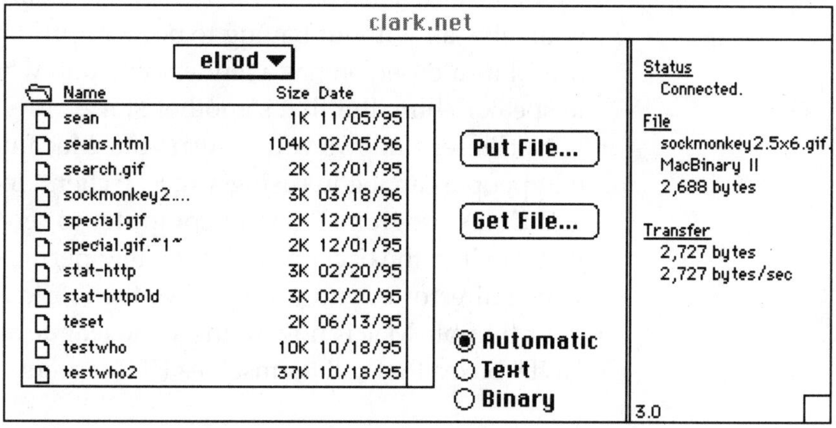

Figure 15-4: Uploading a file with Fetch.

Program Name:	Fetch
Type:	FTP client
System:	7.5 or later for all features
Special Features:	Drag-and-drop file uploading and downloading. Automatically sets file types. Allows saving of bookmarks for frequently accessed sites. Able to parse directory structures that Anarchie can't handle. Good for transferring files to Windows NT servers. Scriptable with AppleScript or Frontier.
Where to get the latest version:	http://www.dartmouth.edu/pages/softdev/fetch.html

Table 15-2: A brief review of Fetch.

NetPresenz

Say you're sitting at your computer writing a book. You get to a certain point in the chapter when you remember that your co-author (we'll call him Gareth) has a file that you need. Now, you could call him up (or send him e-mail) and ask him to attach the file to a mail message and send it to you. But why bother? If he's running an FTP server on his computer, you can just fire up Anarchie or Fetch, connect to his computer, and grab the file yourself—all without having to bother him. This becomes really useful if said person has a tendency to nap when you really need to speak to him. But that's another story.

NetPresenz allows you to turn your Mac into an FTP server so that people can log in (using any FTP client, including Windows and UNIX programs) to your computer to send and receive files. Just run it in the background, set a few permissions, designate which directories you want to give the world access to, and poof! Your humble Mac is now in the same league as any of those fancy UNIX boxes that call themselves FTP servers.

Server Security

Just a note on security before we go any further. Normally, when you're online, your Mac is pretty much impervious to wiley crackers. Since Macs don't use a command-line interface (like UNIX or DOS machines), there are no secret security holes, background processes, or ways that a malicious person can use TCP/IP to hack your computer and gain access to your files. That all changes when you set yourself up as an FTP (or other) server.

Once you set up as a server, you're inviting people into your machine. To make sure they behave themselves, you should take a few precautions. First, don't allow unlimited access to your hard drive to anonymous users. Designate a special folder for Internet access, and make sure you restrict anonymous user access to only that directory. If you must give someone access to your entire drive, make sure you trust that person, and protect their access with a hard-to-hack password.

Second, unless you know the identity of every person who uploads a file to your computer, check each file for viruses before you open it. You never know what might be hidden inside.

Finally, don't tell the world about your server unless you're prepared to deal with the hassles that come from running a publicly accessible site. Security-through-obscurity is sometimes the best security of all.

The greatest feature of NetPresenz is that it's incredibly easy to set up and use. With a few clicks of the mouse (see Figure 15-5), not only can you set up your own spiffy FTP server, but you'll also be online with your own Gopher and WWW servers, too. While NetPresenz doesn't support all of the advanced features supported by a full-fledged Web server like StarNine's WebStar, it does get the basic job done. It's a great way to share files with other people, test your Web pages, and gain remote access to your machine if you have to.

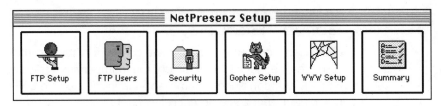

Figure 15-5: Setting up NetPresenz—a virtual piece o' cake!

Program Name:	NetPresenz
Type:	FTP, HTTP, & Gopher server
System:	7.5 or later for all features. Requires prior installation of Mac networking software, particularly Users&Groups.
Special Features:	Very easy to configure, multiple server solution. Great for small businesses/home users who want to let others connect to their Macs to share information. Supports custom FTP commands for dealing with Mac files. Good documentation and simple interface. Uses InternetConfig for most preferences.
Where to get the latest version:	ftp:// ftp.share.com/pub/peterlewis/

Table 15-3: A brief review of NetPresenz.

Easy Transfer

The only problem with setting up an FTP server on your Mac to share files with your friends is that, well, it's an FTP server. And while programs like NetPresenz make setting up an FTP server pretty simple, it still doesn't offer all the point-and-click, drag-and-drop ease that most Mac users are used to.

If you want to share files across the Internet with other Mac users, Easy Transfer is the solution. Using a proprietary file transfer protocol and offering up a simple-to-use setup and interface, Easy Transfer makes sending and receiving files as easy as dragging files into a folder. On top of that, Easy Transfer is quick. It uses its own on-the-fly compression technology to speed file transfers— no need to use StuffIt before you send them.

Because Easy Transfer is a Mac-only program, it also eliminates many of the security problems you could have with setting up an FTP server on your Mac. In fact, Easy Transfer lets you set permissions based on unique Mac ID numbers, so you can control who connects to your machine and reduce the possibility that someone could hack a password or spoof a connection.

Setting up Easy Transfer is simple. Just start the program, assign user names and passwords, decide how much of your hard drive you want people to have access to, and you're ready to go. Figure 15-6 shows the Easy Transfer setup window. In this example, we're configuring the server section of Easy Transfer.

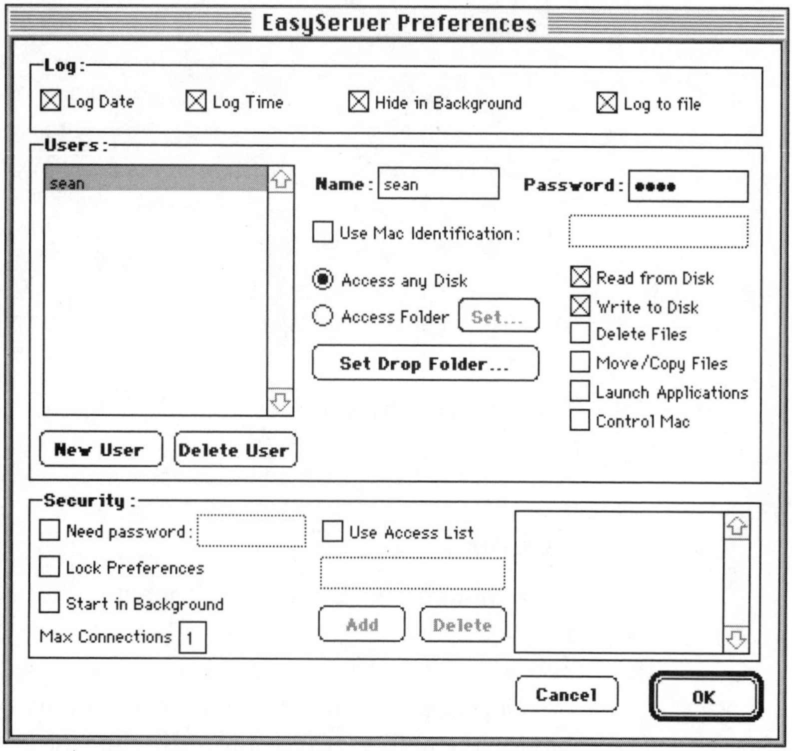

Figure 15-6: Setting up Easy Transfer.

Sending files is even easier. In fact, if you're going to be sending files to the same machine all the time, a nifty utility called Easy Drop Primer (included) helps you create aliases for a remote machine so that you can transfer a file just by dragging and dropping it onto an Easy Drop alias (see Figure 15-7). Transferring files across the Net doesn't get much easier!

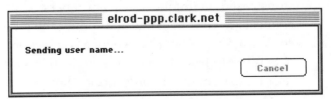

Figure 15-7: Using an Easy Drop alias to send a file to Gareth.

Program Name:	Easy Transfer
Type:	Proprietary TCP/IP Mac file transfer program
System:	7.5 or later for all features
Special Features:	Good security options. On the fly compression. High-speed through-put. Very easy to use. Utilizes Finder drag and drop for file transfer. PowerPC native.
Where to get the latest version:	ftp://mac-ftp.cs.strath.ac.uk/macstuff/EasyTransfer/

Table 15-4: A brief review of Easy Transfer.

TELNET TOOLS

Even though you can do just about everything you need to do on the Net with your Mac, there still may be times when you need to access a remote UNIX machine to get some work done. If you develop Web sites and just want to get in to do some simple editing, having the ability to Telnet in, edit your file online, and save it can make life a lot easier. Why should you have to download the file, edit it on your Mac, and upload it again? You shouldn't.

Besides giving you the ability to edit files in place, Telnet also allows you to use a remote machine's resources. If you have to do any CGI programming for a Web site you're working on, play on a MUD or MOO, or even just have a quick and dirty way to check your e-mail, Telnet can be an invaluable tool.

NCSA Telnet

NCSA's version of Telnet is probably the most popular version for the Mac. It's had a long shelf life, it's been tested by probably hundreds of thousands of people, and it provides nearly every feature that you could want in a simple Telnet program. On top of that, it also provides a simple FTP server/client interface so that you can easily work on a file on a remote machine and then transfer it back to your Mac—all within the same program. Add to this the ability to emulate several popular terminal types and save connection aliases for quick point-and-click connections to Telnet sites, and you've got yourself a nice tool. Here's a complete list of the features.

- ❏ Multiple terminal emulations: VT102, VT220
- ❏ FTP client and server
- ❏ Multiple simultaneous connections
- ❏ Scrollback buffer with print and copy
- ❏ Macros for automating repetitive keystrokes
- ❏ Fonts, colors, font size, number of lines all configurable

NCSA Telnet is your bare-bones application. All you have to do is select Open Connection from the File menu, type the address of the machine you want to go to, and you're there (see Figure 15-8). You can even save your connections as separate files. Later, if you want to connect to a remote machine, all you have to do is double-click on the Telnet file in the Finder, and NCSA Telnet will launch itself and make the connection.

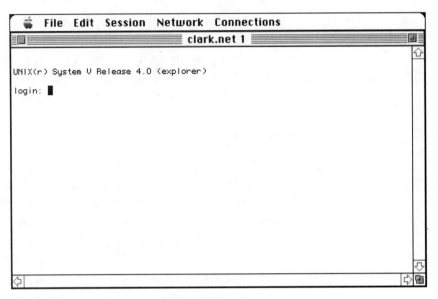

Figure 15-8: Connecting with NCSA Telnet.

Program Name:	NCSA Telnet
Type:	Full-featured Telnet client. Also includes FTP client/server.
System:	7.5 or later for all features.
Special Features:	Good, clean, easy to use. Does not support all terminal emulations, but it does include the main ones. Uses internal FTP client and server for easy file transfer. Can save connection files as aliases for easy connection straight from the Finder.
Where to get the latest version:	http://www.ncsa.uiuc.edu/SDG/ Software/Brochure/ MacSoftDesc.html#MacTelnet

Table 15-5: A brief review of NCSA Telnet.

DataComet

If you're looking for a real Telnet power tool, DataComet is it. Sure, NCSA Telnet lets you connect to most computers out there, but if you need a special terminal type or connection emulation, chances are DataComet can handle it.

We do have to say one thing, though—as Mac programs go, DataComet is ugly. It's based on the old Mac Telnet client, Comet, and still sports the same clunky black and white interface, monochrome icon, and multi-button screens (see Figure 15-9).

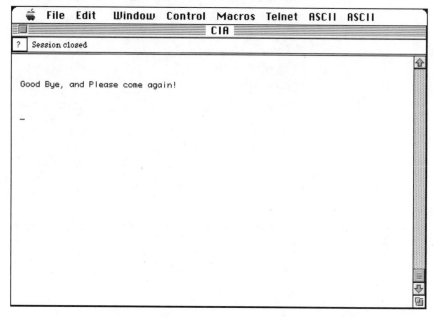

Figure 15-9: DataComet—not a pretty sight, but it gets the job done.

As we pointed out, DataComet's strength is its ability to emulate many different terminal settings:

- ❐ PC-ANSI
- ❐ VT52 (Heath H19)
- ❐ Digital VT102
- ❐ IBM 3278

It can do so using any font size and color. DataComet can maintain up to 50 simultaneous connections, use macros to simplify most repetitive and complex commands, and transfer files using IBM's FT3270 and TFTP protocols. And if you're using 3270 to connect, Data Comet will even support the various extended character types used by these systems (the NOTIS library card catalog system, in particular).

DataComet is a serious geek tool for Telnet geeks (and we mean that in a nice way). If your connections to the Net include hooking up to anything beyond plain-vanilla VT100 or ANSI systems, you might need Data Comet.

Program Name:	Data Comet
Type:	Telnet client
System:	7.5 or later for all features
Special Features:	Supports many terminal emulations: PC-ANSI, VT52, IBM 3278, VT102, IBM 3270. Allows serial connections. Works well with OpenTransport. Can have up to 50 simultaneous connections in separate windows. Includes many, many other features.
Where to get the latest version:	ftp://ftp.databeast.com/pub/datacomet/

Table 15-6: A brief review of Data Comet.

DATA-FINDING TOOLS

These days you can find just about anything you want to find using the Web. Between all the Web-walking search engines, comprehensive indexes, and file repositories, the Web has become our doorway to a world of information on the Net. Add to that the ability that most Web browsers have to access information on other data sources—like Gopher and FTP—and you might wonder why you'd ever need another tool to find what you're looking for.

The truth is, you really don't need another data tool if you're content with using your Web browser for everything. But, for the same reasons that you probably don't want to always use Netscape Navigator or Microsoft's Internet Explorer for reading your mail and Usenet news, you may want to use a separate client for your data searches.

Using a separate data-finding tool has several advantages. First, because the tools are designed for one thing and one thing only, they usually take up less memory and perform their functions faster without the extra overhead of a browser. Second, because Web clients can't be all things to all people, their abilities are often limited when it comes to browsing non-Web sources of information. A dedicated client can do many things that a browser can't, providing many special features and streamlining your searches.

TIP

For more information on Internet search tools and techniques, see Part VIII, "Netsearching: Unleashing Your Code Hound."

TurboGopher

Gopherspace is a section of the Internet accessible through Gopher clients. Users can browse menus of information, select documents that they want to view, and then either download them or view them through the Gopher client.

One main difference between Gopherspace and the Web is that Gophers don't use hypermedia links. On the Web, you can link to other documents from within a document, setting up contextual links to source materials, pictures, sounds, and other data. In Gopherspace, the linking takes place on a document level—once you're inside a document, you have to go back to the menu to get to another document. However, as a precursor to the Web, Gophers did allow you to view and/or save multimedia data, search for documents you wanted to read, and get information from the far reaches of Cyberspace.

TurboGopher is the product of the Gopher Team at the University of Minnesota and represents the best way for you to go-fer information with your Macintosh. TurboGopher is a fast, easy way to browse through GopherSpace using a well-constructed interface (see Figure 15-10). While today's Web browsers allow you to browse Gopher servers, TurboGopher offers several advantages over using your browser.

❏ Speed: TurboGopher is fast—most operations take place almost instantly, even over a 28.8 Kbps modem.

❏ Ease of use: Everything that you need to do when searching can be done with the click of a mouse button. If you need to enter information (for instance, if you're doing a search), TurboGopher provides dialog boxes.

❏ Pre-set Gopher servers: A nice Bookmark Worksheet form lets you build your own customized Gopher menus to quickly access data you need.

❏ Low overhead: TurboGopher only needs 700K to run. It's great for finding data when you've got lots of other programs open or are using an older Mac.

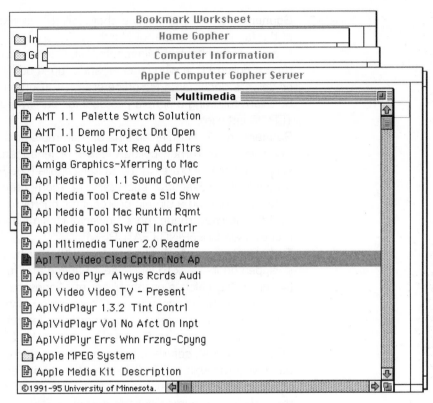

Figure 15-10: Go TurboGopher go!

A Little Gopher Humor

The Gopher team at the University of Minnesota must know by now that the Web has pretty much taken over the online world. But that doesn't stop them from having a sense of humor about their work. The following definitions of Gopher are taken from the TurboGopher help file. It may help you get a better idea of the genesis of the Gopher program:

❑ **Gopher** n. 1. Any of various short-tailed, burrowing mammals of the family Geomyidae, of North America. 2. (Amer. colloq.) Native or inhabitant of Minnesota: the Gopher State. 3. (Amer. colloq.) One who runs errands, does odd-jobs, fetches or delivers documents for office staff. 4. (Computer tech.) Software following a simple protocol for burrowing through a TCP/IP internet.

❑ **Gopher+** n. 1. Hardier strains of mammals of the family Geomyidae. 2. (Amer. colloq.) Native or inhabitant of Minnesota, the Gopher state, in full winter regalia (see PARKA). 3. (Amer. colloq.) Executive secretary. 4. (computer tech.) Software following a simple protocol for burrowing through a TCP/IP internet, made more powerful by simple enhancements (see CREEPING FEATURISM).

❑ **TurboGopher** n. 1. A small rodent with a turbocharger strapped on its back to increase its speed and ferocity. 2. (Amer. colloq.) Native or inhabitant of Minnesota after consuming three double espressos. 3. (Amer. colloq.) An Olympic sprinter who runs errands, does odd-jobs, fetches or delivers documents for office staff. 4.(computer tech.) Speed-optimized Macintosh software following a simple protocol for burrowing through a TCP/IP internet; network speed is achieved by using turbocharged software; incoming bits spin the turbine that pumps out the outgoing bits.

Program Name:	TurboGopher
Type:	Gopher client
System:	7.0 or later for all features
Special Features:	Basic Gopher client. Presents a nice graphical interface for a fairly plain subject. Uses helper apps to view multimedia data and e-mail.
Where to get the latest version:	gopher://boombox.micro.umn.edu:70/11/gopher/Macintosh-TurboGopher

Table 15-7: A brief review of TurboGopher.

TurboGopherVR

This program is mainly an oddity, and we're gonna admit right now that we're including it for its novelty value. It won't let you get to data any faster, probably won't make your life any easier, but it can make things more fun.

TurboGopherVR is a 3D, PowerMac only, virtual reality interface for Gopherspace. Instead of merely representing Gopher menus as directories, TurboGopherVR transforms boring ol' 2D Goperspaces into a 3D world of data monoliths, reminiscent of a Technicolor Stonehenge. You can fly through the views using your mouse, and you can select directories and documents just by clicking on their representations. See Figure 15-11 for an example.

Figure 15-11: Cruisin' Gopherspace with TurboGopher VR.

The biggest drawback of TurboGopherVR is that it's slow. On Sean's PowerMac 6100/66 (admittedly a low-end machine), moving through the menus felt like swimming through taffy. Also, the 3D interface took some getting used to, and we often found ourselves overshooting a data monolith that we meant to click on. But still, it is fun to play with and perhaps a harbinger of the VRML worlds to come on the Web. Then again, it may just point out the silliness of forcing an elaborate unneeded interface.

Program Name:	TurboGopherVR
Type:	Gopher client using 3-D interface
System:	PowerPC only
Special Features:	Does the job of a basic gopher client, but with a flythrough 3D interface. It's slow.
Where to get the latest version:	ftp://boombox.micro.umn.edu/ pub/gopher/Macintosh- TurboGopher/TurboGopherVR/

Table 15-8: A brief review of TurboGopherVR.

MacWAIS

Another service that's quickly being taken over by the Web is WAIS, or Wide Area Information Server. Originally, WAISes were used to link large collections of documents and make them searchable by content, not just by title.

These days, WAIS engines still enjoy wide usage, but they're accessed mainly through the Web and not with stand-alone clients. However, for many documents, especially education documents, government information, and historical documents, a WAIS client might be your ticket.

MacWAIS is pretty much the only WAIS search client available for the Mac. However, it hasn't been updated since 1994, so it's getting a bit long in the tooth. If you have the need to search WAIS, it's your only way to go.

Basically, it works like this: first, you select a list of servers from the ones supplied in the program you want to search, and then you ask WAIS a question such as "weather." It bops onto the Net, queries the search engines, and returns the documents matching your criteria back to you. Figure 15-12 shows a search under way with MacWAIS.

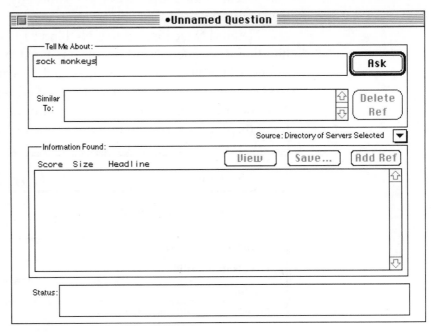

Figure 15-12: A MacWAIS search.

Program Name:	MacWAIS
Type:	WAIS database search client
System:	6.0 or later
Special Features:	Simple, clean interface for WAIS searches.
Where to get the latest version:	http://hyperarchive.lcs.mit.edu/HyperArchive.html

Table 5-8: A brief review of MacWAIS.

NetFind/Mac

Searching for data is one thing. What do you do if you want to find a person? Use Netfind/Mac!

NetFind/Mac is a program written by Jason Bernstein that accesses SUN NetFind servers located across the Internet. It allows you to search for people based on name, city, state, and university (see Figure 15-13). Once you provide as much information as you can, NetFind/Mac logs on to a NetFind server (accessible from a handy pop-up menu) and begins its search. NetFind/Mac uses a variety of methods to narrow the search down and uses finger and SMTP to search for a person's name and e-mail address. Once NetFind/Mac gets as close as it can to finding who you're looking for, it displays the information on your screen.

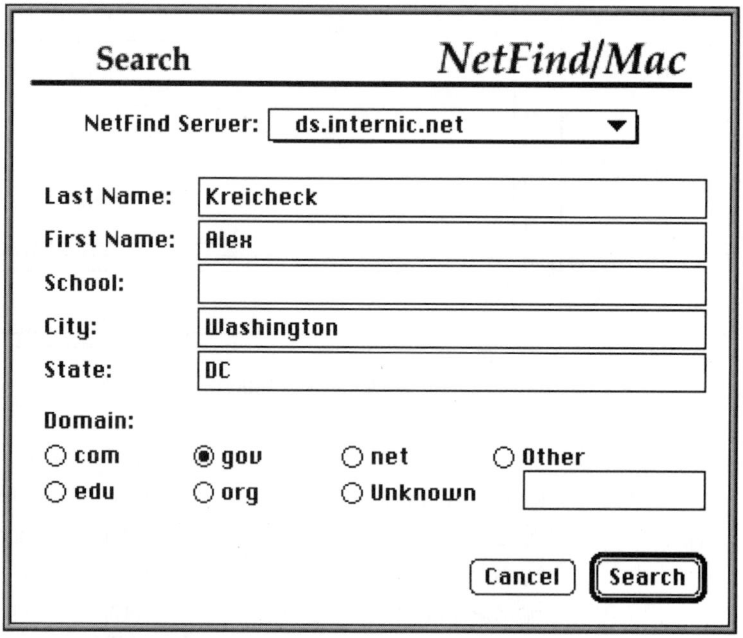

```
  Search                    NetFind/Mac

       NetFind Server:   ds.internic.net        ▼

   Last Name:    Kreicheck
   First Name:   Alex
   School:
   City:         Washington
   State:        DC

   Domain:
   ○ com     ◉ gov      ○ net      ○ Other
   ○ edu     ○ org      ○ Unknown  [          ]

                            [ Cancel ] [ Search ]
```

Figure 15-13: Setting up a search with NetFind/Mac.

NetFind/Mac is a great idea, but in practice, it usually has a hard time finding anyone who's not at a university. That aside, it's still a handy tool to have around should you need it.

Program Name:	Netfind
Type:	Searches for people on the Internet using NetFind servers.
System:	7.0 or later
Special Features:	None. Just a quick and dirty way to search for e-mail addresses.
Where to get the latest version:	http://hyperarchive.lcs.mit.edu/ HyperArchive/Archive/comm/tcp/

Table 15-9: A brief review of Netfind.

MISCELLANEOUS NET UTILITIES

Sometimes you just need to grab a quick bit of information about someone, have a quick chat, or let other people know what you're doing while you're online. These utilities address those needs.

Finger

The finger daemon and client were originally UNIX programs that let a person on one machine check up on someone on another. By "fingering" someone you can find out information about his or her online status, the last time he or she logged in, what his or her full name and contact information is, the local time, and how long he or she has been online. Until finger for the Mac was released, the only way to finger someone was to log in to a UNIX shell account using Telnet, finger the person, look at the information, and log out. If you were using your Mac with a TCP/IP connection to access the Net, you were out of luck. There was no way anyone could finger you.

Peter Lewis changed all that when he released finger for the Mac. Now, not only can you finger someone on a remote machine, but you can actually run a finger daemon on your Mac so that others can finger you. And, as an added bonus, you can fully configure your finger plan file to display various tidbits of information about your status, your Mac, and anything else you'd want to display to the world.

In typical Peter Lewis fashion, finger is a clean, extremely well-written program that gets the job done with a minimum of fuss. Just enter a username, type the machine the user is on, and the info comes screamin' back. See Figure 15-14 for finger in action.

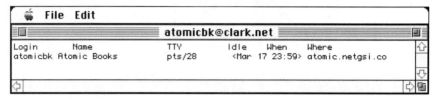

Figure 15-14: Fingering the fringe—Atomic Books finger information.

Program Name:	finger
Type:	finger client and daemon
System:	7.0 or later
Special Features:	Nice, simple, easy to configure program. Provides features for providing custom information via finger.
Where to get the latest version:	ftp:// ftp.share.com/pub/ peterlewis/

Table 15-10: A brief review of finger.

Talk

Sometimes you just gotta chat with someone. While IRC (Internet Relay Chat) is the place to go for real-time chat with hundreds of people, if you just want to talk to a single person, and you don't want to pick up the phone, you can use the program Talk.

Talk is a client that lets you hook up with a talk daemon on a UNIX machine, providing you with a nifty split-screen way to have text conversations over the Net. And, with the talk daemon (provided with Talk), people can "call" you while you're using your computer if they need to chat.

In this day of Internet phones, IRC, and powerful multiuser chat software, why use Talk? Several reasons. First, if you only have one phone line, it provides a way for your wired friends to reach you while you're online. Second, if you ever need to reach someone who's logged in at the school or company computer lab, he or she might not have a phone nearby. Now you can talk in real time as long as his or her computer has Talk capability.

To use Talk, you just type the name of the person you're trying to reach, enter the address for the computer the person uses, and wait. When the person answers, a split-screen window appears. Everything that you type appears in the top of the screen, and everything that the person you're talking to types appears at the bottom. Figure 15-15 shows a conversation in progress with Talk.

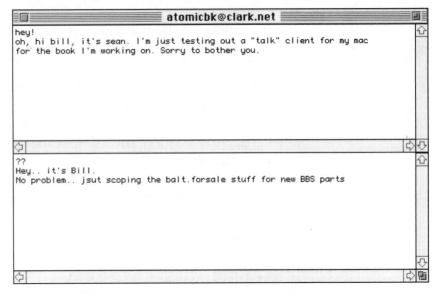

Figure 15-15: Sean chatting with his friend Bill using Talk.

Program Name:	Talk
Type:	Macintosh version of UNIX talk client and daemon
System:	7.0 or later
Special Features:	None. A simple talk client.
Where to get the latest version:	ftp:// ftp.share.com/pub/ peterlewis/

Table 15-11: A brief review of Talk.

Daemon

If you really want to play with the big boys, and provide your Mac with many of the services UNIX users enjoy, you need Daemon.

Pop Daemon in your Startup Items folder, and every time you start your Mac, you'll be running finger, whois, ident, daytime, and NTP (Network Time Protocol) servers. Once you've got these puppies running, anyone who wants to find out what you're up to can use his or her own finger or whois clients to connect to your machine. Once connected, he or she can find out anything from what kind of Mac you're running to how long you've been on, and even view any files you specify. At the same time, because you're running the show, you can serve or restrict whatever information you want through the configuration of your plan and whois files.

To set up Daemon, create a plan file, and place it in the Files folder in your Preferences folder. As soon as you start Daemon, you're ready to go. You can provide any of the following information to people who finger you using simple programming tokens that you place in your plan file:

- ❒ Startup Date & Time
- ❒ Current Date & Time
- ❒ Idle Date & Time
- ❒ Machine Name
- ❒ Owner Name
- ❒ Latitude and Longitude
- ❒ Mac Specifications
- ❒ Mac Icon
- ❒ Text Files
- ❒ A Random Fortune

Daemon even comes with a simple lookup feature so that you can provide people with different types of information based on what name they use when they finger your machine. Some people even use this feature to serve up price, availability, e-mail, or list database information. Use your imagination!

Ordinarily, we'd show you a screen shot of some aspect of Daemon, but since everything runs in the background, there's nothing to see!

Program Name:	Daemon
Type:	finger, whois, ident, daytime, and NTP (time) server /daemon
System:	Runs on nearly any Mac which supports MacTCP 1.1 or later.
Special Features:	Allows users to configure their own plan and whois files which provide scads of information with easily-programmable imbedded tokens.
Where to get the latest version:	ftp:// ftp.share.com/pub/ peterlewis/

Table 15-12: A brief review of Daemon.

MOVING ON

Well, your toolbox is now chock full of Internet power tools. "The right tool for the job," as they say. We've covered a variety of tools because users have different needs. Some want lean, mean, and small tools that specialize in one thing. Others won't be happy 'til someone develops the ultimate Net tool that does everything with equal élan. It's a matter of personal choice. Whatever you choose, make sure you're using tools you're comfortable with and that perform well for you. Experiment. Don't be afraid to try new features of the programs you're already using and to try new programs as they become available. As the Net expands, new and better stuff is coming out every day. The tools we covered in this chapter will help you learn about the tools that will replace them.

So what's ahead at this point? The wonderful world of UNIX! Now, don't get scared and run off to Chapter 20. Why not geek out with us as we dissect UNIX and explain how you can use its powerful features to access the Net? We'll cover everything from logging in to reading e-mail to browsing the Web from your shell account.

If you just don't have the stomach for it (the few, the proud, the UNIX savvy), skip ahead to Part V and learn about using e-mail more effectively. We'll tell you, among other things, what all that gibberish is in your e-mail headers and how to keep your e-mail private and secure.

UNIX Power User's Tools

## Chapter 16

Getting Connected With a Shell Account

Back in the mists of time (oh, say five years ago), no one but a few privileged hackers had direct Internet TCP/IP connectivity. Instead, if you wanted to get on the Net, you had to use a dial-up shell account where you dialed another computer system, logged in, and used its resources to get around. Your computer acted as a mere "dumb terminal," a conduit for your commands to get from your keyboard into the remote computer. And, because all of this was done with simple terminals, there was little or no graphics online—instead, Net surfers saw the Internet as a land of text-based menus and command-line control.

Things have changed a lot since then. Newcomers to the Internet don't have to deal with remembering obscure commands, command lines, or strange text-based interfaces. Instead, most of us (your humble authors included) surf the Net with dial-up TCP/IP accounts, using programs directly on our computers. If you want to read e-mail, you fire up your own, easy-to-use, graphical e-mail client. If you want to read Usenet news, you use an equally powerful graphical interface newsreader and just point-and-click your way through the news. And don't even think about browsing the Web without a graphical client!

So if we've come so far, why would we want to turn back the clock and go back to using dial-up terminal accounts? Several reasons. First, since you may have access to a shell account (through a direct Internet connection or a dial-up account), you might want to see what options a shell account offers. As we've said a number of times throughout this book, options are key to power using. There are so many things that can (and do) go wrong when you can't afford for them to. Your PPP connection fails, your FTP client becomes corrupted, or you're on vacation and have no access to the Internet other than a university UNIX machine. Under any of these circumstances, being able to log into your shell account, read your mail, access newsgroups, and transfer files can be a godsend. And let's not forget—even though most people have dial-up TCP/IP these days, many people don't. If you're one of those people with just a shell account, then this chapter is definitely for you.

A shell account does not have anything directly to do with the Internet. It normally doesn't use any of the Internet protocols (although there are some special exceptions to this). Rather, it is simply a way to connect to a UNIX system using a dumb terminal or, more commonly, terminal emulation software that makes a PC or Mac act like a dumb terminal. This type of connection is called a shell account because access to the system is accomplished through a shell program. Shell programs simply wait for a keystroke to be entered, put together a sequence of these keystrokes to construct user commands, and then execute the commands. (On DOS/Windows, for instance, the program command.com is a shell program.) In this way, users can do all the things the system will give them permission to do. Once you log in to a UNIX system that has Internet access, you can use UNIX's Internet utilities just as if you were logged in locally. However, it is the UNIX system that is on the Internet; you're simply connected to it in that ol' dumb terminal sorta way.

There are Internet service providers from which you can rent UNIX shell accounts. Most PPP and SLIP connections through an ISP come with a shell account as well, and a shell account gives Internet users some capabilities that they would not otherwise have. There's disk space available for you to keep your mail and anything else that suits your fancy. You can maintain a Web page or an FTP site there. Some shell account hosts are even equipped with compilers and linkers so that users can log in and do software development. (For years, modems have been set up by companies so that employees, and others, would be able to dial in to shell accounts to get work done.)

SHELL ACCOUNT BASICS

People have been logging into shell accounts since UNIX was a pup. This has traditionally been done with dumb terminals attached to modems. The user would simply set the modem switches to the configuration that matched the kind of connection and the terminal, type in the phone number for the modem to dial, wait for the connection, bang the Return key a few times to wake up UNIX, and log in whenever the prompt appeared. These were simple character-based terminals, so there were no large mysteries once the communications got going. It seldom got more exotic than the function and arrow keys.

UNIX hasn't changed. Remote logins still are treated as if they were being executed through a dumb terminal. Here's a quick lesson in how UNIX operates a login port. There's a little program called "getty" that is started by the UNIX operating system when it boots up. The name getty (rhymes with Betty) is short for "get tty." Now, tty is an acronym for teletype (see, we *told* you this was old stuff) and has become the UNIX name for a serial port. Anyway, the getty sits there like a ferret watching a hole, waiting for something to come in through the port. Whenever something does, the getty tries to make sense of it. It starts gathering up characters and tries to find a carriage return or something else it can recognize in the incoming stream. If it can't make sense out of the input, it will try different baud rates and data formats in all sorts of different combinations until a (usually empty) string followed by a carriage return is found. This is its whole purpose in life. This thrashing around is why, on some older systems, it was necessary to hit the Return key forever before any signs of life appeared. But, back to our story. Once the getty finds the carriage return, it sort of shouts "Eureka" and spawns a login program on that port. The getty, having done its work, performs a kind of digital hara-kiri.

The login program (which was given the port configuration by the getty) sends out the magic word "login:" and waits. It waits impatiently, however, and will eventually time out. It waits for some sequence of keystrokes that ends with a Return key. Whatever it receives, it keeps, and then it says "password:" and starts waiting again. If it successfully receives another string of keystrokes followed by a carriage return, it assumes that it's a password. It tries to find the login name and the password in the /etc/passwd file. If it finds an appropriate entry, it will also find the name of the shell program that is to be executed. At this point, everything is turned over to the shell program. The user is logged in and can start issuing commands for the shell program to obey.

TIP

UNIX has more than one version of these shell programs, and a user can choose the one he or she wishes. As a matter of fact, there are the same sorts of holy wars over shell programs as there are about computer languages, text editors, and operating systems. The original UNIX shell is the Bourne shell, which has the executable name sh. Its main two modern successors are the Korn shell, ksh, and the C shell, csh. There are any number of special-purpose shells, too.

As you can imagine, there's a bit more to all this, but we're sure you get the general idea. To get logged in, you have to get through the getty, then through the login, and finally to the shell. You notice there was no mention at all on the UNIX end about whether there's a modem or a simple terminal connected to the port. As shown in Figure 16-1, except for the modem, there's no real difference between a remote and local login. The getty doesn't care whether the incoming string of characters is from a modem or from a dumb terminal connected to the tty port.

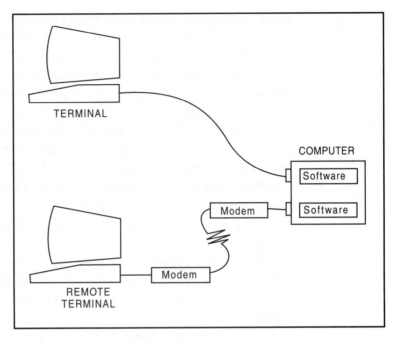

Figure 16-1: Remote and local logins to a shell account.

TERMINAL EMULATORS

To make a connection into a shell account, you either have to have a dumb terminal or software that will make your PC or Mac act like one. Of course, these days, almost no one uses dumb terminals. The cost of personal computers has dropped to the point that a plain ol' terminal is a dumb investment. A terminal emulator is a program that, through modern advances in computer science, has the capability of converting a high-speed multimegabyte modern desktop computer into a dumb terminal of about 20 years ago. Just set this puppy up by telling it which port the modem is on, give the number a dial, and watch it go to work. If the PC is networked on a LAN, it is just a matter of bringing up the software and addressing the desired host computer.

Once connected, commands can be typed from the keyboard and sent out over the modem to the shell program on the host end. The shell program on the host needs to know just what each keystroke means. To this end, the shell program needs to be told just what type of terminal is being used (or emulated). There's no problem recognizing the standard set of ASCII characters, but things like the arrow keys and function keys, which may be defined differently for different terminal types, need to be correctly recognized as well. This is done by having the shell program read an initialization file when it starts running. This startup file (the UNIX equivalent of autoexec.bat in DOS) will define the terminal type. The terminal type is set in the UNIX environment variable called TERM. There is a file that holds a description of all the terminal types that are likely to log in. For years, this was an ASCII file named "termcap" (terminal capabilities), but it has been changed to a compiled form that holds the same information and is now called "terminfo." Anyway, the environment variable TERM is set to the name of one of the entries in this file (see the section "Logging In & Looking Around" for more on setting the TERM variable).

All terminal emulation programs have facilities to do file transfer. This is a very manual, and sometimes cumbersome, process. You're better off if you can make a TCP/IP link and use FTP if you're really serious about getting your files transferred. However, there are times when you just need a quick text file or something, and the convenience of having file transfer at your fingertips is the overriding concern. To do a file transfer, there must be a protocol match on both ends. If both ends have Xmodem or Zmodem, you're set. Most often, with a connection between a personal computer and a UNIX system, you'll find that Kermit (the protocol, not the frog) is the one they all have in common. In any case, you start the UNIX version of the program on the remote machine and then start the terminal emulator version on the local machine. If all goes well, the two of them will transfer the file and then turn the connection back over to you. If the connection and handshaking aren't all they should be, you could wind up with a deadlock situation and only get out of it by breaking the connection. This is especially true of Kermit. Make sure you know the secret handshake to get Kermit to shut down on the remote system before you start the file transfer. It's right there with the other interface instructions.

Windows Terminal Programs

There are lots of shareware terminal emulators for DOS and Windows. There are commercial packages as well. The commercial versions can get very fancy, with lots of other utilities and very sophisticated scripting languages. There are some basic things to look for in terminal emulators. A good terminal emulator is able to emulate several different kinds of terminals, has a scripting language that can be used to automate complex and repetitive sequences, and should be able to handle several different protocols for copying files to and from the host computer.

Hyperterminal

Hyperterminal is a simple-to-use terminal emulator that comes with Windows 95. To operate, it's just a matter of locating it on the Start menu and selecting it. What comes up first is a window containing a selection of previously configured connection icons. This serves as a dialing directory. Each icon is associated with a telephone number and other dialing prerequisites. There's one icon in the bunch that brings up a window for the user to define a new member for the dialing directory icon group (this one may be labeled hypertrm or hypertrm.exe—it depends on your system settings). Before a connection is made, there must be an entry for that connection in the iconized directory listing. Figure 16-2 shows the Hyperterminal window as it appears immediately following a dial-up connection with MCI Mail.

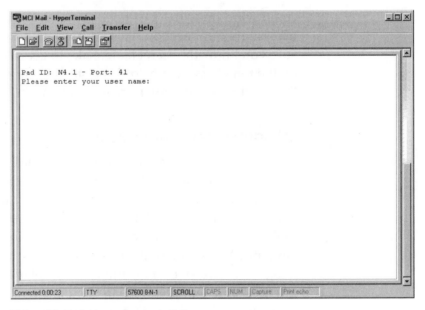

Figure 16-2: A Hyperterminal window.

TIP

The settings for the modem are not found in the terminal emulator, but instead are a part of the Windows system configuration. The terminal emulator just remembers the name of the entry in the list of configured modems.

Windows 3.1 Terminal

There's a terminal emulator in Windows 3.1 called, simply, Terminal. As far as bright little programs go, this one is a pretty dim bulb. It will do all the basic stuff, but there's nothing automatic about it. It will keep one setup (phone number, baud rate, etc.), and only one. It has to be reconfigured each time you make a connection. It's a very simple little terminal emulator, but it does come with the system so it's always there. We've used it ourselves in situations where nothing else was available.

Crosstalk

Crosstalk for Windows is a commercial product that's been around for a long time. It started as a DOS application and has maintained a very loyal following. When you start to use it, you'll quickly see why people like it. It supports a wide range of terminal types and has file transfer software for any protocol you would want to use. As a matter of fact, if you need some type of file transfer protocol that doesn't seem to exist in any other terminal emulator, you'll probably find it here.

This is quite a sophisticated package. In addition to the regular terminal emulation operations, it can also be used over different types of networks. It will work with NetWare, NCSI, the redirected BIOS interface, and others. It can be set up to make several different types of connections so that it can be used for direct serial connections, dial-up connections, and a LAN.

The configuration is done using menu selections or by selecting options on a toolbar. Like most toolbars, it's mostly useless until you've figured out what some of the little hieroglyphs mean.

One of the outstanding features of Crosstalk is the very sophisticated scripting language CASL (Crosstalk Application Scripting Language). Entire applications are written using it. Crosstalk is a mature product and it has always had a very good scripting language. With each new release it becomes more extensive. Programming in CASL is not difficult. You'll find yourself writing working code very quickly.

Procomm Plus for Windows

This package started out as a DOS shareware package simply called Procomm. By the time it became Procomm Plus for Windows it was a full fledged, honest-to-goodness shrink-wrapped product. It was one of the packages that started the era of ease of use by being the first communications package with a simple and intuitive interface. Its ease of use was a prime reason for its success. It's the only DOS package that I know of that's had a UNIX copycat version. The UNIX version is not in common use today, but for a while there it was quite popular.

There are two commercial versions of Procomm: one for DOS and one for Windows. The Windows version has menus and a toolbar. Departing from the normal way of doing things, the Procomm toolbar is composed of buttons that are large enough to actually see. Most of them have graphics on them that make sense. This is a radical departure from the traditional method of tiny little cryptic icons of unknown purpose that can be remembered only by people who use the package four hours a day.

There are pop-ups that hold phone lists and configurations. Like all Windows programs, there are some confusing points and a few buttons that have mysterious purposes, but all in all they've kept most of the clear and intuitive interface that made Procomm famous. In a couple of places, they did give in to the non-obvious secret handshake mode of requiring a double mouse click to cause something to happen.

Procomm is fancy. It looks good, and has lots of stuff in it. It includes complete FAX software. It has an automatic graphics viewer that pops up a display whenever it receives a graphics file. There's DDE support so that data from other applications can be transmitted and received. And it has just about every data transfer protocol a practical-minded person would ever need.

Chameleon/X

Chameleon/X, from Netmanage, is an X server for Windows. This is quite a bit more than just a dumb terminal. The X system is a complete GUI and windowing interface to UNIX, so it requires a shell account with some special software on the UNIX side. (By the way, when it comes to X windowing, we can see some of the terminology drift. The software that operates the terminal, keyboard, and mouse is called an X server. On almost all other systems, the user side of the software is called a client.) Anyway, for the Chameleon X server to run on Windows, some Netmanage software must also be running on the UNIX end. This means that the UNIX software will have to be purchased and installed by the UNIX system administrator. The home page of Netmanage is at http://www.netmanage.com, where you'll find demonstration versions of this and other software.

Hooking up the Chameleon to an X windowing UNIX network opens up a whole new world of graphical interfacing. There are several different windowing "looks and feels" that can be used. The "look and feel" is determined by whichever window manager is being used by the person logging in. The most common remote window managers are Motif and Open Look, but there are others (X is very open in regard to look and feel). You can also use a local window to give X the look and feel of Microsoft windows. X is a networking system (it uses TCP/IP for everything), so applications all over the UNIX network can be executed. There are any number of UNIX programs for e-mail, news, FTP, and everything else. The mother lode of Internet software is available to you.

Chameleon is a very complete software package. This software includes full terminal emulation, and it supports Telnet, FTP, and so on. You can launch any number of local sessions, so unlike simpler terminal emulators, Chameleon supports several simultaneous sessions. This is mature software. It has been a workhorse in this area for several years.

Macintosh Terminal Programs

ZTerm

ZTerm is a shareware terminal emulator for the Mac. It emulates two terminal types: VT100 and ANSI. It's common for both of these to be supported by a UNIX host, but VT100 is the most common. The shareware fee is $30. Figure 16-3 shows the main window of the shareware version of Zterm.

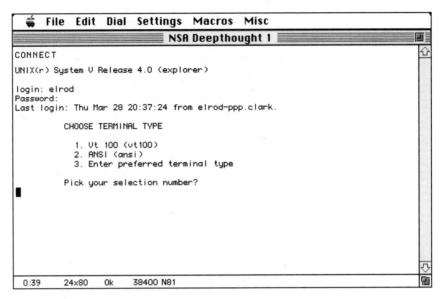

```
  File  Edit  Dial  Settings  Macros  Misc
                    NSA Deepthought 1
CONNECT

UNIX(r) System V Release 4.0 (explorer)

login: elrod
Password:
Last login: Thu Mar 28 20:37:24 from elrod-ppp.clark.

        CHOOSE TERMINAL TYPE

        1. Vt 100 (vt100)
        2. ANSI (ansi)
        3. Enter preferred terminal type

        Pick your selection number?



0:39    24x80    0k    38400 N81
```

Figure 16-3: The main window of ZTerm.

The shareware version can be found on almost any Mac software site. One location to find it, along with its latest FAQ, is the FTP site usit.net, in the directory /pub/lesjones. It can do file transfer using Xmodem, Ymodem, Zmodem, and Kermit.

TIP

The Xmodem, Ymodem, Zmodem, and Kermit protocols aren't standard with UNIX, but any or all of them could possibly be available on a UNIX system. Kermit is probably the most common, but if Zmodem is available it should be used (it's much faster, and much less error-prone). It has some special features, too. For example, it can be configured to automatically detect when a MacBinary file is being received, and it will convert the file back to its original form. It can also be configured to convert outgoing files into MacBinary format. Perhaps most important, it can be configured to automatically pick up a download where it left off, should your connection crash in the middle of a large transfer.

ZTerm's scripting facility can be used for various purposes. Here's a simple example of a login script. The values for name and password have already been entered into the Connection dialog .

```
wait prompt "login:"
send $name "^M"
wait prompt "password:"
send $password "^M"
```

Once the connection is established, this script will wait until it receives the string "login:" and then send the login name (the one that was entered into the Connection dialog). It will then wait until the string "password:" arrives and respond with the password (the one from the Connection dialog).

VT100 Emulation on the Mac

Some notes about VT100 emulation. While this emulation is turned on, all the keys operate as if they were VT100 keys. To be able to use them as Mac keys, you'll need to hold down the Shift key. The function keys are assigned to VT100 also, so you'll need to use the command key shortcuts or the Edit menu to simulate the function keys. To emulate the Control key and Escape key (which you'll need for vi and some other utilities), check Option for Control in the Terminal Preferences. The "accent grave" key will emulate the Escape key. On a Mac, all 8 bits are used for characters. A VT100 uses 7-bit ASCII. You can paste text directly into the VT100 emulation, but care must be taken that only standard ASCII characters are used; the others will present you with garbage on the display (for example, don't try to use "curly quotes" on a VT100 system—you won't get what you want).

White Knight

White Knight started as a popular shareware package known as Red Ryder. When it moved from version 10 to version 11, it got a name change and became the commercial product of a company named Freesoft. White Knight is very good about sticking with the

Macintosh interface standards, and is easy enough to use that you never need to open the manual. Of course, those who do read the manual will have a better time of it, since they'll understand how to use all of White Knight's many features.

White Knight has a very extensive scripting language (and you'll certainly need the manual for that). This language becomes intuitive after a bit, since many of the functions in it perform the same functions that appear on the menu. This way, you can automate a procedure that you already know how to do manually. Even the scripting language has adhered to the interface standards in that you can write a script and add it to the menu bar. You can also define onscreen objects. The language will do just about everything you need to do, but in case you want to get real fancy, the language can even access external programs. You can, for example, write a script that connects up with MacInTalk so that it can speak your messages.

MicroPhone Pro

MicroPhone Pro, from Software Ventures, is available for both the Macintosh and Windows. Like White Knight, MicroPhone Pro has a complete scripting language. You can easily write scripts that let you automatically log on, transfer data, and log off. A "Watch Me" feature has MicroPhone Pro build a script while you perform the tasks manually. It's like a tape recorder. You turn it on, and do whatever the tasks are that you want to automate in the future. When you're done, you turn Watch Me off, assign a button, a menu item, or a keyboard command to your new script. If the script doesn't work, you can "rerecord" it or go into the script window and tweak the script yourself. MicroPhone has a quick and dirty text editor, a sophisticated but not overwhelmingly complicated interface, and lots of useful special features. Gareth's son likes to play around with making MicroPhone Pro interfaces 'cause he likes all the cool custom icons it comes with.

TIP

This chapter is about modems and terminal programs as they relate specifically to accessing a shell account. If you're looking for more general information about modems and how they work, check out Chapters 1 and 2.

CONFIGURING YOUR MODEM

There are three basic ways to log in to a shell account. The first, and most traditional, is to log in to a terminal connected directly to the system. The second, which is becoming more common, is to log in through another computer on the same LAN. The third method is to dial up through a modem. With the first two, there is usually a system administrator who sets up everything. With a modem, as often as not, the setup is done by a person who has little or no background in setting up data links. Fortunately, modern modems have gotten smart enough that most of the setup knowledge is built into them. Most, but not all.

The purpose of a modem is to have your computer communicate over a telephone line to a modem connected to another computer. To communicate with 70 percent of the world out there, modems are set to N81 (no parity, 8 data bits, 1 stop bit). For the next 20 percent the settings are to E70 (even parity, 7 data bits, no stop bits). The last 10 percent use random modem settings and are probably not worth communicating with. But if you must, take heart in the fact that there is a finite number of combinations of these three settings. The only way to find out (unless somebody writes it down or tells you) is to try the different settings until all of a sudden you get something besides a bunch of unsightly garbage. Any responsible provider of a shell account will tell you what the settings are.

Until Windows 95, every DOS/Windows application had the responsibility of configuring its own modem connection, and each program had its own way of doing things. The Mac OS still works this way. In Windows 95, we have unity. Each modem is configured in one central configuration file. Now all the software can be written to communicate through this standard system of defined modems. Of course, for backward compatibility, older software can still go around this feature.

There's a huge list of modems in Windows 95. If you pick your modem from this list, all the settings will be made for you. If your modem is not in the list, and if the defaults don't work, you'll need to start setting things up yourself. Figure 16-4 shows the Modems Properties window (located in the Modems Control Panel) for the basic connection settings of data, parity, and stop bits that we discussed above.

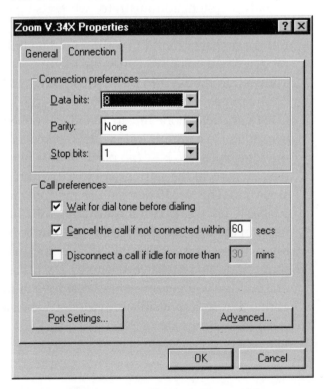

Figure 16-4: Basic modem setup in Windows 95.

Selecting the Advanced button will bring up the window in Figure 16-5 so that handshaking can be set up. If your modem needs some sort of special command string for initialization, it can be included here as Extra settings.

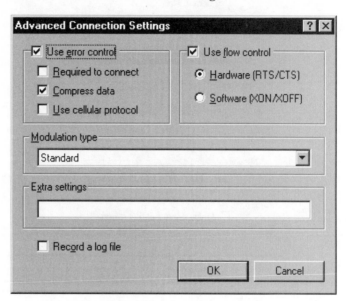

Figure 16-5: Advanced modem setup in Windows 95.

Figure 16-6 shows the window used to select the port and the baud rate. If there are several modems available, it will be possible to configure them all. This will cause a selection window to appear whenever an application needs a modem.

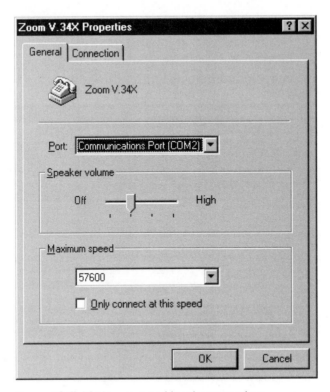

Figure 16-6: Modem port and baud rate settings.

On both Mac and Windows, the baud rate you'll be able to get away with depends on a lot of factors. One simple rule is that you want it to run as fast as it can and still get clean data across the line. You have to deal with the speed limitations of the serial port in your local computer, and the capabilities of your modem, the quality of the telephone connection, the capabilities of the modem and serial port on the other end. First, try setting the baud rate at the highest speed your serial port can handle. The reasoning is that if you have, for example, a 28.8 modem, it may still be able to communicate with your computer at 115.2, and on a clear telephone line, with the wind at its back, you'll get bursts of data in and out that are well above 28.8 and your serial port will be ready to handle them. If this just does not work, reduce the baud rate setting until you find the highest speed that both of the devices can handle. You really want to experiment with this a bit because the time spent here could save you all sorts of time later. There are circumstances where a higher baud rate will slow down communications because the modems are spending an inordinate amount of time in error correction, so you'll need to check some different speeds. It does no good to send the data twice as fast if you have to send it three times to get a clean transmission.

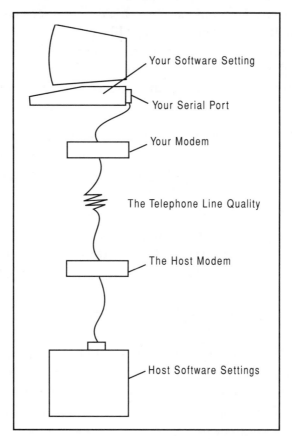

Figure 16-7: Things that determine maximum baud rate.

LOGGING IN & LOOKING AROUND

You may need to search around a bit to find a terminal type that makes both your terminal emulator software and the UNIX shell happy. The terminal types must be the same on both ends. When everything is set right, you can start to use the special cursor-control features built into UNIX. All this is defined in the standard UNIX cursors library. The functions from this library are linked into many UNIX utilities and they control cursor movements and character displays on the screen. This is all configured by setting the environment variable TERM. The screen control can get very sophisticated and do things like clear the screen and draw lines, and even do overlapped character windowing.

There are some things you must know to be able to log in, and there are other things that it would be very convenient for you to know:

❏ Username. You must know this. It's usually also the name of your home directory. Your home directory is where you'll find yourself whenever you log in.

❏ Password. You must know this. You may have had this automatically assigned to you or you may have created it yourself. If you get a temporary password assigned, you'll want to change it as soon as you log in for the first time.

❏ Telephone number. This is the telephone number for the computer you're trying to connect to. You must know this. There may be more than one number, but you must have at least one.

❏ Modem settings. It would be very nice to know these. With modern modems it isn't as crucial as it used to be, but it could still save you from several wrong guesses.

❏ Shell. It would be very nice to know this. There are several shells that can be configured for a shell account.. There's the Bourne shell (sh), the C shell (csh), the Korn shell (ksh), and the Bourne again shell (bash). There are others, but these are the main players.

Login Procedures & Initial Account Setup

Here's a typical sequence to follow the first time you log in to a new shell account. The account should have been set up for you with a login name and a password. That, and the modem connection information, is all you need to know. Follow these steps to get in and get set up. (This list is not intended to list all the things you may want to do to customize your account. This is a list of the basics to help you make a clean and usable login.)

1. Make sure the Caps Lock key is off. Logging into a UNIX system with all caps causes the shell to operate in a different mode. It thinks you're on an exceptionally dumb terminal that has no lowercase and, since all UNIX commands require lowercase, it will kindly translate everything to lowercase internally and translate everything it sends back to you into uppercase. This will cause no end of weird little problems.

2. Do whatever you need to get your terminal emulator software to dial the number and make a connection (a number of good shareware packages are available on the Net).

3. Once the modems have connected, you may need to tap the Return key a few times depending on how sleepy the getty is. When you see the prompt "login:" enter your account name.

4. When you see the prompt "password:" enter the password. Don't worry—if you get either the name or password wrong, it will pause for a bit and come back around again. It has a time-out, but it's friendly for a while.

When you get the login and password correct, you should see a command-line prompt of some sort. Depending on how the system is configured it could be any one of a number of things. It's normally a single character like % or : or even $. It could be set up so that it shows the host name and/or the current directory path. If you don't know what shell you are using, type **grep <name> /etc/passwd**, where <name> is your login name. The grep command reads through files searching for strings; in this case it is searching for your login name. This will display a line of text that has the name of the shell at its far right. The C shell is csh, the Korn shell is ksh, and the Bourne shell is sh. If it's anything else, treat it like the Bourne shell. If you want to change your password at this time, enter the command **password**, and you'll be asked to enter your existing password and then a new one. You'll then be asked to verify the new one by entering it again. This will replace the password that may have been assigned to you when the account was created.

Special Keys & Settings

Once you've gotten logged into your account, you'll need to spend a few moments configuring your shell correctly. Many times, university and corporate UNIX systems set up user accounts in line mode, which means that you can't readily back up to see what's scrolled off the screen and you can't use any full-screen editors that allow you to move around the screen with the cursor keys. On top of that, many commands that you're used to on your home PC — backspace, delete, break—are completely different.

What do you do about this? Change things to your liking! See, we told you that UNIX was flexible! To set your account to the nice VT100 format, you're going to have to add some information to your login or profile file. These files can be found in the top-level directory of your UNIX account and are used to store system configuration information and login scripts.

First, check with your system administrator to see what kind of shell your account is running. If your sysadmin is too busy, you can often tell what kind of shell it is by looking at your prompt. It's important to know what type of shell you're using so that you can be sure to use the correct commands. Most, if not all, of the commands we'll cover in this chapter will work with any shell, but if you have any questions, ask your systems administrator. See Table 16-1 for some examples.

Prompt	Usual Shell
$	ksh (Korn shell)
%	csh (C shell)
>	tcsh

Table 16-1: Some common UNIX shell prompts.

If you're running a Korn shell or Bourne shell, add the following to your profile file:

```
eval 'tset -m sun:\?hp -s -e -k -Q'
```

The "sun" is for the type of host you're using. You can pretty much use whatever you want here. This line will set your terminal to VT100 when you log in.

Editing Your Files: A Very Brief Intro to UNIX Editors

In order to add or modify your .login or .profile files, you'll need to open them in a text editor. A text editor is like a simple word-processor, providing you with a way of making changes to text files. There are many different types of text editors available, and describing how to use each would take much more space than we have here.

Here's a brief rundown of UNIX text editors:

Pico: A full-screen text editor that works much like the word processor you're probably used to. Just move the cursor with the arrow keys, use the backspace to delete, and add new lines by hitting Enter. If you have this on your system, use it—it's perfect for simple editing. Try typing *pico* at the command line and see what happens. **Note:** if you have the Pine e-mail program installed, you have Pico.

EMACS: A very complicated text editor for programmers. Not for the faint-hearted or for beginners. In fact, EMACS is so powerful that it includes its own programming language.

vi: A slightly less complicated full-screen text editor. While vi isn't quite as powerful as EMACS, it can run circles around Pico. However, it is fairly complicated to learn. If you can, stick with Pico.

If you're running a C shell, then you may just be able to add the following line to your login file:

```
setenv TERM vt100
```

Give it a try.

Once you've got that settled, you'll want to configure the terminal to use some custom keys. You can either type this line at the prompt after you log in or you can add it to your login or profile file so that it's set automatically:

```
stty erase "^H" int "^C" kill "^U"
```

Doing this will set the Backspace key to the same as the Delete or backspace key on your keyboard. It's the one usually located above the Enter or Return key—not the smaller "Del" in the keygroup between the alpha keys and the keypad. This stty command will also set the interrupt command to Control+C and the kill or "discard this line I'm typing" command to Control+U.

TIP

If you really start hacking with stty, you can do some wacky stuff to your keyboard mappings. If things get too weird, just type **stty sane** and the settings will go back to the system defaults. It may not be exactly what you want, but at least you've got a spot of normalcy to go from.

Those are pretty much the basics of setting up your UNIX terminal. Simple stuff, really. For a quick reference, Table 16-2 shows you the special terminal "control" characters often used on UNIX systems. Yours might be different. Type **stty** by itself and hit Enter to see what they are on your system.

Key	stty name	Action
Control+C	int	Interrupt key. Stops current program.
Control+D	eof	Represents the end-of-file character.
Control+H	erase	Deletes previous character. Often the same as backspace.
Control+Q	n/a	Resumes command halted by Control+S.
Control+S	n/a	Halts command being executed.
Control+U	kill	Deletes current line of text.
Control+\	quit	Quits current program. Dumps a "core" file on some systems.

Table 16-2: Typical UNIX terminal control characters.

MOVING ON

Now that we've covered the basics of the software needed to get into a UNIX account and how to get through the front door and turn on the house lights, it's time to look at what UNIX offers by way of Internet tools. It may seem odd to some that we're even bothering with all that UNIX stuff. Isn't UNIX your father's operating system? Not at all—UNIX is still a critical part of the Internet's infrastructure. It's a big part of the Internet's backbone, and it's still in wide use in many schools, businesses, and research centers. It's also an integral part of online culture, so that culture will be richer to you if you understand some of the UNIX legacy.

In the next chapter, we'll start our tour of UNIX Internet programs by looking at e-mail programs. There are a number of them to suit your needs and interface tastes. Regardless of whether you plan to use your shell account for news reading, Web browsing, file transfer, and other functions better served by more user-friendly, menu-driven programs, knowing how to use UNIX e-mail can always come in handy.

## Chapter 17

UNIX E-Mail Tools

In this and the next two chapters, we're going to focus on UNIX Internet communications tools. Because there's so much ground to cover, we aren't going to go into great detail on each and every program.

Here, we'll cover the three most common UNIX e-mail programs—elm, Pine, and mailx. We'll show you how to get into each program, read your e-mail, send e-mail, and do some fancy tricks that should make your life easier.

Remember, if you're a little unsure of how to use your shell account, turn to Appendix D, "UNIX Boot Camp," for a bracing refresher on UNIX and navigating around a UNIX account.

UNIX E-MAIL COMMUNICATIONS

Who can ever forget how exciting it was to log on to an Internet account to discover their first e-mail message? E-mail is probably now a routine and essential part of your life. You rely on it to conduct business, stay in touch with friends, keep up on interoffice gossip, send news to family members, or just chat with people you meet online. No matter how you slice it, if you're like most Internet users, you probably use e-mail a lot.

If you're accustomed to getting your mail through America Online, CompuServe, or Prodigy, or if you use a graphical e-mail reader with your SLIP or PPP connection, you'll probably be pleasantly surprised when you discover how quick and easy it is to use your e-mail in UNIX.

Even though many UNIX commands and programs can repel the new user, most UNIX e-mail programs are relatively user-friendly. elm and Pine, the two most popular UNIX e-mail programs, use a simple menu-driven interface that allows you to read and send mail just by selecting options with your arrow keys. The other mail program that we'll cover—mailx—isn't as pretty, but it's remarkably easy to use. You just type your message, press a few keys, and off goes your mail!

Using your UNIX account to get your e-mail can have several advantages. First, as we've said before, it's fast—just a quick dial in, a few keystrokes, and your message is mailed. Second, because it's UNIX, you can do a lot of fancy stuff with your mail by piping and processing messages through other programs. Third, since your UNIX account is always online, you can set it to process, respond, and filter your mail, even when you're not there!

Interested? We hope so, otherwise we slaved over this chapter for nothing. Let's take a look at basic UNIX e-mail communications.

Elm

Elm is probably the most popular UNIX e-mail communications program, mainly because it's quick, uncomplicated, and versatile. As a screen-oriented program, it's very easy for people who are unfamiliar with UNIX and command-line interfaces.

Screen-oriented programs use the entire screen to display information. Unlike line-oriented programs, which display information line-by-line, screen-oriented programs usually keep a constant display on the screen and allow you to move around to the various parts of it by using the arrow keys on your keyboard. The standard DOS editor program is a good example of a screen-oriented program.

Since elm is a screen-oriented program, you have to use a terminal type that supports screen-oriented programs to use elm. If your account is set up as a VT100 or ANSI terminal (and most are), then you're fine. If not, go back to in Chapter 16, "Getting Connected With a Shell Account," and read the section on setting up your terminal for directions on how to get into the correct terminal mode.

OK, enough introductions—let's get started.

Starting elm

To start the elm program, type **elm** at the command line, and press Enter. If you get the following message, or something similar, elm may not be installed on your system:

```
elm: Command not found.
```

Elm has been placed in the "public trust" and is freely available, so there's really no excuse not to have it. Call your system administrator, and demand it! Well, ask nicely, actually.

After you begin elm, you should see a screen that looks similar to the one shown in Figure 17-1.

```
      Mailbox is '/var/mail/elrod' with 98 messages [ELM 2.4 PL24alpha3]


->N   1   Nov 7   Matthew Wood      (46)   wildcards
  N   2   Nov 7   Linda Reynolds    (47)   Re: YKYACH When :
  N   3   Nov 7   Meredith Foster   (35)   Re: updating Quark
  N   4   Nov 7   Jim Leftwich      (89)   Re: hey waaaaaard
  N   5   Nov 7   Trevor            (32)   Chile Today - Hot Tamale
  N   6   Nov 7   Lauren Chung      (44)   Jerk Seasoning - Bakayawd Jerk Seaso
  NM  7   Nov 7   Alan Benson       (45)   Step and Repeat
  N   8   Nov 7   Era Eriksson      (49)   Re: quark import acrobat
  N   9   Nov 7   Larry Hunter      (74)   Re: YKYACH When :
  NM 10   Nov 7   Era Eriksson      (46)   Re: Quark  to HTML?



         |=pipe, !=shell, ?=help, <n>=set current to n, /=search pattern
    a)lias, C)opy, c)hange folder, d)elete, e)dit, f)orward, g)roup reply, m)ail,
      n)ext, o)ptions, p)rint, q)uit, r)eply, s)ave, t)ag, u)ndelete, or e(x)it

Command: █
```

Figure 17-1: Initial elm screen.

If you don't have any mail, you obviously won't see any messages on the screen. Skip ahead to the "Sending Mail with elm" section, send yourself a message so you have something to work with, and come on back.

The top line of the initial elm screen (Figure 17-1) tells you where your system mailbox is located. At this point we won't do anything with that information, but it is useful. This line also tells you what version of elm your system's running. The next few lines contain all the important stuff—your mail! In the first column on the left, you'll see one of several different codes. Table 17-1 sums them up.

Code	Description
N	New message—one you haven't read yet.
E	Expired message—some systems allow you to set an expiration date for old messages.
O	Old message—one that was listed the last time you listed your messages but hasn't been read yet.
D	Deleted—one that has been marked for deletion.

Table 17-1: Elm message codes.

Occasionally, you may see an M next to one of these codes. The M code means that your message has a file attached to it via MIME. If you encounter this, refer to Chapter 20, "Inside E-Mail" and look at the section on MIME and e-mail.

Moving to the right, the number is the message number for each message. As each message comes in, elm assigns it a number in numerical order. The next column contains the date that the message was sent. Next to the date field is the e-mail address or name of the sender (depending on how the sender's e-mail program is configured). Following the address of the sender is a number in parentheses representing the number of lines (including header information) of the message. The last column shows the subject of the message.

Right below the list of mail is the elm menu, which stays on the screen as long as you're viewing the list of messages. If you're set to the beginner user level (which you probably are), you'll see a menu like the one in Figure 17-1. If you see something different, don't fret—your elm program may have been set to a higher user level. Just ignore any extra stuff you see, and follow along here. Finally, at the bottom of the screen, you'll see Command: patiently waiting for your input. Let's not keep it waiting.

Reading Your E-Mail

You may notice an arrow (->) pointing at message 1 on your elm mail list. If you don't see the arrow, no big deal—it just means that your elm mailer hasn't been configured to use it. Either way, when you first start elm, you should be at the first message.

To read your mail, press Enter or space. Your mail should appear on your screen in a format similar to that shown in Figure 17-2. On the top line, you'll see text describing the message number you've selected and how many more messages are in the list. In this case, we've selected message 1 of 5. This line also tells you who the message came from and when it was sent. The next four lines are called the header, and it tells you when the message was sent, who it's from, and the subject of the message. There may be more information up there, depending on your setup and the content of the message, but these four lines should always be there.

```
Message 5/5  From Automatic digest processor        May 11, 96 09:48:02 am +2000

Date:      Sat, 11 May 1996 09:48:02 +2000
Reply-To: Net-Happenings <NET-HAPPENINGS@LISTS.INTERNIC.NET>
Sender: Net-Happenings <NET-HAPPENINGS@LISTS.INTERNIC.NET>
Subject:  NET-HAPPENINGS Digest - 10 May 1996 to 11 May 1996 - Special issue
To: Recipients of NET-HAPPENINGS digests
          <NET-HAPPENINGS@LISTS.INTERNIC.NET>

There are 15 messages totalling 663 lines in this issue.

Topics in this special issue:

  1. SCOUT> The Scout Report -- May 10, 1996
  2. WWW> To all the Moms on the List
  3. <No subject given>
  4. WWW> Big Yellow (NYNEX Business Listing)
  5. WWW> The Zipper (GOVT)
  6. WWW> A Journalist's Guide-Finding Data Online
  7. WWW> CyberHound Homepage
  8. WWW> Blue Cares
  9. SEM> LAN/Network managers
 675 lines more (you've seen 3%)
```

Figure 17-2: Reading a message with elm.

Next comes the body of the message. If the message takes up only one screen, you'll see text at the bottom of the screen indicating that you can press the letter i to return to the index or list of messages. If the message takes up more than one screen of text, you'll see text at the bottom of the screen that indicates how many more lines are left in the message and what percentage of the message you've seen so far. Just like the more utility, if you press Enter, you'll see the rest of the message, one line at a time. If you press space, you'll get another screenful of text. When you're finished reading, type **i** to return to the index.

Once back at the index, you can type **j** or press the Down arrow key to move down through the list of messages, type **k** or press the Up arrow key to move up through the list, or just type the number of the message and press Enter to move to the message that corresponds to the number. Once you've selected a message, press Enter or space to read it. See Table 17-2 for a list of commands you can use to read mail in elm.

Key	Description
space or Enter	Reads message selected in index.
Up arrow or k	Moves up one message in the index.
Down arrow or j	Moves down one message in the index.
d	Marks current message for deletion.
Number	Moves to message with corresponding number.

Table 17-2: Commands to Read Mail in elm.

Sending Mail

Okay, you've done it. You've read your first message with elm! Sending messages is even easier.

When you tell elm that you want to send a message, it puts you in the editor that you've specified in the Options menu. Depending on the system you're using, this editor could be either vi or Pico or a different editor. If Pico has been installed on your system, use it—it's much simpler to learn than vi.

If you want to check your editor, press **o** from the index screen. You should then get an Options menu as shown in Figure 17-3.

```
                    -- ELM Options Editor --

C)alendar file        :  /homec/elrod/calendar
D)isplay mail using   :  builtin+
E)ditor (primary)     :  pico
F)older directory     :  /homec/elrod/Mail
S)orting criteria     :  Reverse-Sent
O)utbound mail saved  :  =sent
P)rint mail using     :  /bin/cat %s | /bin/lp
Y)our full name       :  Sean Carton
U)isual Editor (~v)   :  /opt/local/bin/pico

A)rrow cursor         :  ON
M)enu display         :  ON

U)ser level           :  Expert User
N)ames only           :  ON


      Select letter of option line, '>' to save, or 'i' to return to index.

Command: █
```

Figure 17-3: Elm Options menu.

To set your editor to Pico (if your system has it) or vi, type **e** and then enter **pico** for the pico editor or **vi** for the vi editor. Then press Enter. If you've typed everything correctly, press the greater than symbol (>) to save your changes and return to the index. If you've decided that you don't want to change the editor, press **i** to return to the index without changing anything.

Now let's send some mail. You can send mail one of two ways. If you're already in elm, just type an **m**. You should then get the following prompt:

To:

Enter the e-mail address of the person you want to mail, and press Enter. If it's someone on your system, you can just enter his or her username. If you want to send mail to several people at once, just enter their email addresses separated by commas. Elm will prompt you for the subject. Type the subject of your message, and press Enter. Elm will ask you to enter the e-mail address of anyone you want to send copies to. Again, if you want to send e-mail to several different people, just separate their e-mail addresses by commas.

If you enter an e-mail address here, your message will be copied and mailed to the person or persons you specify. If you don't want to send a copy, just press Enter. Elm will put you in the editor you specify. If you've set up elm to use the Pico editor, you'll see something like the screen shown in Figure 17-4. If you use vi, you'll be placed in the vi editor.

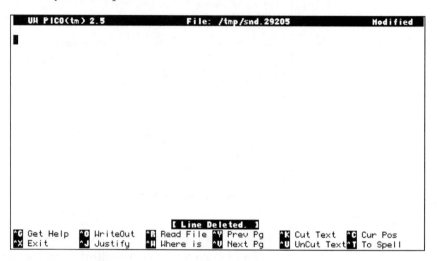

```
  UH PICO(tm) 2.5              File:  /tmp/snd.29205              Modified
█
 




 


 



                            [ Line Deleted. ]
^G Get Help  ^O WriteOut  ^R Read File  ^Y Prev Pg  ^K Cut Text   ^C Cur Pos
^X Exit      ^J Justify   ^W Where is   ^V Next Pg  ^U UnCut Text ^T To Spell
```

Figure 17-4: The Pico editor waiting for you to type a message.

The two lines of text at the bottom of the Pico screen are the menu of commands. Each command can be invoked by typing its corresponding letter and the Control key. As you'll notice, the letter has the caret character (^)in front of it. That's the techie notation for the Control key. So if you wanted to spell check your message, you'd type **Ctrl+t**.

Type your message. Pico works like a simplified version of many popular word processors, so it shouldn't take you long to get acclimated. Use the arrow keys to move around and the backspace key to delete stuff. When you're finished typing your message and you want to send it, press Ctrl+x to exit the Pico editor. You'll then see a message similar to this one:

```
Save modified buffer (ANSWERING "No" WILL DESTROY CHANGES) ?
```

If you want to exit without sending your message, press **n** for No, and when the next menu appears, press **f** to tell elm to forget it. If you want to send your message, type **y** for Yes. Pico will ask you to confirm the name of the message that it's saving. Do so by pressing Enter. You'll get a menu that looks like this:

```
e)dit message, h)eaders, c)opy, i)spell, !)shell, s)end, or
f)orget
```

We want s. Press **s**, and your message will be on its way. Elm will then place you back at the index. If you need any more help with sending e-mail, refer to Table 17-3.

Key	Description
m (from index)	Begins actions to create new mail message.
E	Goes back and edits message in editor.
H	Edits header information.
c	Saves a copy of the current message to a file.
i	Spell checks message.
!	Allows you to issue a UNIX command without leaving elm.
s	Sends message.
f	Forgets (trashes) message.

Table 17-3: Commands to send mail with elm.

Replying & Forwarding

Replying to mail is similar to sending mail, except that you can only reply to a message that you've selected or a message that you're currently reading. If you've selected a message that you want to reply to or if you're reading a message and want to reply to it, press **r**. Elm will ask you if you want to copy the message.

If you want to include the message you're replying to in the text of your own message, press **y**. If not, type **n**. If you decide to include the message in your new message, it will be set off from your message with greater than symbol (>)—using the greater than symbol to set off a message you're replying to is called *commenting* or quoting. Since elm usually includes the entire header of the message in your new message, you may want to edit some of the information (particularly extraneous header information) so things don't get too confusing. When you're finished editing the message and adding your own words, press Ctrl+x to send the message.

Sometimes you may want to forward a message that you've received. If so, just use the f command in the index or while you're reading the message. Again, if you want to forward the message to several people, just type in all their e-mail addresses separated by commas. Elm will ask you who you want to forward the message to and if you want to edit the outgoing message. If you choose to edit the outgoing message, you'll be sent into the editor where you can add your comments before sending the message. See Table 17-4 for a summary of elm's commands for replying and forwarding mail.

Key	Description
r	Replies to current message.
f	Forwards current message.

Table 17-4: Commands to reply to and forward mail.

Deleting (& Undeleting) Mail

Elm doesn't delete your mail 'til you tell it to do so. In fact, you almost have to go out of your way to delete a message.

To remove a message from your list, select it in the index, and press **d**. A d will appear in the far-left column, indicating that your mail has been marked for deletion. If you delete a message by mistake, just select it again by typing its number. Once it's selected, press **u** to undelete it. The d in the left column will disappear. When you exit elm (by using the q command), you'll be asked if you want to delete the marked messages. If you do, answer Yes. Table 17-5 provides a summary of deleting and undeleting commands in elm.

Key	Description
d	Marks selected message for deletion.
u	Unmarks message selected for deletion.

Table 17-5: Deleting and undeleting messages in elm.

Batch Operations: Tagging, Deleting & Searching Mail

Elm allows you to tag messages manually or based on a pattern that you specify. You can save a tagged message to a folder or print it. It's a great way to save a bunch of messages to a folder.

To tag messages manually, go the message you want to tag from the index, and press **t**. Elm places a + next to the tagged message. If you want to tag messages from the same person or with the same subject, you can use Ctrl+t. After you pressing Ctrl+t, elm will ask you to enter a pattern. The pattern can be any string of characters that you want to search. Elm will then search in the header information of each message for a match. Messages that contain the information you're searching for will be tagged. Once you've tagged messages, you can use the vertical bar character (|) to pipe (send) the selected messages to a system command for processing, or you can type **s** or **>** to save them to a directory.

- -

TIP

If you want to view a bunch of messages containing similar subjects all at once, you can use the Ctrl+t command to tag them all and then type I to pipe them to the more command for viewing. For example, if you had several messages with "Netscape" in the Subject, you could type Control+t, enter the word Netscape to tag all the messages with "Netscape" in the header, and the type I and then more to read them all with the "more" shell command.

- -

If you want to delete a bunch of similar messages at once, you can use Ctrl+d to do it. From the index, just press Ctrl+d, enter the search pattern, and any messages that match that pattern will be marked for deletion.

Key	Description
t	Tags messages manually.
Ctrl+t	Tags messages based on pattern.
>	Saves tagged messages to a folder.
s	Saves tagged messages to a folder.
l	Pipes tagged messages to a system command.
Ctrl+d	Deletes messages based on pattern.

Table 17-6: Commands to batch tag, delete, and save Messages in elm.

Quitting elm

When you want to exit the elm program, you have two options. If you want to quit quickly, just type Q. Elm will shut down without making any changes to any of the messages. However, if you've marked messages for deletion, quit by using q. Elm will allow you to save your read messages to the received folder, as well as give you the option to delete any messages you've marked for deletion. Table 17-7 shows the commands you need to use to quit elm.

Key	Description
q	Quits and prompts for deleting and moving to received directory.
Q	Quits with no prompting and no modification to messages.

Table 17-7: Quitting elm.

Pine

Like elm, Pine is a screen-oriented mail program. Almost everything you need to do in Pine can be accomplished either by selecting items on a menu or by moving the cursor around with arrow keys and by selecting items. Overall, it's easy to use and an ideal mail program for beginners.

Pine was originally developed at the University of Washington to fill the need for a simple menu-driven mail program that could be quickly mastered. There's online help, and all the commands that you need are always available from the menu at the bottom of the screen.

On top of being a popular mail reader, Pine has the distinction of functioning as a newsreader, too. In fact, Pine is an acronym for Program for Internet News and E-mail. A lot of people who use UNIX accounts have found Pine a great way to consolidate their two major time wasters . . . err . . . activities . . . into one program. We're only going to cover Pine's mail-reading features in this section, but if you want to learn how to read Usenet news with Pine, check the online help, it's fairly extensive.

Starting Pine

Starting Pine is easy. Type **pine** at the command line. The following message means that Pine has not been installed in your system:

```
pine: Command not found.
```

Just as with elm, Pine is freely available on the Internet, so you should get your system administrator to install it. If Pine is installed on your system, its opening screen should appear. See Figure 17-5.

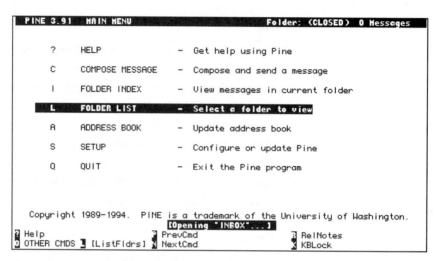

```
PINE 3.91   MAIN MENU                      Folder: (CLOSED)  0 Messages


      ?     HELP              -  Get help using Pine

      C     COMPOSE MESSAGE   -  Compose and send a message

      I     FOLDER INDEX      -  View messages in current folder

      L     FOLDER LIST       -  Select a folder to view

      A     ADDRESS BOOK      -  Update address book

      S     SETUP             -  Configure or update Pine

      Q     QUIT              -  Exit the Pine program



   Copyright 1989-1994.  PINE is a trademark of the University of Washington.
                              [Opening "INBOX"...]
 ? Help                      ? PrevCmd                     ? RelNotes
 O OTHER CMDS ] [ListFldrs] ? NextCmd                     ? KBLock
```

Figure 17-5: Pine's opening screen.

Right away, you can get an idea of Pine's friendliness. All the commands you need to get started are there right in front of you. You can select each option by using the Up and Down arrow keys on your keyboard. As you press these arrow keys, you'll notice that the current selection is highlighted in reverse text. Once you've decided what option to use, press Enter.

Let's take a brief look at the main menu options. The first command, ?, brings up the help system. In here, you'll find detailed information on just about every aspect of Pine. Next, command C is used for creating a new mail message. If you want to send new mail, choose this. The command I allows you to view an index list of the currently selected mail folder. The default folder is the incoming mail folder. If you start Pine and select this option, you'll be presented with a list of your current incoming messages.

Moving down, the command L is used to get a list of the mail folders available in Pine. One of the nice features of Pine is that it is easy to sort and organize your mail into different folders. Pine can even automatically filter mail. The A option is for the Address Book. Another nice feature of Pine is that you can set up lists of e-mail addresses in Address Books. S takes you to Pine's setup screen. From here you can configure over 70 options that control how Pine handles your mail. Now that's flexibility! Finally, Q allows you to quit the program. Table 17-8 summarizes the main-menu features of Pine.

You'll also notice another menu of choices along the bottom of the screen. This menu allows you to navigate through your list of commands, read the Pine release notes, get help, and access other commands.

Pine is also context-sensitive, which may be hard to get used to. Pine only displays commands that can be used in the section you're in. You'll never waste your time looking for the right command to use—just look at the bottom of the screen.

Key	Description
?	Brings up help menu.
C	Creates a new mail message.
I	Displays index mail from currently selected folder.
L	Lists mail folders.
A	Displays Address Book of e-mail addresses.
S	Configures options.
Q	Quits Pine mail reader.

Table 17-8: Main menu commands in Pine.

Reading Your E-Mail

To get a list of the messages that you've received, type **I**. The default mail folder in Pine is the INBOX, so if you've just started Pine, this command should give you a listing like that shown in Figure 17-6.

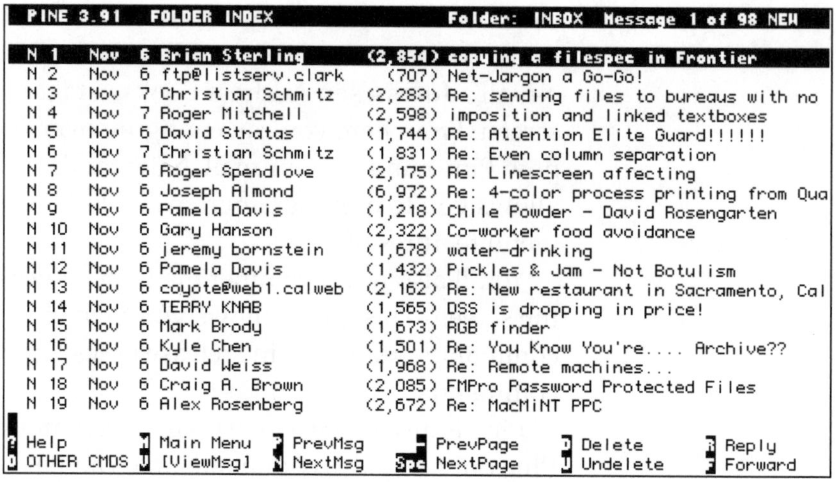

```
┌────────────────────────────────────────────────────────────────────────────┐
│ PINE 3.91   FOLDER INDEX                    Folder: INBOX  Message 1 of 98 NEW│
├────────────────────────────────────────────────────────────────────────────┤
│ N 1   Nov  6 Brian Sterling        (2,854) copying a filespec in Frontier    │
│ N 2   Nov  6 ftp@listserv.clark      (707) Net-Jargon a Go-Go!               │
│ N 3   Nov  7 Christian Schmitz     (2,283) Re: sending files to bureaus with no│
│ N 4   Nov  7 Roger Mitchell        (2,598) imposition and linked textboxes   │
│ N 5   Nov  6 David Stratas         (1,744) Re: Attention Elite Guard!!!!!!    │
│ N 6   Nov  7 Christian Schmitz     (1,831) Re: Even column separation        │
│ N 7   Nov  6 Roger Spendlove       (2,175) Re: Linescreen affecting          │
│ N 8   Nov  6 Joseph Almond         (6,972) Re: 4-color process printing from Qua│
│ N 9   Nov  6 Pamela Davis          (1,218) Chile Powder - David Rosengarten  │
│ N 10  Nov  6 Gary Hanson           (2,322) Co-worker food avoidance          │
│ N 11  Nov  6 jeremy bornstein      (1,678) water-drinking                    │
│ N 12  Nov  6 Pamela Davis          (1,432) Pickles & Jam - Not Botulism      │
│ N 13  Nov  6 coyote@web1.calweb    (2,162) Re: New restaurant in Sacramento, Cal│
│ N 14  Nov  6 TERRY KNAB            (1,565) DSS is dropping in price!         │
│ N 15  Nov  6 Mark Brody            (1,673) RGB finder                        │
│ N 16  Nov  6 Kyle Chen             (1,501) Re: You Know You're.... Archive??  │
│ N 17  Nov  6 David Weiss           (1,968) Re: Remote machines...            │
│ N 18  Nov  6 Craig A. Brown        (2,085) FMPro Password Protected Files    │
│ N 19  Nov  6 Alex Rosenberg        (2,672) Re: MacMiNT PPC                    │
│                                                                              │
│ ? Help        M Main Menu    P PrevMsg        - PrevPage    D Delete    R Reply│
│ O OTHER CMDS  V [ViewMsg]    N NextMsg      Spc NextPage    U Undelete  F Forward│
└────────────────────────────────────────────────────────────────────────────┘
```

Figure 17-6: Index screen in Pine.

The next message that's waiting to be read should be high-lighted. If you're starting Pine for the first time or you deleted all your mail the last time you used Pine and new mail has arrived in the mean time, the first message on the list will be highlighted.

Let's take a look at what each column means. The column on the left contains a character indicating the message status. New messages are marked with an N, messages that you've read and replied to are marked with an A, and messages that you've marked for deletion have a D next to them.

Some messages may be marked with a plus sign (+). This means that the message was sent directly to you rather than being bounced to you from a mailing list or sent as a carbon copy from someone else. This is a handy indicator if you subscribe to several mailing lists because it clearly indicates if a personal message has arrived for you. Table 17-9 lists the message status codes you'll see when using Pine.

Code	Description
N	New, unread message.
D	Message marked for deletion.
A	Message that you've read and replied to.
+	Message sent directly—not a copy or from a mailing list.

Table 17-9: Message status codes in Pine.

The next columns are self-explanatory. Following the status codes is the message number, the date the message was sent, who sent it, the size (in characters) of the message, and the subject.

So, let's read some e-mail. Using the arrow keys, highlight the message you want to read. If you want to read the first message on the list, leave the arrow keys untouched.

To view a message that you've selected, press **V** or press the Enter key. The message will be displayed as shown in Figure 17-7.

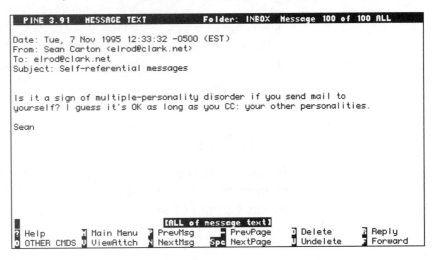

Figure 17-7: An e-mail message in Pine.

You'll notice that the line at the top of the screen indicates the folder you're in and the number of the message you're viewing. You'll also notice a percentage value—that's the percentage of the message you've read so far.

In the middle of the screen, you'll find the body of the message. Once you've read the first screenful, press the spacebar to display another page. If you want to go through the message line-by-line, just press Enter, and Pine will display your message one line at a time. If you want to back up to a previous page, press the hyphen key.

When you're finished reading the message, you can return to the index screen by pressing I. Refer to Table 17-10 if you need help remembering Pine's mail reading commands.

Key	Description
(from the index) V	Displays selected message.
(from the index) Enter	Displays selected message.
Space	Displays next page of message.
Enter	Displays message one line at a time.
- (hyphen key)	Displays previous page of message.
I	Returns to message index.

Table 17-10: Commands to read mail in Pine.

Sending Mail

To send a message in Pine, you need to press C, from either the main menu or the message index, to access the compose message screen. Figure 17-8 shows you what you'll see.

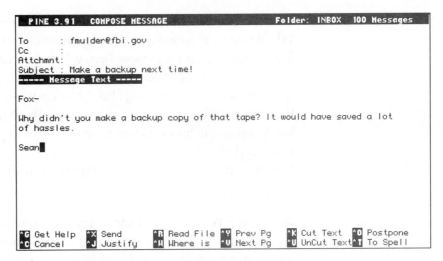

Figure 17-8: Composing a message in Pine.

As you can see, it's fairly straightforward. First, you need to enter the e-mail address of the person you're sending a message to in the To: field, and press Enter. Just as with elm, if you're sending a message to someone on your system, all you need to do is type his or her username, and Pine will fill in the correct e-mail information. Also, just like with elm, if you want to send or CC to several different people, just enter their e-mail addresses separated by commas.

Next, if you want to send a copy of the message you're mailing to someone else, enter that name in the cc: field, and press Enter. If you don't want to mail a copy to anyone, just press Enter.

The next field, Attachment:, is a special feature of Pine. It allows you to attach a file to a mail message. Actually, even cooler than that, Pine doesn't even really send the file. Instead, when you add an attachment, Pine just mails a link to the file. When someone receives your message and opens it with Pine, the file is transferred across the Internet to that person. More about attaching in the section "Attaching Files to Your Pine E-Mail." For now, just press Enter.

In the Subject: field, enter the subject of your email message. When you're finished, press Enter. Your cursor should now be in the section labeled Message Text, where you can enter your message. Pine uses the Pico editor (the one we suggested you use in the elm section), so editing should be easy — just move around the screen with the arrow keys, and use the Backspace or Delete key to erase mistakes. When you're finished typing your message, press Ctrl+X.

Finally, Pine will ask you the following question:

    Send message?

Press Y for Yes, or press Enter. Pine will send the message and return you to where you were before you entered the compose message screen.

Replying & Forwarding

As you could probably tell if you snuck a peek at the menu at the bottom of the screen when we were viewing our first mail message, replying to messages or forwarding them is easy.

If you want to reply to a message, you can do so from either the message index or within the message that you're currently reading by typing **R**. If you're in the message index, Pine assumes that you want to reply to the currently selected message.

After you press R, Pine will ask you:

    Include original message in Reply?

If you press Y for Yes, Pine will place the message, along with the headers, into the compose editor. If you answer N, you'll be placed in the compose editor, ready to type your message. See Figure 17-9.

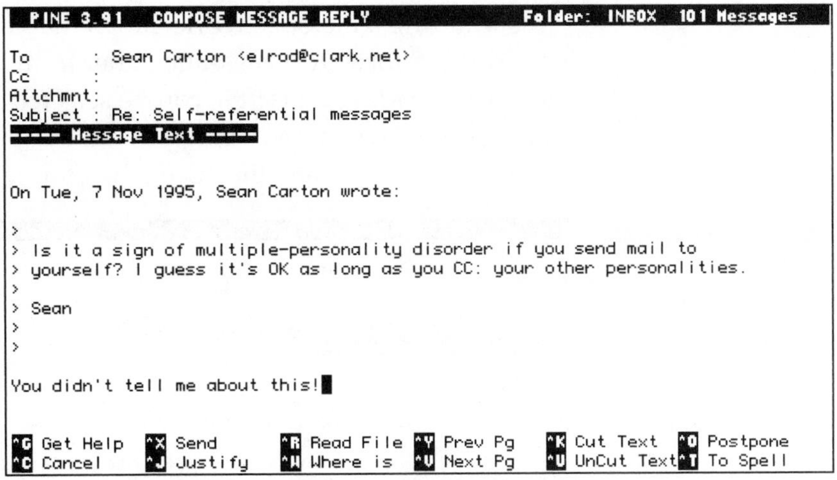

```
PINE 3.91   COMPOSE MESSAGE REPLY              Folder: INBOX  101 Messages

To      : Sean Carton <elrod@clark.net>
Cc      :
Attchmnt:
Subject : Re: Self-referential messages
----- Message Text -----


On Tue, 7 Nov 1995, Sean Carton wrote:

>
> Is it a sign of multiple-personality disorder if you send mail to
> yourself? I guess it's OK as long as you CC: your other personalities.
>
> Sean
>
>

You didn't tell me about this!█



^G Get Help   ^X Send        ^R Read File ^Y Prev Pg   ^K Cut Text   ^O Postpone
^C Cancel     ^J Justify     ^W Where is  ^V Next Pg   ^U UnCut Text ^T To Spell
```

Figure 17-9: Replying to a message in Pine.

TIP

If you're replying to a message from a mailing list, after you decide whether to include the original message in your reply, Pine asks you another question:

> Reply to all recipients?

If you answer Yes, your message is sent to the person who wrote the message as well as all the members of the mailing list. If you answer No, only the person who wrote the message receives your reply. This helpful feature allows you to choose whether you want to continue a public mailing list discussion in private or if you want to take it public and send it out to the rest of the list.

Once you're in the compose message section, you'll notice that all the headers have already been filled out for you, but this doesn't mean that you can't change them. Simply use the arrow keys to move upward into the header section if you want to edit the headers. When you're finished with your reply, press Ctrl+X to send the message, and then type **I** to return to the index.

Forwarding a message works much the same way as replying to one. You can forward a message either from within the message, as you are reading it or after you've selected it from the message index. Press **F** when you've chosen a message to forward. Figure 17-10 shows you what you'll see when forwarding a message.

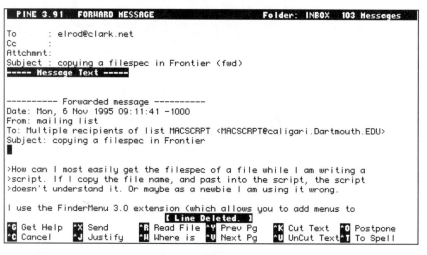

```
  PINE 3.91   FORWARD MESSAGE                Folder: INBOX   103 Messages

To       : elrod@clark.net
Cc       :
Attchmnt :
Subject  : copying a filespec in Frontier (fwd)
----- Message Text -----


---------- Forwarded message ----------
Date: Mon, 6 Nov 1995 09:11:41 -1000
From: mailing list
To: Multiple recipients of list MACSCRPT <MACSCRPT@caligari.Dartmouth.EDU>
Subject: copying a filespec in Frontier


>How can I most easily get the filespec of a file while I am writing a
>script. If I copy the file name, and past into the script, the script
>doesn't understand it. Or maybe as a newbie I am using it wrong.

I use the FinderMenu 3.0 extension (which allows you to add menus to
                          [ Line Deleted. ]
^G Get Help  ^X Send       ^R Read File  ^Y Prev Pg   ^K Cut Text   ^O Postpone
^C Cancel    ^J Justify     ^W Where is   ^V Next Pg   ^U UnCut Text ^T To Spell
```

Figure 17-10: Forwarding a message in Pine.

Once you've pressed F, you'll be placed back in the compose screen and the message that you're forwarding will be automatically loaded into the message text area with a header that reads:

```
---------- Forwarded message ----------
```

so that the person receiving your message knows that it was forwarded.

You'll need to fill out the To: , Cc: , and Attachmnt: fields yourself, but notice that the Subject: field has already been filled with the subject of the message you're forwarding followed by "fwd" in parentheses. The (fwd) clearly indicates that the message has been forwarded.

If you want to add your own comments to the forwarded message, use the arrow keys to move down into the message text area. Press Enter a few times to make space for your message, and begin typing. When you're finished, press Ctrl+X, confirm that you want to send the message, and you'll be returned to where you were before you entered the message text area.

Key	Description
r	Replies to current message or message selected in index.
f	Forwards current message or message selected in index.

Table 17-11: Commands to reply to and forward messages in Pine.

Deleting Mail

You can mark a mail message for deletion while in the message that you're reading or by selecting the message from the index.

If you're reading a message and you want to mark it for deletion, type **D**. Pine will mark the message and then display the next message in line. If you're in the index, pressing D will mark the currently selected message for deletion. Notice that a D will appear in the far-left column, indicating that the message is marked for deletion.

If you mistakenly delete a message, don't panic! Just select it again from the index, and press **U** for Undelete. The status of the message will change from D to what it was before the message was marked.

Key	Description
D	Deletes currently selected message.
U	Undeletes currently selected message.

Table 17-12: Commands to delete and undelete Mail in Pine.

Attaching Files to Your E-Mail

One of Pine's greatest features is that it allows you to easily attach files to e-mail messages that you send. These files can be anything that you've got stashed in your directory on the host—pictures, text files, spreadsheet documents, or binary programs. (Notice that the file has to be on your host machine, not your PC at home.) How, you ask? Actually, it's quite ingenious. Pine uses the MIME (Multipurpose Internet Mail Extension) protocol to attach mail messages. We'll cover MIME and attaching files in much greater detail in Chapter 20, "Inside E-Mail," but for now, it's enough to say that MIME is a rapidly developing standard for file attachment no matter what mail program you're using.

The neat part is that Pine doesn't actually clog up the Internet (and the recipient of your message's account) by sending the actual file along with the message. Instead, Pine sends a pointer back to the file on your ISP's computer. When someone receives the message, he can decide if he wants to transfer that file to his computer or not. If he decides to nab it, the file is jetted across the Net to him. If not, he just deletes the message and <HLbandwidth<HL> is saved for another day!

Here's how to attach a file to a mail message you're sending:

1. Start a new message by entering the compose message section, either by pressing C in the index or from the main menu. Pine brings up the compose message screen you now know and love so well.

2. Enter the information that designates who you want to send the message to and who's getting copies in the To: and Cc: fields, respectively.

3. When you get to the Attchmnt: section, that's where the fun begins. Once you've reached this field, press Ctrl+J. You'll notice from the menu at the bottom of the screen that that's the command for Attach.

4. Pine will ask you what file you wish to attach. (See Figure 17-11.) If you know the exact name of the file, enter it here. However, if you don't know the exact name, you can get a listing of

your home directory by pressing Ctrl+T. Pine will build a listing of the files in your directory and display it onscreen. See Figure 17-12.

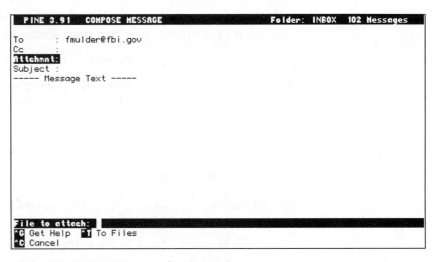

Figure 17-11: Pine asks what file to attach.

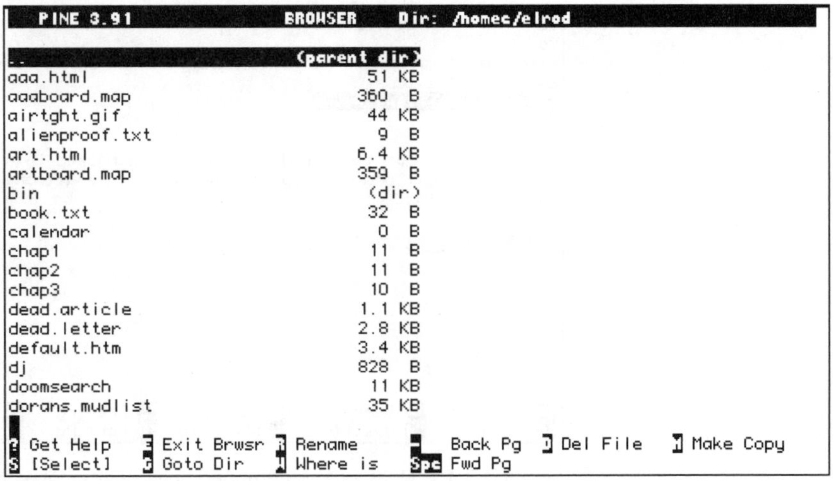

Figure 17-12: A file listing for attachment.

You can see from Figure 17-12 that the sizes of the files are indicated in kilobytes. Notice also that any directories you have in your account are indicated by (dir). See Table 17-13 for a review of Pine's attaching commands.

If you want to move to another directory, select the directory name with the arrow keys, and press Enter. Pine will ask you:

```
A directory is selected, enter it ?
```

If you have correctly selected a directory, press Y or Enter. Pine will displays the new directory. To move up to the previous directory, select

```
..                        (parent dir)
```

and press Enter twice.

5. To attach a file, select it from the list of files using the arrow keys, and then press Enter to attach it to your mail message. You'll be placed back at the compose message screen. See Figure 17-13.

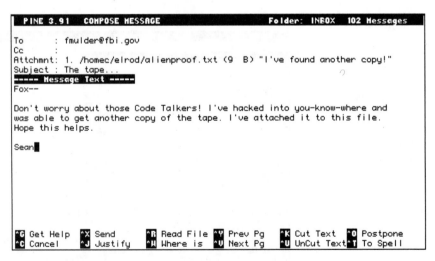

Figure 17-13: Back at the compose screen after attaching a file.

6. If you want to enter a description so that the person you're sending the file to knows what it is, type a short description at the prompt:

    ```
    Attachment comment:
    ```

    and press Enter. If you don't want to include a comment, press Enter. Pine will list your file, its path, and the comment in the Attachmnt: field of your header.

7. If you want to attach multiple files, go ahead! Just press Ctrl+J, and follow the steps for attaching each file.

8. When you're finished attaching files, use the arrow keys to move down, enter a subject in the Subject: field, and type your message. When you're ready to send your message, press Ctrl+X.

Key	Description
Ctrl+J	Attaches file to current message.
Ctrl+T	Gets list of files to attach.

Table 17-13: Commands to Attaching files in Pine.

Quitting Pine

When you want to quit Pine, type . . . you guessed it . . . Q. You can do so from within a message that you're reading, from the main menu or from the message index. When Pine asks if you really want to quit, press Y. If you've marked any messages for deletion, you'll be asked:

```
Expunge the <number of messages> deleted messages from
"INBOX"?
```

where <number of messages> is a number indicating the number of messages you've marked for deletion. If you answer Y for Yes, those messages will be deleted. If you answer N, Pine will keep the messages marked for deletion and doesn't actually delete them.

Mail & mailx

After reading about two easy-to-use, menu-driven, screen-editing mail programs, going to a line-oriented, command line-driven mail program may seem like a step back. *Au contraire, mes aimes!* Even though mail and mailx might not look like much, their simplicity hides an amazing set of flexible features perfect for the power user!

Mail and mailx are actually two of the oldest UNIX mail programs. Even though they have different names, they operate almost identically. Chances are, you have both installed on your UNIX system. To keep it simple, we'll refer to them as mailx throughout the rest of this section. If you find that you only have mail installed, don't worry. Most of the basics are the same.

Starting mailx

The simplest way to start mailx from the command line is by typing **mailx** at the prompt. You should see a screen similar to that shown in Figure 17-14.

```
explorer:[/homec/elrod] mailx
mailx version 5.0 Fri Jul 15 21:21:05 PDT 1994  Type ? for help.
"/var/mail/elrod": 106 messages 96 unread
  O   1 Brian Sterling     Mon Nov  6 21:48    61/2889   copying a filespec in Fro
 >U   2 ftp@listserv.clark Tue Nov  7 01:44    19/768    Net-Jargon a Go-Go!
  U   3 Christian Schmitz  Tue Nov  7 01:49    46/2331   Re: sending files to bure
  U   4 Roger Mitchell     Tue Nov  7 01:50    49/2643   imposition and linked tex
  U   5 David Stratas      Tue Nov  7 01:51    39/1789   Re: Attention Elite Guard
  U   6 Christian Schmitz  Tue Nov  7 01:52    36/1889   Re: Even column separatio
  U   7 Roger Spendlove    Tue Nov  7 01:53    46/2223   Re: Linescreen affecting
  U   8 Joseph Almond      Tue Nov  7 01:53   137/6929   Re: 4-color process print
  U   9 Pamela Davis       Tue Nov  7 01:57    26/1291   Chile Powder - David Rose
  U  10 Gary Hanson        Tue Nov  7 01:57    44/2377   Co-worker food avoidance
  U  11 jeremy bornstein   Tue Nov  7 01:57    38/1739   water-drinking
  U  12 Pamela Davis       Tue Nov  7 01:57    29/1502   Pickles & Jam - Not Botul
  U  13 owner-chile-heads@ Tue Nov  7 01:59    42/2219   Re: New restaurant in Sac
  U  14 TERRY KNAB         Tue Nov  7 02:04    37/1612   DSS is dropping in price!
  U  15 Mark Brody         Tue Nov  7 02:07    35/1732   RGB finder
  U  16 Kyle Chen          Tue Nov  7 02:16    35/1565   Re: You Know You're.... A
  U  17 David Weiss        Tue Nov  7 02:18    38/2025   Re: Remote machines...
  U  18 Craig A. Brown     Tue Nov  7 02:19    34/2146   FMPro Password Protected
  U  19 Alex Rosenberg     Tue Nov  7 02:19    54/2704   Re: MacMiNT PPC
  U  20 Roger Mitchell     Tue Nov  7 02:19    50/2723   output to non-postscript
? █
```

Figure 17-14: Mailx, as started from the command line.

Not much to it, eh? When you first invoke mailx, you'll probably see a listing of your mail, much like the list shown in Figure 17-14. Across the top of the screen, mailx displays a listing of the mailbox it's reading your mail from. Usually, this defaults to your main mailbox. In this case, it's Sean's mailbox, /var/mail/elrod.

TIP

It's possible to read mail from another mailbox. Just use the -f option to specify which mailbox you want to read. For example, if your old mail is stored in a file called mbox in your directory, starting mailx with the command mailx -f mbox will start mailx with mbox as the mailbox file.

Let's take a look at what those columns in the listing mean. In the second column (reading from the left), you'll see a code indicating the message's status. It may look like the first column to you, but the first column actually contains a character indicating the current message. U means unread, N means new, and O means old or a message that you've already read.

Code	Description
N	New message
U	Unread message
O	Old, already read message saved to a folder
blank	Read but not saved to a folder
*	Unsaved

Table 17-14: Message status codes in mailx.

The next column is the message number. Just as in elm and Pine, mailx assigns each message in the mailbox a new number as it comes in. You'll use these numbers later to select the message you want to read or operate on.

The next column lists the sender of the message. Depending on how mailx reads the headers of the message, either the person who sent the message or the mailing list it came from will be displayed here.

The next three columns contain information about the day, date, and time that the message was sent. There's no year, because if you need to know, it's time to clean out your mailbox and go home!

The next column indicates the number of lines each message contains as well as the number of characters. The last column displays the subject of the message.

As you can tell so far, even though the interface might be a little different than elm or Pine, the ideas are basically the same. This is true of a lot of things in UNIX—once you get the gist of one program, other programs will be easier to learn.

Reading Your E-Mail

Reading your mail in mailx isn't all that different than reading mail in any of the other programs we've looked at. Basically, just select a message to read, and it'll be displayed.

Let's read message 1. If you look at the bottom of the screen, you'll see that mailx is displaying a question mark. At this point, you might think that it stands for your state of mind. It doesn't. The question mark is mailx's friendly prompt asking, "What do you want me to do now?"

The messages marked with N have greater than symbols (>) next to them in the first column. This symbol indicates the first new message in your list. At this point, if you just press Enter, mailx will display the message marked with the >. However, if you want to display a specific message, just type its number at the ? prompt, and press Enter. Figure 17-15 shows how the message is displayed.

```
Message 100:
From elrod Tue Nov  7 12:33 EST 1995
Date: Tue, 7 Nov 1995 12:33:32 -0500 (EST)
From: Sean Carton <elrod@clark.net>
To: elrod@clark.net
Subject: Self-referential messages
MIME-Version: 1.0
X-Status: A


Is it a sign of multiple-personality disorder if you send mail to
yourself? I guess it's OK as long as you CC: your other personalities.

Sean

?
```

Figure 17-15: A mail message displayed in mailx.

As you can see, it's not too complicated. At the top of the message is the header information, displaying who the message is from, who it was sent to, the date it was sent, and the subject. Next comes the body of the message. At the end, you'll see the ? prompt, waiting for your next command.

Pressing Enter again will display the next message and on and on until you reach the last one. You'll know when you've come to the last message when mailx displays :

```
At EOF
```

This is just a nice way of telling you you've reached the end of your message list file.

As you're reading messages, you can access a list of your messages again by typing **h** to get a list of mail headers. mailx will display 20 message headers at a time (some systems display 10). If you want to return to the beginning of the list, just use h and a number indicating which header number to display. Since mailx lists your mail headers 20 at a time, any number between 1 and 20 will display the first 20 headers, any number between 21 and 40 will display the next 20, and so on.

The other, more elegant way to display one screenful of messages at a time is to use the z command at the ? prompt. Every time you type **z** and press Enter, mailx will display another screenful of headers. See Table 17-15 for a review of mailx's reading commands.

TIP

You may have noticed that when mailx displays a message, the message scrolls up the screen, regardless of its length. Unless you're Mr. Spock or maybe Lt. Commander Data, you probably can't read that fast. If you want to read the message one screenful at a time, use our old friend more. Mailx allows you to pipe messages through to system commands, so to get your message to more, use the following command at the ? prompt:

```
pipe [message number] more
```

Mailx will send the message through to the more command, allowing you to read a long message one screen at a time.

Key	Description
Enter	Displays first message marked with a greater than symbol (>).
[message number]	Displays message [message number].
H	Displays a list of message headers.
Z	Displays one screenful of new headers.
Pipe [message number] more	Pipes message through system more command for easier-to-read display.

Table 17-15: Reading mail with mailx.

Sending Mail

OK. Now we can read mail, but how do we send it? There are two main ways. One is to use the m command at the ? prompt while you're in mailx:

```
?m e-mail address
```

Don't type the words "e-mail address." Instead, substitute the e-mail address of the person you want to send mail to, and press Enter.

You can also send mail from the UNIX shell prompt, even before you enter mailx. You can start sending a message by using the command:

```
mailx e-mail address
```

If you want to send mail to several people, just enter their e-mail addresses separated by commas. With both the m and mailx commands, after you press Enter, mailx will prompt you for the subject.

Enter the subject of the message, and press Enter. You'll get a blank line where you can type your message.

You've now entered the wonderful world of the mailx line editor. Until you type a period on a line by itself, mailx will put anything you type at this point into your message. When you're finished typing your message, type a period on a line by itself, press Enter, and your message will be sent. If you decide you don't want to send the message after all, press Ctrl+C to cancel the message.

The default editor for mailx is a line editor, and it can be maddening to say the least. First of all, mailx uses a line editor, so there's no word wrap as with a traditional full-screen editor. For as long as you don't press Enter, your line just keeps going and going and going. When you do press Enter, that line is saved just the way it is. Also, if your system's like many, you won't be able to use the Backspace key to delete. You'll have to use Ctrl+H. Not fun.

So what can you do? Well, the mailx editor has some powerful features called tilde commands. They're called tilde commands because they can be invoked from within the mailx line editor by prefacing them with a tilde character (~). We'll go over some of the most useful commands here, but you should consult the Table 17-20 for a complete list.

We can use a tilde command to exit the line editor, and use our old friend Pico. You can do this by typing ~e and pressing Enter while you're in the line editor. As long as Pico has been set up as your system editor in your .login or .profile file, you should see something similar to the screen shown in Figure 17-16.

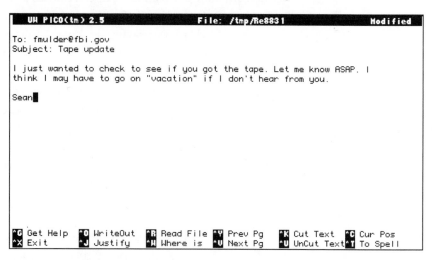

Figure 17-16: Editing a message with Pico in mailx.

Just as you did in elm and Pine, you can type to your little heart's content, and then press Ctrl+X to finish. Unlike Pine and elm, when you type Ctrl+X, mailx doesn't automatically send your message. You still need to type a period on a line by itself, and press Enter to signal that you want your message sent. See Table 17-16 for a list of commands you can use to send mail with mailx.

Command	Description
m	Use at the ? prompt to begin a new message.
mailx [e-mail address]	Use at the command line to begin a new message.
~e	Brings up a full-screen editor (as defined in the .login or .profile file) for editing messages in mailx.
Ctrl+H	Types backspace in mailx line editor.
Ctrl+C	Cancels message in mailx line editor.
.	Ends editing session, sends message.

Table 17-16: Commands to Send mail with mailx.

Replying & Forwarding

If you want to reply to a message, you have two choices. Both work the same way but differ in who they send the reply to.

If you're reading a message and want to reply, you first need to decide who you want your reply to go to. If you're replying to a message that doesn't include any carbon copies (cc:s), it doesn't matter. However, if you're reading a message posted to a mailing list, it's very important that you decide whether you want the reply to go to the whole list or not.

If you want to reply to just the person who sent the message and don't want your reply to go to the list, type the following at the ? prompt:

```
R [message number]
```

where [message number] stands for the message number corresponding to the message you're replying to. Mailx will automatically fill in the Subject: field for you by placing Re: before the subject of the message you've replied to:

```
Subject: Re: The check's in the mail
```

Mailx then dumps you into the editor where you can type your message, as we discussed earlier in the "Sending Mail with mailx" section. If you want to quote a message when replying to it, you'll have to save it to a file first (using the s command) and then read it back into your message as you reply using the ~r *filename* command.

If you want to send a reply to the entire mailing list, use a lowercase r. Everything else works the same, but your reply will be sent to everyone on the list, as well as to the person who actually wrote the message.

TIP

Pay close attention when you reply to a message on a mailing list! While most mailing lists only reply to the list as a whole, some allow you to reply to the sender of the message. If you send a snide comment to a friend about someone else on the list by using the r command instead of the R command, you could be public enemy number 1 in no time when everyone on the list reads what you meant to be private. Take care!

If you want to forward a message, begin sending a message as you normally would. When you're finished typing your introduction but before you type a period, type:

```
~f [message number ]
```

The editor will add the specified message number to your message. You won't see it appear on the screen, but it's there. If you want to check to make sure, use the ~p command to print your message to the screen. When you're satisfied that the message is okay, type a period to send it. See Table 17-17 for a review of forwarding and mailing commands.

Command	Description
r	Replies to entire mailing list.
R	Replies only to author of message.
s	Saves message to file.
~f [message number]	Puts text of messages in [message number] into message.
~p	Displays outgoing message in mailx editor.

Table 17-17: Commands to reply to and forward mail in mailx.

Deleting & Undeleting Your Mail

To delete messages in mailx, simply use the following command at the ? prompt:

```
delete [message list]
```

Message list can be a range of message numbers (1-10, for example) or an e-mail address. If you want to wipe out all the messages in your mailbox, use the following command at the ? prompt:

```
delete *
```

If you want to undelete messages (*before you quit out of mailx*), just use the following command at the ? prompt:

```
undelete [message list]
```

If you want to undelete all the messages that you'd deleted during that session, use the following command at the ? prompt:

```
undelete *
```

A word of caution about deleting messages. Even though you can undelete messages, as soon as you quit out of mailx, the messages that you've marked for deletion are gone. History. There's no way to get them back. So, make sure you know what you're deleting when you delete. Refer to Table 17-18 if you need a refresher on how to delete and undelete mail in mailx.

Command	Description
delete [message list]	Marks messages in [message list] for deletion.
delete *	Mark all messages for deletion.
undelete [message list]	Removes deletion from messages in [message list].
undelete *	Undeletes all messages.

Table 17-18: Commands to delete and undelete mail in mailx.

Mailx Quick Reference

Mailx has a lot of options—much more than we have space to go into in this book. Tables 17-19 and 17-20 are guides to more mailx functions for you to explore on your own.

Option	Description
[e-mail address]	Sends mail to [e-mail address].
-e	Tests to see if you have mail.
-f <filename>	Opens mailbox specified in <filename>.
-F	Saves message to file named for recipient of message.
-H	Prints headers only and exits.
-s [string]	Sets Subject: to string specified after -s.

Table 17-19: Command-line options in mailx.

Command	Description
~a	Inserts a signature specified in the .mailrc file sign variable.
~A	Inserts a signature specified in the .mailrc file Sign variable.
~b <e-mail addresses>	Allows blind carbon copies.
~c <e-mail addresses>	Adds <e-mail addresses> to cc: field.
~d	Puts dead letter (canceled message file) into message.

➡

Command	Description
~e	Calls up editor specified in EDITOR system variable.
~f [message list]	Inserts messages in [message list] into new message.
~h	Allows you to change headers.
~i [variable]	Inserts text defined in [variable] into message.
~m [message list]	Inserts messages in [message list] into new message, indents them one tab.
~p	Prints current message to the screen.
~q	Cancels message.
~r <filename>	Inserts file <filename> into message.
~s [string]	Changes the Subject: field to [string].
~t <e-mail addresses>	Inserts <e-mail addresses> into To: field.
~v	Switches to full-screen editor.
~w	Saves message to a file without headers.
~x	Completely cancels and deletes current message, without saving to dead letter file.
~! [system command]	Executes [system command].
~.	Ends message.
~: [mailx command]	Runs [mailx command].
~_ [mailx command]	Runs [mailx command].
~?	Accesses tilde command help screen.
~l [system command]	Pipes current message through [system command].
~~	Puts a tilde in message.
~< <filename>	Puts <filename> in message.
~<~ [system command]	Runs [system command], and places the output into current message.

Table 17-20: Tilde commands in mailx.

Quitting mailx

Once you're all finished, quitting mailx is the easiest part. Just type **q** at the ? prompt. All the files that you marked for deletion will be removed, and you'll be back at the system prompt.

SIG FILES: THE GOOD, THE BAD & THE UGLY

If you're going to send mail, it's probably a good idea to let the recipients know where it's coming from. Some systems don't put a person's real name in the From: header; all they put is an e-mail address. And most e-mail addresses are fairly cryptic. Would you know who elrod@clark.net was if it didn't have (Sean Carton) appended to it? Probably not.

Of course, if you wanted to you could always just put your name at the end of every message. That's what most people do. But the best way to make sure that the world knows who you are is to use a stunning signature file.

The Signature File

Elm and Pine (as well as most Usenet newsreaders) append whatever you've written and stored in a signature file to any message you send. With mailx it's a little more complicated—you have to use the ~a or ~A command to append a signature file. However you do it, the principle's the same. Anything in a file called signature is appended to the end of messages that you send.

People use signature files (or *sig files* as they're known) to tell the world about themselves (name, name of business, address, slogan), to push their agendas ("President, Ren and Stimpy Fanclub"), publish their PGP (encryption) keys (more about this later in Chapter 21 when we discuss e-mail privacy), and share recipes, witticisms (or not), ASCII art, and other stuff. Think of a sig file as a calling card, billboard, or soapbox that can be attached to the end of all your e-mail messages and Usenet posts. Sig files allow to you personalize your messages so that you stand out from the crowd.

To create a sig file, all you have to do is open a file called signature in your favorite text editor, enter the information, and save it in the top level of your directory.

683

■ ■

Uncle Sig's Sig File Etiquette

As you can imagine, it's a little too easy to go crazy with sig files. That's why we've enlisted the help of our favorite Uncle Sig, the sig file master, to gain some insight into the etiquette of sig files. Here's an excerpt from a brief Q&A session we conducted while writing this book. In case you're wondering, IPTK is us, your humble authors, Gareth and Sean.

IPTK: Uncle Sig, how big should a sig file be? We've seen some whoppers, and we were wondering if you could give us a brief rule of thumb.

Sig: Well boys, I've seen it all. Sig files two and three screens long. Whole maps of the earth done up in ASCII text. I remember the .sig glut of '89 when not a day went by that I didn't see...

IPTK: [interrupting] Uh, yeah. That's great. Could you just give us your rule of thumb?

Sig: OK. OK. Hold on to your ergonomic armrests, pal. I was comin' to that. I guess if I had to give one rule of thumb it would be: A person's IQ is inversely proportional to the size of his/her sig file.

IPTK: So keep it short, eh?

Sig: Yup.

IPTK: What about subjects? What should we tell our readers to put in their sig files?

Sig: [stroking his pixelated beard] Good question! You guys aren't as dumb as you look in those CU-SeeMe windows. Sig files are out there for all the world to see. Giving away too much information is not always advisable.

IPTK: So, what wouldn't you put in a sig file?

Sig: A picture of you two, that's for sure!

IPTK: [silence]

Sig: I wouldn't recommend putting home phone numbers, home addresses, and any information that someone might be able use to make trouble.

IPTK: Such as?

Sig: Well, there's a clever lot of crackers and naughty kids cruising around in Cyberspace. They look for anything in a sig file or other globally readable files (such as a finger file) that can give them an edge. For instance, many people use passwords taken from their favorite pastimes and then publicize those pastimes in their sig files. If you put too much stuff about yourself in a sig file, who knows what crackers could figure out about you. Which reminds me of a story . . .

IPTK: Uh! That's okay, Sig. Maybe next time. I guess that's the best advice we could leave people with: Keep your sig files short and to the point, don't waste bandwidth with too much junk, and don't give away too much personal information. Is that about right?

Sig: Sounds good, son. Now I gotta go, I haven't edited my sig file in several hours!

Sig File Wall o' Shame

No discussion of signature files would be complete without some examples of sig file mania. Here's some of most gonzo signatures we've encountered. The names and e-mail addresses have been changed to protect the guilty.

```
                                            xxxxxxxxxxxxxxxxx          ( O )
    Firefighter                        +——————————+
    First Responder                    º  _____                º
    Biology/Education         ___      º  /\  xxxxxxxxxxxxxxxxxxxxxxxxx    \      º
    And all around         _____(_O_)___º  \/_____/   º
       great guy!        / +———+  º                                           º
                        / /   ~~~~    º º         Or xxxxxxxxxxxxxxxxxxxxxx        º
                       / /  /* )º     º º    _____  _____  º
    _____/ (     º_  º  º º   º        º  º::       º  º      º º
    º  (*)           : +-+-+-+ :  º::            º  º::     º  º::       º º
    º  Rescue 34     :    ——     "  :  º::             º    ——   º::       º º
    º                :    BVFD      :  º              º              º      º º
    º   _____   /  ——           :  ———————  /  ____  \     ———— º_
    º===/ /    \  \========================================/ /    \  \==============º___
       (  ::  )                                            (  ::  )
        \____/                                              \____/


    (C) Big Sigs - 1993   (sike!)
```

```
                  -.                                          .-
            _..-'(                        ACK!        )'-.._
          ./'. `ºº\\.              _ _ _ _/º    .//ºº` .`\.
        ./'. º'.'ºººº\\º..     \'o.O'/   ..º//ºººº'.'º.'\.
      ./'..º'.ºº ºººº\"""   =(___)=   """/ººººº ºº.'º..'\.
    ./'.ºº'.ºººº ººººººººººº.  U  .ººººººººººº ºººº.'ºº.'\.
   /'ººº'.ºººººº ººººººººººº       ºººººººººººº ºººººº.'ººº'\
   \.ºººº'.ºººººº ºººººººººººº      ºººººººººººº ºººººº`.ººº.`
    \.ººº ºººººººº º/'    ``\ºº``     ''ºº/''    `\º ºººººººº ººº.`
   º/' \./'       '\./         \!º\  /º!/          \./'       '\./ '\º
   V     V       V        }' '\ /' '{        V        V    V
    '      '         '              V              '      '    '
           See you next time—same bat.time, same bat.computer!!



         _                ____                   _                    ___
        º  º             º    º_            /    \            __{  H  }__
       / ŸÙ \          __º    º#º     º__   /  Ÿ+Ù  \     ____+____    {   ŸÙ ŸÙ   }
      /  ŸÙ  \      º   º#º º #º    º  /       \   .<_O_>.  \  º ŸÙ ŸÙ ŸÙ ŸÙ º
     I==========IO=o=o=o=O=O=o=o=o=OI=I=I=I=I=I=I  ============  {=o=o=o=o=o=o=}
     º ŸÙ ŸÙ ŸÙ  ºº#º#º#ºŸÙ ŸÙºº#º#º#ºº+º+º+º º+º+º+º ºº++º º  º ºº++º  º ŸÙ ŸÙ ŸÙ ŸÙ º
     º ŸÙ ŸÙ ŸÙ ºº º º ºŸÙ ŸÙ ºº#º#º#º#ºº+º+º+º º+º+º+º ºº++º º  º  º++º  º ŸÙ ŸÙ ŸÙ ŸÙ º
     º ŸÙ __ ŸÙ ºº#º#º#ºŸÙ_ŸÙºº#º#º#ºº+º+º+º º+º+º+º ºº++º º  º º++º  º ŸÙ ŸÙ_ŸÙ ŸÙ º
     º  /   \   ºº#º#º#º_º_º_ºº#º#º#ºº+º+º+º_º+º+º+º ºº++º_º_º_º++º º ŸÙ _º_º_ ŸÙ º
     º___º_º___ºº_____/I_I_I\_____ºº_____/I\_____º º__/H_H_H\__º º___/I_I_I\___º
     ====================================================================
     º XXXXXXXXXXXXXXXXX    ºº XXXXXXXXXXXXXXXXX  fax: + XXXXXXXXXXXXX       º
     º phone:  +XXXXXXXXXXXXX ºº department of ALFA-INFORMATICA Faculty of Artsº
     º History & Computing    ºº University of Groningen, The Netherlands    º
     ====================================================================
     º                        ºº http:/xxxxxxxxxxxxxxxxxxxxxxxxxxxxxxxxxxxxx  º
     ====================================================================
```

```
         *               * * * * * * * * * * * * * * * * * * * * * * * *           *
   *           *                                                         *                *
   *      * * * * * * * *         PUT YOUR MESSAGE HERE!                  * * * * * * * *  *
   *           *                                                         *                *
   *           *          Blah, blah, blah, and more blah.       *                *
   *                                   mm/dd/yy                                          *
   *                                     time                                            *
   *                                    place                                            *

=-=-=-=-=-=-=-=-=-=-=-=-=-=-=-=-=-=-=-=-=-=-=-=-=-=-=-=-=-=-=-=-=
% Name                              %   Phone #'s                          %
% Place                             %   email address(s)                   %
% Univ                              %                                       %
% Address (snail mail)              %                                       %
%                                   %                                       %
%...............................................................................%
% Saying:....                                                               %
%                                                                           %
=-=-=-=-=-=-=-=-=-=-=-=-=-=-=-=-=-=-=-=-=-=-=-=-=-=-=-=-=-=-=-=-=
```

MOVING ON

Mastering e-mail is only part of learning to communicate on the Internet. The next step is learning how to step into the global free-for-all that is Usenet, armed with the appropriate tools and understanding of how newsgroups work.

In the next chapter, we'll cover the basics for reading and posting news to Usenet with UNIX news readers. We'll cover the two most popular and easiest to use programs—tin and trn—and show you how to read and post netnews with the best of 'em. We'll also look into juggling your newsrc file so that you can read what you want, when you want.

## Chapter 18

UNIX Usenet Tools

As we've rattled on about in the previous chapters, using UNIX utilities via a shell account to get on the Net can sometimes be faster and easier than using a graphical user interface (that's GUI to you). The power user doesn't always want to be confined by predetermined windows and menus when something more flexible is needed.

In this chapter, we'll explore the two newsreader programs known as tin and trn. We'll cover the basics of subscribing, reading, posting, and searching Usenet news, as well as program-specific goodies we encounter along the way.

First, let's take an in-depth look at the heart of any UNIX newsreader—the newsrc file. No matter which newsreader you use, you'll have to deal with this sooner or later. So we might as well master it from the start.

THE NEWSRC FILE

With all of these newsgroups floating around, how does anyone keep track of them? Meet the newsrc file!

In a UNIX shell account, a list of all the newsgroups to which you subscribe is stored in your directory in a file called .newsrc. Unfortunately, there's no way of telling how your newsrc may be initially set up. When you first decide to start reading Usenet news with your UNIX account, your newsrc file may not contain any newsgroups. On the other hand, the first time that you fire up your UNIX newsreader, you may have the fun (that's sarcasm, kids!) task of deciding what newsgroups you want to subscribe to. This may take a long time to do by hand. A very long time. Read along if you want to find out how to avoid this task.

After you've subscribed to what you want to read, your newsrc will contain the groups that you've subscribed to. When you begin reading your news, you'll see the groups listed in the order in which they've been placed in your newsrc file.

The good news is that since the newsrc file is a text file, if you don't like the order you see your news listed in, you can just open up your newsrc with your favorite editor and move the news-groups around.

At this point, it's enough that you know what a newsrc file is. Also, because it contains all the information about the newsgroups that you've selected, it's probably a good idea to make a backup copy of this file. You can do so by using the command:

```
cp .newsrc backup.newsrc
```

If your newsrc file ever gets corrupted, you can restore it from the backup by typing:

```
cp backup.newsrc .newsrc
```

So now that you know what your newsrc is, let's read some news!

TIP

In your newsrc file, newsgroups are marked as either subscribed or unsubscribed. Newsgroups that you are subscribed to are followed by a colon (:), and newsgroups that you've unsubscribed from are followed by an exclamation point (!).

Depending on how your system administrator has configured your newsreader, you may be subscribed to all the newsgroups available the first time that you use your newsreader. Being subscribed to all the newsgroups might be considered a very charitable act by some, but it becomes a big pain when you're trying to read a specific newsgroup. What do you do?

The trick is to unsubscribe yourself from all the newsgroups and then go back and subscribe to only the newsgroups that you want. Here's how. If you are originally subscribed to all the newsgroups on your system when you first use your newsreader, you can unsubscribe from all of them by using the following sequence of commands. Type them at your regular UNIX system prompt, and press Enter at the end of each line.

```
tr : ! <.newsrc>newnewsrc
cp .newsrc .old.newsrc
mv newnewsrc .newsrc
```

This sequence of commands first uses the tr (translate) command to change all the subscribed characters (:) into unsubscribed characters (!) in your .newsrc file, saving the result in a file named newnewsrc.

Next, we make a backup copy of the original .newsrc file in case something goes awry. Finally, we copy the new, unsubscribed newnewsrc over the old, everything-subscribed .newsrc. Finished! Everything unsubscribed to! Now when you enter your newsreader, you can subscribe only to the newsgroups *you* want.

■ ■

USING TIN

For anyone moving from the GUI (graphical user interface) world into the text-based UNIX world, tin probably provides the smoothest transition. No, you won't be using your mouse to enter commands, but you can use the arrow keys on the keyboard to move your cursor around to read articles. In fact, if all you ever want to do is read news, you'll never have to touch any other keys.

Also, like Pine, tin provides a handy menu at the bottom of each screen. If you ever forget a command (or leave this book on the bus), you can glance down at the menu to see what to do.

Starting tin

To start tin from the command line simply type **tin**, and press Enter. The program will run through its startup procedure, connecting to your system's news server and opening all the newsgroups to which you've subscribed. If this is the first time you've used tin, this process may take a while because tin is often configured to subscribe to all the newsgroups available on the server.

Whether your version of tin is configured to subscribe to all the newsgroups or configured to subscribe to none of the newsgroups, once tin has finished its startup procedure, you'll be placed in the Group Selection page (see Figure 18-1).

Let's take a closer look at Figure 18-1. It'll help keep things straight for later. The first column on the left contains the index number for each newsgroup. The next column contains the number or unread articles in each newsgroup. Finally, the third column contains the name of the group.

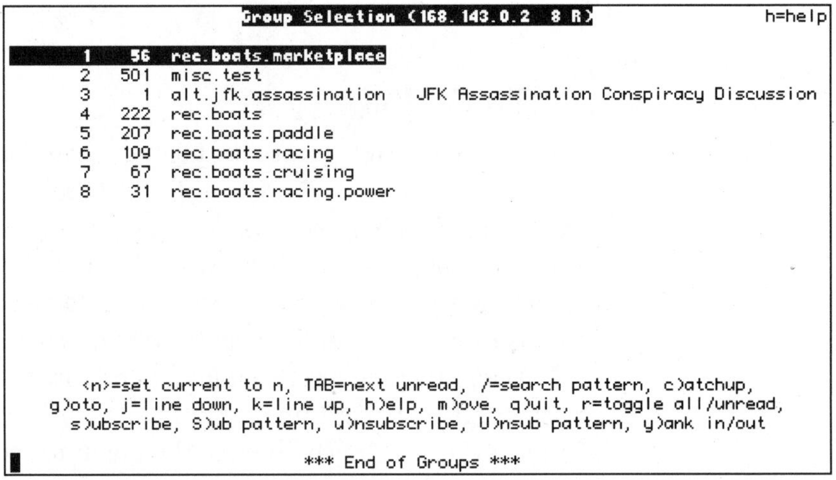

```
            Group Selection (168.143.0.2  8 R)                      h=help

    1    56   rec.boats.marketplace
    2   501   misc.test
    3     1   alt.jfk.assassination    JFK Assassination Conspiracy Discussion
    4   222   rec.boats
    5   207   rec.boats.paddle
    6   109   rec.boats.racing
    7    67   rec.boats.cruising
    8    31   rec.boats.racing.power






        <n>=set current to n, TAB=next unread, /=search pattern, c)atchup,
      g)oto, j=line down, k=line up, h)elp, m)ove, q)uit, r=toggle all/unread,
        s)ubscribe, S)ub pattern, u)nsubscribe, U)nsub pattern, y)ank in/out

                          *** End of Groups ***
```

Figure 18-1: Group Selection page in tin.

If you're subscribed to every group, they'll appear here. If you're not subscribed to any newsgroups, the middle part of the screen will be blank. Along the bottom of the screen is the menu that we mentioned earlier. It contains all the commands you need to do most of the common tasks with tin. Table 18-1 briefly describes the commands you can use on the Group Selection page.

Command	Description
c	Marks articles in selected newsgroup as read, and asks you to confirm the change before saving.
C	Marks articles as read in currently selected newsgroup. Does not ask you to confirm the changes.
G	Goes to newsgroup by name.
M	Moves location of currently selected newsgroup in list.
N	Selects next newsgroup.
n	Moves to next newsgroup, and displays articles.
q	Quits tin.
r	Toggles display between all subscribed groups and only subscribed groups containing unread articles.
s	Subscribes to currently selected newsgroup.
y	Yanks in all newsgroups. Subscribes you to all the newsgroups on the news server.
Enter	Goes to newsgroup index page for currently selected newsgroup.
[number]	Selects newsgroups by index number.
Tab	Looks at next newsgroup containing unread news.

Table 18-1: Commands on the Group Selection page.

Subscribing & Unsubscribing

If you're subscribed to all the newsgroups, you'll probably want to unsubscribe from at least some of them. It's not uncommon for a news server to carry thousands of groups, and finding and reading the ones you want in such a huge list every time can be a giant pain.

When you start tin, you'll notice that the topmost newsgroup on the list is in reverse type (white on black). This indicates that it is the currently selected newsgroup. You can move the selection bar (the reversed area) through the list of newsgroups by pressing the Down arrow. If you want to move backward through the list (back to the top), press the Up arrow key.

■ ■

TIP

If you think about tin spatially, you'll have a much easier time remembering how to move around. "Think about it how?" you're asking. It's easier than it sounds.

Tin has several levels of operation: a newsgroup selection level for selecting newsgroups to read, a newsgroup index level for selecting articles within a newsgroup, and an article page level to read a specific article. If you think about them like nested boxes, it becomes easier to remember how to get around. The big box that tin sits in is UNIX. Once you start tin, you're moved "into" the first level. In that level you can move up and down though a list of newsgroups or you can move back "out" to UNIX. As you've already seen, moving the arrow keys up and down moves you up and down the list of newsgroups. However, if you use the Left arrow key when you're at this level, you'll move "out" of tin and back into UNIX. Conversely, using the Right arrow key will move you deeper into the program to the newsgroup index level.

In the newsgroup index level, you can move up or down a list of the articles, you can move "out" (left) to the newsgroup selection level, or you can move further inward (right) to the center of the program—the article itself.

Once you're in the article, you can move up or down though the text (using the Up and Down arrow keys) or you can move "out" to the newsgroup index level. At this level, since you've reached the "center" of the program, moving deeper with the Right arrow key takes you to the next message in the thread you're reading. Continuing to press the Right arrow key will move you to the next thread, then to each article in the thread, and so on until you've read all the articles. When you reach the end of all the articles, you'll be put back at the newsgroup index level.

Once you've mastered this "spatial" concept, moving around through tin will become second nature. Like we said before, if you just want to read articles, you can do it by using the arrow keys.

■ ■

Once you've selected a newsgroup, you can unsubscribe from it by pressing the u key. You'll see that the name of the newsgroup is marked with a u in the far-left column. If you decide that you really didn't mean to unsubscribe from it, select the newsgroup again, and press **s** to subscribe to it. The u will disappear.

If you want to subscribe to a newsgroup, you have a couple of options. If you know the name of the group that you want to subscribe to, press **S**. Tin will prompt you:

```
Enter regex subscribe pattern>
```

Type the name of the newsgroup that you want to subscribe to, and press Enter. It will be added to your list of subscribed groups (provided that it is a group carried on your news server). If you don't know the exact name of the group you want to subscribe to, but you've got a general idea of its name, type **S**. At the following prompt:

```
Enter regex subscribe pattern>
```

enter a word you think occurs in the name of the newsgroup, surrounded by wildcard characters (*). For example, if you wanted to subscribe to a newsgroup with "mac" in the name, you'd type the following and press Enter:

```
Enter regex subscribe pattern> *mac*
```

The only problem with this method is that it's inexact—it subscribes you to *all* the newsgroups with "mac" in the name. If you use this kind of broad selection, you'll probably end up subscribed to alt.women.supremacy, alt.music.fleetwood-mac, and alt.news.macedonia along with the newsgroups about the Macintosh. To narrow your search, you'll have to use regular expressions. Refer to the section "Regular Expressions for Regular Folks" in Chapter 26, "Data Tracking," for more details. As you're winding your way through the process of subscribing and unsubscribing, use Table 18-2 as a reference.

Command	Description
s	Subscribes to newsgroup that's been marked unsubscribed.
S	Subscribes to newsgroups matching specified pattern.
U	Unsubscribes from selected newsgroup.

Table 18-2: Commands to subscribe to and unsubscribe from newsgroups in tin.

Reading News

Using the arrow keys, move the selection bar to the name of a newsgroup you want to open. Once you've selected the one you want, press Enter (or the Right arrow key) to see the list of articles in the newsgroup. Figure 18-2 shows an article index page in tin.

```
                    alt.ufo.reports (13T 14A OK OH R)          You have mail
     1  +     Donald R. Schmitt in Las Vegas               Randomity
     2  +     Femdom In Search of Naughty Boys             Anne Schoofs
     3  +     Some difficult questions for believers to ans Gwa Mcmurphy
     4  +     Triangular UFO in southern England           Piers Sherwood
     5  + 2   A New Book, by Mark Dean                     Mark Dean
     6  +     UFO Sighting(?)                              Richard Caldwell
     7  +     just cuz i was abducted dont make me alien   William C. Kelton
     8  +     Abduction For Sex???? Again?                 The J Man
     9  +     Please translate this Quatrain...            Greg Long
    10  +     *MELT*ing Windshields in Seattle?            Greg Long
    11  +     ufo sited in oz??                            Greg Long
    12  +     Pyramid Energy is alive                      dtmc
    13  +     PHILIPPINES/KOREA UFO SIGHTINGS?             The J Man



     <n>=set current to n, TAB=next unread, /=search pattern, ^K)ill/select,
   a)uthor search, c)atchup, j=line down, k=line up, K=mark read, l)ist thread,
    |=pipe, m)ail, o=print, q)uit, r=toggle all/unread, s)ave, t)ag, w=post

                         *** End of Articles ***
```

Figure 18-2: Article index page in tin.

This list looks much like message lists you may have seen in Pine and elm. The far-left column contains the index number for the article. Moving right, a + indicates that the article is unread. Next to the + is a number. Tin is a "threaded" newsreader, which means that each article is grouped with any articles posted in reply. The number indicates how many total articles are in the thread. Moving right once again, the middle column contains the subject of the thread. Unless the original post has already been read, you won't see a "Re" indicating a reply in this list. Tin removes them from the message list. Finally, the far-right column gives the name of the person who posted the article.

You can move up and down through the list of articles using the arrow keys. To move back to the newsgroup page at the beginning of the program, use the Left arrow. Table 18-3 lists the commands you can use to select an article to read with tin.

Command	Description
Ctrl+K	Goes to kill menu. This function allows you to select certain "kill" criteria for your newsreader. Articles matching the criteria you set will be "killed" — not shown in your Article index.
a	Searches forward through the list for a specific author.
A	Searches backward through the list for a specific author.
l	Lists the author of each article in the thread, and allows user to select specific articles.
m	Brings up mail command. You can mail a single article, a whole thread, a group of tagged articles, or a group of articles matching a pattern.
o	Prints a single article, articles in a thread, tagged articles, or articles matching a pattern.
q	Quits tin.
s	Saves a single article, articles in a thread, tagged articles, or articles matching a pattern to a file.
t	Tag articles or a thread of articles for printing, saving, or piping.
w	Posts a message to this newsgroup.
Enter or Right arrow key	Reads selected article.
I	Pipes (processes) a single article, articles in a thread, tagged articles, or articles matching a pattern through a system command. Useful for uudecoding binary files.

Table 18-3: Article index page commands in tin.

To read a thread or a single article, select it using the arrow keys, and press Enter or the Right arrow key. tin will place you in the article display page, where you can read the article (see Figure 18-3).

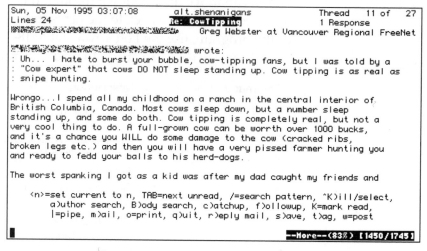

```
Sun, 05 Nov 1995 03:07:08        alt.shenanigans           Thread   11 of   27
Lines 24                         Re: CowTipping               1 Response
█████████████████████████    Greg Webster at Vancouver Regional FreeNet

████████████████████████ wrote:
: Uh... I hate to burst your bubble, cow-tipping fans, but I was told by a
: "Cow expert" that cows DO NOT sleep standing up. Cow tipping is as real as
: snipe hunting.

Wrongo...I spend all my childhood on a ranch in the central interior of
British Columbia, Canada. Most cows sleep down, but a number sleep
standing up, and some do both. Cow tipping is completely real, but not a
very cool thing to do. A full-grown cow can be worrth over 1000 bucks,
and it's a chance you WILL do some damage to the cow (cracked ribs,
broken legs etc.) and then you will have a very pissed farmer hunting you
and ready to fedd your balls to his herd-dogs.

The worst spanking I got as a kid was after my dad caught my friends and

    <n>=set current to n, TAB=next unread, /=search pattern, ^K)ill/select,
        a)uthor search, B)ody search, c)atchup, f)ollowup, K=mark read,
        |=pipe, m)ail, o=print, q)uit, r)eply mail, s)ave, t)ag, w=post

█                                              --More--(83%) [1450/1745]
```

Figure 18-3: Article page level in tin.

Once you're in the read article mode, you should first look at the upper right-hand corner of the window. It'll tell you which thread you're currently reading, how many more there are to go, and if there are any responses to the article you're currently reading.

If the article you're reading takes up more than one page, you'll have to use the Up and Down arrow keys to scroll through the message. If the article you're reading has any replies to it in the thread, pressing the right arrow key will move you to the next response. However, if you've reached the end of the thread, pressing the Right arrow key will move you to the next thread.

Once you're done reading articles, pressing the Left arrow key will return you to the article index page. In case you need a handy reference for your tin article-reading commands while you're perusing your newsgroups, Table 18-4 should help.

Command	Description
a	Searches for author specified in list of articles.
c	Marks all articles in newsgroup as read.
F	Posts reply to article, and doesn't include current article in reply.
f	Posts reply to article, and includes article in reply.
h	Gets help.
K	Marks single article as read.
q	Goes back to newsgroup index page.
Q	Quits tin.
r	Replies to article through e-mail. Includes copy of article.
R	Replies to author of article through e-mail, and does not includes copy of article.
Enter	Opens next article.
I	Pipes article through system command.

Table 18-4: Commands at the Article Page in tin

Posting News

If you want to post an article to a Usenet group using tin, you can do so by using only a few simple commands.

If you're in the newsgroup selection level, you can post a message to the currently selected newsgroup by typing **w**. Tin will respond:

```
Post subject []>
```

Type the subject of your message at this prompt, and press Enter. Tin will place you in your system editor. Type your message, and exit the editor. Tin will treat you to some important advice and ask you if you really want to post your message (see Figure 18-4).

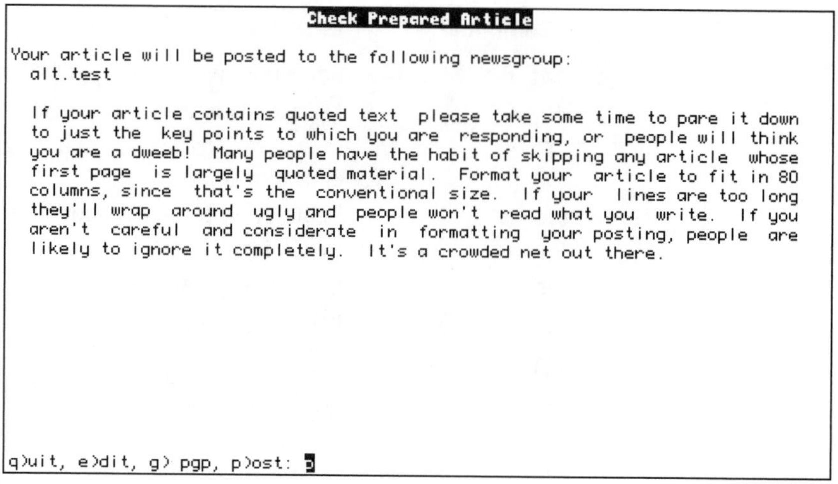

```
                        Check Prepared Article
Your article will be posted to the following newsgroup:
  alt.test

  If your article contains quoted text  please take some time to pare it down
  to just the  key points to which you are  responding, or  people will think
  you are a dweeb!  Many people have the habit of skipping any article  whose
  first page  is largely  quoted material.  Format your  article to fit in 80
  columns, since  that's the  conventional size.  If your  lines are too long
  they'll  wrap  around  ugly and  people won't  read what you  write.  If you
  aren't  careful  and considerate  in  formatting  your posting, people  are
  likely to ignore it completely.  It's a crowded net out there.




q)uit, e)dit, g) pgp, p)ost: ▊
```

Figure 18-4: Confirming a post in tin.

If everything's up to snuff, press **p** to post your article to the world! You'll be returned to the Group Selection page. If you're at the article index page of tin, everything works the same as in the Group Selection page. Press **w** to post an article.

If you're reading an article at the article page level, you have several options. If you want to reply to the article directly to the author through e-mail, just press **r**. Tin will place you in the editor, along with a copy of the message you were reading. Add your comments, save the message, and off it goes. If you want to reply to the author without including the article, type capital **R** instead.

If you want to post a follow-up message to the newsgroup, doing so works much the same as the reply function we just described. Instead of mailing to the author, you're adding your reply to the newsgroup postings. To reply without including the article you're reading, press **F**. Edit your message, close the editor, and send it. If you want your reply to include the article you're reading, type **f** instead. We've provided Table 18-5 as a reference in case you need help remembering which commands to use when replying.

TIP

A note on replies that include the text of the original message. tin actually has some sage advice on the subject:

> If your article contains quoted text please take some time to pare it down to just the key points to which you are responding, or people will think you are a dweeb! Many people have the habit of skipping any article whose first page is largely quoted material. Format your article to fit in 80 columns, since that's the conventional size. If your lines are too long they'll wrap around ugly and people won't read what you write. If you aren't careful and considerate in formatting your posting, people are likely to ignore it completely. It's a crowded net out there.

Listen to tin. There's nothing worse than trying to follow an article that's been quoted and quoted and quoted *ad infinitum*. It becomes unreadable!

Command	Description
w (in Group Selection page)	Posts article to selected newsgroup.
w (in article index page)	Posts article to newsgroup.
r (in display page)	Replies to author through e-mail, and includes copy of article.
R (in display page))	Replies y to author through e-mail, and does not include copy of article.
f (in display page))	Posts follow-up article, and includes copy of article.
F (in display page)	Posts follow-up article, and does not include copy of article.

Table 18-5: Commands for posting articles in tin.

Searching News

With the sheer volume of news being posted to Usenet these days, being able to search newsgroups for articles of interest is more important than ever. Tin offers several features for searching newsgroups.

At the Group Selection page, you can search forward through your list of subscribed newsgroups by typing a forward slash (/). Tin will prompt you for a pattern. If you wish to search backward through the list, type **?**.

At the article index page, you have several more options. You can search forward through the list of threads for a specific author by typing **a**. If you want to search backward for an author, type **A**. If you want to search forward by subject, just type **/** as with the Group Selection page. If you get far down in the list and want to search backward, type **?**.

Once you get into reading a specific article, you have several additional options. As in the other levels, you can type **/** and **?** to search forward and backward in the body of the text for a specific string. Refer to Table 18-6 for a list of search commands in tin.

Command	Description
/	Searches forward for string.
?	Searches backward for string.
A	Searches forward for author.
A	Searches backward for author.

Table 18-6: Commands to Search in tin.

Quitting tin

No matter where you are in tin, pressing **Q** will allow you to quit the program immediately. If you're at a "lower" level within the program, pressing **q** will quit the level you're in and move you to the next higher level. If you are at the top level (newsgroup selection), typing **q** will quit tin.

USING TRN

Considerably more complex than tin, and probably more common, trn is an expanded version (written by Wayne Davison) of the old UNIX newsreader rn.

Basically, most of the major commands are the same, and the user interfaces in the two programs are similar. If you find that you don't have trn installed on your system, don't worry—most of what you'll learn in this section can be applied to rn as well.

Trn is a threaded newsreader. Like tin, trn groups messages with similar subjects into threads for easier reading. It's a major improvement over the old rn, which basically functioned like a lot of mail programs, presenting a long list of articles to be read. This wasn't a problem in the old days when a hundred messages a week for a newsgroup was considered heavy traffic. These days, some newsgroups get that many messages in an hour!

TIP

Trn has several "universal commands" that work no matter where you are in the program:

space bar	Executes first command in the list of command choices.
Q	Quits what you're doing and moves you up one level in the program. If you're at the top level, this command will quit trn entirely.
H	Gives you help on the commands available at the current prompt.

Starting trn

To start trn, type **trn** at your UNIX prompt. What you'll see next depends on how your system is set up. If you've been automatically subscribed to all the newsgroups, you will see a screen similar to the one shown in Figure 18-5.

```
explorer:[/homec/elrod] trn
Unread news in rec.boats.marketplace                    56 articles
Unread news in misc.test                               253 articles
Unread news in alt.jfk.assassination                     1 article
Unread news in rec.boats                               120 articles
Unread news in rec.boats.paddle                        102 articles
etc.

======  56 unread articles in rec.boats.marketplace -- read now? [+ynq] ▊
```

Figure 18-5: Newsgroups ready to be read in trn.

If you haven't been subscribed to any newsgroups, you may see a screen similar to the one shown in Figure 18-6.

```
explorer:[/homec/elrod] trn
No unread news in subscribed-to newsgroups.  To subscribe to a new
newsgroup use the g<newsgroup> command.

****** End of newsgroups -- what next? [qnp] ▊
```

Figure 18-6: No newsgroups to read in trn.

If you've already been subscribed to some newsgroups and new newsgroups are available on the system, you'll see a screen similar to the one shown in Figure 18-7.

```
well% trn
Unread news in well.general                              5 articles
Unread news in ba.food                                  52 articles
Unread news in ba.general                            11263 articles
Unread news in ba.motss                                 10 articles
Unread news in ba.mountain-folk                         18 articles
etc.

Checking for new newsgroups...

Newsgroup alt.bonehead.dave-williams not in .newsrc -- subscribe? [ynYN] ▊
```

Figure 18-7: New newsgroups to subscribe to in trn.

- -

TIP

Like tin, trn has three main levels: the newsgroup selection level where you enter the program, the thread selection level where you can choose the threads within a newsgroup that you want to read, and the article-reading level where you actually read the articles.

- -

Subscribing To & Unsubscribing From Newsgroups

If you see a screen similar to the one shown in Figure 18-5 when
you start trn, you can do one of two things. First, you can quit trn
by using the q command and then use the Tip described earlier to
unsubscribe yourself from all the newsgroups. When you re-enter
trn, you can use the g command to subscribe to the newsgroups
you want, like so:

```
g news.group.name
```

at the following prompt:

```
****** End of newsgroups - what next? [qnp]
```

If the newsgroup name that you type is in your newsrc file,
you'll then be asked:

```
Newsgroup news.group.name is unsubscribed - resubscribe? [yn]
```

If you answer y for Yes, you'll be able to read the newsgroup. If
you answer n, the newsgroup won't be subscribed to in the
newsrc.

If you don't choose to exit and unsubscribe from the newsgroups in your newsrc file at the start, you'll have to go though
each and every newsgroup in trn and choose y or n. With thousands of newsgroups on the average server, this process could
take a *very* long time.

If you've already been subscribed to some newsgroups but new
groups have been added since you originally subscribed (see
Figure 18-7), you'll have to decide which new groups you want to
subscribe to.

When you enter trn and there are new newsgroups, you'll be
prompted for whether you want to subscribe to each new group:

```
Newsgroup not in .newsrc-subscribe? [ynYN]
```

Typing y for Yes will bring up the following prompt:

```
Put newsgroup where? [$^.Lq]
```

At this point you have several more choices. Table 18-7 describes them. You should get used to this prompt, especially if
your system adds newsgroups frequently.

Command	Description
$	Places newsgroup in the last position in the newsrc file.
^	Places newsgroup first in the newsrc file.
L	Lists current newsgroups.
Q	Quits–aborts adding newsgroup.
Number	Places newsgroup in newsrc at position indicated by number.
-newsgroup	Places newsgroup in front of newsgroup specified.
+newsgroup	Places newsgroup after newsgroup specified.
	Places newsgroup before current newsgroup.

Table 18-7: Commands to arrange newsgroups in trn.

The g command is great if you already know the name of the newsgroup you want to subscribe to. If you don't, use o. The command o typed at the following prompt with a string will subscribe you to all the newsgroups containing that string:

```
****** End of newsgroups - what next? [qnp]
```

For example, if you wanted to add all the newsgroups with the word "boat" in the title, you could enter this:

```
****** End of newsgroups - what next? [qnp]o "boat"
```

You will be asked whether you want to subscribe to each newsgroup matching the pattern.

Sometimes you may encounter many, many new newsgroups to subscribe to when you enter trn. What do you do if you don't want to have to answer N to each one of them? Or, what if you want to subscribe to them all? Well, you could select each one individually. Or you could use the uppercase versions of the y or n commands (Y or N) to subscribe or not subscribe to them as a batch. Pressing **N** will not subscribe you to any of the new news-groups, while pressing **Y** will sign you up for all the new groups.

Once you've gotten all the preliminaries worked out, you may need to unsubscribe from a specific newsgroup. To do so, press **u** at the newsgroup selection-level prompt:

```
====== 100 unread articles in some.news.group - read now?
[+ynq]u
Unsubscribed to newsgroup some.news.group
```

Keeping track of all these commands can get confusing. If you get lost, please refer to Table 18-8.

Command	Description
g newsgroup	Subscribes to newsgroup.
U	Unsubscribes from newsgroup.
Y	Subscribes to new group.
Y	Subscribes to all new groups.
n	Doesn't subscribe to group.
N	Doesn't subscribe to all new groups.
o string	Subscribes to all newsgroups matching string.

Table 18-8: Subscribing to and unsubscribing from newsgroups in trn.

Reading News

Once you've subscribed to a newsgroup, we bet that you'll probably want to read some of the articles in it. While you're in the newsgroup selection level, you'll get a prompt like this for each newsgroup you've subscribed to:

```
====== 1619 unread articles in news.group.name - read now?
[+ynq]
```

Again, more choices. If you press the plus sign (+) (or the spacebar—which always invokes the first command in the list), you'll be placed in the thread selection level (see Figure 18-8).

```
alt.shenanigans          58 articles

a Len Smith          2  >Toilet trick experience
  Marc Dufour
b Timothy B. Black   1  >Fun halloween handouts
d freddy1@indy.net   3  >Religious Shen I Have Pulled
  levendis
  ron walker
e Mike Kuhn          5  >Cake!!!!!!!
  Greg Webster
  Barney t C Dino
  Ian M. Schirado
  Jonathan D Rowe
  Charles Eicher     4  >tires/valve stems
  Steve Thomas
  Daniel J Stern
  Daniel
f Steven J. Tella    1  >Bhuddist? (sic)

(Mail) -- Select threads (date order) -- Top 27% [>2] --
```

Figure 18-8: Thread selection-level screen in trn.

If you press **y**, you'll be placed in the article-reading level, where you can read the first article in the newsgroup (see Figure 18-9).

```
alt.shenanigans #19769 (5 + 49 more)        ( )+-(2)--(2)--(2)
                                            |-( )--( )--( )+-[1]
[1] Re: tires/valve stems                   |            \-[1]+-[1]
Date: Sat Nov 04 14:58:28 EST 1995          |                  \-[1]
Organization: Society For Putting Things On \-( )--( )--[2]
+              Top Of Other Things          ( )--[2]
Lines: 28
X-Newsreader: Value-Added NewsWatcher 2.0b27+

In article <Pine.SOL.3.91.951103235122.15339D-100000@gladstone>, Daniel
Joshua Stern <dastern@gladstone.uoregon.edu> wrote:

> Better: take a utility knife to the inner side of the valve stems.  Cut
> them about 1/2 to 2/3 of the way through.  They have enough rigidity to
> spring back straight when you remove the knife, sealing the leak. . .

That is NOT a shen.. It causes permanent damage, and costs real money to
repair. A true shenner would NEVER do such a thing.

A REAL shenner knows how to do this properly. Take off the valve cap, put
a BB pellet in it, and screw the cap back on just enough for the BB to
depress the valve stem slightly. The mark will now have a slow leak. If
you do this right, with enough finesse, the slow leak will take days to
--MORE--(73%)
```

Figure 18-9: Article-reading level in trn.

If you press **n**, you'll go to the next newsgroup that you've subscribed to. Pressing **q** will quit trn, and send you back to the UNIX shell.

Let's go back and look at the thread selection-level screen shown in Figure 18-8. At the top of the screen you'll find information describing the newsgroup you're reading as well as how many articles are in that newsgroup. But look at that list! Sure, the second column containing the author's name looks familiar, the next column showing the number of articles in the thread resembles the same feature in tin, and the subject column on the far right looks like everything else we've seen in news- and mail-reading programs. So, what's that alphabet soup in the far-left column?

Those are the thread selection letters, and they're an integral part of how trn works. Instead of selecting threads with the arrow keys like you did in tin, you select threads in trn by typing the selection letter next to the thread you want to read. When you do, a plus sign will appear between the selection letter and the author's name, indicating that the thread has been selected.

If you're wondering why the letters skip around, the answer is simple: trn can't use selection letters that would be confused with commands. In trn, you won't read a thread until it's selected, and you can select multiple threads before deciding to read them. Figure 18-10 shows a thread selection screen with several threads selected. If you want to select all the threads on the screen, type @.

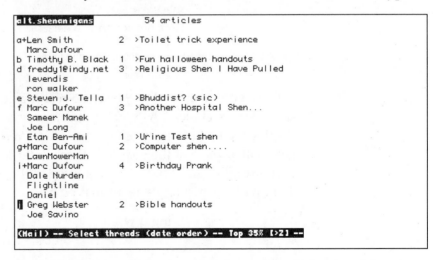

```
alt.shenanigans          54 articles

a+Len Smith         2  >Toilet trick experience
  Marc Dufour
b Timothy B. Black   1  >Fun halloween handouts
d freddy1@indy.net   3  >Religious Shen I Have Pulled
  levendis
  ron walker
e Steven J. Tella    1  >Bhuddist? (sic)
f Marc Dufour        3  >Another Hospital Shen...
  Sameer Manek
  Joe Long
  Etan Ben-Ami       1  >Urine Test shen
g+Marc Dufour        2  >Computer shen....
  LawnMowerMan
i+Marc Dufour        4  >Birthday Prank
  Dale Nurden
  Flightline
  Daniel
  Greg Webster       2  >Bible handouts
  Joe Savino

(Mail) -- Select threads (date order) -- Top 35% [>2] --
```

Figure 18-10: A thread selection screen in trn with multiple selected threads.

Once you've selected which threads you want to read, you have several options. First, if you don't want to read any of the threads that you haven't selected, type **X**. It'll mark all the unselected articles as read and start you reading the first article in the first thread that you've selected.

If you just want to read the articles you've selected, press the spacebar or type **Z**. You'll be placed in article-reading mode, accessing the first article in the first thread you've selected.

Command	Description
letter	Marks thread letter to be read.
<	Goes to previous thread page.
>	Goes to next page of threads.
^	Goes to first page of threads.
$	Goes to last page of threads.
@	Marks all visible threads to be read.
X	Marks all unselected articles as read so you can begin reading selected articles.
D	Marks unselected articles as read. If any threads have been selected, you can begin reading. If not, go to the next page of threads.
J	Marks selected articles as read.
L	Leaves newsgroup without changing the status of any message.
h	Gets help on thread selector screen commands.

Table 18-9: Commands for selecting threads in trn.

Once you've moved to the article-reading area, you'll have several more choices. As you'll notice, trn uses our buddy more to display the text of the messages you read. Press the spacebar to get another page of the message. Press Enter to read it line by line. If you want to go back to the beginning of the article, press Ctrl+R. To move back just one screenful, type **b**.

If you finish reading an article, you can press the spacebar or type **n** to move to the next article in the thread. While you're reading, if you decide that a thread isn't worth reading, you can use the Junk command, J, to mark all the other unread articles in the thread as read and then move to the next article. If you're reading the last thread when you use J, you'll be placed back at the thread selection screen. Please refer to Table 18-10 for a list of commands if you get lost.

Command	Description
spacebar	Displays next page of article.
Enter	Displays next line of article.
Ctrl+R	Moves to beginning of article.
B	Moves back one page in article.
N	Moves to next article in thread.
J	Marks all unread articles in thread as read, and moves on to next thread.
+	Goes back to thread selection screen.
Down arrow	Goes to next article in thread.
Up arrow	Goes to previous article in thread.

Table 18-10: Commands to read articles in trn.

Posting News

If you want to post an article using trn, you have several choices.

You can post articles from the newsgroup selection level by using the .f command:

```
====== 10 unread articles in some.news.group-read now? [+ynq]
.f
```

Trn will respond with:

```
Subject:
```

Type the subject of your message, and press Enter. Next you should see this:

```
Distribution:
```

If you want your article to be distributed to the whole world, type **world**. If you want it to circulate just within the United States, type **usa**. If you want your message to go to just the system you're currently on, type **local**, and press Enter.

Next, trn will ask you an ominous question:

```
This program posts news to thousands of machines throughout
the entire civilized world. Your message will cost the net
hundreds if not thousands of dollars to send everywhere.
Please be sure you know what you are doing.
Are you absolutely sure that you want to do this? [ny]
```

Even though it sounds scary, as long as you're sure that you want your message to go out, press **y**. trn will respond:

```
Prepared file to include [none]:
```

At this stage, you probably don't have a file you want to send out with your message. If you do, here's where you can type the filename of the file you wish to include in your message. If you don't have a file to include, press Enter. You'll now find yourself in your system's text editor once again. Type your message, save it, and you should see the prompt:

```
Your article's newsgroup:
some.news.group          some witty description
Check spelling, Send, Abort, Edit, or List?
Type the first letter of the choice you want, and press
Enter. If you want to send your message on its way, type S.
That's it! You've sent a message.
```

You can also post a follow-up to an article or thread that you've read. If you're in article-reading mode, and you press **F**, trn will place a copy of the article that you're reading into your editor. If you simply type **f** by itself, you'll be able to post a follow-up that doesn't quote the original article. If you're in thread selection mode, pressing **u** by itself will allow you to post a new article.

Just like in tin, using r and R allows you to reply directly through e-mail to the author of an article. Using r will send a reply without quoting the original article. Using R will include a copy of the original article with the e-mail. Table 18-11 provides a reference for the commands you need to post news in trn.

Command	Description
.f (in newsgroup-selection mode)	Posts new article to newsgroup.
f (in article-reading mode)	Posts follow-up to current article, and doesn't quote current article.
F (in article-reading mode)	Posts follow-up to current article, and quotes current article.
f (in thread selection mode)	Posts new article to current newsgroup.
R (in article-reading mode)	Replies to author of current article, and includes copy of article.
r (in article-reading mode)	Replies to author of current article, and doesn't include copy of current article.

Table 18-11: Commands for posting news in trn.

Searching News

Since Usenet's volume is up tremendously (and shows no signs of slowing down), learning how to search news for what you want is important. In the newsgroup selection level, trn offers several nifty ways to search newsgroups. Table 18-12 gives some examples.

Command	Description
g newsgroup	Goes (and subscribes) to newsgroup.
/pattern	Searches forward for newsgroup name matching pattern.
?pattern	Searches backward for newsgroup name matching pattern.
l pattern	Lists unsubscribed newsgroups that match pattern.
o pattern	Displays only newsgroups that match pattern.
O pattern	Displays newsgroups that match pattern and omits empty newsgroups.
a pattern	Displays newsgroups that match pattern and scans for unsubscribed newsgroups that match pattern.

Table 18-12: Commands to search newsgroups in trn.

Once you enter the thread selection level, trn gives you the capability to do powerful searches. The following command allows you to scan all the articles for a subject containing the string found in the pattern:

`/pattern/modifiers`

Use the modifiers listed in Table 18-13 for better results.

Modifier	Description
a	Scans entire articles.
c	Makes scan case-sensitive.
f	Scans from line.
h	Scans whole header.
r	Scans articles that have been read.

Table 18-13: Commands to scan in trn.

Once you're in article-reading mode, you can use the commands described in Table 18-14 to search the article you're currently reading as well as search for articles with similar attributes.

Command	Description
g pattern	Goes to pattern within message text.
G	Searches again for pattern.
Ctrl+G	Searches for next line beginning with the word "Subject:"
Ctrl+N	Searches for next unread article with the same title as current article.

Table 18-14 Commands to search articles in trn.

Quitting trn

To quit trn, type either q or Q, depending on where you are in the program. If you're at the top newsgroup selection level, pressing either **q** or **Q** will quit the program. However, if you're deeper into the program, pressing **q** will take you up one level. If you want to quit trn and go back to UNIX, type **Q**.

MOVING ON

Now that you've mastered Usenet with UNIX, let's get on to the rest of the Internet. In the next section, we're going to tackle the basics of all the tools that you need to get all your *other* work (and play!) done on the Net.

First, we'll cover the UNIX file system and how to transfer files to and from remote computer systems using FTP. Along the way, we'll also take a brief look at how to find files with Archie so that you'll actually have some stuff to transfer.

Next, we'll move on to Gopher. With the explosion of the Web during the past year or so, Gopher has kind of languished in its own little corner of Cyberspace, nearly forgotten as everyone rushes to goggle the graphics on the Web. We're going to teach you how to dust off this very useful (and nearly forgotten) Net tool to find the info you need.

Of course, we can't ignore the Web. We'll also cover lynx, a text-based UNIX Web browser. It's not quite as pretty as Netscape, but it'll get the job done. Check it out.

Finally, we'll push through a plethora of UNIX Net tools for chatting, tracking down people, checking your connection, and using remote systems.

## Chapter 19

UNIX Net Tools Gallery

Now that you've mastered UNIX basics, delved into e-mail, and tried your hand at newsgroups, it's time to move out onto the rest of the Net.

No matter what kind of data you're manipulating with your UNIX account, the basis for all that information moving is the UNIX file system and various file transfer programs. While you're online, it doesn't matter if you're downloading a new game, looking up a book at the Library of Congress, or checking out a new Web site—all of these processes involve transferring files.

We'll begin our journey into the wilds of the Internet with a short discussion of file transfer, specifically looking at the two programs most UNIX users employ: FTP and FSP.

Next, it's on to finding files with Archie. After that, we'll employ Gopher to find information, download weather reports, and even sneak a peek into a university computer or two.

Then, we'll take a look at lynx, that wily little text-based WWW program that you can use on a UNIX account. We'll discover the basics of getting around the Web, using bookmarks to find our way back, and how to download files and pictures.

Finally, we'll go on a whirlwind tour through a rogues gallery of UNIX tools. We'll learn how to connect to other computers with Telnet, how to chat with friends using talk and write, and we'll even track some people with whois, who, and finger.

FILE TRANSFER IN UNIX

Transferring files is one of the most basic and important functions you can do when you're online. And, if you think about it, almost every Internet activity—browsing the Web, reading e-mail, and surfing Usenet newsgroups—involves transferring files, or moving information from one place to the other.

In this section, we'll examine how you can move files that you've saved or created to other computers on the Net. Also (and probably more importantly), we'll look at ways that you can transfer files from remote computers to your computer.

FTP

One way to grab files from other computers on the Net (and to put your files on other computers) is to use a program called FTP. FTP stands for File Transfer Protocol, and there's probably not a UNIX system out there on the Internet that doesn't use it.

In a nutshell, here's how it works. FTP allows you to connect to another computer, get a listing of files that are available, change directories on the remote machine, and then transfer the files you want to your account.

Why use FTP? Because it's the best way to get free stuff off the Net! Many generous people from all over the world have put software, FAQs, electronic books and publications, and other useful files on what are called "anonymous FTP servers," which are FTP sites that allow anyone to log on and snarf what they want—for free!

Shareware, program demos, graphics files—they're all out there waiting for you to snag 'em with FTP. Here's how. First, let's log on to a site. Since you purchased this book from the fine folks at

Ventana, let's go grab some goodies from their site. The address for Ventana's FTP site is ftp.vmedia.com. So, to connect to it, type **ftp ftp.vmedia.com** at your UNIX prompt. You should see something similar to the screen in Figure 19-1.

```
explorer:[/homec/elrod] ftp ftp.vmedia.com
Connected to kells.vmedia.com.
220 kells FTP server (Version wu-2.4(2) Thu May 4 15:17:17 EDT 1995) ready.
Name (ftp.vmedia.com:elrod): █
```

Figure 19-1: Logging on to ftp.vmedia.com with FTP.

Okay. You've made the initial contact. Since this is an anonymous FTP server, just type the word **anonymous** when the server asks for your name, and press Enter. You'll then be prompted for a password. Enter your e-mail address, and press Enter again. You should see something similar to the screen in Figure 19-2.

```
220 kells FTP server (Version wu-2.4(2) Thu May 4 15:17:17 EDT 1995) ready.
Name (ftp.vmedia.com:elrod): anonymous
331 Guest login ok, send your complete e-mail address as password.
Password:
230-
230-
230-Tue Nov  7 13:09:24 1995
230-
230-Welcome to the Ventana Online Anonymous FTP Server.
230-
230-If your FTP client crashes or hangs shortly after you login, try
230-inserting a dash (-) before your password.
230-
230-Remote host name: clark.net
230-
230-You are user 17 out of a maximum of 60 users.
230-
230-If you have problems with or questions about this service, send e-mail
230-to help@vmedia.com.
230-
230-IMPORTANT NOTICE: All transfers to and from Ventana Online are logged.
230-
230 Guest login ok, access restrictions apply.
ftp> █
```

Figure 19-2: Logged on to the Ventana FTP site.

You're in! Let's have a look around. Remember all those UNIX commands you learned? (You don't? Turn to Appendix D, "UNIX Boot Camp," for a refresher.) Here's where they come in handy. FTP servers use **ls** and **cd**, just like your UNIX account. Let's try it out by getting a listing of what's available. Type **ls**, and press Enter. You'll see a directory listing like that shown in Figure 19-3.

```
ftp> ls
200 PORT command successful.
150 Opening ASCII mode data connection for file list.
pub
dev
etc
usr
outgoing
bin
welcome.msg
incoming
current_books
usergroups
welcome.txt
226 Transfer complete.
98 bytes received in 0.0027 seconds (36 Kbytes/s)
ftp> ▮
```

Figure 19-3: The ftp.vmedia.com directory listing.

Hmmm . . . it's kind of hard to tell what's a directory and what's a file. Remember how we got a detailed directory listing before? Type **ls -la**, and press Enter. Figure 19-4 shows what you'll see.

```
ftp> ls -la
200 PORT command successful.
150 Opening ASCII mode data connection for /bin/ls.
total 30
drwxr-xr-x  10 0        1          512 Jul 14 13:55 .
drwxr-xr-x  10 0        1          512 Jul 14 13:55 ..
lrwxrwxrwx   1 0        1            7 May  1  1995 bin -> usr/bin
drwxrwxr-x  23 183      100        512 Nov  1 20:35 current_books
dr-xr-xr-x   2 0        1          512 Jan 16  1995 dev
d--x--x--x   3 0        1          512 Jan 16  1995 etc
drwxrwx-wx  17 0        100       2560 Nov  6 19:52 incoming
drwxrwx--x  19 0        100        512 Oct 24 15:18 outgoing
dr-xr-xr-x  13 30000    1          512 May 11  1995 pub
drwxr-xr-x   2 130      100        512 Jan 31  1995 usergroups
dr-xr-xr-x   6 0        1          512 Jun 27  1994 usr
-rw-r--r--   1 0        1          401 Sep 27  1994 welcome.msg
-rw-r--r--   1 0        1          328 Apr 21  1995 welcome.txt
226 Transfer complete.
remote: -la
828 bytes received in 0.67 seconds (1.2 Kbytes/s)
ftp> ▮
```

Figure 19-4: Detailed directory listing.

Now that's more like it! We can see that pub is a directory. Let's see what's inside. Type **cd pub**, press Enter, and then type **ls -la** to get a full directory listing. Your listing should look something like the one shown in Figure 19-5.

```
ftp> cd pub
250 CWD command successful.
ftp> ls -la
200 PORT command successful.
150 Opening ASCII mode data connection for /bin/ls.
total 76
dr-xr-xr-x  13 30000     1          512 May 11  1995 .
drwxr-xr-x  10 0         1          512 Jul 14 13:55 ..
drwxr-xr-x  14 0         1          512 Jun 28 14:43 Mac
drwxr-xr-x   2 198     100         1024 Jun 29 19:05 PR
drwxr-xr-x   3 0         1          512 Feb 22  1995 Unix
drwxr-xr-x  20 0         1          512 Jul 12 18:01 Windows
drwxr-xr-x  15 0         1          512 Oct 30 20:52 companions
drwxr-xr-x   5 0         1          512 May  2  1995 dtp
drwxr-xr-x  15 0         0          512 Oct 21 03:12 infosystems
d-wx--x--x   5 0         1          512 Nov 22  1994 mirror
drwxr-xr-x   3 0         1          512 Aug 23  1994 multimedia
drwxr-xr-x   2 0         1        26624 Nov  7 04:01 rfc
drwxr-xr-x  10 0         1          512 Aug  9 20:06 users
226 Transfer complete.
remote: -la
805 bytes received in 0.004 seconds (1.9e+02 Kbytes/s)
ftp> █
```

Figure 19-5: Pub detailed directory listing.

Let's change to the Windows directory and see what's in there. Type **cd Windows**, press Enter, and then get a directory listing by typing **ls -la** again, and pressing Enter. Figure 19-6 shows the listing.

TIP

If you ever get a listing that's too long to fit on your screen, you can pipe the ls command through more to get the directory listing to pause. Just type **ls -la |more**.

```
ftp> ls -la
200 PORT command successful.
150 Opening ASCII mode data connection for /bin/ls.
total 5220
drwxr-xr-x  20 0         1          512 Jul 12 18:01 .
dr-xr-xr-x  13 30000     1          512 May 11  1995 ..
-rw-r--r--   1 0         1          313 Oct 14  1994 MOSAIC-IMPORTANT
lrwxrwxrwx   1 0         1           41 May  1  1995 Mosaic -> ../infosystems/M
osaic/Mosaic-NCSA/Windows
drwxr-xr-x   2 0         1          512 Sep 14 12:15 PGP
drwxr-xr-x   2 0         1          512 Nov 12  1994 WWW
drwxr-xr-x   2 0         1          512 Nov 12  1994 archie
drwxr-xr-x   2 0         1         1536 Feb 22  1995 autocad
drwxr-xr-x   2 0         1          512 Nov 30  1994 email
drwxr-xr-x   2 0         1          512 Nov 18  1994 ftp
drwxr-xr-x   2 0         1          512 Nov 12  1994 gopher
-rw-r--r--   1 0         1          375 Nov  4  1994 internet.txt
-rw-r--r--   1 0         1      2367191 Nov  4  1994 internet.zip
drwxr-xr-x   2 0         1          512 Feb 15  1995 irc
drwxr-xr-x   2 0         1          512 Feb 22  1995 mud
```

Figure 19-6: Windows directory listing.

Sheesh! Look at all those directories! Since we're doing FTP right now, let's change to the FTP directory and get a listing. Type **cd ftp**, press Enter, type **ls -la**, and Figure 19-7 shows what you should see.

```
ftp> ls -la
200 PORT command successful.
150 Opening ASCII mode data connection for /bin/ls.
total 724
drwxr-xr-x   2 0         1            512 Nov 18  1994 .
drwxr-xr-x  20 0         1            512 Jul 12 18:01 ..
-r--r--r--   1 0         1         113252 Nov 12  1994 ws_ftp.zip
-r--r--r--   1 0         1         233719 Nov 18  1994 wsftp32.zip
226 Transfer complete.
remote: -la
259 bytes received in 0.002 seconds (1.3e+02 Kbytes/s)
ftp> ▊
```

Figure 19-7: FTP directory listing.

You can see that two files are in this directory: ws_ftp.zip and wsftp32.zip. They're both Trumpet Winsock ftp clients, one for 16-bit PCs and the other for 32-bit computers. Let's grab the ws_ftp.zip file.

First, you'll need to set the file transfer mode to binary, because zip files are binary files (normally, FTP works in ASCII mode). Type **binary** at the FTP prompt, and the FTP server should respond with the following:

```
Type set to I.
```

Good, that's what we want. Now, to get the file, type **hash**, and press Enter. The server will respond:

```
Hash mark printing on (8192 bytes/hash mark).
```

Hash gives you a visual indication of how a file transfer is progressing by outputting a hash mark (#) every so often. It's not necessary, but it helps promote peace of mind.

Next, type **get ws_ftp.zip** and press Enter. Figure 19-8 shows what you should expect.

```
ftp> hash
Hash mark printing on (8192 bytes/hash mark).
ftp> get ws_ftp.zip
200 PORT command successful.
150 Opening ASCII mode data connection for ws_ftp.zip (113252 bytes).
###############
226 Transfer complete.
local: ws_ftp.zip remote: ws_ftp.zip
113782 bytes received in 4 seconds (28 Kbytes/s)
ftp> █
```

Figure 19-8: Transferring a file with FTP in hash mode.

That's it. The file's in your account.

TIP

Many FTP sites include index files that allow you to read descriptions of files before you download them. If you encounter a site with an index file (often called 00Index), you can read it right there without leaving FTP by using the following command:

```
get 00Index |more
```

At this point, you can do several things. You can keep transferring files using the get command. Or you can use cd. to move up one directory and keep poking around. If you want to leave FTP and go back to your own account, just type **bye**, and press Enter. You'll leave FTP and return to your own shell account. To get the files from your directory on the host computer to your desktop computer, you'll need to follow the instructions available from your dial-up account provider and in your terminal program documentation. See Chapter 16, "Getting Connected With a Shell Account," for more help. If you need a quick reference for ftp-ing, see Table 19-1.

Command	Description
cd <directory>	Changes directory to directory.
cd	Moves up one directory.
cdup	Moves up one directory.
Ls	Gets a directory listing.
dir	Gets a directory listing.
put filename	Puts file from your account on to FTP server.
mput file list	Puts multiple files on server.
get filenam>	Gets file filename.
mget file list	Gets multiple files.
FTP commandsystem command	Pipes output from FTP command to system command.
binary	Sets transfer mode to binary.
ascii	Sets transfer mode to ASCII.
!	"Shells out" to remote machine.
bye	Leaves FTP.
quit	Leaves FTP.

Table 19-1: FTP quick reference.

FSP

In the last few years, a growing number of people have been pushing a file transfer protocol called FSP. It's a protocol specifically designed for use with anonymous file archives and has the advantage of being designed to avoid the overload problems to which FTP is prone. As FSP proponents are fond of saying, "FSP is what anonymous FTP *should* be."

Unfortunately, FSP is excruciatingly difficult to use for most people. It uses a complicated syntax consisting of C-shell aliases. Several FTP-like FSP clients have been devised to make it easier, but most people usually find FSP too difficult to use.

As a power user, you should at least know what FSP is, even if you don't have to actually use it. There are very few public FSP servers, and learning the syntax of FSP isn't worth the effort (in our not-so-humble opinions).

But if an alternative to FTP piques your interest, you may be a real hacker dude (or dudette) at heart! You can find out more about FSP by visiting the official FSP FAQ site at http://itu.rdg.ac.uk/misc/fsp/faq/faq.htm.

Finding Files With Archie

Once you've played around with FTP, you'll probably be itchin' to download everything you can get your hands on. Having the power to easily find free stuff on the Internet, and bring it back to your computer can be addicting.

What do you do if you want to find a file on the Internet, and you don't know where to look? Use Archie.

■ ■

TIP

This section is intended to be a brief introduction to Archie. If you really want to kick your data-searching skills into high gear, head over to Part VIII, "Netsearching: Unleashing Your Code Hound" for an in-depth look at finding data on the Internet.

■ ■

Archie is a program specifically designed with your FTP needs in mind. It tirelessly searches the globe for new FTP sites and files, updating its database as it finds them. Archie servers are located all over the world for easy access no matter where you are. Table 19-2 lists several popular Archie servers.

Archie Server Address	Physical Location
archie.au	Australia
archie.ad.jp	Japan
archie.ans.net	New York
archie.rutgers.edu	New Jersey
archie.sura.net	Maryland

➡

Archie Server Address	Physical Location
archie.unl.edu	Nebraska
archie.mcgill.ca	Canada
archie.funet.fi	Finland
archie.luth.se	Sweden
archie.doc.ic.ac.uk	United Kingdom
archie.kuis.kyoto-u.ac.jp	Japan
archie.nz	New Zealand
archie.ncu.edu.tw	Taiwan
archie.songang.ac.kr	Korea
archie.univie.ac.at	Austria

Table 19-2: Archie servers around the world.

You may even have Archie on your host machine if you're lucky. Try typing **archie** at your UNIX prompt. If you get the following response, you're out of luck:

```
archie: Command not found.
```

However, if you type **archie** and get a description of all the command options, you're in luck! Archie has been installed on your host computer, and you won't have to go out on the Net to use Archie. Just type the following, and press Enter:

```
archie optionsearch string
```

Archie will return a list of all the files it has found matching your *search string*. Table 19-3 lists some of the command-line options for using Archie from your UNIX account.

Option	Description
-c	Makes search case sensitive.
-e	Makes search match exact string.
-h	Uses specific Archie server.
-l	Lists only one match per line of output.
-L	Displays list of Archie servers.
-m [number]	Lists only [number] of matches.
-s	Uses substring search method.
-t	Displays output sorted by date.

Table 19-3: Command-line options in Archie.

If you don't have Archie installed on your system, you must first connect to an Archie server. Select one that's located close to you from the list in Table 19-2. In our case, we'll pick the server named archie.sura.net.

We'll use Telnet to connect to an Archie server From the UNIX prompt, type the following, and press Enter:

```
telnet archie.sura.net     <- substitute your nearest archie
                              server here.
```

Figure 19-9 shows what you should see.

```
explorer:[/homec/elrod] telnet archie.sura.net
Trying 192.239.16.130 ...
Connected to kadath.sura.net.
Escape character is '^]'.


SunOS UNIX (kadath.sura.net)

login: archie█
```

Figure 19-9: Connecting to archie.sura.net.

You'll notice that the server is asking you to log in. At the login prompt, type **archie**, and press Enter to start an Archie session. Archie will now scroll a welcome message on the screen. Your screen should resemble the one shown in Figure 19-10.

```
                    Welcome to Archie!
                      Version 3.3

                 BBN Planet Southeast Region

For Information or questions about this archie server,
please send mail to:

        archie-admin@sura.net


# Bunyip Information Systems, Inc., 1993, 1994, 1995

# Terminal type set to `vt100 24 80'.
# `erase' character is `^?'.
# `search' (type string) has the value `sub'.
archie> █
```

Figure 19-10: Archie awaits your commands.

At this point, you can begin your search. To search for a file, you'll need to use the **prog** command. For example, if you wanted to search for a file named subgenius (or a filename containing the string "subgenius"), type **prog subgenius** at the prompt. Archie will respond with some information about your type of search, what number your request is in line, and an estimate of how long your search will take. Once Archie has found some files matching your description, it'll output their locations as shown in Figure 19-11.

```
archie> prog subgenius
# Search type: sub.
# Your queue position: 1
# Estimated time for completion: 5 seconds.
working... =

Host lysita.lysator.liu.se    (130.236.254.153)
Last updated 02:02 11 Jul 1995

    Location: /pub/religion/discordian
        DIRECTORY    drwxr-xr-x    1024 bytes  09:19  4 Apr  1995  Subgenius


Host quartz.rutgers.edu    (128.6.60.6)
Last updated 01:45 16 Sep 1995

    Location: /pub/QUARTZ.BY.TOPIC/fun
        FILE    -rwxrwxrwx        14 bytes  14:58 31 Jul  1994  subgenius

    Location: /pub/.cap
        FILE    -rw-r--r--        43 bytes  18:00  3 Oct  1993  subgenius
```

Figure 19-11: Archie output.

Let's examine what that output means. On the first line, Archie tells you the hostname of the anonymous FTP server where the file is located. Right below that, Archie tells you last time the file was updated.

The meat of what we're looking for is on the next few lines. That's where Archie tells you the names of the files it found and the directory path where to find them. This is the information you need to actually get the files.

Once you've done one search, continue doing as many as you wish. When you want to quit Archie, type **quit**.

That's pretty much the basics. Just log on to Archie, do a search, and away you go! We'll cover Archie in much greater depth in Part VIII, "Netsearching: Unleashing Your Codehound." For now, though, what you've learned should do you fine if you just want to poke around and find a few files.

GOPHER IN UNIX

Long before there was the World Wide Web, Gophers ruled the Net. Much like it is today with the Web (though on a smaller scale), any organization worth its salt had its own Gopher server on the Internet displaying information about itself, providing links to other servers and allowing people to download pictures, files, and programs.

When the Web burst on to the scene with its fancy graphics, flashy interface, and other high-falutin' multimedia features, Gophers were pushed into the background.

In the mad rush to get on the Web, many people have forgotten what a great resource Gopher was in the first place. Even though it didn't use hyperlinks to move from one document to another, it did provide a neat and tidy way of easily accessing gobs of information, no matter where it existed on the Net.

Now we're not saying that everyone should dump the Web for the nostalgia of Gopher. All we're saying is don't neglect this (or any other) useful resource. There's still lots of information to be had out there in Gopherspace. Oftentimes it's faster to use Gopher to find the information that you want than it is to navigate the click-and-wait maze of the World Wide Web. Always remember, your power user's credo: "the right tool for the job."

Connecting

Gopher's been around for so long that it's probably a safe bet to say that you've got it installed on the UNIX system that you use. To access Gopher on your system, type **gopher** at the UNIX prompt, and press Enter. If all goes well, you'll see an opening menu like that shown in Figure 19-12.

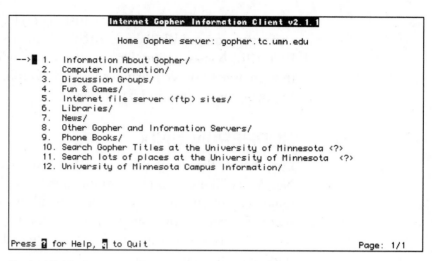

```
         Internet Gopher Information Client v2.1.1

              Home Gopher server: gopher.tc.umn.edu

-->  1.  Information About Gopher/
     2.  Computer Information/
     3.  Discussion Groups/
     4.  Fun & Games/
     5.  Internet file server (ftp) sites/
     6.  Libraries/
     7.  News/
     8.  Other Gopher and Information Servers/
     9.  Phone Books/
    10.  Search Gopher Titles at the University of Minnesota <?>
    11.  Search lots of places at the University of Minnesota  <?>
    12.  University of Minnesota Campus Information/




Press ? for Help, ? to Quit                            Page: 1/1
```

Figure 19-12: A top-level Gopher menu.

However, if you don't have Gopher installed on your system (and the chances of this are pretty small), you'll probably get a "command not found" error. In this case, contact your systems administrator and ask that Gopher be installed.

That's what you should notice first about Gopher—it's all menus. In fact, that's what made Gopher the information retrieval tool of choice when it was first introduced. You never have to remember any complicated commands to get to the information you're looking for. Just follow the menus.

Let's take a closer look at the menu in Figure 19-12. We'll be seeing a lot more of these menus, so it's best that we get a good idea of how they work right off the bat.

First, look at the top of the screen. Here's where Gopher displays the name of the Gopher server you're currently using. Not all sites have their own Gopher server. If you're on a site that doesn't have its own server, it'll connect you to a server on a remote machine. If you know a particular Gopher server that you want to connect to before you start, just type the following at your UNIX prompt:

```
gopher [gopher server address]
```

Below the name of the Gopher server, you'll see a numbered menu listing different types of information. Each line of information represents a Gopher "object" or specific information type. You can tell the kind of object a menu choice represents by looking at the end of the line it's listed on. Table 19-4 shows you the types of Gopher objects you can expect to encounter on your travels through Gopherspace.

Object Indicator	Object Type
(nothing)	Text file
/	Directory (menu)
<)	Sound file
<Picture>	Image file
<Movie>	Movie file
<HQX>	BinHexed Macintosh file
<Bin>	Binary file
<PC Bin>	DOS binary file
<CSO>	CSO phone book server
<TEL>	Telnet connection
<3270>	Telnet connection using IBM 3270 emulation
<MIME>	Multipurpose Internet Mail Extension file
<HTML>	HTML (Hypertext Markup Language) file
<?>	Index search
<??>	ASK form

Table 19-4: Gopher object types.

As you can see, you can access quite a number of different types of information through Gopher. However, since this is the top level of the server, you'll notice that most of the menu objects end in /. That's because selecting them will move you on to other directories (menus) of information. Two of the menu choices are marked with <?>, indicating that they are places you can select to search Gopherspace. If you select one of the remote selections, you'll "tunnel" through "Gopherspace," accessing the server you've selected.

Along the bottom of the screen, you'll see a simple menu. Just press **?** for help on how to use Gopher or **q** to quit Gopher and return to UNIX. In the far-right corner of the screen is an area that doubles as both a message area and an indicator of where you are. You can tell where you are in Gopher by looking at what looks like a fraction. At the top level (where you are now), it reads Page: 1/1 indicating that you're at the top page of the first server you've visited. If you were to move to the top page of a second server, the indicator would read 1/2 for "first page of second server."

Navigating

Getting around with Gopher is easy. All you mainly have to do is use the arrow keys.

The arrow (–>) on the left of the Gopher menu indicates which object is currently selected. You can move the arrow up and down by using the Up and Down arrow keys. Watch as the arrow on the screen responds to your movements.

Once you've selected an item that you want to view, you can either press Enter or the Right arrow key. If you've selected a directory, Gopher will display the new directory on the screen. If you've decided to view a text file, Gopher will display it on the screen as shown in Figure 19-13.

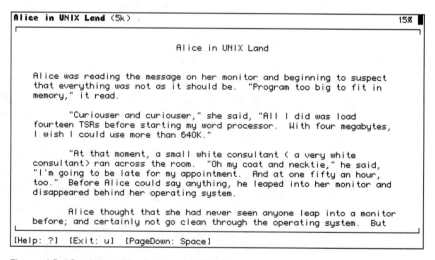

Figure 19-13: A text file displayed in Gopher.

If the item you've selected is a file of a type that Gopher can't display (like a picture, movie, or binary file), Gopher will ask you if you want to save the file to your account (see Figure 19-14). If you do, just press Enter, and Gopher will transfer the file. If you don't want to save the file, just press Ctrl+G to cancel.

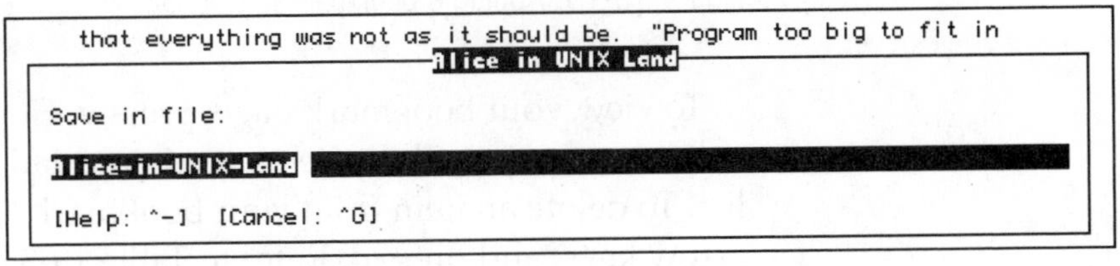

```
  that everything was not as it should be.   "Program too big to fit in
                          Alice in UNIX Land

Save in file:

Alice-in-UNIX-Land

[Help: ^-]  [Cancel: ^G]
```

Figure 19-14: A Save dialog box in Gopher.

Once you've moved down a few levels into Gopher, just use the Left arrow to move backward. Gopher will step you back through all the menus you'd previously visited.

Organizing Bookmarks

Once you start bouncing around in Gopherspace, you'll probably wish that there was some way that you could get back to a place you found useful without going through all the menus. Guess what? There is a way—bookmarks.

Bookmarks are Gopher's way of saving references to places that you want to visit again. Since everything in Gopher is menu-driven, bookmarks are, too. When you view your bookmark page, it looks and acts just like a Gopher menu. You never have to learn anything complicated to use your bookmarks. Once you've mastered the main part of Gopher, bookmarks are a breeze.

If you want to add an item that you've currently selected, just press **a**. Gopher will display a dialog box (see Figure 19-15) asking you what you want to name that bookmark. The default name is the same name as the item you've selected. To accept the name and add that object to your bookmark list, just press Enter. If you don't want to add the bookmark, press Ctrl+G. If you want to add an entire directory to your bookmark list, press A.

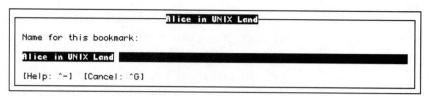

Figure 19-15: Adding a bookmark in Gopher.

To view your bookmark page, press **v**. Gopher will display a menu containing all the items you've added to your bookmark list. To delete an item from your bookmark list, select it using the arrow keys, and press **d**. Refer to Table 19-5 if you need a refresher on your Gopher bookmark commands.

Command	Description
a	Adds current item to bookmark list.
A	Adds directory or search results to bookmark.
v	Views bookmark list.
d	Deletes item from bookmark list.

Table 19-5: Bookmark commands in Gopher.

Searching: Using Veronica & Jughead

After spending some time in Gopherspace, you'll start to get an idea of how enormous it is. Finding what you want can turn from a quick exercise in menu-walking into a tedious slog through an endless maze o' menus.

To alleviate this problem, Veronica and Jughead were developed. What's with the goofy names? Both are plays on Archie, the first of these file-finding programs. Like Archie, Veronica and Jughead are Internetwide search engines. Unlike Archie, Veronica and Jughead search Gopherspace, not anonymous FTP sites.

TIP

If this information isn't quite detailed enough for you and you really want to get intimate with Veronica and Jughead, check out Chapter 26, "Data Tracking."

Veronica and Jughead operate much the same way—both search Gopherspace using regular expression search strings. How they differ is in what they search. Jughead searches all of Gopherspace for the string that you define. Veronica merely searches menu titles.

To use Veronica and Jughead, you need to find them on the Gopher server you're using. Many servers have a menu item entitled Other Gopher and Information Servers/ that provides access to Veronica and Jughead searches, as well as to a menu of many other Gopher servers around the world. Figure 19-16 shows a typical menu.

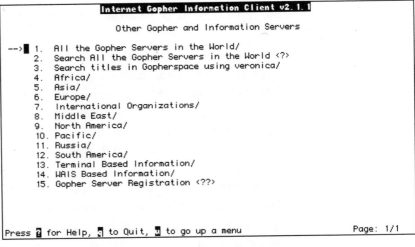

```
            Internet Gopher Information Client v2.1.1

                  Other Gopher and Information Servers

  -->█ 1.  All the Gopher Servers in the World/
        2.  Search All the Gopher Servers in the World <?>
        3.  Search titles in Gopherspace using veronica/
        4.  Africa/
        5.  Asia/
        6.  Europe/
        7.  International Organizations/
        8.  Middle East/
        9.  North America/
       10.  Pacific/
       11.  Russia/
       12.  South America/
       13.  Terminal Based Information/
       14.  WAIS Based Information/
       15.  Gopher Server Registration <??>



  Press █ for Help, █ to Quit, █ to go up a menu         Page: 1/1
```

Figure 19-16: A typical Gopher and Information Servers menu.

To use Veronica from the menu in Figure 19-16, we'll select item number 3, Search titles in Gopherspace using veronica/. Doing so will display a list of Veronica and Jughead search engines as shown in Figure 19-17.

```
                        Internet Gopher Information Client v2.1.1

                         Search titles in Gopherspace using veronica


-->  3.  Find GOPHER DIRECTORIES by Title word(s) (via NYSERNet    ) <?>
     4.  Find GOPHER DIRECTORIES by Title word(s) (via PSINet) <?>
     5.  Find GOPHER DIRECTORIES by Title word(s) (via U. Nac. Autonoma .. <?>
     6.  Find GOPHER DIRECTORIES by Title word(s) (via UNINETT..of Bergen) <?>
     7.  Find GOPHER DIRECTORIES by Title word(s) (via University of Koe.. <?>
     8.  Frequently-Asked Questions (FAQ) about veronica - January 13, 1995
     9.  How to Compose veronica Queries - June 23, 1994
    10.  More veronica: Software, Index-Control Protocol, HTML Pages/
    11.  Search GopherSpace by Title word(s) (via NYSERNet    ) <?>
    12.  Search GopherSpace by Title word(s) (via PSINet) <?>
    13.  Search GopherSpace by Title word(s) (via U. Nac. Autonoma de MX.. <?>
    14.  Search GopherSpace by Title word(s) (via UNINETT/U. of Bergen) <?>
    15.  Search GopherSpace by Title word(s) (via University of Koeln) <?>
         Simplified veronica chooses server - pick a search type:
    17.  Simplified veronica: Find Gopher MENUS only <?>
    18.  Simplified veronica: find ALL gopher types <?>

Press ? for Help, q to Quit, u to go up a menu              Page: 1/1
```

Figure 19-17: Veronica and Jughead search engines.

To search, just select the Veronica search engine you want to use with the arrow keys, and press Enter. Veronica will display a dialog box asking for the string you want to search for. At this point, just type in the word representing what you're looking for. In reality, Veronica and Jughead searches can be much more complex, but we're saving that discussion for Chapter 26, "Data Tracking."

If your search is successful, Veronica will serve a directory of directories matching your search terms (see Figure 19-18). If not, you will get an error message. Start over. Remember, there's a lot of ground for these engines to cover, particularly Veronica— searches can take a while.

```
┌─────────────────────────────────────────────────────────────────┐
│             Internet Gopher Information Client v2.1.1             │
│                                                                   │
│        Find GOPHER DIRECTORIES by Title word(s) (via PSINet): ufo │
│                                                                   │
│  -->█ 1.  ufo                 (A:)/                               │
│      2.  UFO                           *DIR*   /                  │
│      3.  UFO                           *DIR*   /                  │
│      4.  ufo/                                                     │
│      5.  UFONet - UFO and Alien information/                      │
│      6.  ufo/                                                     │
│      7.  ufo/                                                     │
│      8.  ufo/                                                     │
│      9.  ufo/                                                     │
│     10.  UFONet - UFO and Alien information/                      │
│     11.  ufo/                                                     │
│     12.  UFO/                                                     │
│     13.  UFO/                                                     │
│     14.  UFO/                                                     │
│     15.  UFO/                                                     │
│     16.  UFO/                                                     │
│     17.  UFO/                                                     │
│     18.  ufo/                                                     │
│                                                                   │
│ Press ? for Help, ? to Quit, ? to go up a menu      Page: 1/2     │
└─────────────────────────────────────────────────────────────────┘
```

Figure 19-18: A successful Veronica search.

WEBWALKING WITH LYNX

Ah, the World Wide Web. These days, it's hard to imagine that just a few years ago, only a few no-life computer geeks, university students, and researchers knew what it was. Now, URLs (World Wide Web addresses) are appearing everywhere, from business cards to billboards, to car ads on TV.

Many people confuse the World Wide Web with the graphical browser that they use to access it. Let's straighten something out right now—Netscape is not the World Wide Web. Mosaic is not the World Wide Web. Browsers in CompuServe, Prodigy, and America Online are not the World Wide Web. All of these are merely windows onto the Web. The Web itself is actually a highly sophisticated and standardized way to pass information between computers using the Hypertext Transport Protocol (HTTP).

What does this mean to you, the command-line jockey? It means that you don't have to fire up your SLIP or PPP account to find information on the World Wide Web. If you're running UNIX, you can use lynx.

737

What is Lynx?

Lynx is a text-based Web browser that you can use from your UNIX account. Now you won't see any pretty pictures or movies, and you won't hear any sounds (unless you download them to your own computer). What you will see is lots and lots of information that's yours for the browsing.

If you've used a graphical Web browser such as Netscape Navigator or Mosaic, using lynx might take a little getting used to. Instead of the graphics you'd normally see in your browser window, you'll see a tag that looks like this:

[Image]

or, if someone has been kind enough to use the ALT tag when defining images, you'll see tags that look like this:

[this represents an image that you'd see with a graphical browser]

See Figures 19-19 and 19-20 for a comparison of a Web page viewed with lynx and the same one viewed with a graphical browser.

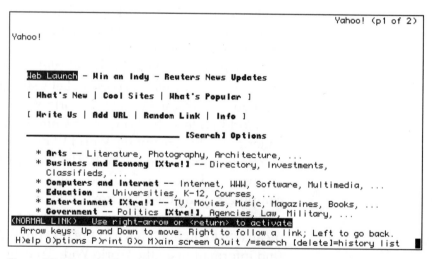

Figure 19-19 : http://www.yahoo.com viewed with lynx.

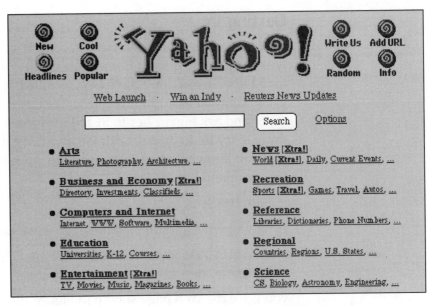

Figure 19-20: http://www.yahoo.com as seen with Netscape Navigator.

Since you can't view pictures in lynx, you may be asking yourself what good is it? If you want to browse just for text-based information, lynx is great. Rather than having to wait for big images to download, lynx takes you right to the info. However, as more and more people make pages that depend heavily on graphics, lynx users are becoming an endangered species. Basically, it comes down to this: lynx is great if you're in a hurry and text is what you're after.

TIP

If you're using a UNIX account, you can think of lynx and Gopher as complimentary programs. Both are great ways of getting at information quickly and easily. In fact, some new versions of Gopher also recognize this synergy. Try pushing w in Gopher. If it's a newer version, you'll be prompted for a URL to enter. Try http://www.yahoo.com to go to a great list of Web services. Press Enter, and Gopher will launch lynx. Quitting lynx will return you to Gopher. Or, if you come to a Gopher object of type <HTML>, selecting it will also launch lynx. Experiment, and see what happens.

Getting In

There are basically two ways to start up lynx. First, if you want lynx to open the default home page, just type **lynx** at the command line. If you don't have lynx installed on your system, you'll get a "command not found" error. Contact your systems administrator and ask him or her to install lynx for you. It's a pretty hairy thing to try to do by yourself. We know. We tried. We failed.

If you know what URL you want to view, type the following at the command line:

```
lynx [URL]
```

Lynx will open and display the page. For example, if you enter:

```
lynx http://kufacts.cc.ukans.edu/lynx_help/
lynx_help_main.html,
```

you'll see the Web page shown in Figure 19-21.

```
                          www.ukans.edu default index (3/15/95) (p1 of 2)

                        WELCOME TO THE UNIVERSITY OF KANSAS

     This server is operated by Academic Computing Services at the
     University of Kansas, which is the home of

          * KUfacts, the KU campus wide information system,
          * KANREN Info, the KANREN information system,
          * HNSource, the central information server for historians, and

          * the Lynx and DosLynx World-Wide Web (WWW) browsers. The current
            version of Lynx is 2.4. If you are running an earlier version
            PLEASE UPGRADE!

     OTHER UNIVERSITY OF KANSAS SERVERS
          * The University of Kansas Medical Center--Pulse
          * Atmospheric Science
          * Electrical Engineering and Computer Science
          * Mathematics
          * Physics
     -- press space for next page --
      Arrow keys: Up and Down to move. Right to follow a link; Left to go back.
     H)elp O)ptions P)rint G)o M)ain screen Q)uit /=search [delete]=history list
```

Figure 19-21: Lynx displaying the University of Kansas home page at http://kufacts.cc.ukans.edu/lynx_help/lynx_help_main.html.

Let's take a closer look at Figure 19-21. Along the top of the screen, you'll see the title of the document you're viewing. Here the page is called www.ukans.edu default index (3/15/95). Right next to the title, lynx displays how far we are through the document. In this case, we're viewing page 1 of 2.

What probably jumps out at you right away are the boldfaced words. These are hyperlinks, links to other documents. Sometimes hyperlinks can lead to files, images, or other parts of the same document.

The bottom of the screen displays a menu of frequently used commands. If you want to find out about more of the commands, press **H** to get help. Lynx will take you to the help page (shown in Figure 19-22) where you can find out more information about the commands available in lynx.

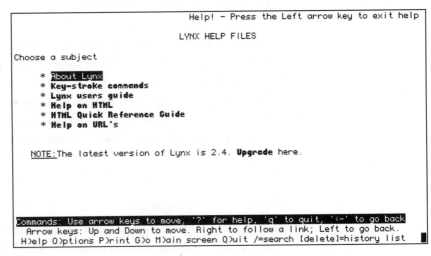

Figure 19-22: The lynx help screen.

Navigating

To move around within lynx, use the arrow keys. If you look at the bottom of the screen, you'll see the following helpful hints:

```
Arrow keys: Up and Down to move. Right to follow a link; Left
to go back.
```

Most of the navigating you'll do in lynx involves moving from hyperlink to hyperlink. As we noted before, hyperlinks are indicated with boldface type.

When you first access a page, the topmost hyperlink on the screen will be selected with inverse text (see Figure 19-23). From here, you can choose several actions. First, if you want to follow the hyperlink, press the Right arrow key. The screen will clear, and the contents of the page that the hyperlink points to will be displayed. To return to the page you just left, press the Left arrow key.

```
OTHER UNIVERSITY OF KANSAS SERVERS
    * The University of Kansas Medical Center--Pulse
    * Atmospheric Science
    * Electrical Engineering and Computer Science
    * Mathematics
    * Physics
```

Figure 19-23: A hyperlink selected in lynx.

If you want to go to a link further down the page, press the Down arrow key. If you want to move back up again, press the Up arrow key.

Sometimes, though, you may want to go to a specific Web page. To do so, press **g**. Lynx will then prompt you for the URL. Type it at the prompt, and press Enter. Lynx will load the Web page you've asked for. See Table 19-6 for a summary of lynx navigation commands.

Key	Description
Up arrow	Moves up to a hyperlink on a page.
Down arrow	Moves down to a hyperlink on a page.
Right arrow	Follows a hyperlink.
Left arrow	Returns to previous page.
g	Goes to a URL.
Spacebar	Displays next page.

Table 19-6: Navigation keys in lynx.

Organizing With Bookmarks

Just like Gopher, lynx allows you to keep a bookmark page of sites that you frequently visit. This feature is just like the personal "hotlist" functions in most graphical browsers.

To add a bookmark to your bookmark page, press **a**. Lynx will then ask you if you want to:

```
Save D)ocument or L)ink to bookmark file or C)ancel? (d,l,c):
```

If you select **d**, lynx will save the URL associated with the document you are currently viewing to your bookmark list. Selecting **l** will save the current hyperlink you've selected. If you made a mistake and don't want to save either one to your bookmark page, just press **c** to cancel without adding the bookmark.

Once you've saved a bookmark or two, you'll probably want to view them. Press v to view your bookmark page. Figure 19-24 shows a typical bookmark page. While in your bookmark page, select the bookmark links just as you would select hyperlinks in other documents. Table 19-7 summarizes lynx bookmark commands.

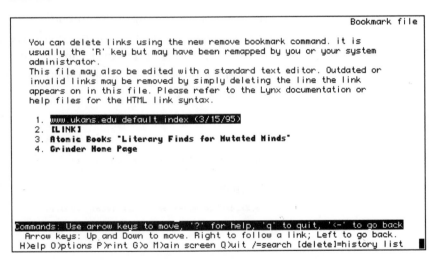

Figure 19-24: A bookmark page viewed with lynx.

Command	Description
a	Adds to bookmark page.
V	Views bookmark page.

Table 19-7: Bookmark commands in lynx.

743

Viewing & Downloading Files

Since lynx is a text-based browser, you may be wondering how to view an image or a sound file. Basically, it comes down to this: lynx will allow you to save images, sounds, or other multimedia files to your account so that you can download them to your PC and use the tools you have there to view them. In some cases, you can skip a step and download the files directly to your PC using a terminal program transfer protocol.

Let's say that you're at an "art gallery" page and you want to view a picture. First, select the link to the picture with the arrow keys. Then, press Enter or use the Right arrow key to follow the link. If it's a file that lynx can't display, you'll see the message:

```
This file cannot be displayed on this terminal:  D)ownload,
or C)ancel
```

If you don't want to bother downloading the file, press **c** to cancel. Lynx will place you back at the page you were viewing.

If you decide that you want to get the picture so that you can download it, press **D**. You should then see a screen similar to the one in Figure 19-25.

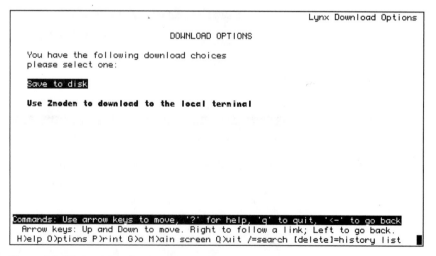

```
                                              Lynx Download Options
                         DOWNLOAD OPTIONS

    You have the following download choices
    please select one:

    Save to disk

    Use Zmodem to download to the local terminal




Commands: Use arrow keys to move, '?' for help, 'q' to quit, '<-' to go back
  Arrow keys: Up and Down to move. Right to follow a link; Left to go back.
  H)elp O)ptions P)rint G)o M)ain screen Q)uit /=search [delete]=history list
```

Figure 19-25: Lynx File Downloading page.

In this case, we have two choices. We can download the file to our account by selecting the first choice, Save to disk. Selecting this option will save the file in your UNIX account. You can then use a terminal program transfer protocol like Xmodem or Zmodem to transfer it to your PC for viewing.

If you select the second choice, Use Zmodem to download to the local terminal, be careful. If you're using a SLIP or PPP account and a Telnet client to log in to your UNIX account, you'll probably hang your login while lynx tries to transfer the file via Zmodem. However, if you're using a dial-up terminal program to log in, the file should begin transferring to your computer. A brief note here: many accounts provide only the option of saving the file to disk. The options you have depend on how your account was set up by your system administrator.

OTHER UNIX NET TOOLS

Now that we've covered the major tools available to the command-line user, it's time to look at some of the minor tools that can help make your Internet communications easier. Most of these tools have functions far more complex than we're going to cover in this section. This section is intended as a quick reference for you to use when you encounter one of these tools during your online travels.

Telnet

We've used Telnet once before when we connected to Archie. However, at that point we didn't go into too much detail about what Telnet is and how to use it. Look no further.

When you want to connect to another computer on the Internet, use Telnet. When you connect with Telnet, you are able to use the resources of the other computer just as if you had logged in to it using an ordinary dial-up program. However, when you log out of that remote computer, you won't be disconnected, you'll just be returned back to your account.

Telnet can be used in one of two ways—from the command line with arguments or interactively from within the Telnet program.

To use Telnet from the command line, use the following syntax:

```
telnet host name port
```

The *hostname* refers to the actual Internet name of the computer you want to connect to. When we wanted to connect to an Archie server earlier, we used the hostname archie.sura.net. The *port* is usually not necessary if you're just connecting to another computer to use its ordinary services. However, some computers, notably those serving online games (MUDs and MOOs), Internet Relay Chat servers, and other specialized computers, require that you Telnet to a specific port. Check the computer that you're connecting to for details.

If you want, you can also use Telnet in interactive mode in which you can type commands at a telnet> prompt. Ordinarily, you won't have to use this mode. If you do, Table 19-8 gives a summary of interactive Telnet commands.

Command	Description
close	Closes current connection.
Display	Shows operating parameters.
Mode	Changes to line-by-line or one-character-at-a-time mode.
Open	Connects to a remote site.
Quit	Exits the Telnet program.
Send	Transmits special characters.
Set	Sets operating parameters.
Status	Prints current status to the screen.
Toggle	Toggles status of operating parameters.
Z	Suspends Telnet program.
?	Accesses help.

Table 19-8: Interactive Telnet commands.

Finger

If you're the snoopy type who always wants to know what your friends are up to, finger is the command you've been looking for. Using finger, you can find out such fun information as someone's real name, what shell he or she is using (always great info to know when you meet someone face to face for the first time!), how long he or she has been logged on, what kind of projects he or she is working on, and any other information that he or she wants to give out. Sound like fun?

To use finger, type the following command at your UNIX prompt:

```
finger options user
```

where *option* represents one or more (separated by spaces) of the fingering options listed in Table 19-9, and *user* is the e-mail address of the person you want information on.

Option	Description
-b	Does not display user's home directory and shell.
-h	Does not show user's .project file.
-p	Does not show user's .plan file.
-q	Accesses quick format.
-s	Accesses short format.

Table 19-9: Command line options in finger.

Once you finger someone, you should see something like the information shown in Figure 19-26 (well, maybe without the Zippy the Pinhead quote). Most of this information is pretty self-explanatory. However, you may be wondering about how the information in the Project: and Plan: fields got there. Is finger psychic?

```
explorer% finger doug@polarmet1.mps.ohio-state.edu
[polarmet1.mps.ohio-state.edu]
Login name: douglist                     In real life: Doug Stevenson
Directory: /home/doug                    Shell: /usr/local/etc/nologinsh
Last login Sat Sep 30 15:15 on ttyp0 from slip5-6.acs.ohio
No unread mail
Plan:

Hello, elrod from 168.143.0.7!
Your hostname is clark.net.
This is visit #2 from your particular host.

Congratulations, you are visitor #2256 to my .plan!

Here's your random Zippy the Pinhead quote for today:
-----
Send your questions to ``ASK ZIPPY'', Box 40474,
 San Francisco, CA 94140, USA
-----
If you didn't like that one, finger me again!
```

Figure 19-26: Information returned from fingering someone.

Not really. The information in these fields comes from information that the person being fingered put in his or her .plan and .project files in his or her account. Many people you finger won't have any information in these files. Others use them as a place to distribute their public PGP encryption keys, information about their favorite TV shows, and even the weather!

TIP

Sometimes when you try to finger someone, finger will fail to display any information. This happens for several reasons. First, if the person isn't on the Internet with a UNIX account, they probably aren't fingerable. Some people using SLIP or PPP accounts at home, run finger servers on their home computers, but that's kind of rare.

Many times finger will fail because the system administrator on that remote machine has disabled it. finger gives out a lot of information about a person, and many sysadmins feel that it's a breach of their users' privacy to provide finger information to the world. The Well BBS, a popular Cyberspace watering hole, is one example of a system that blocks finger requests.

Whois

Whois used to be a much more useful command. In theory, using whois [username] would display information about a specific person. This was a viable idea when the Internet consisted of a few thousand military and university researchers. Now that the Net has expanded to millions of users, whois isn't used much for looking up people anymore.

Nevertheless, whois is still useful for looking up information about who owns a particular computer or Internet domain name. To use whois in this way, type the following, and press Return:

whois *domain name*

If *domain name* is owned by someone already, you'll see a display much like the one in Figure 19-27, telling you who or what company owns the name, the contact person for that domain, and some other technical information. If no one owns that domain name, you'll see a display like Figure 19-28.

```
explorer:[/homec/elrod] whois emerald.net
EmeraldNet (EMERALD2-DOM)
   1718 E. Speedway, Suite 315
   Tucson, AZ 85719

   Domain Name: EMERALD.NET

   Administrative Contact:
      Fisher, Mike  (MBF2)  fisher@EMERALD.NET
      (520) 670-1994
   Technical Contact, Zone Contact:
      Krawitz, Matthew S.  (MSK2)  MatthewK@EMERALD.NET
      (520) 670-1994

   Record last updated on 23-Oct-95.
   Record created on 19-Aug-94.

   Domain servers in listed order:

   NS1.ACES.COM              192.195.240.1
   ARIZONA.EDU               128.196.128.233
```

Figure 19-27: Whois information on emerald.net.

```
explorer:[/homec/elrod] whois whubbawhubba.com
No match for "WHUBBAWHUBBA.COM".

The InterNIC Registration Services Host contains ONLY Internet Information
(Networks, ASN's, Domains, and POC's).
Please use the whois server at nic.ddn.mil for MILNET Information.
```

Figure 19-28: A failed whois lookup. Quick! Get out there and register that domain name!

Why would anyone want to look up a domain name? Curiosity for one thing, but commerce is usually the main reason these days. Domain names are hot property as more and more companies get on the Internet, and the pool of good names is rapidly being used up.

Ping

Sometimes, if you can't get through to an Internet site, you may wonder if the computer you're trying to Telnet or FTP to is still up and running. You can get a good idea by using ping.

Ping is a powerful tool for the hacker who wants to dig in to the inner workings of the Internet. With over 14 different options to choose from, it's possible to get incredibly detailed info about how fast the Internet's transferring information in your area, packet transfer data, and multicast info. However, for the average power user, just knowing if a computer's up and running is usually enough.

To use ping, type the following at the UNIX prompt, and press Enter:

```
ping host name
```

If the remote computer [host name] is still up and running, ping will return :

```
host name is still alive.
```

If the remote computer is down, ping will respond:

```
no answer from host name.
```

Talk & Write

Sometimes you might feel a little chatty while you're working in your UNIX account, but you're stuck at a terminal without a telephone anywhere in sight. Or, maybe you just want to save on long distance phone calls. Whatever your reason, if you want to chat with someone through your account, you can do it with talk and write.

Write is useful if you just want to send a quick, one-way message to someone. Because you have to use the write command every time you want to send a new message, it's not practical for interactive chatting. To write to someone, use the following syntax:

```
write username
```

If the user you are trying to contact is not logged in, you'll get the message:

```
useris not logged in
```

If the user is logged in, you may be surprised at the response you get—a blank line. This doesn't mean that your account is hung, it just means that write is waiting for your message. Type your message, and then press Ctrl+C (or enter your system's End of File command) to end it. It'll be sent lickety split.

TIP

To find out if someone is logged in before sending them a message with write, finger them first.

If the person you're writing to responds, you'll hear a beep, and then a message similar to the one in Figure 19-29 will appear on your screen. This is a signal that someone is using write to respond. As he or she types the message and presses Enter, it will appear on your screen.

```
Message from elrod on explorer (pts/23) [ Tue Nov  7 13:36:07 ] ...
```

Figure 19-29: An incoming message from write.

For real interactive chatting, use talk, which opens a split-screen chat window. See Figure 19-30.

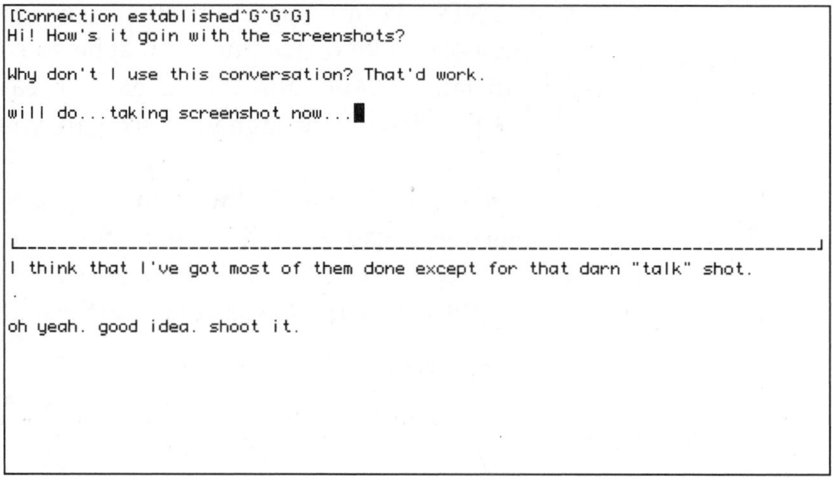

```
[Connection established^G^G^G]
Hi! How's it goin with the screenshots?

Why don't I use this conversation? That'd work.

will do...taking screenshot now...█




L_____J
I think that I've got most of them done except for that darn "talk" shot.
.

oh yeah. good idea. shoot it.
```

Figure 19-30: An ongoing conversation using talk.

To talk with someone, use the following command:

talk *user name or address*

If that user is logged in, you'll see a window similar to the one shown in Figure 19-31. If the user decides to talk to you, you'll be notified in the upper-left corner of the screen. Once the connection's made, just type. Your words will appear in the upper half of the screen, while the other person's words will appear in the bottom half of the screen. As you reach the end of your half of the window, your words will begin to appear at the top of the window, overwriting what you typed before. If the display gets too confusing, just press Control+L to redraw the screen. When you're finished, press Control+D to exit the talk screen.

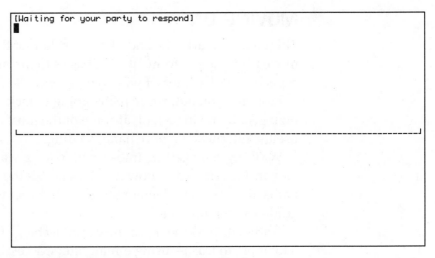

Figure 19-31: Setting up a conversation in talk.

```
explorer:[/homeh/elrod]

Message from Talk_Daemon@explorer at 20:36 ...
talk: connection requested by order@clark.net.
talk: respond with:  talk order@clark.net

```

Figure 19-32: Someone wants to talk to you.

If someone wants to initiate a talk conversation with you, a message will appear on your screen similar to the one shown in Figure 19-32. If you want to talk back, type the following, and you'll be connected:

talk *user name or address*

If you don't want to be bothered, just ignore the summons.

MOVING ON

This chapter marks the end of the first half of the book. It's time to move from the platform-specific basics to the more general concepts of how we interact with cyberspace.

From here on out, we're really going to kick our discussion into high gear by taking a look at some of the most powerful ways to use the Internet. No more hand-holding.

We'll begin by getting into e-mail in a big way. First, we'll take a look inside e-mail and how it moves across the Internet: headers, paths, routing, mail daemons, and an Internet working mail guide—you'll find it all.

And that's just the tip of the e-mail iceberg. There'll be a heck of a lot more to learn—using e-mail filters, accessing mailing lists, transferring files, using MIME types, and even getting FTP files by e-mail. Finally, we'll wrap up with an in-depth look at e-mail security and privacy.

## Part V

The Power User's Guide to E-Mail

## Chapter 20

Inside E-Mail

E-mail is the one function that everyone with access to the Net uses, and the one that most people get the most practical utility out of. E-mail is vital to your online life. In Chapters 7, 12, and 17, we covered the nuts and bolts of how to set up specific e-mail programs for specific platforms, and how to send and receive mail. What we didn't cover is what happens to those messages once they leave your computer. Often, what happens behind the scenes as that message leaves your mailer and heads off into the Net is just as important as anything you do to create the message or read it once it arrives.

In this chapter, we'll take a look inside the e-mailing process, covering all the advanced aspects of e-mail that we glossed over in earlier chapters. First, we'll lay an e-mail message out on our virtual dissecting table, labeling and examining all the parts of the message. Next, we'll open up the hood of your local mail server so that we can learn what goes on underneath. Along the way, we'll discover important details of how messages are sent and received and learn how we can use these features to our advantage. After that, we'll step out into the Net and look at some more advanced ways of communicating—getting messages out to other networks, and getting messages to (and from) groups of people with e-mail lists. We'll wrap up with a look at one of the more beguiling aspects of e-mail, and the one aspect that so often vexes anyone who's tried it—sending and receiving files via e-mail. We'll learn how mailers attach programs using MIME and take a look at the advantages and disadvantages of the two most common text-based encoding programs, uuencode and BinHex.

As you can probably tell by now, we've got a lot of ground to cover. And while it may seem like a lot to get through all at once, the journey will be worth it. When you're done, you'll be more successful at doing what we all got online for in the first place—communicating.

THE MAIL MUST GO THROUGH: INSIDE SMTP, SENDMAIL & POP

A lot of times, e-mail seems like magic. We type in our message, tell our mailer who the message is supposed to be delivered to, click a mouse, and within minutes, our message can travel half-way around the world, right to the person we wanted to send it to.

But how does our message get to where it's supposed to go? Basically, it comes down to this—just like a snailmail letter, the address and its format are vital for making sure that all the postal stops along the way know how to deliver the message. In the case of e-mail, the addressing functions aren't handled by people but by automatic mail handlers or servers, which look at the addressing information and figure out how to send the message to where it belongs.

It's very interesting to see how your message interacts with all the different servers that move it along the way. In the following sections we'll examine how outgoing mail works on the SMTP (Simple Mail Transport Protocol) server. Once we get a basic understanding of how the server handles the mail, we'll take a look at how the header information in the message makes sure it gets through. Finally, we'll take a look at how mail is delivered by digging into sendmail (UNIX's mail transport mechanism) and POP (Post Office Protocol) servers.

Simple Mail Transfer Protocol (SMPT)

Whenever you receive e-mail, there's always that cryptic bunch of stuff at the top of it. These lines are the actual protocol that controls the routing and delivery of the message. It is the e-mail delivery information in the form of an SMTP header. This header is all the information necessary for the e-mail to travel across the Net, and to return if necessary. You can receive a quick little one-line note from someone, and you'll still find several lines of gibberish at the top of it. As far as the mail delivery system is concerned, the header is the only really important part. The technical specification of SMTP actually contains the statement, "A message consists of header fields and, optionally, a body." That's right. According to the specification, the text of the message is completely unnecessary. Yeesh.

Delivery of mail is one of the first things that was done on the Internet. SMTP was a very robust and well-conceived design from the beginning. The original specification was written in 1982. There have been no changes to it since then, although there have been a few extensions. These extensions in no way modified the original format—they only added to it. A mail server from the early '80s would be able to process any mail message being sent today. It wouldn't know what some of the newer header commands are, but the mail would go through (insert background noise of sleet and snow).

As originally conceived, this basic mail protocol was designed to only carry text. Luckily, any file of any type can be converted to text. The basic format of a message is several lines of routing stuff at the top (that gibberish that we see every day and mostly ignore) followed by a line with nothing on it, and finally the "optional" message body.

SMTP is a UDP (User Datagram Protocol—see Chapter 3 if you need a refresher on your TCP/IP terms) animal. Much of what happens over the Internet is done through TCP. So much so that TCP got top billing (TCP/IP) while UDP has been relegated to relative obscurity. They are really quite similar, except for one major difference: TCP is a two-way communication protocol; messages pass in both directions interactively. E-mail doesn't need all this. It uses UDP for a one-way communications link.

An e-mail message is sent off on its way with no response expected by the sender. This is one of the main reasons that there's a return address in the header. If the mail's target address is invalid, the message will be bounced back to the sender by an Internet mail server as quickly as its little bits can carry it. If, however, the address is valid but the routers can't find the receiver, it will take up to 24 hours or more for the mail to bounce. There are even some mailers that will continue trying to deliver mail for several days while, about once a day, sending mail to the originator saying, "It isn't there yet, but I'm still trying."

SMTP Header Format

Each line of the SMTP header is made up of a field name followed by a field body. For example, the date line has a field name "Date," followed by a colon, and then the date:

```
Date: Wed, 20 Mar 96 15:53:35 -0600 (CST)
```

All lines of the header must begin in the first column. A long line can be broken and continued by spacing it to the right so it doesn't begin in the first column. The date example could also be in the following form:

```
Date: Wed, 20 Mar 96
      15:53:35 -0600 (CST)
```

Or even this:

```
Date: Wed,
   20 Mar 96
   15:53:35 -0600 (CST)
```

The only requirement is that the line be broken wherever there would have been a space anyway. The line may even be broken inside a quoted string, as long as there was a space at the breakpoint. You may happen to look at the header information displayed in your mail software and see continued lines that are jammed up against the left. Some mailers display the lines this way. Still other mailers will reformat the lines into something the programmer liked better. A lot of mailers simply hide them from us altogether. It all depends on the software used.

The data format of the header is really quite simple. There are only a couple of special cases, such as comments and continuation lines. Anything included in parentheses is a comment, except in quoted strings, and is there only for human consumption. The e-mail software does not process comments. In the date example above, the time zone is a comment. Any line not beginning in the first space of the line (column one) is a continuation of the previous line. The backslash character is used to delimit the character that follows it. For example, if you had a left parenthesis that was not intended to start a comment, it would appear as "\(." The backslash does to characters what kryptonite does to Superman; it removes any special powers.

A Rosetta Stone of an E-Mail Header

Below is a sample hypothetical SMTP header. Notice that every line begins with a field name followed by a colon. This is not a real header. It's a composite of information from some real headers. No header would actually contain all these lines. They are included here for explanation purposes only. Following the header is a line-by-line description of it.

```
Return-Path: <elephant@animals.com>
Received: by airmail.net
      (/\##/\ Smail3.1.30.16 #30.59)
      id <m0tzAxt-000FEqC@airmail.net>;
   Tue, 19 Mar 96 17:37:21 -0600 (CST)
Received: from pachy by animals.com
      with SMTP (Infinet-S-3.3) id SAA14781;
      Tue, 19 Mar 1996 18:38:00 -0500 (EST)
Date: Tue, 19 Mar 1996 18:38:00 -0500 (EST)
Message-Id:
      <199603192338.SAA14781@animals.com>
X-Mailer: Windows Eudora Light Version 1.5.2
Mime-Version: 1.0
Content-Type: multipart/mixed;
      boundary="=========_827275937==_"
Content-Type: text/plain; charset="us-ascii"
To: wombat@downunder.net (Billy Joe Wombat)
```

```
Resent-To: wally@walrus.net
Cc: white_bear@kodiak.net
Bcc: ocelot@jungle.net
From: Johnny Dumbo <elephant@animals.com>
Subject: Roaming the verdant plains.
In-Reply-To: Where's the beef?
References: Ecology and you.
Keywords: animals, dirt, filth
Encrypted: globbing,4
X-Attachments: C:\DOC\RAINFALL.DOC;
```

Return-Path

```
Return-Path: <elephant@animals.com>
```

This is the return address that's added at the very last stage of delivery. This is the path back to the originator of the message. It's optionally placed between a pair of angle brackets. It can be the complete path back to the sender, but it is more often just the return address.

Received

```
Received: by airmail.net
        (/\##/\ Smail3.1.30.16 #30.59)
        id <m0tzAxt-000FEqC@airmail.net>;
        Tue, 19 Mar 96 17:37:21 -0600 (CST)
Received: from pachy by mh004.animals.com
        with SMTP (Infinet-S-3.3) id SAA14781;
        Tue, 19 Mar 1996 18:38:00 -0500 (EST)
```

A Received line is inserted by each mail server that receives a copy of the message. If, for some reason, the mail had been routed through several mail servers, there would have been several of these lines. Two is normal. Four or five is not uncommon. The information here varies quite a bit, but these lines always end with a semicolon followed by the current date and time. Since each mail server adds its line to the beginning of the message, the history of mail servers can be read in order by starting with the one farthest down on the list.

There are quite a few things that can be included here on the "Received" line, and each is identified by its own keyword. All of them are optional. Different mail servers will include different things. As you can see from the examples, comments can be slipped in anywhere by simply putting a string inside parentheses. Here are some common keywords and what they mean:

- ❏ *from* This is the name of the sender. This could be the name of a sending mail server. In our example, the first originating mail server received this message from a user named pachy.

- ❏ *by* This is the domain name of the mail server creating the entry.

- ❏ *for* This is a copy of the incoming address as received by the mail server creating the message. In other words, there was an address that got the mail to the server and it is reproduced here. The address will be modified by the server before sending the message on.

- ❏ *id* Some mail servers use queues for the mail messages. This is the ID that the message was given in the queue. Different mailers will use different ways to arrive at these ID names. It makes no difference, as long as it is unique.

- ❏ *via* The medium over which the message was received. This could specify an Ethernet technology, a serial line, or whatever.

- ❏ *with* This can be used to specify the incoming protocol. This would normally be SMTP, but it could be X.25, Novell, or some other system that supports its own e-mail protocol. There can be several of these "with" statements in the case of nested protocols.

Date

```
Date: Tue, 19 Mar 1996 18:38:00 -0500 (EST)
```

This is the date and time that the message arrived at the mail server. This data format is quite obvious with the possible exception of the number -0500. This is the offset of the specified time from Greenwich Mean Time (GMT)—Eastern Standard Time is 5 hours behind GMT. The time zone specifier (EST)—for Eastern Standard Time—is simply a comment to make it a bit easier for a human to read.

Message-Id

```
Message-Id:
     <199603192338.SAA14781@animals.com>
```

This is the unique identifier for this message. This ID is generated by the mail server that initiates the message. It includes the domain name of the mail server, so it is guaranteed to be unique all over the world. This name is intended to be machine readable and is not designed for human consumption, so if you looked at it and made sense out of it (like, you thought it was a date or something), you may be experiencing hallucinations and should consider a decaffeinated coffee.

X-Mailer

```
X-Mailer: Windows Eudora Light Version 1.5.2
```

The "X-" prefix is a standard method of including something that is nonstandard. The prefix allows mailers to include things that are outside the SMTP specification. Someone could write a mail server that has some sort of special extension that requires information to be inserted into the header. This way the mail servers could do special secret stuff that only they know about. Any mail servers that don't know about it will ignore it and pass it on. In our example, we have a boastful mailer that has deemed it necessary to identify itself. (Makes one wonder if there's a Dark version of Eudora. Or maybe a heavy version. Or a high-fat version.) The reason this special prefix was used is to allow special keywords to be added to the standard without fear of conflict.

Mime-Version

```
Mime-Version: 1.0
```

This is the version number of MIME that was used to attach any documents. This will tell the receiving e-mail software that the sender was capable of sending MIME-attached data, and what version of the MIME standard would be used to do that. This line is usually sent whether or not there is an actual attachment. This is an extension to the original SMTP specification.

Content-Type

```
Content-Type: multipart/mixed;
     boundary="========_827275937==_"
Content-Type: text/plain; charset="us-ascii"
```

Two of these appear in our hypothetical header for purposes of explanation. In reality there would be only one. The first example indicates that we have a multipart message of mixed data types. The parts of the message are separated with the specified string of characters. This multipart/mixed thing will occur if a file of some data type other than plain ASCII is included, such as with MIME. The second example is the more normal case and specifies that the entire message consists of plain ASCII text.

To

```
To: wombat@downunder.net (Billy Joe Wombat)
```

This is the address of the recipient. The name in parentheses is added as a comment. There are two forms of this address specification. The other form is shown in the "From" example. There can be several addresses on this line, separated by commas.

Resent-To (-Cc, -Bcc or -Message-Id)

```
Resent-to: wally@walrus.net
```

The "Resent-" prefix indicates that the mail was forwarded from the original destination to this new destination. Our example only shows one of the Resent prefixes, but there are several. All of them have to do with messages being forwarded from the original target recipient to a new target recipient. The secondary addresses can also be forwarded by using "Resent-Cc" and "Resent-Bcc." There's even "Resent-Message-Id," for the case of the forwarding station changing the text of the ID.

Cc

```
Cc: white_bear@kodiak.net
```

This is a secondary recipient. A copy of the complete mail message will also be sent to this address.

Bcc

```
Bcc: ocelot@jungle.net
```

This is a secondary recipient just like Cc, except that the primary receiver and the secondary receiver will never have this line included in their e-mail headers. This is so that the originator can conveniently send an extra copy to someone else without the primary recipient knowing about it. Sneaky, huh?

From

```
From: Johnny Dumbo <elephant@animals.com>
```

This is the address of the sender. The name on the left is ignored as far as addressing is concerned and only the portion between the angle brackets is used. This could just as well have been put in the form of the "To" example above.

Subject

```
Subject: Roaming the verdant plains
```

This is the subject line provided by the user. It's just free-form text containing whatever. When the mail being sent is a reply, most mailers will prepend the original subject line with a "Re:" to use as the new subject line.

In-Reply-To

```
In-Reply-To: Where's the beef?
```

This is used in a response message to include the message ID of the e-mail being answered. In practice this is seldom used because most mail readers display the Subject line as a way of identifying the mail, and responders simply prepend that line with a "Re:". It's nice to see that something unnecessary was included in the original specification; we were beginning to think these guys were perfect.

References

```
References: Ecology and you.
```

This is a convenient way of referring to other e-mail. Actually, you can reference anything here, but it was intended to allow the sender to refer to other specific correspondence by message ID or subject.

Keywords

```
Keywords: animals, dirt, filth
```

This is a comma-separated list of keywords that may be used by a mail browser to locate information by subject.

Encrypted

```
Encrypted: globbing,4
```

This indicates that the message has been encrypted. In this example, the algorithm used for the encryption is called "globbing." There can also be some added information (in this case "4") to aid the recipient in figuring out how to decrypt the message. This is usually an index into an array of passwords, but it can be any number of things. The format is formalized this way to make it possible to have the sending and receiving software automatically encrypt and decrypt messages.

X-Attachments

```
X-Attachments: C:\DOC\RAINFALL.DOC;
```

This is the list of MIME attachments. This line shows one, but there can be several of them all separated by semicolons. If there's no attachment, this line will simply not be included in the header. There may or may not be a full path name. If there is, it will be the path name of the file on the originating client system. Also, many e-mail client programs will store the attached file in a local directory and add some sort of header entry that indicates the local path name.

Sendmail

Sendmail is a program that resides inside a UNIX server and has the job of receiving mail and delivering it to the intended recipient. Neither rain, nor hail, nor . . . (Oops. Wrong mail.) There are some other mail servers around, but the world seems to be pretty much settling on sendmail as the standard.

Sendmail is a complicated program. One could ramble on for hundreds of pages discussing the labyrinth of algorithms and configuration files that are needed to operate it. But that's a problem for system administrators. Sendmail handles more than just the Internet mail protocol, SMTP, that we all know and love. It also handles the UUCP (UNIX to UNIX Copy Protocol) mail format, as well as handling its own local mail delivery system. A group of configuration files tells sendmail how it is to operate. These files include information on everything from port numbers to instructions on editing mail headers. Sendmail also has access to the disk on the computer where it runs so it can store-and-forward mail to be delivered later to dial-up users.

It's normal to have sendmail run as a daemon whenever a UNIX system boots up so it will always be there to accept and process mail. Whenever mail arrives at sendmail, its header is examined to determine the destination. The header is then updated appropriately and the mail is sent to its next stop. The next stop could be a user's mailbox directory (if this is local mail), another mail server somewhere on the Internet, or a file on disk to wait for a user's e-mail software to call in and request the mail over a remote connection. A remote user can instruct his or her e-mail program to log in and, using the mail protocol, request his or her mail. In response, the sendmail daemon will then look at the files it stored earlier and deliver any mail it finds that is addressed to that user.

Sendmail doesn't really do all this work itself. There are other programs for the low-level stuff, like handling the different mail routes. These programs are called "mailers" and there can be several of them configured into one system. This flexibility is the main reason that sendmail is becoming the standard. The penalty to be paid for the flexibility is that it takes a hairy-legged system administrator to configure sendmail so it will operate smoothly.

Going Postal: Post Office Protocol

Since we have sendmail operating the mail server, and you have your own e-mail software on your PC or workstation, it's obvious that the two need to talk to one another. Mail is sent back and forth between them in the SMTP format. What we also need is some way for the e-mail program to ask, "Do I have any mail?" and some way for the mail server to answer, "Yes. Do you want it now?" and so on.

That's what POP (Post Office Protocol) does. The original design was intended to be used from a workstation on a LAN, with a mail server on the same LAN and the mailbox (mail-holding area) on the server. The workstation could ask for mail whenever it wanted it, and the user could log in from any work-station and get his mail. Luckily, there was enough flexibility built into the POP design that it does just fine over a dial-up link, too. Your mail is addressed with your name, and the name of the server, with an at sign (@) in between them. The server receives the mail and holds onto it until you call for it.

POP is not intended to be a user-friendly protocol. It likes to talk to software, not to humans. The protocol is designed to be run as a series of questions and answers sort of like those in Figure 20-1. Basically, the mail server sits and waits until a connection is made, then answers with the POP version of "Howdy." The conversation proceeds with the user's e-mail software sending requests, and the server responding. The protocol is very simple— its solution to most problems is to simply hang up (haven't we all experienced that!).

```
Client                        Server
———                           ———
                              Wait for Connection
Open Connection
                              "POP Server Ready"
"Hello, I'm fred"
                              "I have 2 messages for you, fred"
"Send me one"

                              "Ok, 537 characters"
"Could we retry that?"
                              "Sure. Here it is"
"Got it. You can
delete it."
                              "Ok. I have 1 message."
"Send me one"
                              "Ok, 134 characters"
"Got it. But don't
delete it"
                              "Ok. I have 1 message."
"Quit."
                              "Ok."
Close connection              Close connection
```

Figure 20-1: A POP client-to-server conversation.

INTER-NETWORK MAILING GUIDE

Moving e-mail through the Internet is a pretty easy and standardized procedure (at least as easy and standardized as these things get!). But what if you want to send a message to someone on another network not on the Internet proper (like MCI mail, for example)? While you can pretty much count on a standard format for most addressing on one network, how can you keep the various and sundry addressing methods for other networks straight? Just use our handy mail guide. It lists all the addresses you need to be able to use the various gateways that exist between the Internet and most commercial e-mail services.

TIP

The following table is based on the super-handy "Inter-Network Mail Guide," which can be found at http://alpha.acast.nova.edu/cgi-bin/inmgq.pl. It goes into much greater detail than our humble chart can and has the advantage of being an electronic document so it can be constantly updated to remain current.

Here's how to use this table. If you're sending mail from the Internet to another network, you need to know how to format your address so it arrives in the mailbox of the person you're trying to reach on that other network. To find how to send the message, just go down the left side of the chart till you find the network the person you're sending the message to uses. Then move right one column and look at the e-mail address template. In most cases, the format of the address template will contain the username of the person you're trying to reach followed by the format for routing the message.

Network	Address Form From Internet
AlterNex	user@ax.apc.org
America Online	user@aol.com
AppleLink	user@applelink.apple.com
ArCom	/G=test/S=user/O=organization/A=arcom/C=ch/@chx400.switch.ch
AT&T Mail	user@attmail.com
BITNET	user@site
Byte Information eXchange	user@bix.com
Berkeley Macintosh User's Group	Full.Name@bmug.org

➡

Network	Address Form From Internet
BULMAIL	Full.Name/O=organization/ @BULMAIL.Sprint.com
Calvacom	usercode@calvacom.fr
Chasque	user@chasque.apc.org
ComLink	user@oln.comlink.apc.org
CompuServe	user.number@compuserve.com (substitute a period for the comma in the CompuServe user code)
Connect Professional Information Network	NAME@connectinc.com
EasyLink	usermailnumber@eln.attmail.com
Easynet	user@host.enet.dec.com
EcoNet	user@igc.apc.org
Envoy-100	/G=firstname/S=lastname/P=company/ @tc.resonet.com
Francomedia	If Sean Carton is a user at node 101:2/ 3.4, the address would be: Sean.Carton%101-2-3- 4@absint.login.qc.ca
FR/ATLAS	fullname.name@org- unit.organization.atlas.fr
GEnie	user@genie.geis.com
GeoNet	user@host.geonet.de
GlasNet	user@glas.apc.org
GNS Gold 400	full.name@org_unit.org.prmd.gold-400.gb
GoldGate Telecom Gold	User.designation@goldgate.ac.uk
GreenNet	user@gn.apc.org
GSFCmail	user@gsfcmail.nasa.gov
VNET	user@vmnode.tertiary_domain.ibm.com
KeyLink	Full.Name@organization.telememo.au
Mausnet	full_name@box.maus.de
MCIMail	mbx1%mbx2%EMS_Name@MCIMail.com
Nicaro	user@nicarao.apc.org
Nifty Serve	user@niftyserve.or.jp
NordNet	user@pns.apc.org
NASA Science Internet	user@host.dnet.nasa.gov
PeaceNet/EcoNet	user@igc.apc.org

Network	Address Form From Internet
Pegasus	user@peg.apc.org
Prodigy	userid@prodigy.com
Pro-Net Australia	user@tanus.oz.au
Argentina SatLink Internet Services	user@node.satlink.net
Schlumberger Information Network	user@node.SINet.SLB.COM
SprintMail	/G=First name/S=last name/ O=organization/ADMD=TELEMAIL/C=US/ @sprint.com
Telecom Australia	user@viatel.pronet.com
Telkom 400	full.name@X400.telkom400.inca.za
Texas Higher Education Network	user%host.decnet@utadnx.cc.utexas.edu
The Web	user@web.apc.org
WWIVnet	number-node@wwiv.tfsquad.mn.org

Table 20-1: Inter-network mail guide.

MAILING LISTS

One of the great things about publishing through e-mail and conducting a discussion with an e-mail list is that it's a forum that's both open to many people while retaining some semblance of privacy (or manageable size). Unlike the anarchy of Usenet, a mailing list can be a small, intimate group of people interested in a similar topic carrying on discussions without worrying about thousands of people lurking in the background.

Besides the more entertaining and educational aspects of lists, many businesses are realizing that, as their customers go online, mailing lists are a great way to stay in touch with them. They can send out product updates, breaking news, or technical newsletters to customers at a fraction of the cost of a conventional mailing.

Finding Lists

One drawback with mailing lists is finding out what's available. There are literally thousands of e-mail lists on the Net today, but since they aren't as open as Usenet discussion groups, most go about their business unknown to everyone besides subscribers.

Fortunately, several different "lists of lists" exist which allow you to search for e-mail lists of interest. Table 20-2 should point you toward all of the lists that are available.

List Search Site	Web Address
Active Mailing Lists	http://www.oai.org/External/ActiveMailLists.html
E-mail Discussion Groups	http://www.nova.edu/Inter-Links/listserv.html
Search the List of Lists	http://catalog.com/vivian/interest-group-search.html
Tile.Net/Lists	http://tile.net/listserv/
Liszt (has over 32,000 entries!)	http://www.liszt.com/

Table 20-2: Places to search for e-mail lists.

How to Subscribe & Unsubscribe

To get on a mailing list, you'll have to know how to "subscribe" to it. Most lists are maintained by automatic list software. (A few are done by hand, where you subscribe simply by e-mailing the list editor.) Automated list subscribing must be done using the proper form.

Getting on a mailing list (and getting off when you're done) is pretty straightforward. Generally, you send a "subscribe" message in the body of a message (SUBSCRIBE *list your name)* with your name and e-mail address to the server software. Most lists have two addresses, the administration address and the actual list address. The former you use to talk to the list server (to subscribe, get archives, get help info, etc.), the latter you use to post messages to the group. Once the server software receives your subscribe request, it adds you to the list, and any message posted to the list will now show up in your mailbox. Likewise, any message you send to the list gets distributed to everyone else on the list. To get off the list, all you need to do is send an "unsubscribe" message to the server address and you'll be removed.

Once you get on a mailing list or two, it's good to remember a few simple tips. First, if your e-mail software has mail filtering functions, learn how to use them. It's much easier to deal with your mailing lists if you can automatically shuffle them off into folders. However, once you have the filter set up, don't forget about it—the mail can pile up pretty quickly in a forgotten folder. Most important of all—*save the administration message you'll receive from the mailing list server when you subscribe!* Usually, it contains all the information you need to know in order to later get off the list, and the addresses of the list moderators in case you need to take care of a problem. Whatever you do, don't try to subscribe and unsubscribe to a list by mailing a message to the list itself—it's both impolite and unhelpful. The unsubscribe message must go to the list server software.

Generally, there are three major mailing list servers you'll come in contact with. Knowing how to control each one with the various commands available can make your life a lot easier. Table 20-3 lists the most common mailing list server commands:

Command	Listserv	Majordomo	Listproc
Subscribe	SUBSCRIBE [listname] [yourFirstName yourLastName]	SUBSCRIBE [listname] [yourFullEmailAddress]	SUBSCRIBE [listname] [yourFirstName yourLastName]
Unsubscribe	UNSUBSCRIBE [listname]	UNSUBSCRIBE [listname] [yourFullEmailAddress]	UNSUBSCRIBE [listname] [yourFirstName yourLastName]
Help	help	help	help
Subscription options	QUERY [listname]		QUERY [listname]
Obtain a List of Files in the Archive	INDEX [listname]	majordomo:INDEX [listname]	INDEX [listname]
Get a particular file	GET [filename] [file-type] [listname]	GET [listname] [filename]	GET [listname] [filename]
Change to digest/index version	SET [listname] DIGEST	SUBSCRIBE [listname]-DIGEST. In the same message, unsubscribe from the undigested version: UNSUBSCRIBE [list-name] [fullEmailAddress]	SET [listname] MAIL DIGEST
Change back to regular version	SET [listname] MAIL	unsubscribe [listname]-digest (then resubscribe)	SET [listname] MAIL ACK
Stop temporarily (for vacation, etc.)	SET [listname] NOMAIL	not supported	SET [listname] MAIL POSTPONE
Start again after temporary stop	SET [listname] MAIL	not supported	SET [listname] MAIL ACK
Get a list of other subscribers	REVIEW [listname]	WHO [listname]	RECIPIENTS [listname]
Hide yourself from the request for list of subscribers	SET listname CONCEAL	not supported	SET listname CONCEAL YES
Get a copy of your posts	set [listname] repro	not supported	SET [listname] mail ack

Table 20-3: Common commands in the major list server programs. (Commands should be typed as one line with no returns.)

E-MAIL ATTACHMENTS: SENDING & RECEIVING FILES

One of the most perplexing things about e-mail, and the one thing that most people don't *really* know how to do, is attaching files to messages and sending them so that they arrive in one piece. If you can get attachments working, it can be one of the handiest things about e-mail. However (and this is usually what happens), if you don't know how to send files through e-mail, you'll drive yourself absolutely nuts with misplaced attachments, corrupted files, and files that never arrive.

In Chapters 7, 12, and 17, we covered the "what button do I push" basics of sending and receiving attached files, but we didn't explain why things work the way they do. Now's our chance to set the record straight. In this section, we'll take a closer look at the various ways you can attach, send, and receive files with your e-mail program. We'll examine MIME, uuencode, and BinHex—the most popular ways of attaching files to e-mail. We'll learn how to attach a file to an outgoing message and what to do with an attachment once you receive it.

MIMEs Invade Cyberspace—News at 11

SMTP (Simple Mail Transfer Protocol) is the standard that's used to transmit e-mail message across the Internet. These messages, according to the basic standard, are plain ASCII text. In order to transmit file types other than plain ASCII text via e-mail, some extensions were added to SMTP. These extensions are called MIME (for "Multipurpose Internet Mail Extensions").

The existing SMTP formats were left unmolested so the entire Internet mail system would continue to operate exactly as it did before except that the new capabilities would be available. Some new header fields were added to the standard format. In the previous discussion of SMTP, we described the format of the fields in the header, and even touched on some of the MIME options. We now look at MIME more carefully.

There is one header field that determines whether the message is indeed a MIME message or not:

```
MIME-Version: 1.0
```

If this line is present, you've got a MIME on your hands. As you can see, this format allows for upgrades to newer version numbers, but since 1992, everything has been doing just fine on version 1.0. The reason that 1.0 has held out for so long is that the specification was written to be extensible enough to handle all the file formats and data types we have needed so far.

Content-Type

Whenever MIME is used to include data inside an e-mail message, it's necessary that the receiver know something about the data that's being included. The content-type field does it using this format:

```
Content-type: type / subtype [;parameters]
```

The type is sort of like the general category of the transmitted data. There are seven of these categories. On every content-type line, there are always both a type and a subtype. The type is just a general category. Each type has a sort of standard subtype. This standard subtype is the one that was in the mind of the designers of MIME. However, it was divided into type and subtype so that any other data formats could be included. Beyond the type and the subtype, over to the right following the semicolon, there's a provision for parameters to be set. Some types require a parameter setting, others don't. (And still others really don't care.) An example of a required parameter is the definition for regular ol' plain ordinary ASCII text:

```
Content-Type: text / plain; charset=us-ascii
```

Following is a list of the types and a brief description of each:

❏ *application* This is used to transmit raw binary data. This can be used to do file transfers where the content is considered binary and is not to be interpreted except by some application program on the receiving end. The subtype is normally "octet-stream," and the receiving mailer simply writes it to disk. Friendly mailers will ask something like, "Ok buddy, where do you want it?" Another common subtype is "postscript," which is really a programming language.

❏ *audio* This type has the standard subtype "basic" for simple audio. The simple audio format is 8-bit with a sample rate of 8000 Hz and a single channel.

❏ *image* This is used for still-picture transmission. The initial subtypes defined here were "GIF" and "JPEG." There are now others. The ability to send these around has probably gotten the Internet into more trouble than anything else. Congress seems to be saying, "I don't know what the Internet is, but I know a dirty picture when I see one!"

❏ *message* This can be used to encapsulate a mail message inside the one being sent. There were three original sub-types: "rfc822," "partial," and "external-body." The subtype "rfc822" specifies that the embedded message is another standard mail message complete with header. (We're sure there's a good reason for doing this, we just don't know what it is.) The subtype "partial" indicates the message is incomplete and should be combined with other e-mail messages to reconstruct the complete message. This allows for the transfer of very long messages, since they can be sent in multiple parts. The required parameters for a "partial" subtype are "id," for unique identification of the message, "number," specifying where this part will fit back into the whole, and "total," specifying how many parts there are. The subtype "external-body" means that the actual message was not sent with the e-mail. What was sent is information about the location of the message. The "external-body" message could be a filename, an Internet URL, or a database key.

❏ *multipart* This is used to send multiple messages of varying types as a single e-mail message. This is a bit more complicated than the other types, so it's explained below.

❏ *text* The most common subtype for this is "plain," which means that we're dealing with plain, unformatted text. It should be immediately readable by the receiver without using any special software, other than something that will interpret the specified character set. This always requires that the parameter "charset" be included so the receivers will know just what sort of characters they're letting in through their ports.

❏ *video* This is the transmission of a file that contains moving pictures and audio. The initial video subtype was defined as "MPEG."

❏ *x-* This is one you can make up. If you wish to invent a type, simply start it with the two characters "x-" and go ahead and use it as a header in your e-mail. It will pass through the system unaltered. It will be necessary, however, that the receiver be let in on your little secret so he or will have some idea what to do with it once it is received.

The MIME Multipart Type

A "multipart" e-mail message contains one or more of the other types in a single message. An example of this would be sending e-mail that has a description of a picture, and sending the picture along with it. ("Senator Exon, look at this filth I found on the Internet!") The description could be normal e-mail in plain text, and the picture could be JPEG or GIF.

The primary "multipart" subtype is "mixed." The mixed subtype signifies that the parts of the multipart message are just a collection of separate and independent items that have no real relationship to one another other than the order in which they appear. Whenever there is one (or more) parts of a message that are of unknown type, the only subtype that is valid is "mixed." You can think of all the other subtypes as being special cases of "mixed."

The subtype "alternative" is used to mean that all the body parts are the same information in different forms. For instance, this could be used to send the same document in a word processor file, a PostScript file, and a plain ASCII text file. This way the recipient will get the message, and have the option of choosing from the most suitable format.

The subtype "digest" means that the parts are a combination of related things, often in the same format. For example, they could be a group of e-mail messages generated by a bunch of people discussing a specific subject. This e-mail could be gathered together into a "digest" document and distributed in one piece. There's a logical relationship among the included items, and their order is important.

The subtype "parallel" is the same as the "mixed" subtype, except that the order is not important. Conceptually, the receiver would display (or otherwise process) all the body parts simultaneously. At the very least, they can be handled in any convenient order.

Even though a multipart message contains several body parts, there's still only one header at its top. Here we have stripped-down a mail message to just the multipart stuff.

```
Mime-Version: 1.0
Content-Type: multipart/mixed; boundary="=== new message ==="
X-Attachments: E:\DOC\IPT\GLOSNOTE.DOC;


-=== new message ===
Content-Type: text/plain; charset="us-ascii"
<Plain text message body goes here>
-=== new message ===
Content-Type: application/octet-stream;  name="WORDPROC.DOC";
     Content-Transfer-Encoding: base64
     Content-Disposition: attachment;filename="WORDPROC.DOC"
     <Encoded wordproc.doc goes here>
```

This message uses the subtype "mixed," indicating that several messages of various content-types can follow. There's the required parameter "boundary," which is used to define the character string that divides one body part from another. The result of all this, in effect, is that there are two or more e-mail messages included under one header. The above example shows a multipart e-mail message that has plain ASCII text followed by some sort of word processor document. The type of document is not known to the MIME standard, so it is simply transmitted as an "octet-stream." Notice that the only part of the header that is repeated for each body part is the

Content-Type specifier that follows each boundary separator. In our example, the document of unknown origin was converted into ASCII by using the old base64 encoding trick.

What is the old base64 trick? Binary data can be converted to character data by using base64 notation. It is sort of like base 16 notation, except that the entire alphabet is used. To represent base64, we need 64 unique ASCII characters. Using the 10 digits, the 26 lower case and 26 upper case letters gives us 62. Throw in the plus sign and the slash and we have 64. Converting the binary data to base64 ASCII gives us a much more compressed form than simply using hex, since each character represents 6 bits instead of 4.

By the way, the boundary string in a multipart message can be anything that the mail software wants it to be. Well, almost. It can't be any string that appears anywhere inside any of the body parts because confusion would set in. Also, it can't be dirty words because Congress has put a stop to that.

MIME & IANA

MIME is defined as an extensible standard. That is, it has been designed in such a way that new data type names and definitions can be added to it. A new data type can be added by everyone agreeing on a new subtype for one of the seven basic types. There are a couple of hitches in doing it this way. First, two people could come up with the same name for two different things. Second, whenever a new name is added, its specifications need to be known to the world so the various implementations of e-mail software can start to process the data in the manner intended. After all, the entire purpose of this exercise is to send readable data from one location to another.

To solve this problem, the Internet Assigned Number Authority (IANA) was enlisted to keep track of the names being added. The IANA is a central registry for numbers and names that need to be universally known to the Internet. Since file formats are specified in the standard, and new file formats are springing up all the time, it's expected that there will be any number of new definitions of MIME fields.

There have been a few subtypes added in the years since MIME was first introduced. Table 20-4 is the current list at IANA. Of course, the list is always growing and by the time you read this it will likely have changed. Updates to the list, as well as specifications of what the list members mean, can be retrieved by FTP at ftp.isi.edu/in-notes/iana/assignments/media-types. In this directory you'll find an up-to-date list of all the defined subtypes. There's a directory for each type, and in each directory you'll find the specifications of the subtypes.

Type	Subtype	Type	Subtype
application	activemessage	image	cgm
	andrew-inset		g3fax
	applefile		gif
	atomicmail		ief
	cals-1840		jpeg
	commonground		naplps
	cybercash		tiff
	dca-rft	message	external-body
	dec-dx		news
	eshop		partial
	iges		rfc822
	mac-binhex40		
	macwriteii	multipart	alternative
	mathematica		appledouble
	msword		digest
	news-message-id		form-data
	news-transmission		header-set
	octet-stream		mixed
	oda		parallel
	pdf		related
	postscript		report
	remote-printing		voice-message
	riscos	text	enriched
	rtf		richtext
	sgml		plain
	slate		sgml
	wita		tab-separated-values
	wordperfect5.1		
	x400-bp	video	mpeg
	zip		quicktime
audio	basic		
	32kadpcm		

Table 20-4: The MIME types and subtypes.

uuencode & BinHex

Long, long ago, in a land far away (well, it was 1976 at Bell Labs), it was concluded that it would be a good thing to be able to copy files from one UNIX system to another over Usenet. Out of this was born UUCP (UNIX to UNIX Copy Protocol). It was very successful and for years was the mainstay of UNIX communications. As a matter of fact, it's still in use today where automated transfer of lots of data is required. As time went by, the transfer of simple text files was not enough. The capability was added to execute a program on a remote computer by using a program called uuxqt (pronounced "you you execute").

This still wasn't enough. Folks wanted to be able to transfer binary files as well as text. The problem with this was that many connections were set up to handle 7-bit data. This is fine for sending ASCII text, which is 7-bit data, but useless for sending binary data where all 8 bits are important. Transmitting binary data through a link could just strip off the high-order bits. Not good. Undaunted, Internet gurus added the programs uuencode and uudecode so that binary data could be transformed into and out of a 7-bit format. These are pronounced "you you encode" and "you you decode." (There was the Southern version, "ya'll ya'll encode," but it ran a bit slow in the summer.)

It turns out that even those who don't use UUCP can make use of uuencode and uudecode to convert binary data to 7-bit ASCII data, and then back to binary data. Until MIME came on the scene, uuencode was used by almost everyone to send binary files via e-mail. It required a manual operation on the part of the sender to uuencode the file to be mailed, and another manual operation on the part of the receiver to uudecode it. MIME has simply automated the procedure. However, there are still people out there who have old e-mail software that doesn't know about MIME, so you will need to do something like this to send files to them. The most common use I know of today for uuencode is to post graphics to newsgroups.

Besides the uuencode and uudecode programs, there's another commonly used program, called BinHex, that does essentially the same thing. BinHex has the added capability of preserving the Macintosh two-part program structure (the resource fork and the data fork).

TIP

A rule of thumb about encoding files. Rules were meant to be broken (especially rules of thumb), but generally speaking, you should use BinHex to convert Macintosh executable programs, and use uuencode/uudecode to handle everything else, such as GIF or JPEG files. Text files need no conversion since they are already in a 7-bit format.

uuencode

The uuencode program is the easiest thing in the world to run. It has one input (the file to be encoded) and one output (the encoded file). There are any number of implementations, but normally you simply type in **uuencode** <filename> and the encoded file is generated. It is normally a file of the same name as the input file, but with a different extension (such as UUE). The following example shows the format of a uuencoded file:

```
begin 644 isit.exe
M34E-1OT*24%.00T*26YT97)V80T*N97970@3G5SM8F5R#OHX,C
M"F@@:69?;5T8GET9OT:"!7:&A95EA=#HX,5R95EEA=#HHZ<F5A9&
M=',,-"F@@;95M8F5R,G=0<F0-YU;6)E<(CW:W)D#OIH
M(&ES7V0T*":I(<U]S>6UB;;7Q?8Y]U;;GG%Q6G.;"F@@:U: 7-
M<WEM8F]]7L7W=87W-87T;?#IHI0%$Q%.EQU=='!!]!1%Q53%I)
M4%QQ96%D;#;64N='T*AT#0I%.E%'0-"D0=$Z7&5Z5&QQQ9UF-I
?;IE=>"YT>']I1R#0I%EQD-<<F9C,,34R,,2YT
`
end
```

As you can see, it is plain text and can be slipped right in the body of an e-mail message without any problem. The encoded data character strings are between the lines "begin" and "end." The "begin" line has the number 644 (or possibly some other three-digit number) that is a file type and version identifier needed by uudecode, followed by the filename. The uudecode program will accept this text as input, decode everything between the beginning and ending lines, and create a binary file named isit.exe, in this example.

You'll often see pictures, programs, and other data items posted to newsgroups in this format. When one is too large for a single posting (or single e-mail message), it can be split into parts. This is done by simply chopping the uuencoded form of the text into pieces (a good uuencoder will do that for you). The first of these pieces will have the "begin" line at its top, and the last will have the "end" line at its end. All the ones in the middle have no tags on them at all. The sender normally names them with part numbers in the title of the message, like:

```
My Chevy jpeg (0/3)
My Chevy jpeg (1/3)
My Chevy jpeg (2/3)
My Chevy jpeg (3/3)
```

By looking at the titles, one could assume that this is a JPEG encoded picture of someone's car. It is a message in four parts, with a picture in three parts. Part 0/3 is optional and contains only a description of the contents of the other parts ("Check out my totally smokin' wheels, dudes!"). If it is uuencoded, part 1/3 will have something like "begin 644 chevy.jpg" at its top, and part 3/3 will have an "end" line at its bottom. Simply take these parts and load them into a text editor and paste them together (again, there are several good uudecoders out there to do this part for you). You'll need to remove any extraneous matter that appears between the parts, since uudecode will try to decode it. Run the results through uudecode and you'll be rewarded with an image, in this case, of some guy's ol' rusty Chevy Impala.

You can get uuencode and uudecode programs from almost any software site. These programs are like navels; everyone's got one. There is a selection of them from plain to fancy (including Windows and Mac versions) on the Web site http://www.infocom.net/~elogan/wuudoall.html. If you want specific recommendations about programs, check out Chapter 23.

BinHex

A BinHex file, as shown in the following example, begins with the line "(This file must be converted with BinHex 4.0)." The line right under it always begins with a colon. The very last line always ends with a colon.

```
(This file must be converted with BinHex 4.0)
:$&"Kj$F*[G(jMP4"+8%"@!!%'IrfrJ""+4P'!!%#!J!
Y-jT@RpjaD%PrRF*f(+'p@3L5)Cfp-HTrr99Qa%VlVLi
IIOKTpl$X1'[IX([J"#Rm1YIOiQ')DNGYTD)rpQkM3!:
```

The same split apart and put back together naming conventions apply here that apply to uuencoded messages described above.

There are a few versions of the BinHex program for the Macintosh. There is a shareware version, called StuffIt Lite, available from Aladdin Systems at http://www.aladdinsys.com.

A Question of Compression

Some files can be compressed before they are BinHexed or uuencoded. For other files, this is fruitless. Some files are already inherently compressed and just won't squeeze down any further. Ever tried to ZIP a ZIP file?

The graphical files formats GIF, JPEG, and MPEG have data compression already built into them. There's also the frustrating thing about audio. To a compression program, audio appears as random data. For compression to succeed, there must be some predictability to the data pattern. They can be compressed some, but probably not enough to worry about. Also, there's some built-in compression for Windows WAV files and for Macintosh system sounds, so don't bother.

If you have a file that's large enough that compressing it could help you out, and you aren't sure about whether or not it will compress, just try it and look at the before and after sizes. If there's no appreciable difference, skip it.

MOVING ON

E-mail doesn't have to be complicated, especially after you understand all of the information that's built into every message. Now that you've made it through this chapter, we hope you'll feel more comfortable dealing with e-mail headers, mailing lists, internetwork transmissions, and attachments. Having this knowledge will make your life a lot easier when things go wrong, and streamline your everyday e-mail operations.

Now that you know how to make sure your messages arrive intact, what can you do to make sure that they stay private as well? In the next chapter, we'll examine such things as encryption, anonymous remailers, and security software. These days, as more and more information about our lives becomes public, it's nice to know that there are some powerful tools and techniques that can keep your e-mail away from prying eyes. Protect your privacy!

## Chapter 21

E-Mail Privacy & Security

There are times when things just need to be private. In this chapter, we'll discuss some ways of keeping your e-mail and other online files that way. Of course, it's not difficult to keep something *totally* secret. The trick is keeping something secret in such a way that you have control over which parts are made available and to whom. It's this controlled access that brings about all the difficulties. Sometimes you want to transmit data so that only those it is intended for can read it. Sometimes you want to keep data private and not let outsiders get to it, but it needs to be available to insiders. Sometimes you want some of the information to be public and the rest of it to be private. There are all sorts of situations and all sorts of methods for addressing them.

Here is a list of basic e-mail privacy tips. Each aspect of this list (password creation, e-mail encryption, anonymous remailers, and so on) is discussed in greater detail throughout this chapter. If such topics as cryptographic algorithms and the specifics of computer security leave you cold, you can skip over those sections. The important information every e-mail user should know is contained in this list and the do's and don'ts of password making that follow.

1. Most computer intrusions happen through insecure passwords. Take special care when generating your passwords and change them frequently.

2. Make sure your mail gets to the person for whom it is intended. This is a detail you can't be too careful about.

3. If you're paranoid about having your password intercepted because you've sent it over an unsecure network, change it immediately.

4. If you need to send a message, and you don't want your name attached to it, use an anonymous remailer.

5. If you want to encrypt your mail, you can use a program like PGP, RIPEM, or crypt, depending on what platform you're on and how much protection you think you need.

6. Remember: your e-mail is not really private, so take precautions accordingly.

7. If you don't want people reading your deleted messages and other files on your machine, you can use a program like Norton Utilities (for both Mac and Windows) to zap all of the hidden, deleted files. A program such as this can be used to remove all traces of the deleted files from your drive by completely erasing and *zeroing out* all space on your disk that is marked as free.

8. If you suspect that your e-mail account has been tampered with, contact your ISP or systems administrator immediately.

BFLSPK: PASSWORD TRICKS

The password is the first layer of protection. This is far and away the biggest security hole in any computer system. Most computer intrusions happen by hacking users' insecure passwords. You should put a great deal of thought into your password to make sure that it cannot be easily cracked. Although it is rare, all the heavy technical news you hear about security breaches and brilliant crackers is true.

The number one thing you need to do to keep your e-mail private and secure is to change your passwords frequently. Some systems age the passwords and tell users when the time comes to make a change. This only sort of works; people become emotionally attached to their passwords (we know we do) and take delight in trying to fool the system administrator. They simply change their password and then change it right back again. To deal with this sort of childish chicanery, old passwords have to be archived so they can be compared to current passwords. This is tedious for the systems administrator, but necessary if security is a real concern.

How *Not* to Construct a Password

There are certain passwords that people use over and over. Crackers know this. If you consider the following suggestions, you can maximize the security of your passwords:

❐ Don't set up an account and use the account name as the password, even as a temporary measure. This happens frequently when new users are added to a system.

❐ Don't use a word you find in a dictionary. There is a common trick used by crackers—they simply set up an automatic loop to apply the words of a dictionary to the account until one of them opens it up. This goes for foreign words and common abbreviations, too.

❐ Don't use short passwords of three or four characters. There are not enough of these to prevent a scan from being made (in a very short time) of all the possible combinations. Never use a password of less than six characters.

❏ Don't use the name of a person. There are two ways this can be broken. One is simply by using a dictionary of names. The other is by using the names of the people you know.

❏ Don't use your birthday (or some other special date). This is such a common password scheme that it is one of the first ones checked by someone breaking in. Don't use your social security number or phone number, either. It's best not to use any number that can be looked up.

❏ Don't use common words or dates (or anything) spelled backwards. The cracker simply tries each one in both directions.

❏ Don't use all letters or all numbers.

❏ No matter how good it may seem, don't use a password that you find in this book or in any other book. The people that break in to computers also read books. Where do you think they get all the ideas about bad passwords?

❏ Ideally, don't even write your password down. If you have to, store it in a safe place, away from your computer. Don't write it in the back of your MS Word manual or leave it on the bulletin board behind your desk or in other obvious places.

❏ If you're signing on to a new system, think up your new password before you log on. Sometimes, people feel like the meter's running and they need to think up something quick when prompted for their password. So, they look at their surroundings and choose the first thing they see. Not smart. Someone wanting to break in will often visit the site of the target system and look for these clues.

❐ Finally, something not directly related to construction, but which should be pretty obvious—never tell anyone your password. As the little man at the door of the Emerald Palace said, "Not nobody, not nohow!" You would be positively amazed at how many crackers can barely string two lines of code together, but are adept social engineers. They're very good at coaxing someone's password out of them with some sob story or tale of woe. Don't go for it. Your password should be absolutely secret.

TIP

If you suspect that someone has gained unauthorized access to your e-mail account contact your ISP or systems administrator immediately.

How to Construct a Password

What you want for a password is a random selection of letters and numbers and punctuation. Along with this, you will need some way to remember it without writing it down. Most of the "great safe crackers" in history have simply been astute enough to look in certain hiding places for the written combination. Here are some ways to create a secure password that you can remember:

❐ Come up with some fictional word that you can pronounce and spell in some personal way. For example, say "for drum lee" in your mind and type "4drumly." Or, say "oh but yes they are too" in your mind as you type "Obytr2." Or, say "base on balls" while you type "B@snBalls."

❐ Take a couple of words and insert some punctuation such as "hen&fruit" or "Yall*drill."

❑ Make up a multisyllable word and leave out the vowels (or the consonants, or anything else you like). For example, the word "BaffleSpeak" could become "BflSpk."

❑ There are random password generators available on the Internet. They generate passwords that are pronounceable so you can remember them as sounds after a few repetitions.

❑ Pick some sort of phrase or saying and use the first letter from each of the words—for example, "The traveling salesman and the farmer's daughter." While you say this in your head, type "ttsatfd." It would be even better to add a couple of capital letters, as in "TtsaTfd," or add some numbers as in "1ts1fd" (for "one traveling salesman, one farmer's daughter").

❑ Construct a password from some sequence that you can reconstruct if you forget the word. For example, if you have a personal address book you carry with you, take the last letter from the first name of the first 8 people in the book. We just did this and got "kjjsjscc." This gives a bit of a convoluted password that could be hard to remember, but it can always be recreated. Just don't lose your address book!

ANONYMOUS REMAILERS

Normally, when e-mail is sent from one person to another, every effort is made to include the name and address of the sender. You may find yourself in a position in which you'd like to send mail but you don't want the receiver know where it came from—there are ways to do that.

The simplest (and least effective) method to achieve anonymity is to simply change the name of the sender in your e-mail software. But this is only a facade since the sender can be traced directly by the other information in the header of the message. All received e-mail has the address of the sender. The only way to not have your return address appear on the mail is to have someone else send it so that their return address will appear there instead. That's exactly what an anonymous remailer does. You send the mail to the remailer, it strips off all of the return address information and inserts its own return address by sending the mail on to the intended recipient.

TIP

This may seem obvious, but when sending mail that *does* include your address, be careful about who exactly you're sending it to. People have actually lost their jobs because they've accidentally sent a message about the boss *to* the boss. We've seen a number of embarrassing incidents where someone on a group list intends to veer off from the list and complain about one list member to another, but they've used the "Reply to All" command by mistake. Oops.

Some people say all reasons for using a remailer are suspicious (illegal activities, terrorism, child pornography). But there are legitimate reasons. For instance, there are mailing list discussion groups on sensitive and personal subjects. Anonymous remailers allow the bashful to participate. Sometimes a corporate or government spokesperson wants to say something "off the record." For example, an anonymous remailer would have simplified the communications between the *Washington Post* and Deep Throat during the Watergate incident. In technical and intellectual discussions that may be over your head, remailers allow you to "think out loud" without publicly embarrassing yourself if your brilliant idea turns out to be a dim bulb.

There are security reasons for wanting anonymity, too. If sensitive information is to be sent from one place to another, it may be advisable to obscure the sender as well as the message so that snoopers won't know the message may be worth reading. If a message is taken out of the context of the identity of the sender this way, the contents mean very little. A combination of a remailer and encryption can be used to make messages even more secure.

There are a number of anonymous remailers (also called anonymous servers) around the world. There are a few remailers that have been in operation for a while, and there are new ones appearing and old ones dying all the time. There's a tendency for remailers to be short lived because there's no profit in them. An anonymous remailer allows mail to be sent to an individual, or to a newsgroup, and have the sender remain anonymous. With a couple of special exceptions (which we'll discuss in a minute), the sender information is discarded completely by the remailer, making it difficult to collect fees from a list of anonymous clients.

There are three classes of anonymous servers: the penet class, the cypherpunk class, and the mixmaster class. The classification of remailers is quite informal. The whole thing has such a short history and sites come and go so quickly, it's difficult to formalize anything. There is a new class of remailers just appearing that are constructed to work as Web pages. An example can be seen in Figure 21-1. Although these pages are simply front ends for existing anonymous remailer classes, they're very easy to use via a simple input form.

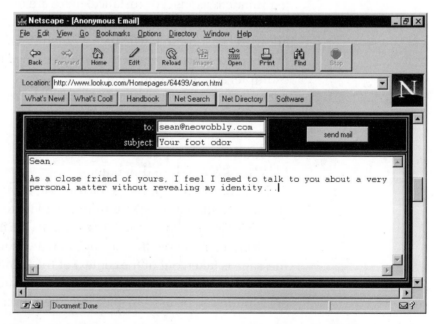

Figure 21-1: The no fuss/no muss anonymous remailer at Noah's Place.

The Penet Class

Anon.penet.fi is one of the oldest, most well known, and most-used anonymous servers. It's in a class all by itself. In 1995, it grew from 200,000 users to 500,000 users and the message traffic increased from 7,000 to 8,000 per day. Located in Finland, it was originally intended for use by Scandinavians, but it quickly became a worldwide service.

Anon.penet.fi keeps a database of users with a special ID for each one. Whenever a user sends mail to be forwarded, the sender's name is replaced with their ID and the sender's address is replaced with the address of anon.penet.fi. In the opposite direction, any mail arriving at anon.penet.fi that's addressed to one of the IDs in the database is readdressed and forwarded to the receiver with that ID. You can also assign yourself a password so that no one else can use your ID to send mail.

The service does have security holes. The addresses of all its users are kept in a database. There was one instance in early 1995 in which the Helsinki police raided the database and took one name and ID. The person was purportedly the member of a group that had used the anonymity for illegal purposes. The service does not use encryption, which is another security consideration. You can, of course, use your own encryption. If you don't, your plain text messages are open for perusal traveling to and from anon.penet.fi.

To subscribe to the service (that is, to get an ID), send a message to ping@anon.penet.fi. To get a copy of the current text file describing the service and how to use it, send a message to help@anon.penet.fi. The help file contains all the information you need to use the service. There is also an excellent Unofficial anon.penet.fi Web site (http://www.stack.urc.tue.nl/~galactus/ remailers/penet.html), which has lots of information and links covering all aspects of anonymity, privacy, and security. Figure 21-2 shows you the privacy page.

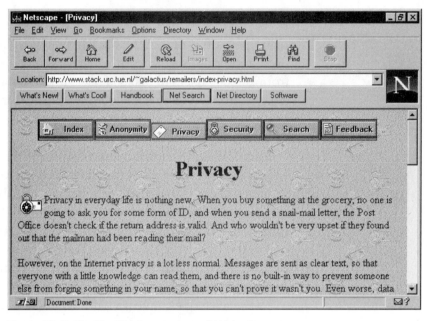

Figure 21-2: The Unofficial anon.penet.fi Web site.

The Cypherpunk Class

The largest of the cypherpunk class of remailers appears to be the alpha.c2.org server. This is a more secure server than anon.penet.fi. Whenever a message is sent through alpha.c2.org, it must begin with an encrypted reply block. The service then replaces the sender's address with its own and forwards the message to the recipient, original reply block included. Upon responding, the recipient includes the original reply block, which alpha.c2.org then decrypts to the original sender's actual address and forwards the mail to that address. This way, there are no files kept on the server, which means that not even the systems administrator can find the addresses.

There's one problem. The price paid for the higher level of security is reflected in the difficulty of use. You have to be able to do some fancy (and very specific) juggling to set up the encryption format part of the message. Fortunately, most of the difficulties come about when setting things up. Once you are up and running on the service, it's fairly easy to use. Getting yourself set up to use a cypherpunk remailer will certainly be educational and can approach becoming a hobby. With all of the crackers, hackers, and guys in trenchcoats playing cloak and dagger games on the Internet, boning up on encryption is not such a bad idea (see "Encryption" later in this chapter).

We won't attempt to describe the whole process here, but we will give you an idea of what has to be done and how the thing works. To set up an account, first you'll need to send for the instructions by sending a message to help@alpha.c2.org. Once you get the instructions, which includes the server's PGP public encryption key (see "PGP," later in the chapter), you will send the server a username, password, and an encrypted reply block. The name is, of course, any name you choose. The password is the one that will be used by the server to encrypt the alias before it's sent back to you. A reply block must be constructed by you. It is an encryption of your address with PGP, using the server's public key. Its exact format is in the instructions you receive from the server.

The Cypherpunks Home Page (http://www.csua.berkeley.edu/cypherpunks/ Home.html) contains links to rants, papers, articles about privacy and cryptography, a link to their FTP server, and pointers to other sites of interest, to name a few of its features (See Figure 21-3).

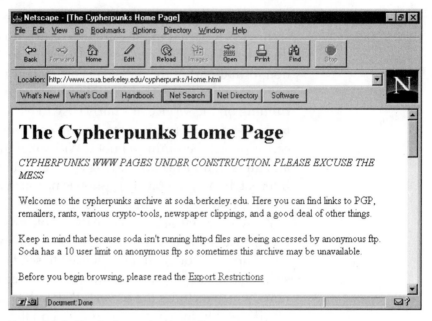

Figure 21-3: The Cypherpunks Home Page.

The Mixmaster Class

This is the cutting edge of high-tech anonymity. The mixmaster class of remailers uses the latest in security technology—software based on the cypherpunk software (so it has the security of that class)—but it's not nearly as difficult to use. There is a trade-off, however. Since the security comes from using a special message format, there is special software used to create the messages. The message-formatting software comes as compilable source code for UNIX (it does not run on PCs or Macs). You should be able to run this software from a shell account on almost any UNIX system. It has been verified on a number of platforms including SunOS, Solaris, Linux, and FreeBSD. The original release of mixmaster was in the summer of '95, so it is the newest of the three classes.

The software can be acquired from FTP at obscura.com in the directory /pub/readmail, or ftp.ipunix.com. There are some restrictions on the mixmaster software. The software uses cryptography that cannot be copied outside of the United States. There are some instructions about this at the FTP sites. The client software and the server software are one and the same. The system configuration determines which is which. A server is a bit more difficult to set up. The mixmaster software does not use PGP encryption; it uses the RSAREF package from RSA.

Here is a list of the mixmaster remailers. You can get an updated list via FTP at obscura.com/pub/no-export or on the World Wide Web at http://www.obscura.com/~loki/remailer/active.remailers.html. To get the mixmaster public encryption key for any of these remailers, just send mail to it with the subject remailer-key.

```
mixmaster@obscura.com
mixmaster@vishnu.alias.net
mixmaster@aldebaran.armory.com
robo@c2.org
syrinx@c2.org
remailer@replay.com
remailer@utopia.hacktic.nl
remailer@crynwr.com
remailer@spook.alias.net
remailer@flame.alias.net
remailer@armadillo.com
mixmaster@anon.alias.net
secret@secret.alias.net
mixmaster@remail.ecafe.org
anon@ad.org
remailer@shinobi.alias.net
amnesia@chardos.connix.co
q@c2.org
mixmaster@mix.precipice.com
```

ENCRYPTION

There has been data encryption since there's been communication. It almost seems to be instinctive. Grade school children invent ciphers to map the letters of the alphabet to numbers so they can write secret messages. Throughout history, nations have devised cyphers to hide information from one another. It all comes down to, "I know what it says, and you know what it says, but *they* don't know what it says." Encryption is simply the conversion of data from a commonly readable form into a form that is only readable by certain people.

In its most basic form, encryption is a combination of input data (the text to be encrypted) and an algorithm that is used for the encryption. Since the text will eventually need to be made useful again, there is also a decryption method that reverses the actions of the encryption. To make the encryption more secure, there can be a key included with the input text. The key is a value of some sort thrown into the mix. It works just like a key in the real world. If you don't have the key, you cannot "unlock" the message. This means that the one doing the decryption will need to know the decryption key.

There are three basic types of encryption; each has its own purposes. There is one way to encrypt that is not intended to be decrypted. It is ideal for things like passwords that just need to be encrypted and compared to that which was previously encrypted. There is single key (or conventional) encryption, which uses the same key to decrypt the data as it did to encrypt it. Finally, there is public key (or dual key) encryption, which uses one key to encrypt the data and a different key to decrypt it. Single key encryption is also called symmetric, and dual key encryption is called asymmetric.

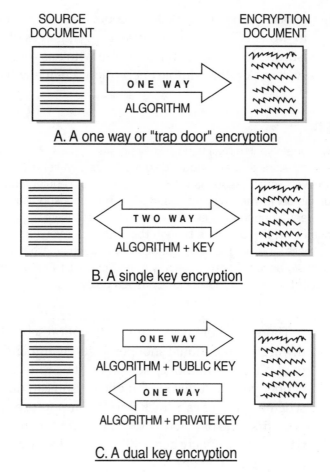

Figure 21-4: The three basic types of encryption.

Encrypting and decrypting can be a lot of work. Before you go to all that trouble, you need to make sure that it's necessary. If it is, you need to make sure that doing it doesn't become an onerous chore.

One valid reason for using encryption is to prevent information from being accidentally discovered. An unauthorized person can, through unforeseen circumstance, wind up with a copy of sensitive information. This doesn't require that the data be deeply encoded in some 500 character key-deep, hairy-legged encryption scheme. Something very simple would work. In this circumstance, nobody is trying it crack the code. Instead, a computer user wants to protect data from the possible prying eyes of a systems administrator, let's say, or someone else who has root-level access to the system. A rather simple encryption scheme will do the trick.

TIP

Remember: your e-mail is not really private. On a network, systems administrators and anyone with root access can read your mail. Moreover, your messages will often be part of regular, routine system backups performed by your sysadmin. These backup files can be and have been subpoenaed as evidence in lawsuits involving employee misconduct. If you feel as though the content of your mail is innocuous, there's nothing to worry about. If you care whether your mail is *potentially* accessible to others, you might want to consider using some of the privacy methods discussed below.

There are more heavy duty encryption schemes designed to thwart the intentional snooper. Just remember the code of the ol' west, "There ain't no horse that can't be rode, and there ain't a cypher you can't decode." If one person can devise an encryption scheme, another can crack it. Use computer security methods as your first line of defense. Of course, if you are going to transmit data across publicly accessible data links, you'll need to encrypt anything that is sensitive.

Can Encryption Be Illegal?

There is all sorts of legal wrangling going on over encryption. And, like most legal situations, the wrangling seems to continue to muddy the water and add to the confusion. The United States, which treats encryption technology as a weapon, has banned the exportation of encryption software. Since encryption is about communications, and since communications is now worldwide, the governments of several countries have gotten involved. Boris Yeltsin issued a formal decree in Russia banning non-government-approved encryption. In the United States, the Clinton administration has been trying to get legislation passed that would put encryption hardware, namely the Clipper Chip, into all communications devices and force everyone to use it so the government could decrypt anything it wanted to. Nongovernmental encryption is flat out illegal in France, Iran, Iraq, and several other countries.

TIP

There are sites on the Internet from which encryption software can be downloaded, and there are Usenet newsgroups for the discussion of encryption. Before accessing any data or software, you should check the laws in your country.

The exportation limitations in the U.S. have been a point of irritation for manufacturers and vendors. The United States export control policy categorizes certain encryption software and hardware as being "munitions-related" and subject to export laws under the Arms Export Control Act. This stuff requires licensing from the Office of Defense Trade Controls at the State Department and the Commerce Department. Export licensing requires a review from the National Security Agency. It has been found in the past that the approval time is greater than the life cycle of the software. Since encryption is built in to many software products, this ban has prohibited export of a lot of software from the United States.

In dual key encryption (one key to encrypt and one to decrypt), the United States government wants to have access to the decryption keys. There is legislation being considered that would require the decryption keys to be held in escrow by one or more government agencies, or possibly a private escrow company, so the government could get them if it wanted them. This would give the government the ability to decipher any transmitted messages it deemed suspicious.

Strong-Arm Tactics

The government's insistence on labeling certain crypto algorithms as unexportable munitions has gotten under some people's skin. In Richard White's case, it has *literally* gotten under his skin. The Los Angeles civil libertarian has had the RSA encryption algorithm tattooed onto his arm (see "RSA," later in this chapter). This officially makes him contraband, living ammo! No word yet if White plans on doing any international traveling soon or whether the Feds have plans to confiscate his arm if he does.

Encryption Programs

Cryptography is a large field. There are thousands of ciphers and hundreds of books written on the subject. It is a science that goes back thousands of years. What we are going to discuss in this chapter are the most current and popular encryption methods and programs. Our list is by no means exhaustive.

crypt

This is a standard encryption utility on UNIX systems. It is in common use and will do a fine job of the low-level, "convenience" type encryption. However, don't use it to try to hide your latest Doomsday weapon plans.

Crypt is one of the oldest encryption methods still being used today. It is a software implementation of the Enigma machine devised by the Germans in World War II. Methods of cracking it are quite well known. It is implemented as a simple command line utility that can quickly encrypt and decrypt disk files. All it needs is a file name and a password. The password is used as the key. It is a symmetric cipher (the same key is used for encryption and decryption). Crypt is known to UNIX text-editing software, and encrypted files can be both read and written by supplying the password to the editor. The crypt utility has one curious feature: it is designed to intentionally use much more CPU time than it really needs when it is doing decryption. When the systems administrator detects unusually heavy use, he or she will be alerted to the fact that someone is attempting to break into something.

DES (Data Encryption Standard)

The other common UNIX utility, DES, was released to the public in 1977, the same year it was established as a United States government standard. DES is a strong, private-key algorithm developed at IBM. It has been repeatedly recertified as a government standard and will remain certified until 1998. There's a good possibility that it won't be recertified after that. Too much is happening in the area of data security.

On UNIX, DES is implemented as a command line tool (called des) that works almost the same as crypt, but the encryption algorithm is a bit more robust. It is des that is used to encrypt the system passwords kept in the /etc/passwd file. It has a variable algorithm that, as yet, doesn't seem to have been broken. (Crackers have other ways of going after the password file). This is a single key, or symmetric system, just like crypt. Both sender and receiver of an encrypted message must know the same key. This single key also makes it handy for use in encrypting and decrypting files by a single person, since the same key is used going in and out.

RSA

RSA is named after its inventors, Rivest, Shamir, and Adelman. Along with DES, it is considered to be one of the most effective encryption algorithms on the market. RSA has become a very popular cryptosystem. It is an asymmetric system, meaning that it has public and private keys.

RSA is not normally a stand-alone encryption method. It is commonly used in conjunction with DES or some other secret key method. To use this dual method, the sender of a message would encrypt the body of the message with DES using an invented key. Then, the intended receiver's public key is used to encrypt the invented key. The two parts together form the message. The receiver uses his or her private key to decrypt the invented DES key, then the DES key is used to decrypt the body of the message.

Skip This. It's Math.

It is a mathematical fact that it is much easier to multiply two prime numbers together than it is to factor them back out. Much easier. Modern encryption methods, like RSA, take advantage of this fact. Choose a couple of prime numbers, p and q, and multiply them together to find the modulus n; that is n = pq. The larger the prime numbers, the better. Now choose another number, e, such that e is less than n and it is relatively prime to (p-1)(q-1). (Two numbers are relatively prime if they have no factors in common.) Find d, which is the inverse of e mod (p-1)(q-1). This means that ed = mod (p-1)(q-1).

Simple, eh? We now have e, which is the public exponent, and d, which is the private exponent. The public key is the pair (n,e). The private key is d. The two large prime numbers that were so hard to come by are now discarded since they could be used to break the cipher.

The prime numbers p and q should be about the same size. The larger they are, the more secure the encryption. Prime numbers can be hard to find, but it isn't because there is a shortage. If primes of 512 bits are used, you can select any two from a group of 10 to the 150th power, which is more atoms than there are in the known universe.

RSAREF

RSAREF is a collection of cryptographic routines in C source code available at no charge from RSA Labs. The code includes, among others, RSA, MD2, MD5, DES. This is a set of both low-level and high-level functions. Included are functions that will generate keys, encrypt, decrypt, operate on multiple precision integers (required for large keys), perform modular exponentiation, and execute verification of digital signatures.

RSAREF is free, but there is limited access. The code is only available to citizens and permanent residents of the United States. It is also limited to personal and noncommercial use. You can find out about all the capabilities and limitations at the FTP site rsa.com or by sending e-mail to rsaref@rsa.com.

The Zip family

The PKZIP utility is one of a family of programs used to compress files. The files can also be encrypted and decrypted while they are being compressed and decompressed. It is simply a matter of entering an encryption key (a password) during the compression process; the same key will be required for decompression. The PKZIP utility is a product of PKware. There is a shareware version for DOS, and a commercial version for DOS and Windows. There are several compatible programs in the ZIP/UNZIP family, such as Infozip.

PKZIP is a very popular utility that resides in one form or another on virtually every DOS and Windows computer. Internet FTP sites use this as a matter of course to compress files to be downloaded. Its primary purpose, however, is compression, not encryption. The encryption method has been broken and anything encrypted using any of the ZIP family of utilities can be decrypted in a matter of hours. It pretty much falls into that category of something that will "keep the honest people honest."

PKZIP is widely available on FTP sites, software libraries, and via online services like AOL and CompuServe.

Huffman Code

Like the ZIP family, Huffman Code is primarily a method of compression, but it can also be considered (and is sometimes used as) an encryption algorithm. It uses a type of encoding known as a "statistical code," since it operates on probabilities.

Huffman Code was designed to encode text, but can easily be extended to handle binary data as well. It works like this: A pass is made through the text to determine the number of occurrences of each character of text. Next, a code is assigned to each character found. To achieve compression, the shorter codes are assigned to the characters that occur the most often, and longer codes to the ones that are more rare. By looking up each character in the code table, the data is then rewritten as a string of these codes. The code table must be combined with the compressed data so the algorithm can be applied in reverse to decompress it. It is a simple matter for the encoder and decoder to use a standard table so that the table does not have to be included in the transmission of data.

As you can imagine, this is not the most secure code in the world. In the final analysis, it is only one step above A=1 and B=2. It can be handy for low-level security though, since it also does some compression.

TIP

Probably the most interesting Huffman code utility is the one found on the Web page http://www.cs.brown.edu/people/amd/java/ill/huffman.html. It is written in Java and operates interactively, demonstrating the steps taken by the algorithm to encode the text you enter.

SKIPJACK & the Clipper Chip

SKIPJACK is the classified encryption/decryption algorithm used in the Clinton administration's proposed Clipper Chip key escrow system. It uses an 80-bit key (as compared to the 56-bit key used in DES). It appears that, for now, Clipper is a dead (or at least dormant) issue.

Clipper is an algorithm in the SKIPJACK family. Clipper is only for voice and other low speed data, while other members of the SKIPJACK family, such as Tessera and Capstone, were designed for data encryption.

These methods were chosen by the NSA and NIST (National Institute for Standards and Technology) because it was assumed that commonly available computer-processing power doubles every eighteen months, making it 36 years before exhaustive search techniques could break a SKIPJACK encoded message in a reasonable time. Also, it was assumed that there was no significant risk of SKIPJACK being broken.

The United States government wanted to put this in place so they would be able to decrypt any message sent by anyone anywhere (telephone, video, digital data, whatever). The actual algorithm itself is classified and has never been released. Some selected individuals who were allowed a limited viewing declared the encryption as secure, but there was this nervous feeling in some quarters that the encryption algorithm has some sort of "back door" and could be decrypted without the key being taken out of escrow. One thing after another went wrong with Clipper. Each Clipper Chip encrypted message includes a LEAF (Law Enforcement Access Field) by which the key could be identified in escrow. Dr. Matt Blaze of Bell Labs discovered a way to create and insert a bogus LEAF that made the escrowed key value useless.

There was also the possibility that some sneaky citizen would simply encrypt with something else, say PGP, before passing their data through Clipper encryption, thus keeping the data encrypted even if the Feds used the key to unlock Clipper. After all of this, and not a small amount of protest from the Internet community, Clipper took on too much water and sank slowly out of sight.

PGP (Pretty Good Privacy)

PGP, created by Phil Zimmerman, is a very secure system for encrypting e-mail. It has successfully resisted even the most sophisticated forms of analysis. It is a public key encryption method, which means that there are two keys required. One key is used to encrypt the message, the other to decrypt it. This way, the encryption key can be published, or made public. Anyone wishing to send you a message simply uses your published key to encrypt the message, so that you're the only one who can decrypt it. Historically, one of the problems with ciphers has been that the 'bad guys' could get their hands on the key. With a public key system, the decryption key is never at risk because it never leaves home. Also, if the private key does become compromised, it is a simple matter publishing a brand new key to everyone who sends you messages.

```
-----BEGIN PGP PUBLIC KEY BLOCK-----
Version: 2.3

mQCPAizgA+EAAAEEAMzQAf9ff0q9tVD5oBxtV1PYAito4RBM+hJvX4irXzYgJWsA
Fhc4b/RfLcbGQVHwm0Q74cp/KhijXqGeLE2Tk62x04u1mjfBevoOHU1tOOWxrIbU
y6roslcThAzVL031kh6OHR3DbfUJW1d9WtmamGWFGHYvt1WSagSzG6zrQn1RABEB
AAG0G1h1bm9uIDxYZW5vbkBhbm9uLnB1bmVOLmZpPg===TNIL
-----END PGP PUBLIC KEY BLOCK-----
```

Figure 21-5: The Mac version of PGP.

PGP is actually a combination of two cryptographic algorithms: RSA (Rivest, Shamir, Adelman) and IDEA (International Data Encryption Algorithm). The text of the message to be transmitted is encrypted with the symmetric IDEA algorithm. The key used to encrypt the text (which is also the one that will decrypt it) is itself encrypted using RSA. The output resulting from these two encryptions are combined to make up the transmitted message.

There is another way to use PGP that has some pretty neat implications for the future, in business and in personal use. It is possible to have PGP add a "signature" to a document. It doesn't encrypt the document; it only adds a bunch of characters at the end of the document that can act as a signature. Actually, it is stronger than a signature on a piece of paper, since the document cannot be changed without a new signature being attached. PGP can be used to verify that the signature and the document match. If even one character of the document is changed, the verification of the signature will fail. This way, signed documents can be transmitted around the world and kept on computers instead of paper. It's better than a paper signature because a signature can't be forged without breaking the PGP encryption.

PGP is available free in the United States for noncommercial purposes. The free version is in so many places on the Net that there are two FAQs on the Internet; one for PGP itself, and the other just for the locations.

A commercial version for use inside the United States can be purchased from:

ViaCrypt
9033 North 24th Avenue, Suite 7
Phoenix, AZ 85021
http://www.viacrypt.com

It is also possible to get a commercial version for use outside the United States by contacting:

Erhard Widmer
Ascom Systec AG
Dep't. CMVV
Gewerbepark
CH-5506 Maegenwil
Switzerland
IDEA@ascom.ch

PEM & RIPEM

RIPEM (Riordan's Internet Privacy Enhanced Mail) is an implementation of PEM (Privacy Enhanced Mail). PEM is a standard for transmitting encrypted e-mail. It uses RSA, so it's considered "munitions" quality encryption and cannot be exported outside the United States and Canada.

RIPEM is available via FTP to citizens and permanent residents in the United States at ripem.msu.edu. Look in the pub/crypt directory, where you'll see a file named GETTING_ACCESS that will explain what to do next. The RIPEM implementation of PEM runs on several platforms, including MS DOS, Macintosh, OS/2, and Windows NT, and has been shown to work on over 15 UNIX systems. RIPEM can be configured to work directly inside many popular mailers. If there is not an interface for your particular mailer, you can create one.

```
-----BEGIN PRIVACY-ENHANCED MESSAGE-----
Proc-Type: 2001,ENCRYPTED
Content-Domain: RFC822
DEK-Info: DES-CBC,2CFB5B1671A4BB20
Originator-Name: gareth
Originator-Key-Asymmetric:
 MFkwCgYEVQgBAQICAgADSwAwSAJBALGFCbQQ9ZtPmCgMeh7Zj24Y62/UL4TzPJlj
 hVWdNekwk07uzrO8bLULjynbn7QXnhQpda0XWe9wz2S9onP3T+ECAwEAAQ==
Key-Info: RSA,
 oCHndajjXeqfHi94FKb6kBfzakgnzaKqop6EVeOHP3F5B8A70YcrOGAWwNzKHE33
 IvPhzbvdfHtZDMd93iJ3ZA==
MIC-Info: RSA-MD5,RSA,
 AUIQn79tEN2auAYFzA1ppZ4JEMje6ND+u6Sv4jMqZ/xthJXs176W1G3rfbB89K7F
 3brXChO3R1dk1NK+wEnxcDK1NyhCN4U+
Recipient-Name: gareth
Key-Info: RSA,
 oCHndajjXeqfHi94FKb6kBfzakgnzaKqop6EVeOHP3F5B8A70YcrOGAWwNzKHE33
 IvPhzbvdfHtZDMd93iJ3ZA==

8fWHNanDACbZ11PQ3Y9kQ/5R5ROWC1x6dCPOmZBk9Cqu6Ktb3qWT4bebcoBvZNQF
xHhyOAWis3t9aLY4DIRY2ipUdvYQl8zWM1ybpXd/o3eFu6YedUi9kghFS68Y7qYD
PngMJc/5bUn09YluqHQw+5kGcOdiwaSZ6nX0Byz2irAPDjiXf3UqvjIxZoXFpqvX
EAUTRfzpG4WtWzSM1T1Oy2vQ5eFr1fJGIF6/8eQ8WrDfBNIGm1W1X++vgMpOicEq
7VFJek7ecGrL9jIkvwvf48MP95/dxQ6iJ9aajV4sdXe3ZF9wqk1SxjQCMidscroV
SdmEV5cKczV8qeXFRJ6YcCQok87JmZDNxut/JZE7IOVXRe6vzI7Qfx68gH65/9S1
/DAPG4EJpkH4Wqc+1rHdhESH5XuEFehyYI3jV1+XxTKPAaX9+d3Ce9SmX+9e8R1c
Lc8U2qRkSmMBe7eFz5iMKM6ciC6R8BBGFiyYCWrfx1YPABxrEL44IbXUuBJkybnY
FqFbuXHwHCIsCbK6/OtjLfGnOs/P5MJZ3ig9d1xKDVV5P1NzjibLViHokF+vFaJz
i4eisGBhqnMyKA5JCxYhiSOEG/L1H4sdklgv5HaZ+gGDQ2kXpFF9Sf0KodEmcRer
OAc9oJe1T9teOExFhHfQMzYYt8rYoi8HGuo4MMBG/OJg+tALJr6AS46hh/Spgp3D
x/Wur41Uqpp6MheNexL4LweYftjlnqScDXeQUhQl4xW4LKwssao2HsNoSBR/RuaJ
Z41FZq/LfugUA78Su4E/tc9xrc2YUhDrCANRTwM+BWu+5E8LdfgibTp/Av1BxWYv
pxCwSXiGWHz9Px4BdcrHGqy4sxyiTC6zmV2rQ+z1fThAuDOCvRqKTUNpW+1L/cHk
Z9zzgtFn3OV9nNEcJR/oRpbuj5SOnIFH4ObTgP9yIpeR9NyvKn1XYNrxAzvHrV1M
```

```
kWQg5nn5iaPHMqR6CyRcZFnSxzRdBSfE/aQLWRKg61/rqqodhNRLBmWzxIrZ9wsV
ORgjYg4iDsxkJjsB81i+z2Ec+dsEB+Xh1ndOuRjZorb/PvbtMTZyksvF66cbLZir
hBfkusCg5T/k3B+tpqlXDxu+cbsvV/t2YjNUYeDS59SY30eY30HmiKt1RvTsRZI2
halnrqNcVrvU4Lc3Grju/IQQ/qeHyNihJlE4ppOTEUaSI7HENyfUzROfRjW8T34v
1xILXTT2H6SrmPKSAQRxBK1GADkUWPW7gRcDz9sBFWZHA33fCe+ISsQ/jGc302Vw
opQuaqnuZBT22bXiZc8mD252cLOdBvei/fr8EzM1HMHYMVXnSRBgSgjfvVAwLNUQ
mA7QEE2aL8K4v6jOhIpzqg4ntcMFtVj4kIAy9uC95SO3iEHLO4sum95aSShuNYaS
nN6zbOrk3/HifJ4HW8SQdnLr78Dd+EkYeUWfOO+/xPdvxyaSP5YAZPitvId5d4ic
-----END PRIVACY-ENHANCED MESSAGE-----
Created with RIPEM Mac.
```

Figure 21-6: RSA's RIPEM program.

MD (Message Digest)

This is a family of three functions designed specifically for cryptographic use. There are three versions: MD2, MD4, and MD5. There has been some theoretical work done on methods for MD, but there's no known attack other that "brute force." The rule of thumb for encryption is that speed of operation and level of security have an inverse relation. In other words, the quicker the encryption, the less secure the result. MD2 is the slowest to encrypt and decrypt; MD4 is the fastest. MD5 is functionally similar to MD4 except that it has added safety features and a more conservative design, which makes it slower.

MD is used for signature and document validation. It uses something called a "hash function," which takes a variable length message and returns a fixed length string. The string is called the "hash value." This is a one-way activity in that there is no decryption method. It's used as a validation method, since the input will generate exactly the same output. If the output is different, the input was different.

All three types of MD are publicly available for unrestricted use. You can find complete and detailed descriptions along with sample C programs in RFC 1319, 1320, and 1321.

SHS (Secure Hash Standard)

This is a hash function and is a United States government standard that was proposed by the NIST. It is intended to be part of the DSS (Digital Signature Standard). DSS is similar to MD5, but since it produces a larger hash value, its security potential is greater.

Kerberos

Kerberos is a secret key network authentication system developed at MIT. It uses DES for encryption and authentication. It's set up to provide real-time authentication of requests for network resources. It can be used to generate keys for a single session so that two parties can communicate privately.

Kerberos runs on a designated server on a LAN or intranet. The server handles all the key services from a single centralized location, using a database of all the keys and usernames. This means that there must be trust in the security of the server since, if it were compromised, its secret would be revealed. However, setting up Kerberos so that it can be easily used makes it functional for folks who need only a low-level security encryption method.

There is a version of Kerberos that is not secure. A flaw has been discovered in the random number generator of version 4 of the server. It allows an intruder to open the database of names and keywords in a matter of seconds. The release of version 5 has fixed the problem; now this sort of break-in would require a brute force attack against DES encryption. Since Kerberos 4 has been freely available on the Internet for several years, there are a number of locations still using it. If you are on version 4, it is important that you switch to version 5.

In Figure 21-7, you will see the Cygnus Network Security page, one of several locations offering information on Kerberos and how to acquire the patch to move from version 4 to version 5:

```
http://www.cygnus.com
http://www.transarc.com
```

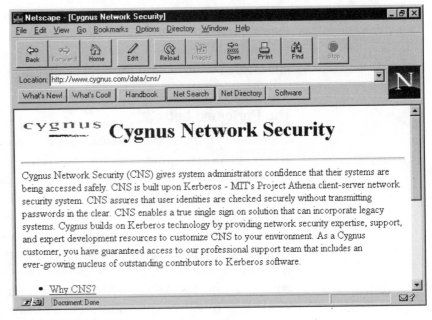

Figure 21-7: Cygnus's Network Security page.

RC2 & RC4

RC2 and RC4 are two ciphers that are functional alternatives to DES. They have a variable length key. Use of the shorter keys renders an encryption that is less secure than DES, but a longer key can make the results more secure than DES. These algorithms are proprietary to RSA Data Security Inc. Several of the RSA Data Security packages are being used in commercial products such as Novell's Netware and PowerTalk from Macintosh. It is also going to be used by Visa and Mastercard for their SET (Secure Electronic Security) system.

There is an agreement between the Software Publishers Association (SPA) and the United States government that gives RC2 and RC4 a special status. The export approval process is simpler and quicker than normal. To be approved for export, the software must limit the size of the key to 40 bits. There can be 56 bits for foreign subsidiaries and overseas offices of United States companies. There can be another 40-bit "salt" value extension to the key thrown in to help thwart a brute force decryption. The salt value is then sent, unencrypted, with the message. This has become popular with software companies wishing to export, since it has some fair level of security and the approval cycle is short.

The Purloined Letter

There are still methods of sending secret messages that are quick and easy. All it requires is a little ingenuity. If the transmitted data doesn't look like it has a secret message embedded in it, it could slip through the fingers of a code cracker with only a glance.

Remember the invisible ink of your childhood? You would use lemon juice to write an invisible message between the lines of some innocuous text and the message would appear only after the paper was heated. The only reason the message was secure was that nobody know it was there. This same sort of thing happened in World War II with the microdot—the message was hidden as periods and commas used as punctuation. In the short story, "The Purloined Letter," by Edgar Allen Poe, a very valuable letter is spirited away by some miscreant. As it turns out, though, the thief had secreted it in plain view amongst a batch of other correspondence on the desk. The whole trick is to make the message not look like a message. The message is not the medium; it is the algorithm.

Take for example a large graphic or an audio clip. Setting the least significant bits to the value required to contain a message would have almost no effect on the displayability or listenability of the data. Since you can get one bit per byte, it wouldn't take a very large multimedia file to hold a sizable message. Of course, the message could be zipped, packed, and tarred and then written backwards. It could even be encrypted first. But the security of the message would primarily come from the fact that no one knows it's there.

This type of cryptography is called steganography (the art of hiding signals inside of signals). There are a number of steganographic programs (such as Stego, Hide and Seek, and StegoDOS). They can all be accessed via the Steganography page at http://www.stack.urc.tue.nl/~galactus/remailers/index-stego.html. See Figure 21-8.

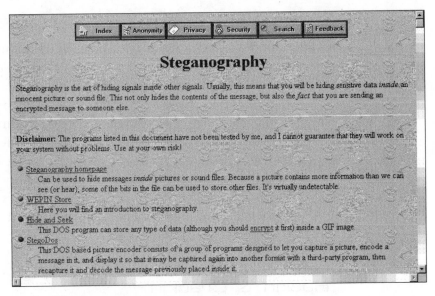

Figure 21-8: The Steganography Web page.

Gone But Not Forgotten

If they're dastardly enough, other people in your office, or others with access to your PC, can perform "undeletes" in the directories on your PC and read the text of mail messages or other files you thought were long gone. On a UNIX machine, this is not as big a threat because the file system is very dynamic. It is conceivable that a file could be recovered after having been deleted, but the odds are against it. The disk space that was the deleted file could be used immediately by some process running in the background that needs a bit of workspace or gets a data block swapped out to disk. On a DOS/Windows or Mac machine, it is very easy to retrieve deleted files. Deleting a file simply marks it as deleted in the directory. If you don't want people reading your deleted mail messages and other files on your machine, you can use a program like Norton Utilities (for both Mac and Windows) to remove all traces of the deleted files from your drive.

PRIVACY & SECURITY CRACKS

All networked systems have holes in them through which unscrupulous, uninvited intruders can slip. The FBI estimates that $7.5 billion is lost annually to electronic attack. The *Wall Street Journal* reported that a Russian cracker successfully breached a large number of Citicorp corporate accounts, stealing $400,000 and illegally transferring another $11.6 million. Here's a very sobering statistic: the Department of Defense says that in 96 percent of the cases where the crackers got in, they went undetected. Hey wait, if they went undetected, how did they know it was 96 percent? Suffice it to say, this poses a significant threat to our increasingly interconnected digital society.

Hackin' & Crackin'

There was once a time when a person who was knowledgeable about programming and worked down at the bit and byte level of computers was called a "hacker." Those who broke into systems, stole data, or destroyed property were called "crackers." The hackers were the good guys and crackers were the bad guys. Somehow, the words hacker and cracker were eventually joined. They probably sound enough alike that the press got them confused. Anyway, the bad guys are now often called hackers and crackers interchangeably. What's left for the good guys? Do we just call them nerds?

If you want to delve into the world of hacking and cracking (and the debate over which is which), there's a notorious magazine called Phrack. It can be found online (where else?) at a number of FTP sites and at http://www.fc.net/phrack/. 2600: The Hacker's Journal is another long-standing print zine dedicated to hacking/cracking and phone hacking (or "phreaking"). It has an active (high noise) newsgroup called alt.2600.

If you know what the holes are in your system, there are things you can do to plug them up. Since most holes appear along with desirable functionality, most of the plugs are some sort of compromise between a level of safety and a level of utility. The only way to be absolutely certain that an unwanted intruder never gets into your system is to cut its wire to the outside world. Those that communicate over a dial-up link are the safest because they are usually offline.

TIP

There is one very important thing you can do for security. In fact, this could turn out to be the most important thing you do to keep your system safe. Keep in touch with your service provider on security issues. These days, everybody has a Web page where they post information, so it has gotten to be very easy to make sure you have the most current information. Service providers and Net software vendors track system break-ins and (usually) keep their customers informed of problems. If you find holes in a system you are using, report them to the ISP or vendor. Remember, at the same time you're reading about a method of corking the bottle, there's a cracker reading a description of how to uncork it.

Holes in a Loosely Connected System

If you are operating a loosely connected system (for example, a PPP or SLIP connection with an ISP), there's virtually no way crackers can get directly to you. You simply don't have the facilities available for them to get in and monkey with stuff. You're not completely immune to danger, however.

One principal source of danger is the fact that your e-mail must pass over the Internet to get to its recipient. About all you can do is encrypt (as we talked about earlier in this chapter), since you have no control over where anything goes once you let it out of its PC cage. It's sort of like a tomcat. E-mail can wander around anywhere before it gets home, and you don't know what sort of adventures it may have had. Encrypting is sort of like having the cat neutered. It can go wherever it wants, but it's not going to get itself into trouble.

You must also consider the danger of downloading files containing a virus. We seem to be adding new viruses at the rate of three or four a day. The best method to avoid viruses is to only obtain files from sites that you suspect to be very clean, and to run a virus scan on the files once you receive them.

A single user dial-up system is under such complete control of the person at the helm, there's little that can go wrong if you take simple precautions. If you recognize the fact that your e-mail can be read and that you can contract a virus, and you take precautions, you should be fine. It's your service provider (or sysadmin on a LAN/WAN) that has all the real security worries.

Network Security Tools

The following section covers some of the software that systems administrators use to keep networks secure and to track down unwanted intruders. While you may not be directly involved in the security of the networks you use, we thought you might benefit from a brief discussion of some of the security issues that keep your systems administrator up at night. If some of the preceding material has already made your eyes glaze over and your palms sweat, you might want to skip over this section.

Packet Sniffing

Packet sniffers are handy dandy little TCP/IP debugging utilities that can monitor the traffic being sent over a network. They are intended to be used by systems administrators to tune and debug networks. But, like guns, they can be turned on the wrong target and used for evil purpose. You know the saying, "It's not sniffers that kill datagrams; it's people that kill datagrams."

A sniffer is a program that sits in a computer and reads all the packets that pass by on the network. Usually the TCP/IP stack ignores any packets or datagrams not addressed to it (or to some other address through it), but a sniffer reads all packets by changing the mode of operation of the TCP/IP stack. A computer that is configured to read all packets is said to be "promiscuous." On a local network, account and password information are passed around in the clear, so a sniffer can pick it up and read it directly.

Sniffers are very popular with crackers. You can see why. A sniffer installed on a system will gather every password and username that's used throughout the time it is installed. This could include the root password for several different systems.

The question is, how can one determine whether or not there's a sniffer running? If a sniffer is only collecting data and not reporting, it is necessary to go around to each machine and make a direct physical check. Whenever a sniffer is being executed, it puts the TCP/IP stack into promiscuous mode. This is so it will accept all the packets and acquire data from the entire network. It is possible to run a sniffer in non-promiscuous mode, but only the traffic in and out of the one host will be captured.

The sniffer sits there logging information to a file that the cracker will come back to and pick up later. If there is a lot of traffic on the network, the log file can swell and fill up the file system, thus shutting down the host and alerting the computer security person.

It is possible to use encryption to thwart sniffing. There are software packages that encrypt the data that passes over a LAN. This will prevent a sniffer from making heads or tails of it. Intruders can still get at the data, but it is of no use to them. During periods when the systems administrator is analyzing the system, the encryption can be disabled so the sysadmin's sniffer can gather useful information. Under normal circumstances, the data is encrypted.

TIP

If you FTP, Telnet, or rlogin across an insecure network, your password has traveled in clear text over communication links that could be littered with sniffers. Change your password as soon as possible after one of these remote jaunts.

Running finger

Outsiders can discover login names if the finger daemon is running. A finger command in the form "finger @host.domain" could return a login name that could subsequently become the target of a password attack. This opening can be closed in the /etc/inetd.conf file by specifying the host names that are allowed access to the finger daemon.

Trojan Horses

A cracker can get in and out of your system very quickly. If successful, they may leave some Trojan horse programs. These are programs that have the same name as some standard utility and work pretty much the same, but have some other features that benefit only the cracker. Examples of commonly replaced programs are sh, ksh, telnet, rlogin, and ifconfig. Things seem to be working OK, but they are really slowly turning toward the cracker.

- -

TIP

Besides Trojan horses, there is an amazing amount of "volunteer" damage that can be done by innocent users adhering to requests that come in the form of administrative e-mail. Things like, "This is the systems administrator. Please temporarily remove your password so I can check your files for bad sectors" or "Please make your local disk sharable so I can run a thorough disk scan tonight." There are cases where the intruder coaxes the user to inflict damage with messages such as "Look for a file named c:\windows\system.ini. If you have this file on your system, delete it." Just because you get a message that says it comes from a systems administrator or other person of authority does not mean it's legitimate. If in doubt, e-mail or call your sysadmin/ISP and ask them to verify the request.

- -

COPS (Computer Oracle Password & Security)

This is a UNIX utility that will scan your system and check for the kinds of security leaks that occasionally will open up during the regular activities of your systems administration. It will also catch a few holes that regular users can open up. It will scan for spots of possible trouble and report them; it doesn't fix them. It can be run manually, but it is best if it is set up so that it will run automatically at regular intervals and catch the holes that accidentally open up. It is very simple to use. It has minimal configuration settings and no command line arguments whatsoever; just run it and it generates a listing of everything it can find that looks the least bit funny.

It checks the access permissions on files, directories and devices. It checks the /etc/passwd and /etc/group files for passwords that are not set properly. It checks the /etc/hosts.equiv file for an opening that would allow someone on another host to override the security on this host. It checks the .rhosts files in each user's home directory since there are settings that can allow anyone onto the system. It checks the UUCP settings since it is possible, among other things, to copy executable programs from remote computers and execute them locally.

It will almost certainly report conditions that are really not a problem on your system. The sysadmin will simply scan its output and make sure that all the things it complains about are things that are not a problem. For example, COPS reporting that the /etc/motd (message of the day) is writable may not be a concern—it could be that it's meant to be used that way. However, things such as missing passwords will almost certainly be a problem.

COPS can be acquired via FTP from any number of sites. The file is normally named cops.tar.Z and contains the full make instructions. Once compiled, it is just a matter of modifying the COPS shell script and setting it up so that it includes the address of the person to whom the report should be mailed.

Could it be...SATAN?

The Systems Administrator's Tool for Analyzing Networks (SATAN) arrived on the Internet on April 5, 1995, at 14:00 GMT. He appeared in a swirl of publicity (both on the Internet and off) about how this evil program was going to be used by all sorts of sneaky and unprincipled people to perform unspeakable acts on computer hosts all over the world. Much to the doomsayer's chagrin, none of the bad stuff happened. What *did* happen was that systems administrators all over the world grabbed a copy of SATAN and used it to find the weak spots in their own defenses. Computer manufacturers (some of which had prior access to SATAN and thus were forearmed) issued bulletins containing patches to be inserted and procedures to be taken to make their systems more secure. The end result of all this: there have been fewer computer break-ins, not more, since SATAN tooled onto the information highway.

SATAN is software that finds holes in the security settings of a computer and then reports those holes. SATAN doesn't run on a PC or a Mac unless you're running some version of UNIX. SATAN is a World Wide Web-based tool that can be set up to gather information about hosts over the network. Along with the report it issues on the security holes, there is a brief tutorial on just what type of problems the hole can cause and what sort of workarounds could be used to close it up. SATAN speaks perl. If you come up with something that is peculiar to your installation and you would like to add it to SATAN, it can be done with a perl script.

There is a primary FTP site for SATAN:

```
ftp.win.tue.nl/pub/security
```

Security Resources

If security is an issue in your situation, you should subscribe to a Net security journal like RISKS Digest (http://catless.ncl.ac.uk/Risks/) and look into security topics at your ISP, Usenet Newsgroup, or BBS for the latest on known holes and security breaches. Usenet groups discussing security and encryption include:

```
comp.risks
comp.security.announce
comp.security.misc
comp.security.unix
alt.security.pgp
alt.security.keydist
```

"Prince Albert" in Cyberspace

A lot of computer break-ins, e-mail intrusions, and phony Net identities are little more than sophisticated, digital age versions of the phone pranks of our youth. Remember making prank calls when you were a kid, asking questions of store owners such as "Do you have Prince Albert in a can?" An affirmative response was rewarded with "Well, you better go let him out!" followed by lots of twittering and knee slapping. These escalated to "Good afternoon ma'am. This is the phone company. We're having a bit of trouble with the lines out your way and need to clear them. Could you please leave your phone off the hook and put it in a paper bag while we blow the dust out from this end? Thank you." Then, more vicious twists developed: "Good afternoon sir. This is the telephone company, and we're going to have to make some minor adjustments to your equipment. This is going to cost you $35 if we do it, or you could do it yourself if you'd like. Really? OK, you'll need a pair of scissors and a screw driver. I'll wait, yes. OK, turn your telephone over and remove the four screws in the corners and take the bottom plate off. Good. Now, the little red wire next to the brass name plate. Yes, that's the one. Cut it." Dial tone. More sinister laughter.

As wily teens have become more and more knowledgeable about computers and the inner workings of the phone system, these pranks have now become highly sophisticated. And, as our society (and the planet) becomes increasingly wired into one grid, these kids can potentially cause big problems, especially if they have malicious intent. The good news is that Net citizens are becoming more aware of these tricksters and, hopefully, are using more good sense online. Computer security types are constantly working on new ways to secure systems so that they'll be virtually impenetrable . . . at least for awhile.

MOVING ON

Well, we've covered a lot of ground and taken a few forays into deep geekdom along the way. Hopefully, you're still with us. The important thing to consider when you start using programs like encryption and remailers is not to be intimidated by them. We did our best here to make these concepts clear to the intermediate user while at the same time offering some meat and potatoes to more seasoned Net vets. If you're curious about cryptography programs like PGP and RIPEM, don't hesitate to download them and give them a try. Once you get the basic key concepts down and learn how to encrypt and decrypt messages, they're really not that hard to use.

In Part VI, we'll take a closer look at Usenet news, how it works, and how you can make the most if it, regardless of whether you're using a Mac or Windows newsreader or accessing news from your shell account. We'll also look at binary files posted to newsgroups, how to make and post them, and how to best decode and view them.

## Part VI

The Power User's Guide to Usenet News

Chapter 22

Inside Usenet News

If you've spent any amount of time on the Net, you've probably at least dabbled with Usenet news. Perhaps you're the wallflower type, lurking around a few newsgroups, reading articles posted by others, but not saying anything yourself. Or maybe you're a real chatterbox, diving right into the fray, posting with abandon.

But what exactly *is* Usenet? The easiest answer is that it's a global bulletin board system, organized by topics and domains of interest (such as science, computers and sports). It's a great place to ask questions, get answers, and be enlightened, enraged, and entertained by the zillions of viewpoints you encounter. So, how does the news you read get to you, anyway? How do the articles you post get out to everyone else? And what the heck does all that stuff at the top of the articles you read (the "header") mean? Fear not, inquisitive friend! That's why we're here.

In this chapter, we'll look behind the scenes of Usenet, moving past the curtain of familiarity to the messy backstage areas of servers, distribution, nodes, backbones, and all the other infrastructure that makes Usenet work. We hope that, in understanding more about the inner workings of Usenet, you'll learn how to use it better, and how to deal with the quirks and idiosyncrasies that come up now and again.

WHAT IS USENET?

The first thing to clear up before discussing Usenet is that it's *not* the Internet. Usenet is a completely separate system of news servers that may use the Internet to transfer articles (though they don't have to) and that run completely independently from the rest of the Internet. Usenet is probably the last bastion of old-time Net anarchy, and has been the one aspect of online life that's resisted the commercialization and control the rest of the Net is starting to come under as it moves into the mainstream.

In a nutshell, Usenet is a global system for distributing discussions on various topics. Ideally, each topic that people want to talk about is segregated to its own area called a newsgroup, a collection of articles on a similar subject. In practice, articles don't always stay exactly on topic, but generally, you can expect the articles in a particular area to stick more or less to the topic the newsgroup's devoted to.

No one owns Usenet. Instead, Usenet exists because systems administrators all over the world agree to use a similar type of software and to voluntarily set aside part of their servers for storing and forwarding the flood of information coming over the wires (approximately 150 megabytes a day!). When you post an article, it goes into a spool area where it's stored until the server "calls up" another server it's connected to, passes off the stored articles, and receives any new articles. All this happens automatically at predetermined intervals, and can use any number of networks, from the Internet TCP/IP network to UUCP modem connections. In this way, articles propagate out from each server, passing from machine to machine until they've gone out to everyone on the Net. (More details on this process later.)

As it stands today, Usenet exists as a global anarchy, with no governing board overseeing its usage, content, or direction. Not that there haven't been attempts to control Usenet—the current Telecommunications Decency Act is the latest of what are sure to become many attempts by governments worldwide to stem the free flow of information and information deemed harmful to society.

Germany, China & the United States Try to Tame Usenet

In early 1996, German officials tried to shut off several "objectionable" newsgroups offered by CompuServe. Not realizing that the newsgroups in question were not the property of a single service provider, these government officials gave CompuServe the order to stop providing these newsgroups (mainly sex-oriented newsgroups) to German citizens. Initially, CompuServe complied, and the outrage could be heard all over the Net.

But then something interesting happened. Taking advantage of the global nature of Usenet, advocates for free speech began making these newsgroups available through alternative channels, effectively circumventing the German attempts at censorship. Eventually, the powers that be got the point, and CompuServe was able to reinstate the groups with a promise to provide more effective "parental controls."

What's the big lesson from this incident? Mainly that it's impossible for any one government or group to bend Usenet (or the rest of the Net, for that matter) to its will. As cybervisionary John Gillmore so succinctly put it, "The Net interprets censorship as damage and routes around it." The Net is so ubiquitous now that any attempts at plugging the flow of information will result in that information merely shifting around the blockage.

The biggest test of this principle is yet to come. The Chinese government, frightened of the effects their subjects might suffer from outside information, have endeavored to construct a "content firewall" around their country to filter out subversive ideas, making it a crime punishable by death to have your own connection to the outside Internet. In the United States, a few legislators (with little or no Internet experience) have tried to pass laws to make the transmission of "indecent" ideas over the Internet a federal crime. We need to make sure that our legitimate concern for the protection of our children does not lead to the suppression of free speech and the abdication of our responsibility as parents.

A BRIEF HISTORY OF USENET

Usenet as we know it today is the product of the Netnews software written by Tom Truscott and James Ellis in 1979 at Duke University. Devised as a way to share information between Duke and neighboring University of North Carolina, the first Usenet programs were merely scripts to pass groups of files back and forth between the two schools. The system became so popular that by 1980, Truscott and Ellis released Netnews Release A, the first system providing wide-spread distribution of articles.

The big breakthrough of Netnews Release A was that not only did it provide a system for moving files around, but it also provided a front end for people to use to read and post articles. Originally, the system had been devised to pass articles back and forth between members of the USENIX Association (a UNIX user's group). Hence, the system became known as Usenet.

Mirroring the early developments in e-mail, people soon began to realize that the system could be used for more than just official discussions. Soon, unofficial interest groups began to become incorporated into the official news server, and by 1982 the system had spread so far and become so popular that new software had to be devised to handle the load. Matthew Glickman and Mark Horton (two users at U.C. Berkeley) took matters into their own hands and developed Netnews Release B. Release B was a major overhaul, including features for adding newsgroup topics and wider distribution.

Release B is obsolete now. These days, most systems are using a variant of Release C or its successor INN (InterNet News). While it'd be almost impossible to get an exact count of Usenet sites worldwide, the number is currently over 250,000, with tens of millions of users. Usenet's come a long way from when it just passed user group info between two schools in North Carolina!

What Usenet Isn't

Chip Salzenberg, the author of "What is Usenet," one of the best overviews of Usenet, provides a wonderful explanation of what Usenet is by giving 13 examples of what Usenet isn't. Here is his list, abridged and annotated by your humble authors. If you want to read the full text, go to http://www.cis.ohio-state.edu/hypertext/faq/usenet/what-is/part1/faq.html.

1. Usenet is not an organization.
   No single organization has control of Usenet. Anyone who can convince a neighboring site to allow it to connect can be on Usenet.

2. Usenet is not a democracy.
   If things go wrong for you, figure it out yourself. There's no board of appeals.

3. Usenet is not fair.
   If you don't like what someone is doing on a newsgroup, put them in your kill file and ignore them. If you don't like it, move on. No one's holding a gun to your head.

4. Usenet is not a right.
   Whoever owns the hardware owns the newsfeed. Don't like which groups your ISP carries? Find another provider. Can't find another provider? Run your own news server.

5. Usenet is not a public utility.
   There is no government control and can be no government control. Now it's up to the governments of the world to realize this.

6. Usenet is not an academic network.
   In the old days, Usenet (and the rest of the Internet for that matter) mainly connected universities. Those days are over.

7. Usenet is not an advertising medium.
   We're not so sure we can still agree with this one. With the explosive growth of the Net has come an explosive growth in advertising spam on Usenet groups. However, because people can respond to these articles in a way they can't with junk mail (and do!), much of this advertising has little positive impact for the advertisers.

8. Usenet is not the Internet.
   Many parts of Usenet do propagate themselves over the Internet. Many use other networks.

9. Usenet is not a UUCP network.
   In the past, many sites did use UUCP for transmitting Usenet articles, and many still do. But Usenet isn't only UUCP.

10. Usenet is not a United States Network.
    Over 50 percent of all the people online in the world are outside of the United States. Even though it seems like the U.S. dominates Usenet, this domination will change over the coming years as more of the world comes online.

11. Usenet is not a UNIX network.
    Usenet started as a UNIX network, but today people are using Windows, Macintoshes, DOS, and even Amigas to run news spools.

12. Usenet is not an ASCII network.
    A lot of the world doesn't use Roman characters. Usenet allows people to post and read articles in their own alphabets (provided they use the right software).

13. Usenet is not software.
    No one program, protocol, or service can be used to define Usenet. It's a system that has truly become more than the sum of its parts.

HOW DO THE ARTICLES GET AROUND?

So we know now that Usenet is a system for transmitting distributed discussion groups. So what does that mean? In this section we'll look at nodes (the interconnected computers that make up Usenet) and propagation (how messages get distributed through the network).

Nodes: Backbones, Intermediate Sites & Leaves

Like the Internet, Usenet is a system of interconnected computers. These computers are interconnected as nodes in the larger network—each Usenet computer or node is connected to one or more other nodes. The designation of each computer on the network depends on how many other nodes it does business with.

Basically, Usenet nodes can be divided into three distinct groups (see Figure 22-1):

❏ Backbone sites

❏ Intermediate sites

❏ Leaf nodes

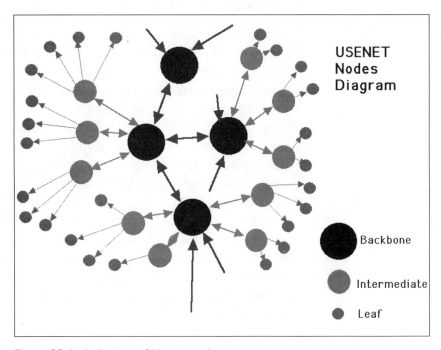

Figure 22-1: A diagram of Usenet nodes.

Backbones

Since no official designating body for Usenet exists, there is some crossover between group definitions, particularly between backbone and intermediate sites. However, for a site to be generally classified as a backbone, it must meet a number of criteria:

1. A backbone must be sufficiently powerful and well connected to be able to gather news that's been posted from several different nearby sites.

2. To qualify as a backbone site, a site must receive and distribute news from at least two other backbone sites.

3. It must be able to forward news coming in from its surrounding region of interconnected computers to at least two other backbone sites.

4. Backbones must be able to pass all the news it receives to all the local sites that ask for it.

If any organization can come close to having any sort of ultimate control over Usenet, it's a backbone site. If a backbone decides not to carry a specific newsgroup or decides to start filtering based on content, it can effectively restrict access to that material to hundreds if not thousands of computers that use that backbone for their newsfeeds. Of course, those sites can choose another backbone, so this isn't usually a problem.

Generally, backbone systems are very big, powerful machines with huge amounts of storage space and the capability to maintain high-speed connections to many other computers. Originally, most backbone sites were at universities or government institutions, and were funded by the National Science Foundation. This restricted the amount of commerce that could be done online because these government-funded sites often enforced their "acceptable use policies," which prohibited commercial use of the Net. However, over the past few years, that funding has been phased out, and most backbones are now firmly in control of private corporations that have no problems with promoting online commerce.

Intermediate Sites

The distinction between backbones and intermediate systems is hazy, but mainly the difference is that intermediate sites feed a series of leaf nodes, or sites that don't pass off news to any other machines. Intermediate sites are usually the larger ISPs or universities and serve as a middle stop-off point for news.

Leaf Nodes

If you think of Usenet as a tree, the backbone sites are the trunk. Off of the trunk, the intermediate nodes pass the news into smaller and smaller branches. Finally, the news reaches a point where it can't go any farther, and this end point is known as a leaf node.

Leaf nodes are the ultimate destinations for Usenet. Leaf nodes read net news from an intermediate site and feed new articles back, but they don't pass off any of the news to any other site. With the number of TCP/IP-connected home PCs in use these days, the whole leaf node distinction enters a new gray area: is the small ISP a leaf node or is the SLIP/PPP-connected computer attached to it the leaf node? A purist would argue that because the home user doesn't download all the newsgroups, they aren't technically leaf nodes even though they can function as one. Others would argue that the distinction doesn't matter that much. We're with the latter group.

Propagation

So how does your article make it out through this web of machines? The best way to understand how the process works would be to look at a semi-real life example following the path of a posted article.

Let's say Sean's at home observing his sea monkey aquarium (that Gareth gave him for Christmas) when he notices that his watery friends just don't seem to have the vim and vigor they usually display when he comes near their tank. He's worried, frantic even—his little brine shrimp friends are sick! He rushes to his computer to post a question to rec.pets.seamonkeys for an answer to his dilemma. The article he posts is this:

```
From: sean@natty.boh.com (Sean Carton)
Newsgroup: rec.pets.seamonkeys
Subject: Help! My 'keys are sick! Need help now!
Keywords: sick, seamonkeys, ill, shrimp, aquarium, contagion
Date: April 1, 1996 01:44:23 EST

Help! I think that my sea monkeys are sick! They've stopped
playing ball, smiling at me when I tap on the tank, and I
just can't get them to swim in formation anymore. I'm not
sure what the problem is, but there seems to be a black film
on the top of the water and they're floating upside down. Can
anyone help me with this?

Sean Carton
```

Frantically, Sean hits the send key and sits back to wait for a response. Here's what happens as his article goes out.

First, the article travels over his PPP connection from his newsreader software to the news server at his local ISP (natty.boh.com—a large enough operation to qualify as an intermediate node, instead of a leaf). The intermediate at natty.boh.com collects his article, along with any other articles that users might post, and forwards them to the local backbone in his region, hal.org. hal.org then adds the articles to its local spool (containing news articles from all its intermediate sites), and then, at the appropriate time, it forwards all the new articles to the other backbones it connects to. At the same time it's sending news out, hal.org distributes any new articles it has received from the other backbones to its intermediate and leaf nodes. Figure 22-2 shows the path the articles take.

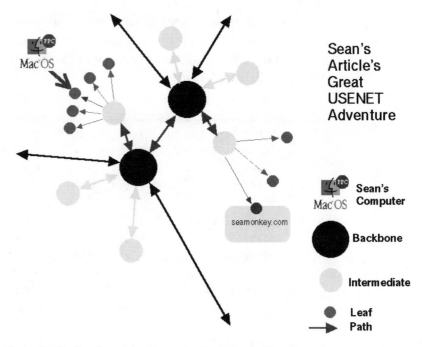

Sean's Article's Great USENET Adventure

Sean's Computer

Backbone

Intermediate

Leaf

Path

Figure 22-2: Sean's article takes a journey across Usenet.

Using this store-and-forward system, each article posted to a leaf node winds its way through the system from leaf to intermediate to backbone and then to other backbones where it's passed along. In this way, articles are transmitted one hop at a time all over the Net. Each article has a unique ID, which allows the servers in the network to keep track of where the article has been delivered.

But back to the story. Sean's article eventually reaches a leaf node in England, which, coincidentally houses seamonkey.org.uk, the server for the United Kingdom International Seamonkey Society (U-KISS). There, the article is answered immediately, propagating outward back through the Net, until the response reaches Sean's ISP (and every other Usenet node that carries the rec.pets.seamonkeys group). Sean's newsreader software checks for new articles, pulls them in to his machine, and displays them on his screen. All this in a matter of an hour or so. Here's the article he received:

```
From: monkeyrx@seamonkey.org.uk
Newsgroup: rec.pets.seamonkeys, rec.pets.dead
Subject: Re: Help! My 'keys are sick! Need help now!
Keywords: sick, seamonkeys, ill, shrimp, aquarium, contagion
Date: April 1, 1996 07:44:23 GMT


>Help! I think that my sea monkeys are sick! They've >stopped
playing ball, smiling at me when I tap on the
>tank, and I just can't get them to swim in
formation>anymore. I'm not sure what the problem is, but
there >seems to be a black film on the top of the water and
>they're floating upside down. Can anyone help me with >this?
>
>Sean Carton

Sean,

They're dead. We'd suggest a burial at sea. Please send
$49.95 for a new starter kit.

Have a nice day,


Nigel Incubator Jones
U-KISS Technical Support, Medical Division
```

Ahh, the wonders of Usenet (and the trials of pet ownership).

ANATOMY OF AN ARTICLE

As you read Usenet articles, you may notice that there's an awful lot of cryptic information posted at the top of the articles you read. You might be able to make out what some of that gobbledygook means. Subject is pretty self explanatory, but a lot of information probably doesn't make any sense at all. This information is called the header information, and it's the control information Usenet servers use to pass your article through the many jumps it has to make while traveling through Usenet. Knowing what to make of the information that appears in a header can help you trouble-shoot a flaky connection, figure out where a forged post really came from, or just give you a little more insight into how Usenet works. Figure 22-3 shows a typical article header.

```
Path:
news.clark.net!netjam!snm.com!netcomsv!uu4news.netcom.com!netcomsv!uu3news
.netcom.com!ix.netcom.com!howland.reston.ans.net!newsfeed.internetmci.com!
in2.uu.net!nwlink.com!usenet
From: alien@ufo.com (alien)
Newsgroups:
alt.alien,alt.alien.research,alt.alien.visitors,alt.paranet.ufo,alt.person
als.aliens,alt.sex.aliens,alt.ufo,alt.ufo.reports,de.alt.ufos
Subject: MIB ACCOUNT on http://nwlink.com/~park/ufo/mib.html
Date: Fri, 22 Mar 1996 08:34:21 GMT
Organization: Northwest Link
Lines: 4
Message-ID: <4ito2r$lle@texas.nwlink.com>
NNTP-Posting-Host: port6.annex4.nwlink.com
X-Newsreader: Forte Agent .99c/32.126
Xref: news.clark.net alt.alien:363 alt.alien.research:16531
alt.alien.visitors:124503 alt.paranet.ufo:57550 alt.personals.aliens:1944
alt.sex.aliens:197 alt.ufo:77 alt.ufo.reports:7406
```

Figure 22-3: A Usenet article header.

If you're the perceptive type, you may notice some similarities between the headers in a Usenet article and the e-mail header information you're used to. (For a discussion on e-mail headers, see Chapter 20, "Inside E-Mail.") There's a reason for that. The creators of the Usenet header information standard (defined in RFC #1036) designed the headers to be compatible with standard mail header information. This way, people would be able to get existing tools to do double duty with both mail and news. In fact, the rules in the RFC are pretty explicit on this subject:

> A standard format for mail messages has existed for many years on the Internet, and this format meets most of the needs of Usenet. Since the Internet format is extensible, extensions to meet the additional needs of Usenet are easily made within the Internet standard. Therefore, the rule is adopted that all Usenet news messages must be formatted as valid Internet mail messages.

To allow simplicity and flexibility in the Usenet system, Usenet headers were divided into two groups—required and optional. Required headers contain the information vital to passing an article between Usenet nodes: From, Date, Newsgroup, Subject, MessageID, and Path are all required for an article to go through. Optional headers aren't vital to the article getting through, but they can provide information to help the server control the distribution of an article: Followup-To, Expires, Reply-To, Sender, References, Control, Distribution, Keywords, Summary, Approved, Lines, Xref, and Organization are all optional headers. And, to make sure Usenet would remain open and flexible for the future, any header information not recognized by the server as either required or optional is simply passed along as part of the article.

TIP

If you can't see any header information in the news articles you're reading, it may be because your newsreader is shielding you from the ugliness that is header information. There's probably a way to toggle the display of header information. Find it and turn it on.

Required Headers

As you probably guessed from the designation "required headers," the header information in this section is required if you want your article to go through. Many servers will reject articles with incomplete header information, and with good reason—what would they do with an article with no Newsgroup information? Most of the time, you won't have to worry about adding all the required fields—your newsreading program should do that for you when you post an article. The following sections explain the headers in the order that they appear.

From

In its most basic form, the From header contains the e-mail address of the person sending the article. This information is used both for identifying the poster as well as providing a way for people to respond to the article via e-mail.

Usenet news servers interpret addresses as follows. The user name (the part before the @) is considered to be case sensitive. sean@ucia.gov is not the same as Sean@ucia.gov. However, the host and domain names are not case sensitive: sean@UCIA.GOV and sean@ucia.gov are considered to be the same address.

The full name of the user can be inserted into the From field in one of two ways. First, the name can be added within parentheses at the end of the e-mail address: sean@ucia.gov (Sean Carton) is valid. In addition, the full name can be included at the beginning of the address, provided that the address is enclosed in brackets: Sean Carton <sean@ucia.gov> is a valid address in the From field.

Your full name can include almost all ASCII characters except the following:

```
(    )  >  <  ,  :  @  !  /  =  ;
```

Date

The date contained in the Usenet news article header indicates the time and date the article was originally posted. Dates should be in the format:

```
Day Name, Date Month Year Hours:Minutes:Seconds Timezone
```

For example, the following would be an acceptable date format:

```
Monday, 13 February 1995 02:32:45 EST
```

While there's no standard way of indicating all the time zones in the world, the most common time zones used in Date fields are Greenwich mean time (GMT), all the North American time zones (EST, EDT, PST, PDT, MST, MDT, CST, CDT), and +/- offsets are all acceptable.

Newsgroups

The Newsgroups field indicates which newsgroups an article should appear in. When you create a new article while reading a particular newsgroup, most newsreaders will automatically insert the name of the group you're reading in the Newsgroups field.

If you want to crosspost your article to several newsgroups, you can do so by adding the names of the newsgroups you want your article to appear in, separated by commas. For example, if you wanted to post an article to alt.test, alt.binaries.sounds, and rec.pets.cats, your Newsgroups field would read:

```
Newsgroups: alt.test, alt.binaries.sounds, rec.pets.cats
```

Take care when crossposting—many newsgroup participants aren't too happy if you crosspost a discussion to other groups, especially a newsgroup on a completely different topic. It's really best to stick to one group.

Since all servers don't carry all newsgroups, you may be wondering what happens if a server receives your crossposted article with a reference for a group it doesn't carry. Actually, nothing. RFC#1036 makes it clear that servers should ignore any unknown newsgroups it encounters in Newsgroups headers containing multiple entries.

Subject

This is perhaps the most free-form line in the entire required headers group. You should use the Subject header to indicate the subject of your article so that people browsing the newsgroup know what your article is going to be about before they take the time to download and read it. However, you can get away with not putting a subject in at all, though we don't know why you'd want to.

Subjects are also used for controlling how responses are grouped. RFC #1036 indicates that "if [a] message is submitted in response to another message . . . the default subject should begin with . . . 'Re: '

and the 'References' line is required." This stipulation insures that threaded newsreaders are able to group related articles together. If you're replying to a previous article, it's best just to leave the subject alone and let the newsreader take care of the rest.

MessageID

The main way that Usenet news servers know whether or not they have an article is by checking the MessageID number in the header. MessageIDs are unique numbers assigned by the server posting the article to the Net. They have the format:

```
messageid@host.name
```

MessageID is a unique number that hasn't been assigned by the host during the past two years and host.name is the name of the computer where the article originated.

Path

If you want to find out how an article got to you, check the Path header. Here you'll find a record of every machine the article you're reading passed through. When an article is posted, the posting machine's name is added to the Path header, and as the article passes through each successive machine, that machine's name is added to the list. For example, the Path header:

```
Path: dogbreath, gobble.com, peanuts.org, ucia.gov
```

indicates that the article originated at ucia.gov, was passed off to peanuts.org, and then made its way through gobble.com and dogbreath before making it to your screen. As the article passes through each computer, that computer's name is added to the left side of the list.

Paths are useful if you suspect that someone has forged a post by changing their information in the From line. Even if they try to hide their identity by changing their e-mail address, you can almost always determine the article's point of origin by examining the Path header.

Optional Headers

While all of the headers in the optional headers category aren't necessary for an article to make it to its intended group(s), they do sometimes add to an article by providing extra information that a savvy server (or reader) can use.

Followup-To

If you must crosspost an article to several newsgroups, try to make use of the Followup-To header. Using the same format as the Newsgroups header, Followup-To is used to indicate to which newsgroup(s) a reply to an article should be posted. If you crosspost an article and don't include a Followup-To header, all replies to your article will be posted to all the newsgroups indicated in the Newsgroups header, and will likely result in a lot of flames directed at you.

Expires

Most news servers have a facility for expiring articles after a certain period of time. If you want your article to go away before this time, or you want it to stick around longer, you can put an expiration date into the Expires field. This date should be in the same format as the Date header. Take care using this field—if you put in long expiration dates, you may incur the wrath of more than a few news administrators who get sick of looking at your message.

Reply-To

The Reply-To header is used by various newsreader packages to figure out to whom e-mail replies to a message should be sent. E-mail addresses should be in the same format as the From header. If you don't include a Reply-To header in your message and someone wants to reply to you by e-mail, the reply will go to the address indicated in the From field.

Sender

If you find yourself using someone else's news account to post articles but you want to make sure replies get back to your mailbox, you can use the Sender header to differentiate between the account you sent the article from and the account you want the attribution to go to. For example, if Sean happened to be over at Gareth's swingin' pad and posted an article from his account, he could set up the headers in the following way:

```
From: sean@natty.boh.org (Sean Carton)
Sender:  gareth@seamonkey.com (Gareth Branwyn)
```

Using this method, people can see both what account the article was posted from as well as the person who posted the message if the two are different.

References

Most people like having their Usenet articles threaded—grouped together by subject—when they browse a newsgroup. Not only is it easier to see the number of messages on a certain subject, but it's also easier to find the articles and subjects you're looking for.

Newsreaders use the information contained in the References header to thread articles into groups. The References header contains a list of all message IDs of the articles referred to by the response, generated when a user uses the Followup command in his or her newsreader.

Control

Here's where you can really work some magic! The Control message header allows you to send messages directly to a Usenet host machine in order to do fun stuff like cancel articles, send articles, receive articles, create a new newsgroup, remove a newsgroup, or get the sys file. Because it's possible for an unscrupulous person to wreak some serious havoc with Control header messages, most system administrators set up their system to reject Control messages from anyone except people with system administration authority. Table 22-1 lists the various Control messages, their syntax, and what they can do:

Control Message	Syntax	Action
Cancel	Control: cancel <messageID>	Cancels message <messageID> on local server.
Ihave/Sendme	ihave <messageID list>*[new line w/in row]* sendme<messageID list>	Controls the sending and receiving of specific messages between servers.
Newgroup	newgroup <groupname> [moderated]	Creates a new newsgroup with the name <groupname>.*
Rmgroup	rmgroup <groupname>	Remove group named <groupname> from every host on the network.*
Sendsys	sendsys	Sends sys file (which lists all network neighbors and the newsgroups they carry) to the e-mail address of the author of the message.
Version	version	Mails the name and version of the server software on the system back to the author of the message.
Checkgroups	checkgroups	When this Control message is included, a list of all newsgroups should be included in the body of the message. The server will compare the list against the list of active groups and e-mail the list of dead groups to the author of the message.

* These Control messages must also include an Approved: <e-mail address> header to take effect.

Table 22-1: Control messages.

Distribution

If you want to control how far your article gets out in the world, use the Distribution header. When a server receives your article, it looks at the Distribution line of the header to figure out if the article should go into the system or not. Only if the locations indicated in the Distribution line match the internal distribution list of the server will the article be posted.

There's no hard and fast rules for what constitutes a valid Distribution location, but the following indicators will often work:

❐ world: message gets posted to all the servers on Usenet.

❐ state abbreviation: MD (for Maryland), VA (for Virginia), and so on usually work to limit the distribution to a specific geographic area.

❐ institution name: the hostname of the institution you want to limit the distribution to.

❐ city name or geographical area: the article will be posted to machines only in the designated city or geographic area.

Keywords

Like Subject, Keywords don't do anything for the server, but they do help a potential reader determine if he or she wants to read a message. Newsgroup search services like DejaNews let you search on the Keywords field. Unfortunately, because most people do not fill in the field, keyword searching is not a very reliable way of finding things in Usenet groups.

Summary

Again, like Keywords, this header usually doesn't get acted upon by anyone but the potential reader. If the header is used by the server or newsreader, it's referred to in the followup to other messages.

Approved

This header is required for certain Control messages (newgroup and rmgroup in particular) and also for approving articles for moderated groups. You should place your e-mail address in this header:

```
Approved: <your e-mail address>
```

Lines

This header includes a count of the number of lines contained in a message. Its automatically generated by the server.

Xref

This field is used for cross references and contains the name of the host the message was posted from as well as a list of corresponding message numbers. The Xref header is only used by the local system to keep track of articles and usually isn't transmitted to remote servers.

Organization

Since it's often tough to tell the name of the organization a person who's posting a message belongs to from the hostname, the Organization line allows you to write a short description of your organization so that others can tell where your articles are coming from.

USENET RESOURCES

Usenet can be a big, confusing place to be wandering around in on your own. At last count there were some 17,000 newsgroups on just about any topic you can imagine. Plus, a dizzying array of newsreaders, server software, and information just keeps getting bigger every day. If you want to get the most out of Usenet, how can you keep up?

Luckily, more than a few altruistic people on the Net realize that Usenet's complexity is a problem. They have put countless hours of time and their own resources into trying to make some sense out of the mess. The result is quite a few useful information archives, search engines, and Web sites where you can easily find out just about anything you'd ever want to know about using Usenet and Usenet-related services.

Archives

A lot of information is out there on Usenet, but not all of it is that useful. A wealth of knowledge is available if you can cut through the chaff. But who has time to?

The folks who maintain these archives must. While they aren't pretty to look at (the pages, not the people! We don't know about them), they do provide an incredible wealth of information. We consider them mandatory reading for any Usenet aficionado. Hop over and check 'em out.

Usenet Info Center

http://sunsite.unc.edu/usenet-i/

If you want a one-stop shop for finding out just about anything you could ever want to learn about Usenet, make your first stop at the Usenet Info Center Launch Pad (see Figure 22-4). Once you're there, browse around a bit—you'll be amazed at what you'll find. There's a great hyperlinked index of Usenet information from across the Net (including many popular FAQs), links to the Ohio State FAQ database, and pointers to Usenet information from around the world. If you want more info on the Info Center before you visit, read the FAQ at http://www.clark.net/pub/usenet-b/www/info-center-faq.html (see Figure 22-4).

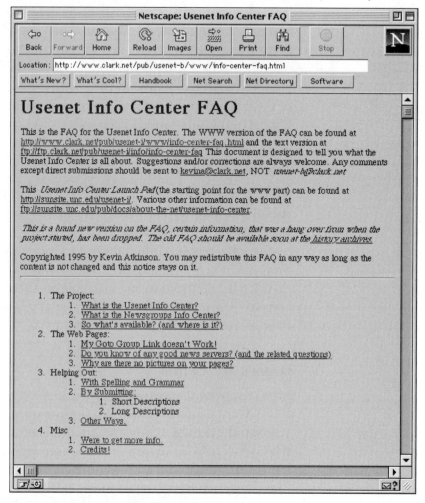

Figure 22-4: The Usenet Info Center FAQ.

MIT RTFM FAQ archives

`ftp://rtfm.mit.edu/pub/usenet/news.answers/index`

Before you post that scathing flame to a newsgroup you've just stumbled across, check out the MIT FAQ Archive first and see if there's an FAQ for the group you're posting to. You'll save yourself a lot of embarrassment and maybe even learn a thing or two. The FAQ Archive is truly one of the wonders of the information world—give it a look.

Search Engines

With over 150 megabytes of information being posted to Usenet every day, keeping track of it all isn't humanly impossible. There are just so many hours in the day you can spend perusing your favorite groups. So how can you know if someone posts something that may interest you, especially if it's in a group you never read? Easy! Use a search engine to cut through the chaff for you! Here's a list of the best.

AltaVista

http://www.altavista.digital.com/

Not only is AltaVista a killer Web searcher, but it includes a simple-to-use Usenet search facility, too. Just type a few keywords into the search field (see Figure 22-5), press Submit, and AltaVista will search its database of recent Usenet articles for any that contain the words you're looking for. See Chapter 26, "Data Tracking," for more information on AltaVista.

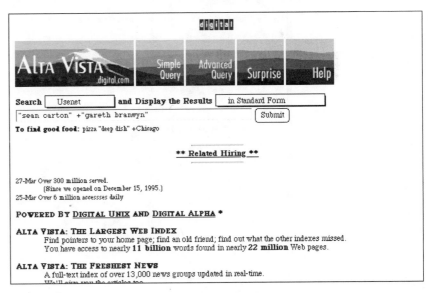

Figure 22-5: Searching Alta Vista for references to your fabulous authors.

DejaNews

http://www.dejanews.com/

It's hard to say enough about DejaNews. Not only does it contain the best and most complete database of Usenet postings available on the Net today, but it also gives you many options just not available anywhere else, including lifetime user profiles of Usenet activity (see Figure 22-6). Its Quick Search feature allows you to blow through simple searches, and its Power Search options provide one of the best online search interfaces on the Web. If you're going to have to search Usenet, stop by DejaNews first.

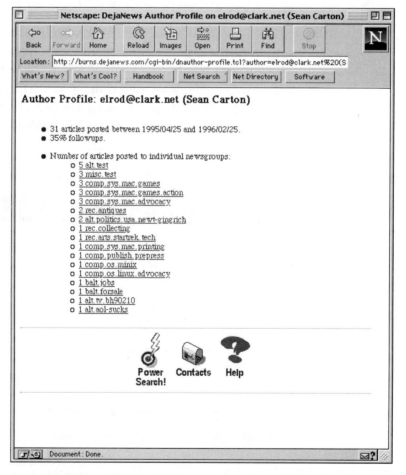

Figure 22-6: Sean's lifetime DejaNews profile. C'mon! Like he has time to post more than that!

Green Eggs Report

http://www.ar.com/ger/

The Green Eggs Report (GER) is a unique combination of a Usenet search engine and the Web. Every day, GER's Rumor Database System scans Usenet groups for URLs. It then sorts the URLs it finds (Web, Gopher, and FTP) by newsgroup and makes them available on the GER Web page, ready for the clicking. It's a great way to find Web pages on topics you're interested in, especially if you want to find semi-private Web pages that aren't generally announced on the Net.

CREATING A NEWSGROUP

So all this information on Usenet has got your juices flowing. You're dying to post something. But there doesn't seem to be a newgroup out there that shares your interests. Why not create your own group?

There are two basic ways of creating a newsgroup. First, if you have access to a server that allows Control messages, you can just add the following headers to your message and send it:

```
Control: newgroup <name of your group>
Approved: <your e-mail address>
```

However, in most cases you'll get a polite note back from the news administrator asking you to submit your requests for new groups to him or her before trying it out yourself. And even if your message does result in a new group, chances are it won't be picked up by most of the news servers out there.

So how do you create a newsgroup that'll stick? Remember how we pointed out that Usenet isn't a democracy? Well, when it comes to creating newsgroups it is . . . kinda. Here's what you have to do.

First, you need to propose your new newsgroup idea to one of the groups related to the new group you want to create. For example, if you wanted to create the rec.pets.seamonkeys group we used in our examples in this chapter, you'd first want to post a proposal to the rec.pets and rec.aquaria newsgroups. After gathering the opinions of the members of these groups, you then should prepare a Request for Discussion proposal about your new group and post it to news.announce.newgroups, news.groups, and the groups you posted your proposal to in the first place—in this case, rec.pets and rec.aquaria. Then sit back for a month and watch the fur fly as your proposal is bandied about on these newsgroups. Prepare yourself for a battle, because a lot of people think that there are enough newsgroups already and will fight tooth and nail against any new proposal. It helps to have a thick skin at this point.

When your month of debate is up, hold an online vote for the creation of your new group. If you get 100 more yes than no votes (and more than twice as many yes votes as no votes), post the results of the vote (including a list of who voted for what) so that everyone can see you're on the up and up. Once the dust settles, e-mail the moderator of news.announce.newgroups (check the FAQ to find out who it is at the moment), and a control message will be sent out to create your new group.

That's the standard procedure for creating a newsgroup in the big seven hierarchies (comp, misc, news, rec, sci, soc, and talk). To create an alt newsgroup, you don't have to follow these rules (though it doesn't hurt). All you have to do is convince your news administrator to issue a control message. However, as we pointed out before, unless your group is something special, there's not much of a chance it'll actually get picked up on the rest of Usenet.

If you aren't scared off by all of this and you still want to create your own newsgroup, here's a list of where to go for more detailed information.

❒ **How to Create a New Usenet Newsgroup**
http://www.cis.ohio-state.edu/hypertext/faq/usenet/usenet/creating-newsgroups/part1/faq.html

❒ **Usenet Newsgroup Creation Companion**
http://www.cis.ohio-state.edu/hypertext/faq/usenet/usenet/creating-newsgroups/helper/faq.html

❒ **How to Create an Alt Newsgroup**
http://www4.ncsu.edu/unity/users/a/asdamick/
www/news/create.html

❒ **So You Want To Create an Alt Newsgroup**
http://www.math.psu.edu/barr/alt-creation-guide/
faq.html

❒ **Emily Postnews answers your questions on how to create a new alt group**
http://www.cis.ohio-state.edu/hypertext/faq/usenet/
alt-hierarchies/emily-alt-advice/faq.html

Good luck! And if you start a sea monkey newsgroup, drop us a line!

MOVING ON

So, now that you know what goes on behind the scenes of Usenet, you'll hopefully be a more informed newsgroup participant. Between all the information you've gathered on newsreaders in Chapters 8, 13, and 18 and the look you just got at Usenet's inner workings, you're well on your way to becoming a real news maven. There's only one thing we haven't covered yet—uploading and downloading files on Usenet.

Even though Usenet was originally conceived of as a way of passing messages and news back and forth between different computer systems—in terms of sheer megabytes—the binaries newsgroups probably take up the lion's share of the traffic these days. Between all the programs, images, clip art, sounds, and movies people are posting, there's enough stuff out there to keep even the most hardened software and multimedia junkie happy for a long time. That is, if you know how to get at it.

In the second part of our power user's look at Usenet, we'll cover binary transfers. You'll learn how to upload, download, and how to decode what you download so that you've got something useful. Even though a lot of people find the concept of turning encoded text messages into binary files confusing, the whole process will be clear as glass after you're finished reading the next chapter.

## Chapter 23

Binary Bonanza! Uploading & Downloading Files to Usenet

While many people use Usenet to debate, talk, and share news, the bulk of information being passed over Usenet isn't talk; it's programs, pictures, and other computer files. Even though thousands of binary computer files are posted to Usenet every day, many people find that downloading and decoding these files can be tricky. On any newsgroup where binary files are posted, you'll be sure to see nearly as many "How do I decode . . . " posts as actual file postings. To make matters worse (at least for the people asking the questions), people in the know who frequent these newsgroups looking for files often have little tolerance for these kinds of questions. "Read the FAQ!" is the most polite response you'll get if you ask how to decode a binary from a newsgroup. We can't even print some of the not-so-polite responses.

So what do you do if you want to get your share of the Usenet binary bonanza? You could find a mentor to teach you, but that's often out of the question. You could try figuring it out for yourself, but you might spend hours and hours before you get it right. You could try reading one of the many FAQs on the subject, but you may end up getting confused by some of the jargon. Or you could read this chapter. We think you should choose the latter option, since you've already read this far.

We'll start with a discussion on the binary newsgroups themselves—what they are, how to get them, what to do if you can't get them—and then move on to the theory behind posting and downloading files. We'll wrap up with a handy resource guide so you can refer to this chapter as more questions come up.

TIP

We're not going to cover any "what button do I push" questions in this chapter—we've covered that stuff in the various newsreader chapters already. What we will do is give you an overall understanding of how binary newsgroups, file encoding, and file decoding work.

BINARY NEWSGROUPS

Binary newsgroups are newsgroups containing computer-readable files that have been specially encoded into text so they can be posted to text-based newsgroups. These newsgroups are usually divided into hierarchies by media type, with each sub-hierarchy divided into topics within that media type.

What kind of files are people posting to binary newsgroups? Just about any kind of file that a computer can generate (other than ASCII). You'll find pictures, PostScript clip art, sounds, movies, games, utilities, applications—you name it, and someone's probably posting it. Table 23-1 lists the major binary newsgroup hierarchies and their contents.

Newsgroup Hierarchy	Contents
alt.binaries	Miscellaneous binary files. Now superseded by alt.binaries.misc. First-level subdomains of the alt.binaries hierarchies contain many miscellaneous file types.
alt.binaries.games	Computer games.
alt.binaries.multimedia	Multimedia files, mainly QuickTime, MPEG, and FLI animations.
alt.binaries.nude	Nude pictures.

➡

Newsgroup Hierarchy	Contents
alt.binaries.pictures	Pictures, including fine art, cartoons, celebrities, and body art.
alt.binaries.pictures.erotica	The dreaded domains of Usenet porn.
alt.binaries.sounds	Sound files. Subdomains include MIDI, MODs, music, and erotica.
alt.binaries.warez	Software, mainly pirated. Several zealous software companies and others have *cancelbots* running on these newsgroups, which prevent most multi-part files from coming through intact.
alt.binaries.zines	Electronic zines.
alt.ham-radio.binaries	Amateur radio utilities.
clari.*	Clarinet, a commercial news service, often includes binaries of news pictures and comics.
comp.binaries	A major binary hierarchy. Contains programs for most computer platforms, including a few obscure computers you've probably never heard of (nor will ever use).
.pictures.	Some sub-hierarchies also include binary groups that carry pictures. Examples are alt.binaries.pictures.animals and alt.binaries.pictures.astro.

Table 23-1: Major binary newsgroups.

Why Don't I Get . . . on My Server (& How Can I Get It)?

When you start to look for some of these binary newsgroups on your local server, you might discover that some of them aren't available. Recent court decisions and the Communications Decency Act hold the service provider potentially liable for any indecent content that their servers contain, whether in e-mail or in Usenet newsgroups. While most ISPs haven't done anything about files and content contained in e-mail messages, many are starting to run scared and are blocking access to all sexually-oriented newsgroups (even the ones on sex education and support groups). As a result, many people are finding that newsgroups they used to have access to are not being carried anymore.

What do you do if you can't access a newsgroup on your server? The first, and most obvious, choice is to find another service provider that carries the full list of newsgroups. Many smaller service providers, in an effort to attract new customers, are beginning to advertise if they carry all the newsgroups or not. If access to everything that Usenet has to offer is a major concern of yours, you may want to consider switching ISPs.

If you've been on one system for a while, switching can be a pain. People know your e-mail address, you may have subscribed to a bunch of e-mail lists, and you may even have a Web page of your own. Switching to a new service provider would mean that you'd have to inform everyone of a new e-mail address, re-subscribe to the mailing lists you're on, and transfer all the files from your current Web server to a new one. Not fun. Fortunately, you have several alternatives.

First, you can get an account on one of the several public-access *freenets*. These ISPs, set up to provide free or low-cost Net access, often carry a full range of newsgroups for their subscribers. Table 23-2 lists several popular freenets.

Freenet	Address
Buffalo Freenet	freenet.buffalo.edu (Accepts only NY residents)
Cleveland Freenet	freenet-in-a.cwru.edu
Denver Freenet	freenet.hsc.colorado.edu
The Spirit of the Night	nyx.cs.du.edu

Table 23-2: Freenets.

You can access these freenets through the Internet by using Telnet. You don't even have to worry about a long distance phone call.

Another option, similar to freenets, is to find a local bulletin board in your area that covers the newsgroups you're looking for. Bulletin boards are still on the edges of Cyberspace, and their administrators often don't mind carrying the more controversial stuff.

But if you want reliable, fast access, nothing beats a commercial news provider. Many ISPs will allow you to pay for just a newsfeed, while other news providers exist only to provide ready access to all the newsgroups on Usenet. The charges are usually low—around $10 or so a month—so using one of these services shouldn't put too large a crimp in your budget. Many people have reported success with zippo.com, a commercial news provider allowing access to every newsgroup in existence. Just hop on over to http://www.zippo.com for a look at their services (see Figure 23-1).

Figure 23-1: The Daily News at zippo.com.

Finally, if you don't mind poking around for a while, you can find an open NNTP server that anyone can use as a newsfeed. These sites are few and far between, and many shut down as quickly as they're found, so we can't give you a list. Check out the How to Receive Banned Newsgroups FAQ (which is available at http://www.cis.ohio-state.edu/hypertext/faq/usenet/usenet/banned-groups-faq/faq.html or is posted regularly to alt.censorship, alt.internet.services, news.misc, alt.answers, or news.answers) for more information on finding open NNTP servers.

Configuring Your Newsreader for Alternate News Servers

So you've found a commercial news provider or an open NNTP server to get your mail from. Now how do you get your software to read it? It's easier than you might think.

If you're using a Mac or Windows newsreader, you can just put the address of the new news server in the News Server section of the Configuration dialog box. Unfortunately, most programs often let you keep only one news server, so if you want to have access to your local news server as well as a remote news server, you may have to run two different newsreaders. One notable exception is Netscape Navigator's news client. While a long way from perfect, it does have the ability to maintain subscriptions to multiple news servers.

If you're using a UNIX shell account to read your news, you'll have to do a bit of simple hacking. First, edit your login file and set the NNTPSERVER environment variable to the address of the news server you want to use. If you're using sh (or a similar shell), you can add the following lines to your login file:

```
NNTPSERVER=nntp.news.server.address
export NNTSERVER
```

If you're using csh, add the following line:

```
setenv NNTPSERVER nntp.news.server.address
```

However, before you add these lines, make sure you check your login file to see if they're already there. Chances are, they aren't. However, if these lines already exist in your login file, replace them with the lines above.

If you don't want to go to the trouble of setting the environment variable and you have access to the tin newsreader, you can start tin by typing:

```
tin -r nntp.news.server.address
```

This command will start tin with the news server you specify.

The only thing that you'll have to remember if you are switching between news servers with your UNIX account is that each site will need its own newsrc file. You can switch newsrc files by renaming the one you're not using to something like .newsrc.onhold and renaming the one you're currently using to .newsrc.

Binary Newsgroup Netiquette

When it comes to Netiquette, binary newsgroups are the places where it's simultaneously most vocally enforced and routinely broken. Binary newsgroups are filled with flames from people complaining that a particular file either isn't appropriate to the newsgroup or shouldn't be discussed in the newsgroup (paradoxically, they are also often full of flames from people complaining that people shouldn't be complaining, but posting more files). Here's what you need to do to remain a Netizen in good standing.

First, before you post anything or ask a question about the files in the newsgroup, read the FAQ! If you don't, your life will be made a living hell as your mailbox fills up with messages from self-appointed net.police telling you that what you asked or posted shouldn't have been. You can save yourself a lot of trouble by making sure you follow the rules.

Second, don't post files that are inappropriate for a group. Posting 1MB, 24-bit pictures of your dog to comp.binaries.mac will get you into trouble fast.

Likewise, don't send your binary uploads to more than one group (*crossposting*). Not only does it eat bandwidth (and server space), but it's almost never appropriate. Chances are, if someone wants to see a file of the type you're going to post, they'll look in the appropriate newsgroup.

If you must discuss the contents of a particular file, don't post your response to the binaries newsgroup! Most binary newsgroups also have a discussion counterpart (indicated by a *d* at the end of the newsgroup name) for text-based discussions of what's found in binary newsgroups. We know that this advice is ignored all the time, but do your part and try to take heed.

Contribute to the newsgroup you read, if possible. No one likes a freeloader. If you have a file to trade, put it up. Usenet only works because not everyone in the world is selfish.

Finally, if you're on the receiving side of a breach of netiquette, hold your virtual tongue. There are enough self-righteous people on the Net without any more self-appointed net.police. A little restraint goes a long way.

POSTING FILES

Newsgroups work fine for 7-bit ASCII text, but what do you do if you want to post a binary file to a newsgroup? You can't just plop the file on Usenet as it is—you have to transform it to a format that newsreaders and news servers can handle. Once you've transformed the file from a binary to a text file, you then have to figure out how to put it up. We're going to tell you how.

Uuencoding

The most common method of posting a file to Usenet is to uuencode it. Uuencode was a program originally developed to allow binary files to be transmitted using the UUCP protocol. (For background information, check out Chapter 20, "Inside E-Mail.") Not surprisingly, because the first Usenet servers used UUCP to transfer news files, people turned to uuencode to post binary files. These days, most of Usenet doesn't use UUCP any more, but many people use uuencode to put messages on Usenet.

Unless you have a newsreader that provides internal support for uuencoding and posting binary files (Yet Another Newswatcher for the Mac is one example, Forte's FreeAgent for Windows is another), posting a file using uuencode usually involves three steps: encoding the file, splitting it into 60K (or smaller) chunks, then posting it to Usenet.

Uuencoding Your Binary File

To uuencode your binary file, you'll have to run it through a uuencoder program. If you're on a UNIX system, that's the easiest part—just run the built-in uuencode program on the file you need to encode. If you're running a Mac or Windows machine, you'll have to get a uuencoder program to do the work for you. If you're on a Macintosh, UUTool-Fat is a great uuencoder (see Figure 23-2). You can find your own copy at http://hyperarchive.lcs.mit.edu/HyperArchive/Archive/cmp/uu-tool-24.hqx. If you're using Windows, try Wpack32. You can download it at ftp://ftp.winsite.com/pub/pc/win95/miscutil/wpack32d.exe.

UUTool-FAT

Platform	Mac68K and PowerMac
URL	http://hyperarchive.lcs.mit.edu/HyperArchive/Archive/cmp/uu-tool-24.hqx

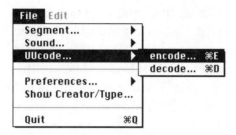

Figure 23-2: Uuencoding a file with UUTool.

Wpack32

Platform	Windows 95. Windows 3.1 version available.
URL	ftp://ftp.winsite.com/pub/pc/win95/miscutil/wpack32d.exe

When you uuencode a binary file, you'll end up with a text file that looks something like this, only probably much longer.

```
begin 0700 hack.gif
MqTEfnc=Aupad'h"'o___P"'bP"""upad"'b_XroJ<OMcZn<kupjkmYp
MiW^'EcAZ@vzyy\zNvvK';RR[\HMR;aOoM=_k\wkdhdQdDHbjObyNQSS]HKrp
MCHKMmuogHg>krfi<1RCMMIIbNR@AUZr;bnoTNEh<Pw_R]KYbg\;wxvvCeuid
M=OAaQNAvmrqx]FoulJFU]jwFv1BGMGmxh[vhNwys=OxirfCfepCVy\Bz^vHJ
MI_BEVhBd=GGDZ'nGYc=1gbL<EE@<JfIg^JF\MRdJFyIhTHA[FZzr?wPimh<J
Mv_FlneM[=^xI]MyFB=muZBq=oDLYsWtoyCZFz_zdsdt;z@eIMvhfkzebv'\d
MLKN@th^J<dGPhmsgP1xNk_^MtkE;T\Mhkcpch=ybMfZ?kbkQ<HUShfIwFG^z
MnkJj^>@FOf<kFnB;M'ZHRGDO?yLZ;dzjfozJGcjm^TB1rGie@XSY<RJkxA[
MLFIUU;bDmI\'cRhA]fNIIhG?jog[eL]yhxKGamg=B=uFndBOXg;kVcxPoKWf
MXIiSvQqFsK<Sr;eARJU;Ufa?ZqVsvEEQB<Q<nwnxWkrCMxZGiHLeS;rAsIzi
MtV;mxErnN[QXNQKq>nLiRZICZOwEZrEzwzkr_adLNZSwfWg@mn[U?ctU]1\1
```

➡

```
MDtVo>eT<sIboMBDgZmGQNiI\av=^RLKTtoswm=dVCnFYUFGhoPi;RsX[qOWx
Ms?hUG__?ephEUuAINoUguGQncx<ymfYdyLEV[r'XtGj_aa>@<]K]TYQ]'?xA
mWX<@mBABBrxrtP"nP
'

end
```

So what does all this gobbledygook mean? All uuencoded files must begin with "begin" followed by a three- or four-digit file permissions code and the name of the file that's been encoded. Everything after this first line and before the end tag constitutes the file information. The end of the file is indicated with a single "end" on a line by itself. Any information that occurs after "end" will be ignored by the decoder program.

If your file is under 60K or so, your next step is to post it to a newsgroup. You can do this by cutting and pasting from a text editor by opening the file you just encoded, selecting the portion you want to post, and using the copy command. Then just paste it into the message you're posting. If you don't want to do a lot of "mousing around," just import your uuencoded file into your message. Check the documentation for your newsreader if you aren't sure how to do this.

When you post the file, make sure that you put an indication in the subject of the message that your file is a one-part binary file. If we were going to post the encoded file above, we'd write something like "hack.gif (1/1)" in the subject line. It's customary to put the number of segments your file is broken into in the subject line so readers (and newsreading programs) can know how many parts they'll need to combine to get a complete file.

Splitting Your File

If your file needs to be split, you have a couple of options. You can use your uuencoding software to split the file (most software provides this option), or you can split the file by hand into sections of approximately 12 single-spaced pages. If you have to split it by hand, make sure you keep track of what segment is what as you save the different text files. When you post your segmented file, make sure you indicate in the subject of your article how many parts you're posting. Take care not to introduce any spurious information into your files. It's customary to put "cut here" lines at the beginning and ending of each segment so that readers know where the data starts and where it ends in the message. See Figure 23-3 for an example.

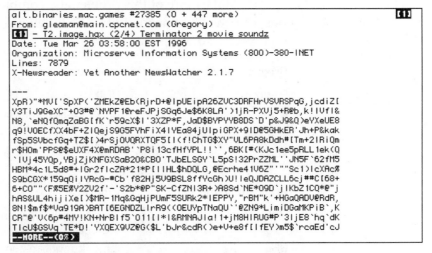

Figure 23-3 An intermediate segment of a uuencoded file.

BinHexing

Uuencode will work for most of the files you encounter, but if you're using a Mac or need to post Mac files, you'll have to use an alternative encoding scheme called BinHex. BinHex files aren't that different from uuencoded files in appearance (a bunch of text-gobbledygook), but they do things in a Mac-friendly way. Most Macintosh files actually contain two parts—a data fork and a resource fork. The data fork holds any internal data needed for the file, such as image information for a graphics file or internally stored data for a program. The resource fork holds all the Mac-specific information for the file, including icons, program code, and other resources needed by the file. If you uuencode a file containing two parts, you'll often just end up with the data fork.

BinHex takes care of this problem by combining the two sections into one text-encoded file. The following programs can help you if you need to BinHex a file:

Program Name	mcvert
Platform	UNIX
URL	ftp://ftp.std.com/customers3/src/macintosh-old/util/mcvert/ (source)

Program Name	Wpack32
Platform	Windows 95. Version for Windows 3.1 is available.
URL	ftp://ftp.winsite.com/pub/pc/win95/miscutil/wpack32d.exe

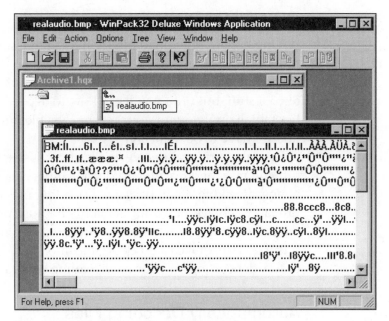

Figure 23-4: BinHexing a file with Wpack32.

Program Name	BinHex 5.0
Platform	Mac68K
URL	http://hyperarchive.lcs.mit.edu/ HyperArchive/Archive/cmp/

MIME

At this point in time, MIME (Multipurpose Internet Mail Extension) files aren't being used on Usenet much, but as more newsreaders come online with MIME support, you may see this situation change.

MIME has several advantages over uuencode or BinHex. While there are no hard and fast standards for these two formats, MIME has been blessed by the Internet standards folks as the attachment method of choice–and with good reason. MIME can be used for every file type, it can include more than one file, and files produced by MIME encoding are smaller than uuencoded or BinHexed files. For a more in-depth discussion of MIME encoding, see the section on MIME in Chapter 20, "Inside E-Mail."

DOWNLOADING FILES

Asking how to download binary files from Usenet groups is probably the number one newbie question on the Internet. Who can blame the newbie? Binary newsgroups hold an amazing range of cool stuff, but until you learn how to decode the files, this stuff lies tantalizingly out of your reach— visible but not readable. It doesn't have to be this way.

Downloading and decoding files from Usenet is often seen as a difficult task, and learning to decode binary files has become almost a newbie rite of passage. Decoding uuencoded files has probably achieved this status mainly because people don't take the time to follow a few simple directions. It's really not rocket science—it just takes a bit of organization and perseverance, more or less depending on your newsreading software.

Automatically Decoding Files

If you have a good newsreader, you probably don't have to worry about how to decode binary files—your newsreader will do it for you. All the popular newsreaders, on every platform, contain features that make decoding files as easy as selecting the different parts and pressing the "decode" key. (See Chapters 8, 13, and 18 for more information about how to use the software.) When newbies run into problems decoding files, it's usually a result of one or more of the three following reasons:

❏ **Lack of patience.** Instead of reading the documentation, most newbies dive right in and expect things to somehow take care of themselves. They won't. Before you start trying to decode files willy-nilly, take a few moments to read the documentation, or visit the appropriate chapters of this book.

❐ **Incomplete posts.** It's a hard fact, but it's something you can't do anything about—if someone doesn't post all the parts of a file (or they don't all make it to your server), you're outta luck. You can wait for the parts to show up, e-mail the poster, or just bag it. It's your choice, but no matter how great a hacker you are, you can't make a complete file out of incomplete parts.

❐ **Incorrectly posted files.** Again, there's nothing you can do about this. If a person doesn't know how to use his or her posting software, if a post has gotten corrupted (a rare event), or spurious information has been inserted into a file, you're going to have to go somewhere else. If you must, e-mail the poster. However, if they can't post correctly to Usenet, there's a slim chance they'll be able to directly e-mail the file to you.

Manually Decoding Files

If your newsreader doesn't give you any facilities for decoding files, you do have one final option—you can assemble the file yourself from its different parts and then run the assembled file through a stand-alone decoder program. It sounds complicated, but it's really not if you follow these steps:

1. Save each posted part to a separate text file.

2. Open each file part, and remove any header or signature information that might have made it into the saved file (see Figure 23-5).

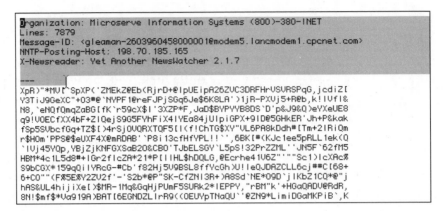

Figure 23-5: Removing extra information from a multi-part uuencoded file.

3. Assemble the parts into one larger file. If you're using UNIX, you can do this by concatenating each part and appending until you've got the whole file assembled. If you're using a Mac or Windows machine, try opening each file in a text editor, and then cutting and pasting each part into a larger master file. Make sure you keep the parts in order! See Figure 23-6.

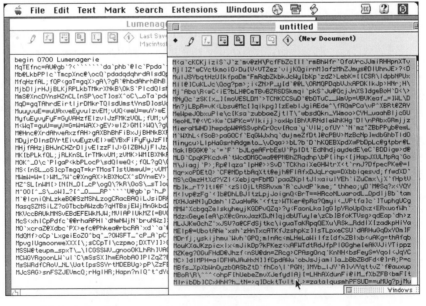

Figure 23-6: Assembling a multi-part uuencoded file.

4. Save the assembled file as a *text* file (if you're using a word processor to assemble the parts, save the file as Text Only with Line Breaks). See Figure 23-7.

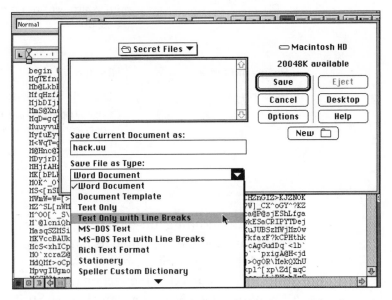

Figure 23-7: Choosing the correct Microsoft Word text setting for saving assembled uuencoded files.

5. Once you've saved the whole file, decode it using the appropriate decoder program.

Uudecode

Decoding a uuencoded file is no more difficult than encoding it—just run it through the appropriate decoder program. If you're using UNIX, you've got it easy—uudecode is included in just about every UNIX distribution on the planet, so you probably already have everything you need. If you're using a Mac or Windows machine, you'll have to use one of the following programs:

Program Name	Wpack32
Platform	Windows 95. Version for Windows 3.1 available.
URL	ftp://ftp.winsite.com/pub/pc/win95/miscutil/wpack32d.exe

Program Name	UUundo
Platform	Mac68K, PowerMac
URL	http://hyperarchive.lcs.mit.edu/HyperArchive/Archive/cmp/uu-undo-10.hqx

BinHex

Just like uudecoding, un-Binhexing a file is as easy as BinHexing it. Just save the file, assemble its parts (if necessary), and run it through the appropriate program. You can use any of the BinHex programs discussed in the section on posting to decode your files (if you're using a Mac, you can also use StuffIt Expander).

Viewing Binary Pictures With Ease: Web Browsers

If you're interested in viewing binary pictures, you don't have to look any farther than your humble Web browser. Both Netscape Navigator 2.0 and the latest version of Microsoft Internet Explorer contain built-in uudecoding and viewing capabilities as part of their newsreading functions. When you choose an article containing a file, Navigator and Explorer will display the picture inline with the rest of the message. You don't have to deal with uudecoders or separate viewers—just click and look. Unfortunately, you can't save the picture or do anything useful with it. See Chapters 9, "Windows Web Power Tools," and 14, "Mac Web Power Tools," for more information. Figure 23-8 shows Netscape Navigator displaying an inline graphic file from a newsgroup.

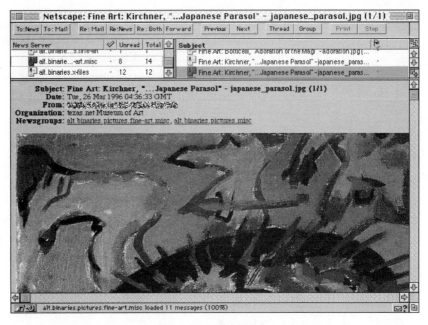

Figure 23-8: Viewing a picture from a newsgroup with Netscape Navigator.

RESOURCES FOR BINARY FILES

Everything we've covered so far should be enough to get you in on the Usenet binary bonanza. However, we realize that power users like you always want more information. As usual, we're happy to oblige. The following list of Web resources should provide everything you need to know about downloading and using binary files from Usenet.

alt.binaries.pictures.d related FAQs

http://www.lib.ox.ac.uk/internet/news/faq/
alt.binaries.pictures.d.html
This page includes links for the AOL Binaries FAQ (detailing how to decode binary files downloaded from America Online), Graphic Utilities' Site &Version FAQ (information on just about every

graphic utility available on the Net), JPEG image compression FAQ (info on JPEG image files), MPEG -FAQ (data on the MPEG compression format), and the ever-so-useful alt.binaries.pictures FAQ, which contains everything you'd ever want to know about decoding what you find on the alt.binaries.pictures newsgroups.

The Usenet-Binary Assemblage

`http://pmwww.cs.vu.nl/usenet/.news.html`

Why bother with decoders at all? Hop over to the Usenet Binaries Assemblage where all the binaries posted to selected newsgroups are already decoded and ready to download. You won't be able to view any nudie pictures here (sorry!), but you will be able to view binaries from the following newsgroups:

alt.binaries.multimedia

alt.binaries.clip-art

alt.binaries.pictures.misc

alt.binaries.pictures.animals

alt.binaries.pictures.vehicles

alt.binaries.pictures.rail

alt.binaries.pictures.astro

alt.binaries.pictures.fractals

alt.binaries.pictures.12hr

alt.binaries.pictures.fine-art.graphics

alt.binaries.pictures.fine-art.digitized

alt.binaries.pictures.cartoons

alt.binaries.pictures.furry

alt.binaries.pictures.anime

alt.binaries.pictures.children

alt.binaries.pictures.teen-idols

alt.binaries.sounds.cartoons

alt.binaries.sounds.midi

alt.binaries.sounds.misc

alt.binaries.sounds.mods

alt.binaries.sounds.movies

alt.binaries.sounds.music

alt.binaries.sounds.tv

Guide to Usenet Binary Attachments

`http://www.europa.com/~tick1845/bin_help.htm`

A nice primer for dealing with binary attachments in Usenet newsgroups, even though this page does have a horrendous background! Included in this concise overview are many links to decoding utilities, viewers, and other programs for dealing with binaries.

PixHelp

`http://www.pixi.com/~keep/page10.html`

Need some more help and links to files? Check out this site. You'll find a good, quick refresher on dealing with picture attachments on Usenet, as well as some links to the programs you'll need (if you're a Windows user) to download and view them.

alt.binaries.pictures utilities archive

`http:// harley.pcl.ox.ac.uk/%7EABPics/`

If you're looking for a one-stop solution to all your binary downloading and viewing needs, look no farther than this absolutely killer Web page. You'll find links here to just about every FAQ, multimedia utility, and decompresser/decoder on the Net (for Mac, Windows, DOS, and UNIX, no less!). We can't recommend this archive enough. In fact, we wish we'd found it earlier—it would have made writing this chapter a whole lot easier! See Figure 23-9 to see what you'll find when you get there.

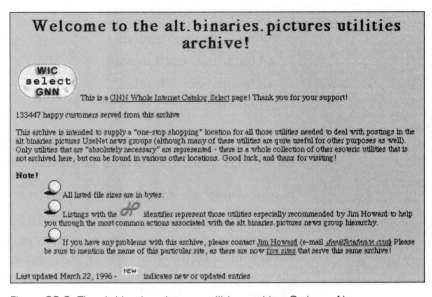

Figure 23-9: The alt.binaries.pictures utilities archive. Go here. Now.

MOVING ON

Well, that just about wraps it up for our power user's coverage of Usenet news. No longer will you quake in fear when you have to download and decode binary files! If you haven't gotten out on Usenet and seen what kind of stuff is available in the binary newsgroups, you should—you'll find all the pictures, sounds, multimedia files, and programs you could ever want, all served up and delivered straight to your newsreader. For the download junky, it's like having a direct line to the source.

Even though you can have a lot of fun with Usenet binaries, up to this point, we still haven't covered where the real action is—the Web. Fear not, intrepid reader—the wait is over! In the next section, we'll dive head first into the site of the Cyberspace gold rush: the World Wide Web. First, we'll cover Web multimedia power tools—all the plug-ins and utilities you need to surf the Web with sound, video, and animation. After you recover from that, we'll move on to tell you what tools you'll need to get your own stuff on the Web.

## Part VII

The Power User's Guide to the Web

Chapter 24

Web Multimedia Power Tools

When HyperText Markup Language (HTML) was designed, no one imagined that this humble page-layout language would become the foundation for one of the biggest media domains of the 20th century. But that certainly looks like the way the Web is headed. Because the original developers of the Web and HTML never imagined that their creation would be used for anything more than sharing documents with fellow researchers, they weren't thinking very far beyond text and links to other text. Of course, at the beginning this wasn't an issue, because most people browsed the Web with text-based browsers. All this changed when Mosaic appeared.

Originally, Mosaic would only display GIF image files and allow controls over text presentation. In order to overcome this shortcoming, *helper applications* were used, allowing people to include links to other data types (like movies and sounds) through their Web pages, which could be displayed by separate programs on the user's machine. Multimedia began to emerge as an adjunct to the Web page design, not as an actual part of the page.

Netscape changed everything once again when it released Navigator 2.0. For the first time, page designers could embed multimedia files right into the page, making the videos, animations, and even sounds part of the overall design, not just a separate media goodie to be viewed as an aside.

Today, the Web is swarming with multimedia. From live video and audio conferencing to animations and VRML (Virtual Reality Modeling Language, for building 3D virtual worlds), the Web has come a long way from the days when a sound file on a page was a big deal. And we're still only at the beginning. As bandwidth increases, graphic technologies become more sophisticated and computers cheaper and faster, media will continue to converge in Cyberspace. By its very nature, the World Wide Web is a meta-medium, a framework where all other media can come together. In a few years, the most advanced, active, media-rich of today's Web pages will look as awkward and quaint as polyester pants, platform shoes, and yellow daisy decals do today.

In this chapter, we'll examine how you can dine on the Web's multimedia stew. Most of the programs we'll cover aren't really programs at all—they're plug-in modules for Netscape Navigator and Microsoft Internet Explorer. If you don't have either one of these browsers, go get one (or both of them) now. Internet Explorer is free (from the Microsoft Network Web site at http://www.msn.com/). They each come in both Windows and Mac flavors.

How to Keep Up

The plug-in craze is insane at the moment. New ones pop up every week or so. How can you keep up? It's easy if you know where to look.

Netscape's home page is probably the best place to find out what new plug-ins have arrived on their doorstep. Go to http://home.netscape.com, and follow the links to the plug-ins section.

Equally as useful (and sometimes more current) is BrowserWatch, an independent resource guide for anyone interested in Web browsers. Once there, bop on over to the Plug-In Plaza!, and check out all the latest wares. BrowserWatch's News page has lots of early announcements and gossip on upcoming browser software. BrowserWatch is at http://www.browserwatch.com.

If you're a Mac user who feels a little left out when it comes to plug-in development, check out *MacWeek*'s plug-in page (http://www.zdnet.com/macweek/mw_1007/plugins.html).

Finally, even though it's not strictly a plug-in resource, make sure you stop by Cool Tool of the Day (http://www.cooltool.com) for the latest in Net tools. Sean takes time out from his job sharpening pencils at the public library to maintain it, so try to support the one useful thing he does with his life by stopping by.

A couple of notes before we press on. This chapter was written in mid-March 1996, and by the time you read this, many of the planned plug-ins may actually be out (and some of the "released" plug-ins may have disappeared). The best policy is to check. Most developers are making an effort to create versions of their plug-ins for Mac and Windows. However, if you see a No designation in the listings that follow, you can be pretty sure that a plug-in for that platform is not going to be developed. But don't fret, someone else will come along and fill the niche in no time.

TIP

Most plug-ins come with fairly good, sometimes surprisingly good, documentation. When in doubt, read it.

As you multimedia-ize your browser, remember that plug-ins and other multimedia viewers suck up memory and often a lot of computing power. If you're having trouble with your browser and a plug-in, try to reduce the load on your system by running as few INITs, TSRs, system extensions, and other programs as possible.

Finally—we can't stress this enough—read the directions! Each plug-in comes with it's own set of installation instructions, instructions that you should follow to the letter. Don't get fancy on us and think that you can wing it—you probably can't.

VIDEO

For sheer impact, it's hard to beat video on a Web page. A 20-second video clip can often provide more information and excitement than 50 pages of text . . . ya know . . . if it's good video. However, video takes up a lot of space, and video files can be huge. At this point, until bandwidth and transmission speeds dramatically increase, we'll have to be content with a lot of either long download times (for quality video) or jerky, grainy *streaming* video that can be viewed as it downloads.

In this section we'll cover all the major forms of online video files—QuickTime, MPEG, and AVI—as well as several proprietary standards for streaming video. All of these plug-ins have different features to recommend them. Since most of them are freeware or shareware, our best advice is to try out as many as you can to find the one that best meets your needs.

QuickTime

QuickTime is Apple's cross-platform standard for digital video and probably the most popular form of online video. As of this time, QuickTime does not support streaming video, but that's expected to change later in 1996 with the introduction of QuickTime 2.3. Keep an eye out for new developments.

KM's Multimedia Plug

This format was kind of a tough one to place, but we decided to put it in the video section because that's probably where you'll get the most use out of it. KM's Multimedia Plug (named for its author, Kevin McMurtrie) is a real workhorse, allowing you to view two types of digital video (QuickTime and MPEG), listen to four different sound formats (MIDI, AU, AIFF, and WAV), and even view inline PICT files.

Macintosh		Windows	
PowerPC	68K	Windows 95	Windows 3.1
Yes	Yes	No	No

Where to get the latest version: ftp://ftp.wco.com/users/ mcmurtri/MySoftware/

MovieStar

This format is about as close as anyone's gotten to producing streaming QuickTime. MovieStar takes QuickTime files specially saved from its Movie Star Maker authoring program and displays them as they download. Technically, it's not streaming video, but it's darn close. The MovieStar plug-in will display QuickTime videos in the native Apple format as well but won't display them during download. Figure 24-1 shows an inline video as displayed by MovieStar.

Figure 24-1: MovieStar—muggin' for the camera.

Macintosh		Windows	
PowerPC	**68K**	**Windows 95**	**Windows 3.1**
Yes	Yes	Yes	Yes

Where to get the latest version: http://www.beingthere.com/

TEC Player

The TEC QuickTime player is a nice, straightforward, 26K QuickTime plug-in. It doesn't do anything fancy (like MovieStar), and it won't display your kitchen sink inline (like KM's plug-in). What it will do is display movies, plain and simple. The Windows 95 version should be ready by the time you read this.

Macintosh		Windows	
PowerPC	**68K**	**Windows 95**	**Windows 3.1**
Yes	Yes	Planned	Planned

Where to get the latest version: http://www.tecs.com/ TEPlayer_docs/

MPEG

MPEG video is a pretty hot commodity these days. Any glance at the Sunday circular of a major newspaper will reveal page after page of ads for new PCs with "MPEG full-screen video" capabilities. And even though most people don't have the foggiest idea what it is, they're rushing to wrestle one of these machine into the family minivan.

MPEG is a way of encoding and compressing digital video that yields relatively small files with very little loss of quality. It does this by using an intelligent algorithm that figures out what changes in a frame of the movie and what doesn't, and then not saving any unnecessary copies of the parts that don't change. What you get is a large (full screen, if you want), high-quality video image. What you don't get is a huge file.

As you can imagine, this kind of compression takes a lot of computing power. But, as computer power goes up and prices go down, the hardware necessary for MPEG viewing is finally becoming affordable to the general public. In fact, this year the video industry will introduce DVDs (digital video discs). These disks use MPEG compression to reduce a full-length movie so that it can fit onto a CD-ROM-sized optical disk.

As MPEG video becomes more popular, we'll probably see a lot more MPEG plug-ins in the coming months. Watch the skies.

PreVU

PreVU is an MPEG video plug-in that provides some really nice features for Netsurfers. First, PreVU movies display a *preview* image on a Web page so that you can see what the movie looks like before you begin to download it. Once the download begins, you can view the movie in a streaming mode, allowing you to watch the movie inline without the wait. Finally, once you download the movie, PreVU plays it from your cache for faster performance. See Figure 24-2 for a preview of PreVU.

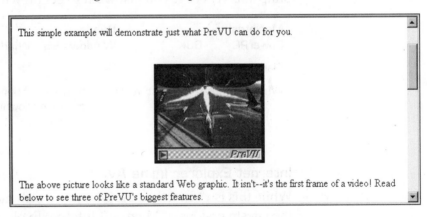

Figure 24-2: PreVU at work.

Macintosh		Windows	
PowerPC	68K	Windows 95	Windows 3.1
Planned	Planned	Yes	No
Where to get the latest version:		http://www.intervu.com/prevu.html	

AVI

Microsoft (of course!) has its own video standard called Microsoft Video or AVI. AVI hasn't been as successful as QuickTime as far as the market's concerned, mainly because there's no real AVI player for the Mac (there are AVI-to-QuickTime converters, however). This doesn't mean that there's not a lot of AVI files out there on the Web. All you need is the right program to view them, which if you've got a Windows machine, is not problem.

Cool Fusion

Cool Fusion by Iterated Systems allows you to view real-time, pseudo-streaming AVI files inside Web pages. While it's not true client-server streaming, Cool Fusion does display files as they download, allowing you to see what you're going to get and decide whether you want to wait another 10 minutes for that Simpsons AVI or if you just want to get on with your life.

Macintosh		Windows	
PowerPC	68K	Windows 95	Windows 3.1
Planned	Planned	Yes	No

Where to get the latest version: http://webber.iterated.com/coolfusn/download/cf-loadp.htm

Internet Explorer Inline AVI

While this isn't exactly a plug-in, it is worth mentioning here that the latest versions of Microsoft Internet Explorer support inline AVI playback. Using a few simple extensions to HTML, Web page designers can size or resize the playback window, loop the video, or control the number of times it plays back. Figure 24-3 shows Microsoft's demo page with an inline AVI coffee cup.

Figure 24-3: Spin a cup o' joe with Internet Explorer's AVI support.

Macintosh		Windows	
PowerPC	**68K**	**Windows 95**	**Windows 3.1**
Yes	Yes	Yes	Yes

Where to get the latest version: http://www.msn.com/

Streaming Video

Streaming video is about as close as the Net comes to television. Using special proprietary file formats, streaming video players overcome the limitations of the Internet to deliver live *streams* of video data between a stream server and a client (either a plug-in or a stand-alone client). The streams of video data can be viewed as they download. If you want more information on the state-of-the-art in "Net TV" and online video, see Chapter 28, "Audio/Video Power Tools."

VDOLive

VDOLive is probably the hottest streaming video software right now. Using a special VDOLive Server on the sending end and either a plug-in (for Navigator 2.01 or Internet Explorer) or a stand-alone helper app (for other browsers), VDOLive allows you to view live video feeds, even with a 14.4 kbps modem! One of the nice features of VDOLive is that it attempts to bring you the best picture quality/frame rate for your bandwidth, so as your connection speed increases, so does the quality of the video. Also, because the data is received and displayed in a stream, no big video file clogs up your hard drive. Figure 24-4 shows what it's like to watch "Net TV" with VDOLive.

Figure 24-4: VDOLive in action.

TIP

The Macintosh client for VDOLive is expected to be released in April, so it should be out by the time you read this. Log on, and see for yourself.

Macintosh		Windows	
PowerPC	68K	Windows 95	Windows 3.1
Planned	Planned	Yes	Yes
Where to get the latest version:		http://www.vdolive.com/	

StreamWorks

This format is another toughie to place. Xing Technology's StreamWorks allows you to watch live video or just listen to live audio. Like VDOLive, StreamWorks is a true streaming format, utilizing a special server and a stand-alone client program. The folks at Xing know that most of us don't have T1 lines or cable modems (yet!), so they've provided the capability to select streams by the speed of your connection. See Figure 24-5.

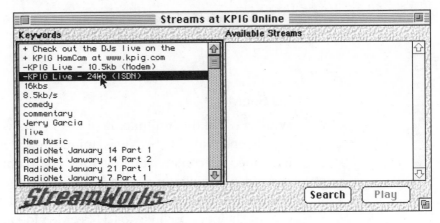

Figure 24-5: Selecting a stream.

There's a lot of programming to choose from, including several commercial radio stations and a few live TV feeds. Figure 24-6 shows NBC-PRO, one of the most popular video streams.

Figure 24-6: Checking up on the biz news with NBC-PRO.

Macintosh		Windows	
PowerPC	68K	Windows 95	Windows 3.1
Yes	Yes	Yes	Yes

Where to get the latest version: http://www.xingtech.com/
streams/index.html

CU-SeeMe

While most of the multimedia players we cover in this chapter are
strictly one-way, CU-SeeMe is unique in that it allows you to do
live video teleconferencing over the Web, complete with sound
and video. Originally, CU-SeeMe was designed as a stand-alone
teleconferencing program, but people have devised ways to
provide helper app links to CU-SeeMe video *reflectors* sites which
allow multi-person video conferences (see Figure 24-7).

Figure 24-7: A CU-SeeMe video conference. Hi Mom!

Macintosh		Windows	
PowerPC	68K	Windows 95	Windows 3.1
Yes	Yes	Yes	Yes

Where to get the latest version: http://cu-seeme.cornell.edu/

Enhanced CU-SeeMe

Cornell University developed the early versions of CU-SeeMe, but now White Pine software has taken over development and is moving CU-SeeMe into a full-blown commercial product. So what do you get if you buy CU-SeeMe? White Pine has included the following enhancements:

❏ Full-color support

❏ A shared white board for exchanging data

❏ Phone books for organizing your connections

❏ Enhanced security

❏ Streamlined user interface

If you're just playing around with video conferencing from home, the freeware version will probably do you just fine. However, if you work for a megacorp, have a high-speed connection, and want to use a color video camera, Enhanced CU-SeeMe might be just the ticket for staying in touch with those far-flung colleagues.

Macintosh		Windows	
PowerPC	68K	Windows 95	Windows 3.1
Planned	Planned	Yes	Yes

Where to get the latest version: http://www.cu-seeme.com

■ ■

CU-SeeMe Addicts, Unite!

Cu-SeeMe is a really cool technology, and if you dabble with it, you may get hooked. If CU-SeeMe addiction creeps up on you, don't blame us. Just give in, and head on over to The Reflector (http://www-bcf.usc.edu/~vanman/reflector.html) for your daily dose of CU-SeeMe info. You'll find reflector lists, information about CU-SeeMe online gatherings, links to the latest software, and a bit of gossip. It's a great way to stay in touch with the burgeoning world of CU-SeeMe aficionados worldwide, as well as a one-stop shop for links to software and information.

■ ■

MUSIC, SPEECH & SOUND

Video's nice, but it eats bandwidth for lunch (and dinner and then breakfast the next morning) and often requires special server software/hardware to use it effectively in your Web pages. If you want to jazz up your pages (or want your life jazzed without as much waiting), sound is a good way to add some excitement.

One of the nice features of sound files is that, depending on what format you use, they can be fairly small. MIDI sounds are the smallest, often taking up as little as 24K for an entire piano concerto. (See the Classical MIDI Archive at http://www.prs.net/midi.html for some examples.) Of course, because MIDI works by recording the method for playback and not the actual sounds, what you hear is entirely based on what MIDI hardware and software you have on your end. Other formats are a bit larger, but you can still squeeze a lot of sound into a little file if you know what you're doing. And now, with the development of streaming audio, even that problem has been solved.

Streaming Audio

Audio developers have also developed streaming formats, allowing large sound files to be played as they download so you don't have to wait to hear them. Two formats—RealAudio and StreamWorks—allow live audio feeds for real Net radio broadcasts (or "Netcasts"). In fact, several commercial radio stations are already on the Net, broadcasting live, 24 hours a day. While the quality of the transmissions doesn't exactly give FM a run for its money, it's at least on par with a cheap clock radio. (Hey, what do you want out of a burgeoning technology?)

RealAudio

By far, RealAudio is the king of Internet audio on demand. A true streaming sound format, it utilizes a special server to deliver reasonable-quality sound files over the Net, in both live and taped formats. You can almost channel surf, clicking between National Public Radio, ABC news, a CD juke box, and even catch special RealAudio Netcasts. What's more, because RealAudio does such a great job of managing to shove a whole lot of sound through a low-speed connection, you can even let RealAudio run in the background while you surf the Web. Figure 24-8 shows the RealAudio player on a Macintosh.

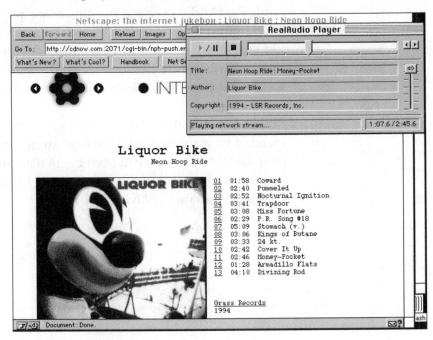

Figure 24-8: Groovin' on RealAudio.

Macintosh		Windows	
PowerPC	68K	Windows 95	Windows 3.1
Yes	Yes	Yes	Yes

Where to get the latest version: http://www.realaudio.com/

Internet Jukebox

One of the coolest applications of RealAudio is the Internet Jukebox, a service of the CDNow store, which allows you to listen to entire selections from hundreds of their CDs. Toss in your quarters, and punch up Hank Williams on http://interjuke.com. Ah . . . don't forget you need the RealAudio player first.

StreamWorks

While RealAudio excels at pushing huge, pre-recorded sound files through the Net, StreamWorks, strength is in delivering live audio. As we discussed earlier in the streaming video section, StreamWorks handles video too. However, until connection speeds go up, you'll probably find StreamWorks more useful for Netcast radio.

StreamWorks allows you to pick your stream based on the speed of your connection. Like RealAudio, StreamWorks works with the Web, and you can even begin listening to a stream and keep browsing without the stream being broken. Figure 24-9 shows StreamWorks playing live radio.

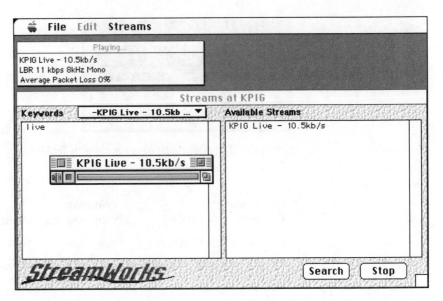

Figure 24-9: Listen to a Netcast with StreamWorks. (Trust us, there's sound coming out of this thing.)

Macintosh		Windows	
PowerPC	68K	Windows 95	Windows 3.1
Yes	Yes	Yes	Yes

Where to get the latest version: http://www.xingtech.com/streams/index.html

ToolVox

ToolVox isn't strictly a streaming protocol, but it uses a 53:1 compression algorithm that's so fast it might as well be. A ToolVox file loads quickly. If you're a Web developer, it gets better. Once you create a ToolVox file with the ToolVox Encoder you'll be ready to serve your files right away. Because the magic of ToolVox is in the compression, you don't need a fancy server to serve ToolVox files on your own Web page—just add it to your page and get your systems administrator to add a new MIME type to your server, and you're ready to go (see Figure 24-10).

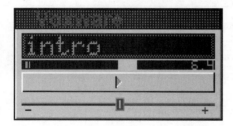

Figure 24-10: Listening to a sound file with ToolVox.

Macintosh		Windows	
PowerPC	68K	Windows 95	Windows 3.1
Planned	Planned	Yes	Yes

Where to get the latest version: http://www.voxware.com/download.htm

TrueSpeech

Even though music makes up a large part of the stored sound content on the Web, recorded speech probably makes up the bulk of the streaming audio. Many organizations are now including spoken greetings on their pages, recorded speeches, or even audio help files. TrueSpeech is a stand-alone helper app optimized for delivering speech. For a great demonstration of the power of TrueSpeech, check out the Banned Books Exhibit at http://www.banned.books.com/. Once you're there, you can hear writers Salman Rushdie and Andrei Codrescu read from their works and Senator Exon read his unsettling "prayer" before the passage of the controversial Telecommunications Decency Act.

Macintosh		Windows	
PowerPC	68K	Windows 95	Windows 3.1
Yes	Planned	Yes	Yes

Where to get the latest version: http://www.dspg.com

MIDI

MIDI is an acronym for musical instrument digital interface. It was developed in 1983 by the International MIDI Standards Organization as a standard to allow electronic instruments and computers to communicate with each other. When you listen to a MIDI file on your computer, you aren't hearing a recording of the actual sounds played by the instrument, you're hearing the sounds generated by your computer in response to the instructions contained in the MIDI file.

Because MIDI codes are simply instructions, a MIDI file can be a lot smaller than a conventional sound recording. It's not uncommon for a 20-minute MIDI song to take up only 25-50K. Because of their small size and their ability to control the computer's playback, MIDI files are very popular with multimedia designers, game developers, and people who generally want high-quality instrumental music with low overhead.

For an excellent introduction to MIDI, read the alt.binaries.sounds.midi FAQ at the R&S Jumpstation (http://www.rsrecords.com/mi_soft.htm). You'll also find loads of MIDI files, resources, and links to other MIDI pages on the Web.

Crescendo

Crescendo is probably the best cross-platform MIDI plug-in for Navigator and Microsoft Internet Explorer. It's small (under 40K) and fast, and it works with every MIDI file we tried. It'll play inline MIDIs as backgrounds for your Web pages as well as any MIDI files you might run across during your travels. Figure 24-11 shows Crescendo playing a stand-alone file.

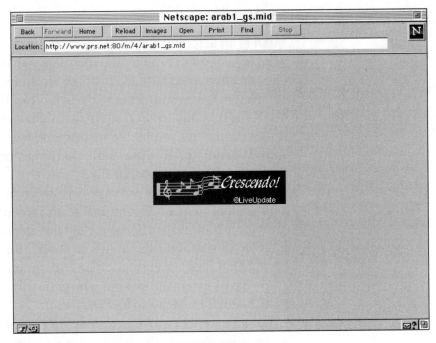

Figure 24-11: Crescendo playing a MIDI file.

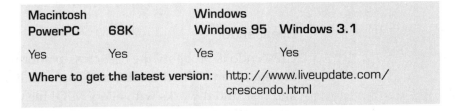

Macintosh		Windows	
PowerPC	68K	Windows 95	Windows 3.1
Yes	Yes	Yes	Yes

Where to get the latest version: http://www.liveupdate.com/crescendo.html

Microsoft Internet Explorer Background MIDI

If you don't want to deal with installing and using plug-ins for MIDI, get yourself a copy of Microsoft Internet Explorer. It can handle background MIDI as well as stand-alone MIDI links and will even play MIDI loops in the background for any Web pages you design. Oh, and by the way, it'll play WAV files, too.

Macintosh		Windows	
PowerPC	68K	Windows 95	Windows 3.1
Yes	Yes	Yes	Yes

Where to get the latest version: http://www.msn.com/

MIDI Plug-in

MIDI Plug-in is a simple plug-in for the Mac written by Arnaud Masson. Don't expect bells and whistles (unless they're part of the MIDI file!)

Macintosh		Windows	
PowerPC	68K	Windows 95	Windows 3.1
Yes	Yes	No	No

Where to get the latest version: http://www.planete.net/ ~amasson/

Speech

Right now, Macs have a lock on Web speech technology, mainly because the Macintosh comes preconfigured with text-to-speech and speech recognition software. However, as more and more PCs come on the market equipped with speech technology (Compaq Presarios, for example), we may start seeing speech plug-ins for Intel computers. Until then, all you Windows users will have to wait.

Speech Recognition

There are two ways to use speech with your computer: you can listen to computer-generated speech, or you can control your computer by talking to it. Macintosh computers come with PlainTalk speech recognition. While it works with most applications through speaking menu choices, it doesn't do diddly if you want to throw away your mouse and surf the Net by voice. Speech-recognition plug-in modules allow you to select links by speaking—good-bye mouse! However, at this point, these plug-ins only work with pages preconfigured for speech recognition.

ListenUp

This first plug-in doesn't generate speech—it listens to yours! Pages that are configured for ListenUp can be navigated by giving spoken commands to your Mac. All you need is PlainTalk installed (available on your system software install disks) and a microphone connected to your Mac.

Macintosh		Windows	
PowerPC	68K	Windows 95	Windows 3.1
Yes	No	No	No
Where to get the latest version:		http://snow.cit.cornell.edu/noon/ ListenUp.html	

ShockTalk

On the slightly more esoteric side, ShockTalk allows you to use your microphone to control multimedia productions created with Macromedia Director that have been enhanced by speech-recognition capabilities. When you encounter one of these speech-enhanced Director files and view it using Shockwave for Director (see the "Shockwave for Director" section later in this chapter), you'll be able to interact with it just by speaking. Pretty cool. Figure 24-12 shows the demo U.S. Capital Quiz , used by Digital Dreams to showcase its ShockTalk technology.

Figure 24-12: Taking a quiz with ShockTalk.

Macintosh		Windows	
PowerPC	68K	Windows 95	Windows 3.1
Yes	Yes	No	No
Where to get the latest version:		http://www.emf.net/~dreams/Hi-Res/index.html	

Computer-Generated Speech

Computer-synthesized speech can add a new, exciting dimension to a Web page. Of course, the speech is just being generated by the computer, which is translating the words on the page, but it's still a pretty cool effect that has some obvious utility for the visually impaired.

Keep in mind that all the plug-ins in this section generate speech directly from the text. When your browser, equipped with a text-to-speech plug-in encounters a talking page, it does all the processing work. Since the computer's doing all the work, there's no lengthy download time as with prerecorded sounds. Talking pages take no longer to load than their mute equivalents.

With most personal computers (Macs included), speech technology is still in its infancy. We're a long way from having computers on our desktops that talk to us like the computers in so many cheap sci-fi films (or certain expensive sci-fi TV shows). Most computer-generated speech sounds downright silly at this point—that's part of its charm.

Speech Plug-in

Using a few simple extensions to HTML you can set up your pages so that anyone visiting your page who has the Speech Plug-In installed will hear your page as well as see it. A basic text reader.

Macintosh PowerPC	68K	Windows Windows 95	Windows 3.1
Yes	Yes	No	No

Where to get the latest version: http://www.albany.net/~wtudor

Talker

Talker is a bit more advanced than the Speech Plug-In. In fact, Talker will even sing or whisper Web pages to you. For an example, try Bananaman's Poem of the Day (http://www.ithaca.edu/shp/shp97/jwhong1/banana/) for a hilarious example of how Talker can be programmed to sing. It's a frightening portent for the rest of the Web (just kidding, Mr. Banana). In case you're wondering if a page has been enhanced with Talker, just look for the Talker logo (see Figure 24-13). Then decide if you want to run away.

Figure 24-13: The Talker warning . . . er . . . we mean logo.

Macintosh		Windows	
PowerPC	68K	Windows 95	Windows 3.1
Yes	Yes	No	No

Where to get the latest version: http://www.mvpsolutions.com/ PlugInSite/Talker.html

Other Sound Formats—Helper Apps

Besides streaming audio, MIDI, and speech, you may encounter loads of other sound formats in your travels. At this point, most of them don't have plug-ins, though that may change soon. KM's Multimedia Plug (see the previous section "KM's Multimedia Plug") is pretty much the only one available for AIFF and AU files. If you don't have KM's plug-in, you'll have to use a helper application.

SoundApp

If you've got a Macintosh, your best bet for a sound helper application is SoundApp. As you can see from the list below, it handles just about everything you can come up against. And, as an added bonus, Netscape Navigator already comes configured for it. You can get SoundApp at http://hyperarchive.lcs.mit.edu/ HyperArchive/Archive/gst/snd/sound-app-151.hqx.

The following formats are supported:

❑ SoundCap

❑ SoundEdit

❑ AIFF and .AIFF-C

❑ System 7

❑ Quicktime Soundtracks

❑ .AU

❑ NeXT .SND

❏ .WAV

❏ .VOC

❏ .MOD

❏ .IFF

❏ Sound Designer II

❏ PSION

❏ .WVE

❏ .DVI ADPCM

❏ Studio Session

CoolEdit

Windows 95 users will want to check out CoolEdit, an excellent utility. Not only does CoolEdit play a whole host of file formats (see list below) but it also allows you to record and edit sounds, too. Not a bad combo. You can get the latest version of CoolEdit from http://www.syntrillium.com/.

The following formats are supported:

❏ .WAV

❏ .SAM

❏ .AIF

❏ .VOX

❏ µ-law

❏ .AU

❏ .PCM

❏ .SMP

❏ .VOC datacomp

SPECIALTY GRAPHICS

There seems to be a graphics file format for nearly every imaginable application. While most browsers support the common graphics formats (GIF and JPEG), this doesn't even scratch the surface of the number of file formats floating around the Net. There are new highly compressed file formats that use special fractal and wavelet techniques to turn large, full-color graphics files into small files that retain most of their detail. Vector formats, used mainly for illustration, maps, and computer-aided design, are really mathematical models of images rather than images themselves. There are even file formats that seem to have no real use except to maintain a proprietary standard. Overall, there are something like 200 different digital graphics file formats.

Fortunately, for just about every file type, there's a plug-in or viewer that can handle it. The problem is keeping track of what plug-in takes care of what file format. Hopefully, this section will straighten things out a bit for you.

High Compression

One of the major problems with high-definition graphics files is that they take up a huge amount of space. It's not uncommon for an 8 x 10-inch full-color (24-bit) graphics file scanned in at 300 dpi to take up over 27MB of space. Even with a 28.8 kbps modem, an image of that size would take up to three hours to download. Obviously, this isn't an option for most people.

Compression can take a large image and make it smaller. Common forms of compression take advantage of one of two techniques, *lossy* or *lossless* compression. Lossy compression does just what it sounds like—it makes a file smaller by throwing away bits of the image that don't make a difference for the viewer. Lossless compression, on the other hand, uses special techniques to retain all the bits of the image while making the file smaller.

Both JPEG and GIF (the two most common file formats) use compression to reduce the size of the image. GIF files use lossless compression, resulting in high-quality images that are somewhat smaller than their uncompressed originals. JPEG, on the other hand, uses a range of compression techniques, from low-loss to high-loss compression, which results in images retaining most of their colors but sometimes losing detail. JPEG images are usually much smaller than GIF images and are becoming more popular as a means of transmitting digital image files.

While GIF and JPEG formats are the standard on the Web these days, there are several highly-compressed formats jockeying for position as the next standard.

Fractal Image

Using new fractal image compression techniques, Fractal Image allows you to view FIF files, which are amazingly detailed and colorful but small. As an extra bonus, Fractal Image's plug-in and viewer allow you to zoom in and out of the image so that you can get the full effect of the detail. Figure 24-14 shows what a zoomed image looks like.

Figure 24-14: Zooming in with Fractal Image.

Macintosh		Windows	
PowerPC	68K	Windows 95	Windows 3.1
Planned helper App available now	Planned	Yes	Planned
Where to get the latest version:		http://www.iterated.com/ cnplugin.htm	

Lightning Strike

Lightning Strike uses wavelet compression to produce files that are over 120 times smaller than their GIF or JPEG counterparts while still maintaining excellent image quality. Lightning Strike is a plug-in, so it allows you to view its images inline as part of a Web page. Don't believe it? See Figure 24-15 for a comparison between a GIF image (on the left) and a Lightning Strike image (on the right).

Figure 24-15: A GIF image compared to a Lightning Strike image.

Macintosh		Windows	
PowerPC	68K	Windows 95	Windows 3.1
Yes	Yes	Yes	Yes
Where to get the latest version:		http://www.infinop.com/html/ infinop.html	

Summus

Summus also uses wavelet technologies to compress images, and the results are just as good as Lightning Strike. The one thing that Summus offers that Lightning Strike doesn't is an incredibly detailed explanation of how the technology works. Go to http://www.summus.com/wavelets.htm for more about wavelets than you could ever want to know. It's *way* over our heads, but the mathematically inclined members of our audience may get something out of it.

Macintosh		Windows	
PowerPC	68K	Windows 95	Windows 3.1
Planned	Planned	Yes	Yes

Where to get the latest version: http://www.summus.com/

Vector Graphics

Most of the images that you view on the Web are one variation or another of bitmapped graphics—each pixel representing one bit of information, with the picture being drawn by placing rows of pixels on the screen. Compression technologies can help, but no matter what you do, bitmapped graphics still must depend on individual pixels displayed together to make a picture.

On the other hand, vector graphics don't contain individual pixels. Instead, they are mathematical models of a picture that instruct the computer on what to draw—what kinds of lines, what colors, in what dimensions, and what thickness. Because you aren't using individual pixels to draw an image, there's virtually no limit to how large or how small you can size a vector graphics image. No matter what size you make it, the level of detail remains the same. Because vector graphics maintain this consistent quality, they're ideal for line illustrations, maps, architectural drawings, and engineering plans.

The most common vector graphics format is PostScript, a language that instructs devices (such as printers and displays) on how to present graphics and text. EPS files (encapsulated PostScript) include both the PostScript version of the image as well as a low-resolution preview image in a format that most computer displays can handle. EPS is the most common vector format, and if you use FreeHand, CorelDRAW!, or Illustrator, you use EPS files. Besides EPS, the other common vector formats are the DXF and DWG formats produced by AutoCAD, FreeHand files produced by Macromedia FreeHand, and Corel CMX files.

FIGleaf Inline

FIGleaf Inline is an incredibly useful plug-in. Not only does it allow you to view CGM (computer graphics metafile—a vector format) images on Web pages, but you can also use it to display any of the following graphic formats:

- Tagged Image File Format (TIFF)
- Encapsulated PostScript (EPSI/EPSF)
- CCITT Group 4 Type 1 (G4) and Type 2 (TG4)
- Bitmap (BMP) and Metafile (WMF)
- Portable Pixmap (PPM)
- Portable Greymap (PGM)
- Portable Bitmap (PBM)
- Sun Raster files (SUN)
- GIF
- JPEG

Macintosh		Windows	
PowerPC	68K	Windows 95	Windows 3.1
Planned	Planned	Yes	Yes

Where to get the latest version: http://www.ct.ebt.com/figinline/

CMX Viewer

If you're an artist, graphic designer, or illustrator who uses a PC, chances are that you use CorelDRAW for some of your work. Wouldn't it be great if you could use some of that art on the Web, without having to translate it into a bitmapped format first? With CMX viewer you can! If you design your own Web pages, CMX Viewer comes straight from Corel and gives you the ability to display CMX vector files in their original format as inline images. Figure 24-16 shows CMX Viewer at work.

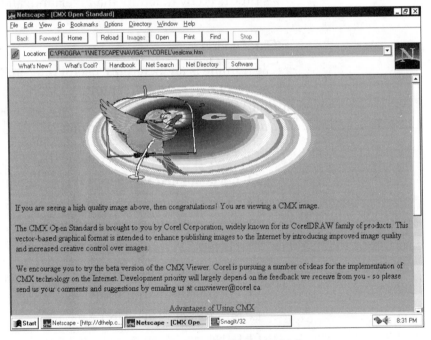

Figure 24-16: Using CMX Viewer to display inline CMX files.

Macintosh		Windows	
PowerPC	68K	Windows 95	Windows 3.1
No	No	Yes	No

Where to get the latest version: http://www.corel.com/

DWG/DXF Viewer/SVF Viewer

If you're an architect, engineer, or anyone who uses AutoCAD, you're going to love these plug-ins. Using the technology SoftSource developed for their Vdraft (Virtual Drafting) program, you can view AutoCAD DWG, DXF files with one plug-in, and SVF files with the other—all inline on the Web without translation. Exchange plans with your clients, communicate with your field engineers, or just show off your works of art. If you use AutoCAD or Vdraft, this is the perfect way to publish your work on the Net. Figure 24-17 shows a puzzle designed in Vdraft and viewed on the Web with SVFViewer.

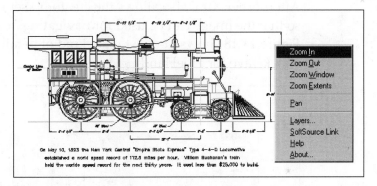

Figure 24-17: The SVF Mystery Puzzle at http://www.softsource.com/softsource/svf/puzzle.html.

| Macintosh | | Windows | |
PowerPC	68K	Windows 95	Windows 3.1
No	No	Yes	No
Where to get the latest version:		http://www.softsource.com/softsource/	

Shockwave FreeHand

FreeHand is one of the most popular PostScript drawing programs, and it's used by nearly every graphic artist who pushes around a mouse. Shockwave for FreeHand now makes all those files available for Web browsing.

Probably the coolest thing about using FreeHand files online is that they can be zoomed up to 25,600 percent! This makes them perfect for highly detailed maps, complex medical or engineering illustrations, complicated diagrams that need to be viewed at various levels of detail, and fancy text effects. On top of the zooming features, Shockwave for FreeHand, in conjunction with the Afterburner Xtra, also allows the creator to set up internal hotlinks so that the image can be used for navigating around the Web. Figure 24-18 shows you just what kind of detail you can get using Shockwave for FreeHand.

Figure 24-18: Zooming in on a map with Shockwave for FreeHand.

TIP

The one problem with Shockwave for FreeHand is that some of the zooming and panning features aren't exactly obvious. If you find yourself viewing FreeHand files with Shockwave, use this handy chart to find your way around:

Action	Macintosh	Windows
Zoom in	Command+click	Ctrl+click
Zoom out	Command+Option+click	Ctrl+alt+click
Original view	Command+Shift+click	Ctrl+click
Pan	Ctrl+click	space+click

Macintosh		Windows	
PowerPC	68K	Windows 95	Windows 3.1
Yes	Yes	Yes	Yes

Where to get the latest version: http://www.macromedia.com/Tools/FHShockwave/

DOCUMENT VIEWERS

While a lot of people are communicating via the Web these days, a lot more are still communicating the old-fashioned way—on paper. Wouldn't it be nice if those same printed documents could be exchanged and published without having to convert them to HTML and deal with all that nasty stuff often involved with putting them on the Web? Portable document formats are the answer.

Portable documents are electronic files generated from word processing and page layout programs that can be viewed without the original program that created them. They retain all the original formatting, layout and design of the original document but are viewable on the screen and easily transmitted over the Net.

To view these documents, you'll need a document-viewer program. Several viewers work inline with your browser, with the documents appearing right in the browser window. Others function as helper apps, automatically opening and displaying any portable documents you download.

But there's a catch (isn't there always?). At this point in time there's no single standard for portable documents. Each vendor has its own proprietary format, requiring its own proprietary viewer. The choices can be confusing, but hopefully after you've perused this section, you'll have a good idea about what you need and where to get it.

Inline Document Viewers

Inline document viewers are the best option if you can use them. Since they allow you to view documents inline, they allow you to keep moving along in your surfing without having to switch back and forth between two different applications. These viewers still give you all the navigation tools you'd get in a stand-alone viewer—they just put the controls right on your Web page.

Acrobat 3.0

Adobe Acrobat currently reigns as the queen of the portable document formats. PDF files (as Acrobat files are called) are just about everywhere on the Web. Until recently, if you wanted to view a PDF file, you had to use a separate PDF reader called Acrobat..

Now, with the Acrobat 3.0 (previously code-named Amber) plug-in, you can view PDF files inline on the Web. Pages appear just as they would if they were printed, and the navigation buttons you need for viewing PDF files appear in a nice row at the top of the document (see Figure 24-19).

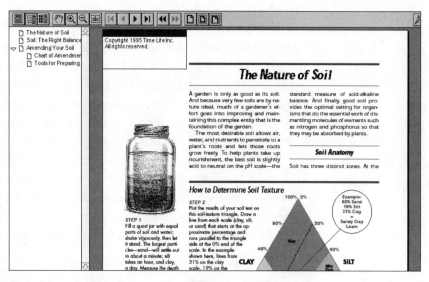

Figure 24-19: Viewing aXcess magazine inline with Acrobat.

TIP

So now that you've got this nifty plug-in, what do you do with it? Go visit the Acrobat examples page at http://www.adobe.com/acrobat/3beta/amexamp.html to find out what Acrobat can do for your Web browsing. You'll be pleasantly surprised.

Macintosh		Windows	
PowerPC	68K	Windows 95	Windows 3.1
Yes	Yes	Yes	Yes

Where to get the latest version: http://www.adobe.com/acrobat/amber/

Envoy

Hot on the heels of Acrobat is Envoy, the new portable document format being promoted by Tumbleweed Software and Novell. Like Acrobat, Envoy documents retain all the formatting and graphics of the original document, while allowing the document to be viewed on nearly any machine. Also, since Envoy is a plug-in, you can use it to view documents inline on the Web.

What's the difference between Envoy and Adobe's PDF format? Not much except that Adobe has the lock on the portable document format world at this point. Both formats accomplish nearly the same task. However, a growing number of sites are starting to use Envoy, so you may want to have it handy on your machine.

Macintosh		Windows	
PowerPC	68K	Windows 95	Windows 3.1
Yes	Yes	Yes	Yes

Where to get the latest version: http://www.twcorp.com/

Word Viewer

Acrobat and Envoy are great if you're a professional designer who uses a page layout program, but what if you're an average Joe or Jane who just uses a word processor for most of your document needs? Have you been forgotten when it comes to putting your publications on the Web? Of course not! Word viewer allows you to view Microsoft Word documents inline. You can include pictures, graphs, and fancy formatting.

Macintosh		Windows	
PowerPC	68K	Windows 95	Windows 3.1
Planned	Planned	Yes	Yes

Where to get the latest version: http://www.inso.com/plug.htm

External Document Viewers

If you don't use Netscape Navigator or Microsoft Internet Explorer, you can use these external viewers to peruse any portable documents you come across while you're online.

Acrobat

Adobe Acrobat was the first portable document viewer, and in our not-so-humble opinions, it's still the best. Not only does it do an outstanding job of rendering portable documents at the best possible quality, but it's also extensible through its own plug-ins that let you do some pretty nifty stuff. You can surf the Web (with the WebLink plug-in), view QuickTime video (with the Movie plug-in), or even link PDF documents with other programs using OLE (with the OLE plug-in).

If you've already downloaded Acrobat Amber, don't bother getting Acrobat, too. Amber comes with its own stand-alone PDF viewer, perfect for viewing PDF files that may come your way off of the Web.

Macintosh		Windows	
PowerPC	68K	Windows 95	Windows 3.1
Yes	Yes	Yes	Yes

Where to get the latest version: http://www.adobe.com/Acrobat/

ANIMATION & INTERACTIVE MULTIMEDIA

While all the other programs we've covered so far are considered multimedia, they usually do only one thing at a time—show movies, play sounds, display documents, or allow you to view highly compressed images. None we've seen so far allow you to do all those things at once.

In this section, we're going to explore the best of the multimedia plug-ins available for the Web. These plug-ins will allow you to display text and animations, listen to sounds, and view presentations all within the Web page you're viewing, often at the same time. Some even let you interact with documents, allowing you to use multimedia menus, view interactive logos, and even play games.

Shockwave for Director

Shockwave is red hot and the object of big hype on the Web right now. By adding the Shockwave plug-in to Navigator or Internet Explorer, you can play files developed in Macromedia Director. So what? Well, these files aren't just simple pictures or animations— they're full-fledged multimedia productions that you can interact with. Shockwave allows mediameisters to create presentations, interactive puzzles, animated title bars, or even full-blown video games that you can play using your Web browser.

How does it work? First, an interactive media designer creates a multimedia program using Director, and then the designer runs it through a special post-processing program called Afterburner (not the same one as the FreeHand Xtra), which combines the file, compresses it, and makes it Web-friendly. If you're familiar with presentation software such as Persuasion or PowerPoint, the concept shouldn't be too alien to you. Afterburner creates a player file that can be run on any machine with the correct playback software. In this case, that software is Shockwave.

If you want to see just what kind of magic Shockwave for Director can do, start your explorations at the Shockwave Gallery (http://www.macromedia.com/Tools/Shockwave/Gallery/ index.html), a list of over a thousand links to "shocked" sites on the Web. Play live games! Control your own Beavis and Butthead! Gag at Boots' Sick and Twisted Shockwave Gallery! Whatever you're looking for, there's probably a Shockwave version of it. Figure 24-20 shows one of the more extreme examples.

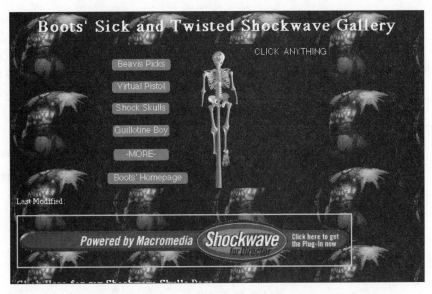

Figure 24-20: Prepare to be shocked (literally!) at Boots' Sick and Twisted Shockwave Gallery.

Macintosh		Windows	
PowerPC	68K	Windows 95	Windows 3.1
Yes	Yes	Yes	Yes

Where to get the latest version: http://www.macromedia.com/Tools/Shockwave/index.html

Animated GIFs

One of the neat features of Netscape Navigator and Internet Explorer is that they support inline viewing of animated GIFs, special GIF files that actually contain several images along with embedded timing and playback information. These GIF files act like regular GIFs, until you view them in a browser that supports their animation features. Then they come to life, playing each stored animation frame. Even though Navigator has supported animated GIFs since release 2.0, surprisingly few people have actually taken advantage of this feature to put animation on their pages. For a killer introduction on how to make animated GIF files and some excellent examples, check out Royal Frazier's Making Animated GIFs page at http://members.aol.com/royalef/gifmake.htm. Animated GIFs don't just have to be window dressing, either. Check out SteveMD's How to Juggle page (http://www.vivanet.com/~stevemd/juggle1.html), where you can watch the animations to learn how to juggle! (See Figure 24-21.)

Learn to Juggle in 6 Steps

Click on image to animate.
Requires Netscape ver 3.0b4 or later.

With a few hours practice, you can learn to juggle. Just follow these steps.

Step 1 - Equipment

Find 3 balls that are heavy for their size. Something about the size and weight of a small apple is about right. You need the weight to properly feel them land in your hand. Lacrosse balls are great and not too expensive. And they come in different colors, which makes them more fun to watch. Tennis balls are too light; golf balls too small; softballs too big. The soft juggling balls they sell are good though a bit expensive. The advantage is they don't roll away when you drop them. But if you practice standing over a bed, the harder balls won't roll away either, AND you don't have to bend over too far to pick them up. Plus if you are practicing with apples, they won't get so smashed up.

Figure 24-21: Watch and learn how to juggle with animated GIFs.

Other Multimedia & Animation Formats

Shockwave and animated GIFs aren't the only animation formats available on the Web, though they are the most popular. If you cruise around for a while, you'll be sure to run into a bunch of other animation formats—some useful, others not, all hyping themselves as a new standard. Some of these animations are based on commercially available presentation or animation products. Others introduce methods for creating files. Each one has some unique features to recommend it, as well as some annoying features. Read on, take a tour through all the different animation formats, and decide for yourself.

ASAP WebShow

If you're a business type who gives a lot of presentations, ASAP's WebShow plug-in may be just the ticket for transforming your favorite presentations into Web pages. Or, if you're a Web browser who wants to be able to view other people's online presentations, ASAP WebShow may be what you need. One of the nice features of the program that creates these animations—ASAP's WordPower—is that you can use it to transform your PowerPoint presentations into Web-playable files. Plus, ASAP WebShow now includes support for RealAudio so you can synchronize your sound files with your presentations. Figure 24-22 shows an example.

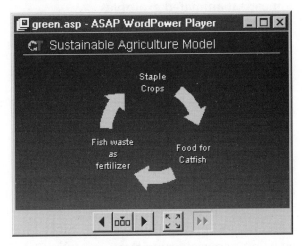

Figure 24-22: An ASAP WebShow presentation on the Web.

Macintosh		Windows	
PowerPC	68K	Windows 95	Windows 3.1
No	No	Yes	Yes
Where to get the latest version:		http://www.spco.com/asap/ asapwebs.htm	

Astound Web Player

Users of StudioM and Astound (supposedly the world's most popular presentation package, but who believes advertising?) will be happy to learn that you can now take those presentations and slap 'em up online where they can be viewed with the Astound WebPlayer plug-in.

Because Astound supports animation, music, sounds, and even movies, pages really come to life with Astound files. It's kinda tough to do justice to the effect in a static book, so if you want to be, um, *astounded* (ugh!) go to GoldDisk's Web site, download the Astound Player, install it in your plug-ins folder, and jump to their demos page (http://www.golddisk.com/awp/demos.html) for some great animated examples.

Macintosh		Windows	
PowerPC	68K	Windows 95	Windows 3.1
Planned	Planned	Yes	Yes

Where to get the latest version: http://www.golddisk.com/awp.html

Emblaze

Emblaze is a new, blazingly fast animation plug-in that displays special Emblaze files right in Web pages. These files are small, load fast, and play within seconds. Since Emblaze works its magic by using a special proprietary animation format, you'll have to download the Emblaze creator program, currently only available for Macs, if you want to create your own Emblaze files.

Emblaze has only one quirk—if your monitor is set to any other setting than 8-bit color, you'll see all the animations in blue. This isn't a huge problem. At least it doesn't crash your browser like a lot of other unfriendly plug-ins, but it did take us a good half an hour of playing round the Emblaze Web site before we figured out what the problem was. That's what we get for not reading the FAQ first.

Macintosh		Windows	
PowerPC	68K	Windows 95	Windows 3.1
Yes	Yes	Planned	Yes

Where to get the latest version:	http://Geo.inter.net/Geo/ technology/emblaze/downloads.html

SCREAM

If you're a Windows user and have a hankerin' for some impressive animation, check out the SCREAM plug-in. Not only does it allow you to view animations through the Web, but SCREAM animators can link WAV and MID files to their animations for a true multimedia experience. SCREAM files play back in 256 colors (8-bit), load extremely quickly, and can even be viewed full-screen. Figure 24-23 shows a great example of a SCREAMing page (http://www.savedbytech.com/sbt/Alt_Home.html).

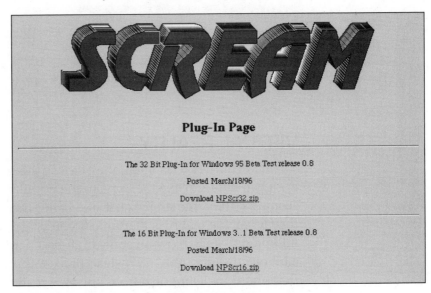

Figure 24-23: Saved by Technology's SCREAMing home page.

Macintosh		Windows	
PowerPC	**68K**	**Windows 95**	**Windows 3.1**
Planned	Planned	Yes	Yes

Where to get the latest version: http://www.savedbytech.com/sbt/ Plug_In.html

Sizzler

Sizzler, from Totally Hip Software, allows you to view inline animation on the Web. While many of the other animation plug-ins out there utilize completely proprietary formats, Sizzler uses PICS animations (a common, cross-platform animation format) and QuickTime to work its magic. If you're feeling particularly creative and have a Mac, Totally Hip Software also provides a version of its Sizzler program on its Web page so that you can make your own Sizzler files.

Macintosh		Windows	
PowerPC	**68K**	**Windows 95**	**Windows 3.1**
Yes	Yes	Yes	Yes

Where to get the latest version: http://www.totallyhip.com/

VIRTUAL REALITY

Virtual Reality (VR) is often one of those things that gives computers a bad name. While the hype in the popular media makes it seem that fully immersive, just-like-being-there VR is just around the corner, the reality is that unless you've got a quarter of a million dollars to blow on some high-end hardware, VR on a PC is a bit of a disappointment. Instead of a computer-generated reality that's hard to distinguish from our own reality, what you'll find most of the time is some crudely shaded polygon graphics, jerky motion, and confusing controls. And that's if you can spring for a head-mounted display. If you're like most folks who have to get their VR through a monitor, you're even more removed from the experience, and the effect becomes even less like reality and more like some poorly rendered video game. Actually, Doom is more like VR than most VR is.

But (and that's a big *but*) VR is in its infancy. Even though most of us haven't had the opportunity to get the full VR treatment with a strap-on, stereoscopic headset, stereo sound, and motion-detecting body circuitry, anyone who has (Sean's one of them), will tell you that the effect is nothing short of amazing. When you enter a fully immersive VR world, the fact that the graphics are a bit rudimentary becomes irrelevant—you actually do feel as if you've entered another world. Unfortunately, at this point, the hardware to get effects like that is not within the average human's price range.

But that's all changing. Computing power doubles every six months or so, prices are continuing to go down, and some consumer-priced VR headsets and glasses have hit the market in the past few years. As technology accelerates, software is getting more sophisticated to utilize the new capabilities. The new combinations of powerful software and fast hardware can do some pretty amazing stuff, as anyone who's nearly tossed their cookies while playing Descent will attest. VR may be pretty lame in general now, but give it a year or so, and we should start to see some amazing stuff show up on our home computers.

So what does this all have to do with the Web? Possibly everything. As anyone who's read William Gibson's *Neuromancer* knows, the idea of surfing the Net by moving through a virtually real 3D representation of the data on a network can be pretty alluring. While people who talk about Cyberspace today are usually referring to the Internet (and other tied-in forms of electronic communication) in the abstract, it may not be long before Gibsonian Cyberspace moves out of our imaginations and onto our desktops.

Why bother? One argument is that humans are spatial creatures. Thousands of years of evolution weren't spent developing binocular vision and 3D hearing so that we could chain ourselves to a flat 2D screen. Done correctly, 3D technology could offer us new ways of navigating the Cyberworld we seem so intent on creating, and even entirely new ways of communicating with each other. Then, of course, the more mundane and perhaps more honest answer is humans just like to have fun. We're constantly looking for new types of stimulation and entertainment, and the idea of creating 3D worlds you can climb into is compelling even if it has no everyday utility.

VRML

VRML (pronounced "ver-mul" by its proponents) is an acronym for Virtual Reality Modeling Language, an ASCII-based graphics description language used for defining and rendering 3D scenes. Once you're "in" a VRML scene, you have a full, 360-degree range of motion—you can zoom in, move up or down, or even rotate completely around. Originally designed by Mark D. Pesce (and others), VRML has the potential for becoming the 3D interface for the Web of the future. Already, Netscape has signed deals with VRML plug-in vendors to provide VRML functionality in future releases of Navigator, and Microsoft already includes rudimentary VRML support in its Internet Explorer browser. While VRML is now in its infancy, it probably won't be long before most of the Web will be engulfed in 3D mania.

Why VRML? It's a perfect fit for the Web. Even though most of us at this point navigate the Web through a 2D, point-and-click interface, the Web actually exists in three dimensions through document hyperlinks. Confused? Think about it this way. When you view a Web page on your screen in a typical browser, you're looking at a 2D object. You can move up and down using the scroll bars. However, when you click on a hyperlink you move "away" from the page you're in and go to another page, which is then displayed on your screen. While most of us don't think of following a link as moving through a third dimension, it's not too hard to visualize it as a 3D move.

Because Web browsing can seem so three-dimensional, VRML is being designed as a more natural, visual way of Web navigation. Pages will still be pages, but you can move among them in Cyberspace through a 3D interface that more naturally mimics the way the movement "feels."

So far, most VRML browsers and plug-ins are painfully slow to use, and complex worlds often take a long time to download and view. However, once you get out on the Web and start playing around with the VRML out there, you'll probably be able to see the potential. Catch a glimpse of what's in store by grabbing one of the plug-ins or browsers we describe in this section.

TIP

For more info on VRML, check out the VRML Format at http://vrml.wired.com/. You'll find links to plenty of information, VRML worlds, and VRML software.

Plug-ins

Navigator (and Explorer) plug-ins allow you to view VRML worlds inline with your Web pages as long as you've got the right plug-ins.

CyberGate

CyberGate may be one of the most assertive first steps in the future development of VRML on the Net. Not only does it allow you to view the myriad VRML worlds you'll run into online, but with the addition of a CyberHub server, CyberGate can be used in real-time, multiuser VRML interactive worlds. You can meet other people, cruise 3D worlds together, and even build your own worlds (with CyberKit, an easy-to-use VRML world builder).

At the time we wrote this, BlackSun (the creators of CyberGate) hadn't released CyberHub or CyberKit, so at this point, CyberGate is just a fine VRML plug-in. However, with the addition of CyberHub, and the additional support for Java (see the "Java & JavaScript" section later in this chapter), CyberGate could become one of the most exciting new VRML products to hit the Web in 1996. We'll have to wait and see. Until then, Figure 24-24 shows you what CyberGate looks like today.

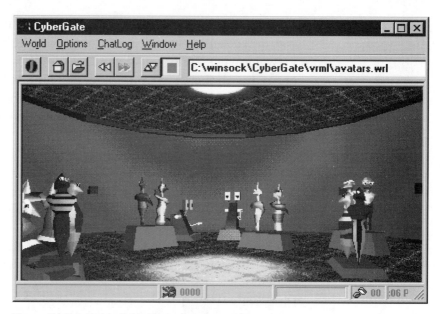

Figure 24-24: Using CyberGate to view a VRML file.

Macintosh		Windows	
PowerPC	68K	Windows 95	Windows 3.1
No	No	Yes	No

Where to get the latest version: http://www2.blacksun.com

ExpressVR

If you've got a Macintosh and want to use a VRML plug-in, ExpressVR is pretty much your only option. But what a great option it is! Unlike many of the stand alone VRML viewers available for the Mac, ExpressVR is small, fast, and, most importantly, it works! While it doesn't include all the bells and whistles of its bigger cousins, it does seem to handle most VRML worlds without crashing browsers. We couldn't say that about most of the other VRML browsers we tried.

What's most amazing about ExpressVR isn't that it works—it's who wrote it. ExpressVR is the creation of one Brad Anderson, a home-schooled high school student fed up with the lack of VRML capabilities on the Mac. In his words:

I am a Mac programmer. Being that I am a homeschooling high school student, I had some time on my hands. Also, being a web person, I have been waiting and waiting for those companies to create a VRML browser that plugs into Netscape for a very long time now.

I got fed up with those companies about 2 weeks ago (1/30/96 or so), and decided to make my own that would be what I wanted it to be.

I wanted it fast. I wanted it to be for both the PowerMac and the older 680x0 machines. I wanted it now.

Now there's the do-it-yourself spirit at work! Figure 24-25 shows a VRML scene from Brad's Web site.

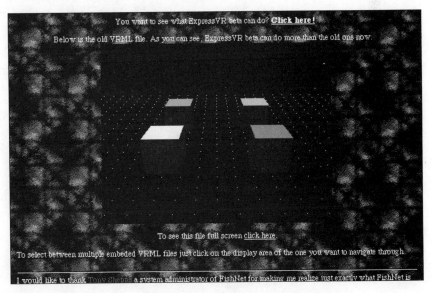

Figure 24-25: A simple VRML scene as seen through ExpressVR.

| Macintosh | | Windows | |
PowerPC	68K	Windows 95	Windows 3.1
Yes	Yes	No	No
Where to get the latest version:		http://www.cis.upenn.edu/~brada/ VRML/ExpressVR.html	

Live3D

Live3D is distributed by Netscape, and if it has anywhere near the success that Navigator did, look for Live3D to become the VRML standard in the near future. As our pal Martha Stewart would say, that's a good thing. Why? Because Live3D supports some of the coolest innovations in VRML yet.

Using Netscape's support for Java and JavaScript, Live3D has the capability of bringing not only 3D worlds to the Web, but actual interactive 3D worlds—worlds that change in response to your actions. And not only can Live3D make VRML worlds come alive through interactivity, but it can really make them sing with its streaming audio and video capabilities.

Live3D also supports a lot of extensions to VRML (it uses the VRML 2.0 Moving Worlds Standard), including multiple camera views, gravity, collision detection, and interactive fly-throughs. These 3D extensions make the virtual Live3D world seem much more "real," putting the reality back into virtual reality. Figure 24-26 shows a typical Live3D scene.

Figure 24-26: Cyberspace, as seen by Live3D.

Macintosh		Windows	
PowerPC	68K	Windows 95	Windows 3.1
Planned	Planned	Yes	Yes

Where to get the latest version: http://home.netscape.com/ comprod/products/navigator/ live3d/download_live3d.html

VR Scout

If you want your VRML quick and simple, check out VR Scout. Touted as "the best implementation of the VRML 1.0 standard," VR Scout will let you browse 3D worlds with ease. And, because VR Scout uses the Microsoft Reality Lab and Intel 3DR graphics engines, anyone with a 3D hardware accelerator card can get really screamin' performance.

| Macintosh | | Windows | |
PowerPC	68K	Windows 95	Windows 3.1
Planned	Planned	Yes	Yes - helper app

Where to get the latest version: http://www.chaco.com/vrscout/

WIRL

Like Live3D, WIRL includes support for Netscape's LiveObjects, a standard that allows for exciting, interactive, detailed multimedia "objects." Unlike most VRML browsers, WIRL supports advanced features like full interactivity (so you can manipulate objects in 3D); gravity, animation, and paths (for animation); Gouraud and Phong shading (for enhanced realism); 8-, 16-, and 24-bit color support (for realistic colors); and speeds up to 100,000 polygons per second on a 90MHz Pentium. All in all, WIRL is one power-house of a VRML plug-in!

| Macintosh | | Windows | |
PowerPC	68K	Windows 95	Windows 3.1
Planned	Planned	Yes	Planned

Where to get the latest version: http://www.vream.com/

Helper Apps

Besides viewing VRML worlds inline, you can also use helper apps to browse 3D worlds. You'll have to set up your browser to launch these programs, as with all helper apps, but if you're using a browser other than Navigator or Explorer, this may be your only option.

One big advantage of using an external VRML viewer is that it allows you to browse through VRML scenes offline. You can download an image, store it on your hard drive, and fiddle with it to your heart's content, while minimizing those nasty online time bills. In addition, if you want to get into developing VRML content, these viewers will give you the opportunity to test your VRML code outside of the application that created it—a second opinion, if you will.

Finally, if you have a Mac and want to take full advantage of VRML, these helper apps are the way to go at this point. While ExpressVR is a wonder of a plug-in, it still doesn't support all of the advanced 3D features you'll find in these apps. Let you own needs decide what you want to use.

VRML Equinox

North Plains Systems' VRML Equinox was one of the first VRML browsers for the Macintosh. Simply, and to the point, it uses Apple's QuickDraw3D technology to render VR worlds. The advantage of this is that drawing will be accelerated if you have a QuickDraw3D accelerator card in your machine. The disadvantage is that Apple hasn't released QuickDraw3D for 68K Macs yet (and may never), so if you don't have a PowerMac, you're outta luck.

Macintosh		Windows	
PowerPC	68K	Windows 95	Windows 3.1
Yes	No	No	No

Where to get the latest version: http://www. northplains.com/

Virtus Voyager

Virtus is the company responsible for Virtus Walkthrough, one of the greatest and easiest-to-use 3D modeling and walkthrough programs on the market. And, just as you'd expect from a leader in 3D modeling, Virtus Voyager is one killer of a VRML browser.

In our tests, Voyager performed better than any other Mac VRML product, accurately rendering many scenes that sent other VRML products down in flames (taking our computers with them). Voyager has a simple, easy-to-use interface that made it a joy to fly around scenes, and we especially liked the ability to change the level of shading (anywhere from simple outlines to rich Gouraud shading), which allowed us to compensate for slow machines.

If you've used Virtus Walkthrough Pro in the past, you'll be happy to know that the new version now supports VRML, making it easy to take any of the models you've created in the past and turn them into VRML worlds. All in all, it's one great package. Slide on over to http://www.virtus.com, and find out for yourself. Figure 24-27 shows a truly romantic VRML scene as viewed through Voyager.

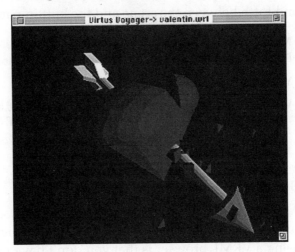

Figure 24-27: It's a Voyager virtual Valentine!

| Macintosh | | Windows | |
PowerPC	68K	Windows 95	Windows 3.1
Yes	Yes	Yes	No
Where to get the latest version:		http://www.virtus.com/voyager.html	

Whurlwind

Whurlwind was the first VRML browser for the Macintosh, and it has been designed to showcase Apple's QuickDraw3D technology. Not only does Whurlwind allow you to view VRML scenes, but it also allows you to view downloaded 3D Metafile formatted files (3DMF), 3D models using Apple's new cross-platform standard.

Whurlwind excels by providing an extremely simple interface. There's no annoying buttons, no complicated Shift-click-Command-Option key combinations—just choose which way you want to go, stick the cursor in the scene, click, and drag. This can get confusing sometimes, but it sure beats having to move back and forth between the scene and the button panel.

Macintosh		Windows	
PowerPC	68K	Windows 95	Windows 3.1
Yes	No	No	No

Where to get the latest version: http://product.info.apple.com/qd3d/QD3D.HTML

Browsers

As VRML moves out into the Web, more browsers that directly support VRML are becoming available. One big advantage of using a VRML browser is that you don't have to worry if that third-party plug-in is going to work—you can be pretty sure that everything will go off without a hitch, or at least without a crash.

Microsoft Internet Explorer

Internet Explorer now includes two types of VRML support. For Mac users (and soon for Windows users), MSIE uses built-in VRML capabilities to display inline 3D images. Windows 95 users must get the VRML Add-In, which adds inline VRML support to the browser. See more about MSIE's VRML Add-in in Chapter 9, "Windows Web Power Tools."

TIP

If you want to browse some VRML worlds guaranteed to work with Explorer, check out the Legit List at http://www.geom.umn.edu/~daeron/bin/legitlist.cgi.

Macintosh		Windows	
PowerPC	68K	Windows 95	Windows 3.1
Yes - browser	Yes - browser	Yes - add-in	No

Where to get the latest version: http://www.msn.com/ie/ie.htm

Silicon Graphics WebSpace

Sporting an absolutely killer-cool interface, excellent rendering capabilities, and great documentation, SIG's WebSpace is the king of all VRML browsers. Of course, all that power takes a lot of power on your computer's end, so for best results, use the fastest machine you can get your hands on.

One of the nicest features of WebSpace is its interface. Eschewing the normal back-and-forth, up-and-down interface of most VRML viewers, WebSpace uses a joystick and control-cube model that allows you quickly and easily cruise through 3D worlds. See Figure 24-28 for a nicely annotated view from SGI's Web site.

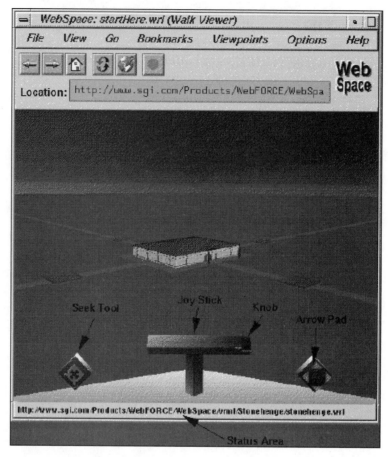

Figure 24-28: WebSpace controls.

If you're one of those people who just can't settle for second best (and you've got the hardware to prove it), download WebSpace today.

Macintosh		Windows	
PowerPC	68K	Windows 95	Windows 3.1
Planned	No	Yes	Planned

Where to get the latest version: http://www.sd.tgs.com/~template/WebSpace/monday.html

Other 3D Formats

While VRML is all the rage of 3D formats right now, that doesn't mean that people aren't working to develop their own formats. While VRML is pretty much geared towards online content, many of these other 3D viewers are designed for looking at models often displayed offline. The field represents quite a variety of formats: chemical models, architectural models, even 3D panoramic pictures that you can walk though.

Chemscape Chime

The Web was originally designed as a place for academic researchers to share data, so it's nice to see that some people are still using it for that. Chemscape Chime is a Navigator plug-in that allows scientists to view chemical information and models on the Web, using Mofile and Brookhaven Protein Data Bank formats, as well as others. If you know what that last sentence means, it's probably a good idea that you download Chime.

Macintosh		Windows	
PowerPC	68K	Windows 95	Windows 3.1
Planned	Planned	Yes	Yes

Where to get the latest version: http://www.mdli.com/chemscape/chime/chime.html

QuickTimeVR

For sheer "gee-whiz!" responses, few programs beat QuickTimeVR's ability to draw gasps from a crowd. QTVR doesn't use computer-generated models in its 3D scenes. Instead, it uses special 360-degree panoramic photographs that are "stitched together" with QTVR software to produce the effect that makes you feel like you're actually standing in the scene.

Apple's QuickTimeVR player is a helper app you'll have to configure your browser to use. It'll play both QuickTime and QuickTimeVR files, so you should have no problem tossing your old QuickTime player in the Trash/Recycle Bin. Give it a try. You'll be blown away.

Macintosh		Windows	
PowerPC	**68K**	**Windows 95**	**Windows 3.1**
Yes	Yes	Yes	Yes

Where to get the latest version: http://qtvr.quicktime.apple.com/

Virtual Space

The Virtual Space plug-in for Windows 95 allows you to view ParaGraph Virtual Home Space Builder files, a kind of alternative VRML 3D standard. These files can include sound, animation, and even movies. It's pretty cool stuff. The only problem is that no one else supports this format. But like everything else on the Net, the market will ultimately decide.

Macintosh		Windows	
PowerPC	**68K**	**Windows 95**	**Windows 3.1**
No	No	Yes	No

Where to get the latest version: http://russia.paragraph.com/vr/ d96html/download.htm

Whurlplug

Apple's QuickDraw3D technology uses a standard file format called the 3D Metafile or 3DMF. Apple recently proposed that it become an Internet standard for the exchange of 3D information, but as of yet, no one really seems all that interested. If you have a PowerMac with QuickDraw3D installed, you'll probably want to get this plug-in, if for nothing else than the ability to play with the models on Specular's Web site (http://www.specular.com/ products/replicas/gallery/3dmf_replicas.html).

Macintosh PowerPC	68K	Windows Windows 95	Windows 3.1
Yes	No	No	No

Where to get the latest version: ftp://ftp.info.apple.com/ Apple.Support.Area/QuickDraw3D/ Test_Drive/Viewers/

JAVA & JAVASCRIPT

The world of the Net now seems like one big horse race in which technologies, and the companies that forged them, rise and fall with the blink of the modem lights. One day it's VRML, the next it's the new Navigator, and the next it's Macromind's Shockwave. The latest craze in Cyberspace is something called Java. Just drop that word into casual conversation, and you'll be instantly hip; slap it on the cover of your latest book, and it will fly off the shelves. So, what the heck is it?

Java

Java is a new programming language developed by Sun Microsystems as an outgrowth of an earlier project to design a small, powerful, portable language for personal digital assistants. Well, the PDA project didn't pan out, but Java was rescued and recast as a cross-platform language with awesome potential for transferring small executable programs over the Web.

The big advantage of Java is that it's completely platform independent. While other high-level languages (such as C and C++) require that you write a different program for each type of computer you're working on, Java doesn't make you get so specific. Java runs on a "virtual computer" that serves as a new layer of abstraction between the hardware (the computer the program must run on) and the software (the Java code). Because of this new layer of abstraction, Java programmers have to write a program only once, without worrying about which platform it's going to run on. With Java, you don't program for a real computer, you program for the virtual computer.

So what the heck does all this mean for multimedia and the Web? Actually, a heck of a lot. Once the folks at Sun realized they could pull off this cross-platform language and that they could use Java to write small programs that did big things, they realized that Java and the Net were a perfect match. Since they're small and can run on any machine with a Java virtual machine on it, Java programs can be passed over the Net much faster than the big, bloated programs we use today.

And speaking of big, bloated programs, that's the other innovation of Java—no more need for big, bloated programs! Because Java applications are modular and object oriented, you don't need one big Java program to do everything. Instead, you just download the Java application to perform the task at hand.

But back to the Web. Because Java applications could be quickly passed over the Net, the engineers at Sun devised a special Java program type called an *applet*. Applets are small applications that are designed not to stand by themselves, but to plug into Java-friendly browsers to extend the functionality of the browser. In fact, Java is so flexible that just about every multimedia function we've covered so far in this chapter could be accomplished with it, without all those plug-ins. Rather than your having to download a plug-in that must stay in your machine, a Java-savvy programmer could design a site that sent the program for viewing the data (in the form of an applet) before it sent you the data. Your browser becomes infinitely extensible.

Right now, a lot of Java is being used to play sounds and animation. That's fine, but it doesn't even come close to scratching the surface of what Java will eventually do. Java hackers all over the world are using this new language to push the envelope of what's possible. One hot area at the moment is (surprise!) interactive arcade games that can be played inline with your browser. See Figure 24-29 for a gallery of the best Java games on the Web.

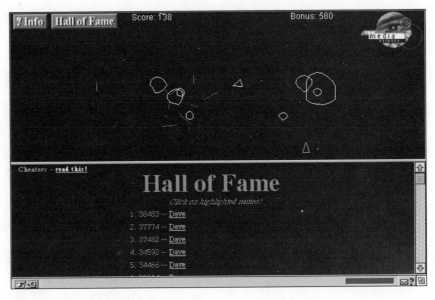

Figure 24-29: A Java arcade game.

So what do you need if you want to put some Java in your cup? Right now, the answer is Netscape Navigator 2.01 for Windows and PowerMac (sorry, no 68K Mac support yet). Microsoft has recently licensed Java from Sun, so look for Java support in Microsoft's Internet Explorer 3.0, which should be out by the time you read this.

Once you've got yourself situated with a browser, start your Java travels at Gamelan, the Java index on the Web (http://www.gamelan.com). It's the Yahoo of the Java world, and you can be pretty sure that if a site using Java exists, it's accessible from Gamelan somewhere. And Gamelan has some pretty nifty Java features of its own, including a helpful floating navigation window (see Figure 24-30) that you can use to quickly access Gamelan's features.

947

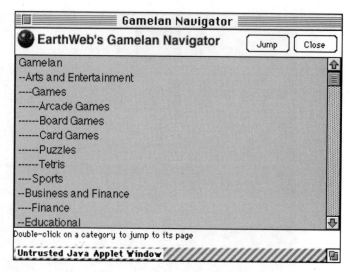

Figure 24-30: Gamelan's Java navigation window.

JavaScript

If you've heard of Java, you may also have heard of JavaScript. The two names are a bit confusing. Because of the unfortunate choice of similar names (JavaScript was originally called LiveScript) and some syntactical similarities to Java, many people have the impression that JavaScript is just a watered-down version of Java. It isn't. The main difference is that, while Java can be used to produce stand-alone applications, JavaScript can't. Instead, JavaScript provides a way for programmers to extend HTML and actually program the behavior of browsers running the JavaScript code.

While this might not sound like a very exciting feature, Web page designers can do a lot of cool stuff with JavaScript. You can create floating button palettes, create interactive forms that react to the user's input immediately, or you can even make a message scroller that sends text crawling along the browser's status bar. If you want to see an example of what can be done with JavaScript, take a look at Figure 24-31, which shows the JavaScript extravaganza that is The Dive (http://www.dream.com/).

Figure 24-31: JavaScript-o-rama at The Dive.

To view JavaScript-enhanced pages, all you need is a JavaScriptable browser, such as Netscape Navigator (all 2.0 versions). Microsoft and Spyglass have both announced commitments to include JavaScript in their new browsers, so keep an eye out for new developments.

MOVING ON

Whew! That was quite a trip through a candyland of cutting-edge applications. If you come away from this chapter with nothing else, realize that most of what we've covered here was developed within the last *year* ! If you're dizzy now, just imagine what will be racing down the ol' data pike a year from now. Our heads will be spinning even faster, so don't forget to take your motion sickness medicine.

Now that you know how to look at what's out there, it's time to find out how to show the world some of your own stuff! In the next chapter, we'll cover the basic tools of getting started in Web publishing. We'll start with a look at the best HTML editors, take a gander at some extra graphical helpers you might need, and wrap up with some deep geek talk about Web server software for those who want to self-serve their Web content.

## Chapter 25

Setting Up Shop on the Web: A Resource Guide

Once you see all the cool stuff on the Web, you might start itching to put your own content online. Maybe you want to publish a magazine on your favorite hobby or erect a shrine to your pet goldfish, Buzz. Or, maybe you want to make a quick million with your own Net-based business. Whatever the reason, there are many simple and inexpensive ways of Web publishing, given the right information and tools.

In this chapter, we're going to make some fast tracks through resources you'll need in order to set up shop on the Web. We're not going to cover HTML or any other programming details—there's enough information out there on that stuff already. What we're going to do is cover the tools you'll need, HTML editors for both Macintosh and Windows and popular Web server software. With our recommendations in hand, you should be able to set yourself up as a new Web publisher.

HTML TOOLS

HTML stands for Hypertext Markup Language and it's the code that forms the foundation for the entire Web. Using a system of markup tags, HTML authors can format text, insert graphics, serve up Java applets, or create user-interface forms. When you browse the Web, you don't see HTML because your browser—Netscape Navigator, Internet Explorer, to name just a couple—transform the HTML codes into the pretty text, pictures, and other stuff you think of as the World Wide Web.

HTML isn't rocket science—it's really just a system of markup tags. If you really want to go at it in a bare-bones fashion, you don't need anything more complicated than a simple text editor and an encyclopedic memory for markup codes and syntax.

Fortunately, there are better solutions. An HTML editor will help you by automatically inserting tags, making sure that your pages are formatted correctly, and providing a way to manage multiple pages and links. In fact, with some of the new WYSIWYG (what you see is what you get) editors, you don't even have to know anything about HTML—you just type your text, drop in your graphics, press Save, and the program automatically transforms your layout into HTML form.

When selecting an HTML editor, you should consider several things. What kind of special features do you need? Do you want to do simple pages, or do you need to be able to incorporate new HTML features as they become available? Are you a visually oriented person who may be easily confused by the HTML code, or do you like to be able to get in there and muck around? Finally, how much do you want to spend? Can you deal with a free or shareware editor with few features, or do you need a lot of special features only available in a commercial product? Whatever your answers, there's probably an editor that fits the bill.

Windows HTML Tools

Windows users are fortunate to have a huge range of HTML editors to choose from. The problem isn't *finding* an editor to use, it's choosing *which* editor. In this section, we've chosen what we feel to be the pick of the litter. What makes these editors so good? Mainly, they're easy to use and flexible. Most can meet the needs of both the beginning writer of HTML code and the professional, all while keeping your stress level down to a slow simmer. So which one is the best? It's hard to say. Try a few, and find out for yourself.

HotDog Web Editor

Created by the authors of Egor Animator (the only Java animation editor), HotDog is a full-featured, easy to use, powerful HTML tool. Professionals will like its support for HTML 3.0 tags, and beginning users will enjoy HotDog Pro's simple drag and drop WYSIWYG interface. The only problem with HotDog is that it's so popular, you may have trouble connecting to the Web page to download it! Figure 25-1 shows what you'll see if you ever connect.

Figure 25-1: HotDog's home page.

HotDog	16 Bit, Windows 3.1, Windows 95
Sausage Software 30-Day Demo HotDog Standard: $29.95 HotDog Pro: $99.95	http://www.sausage.com/
Tables	Yes, built-in table editor.
Forms	Yes, all form elements.
HTML 3.0	Yes, includes all extensions to HTML 3.0, not only Netscape extensions. HotDog Pro also includes support for Microsoft Internet Explorer tags.
WYSIWYG?	Yes, in HotDog Pro.
Preview with Browser?	Yes, will launch a browser to preview HTML code.
Special Features	Includes drag and drop interface, many dialog boxes for special features, converts DOS and UNIX text files, checks for duplicate tags, colored tags, automatically uses FTP to upload files to server, does text-to-HTML conversions.

HoTMetaL

HoTMetaL is the number one choice of professional Webmasters, and for good reason. HoTMetaL includes a full range of support for every HTML tag available—an integrated rules checker to keep you from making any coding boo-boos, a spelling checker, and a full thesaurus. And as HTML keeps advancing, so will HoTMetaL. Its use of rules files allows it to be upgraded as new features become available.

The only problem with HoTMetaL is that its wealth of features can make things a little bit confusing. HoTMetaL employs a dizzying array of tool palettes and icons to provide access to its features, and the complexity takes a little getting used to (see Figure 25-2).

Figure 25-2: HoTMetaL Pro at work.

HoTMetaL Free/HoTMetaL Pro	Windows 3.1
SoftQuad	http://www.sq.com/products/ hotmetal/hmp-org.htm
Freeware: HoTMetaL Free	
Commercial: HoTMetaL Pro, $245	
Tables	Yes, built-in table editor.
Forms	Yes, all form elements.
HTML 3.0	Yes, using rules files, HoTMetaL can be extended to use any new HTML extensions, including frames.
WYSIWYG?	Somewhat—displays images inline with tags.
Preview with Browser?	Yes, will launch a browser to preview HTML code.
Special Features	Uses a built-in rules checker to make sure your code conforms to HTML standards. Pro version includes thesaurus and spell checker.

HTMLed Pro

A nice, full-featured HTML editor, HTMLed is a good editor to start with if you're just getting into HTML. It doesn't do everything, but what it does do, it does well—that's its major strength. As an added bonus, HTMLed includes a feature left out of many HTML editors (but that we feel should be mandatory)—support for using FTP to upload your edited files to your remote server. With this feature, you don't have to save your file, quit your editor, open your FTP program, and then upload your newly created Web page—just send it straight from HTMLed. And, if you need to edit a remote file, HTMLed will even download it for you and then open it up in the editor, ready for editing!

If you're a beginner, you should give HTMLed a try. As you learn more, HTMLed will let you branch out with support for some of Netscape's special tags, so you can be sure that HTMLed will be ready to grow with you.

HTMLedPro	Windows 3.1, Windows 95
Internet Software Technologies 30 Day Demo Available $99.95	http://www.ist.ca/
Tables	Table editor included. Cannot be used to edit previously created tables.
Forms	Yes, form editor included.
HTML 3.0	Yes, includes some HTML 3.0 tags. Also supports Netscape-specific tags.
WYSIWYG?	No. Uses colored text for tag display.
Preview with Browser?	Yes, will launch a browser to preview HTML code.
Special Features	Spell checker, find and replace, customizable tool bar, will open, save, and transfer remote files using FTP, includes preconfigured templates for starting pages.

Netscape Navigator Gold

We would certainly be remiss if we didn't include Navigator Gold in our list of Windows HTML editors. Combining a WYSIWYG HTML editor with a browser, you can accomplish almost all your authoring tasks (except creating graphics) from within a single program. If you want to put some graphics pizzazz in your pages but don't want to deal with creating graphics yourself, don't worry—Navigator Gold lets you steal other people's graphics and plop them right on your pages. Always ask permission before snatching anyone's stuff!

If you want to get started right away, you may want to consider Gold first. It supports all the fancy Netscape tags, allows drag-and-drop editing right from the Windows Explorer, and even lets you download, open, and re-upload files to and from your Web server with FTP. Figure 25-3 shows Gareth editing a Web page with Navigator Gold.

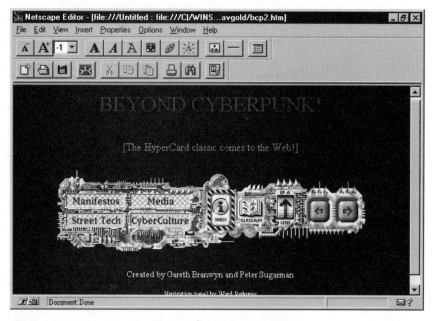

Figure 25-3: Gareth hacking away in Navigator Gold.

HTMLedPro	Windows 95
Internet Software Technologies Free Beta	http://www.netscape.com
Tables	Yes.
Forms	Yes.
HTML 3.0	Yes, including all Netscape tags (what a surprise!).
WYSIWYG?	Yes, drag-and-drop graphics, text, and elements from other Net Web sites.
Preview with Browser?	Yes, integrated with Netscape Navigator.
Special Features	JavaScript support and editor. Supports inline plug-in tags and Java applets. Transfers images and HTML code to remote server via FTP. Multi-level undo.

WebEdit

Some people love WebEdit, others can't stand it. But that's pretty much par for the course with these creatures. You'll have to decide for yourself, but we can say that WebEdit does everything just as well as most of the other editors we've covered and includes a few features the other editors don't have.

WebEdit supports a wide range of HTML tags, implementing not only most of the HTML 3.0 specifications, but Netscape and Microsoft Internet Explorer tags as well. While you have to deal with a mainly text-based interface for most of your editing, WebEdit does allow you to preview your pages before committing them to disk, so you can check your progress at any time. WebEdit also includes a built-in image map editor. Figure 25-4 gives you an idea of what it's like to work with WebEdit.

Figure 25-4: Using WebEdit.

WebEdit	Windows 3.1, Windows 95
Knowledge Works	http://www.nesbitt.com/
Demo Available	
$79.95	
Tables	Yes.
Forms	Yes.
HTML 3.0	Yes, includes some HTML 3.0 tags. Also supports Netscape and Microsoft Internet Explorer tags.
WYSIWYG?	Yes, WYSIWYG preview.
Preview with Browser?	Yes, will launch a browser to preview HTML code.
Special Features	Image map editor included.

Macintosh HTML Tools

Mac users don't have quite the range of HTML editing tools that Windows users enjoy (so what else is new?), but the majority of the HTML editors available for the Mac do a pretty good job. In this section, we'll look at five of the top editors available, from the free WYSIWYG editor, Arachnid, to the new contender for the commercial Mac HTML editor crown—World Wide Web Weaver. Demos are available on the Net for almost all of the examples we'll cover, whether they're commercial, shareware, or freeware, so you can get a taste of each one before you decide which is going to take a bite out of your budget.

Arachnid

Arachnid was originally a project started at the University of Iowa, but now that the developer, Robert McBurney, has left to pursue his own software development career, Arachnid is in its final release. However, the last release of Arachnid fixed a lot of problems with the earlier versions, so at least Bob quit when he was ahead.

Arachnid is written in SuperCard, and even though you're supposed to be able to run it on a 68040 machine, you'll probably find it tortuously slow on anything but a PowerMac. However, if you've got the hardware to run it, Arachnid is a nice freeware editor with a pretty complete WYSIWYG interface that allows you to see pages pretty much as they will look in your browser. It does have a few bugs and seems kind of quirky at times, but, hey! you can't beat the price. Figure 25-5 shows Arachnid's interface.

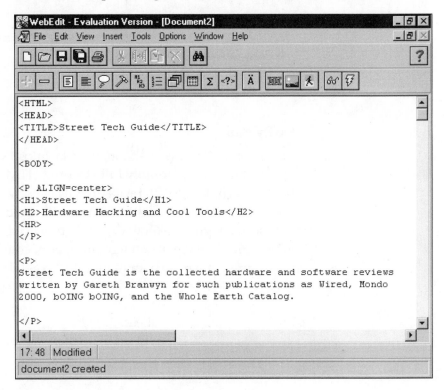

Figure 25-5: Editing with Arachnid.

Arachnid	Mac68K. PowerMac. Almost too slow to be usable on 68K machines.
Second Look Computing	http://sec-look.uiowa.edu/about/projects/arachnid-page.html
Free. Final version released 2/29/96.	
Tables	Table support.
Forms	Yes.
HTML 3.0	No.
WYSIWYG?	Somewhat—displays images inline.
Preview with Browser?	No.
Special Features	Simple.

HoTMetaL

Just like the Windows version, the Macintosh version of HoTMetaL is an incredibly full-featured HTML editor that is the perennial choice of Web professionals everywhere. While Mac users will probably find its Windows-flavored interface confusing at first (see Figure 25-6), with a little practice people often learn to love it. HoTMetaL uses a large number of control palettes, so make sure you've got a large monitor to get the most out of its features.

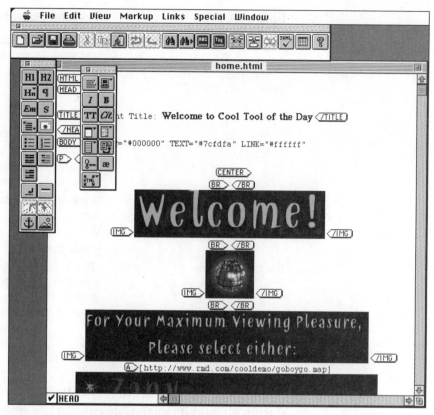

Figure 25-6: HoTMetaL's multi-palette interface.

The best feature of HoTMetaL Pro is that its functions can be extended very easily just by installing new rules files. As new HTML extensions become available, SoftQuad is making them available for HoTMetaL users and installing them just involves copying a few small files.

HoTMetaL combines all the best features of a good text editor — a search and replace feature, a spell checker, and a thesaurus— with just enough WYSIWYG features to let you get an idea of how graphics are going to fit in your document. These capabilities plus a killer tables editor, macro capabilities, and the ability to hotlist commonly used features makes HoTMetaL a joy to use for both big and small projects.

HoTMetaL Pro	Mac68K, PowerMac
SoftQuad	http://www.sq.com/products/hotmetal/hmp-org.htm
Commercial: HoTMetaL Pro, $245	
Tables	Yes, built-in table editor.
Forms	Yes, all form elements.
HTML 3.0	Yes, using rules files, HoTMetaL can be extended to use any new HTML extensions, including frames.
WYSIWYG?	Somewhat—displays images inline with tags.
Preview with Browser?	Yes, will launch a browser to preview HTML code.
Special Features	Uses a built-in rules checker to make sure that your code conforms to HTML standards. Pro version includes thesaurus and spell checker.

PageMill/SiteMill

Adobe PageMill was the first WYSIWYG editor available for the Macintosh, and its incredibly easy-to-use interface and drag-and-drop editing have made it a big favorite with people who just want to be able to knock out basic Web pages. While you can't do a lot of fancy formatting with PageMill—it doesn't support any special Netscape (or Internet Explorer) tags—you can put together the basic outline of a Web page very, very quickly. Figure 25-7 shows PageMill's simple-to-use interface.

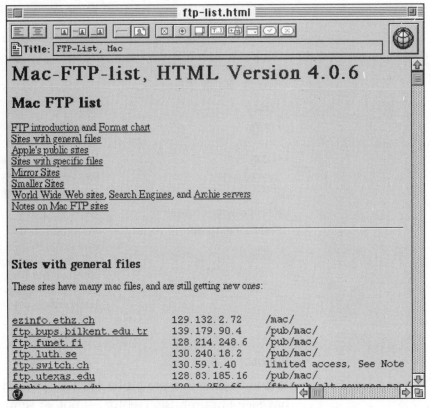

Figure 25-7: Simple page layout is PageMill's greatest strength.

The biggest disadvantage of PageMill is that there's no easy way to edit the raw HTML tags, so you can't use PageMill to take advantage of any cutting-edge features like Java, JavaScript, or Netscape Plug-ins. This may not be a problem if you're developing pages that must be backwards-compatible with simpler browsers like Mosaic, but if you want to do anything that takes advantage of the newest tech, you'll have to add a good text editor to your toolbox if you want to modify your PageMill files.

We've included SiteMill in this section because it still uses PageMill as its HTML editor but combines that functionality with its own site-management capabilities. SiteMill includes a lot of nifty features for anyone who has to manage a large site, including link checking and quick overviews of files.

PageMill & SiteMill	**Mac68K. PowerMac**
Adobe	http://www.adobe.com
Commercial: PageMill: $99.95 (street), SiteMill: $398.99 (street)	
Tables	No.
Forms	Yes, all form elements shown on-screen.
HTML 3.0	No.
WYSIWYG?	Yes. WYSIWYG only. No facility for editing raw HTML.
Preview with Browser?	No.
Special Features	Very easy to use. Enables you to drag and drop images from Finder. SiteMill will check links across pages and work with remote files. PageMill includes both an image map editor and a background color picker.

Webtor

Webtor is only in a pre-alpha release right now, but it seems to have a lot of promise. Webtor is another semi-WYSIWYG editor that allows you to view both your inline images and your HTML code. The current version of Webtor does have its share of bugs, but keep watching—this may become one of the best Mac editors during the next year (see Figure 25-8).

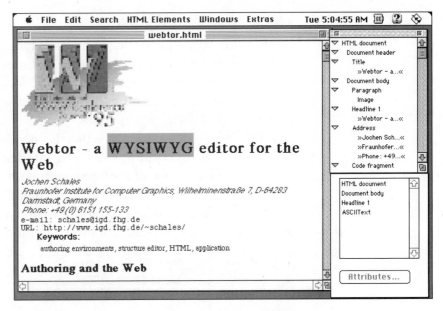

Figure 25-8: Webtor, a rising star in the HTML editor universe.

Webtor	Mac68K
Fraunhofer Institute for Computer Graphics	http://www.informatik.th-darmstadt.de/~neuss/webtor/webtor.html
Free Alpha	
Tables	Yes, built-in table editor.
Forms	Yes, all form elements.
HTML 3.0	No.
WYSIWYG?	Somewhat—displays images inline with tags.
Preview with Browser?	Yes, will launch a browser to preview HTML code.
Special Features	None.

World Wide Web Weaver

World Wide Web Weaver began life as HTML Web Weaver, a not-so-hot HTML editor without much to recommend it. However, in its new incarnation as the super-charged World Wide Web Weaver, this program is fast becoming the Macintosh editor of choice for professional HTML programmers.

WWWW's greatest strength is that it conceals some high-powered features behind a very simple-looking interface (see Figure 25-9). When you click on one of the items in the control panel to access a high-powered feature, WWWW uses a dialog box to let you set the options. Tags are displayed in the main window, and you can edit them at will. HoTMetaL doesn't let you do that.

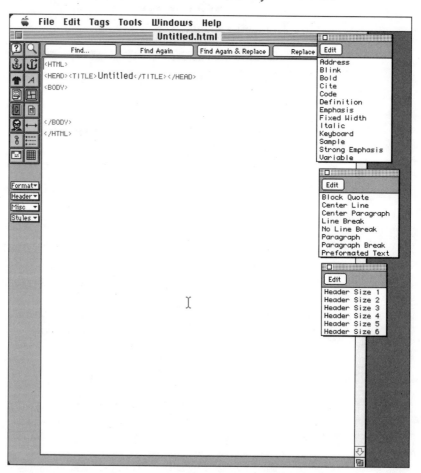

Figure 25-9: World Wide Web Weaver's uncluttered interface.

At this point, the best feature of WWWW is that it's the only HTML editor for the Macintosh that gives you the tools to develop Netscape frames (as shown in Figure 25-10). This is a big deal for a lot of HTML programmers who often find setting up frames to be difficult and time-consuming.

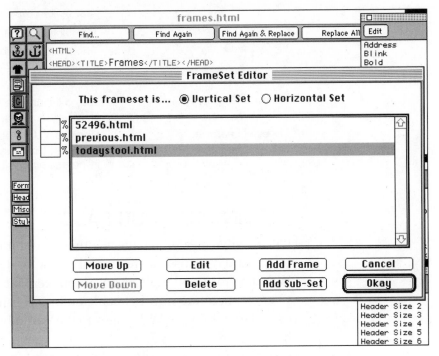

Figure 25-10: Defining frame sets with World Wide Web Weaver.

If you're anything more than a casual HTML hacker, give WWWW a try. It's flexible, powerful, and fast and combines all of that with just enough ease of use.

World Wide Web Weaver	Mac68K
Best Enterprises	http://www.northnet.org/best/Web.Weaver/WWWW.html
Demo Available	
Full version: $50	
Tables	Yes, built-in table editor.
Forms	Yes, all form elements.
HTML 3.0	Yes, most. Also includes the only Macintosh frames support available.
WYSIWYG?	No, text only.
Preview with Browser?	Yes, will launch a browser to preview HTML code.
Special Features	Uses color for setting off tags from imported text. Supports frames. Allows inline editing of all tags.

SERVING UP YOUR PAGES

Once you've created a page, it's time to put it up. For many people, this means transferring files to a local service provider's Web directory, and making an announcement to the world that your creations are now available online. This method is by far the easiest way to serve Web pages to the world because you don't have to maintain anything. Once the pages are up on your ISP's server, all you need to do is sit back, count the hits, and bask in the glory that is Web publishing. No muss, no fuss—your ISP handles all the details of making sure your pages are available. And, don't forget—if all you have is a shell account, there's no other way to serve Web pages except by placing them on your ISP's server.

The disadvantage of using an ISP to serve your pages is that you don't control the server. If you want to add any fancy multimedia stuff, you'll often find yourself on the phone, begging some techie to add a new MIME type to the server's configuration file. Also, because you don't run the server, you don't have any control over when the server's up or down. You're at the mercy of your ISP. This isn't a problem for most folks who just want to put up a Kilroy page (you know, an "I was here!" home page), but if you're using a Web page to advertise your company, publish a 'zine, or for any other mission-critical purpose, you may want to take matters into your own hands with your own Web server.

In this section, we'll cover a few of the most popular Web server packages. Because we've concentrated on personal computer users to this point, we aren't even going to try to touch any of the really complicated stuff—servers that run on high-powered UNIX or Windows NT boxes. Instead, we'll concentrate on servers that you can install and run on the computer you've got on your desk or one that fits the budget (and technical knowledge) of most small-company or home power users, namely Windows 95 and Mac servers.

Connection Considerations

When deciding that you want to use your own computer for serving Web pages, it's important to consider the speed of your connection. Unfortunately, unless you want to run a server just for your friends to log in to every once in a while, you'll have to have a faster connection than your average 28.8 kbps modem. A modem is fine for your single connection going out, but if you plan on having more than one person connecting to your machine at a time, you'll have to get a bigger pipe.

Dual-channel ISDN (see Chapter 4, "Above & Beyond 28.8 Kbps") is probably the lowest point you'll want to start at. With a 156 kbps connection, you can reasonably expect to serve up pages to about three or four people at a time. For many small businesses, home users, and other people expecting a low connection rate, this should work just fine. However, if you run a large company or have a site that may bring in thousands of visitors from all over the world, you'll want to upgrade to at least a T1 line. It's a pretty major expense (easily over $1,000 a month), but if your Web site is a critical part of your life, you may want to check into it. Ask your ISP for details.

Co-location is another method that allows you to have your own server but at a much lower cost than maintaining your own line. Co-location has gained a lot of popularity over the past year or so, and it's a great compromise option for anyone without the cash to spring for a T1. Here's how it works. You buy the hardware (the computer the server is going to run on), and then you pack it in the car and trundle it over to the service provider's offices. Once you hand your computer over to your ISP, they connect it directly to their high-speed line and configure their routing hardware to send requests directly to your server hardware. You get the advantages of having full control over your server and a high-speed connection, without having to pay the high monthly charges. The only drawback is that the box isn't physically at your location, and if you want to put up new Web pages, you'll have to FTP them to your server or carry them on a disk.

Intranets: Serving up Web Pages off the Internet

Many corporations with internal TCP/IP networks are discovering intranets, a new way of publishing information. An intranet uses all the same hardware, protocols, and programs that you'd use to serve pages to the World Wide Web but does so internally, over a company TCP/IP network. Many large corporations are tossing their Lotus Notes in the trashcan and accomplishing all the same tasks—data sharing, publishing, and interoffice communications—by setting up their own internal Web sites that employees on the LAN can access with a Web browser. These intranets aren't connected to the rest of the world through the Internet, so there's no problem with putting sensitive company documents online. And, because much of the software to run an intranet is freely available on the Internet, it's often a cost-effective solution for any company that has to reach a large number of its employees. Some companies are even setting up worldwide intranets on the Internet using a combination of firewalls to shield their computers from the rest of the Net.

Windows Web Server Solutions

A big advantage of using a Windows machine as a Web server is that the setup and administration of the server is usually much easier to deal with than a UNIX machine. The office Windows guru often has enough knowledge at his or her disposal to get the server up and running without having to attend several weeks of expensive classes, and most of the software can be installed just by clicking a mouse. Since Windows Web servers utilize the standard Windows file system, moving files into and out of the server is as easy as dragging icons to the appropriate folders. Better yet, all this ease of use doesn't come at the expense of power—the good Windows Web servers can hold their own against any fancy UNIX server. Let's take a look at some of your options.

ExpressO

ExpressO is the first commercial Web server written in Java (it's not just for applets anymore!). Because it was created in Java, ExpressO shares many of the same advantages of Java—you can extend its functionality with your own Java programs, it's portable to other platforms, and it's fast. ExpressO setup is easy—a graphical user interface guides you through all the steps. Best of all, it includes all the features that you'd expect from any other commercial Web server—full security support, real-time performance measurement tools, proxy support, multiple IP addresses, CGI scripting, and full log entries. You can even take ExpressO on a 60-day test drive if you want, so you can be sure before you buy.

ExpressO	Windows 95
Innovative Desktop Commercial: $295.00 Lite (Personal): $99.00	http://www.capitalcity.com:4321/
Special Features	Extensible through Java programs.

Quarterdeck WebServer

If you're looking to try a server for your own personal use, or you're not sure if your business needs a big, complicated Web server, Quarterdeck's WebServer may be the answer. You don't need any special knowledge to set it up because all the configuration is done with a Windows graphical interface. While it doesn't support a lot of the electronic commerce encryption supported by the bigger, more expensive servers, WebServer does have a range of security features, including full logging and the ability to block access for either a single user or a group of users. Theoretically, WebServer can dish out 25,000 connections per hour or up to 16 simultaneous connections—we weren't able to test it to its full limits, so we'll have to take their word for it. But just because WebServer's cheap ($49) doesn't mean that it doesn't do all the other stuff the big servers do. You can modify MIME types, handle image maps, and even add your own CGI scripts. If you want to get into Web serving in the easiest, cheapest way possible, WebServer may be the answer. Figure 25-11 shows how easy it is to configure.

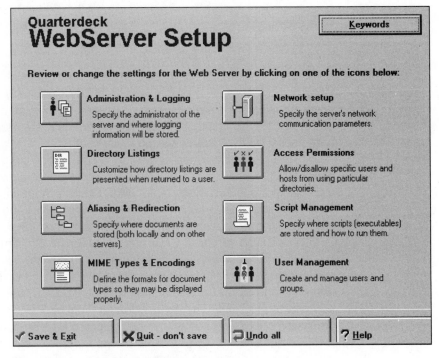

Figure 25-11: Configuring WebServer.

Quarterdeck WebServer	Windows 3.1, Windows 95
Quarterdeck	http://www.quarterdeck.com/
$49 (special introductory price)	
Special Features	Cheap, relatively fast, reasonably secure.

Alternative Server Solutions: Linux

http://www.linux.org   Free

For the true card-carrying geek, there is no higher calling than Linux. Linux is a freely available version of UNIX originally written by Lines Torvalds of Helsinki, Finland. Currently, Linux runs on 386, 486, and Pentium machines. A PowerMac version is in the works, and a beta should be available by the time you read this.

Over the years, Linux has gone from being a geek toy to a full-featured UNIX implementation, and has achieved full-blown cult status with hackers and corporate types alike. Literally thousands of people have contributed to Linux's development, porting just about every UNIX application known to humanity over to run on Linux.

You want Web servers? Linux has at least nine of them, including the standard NCSA server, CERN server, and the powerful APACHE server. You want mail? Linux can run all the standard UNIX e-mail daemons. News? No problem! Several Usenet NNTP servers have been ported to Linux. The same goes for Gopher, FTP, Telnet, X11 . . . you name it, and somebody's probably ported it to Linux (you can even run Doom!). Check out the Woven Goods for Linux page at http://www.fokus.gmd.de/linux/ for pointers to most Linux software.

Sounds great, doesn't it? Rather than spend thousands of dollars on a commercial version of UNIX, you can do it all with Linux, right? Yes, but there are a few things you should know before you dive in. First, Linux must run on its own partition of your hard drive, taking over your machine. You can set up separate partitions for Linux and Windows, but you'll need to reboot if you need to switch. Second, setting up Linux can be a real education in becoming a hacker. You'll need to know all sorts of information about your hardware, and many people find that it takes them as many as 20 hours (or more) before they're up and running. Finally, because Linux is a free product, you're pretty much on your own. Sure, thousands of people on several newsgroups are willing to answer your questions, but if your server goes down in the middle of the night, they might not be much help.

If you know what you're doing and don't mind rolling up your sleeves and digging into the digital guts of your machine, Linux may be the server solution you need. Many people swear by it, and it has definitely become a stable, reliable platform for those who need UNIX. You may want to give it a try, but be ready for some serious commitment.

WebSTAR NT/95

While Quarterdeck's WebServer is a great starter server, WebSTAR NT/95 is what you should move up to once you're serious about getting your pages on the Web. While WebServer has its own internal limitations on the number of hits per hour it can handle, WebSTAR can take as many as your server can handle. It supports multiple Web sites, CGI scripting, image maps, and good security features, though it doesn't handle encrypted security yet. WebSTAR is easy to use, too. You can get going as soon as you install it out of the box, and all the configuration is done with a point-and-click, graphical Control Center. You don't need any UNIX knowledge to set up WebSTAR. Just put it in your machine and go.

WebSTAR NT/95	Windows 95- 486. Windows NT- Pentium recommended.
Quarterdeck Introductory price: $99	http://www.quarterdeck.com/

MacOS Web Server Solutions

If you want a server that's easy to set up and maintain, you can't do any better than a Macintosh Web server. While Mac servers aren't necessarily the fastest servers on the Net, test after independent test has shown that they're by far the easiest to set up, the most painless to maintain, and the most secure from crackers. Anyone with a basic understanding of how a Web server works can get one going in under a few hours, and maintaining the files is a simple point/click/drag affair. Also, using AppleScript or MacPerl, Mac Web servers can do anything the big boys can do—serving up CGI scripts and animations and tracking hits. Plus, many Mac servers can be integrated with easy-to-use Filemaker Pro (and other database) programs, so with a little effort you can get on the Net in a flash.

ExpressO

Just like its Windows 95 cousin, ExpressO is the first commercial Web server written in Java. It's completely extensible with your own Java programs, and it features full security support, real-time performance measurement tools, proxy support, multiple IP addresses, CGI scripting, and log entries. As more Java moves to the Mac, you'll have a wide range of development tools at your disposal (Natural Intelligence, Symantec, and Metroworks are all working on Java development environments), so ExpressO will be able to grow as your Web needs grow.

ExpressO	PowerMac
Innovative Desktop Commercial: $295 Lite (Personal): $99	http://www.capitalcity.com:4321/
Special Features	Extensible through Java programs.

Alternative Server Solutions: MachTen

Tenon Intersystems. http://www.tenon.com/   Cost: $695

If the Mac servers you read about in this section just don't cut it for you or you want to be able to access all the software and support that UNIX users enjoy, MachTen may be the answer.

MachTen is currently the only commercially available UNIX for the Macintosh. It's compatible with BSD UNIX, so most freely available UNIX internet server solutions can be modified to compile and execute. Hundreds of applications have already been ported to MachTen, and Tenon Intersystems even sells the MachTen Ported Applications CD with executable binaries ready to go. Not only can you use MachTen to run a Web server (included), but you can use it for anything UNIX can serve up—mail, Gopher, WAIS, and FTP.

The most amazing thing about MachTen is that it runs as an application under the regular Mac OS, so you don't have to make a difficult decision about whether you should reformat your hard drive and let a new OS take over your machine.

MachTen is also amazingly easy to configure. To install it, all you have to do is copy a folder to your hard drive from the installation CD-ROM, install a few extensions and control panels, throw a few configuration switches, and you're in business with your own UNIX. MachTen's manual steps you through the whole process, which took Sean (not a UNIX guru by any stretch of the imagination!) only 45 minutes from the time he opened the box until MachTen was running.

Besides the UNIX basics, MachTen also includes an X-Windows server and clients (see Figure 25-12), as well as its own robust TCP/IP stack. Overall, if you're looking for ease of use and a powerful solution, MachTen is worth a try.

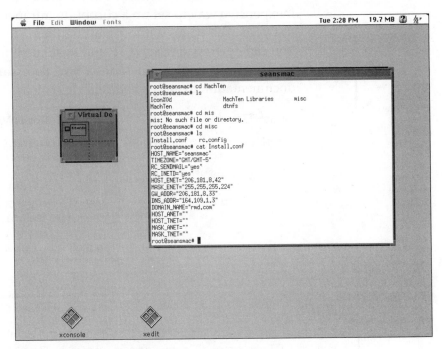

Figure 25-12: MachTen running X-Windows on a Mac.

MacHTTP

MacHTTP is the oldest and most popular shareware Web server for the Macintosh and is now distributed by StarNine software, including full tech support for registered users. If you just want to get into Web serving in a small way, it's the perfect solution because it's easy to configure, simple to use, and easy to administer. In fact, setting up MacHTTP only takes six (!) steps, so you can be on your way to Web serving in under half an hour.

While MacHTTP doesn't support a lot of the fancier server features (there's no special security, for example), it does do all the basic stuff. If you're running a LAN using MacTCP, it's a simple, inexpensive way to set up a corporate Intranet or a nice way to test your Web pages without putting them "live" on the Internet. You can download MacHTTP and evaluate it for 30 days without paying. The download includes all the necessary files and full documentation to get you started right away.

MacHTTP	Mac68K, PowerMac
StarNine	http://www.starnine.com/machttp/machttpsoft.html
Shareware – $95	
Special Features	MacHTTP's lack of special features is its biggest feature. Simple, easy to configure, and to the point. Includes AppleScript support.

TIP

A great alternative to MacHTTP is NetPresenz, the combination Web server, FTP server, and Gopher server written by Peter Lewis. See Chapter 15, "Mac Net Tools Gallery," for details on where to get NetPresenz.

WebStar

WebSTAR is MacHTTP's grown-up alter ego. Based on the original code of MacHTTP and extended to fulfill the needs of the largest Web presence (Apple includes it with all its Web server solution bundles), WebSTAR is the power user's choice for Macintosh Web server solutions. It supports full CGI scripting, image maps, forms, and access controls. Plus, with the new Secure Sockets Layer (SSL) Toolkit, you can now achieve complete secure server status, allowing for electronic commerce with such digital payment systems as First Virtual. WebSTAR also supports remote administration, making it a great solution for anyone who uses co-location for his or her server.

Even though WebSTAR will take care of the job now, look for some exciting new features over the next few months. By the time you read this, WebSTAR should support Open Transport, resulting in a projected speed increase of 40 percent on PowerMacs. But the most exciting feature of WebSTAR is the ability to add new plug-in modules for enhanced functionality. Not to be confused with Netscape Navigator's plug-ins, these extensions (written in C) will allow WebSTAR to be extended as much as the Macintosh architecture allows.

WebSTAR	**Mac68K, PowerMac**
StarNine	http://www.starnine.com/webstar/webstarsoft.html
$795 list	
Special Features	Supports extensions for secure transactions via First Virtual. AppleScriptable. More secure than UNIX.

NEWBIE WEBMASTER RESOURCES

Putting together a Web-server solution can be pretty scary, especially if you've never tackled such a complex technical project before. Don't worry—you're not alone. As more and more people and businesses get on the Web, there's a growing demand for information about how to go about becoming your own Webmaster.

If you're ready to set up a full-time Web server of your own, either on the Web or in your office Intranet, you'll need some good help. Our best advice is to try to find the server software and HTML editor that work best for you. We've tried to pick out the best here, but you may have a different opinion once you try them. Here's a couple of Web pages with links to just about every server and HTML editor on the market so you can discover one for yourself:

❐ **WebCompare**

http://www.webcompare.com/server-main.html

A complete (and we mean complete!) listing of all the Web servers available today.

❐ **Macintosh HTML Editor Reviews at ComVista**

http://www.comvista.com/net/www/htmleditor.html

Reviews of all the shareware, freeware, and commercial Macintosh HTML editors.

❐ **Carl Davis' HTML Editor Reviews**

http://www.ccs.org/htmledit/index.html

The source for excellent reviews, screen shots, and ratings of all the major Windows HTML editors.

MOVING ON

Now that you've gotten a brief overview of the tools you'll need to serve your own Web pages, why not explore a few of your options? Even if you're only connected via SLIP or PPP, try creating a few HTML pages, and installing a demo version of a Web server. Then call (or e-mail) all your friends, and invite them in for an open house on your computer! It's good practice for later if you want to move up to setting up your own full-time server, and as bandwidth becomes cheaper and faster, it may even serve as a dry-run for what you'll be able to do a year or so from now.

Now that we're finished with learning how to get the most out of the Web, we're going to move into a different dimension of Cyberspace, in search of people, ideas, and data. The world is increasingly all about on-demand learning, keeping up with changing technologies and cultures that move at dizzying speeds. Knowing how to stay on top of the flood of information has become more critical. We'll try to point out some of the tools for this.

In the chapter on Data Tracking (Chapter 26), we'll learn how to use agents, Gophers, Web crawlers, spiders, indexes, and other search tools to find whatever you're looking for. Then, in Chapter 27, all about people searching, we'll examine how to track down honest-to-goodness humans on the Net using a number of key resources, including the many white pages that are now becoming available.

## Part VIII

Netsearching: Unleashing Your Code Hound

## Chapter 26

Data Tracking

The Internet: There's information gold in them there hills!

Now that we've recovered from that bit of earth-shattering news, we can start figuring out how to mine the motherlode of info that's out there. Just how do you go about finding what you want in the vast reaches of Cyberspace? Is it possible to be relatively sure that you've found all of the latest and greatest information available? The short answer is no. Even professional information researchers know that there's always more to be found. It's important to find enough of what you're looking for to satisfy the reason for your search. To do that, you need to know enough about the available tools to feel confident that you've found reliable information in a timely manner.

One of the blessings and curses of the Net is that anyone can play. It's a socially constructed world of news, information, and opinion, and *all* of it gets regularly vacuumed into the databases you use when tracking data. This leads to lots of information duplication and some information that only its mother could love (that is, information that's useless to you). Sorting through all this to find the gem you're looking for can be an overwhelming task.

This chapter only scratches the surface of the subject of Net searching and the available tools and resources. Whenever possible, we've tried to point you in the direction of more detailed information. By applying the information here and following up with these pointers, you should be an ace Cybrarian in no time.

DATA TRACKING OVERVIEW

The Internet has grown so quickly that one form of search technology gets quickly overtaken by another. The old tools do not disappear overnight, but rather continue to exist (albeit rusty and creaky) alongside the spiffy new search machines. Many information repositories offer their contents through both old and new access methods. Ideally, power searchers should be knowledgeable about all of these searching methods to get the most out of their online data sleuthing. Let's take a quick look at the main types of search tools:

Web Searches

The World Wide Web has put a pretty face on the powerful search engines that mine the Net's rich information ore. Using simple search expressions, browsing hierarchical menus, and filling out simple forms, Web search sites allow you to quickly fetch documents. The information found is presented with hyperlinks, allowing you to go directly to the found documents with a simple mouse click.

Archie Searches

Archie is an older Net tool used for searching file names on FTP sites. All over the Net, a vast number of programs and text files are stored on these FTP servers. Archie helps you find out where they are.

Gopher Searches With Veronica and Jughead

Gopher is another older Net technology that has been overshadowed by the Web but is still a useful place to track down information. Gophers are menu-driven repositories of information usually presented in text files. Veronica and Jughead are two search tools that allow you to search through Gopherspace, the areas of the Net interconnected by Gopher servers.

WAIS Searches

WAIS (Wide Area Information Server) is adept at searching through the content of its resources. Instead of just searching for document titles, WAIS (pronounced "ways") can actually search for individual words within the document, helping you identify both content and concepts. For example, if you're searching for "puppets," a WAIS search will find "Sock Monkeys And Postmodernity: A Theoretical Dialectic or Just A Lame Grant Proposal?" and "Muppets: Spawn of Satan!" if both documents contain the word *puppets*.

Searching Newsgroups & Mailing Lists

Yes, Usenet newsgroups contain a great deal of useless chatter, but they are also a living information system and repository of collective Net wisdom and expertise. Knowing which groups and lists to follow, and how to globally search newsgroups in general, can be a vital link to getting the information you need.

Searching FAQs (RFCs & STDs)

You can often cut to the chase by quickly laying your hands on the FAQ (Frequently Asked Questions) file for the subject you're exploring. If you're looking for technical information on the Internet itself and the protocols and standards that underlie it, RFCs (Request for Comments) and STDs (Standards) are what you need.

In the rest of this chapter, we'll unpack these various tools and provide a brief starter kit of key Net points for conducting your searches and staying abreast of the latest developments in search technologies.

Are We Searching or Surfing?

It is said that information wants to be free. Well, information also wants to get in your face in every possible way on the Internet. If you're searching for information that you really need, and need fast, it's best to master the fine art of searching *without* surfing. Especially on the Web, there's always another link tempting you to discover what's behind it. If you're looking for a specific file, you might find several tangential ones that look cool. If you're burrowing through a government Gopher, it's easy to get sidetracked by those statistics documents that will help you win that ever-important water cooler debate.

You can find what you need on the Net, but you must be ruthless about staying focused on what you're looking for. Make a note of anything else that looks interesting, or bookmark it, and come back when you have more time. Most people dislike research because they think it takes too long. Stay focused, and Net research will become more manageable.

Remember, you've been warned!. If you click that extra link and find yourself wondering why all of a sudden it's seven hours later and dark outside, you brought it upon yourself.

WEB SEARCH ENGINES & FACILITIES

Search engines on the Web get more powerful and sophisticated all the time, and there are plenty to choose from. Most of your online searching can be accommodated through the Web. We've collected an extensive list of Web search sites in Table 26-1. Each site has different features and slightly different ways to approach a search. Some search by "crawling" the Web, going from link-to-link, cataloging as they go. Others build up their databases by asking Web masters to register their pages. Some can use multiple engines. Familiarize yourself with the inner workings of at least three or four search sites that give you reliable results on a regular basis.

TIP

Don't forget to use the online help. Each of these sites has a help page with useful search tips. We know it's easy to get complacent about reading documentation, but a few moments spent reading the help file during one search can save you lots of time on subsequent searches.

Site	Address/Comments
AltaVista	http://www.altavista.digital.com/ The mother of all search engines, provides tons of hits, attempts to prioritize them. When you want to see everything on a subject, start here.
OpenText	http://www.opentext.com:8080/ Precise search strings get the best results here.
Lycos	http://lycos.cs.cmu.edu/ Another subject-oriented index, or you can search by keyword. Fast.
Inktomi Search Engine	http://inktomi.berkeley.edu/ Tons of useful help information. One of the best.
Yahoo	http://www.yahoo.com Probably the best index site. A great starting point for basic searches. Excellent subject and category listings, or you can search by keyword.
InfoSeek Guide	http://www.infoseek.com:80/Home It costs after 100 queries per month.
InfoMarket	http://www.infomkt.ibm.com/ht3/welcome.htm IBM's offering connects to COMTEX Newswires, NewsBytes, Open Text, and Usenet newsgroups (this service is free for now, but IBM plans to commercialize it sometime during 1996).
WWW Worm	http://www.cs.colorado.edu/home/home/mcbryan/wwww.html Good help for Boolean searches.

➡

Site	Address/Comments
WebCrawler	http://www.webcrawler.com/ AOL uses (and owns) this search tool. It's intuitive. Returns prioritized list.
All-in-One	http://www.albany.net/allinone/ Attempts to put a common interface on many search functions.

Table 26-1: Major search sites.

Web Searches Over Multiple Engines & Data Bases

The Web sites listed in Table 26-2 usually don't have their own internal database but rather access one or more external search engines and such resources as Usenet newsgroups, general databases, and tools such as Archie or WAIS.

Site	Address/Comments
ALIWEB	http://www.nexor.co.uk/public/aliweb/aliweb.html Stronger in general than in specifics.
DejaNews	www.dejanews.com The best way to search Usenet newsgroups.
Galaxy	http://galaxy.einet.net Good listings by subject categories.
Experimental Meta Index	http://www.ncsa.uiuc.edu/SDG/Software/Mosaic/Demo/metaindex.html Searches engines and catalogs. Has facilities for Veronica, Jughead, WAIS.
EZ-Find	http://www.theriver.com/TheRiver/Explore/ezfind.html Just as the name says: easy to use and helpful. Searches many engines, Usenet newsgroups, and Archie.

Site	Address/Comments
Find-It!	http://www.cam.org/~psarena/find-it.html Searches a variety of engines, shareware sites, and Usenet newsgroups.
Internet Exploration Page	http://www.amdahl.com/internet/meta-index.html/ Searches many different engines and other materials from this page.
Internet Searching Center	http://www.lib.umich.edu/chouse/searching/find.html Searches engines, various search facilities, virtual libraries.
MetaCrawler	http://metacrawler.cs.washington.edu:8080/index.html Sends requests to eight of the major search engines.
SavvySearch	http://www.cs.colostate.edu/~dreiling/smartform.html Searches by keyword or subject. Searches several engines. Somewhat slow.
The Internet Sleuth	http://www.intbc.com/sleuth Excellent searches of a number of engines, databases, and other resources.
The Mother-of-all BBS	http://wwwmbb.cs.colorado.edu/~mcbryan/bb/summary.html Tries very hard to be just that. Almost pulls it off.
WebSurfer	http://www.io.com/~derae/ Searches the Web, Usenet newsgroups, and other resources.
Yanoff Special Internet Connections List	http://www.uwm.edu/Mirror/inet.services.html A massive link list and subject-based resource. Web sites, Gophers, and more.
Search.Com	http://www.search.com ClNet's meta-search engine with access to 250 different search facilities.

Table 26-2: Multiple search sites.

Boolean & Other Forms of Searching

Most search sites use some form of Boolean commands to help refine their searches. Boolean commands, or operators, are based upon Boolean Logic which was developed by mathematician George Boole. Programmers and mathematicians use complex Boolean operators, but what you'll use in almost all Net searches is a few simple operators .

Let's look at an example. Say you want to find out more about that wise crackin' cartoon duo Rocky and Bullwinkle. There are four ways you could go about finding the information:

❏ Rocky AND Bullwinkle

❏ Rocky OR Bullwinkle

❏ Rocky NOT Bullwinkle

❏ Bullwinkle NOT Rocky

The OR operator is the broadest—you'll get every listing that includes either "Rocky" or "Bullwinkle."

The AND operator gets you every document or listing that includes "Rocky" and "Bullwinkle." Both words must be present.

The NOT operator helps you further refine your search. If you are interested only in documents that mention "Rocky," you can specifically exclude "Bullwinkle." This operator is very helpful if you are sure you need to exclude a keyword in order to get better results.

Many search engines "weight" their results. This means they give you the best possible matches first, depending on the following criteria:

❏ How often the words are used.

❏ If they're used early in the document.

❏ How close the words in your string are to each other, and other considerations.

If a weighted Boolean search narrows to a dull roar of 1000 matches, you'll most likely find what you're looking for within the first 10 or 20 matches, since these will be weighted highest.

Once you have more than two keywords, the order of them can make a huge difference in the results. At some sites, you can require or eliminate a word by use of the + and - signs. For instance, you could ask such a site to try +Rocky +Bullwinkle -Natasha -Boris. If you loved everything about that show except the storybook segments, you could try +Rocky +Bullwinkle -"Fractured Fairy Tales." The quote marks around words tell the search engine to treat the information in quotes as a complete string, not as separate words subject to and/or selection.

Wildcards are allowed at some sites. If you enter "Bull*", you get every occurrence of words that start with "Bull." We hope you find Bullwinkle before finding bullwhip, bullseye, and other bullwords. You can put further constraints on searches. Some sites will let you search for text in hyperlinks, for instance. Each site has different search features and expressions, so make sure you read the online help.

Searching for "Moose:" A Strange Case Study

Let's take a look at some of these search ideas and strategies in practice. We recently had occasion to search for information about the moose. Don't get us started on why; it's not a pretty story. And, believe it or not, this has nothing to do with our moose and squirrel pals mentioned above.

So, armed with a detailed search strategy–find moose info–off we went. Starting at Yahoo, a popular Web search starting point, we entered "moose" into the main search field (see Figure 26-1).

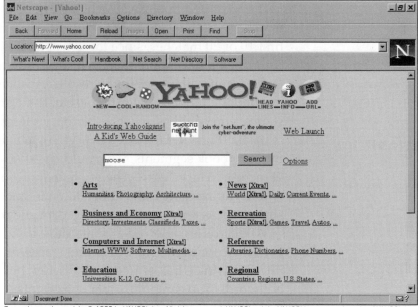

Text and artwork copyright © 1996 by YAHOO!, Inc. All rights reserved. YAHOO! and the YAHOO! logo are trademarks of YAHOO!, Inc.

Figure 26-1: Yahoo's main page loaded for "moose."

We got 51 possible matches in response, most of them with "moose" in the name of a product. A few were about hunting moose. We shuddered at the thought and went back to work.

We chose Options and told Yahoo we wanted to treat "moose" as a whole word, not part of a word or substring. Among the product names were a few interesting tidbits like a cartoon called "Space Moose" and "The Moose's Guide to *Northern Exposure*." We were sorely tempted, but being professionals with steely control of our impulses, we held fast. (Translation: we spent only about five minutes at the *Northern Exposure* page and returned to the quest.)

Before we tried another search site, we took a look at Yahoo's subject categories. We tried choosing the "Science" category from Yahoo's subject menu instead of entering words in the search field (see Figure 26-2).

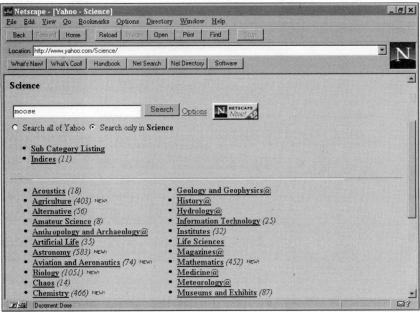

Text and artwork copyright © 1996 by YAHOO!, Inc. All rights reserved. YAHOO! and the YAHOO! logo are trademarks of YAHOO!, Inc.

Figure 26-2: The Yahoo Science section.

From here, we could explore subcategories, such as Zoology, or we could enter "moose" in the search field again. This time we requested that the search go only through the Science listings. We ended up with only one hit, for something called Mooseker Labs at Yale.

Next we tried AltaVista. We chose to search only the Web first, although we could have also searched Usenet newsgroups. See Figure 26-3.

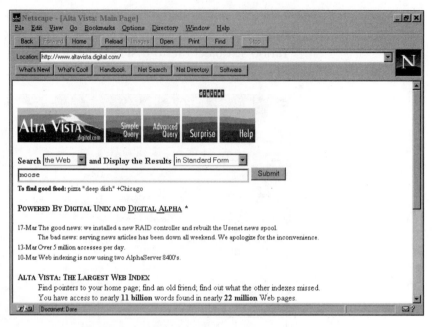

Figure 26-3: AltaVista with "moose" firmly ensconced in the search field.

Holy antlers! We got 30,000 matches! What's going on here; is AltaVista some sort of Mecca of moose info? Well, no. Figure 26-4 shows the first eight matches. (If we had known that at our ages we would be typing "AltaVista moose matches" as part of our job, we would have looked into another line of work.)

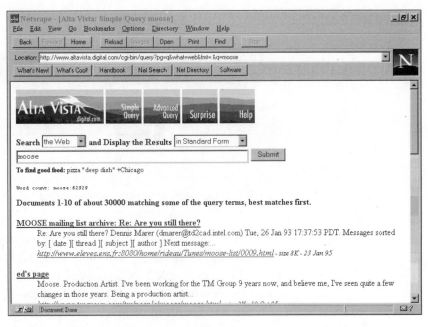

Figure 26-4: The AltaVista moose matches.

As you can see, it isn't until match number eight that we get anywhere near actual moose info. But there it is, a site discussing the majestic Maine Moose. We clicked; we connected. Turns out the Maine Moose site is for a gold medallion (moose jewelry?). It's a perfectly lovely one, we might add, but not what we had in mind.

Using our crack researching skills and deductive reasoning, we soon realized either we were going to read through 30,000 matches that were likely to be the same or we needed to take drastic measures. We went for Boolean operators (see Figure 26-5). Like most good search engines, AltaVista has excellent online help. Using the help screens, we could define our search better. In this case, we could try the following:

```
+moose +animal −macros −membership +Canada −"medallions of gold"
```

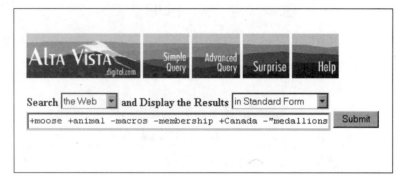

Figure 26-5: Our AltaVista search all decked out with Boolean doodles.

We asked AltaVista to only search for words that were on the matched page: "moose," "animal," and "Canada." Why Canada? Because we once saw a PBS show about Canada, and there were moose everywhere, so we figured what the heck. We specifically excluded any mention of macros (been there, done that) and membership (for some reason, people enjoy naming their clubs and organizations MooseSomething). We also excluded "medallions of gold" as a phrase just in case moose fashion jewelry chose to rear its ugly head again..

We narrowed our search to 800 matches. Within the first few entries, we found scads of useful information about moose. We finally ended our search, armed with scads of info, not to mention particularly informed about moose activities in Canada. We really hope this comes up in conversation at a party sometime soon.

TIP

This is where we bring up a painful truth about online searching: sometimes, offline searches can make more sense. In this case, an old-fashioned encyclopedia would have been a good place to start. For those who can't go cold turkey from the computer, a CD-ROM encyclopedia could have also produced ready access to pithy moose facts and figures. And never forget that indispensable doorstop of a tome, the phone book. Tons of valuable resources are a phone call away. A really handy tool for wired researches are the phone books on CD-ROM, such as PhoneDisc USA, by Database America.

SEARCHING FOR FILES WITH ARCHIE

The Internet has lots of FTP file servers on it, brimming with thousands and thousands of files. Archie was developed to collect the listings on FTP servers into a database searchable by filenames. If you know the name of a file, or part of a name, you have a fairly good chance of finding the file's location(s) with an Archie search. The downside of Archie is that you can't really peruse file listings to see what's on a server. Archie is for finding a file you know you need, and that you know at least part of what the file is called, not for browsing among files to see what's available.

When using Archie, use the Archie server geographically closest to you. If you don't know where to find Archie servers, ask your ISP for the closest locations. Archie client software for use with SLIP/PPP connections usually has a number of Archie sites listed.

For a comprehensive explanation of Archie, go to http://www.sura.net/archie/Archie-Usage.html. If you're a UNIX type with a command-line interface, type **man archie** to access the online Archie manual (if it's been installed in your system).

TIP

FTP file servers and the tools that search them are in high demand these days. Try to use these resources during off-peak hours. Peak hours are typical working hours in the server's time zone. A good rule of thumb is to use sites to the west of your time zone during the morning and early afternoon and sites to the east of your time zone during the afternoon. Using a site during its off-peak evening hours means you're search requests will be handled a lot faster.

Archie Clients

Archie client software, such as WS_Archie for Windows 95 and
Anarchie for the Mac, provides a helpful graphical interface for
doing Archie searches. You'll want to use a program like this for
Archie searches whenever possible. As you can see in Figures 26-6
and 26-7, WS_Archie and Anarchie come with a list of Archie
servers for different continents.

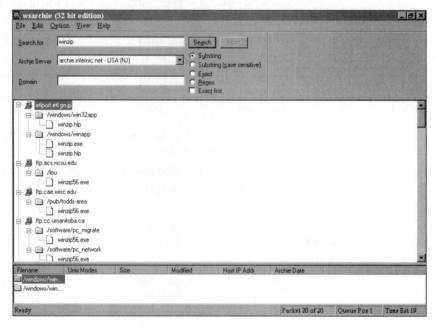

Figure 26-6: The main window in WS_Archie.

Anarchie is a smart combo of both an Archie and an FTP client. With Anarchie, if you're looking for a file, all you have to do is type in what you're looking for, pick an Archie server, and wait. If the server finds the files you're looking for, Anarchie will serve them up to you in a handy list. To download the file, double-click on its name. Cowabunga! File pipeline, dude!

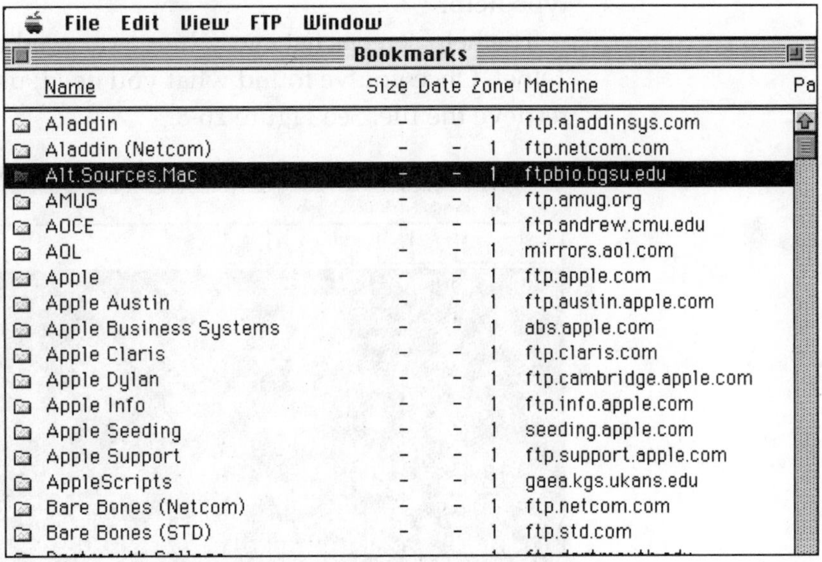

Name	Size	Date	Zone	Machine	Pa
🗁 Aladdin	–	–	1	ftp.aladdinsys.com	
🗁 Aladdin (Netcom)	–	–	1	ftp.netcom.com	
▨ Alt.Sources.Mac	–	–	1	ftpbio.bgsu.edu	
🗁 AMUG	–	–	1	ftp.amug.org	
🗁 AOCE	–	–	1	ftp.andrew.cmu.edu	
🗁 AOL	–	–	1	mirrors.aol.com	
🗁 Apple	–	–	1	ftp.apple.com	
🗁 Apple Austin	–	–	1	ftp.austin.apple.com	
🗁 Apple Business Systems	–	–	1	abs.apple.com	
🗁 Apple Claris	–	–	1	ftp.claris.com	
🗁 Apple Dylan	–	–	1	ftp.cambridge.apple.com	
🗁 Apple Info	–	–	1	ftp.info.apple.com	
🗁 Apple Seeding	–	–	1	seeding.apple.com	
🗁 Apple Support	–	–	1	ftp.support.apple.com	
🗁 AppleScripts	–	–	1	gaea.kgs.ukans.edu	
🗁 Bare Bones (Netcom)	–	–	1	ftp.netcom.com	
🗁 Bare Bones (STD)	–	–	1	ftp.std.com	

Figure 26-7: The main window in Anarchie.

Archie via Telnet

If you do not have a SLIP or PPP account, you can telnet to an Archie server using a shell account. When asked for the login prompt, you would type **archie**.

Do not use an anonymous FTP login. If you're asked for a password, use your e-mail address. As soon as you're connected, type **help**.

The help screens list everything you need to use Archie by Telnet. Once you've found what you need, use anonymous FTP to retrieve the file. See Figure 26-8.

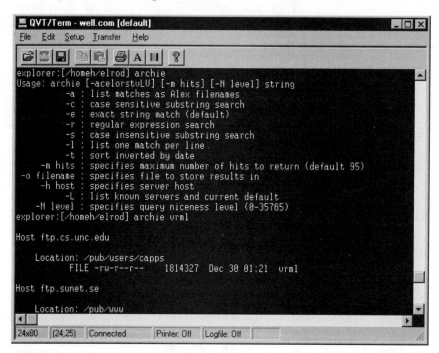

Figure 26-8: An Archie search via Telnet.

Archie on the Web

Several Web pages allow you to do an Archie search. Try the ArchiePlex form at http://www.amdahl.com/internet/archieplex (see Figure 26-9). Once you find the location file, use anonymous FTP to fetch it, either by using an FTP client or by using the "ftp:/ /" URL format in your Web browser.

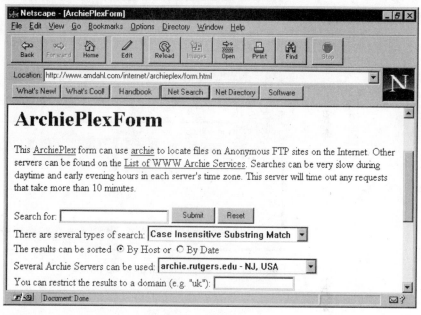

Figure 26-9: Using the ArchiePlex Web page.

E-Mail Archie

You can even do an Archie search via e-mail if you want (see Figure 26-10). Warning: this can be a slow process, as you have to wait patiently for a return e-mail response. Send e-mail to archie@archie.internic.net for instructions.

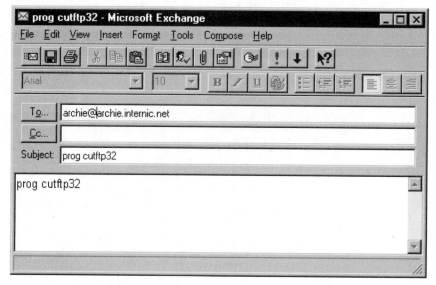

Figure 26-10: An Archie search via e-mail.

SEARCHING BY GOPHER

Gopher is a forerunner of the World Wide Web. It uses a menu-driven interface that allows you to browse through hierarchical menus by subject. While the Web has vastly overshadowed it, Gopher's still a gold mine of information, especially for stuff like University data, scientific reports, or government statistics. Many government and research sites still have a lot of their information on Gophers. Some have both Gopher and Web sites, but it's often easier to get what you need via Gopher. One big advantage is that there are no graphics with Gopher, so access speeds are faster.

Gophers are as good as their menu structure. Some are more thoughtfully designed than others. However, you'll always at least be able to tell if a menu item goes to a document or to yet another menu—directory entries are usually indicated by a forward slash (/).

Ask your ISP for a list of the geographically closest gophers. You can find lists of Gopher servers easily by searching Yahoo subject areas under Computers and Internet.

Gopher Jewels

The best Gopher information is linked to Gopher Jewels. You'll find that a search through this archive is worth the time, and often the only search you'll need to do in Gopherspace. To access Gopher Jewels, head to gopher cwis.usc.edu, and then use the menus to get to Other_Gophers_ and_Information_Resources, Gopher_Jewels. Information about the Gopher Jewels mailing list is given in the "Mailing Lists for Power Searchers" section, later in this chapter.

Gopher Clients

If you have a SLIP or PPP account, you can use Gopher client software, like HGopher and WS_Gopher for the PC, or TurboGopher on the MAC.

Figure 26-11 shows QVT/Gopher with the "home gopher," the original Gopher at the University of Minnesota (home of the "Golden Gophers"), entered as the default.

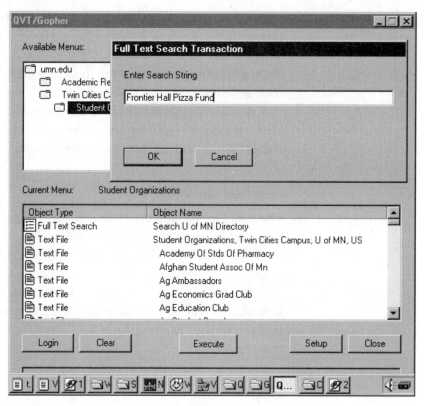

Figure 26-11: QVT/Gopher. Pizza, Anyone?

For the truly adventurous, there's even a 3D VR version of Gopher for the Mac called TurboGopherVR that displays Gopher directories and documents as strange, Stonehenge-esque objects. Go to ftp://boombox.micro.umn.edu/pub/gopher/Macintosh-TurboGopher/TurboGopherVR/ to download it.

Using Veronica

With all those Gophers out there, how can you find out what's on each of them? Why not give Veronica a ring? Veronica is a program that searches Gophers about twice a week and builds a database of the results, much like Archie does for FTP filenames.

Veronica doesn't look for subject matter, it looks for the document's title in the Gopher menus. Once again, information is more easily found if a Gopher site is thoughtfully planned with intelligent menus.

Veronica is built into Gopher programs like WS_Gopher. Or you can use it through the Web at gopher://veronica.scs.unr. edu/11/ veronica. See Figure 26-12.

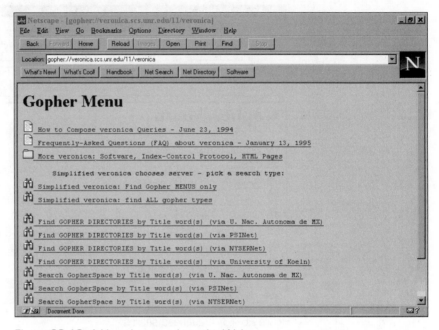

Figure 26-12: A Veronica search on the Web.

Everything you need to know about Veronica is listed in the Veronica FAQ available at gopher://veronica.scs.unr.edu:**70**/00/ veronica/veronica-faq. You get a comprehensive discussion about using keywords and various refinements like Boolean operators and control flags that indicate the type of information sought.

Using Jughead

Jughead searches Gopherspace in a very small area, usually one site, or a particular set of Gopher sites. You can use Jughead by doing a Veronica search for Jughead sites. Or, go to the home of Jughead development, gopher.utah.edu. available at this site are detailed instructions for using Jughead. See Figure 26-13.

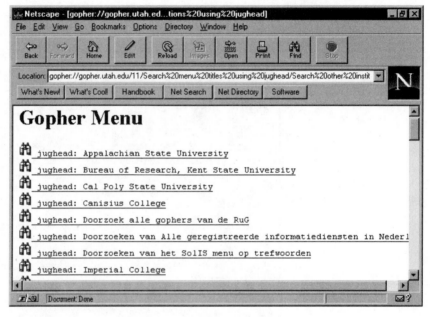

Figure 26-13: A Jughead search.

Comic Book Characters in Cyberspace?

Archie? Veronica? Jughead? Were these designed by someone with a comic book fixation? No, not exactly. Each name means something very different.

- ❒ **Archie:** Legend has it that the name sounded like "archives" to its developers.
- ❒ **Veronica:** Acronym for Very Easy Rodent-Oriented Net-wide Index to Computerized Archives.
- ❒ **Jughead:** Acronym for Jonzy's Universal Gopher Hierarchy Excavation and Display.

SEARCHING FOR CONTENT WITH WAIS

Veronica and Jughead search document titles, but titles don't always adequately represent their documents' content. WAIS is a database server that has collected this content and enables you to search for it using keywords and phrases. It acts as a personal reference librarian, once you become familiar with it and know how to ask for what you're looking for.

WAIS searches a collection of information, an online library called a source, by using keywords. WAIS then presents its findings to you by ranking the responses based on the number of times the keyword appears in the matching document. There is a wide variety of information available for WAIS searching—from the CIA World Fact Book to educational libraries to recipes. In fact, there is so much material, and not enough adequate ways of narrowing down your search, that finding what you want can sometimes be difficult.

There's a newsgroup dedicated to WAIS (comp.infosystems.wais), and a number of WAIS-related mailing lists for further help in using WAIS. You can get more information about these list from the newsgroup.

WAIS Clients

WAIS clients include WinWAIS for Windows, PCWAIS for DOS, and MacWAIS for the Mac. Both free and commercial versions are available.

Web Access to WAIS

You can use WAIS through a Web interface by pointing your Web browser to http://www.ai.mit.edu/the-net/wais.html (See Figure 26-14). From here you can enter in query terms which will search for relevant WAIS databases based on those terms.

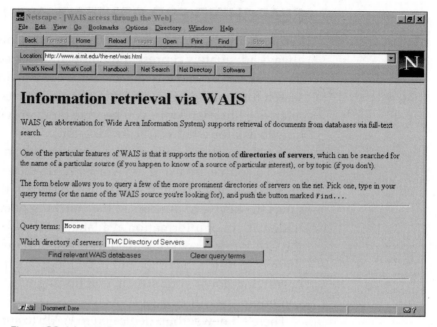

Figure 26-14: WAIS on the Web.

Using Telnet to Access WAIS

You can also use WAIS through Telnet, either via a shell account or with Telnet client software. Try the following sites:

❏ sunsite.unc.edu

❏ wais.wais.com

Follow the login prompts to find out which WAIS program to use. These sites use SWAIS (Simple WAIS), a command-line interface program. You can browse the subjects present or search for what you need using keywords.

LOOKING FOR NEWSGROUPS

A newsgroup exists for practically every subject. With more than 17,000 of them and more popping up every day, how can you find specific information? Try these resources:

- ❏ DejaNews at http://www.dejanews.com is your first stop on the trail of newsgroup content.
- ❏ TileNet News at http://tile.net/news/ lets you search their database of newsgroups.
- ❏ Online services such as America Online have search facilities that look for newsgroups based on subject descriptions.
- ❏ Almost every newsgroup has an FAQ associated with it, and these are stored at ftp://ftp.rtfm.mit.edu/pub. The FAQs are stored by name and newsgroup hierarchy.

LOOKING FOR MAILING LISTS

Mailing lists are discussion groups that use e-mail as their means of exchange. They are great sources of expertise, but they're also common sources of e-mail overload. If you're going to subscribe to a lot of mailing lists, you'll definitely want to use an e-mail program that has filtering capability so that you can sort your e-lists into appropriate folders.

■■

Mailing List Subscriptions: You Are Your Own Secretary

When you subscribe to a mailing list, you'll receive one or more pieces of e-mail that describe what the list is about. Do yourself (and all of the list participants) a favor and save these documents! Print them. They contain all the information you'll need to unsubscribe, put your subscription on hold if you go away, and other functions. It's considered good Netiquette to keep this information so that you don't ask obvious questions on the list.

➡

You are, in effect, your own secretary when it comes to mailing lists. It's considered rude to send messages to the group asking how to do basic functions. It's like treating the group as your secretary instead of being responsible for your own work. While the kinder and gentler power user wouldn't dream of flaming someone for a request for information, the fact is that it's just plain irritating to see these requests on a busy mailing lists.

Most of the mailing lists use several popular list management programs that have standard commands for subscribing/ unsubscribing. See the "Mailing Lists" section of Chapter 21, "E-Mail Privacy & Security," for a listing of these basic commands.

Where to Find Mailing Lists

A number of Web pages let you search for mailing lists. Here is a list of several of them.

- ❏ E-mail Discussion Groups at http://www.nova.edu/ Inter-Links/listserv.html
- ❏ Post Office Central at http://ourworld.compuserve.com/ homepages/djessop/
- ❏ TileNet Lists at http://tile.net/lists/
- ❏ Search the List of Lists at http://catalog.com/vivian/ interest-group-search.html
- ❏ Publicly Accessible Mailing Lists can be found at http:// www.neosoft.com/internet/paml/

Mailing List Archives

Most mailing lists have archives of their messages available through anonymous FTP. You can find information about accessing these archives in the list's basic information mailing sent to you when you joined the list.

Help! Information Overload!

Be careful about setting yourself up for mail overload. If you are short on disk space or have to pay for e-mail, you can often receive a digest version of the mailing list. The digest version collects all of the messages, usually for a 24-hour period on busier lists, and sends it to you in one message. You can find out more about the digest version, if offered, in the list's basic information mailing.

Also, when you find that you're consistently no longer reading a list, unsubscribe to it. Don't just keep deleting it when it arrives or, God forbid, adding it to your e-mail kill file. The Internet doesn't need the unnecessary traffic. Take a morning a month (or whatever schedule is appropriate) and do some list pruning. You'll save yourself time and spare yourself that guilty feeling of not reading all those cool lists you receive.

LOOKING FOR FAQS, RFCS, STDS

The chances are good (and getting better all the time) that a Frequently Asked Questions (FAQ) file is available for the subject you are searching for information on. There's everything from detailed information on Net services, tools, and techniques to expert advice on computer systems to non-computer information on things like fat-free cooking, inline skating, your favorite TV shows, various support groups, you name it! Most Usenet newsgroups have related FAQs. The largest repository of newsgroup and other assorted FAQs is at the FTP site: ftp://rtfm.mit.edu. (RTFM stands for "read the . . . *er* . . . freaking manual!").

RFCs stands for Request for Comments and STD is short for Standards. These documents are loaded with information on the inner workings of the Internet and the technologies, protocols, and standards on which they are based. Sites that have FAQs, RFCs and STDs available by FTP include:

- ❏ ds.internic.net
- ❏ nic.ddn.mil
- ❏ nic.merit.edu
- ❏ ftp.uu.net

You can also find many of these documents at InterNIC's Directory of Directories (http://www.internic.net/ds/dsdirofdirs.html). Online services like America Online make many of these materials available in their Internet areas.

SEARCH STRATEGIES

Timely and successful Net searching is best accomplished if you follow some tried and true guidelines. The following tips should help make your searches easier:

❏ Plan offline. Even if you don't pay a dime for your Net connection or the information you get from it, you're bound to run into time constraints and the occasional slow connection. Conserving Net resources will save you time. Planning offline and sticking to your plan helps prevent you from getting distracted.

❏ Think in broad, general terms about what you're trying to find. Each step of the way, narrow your search. Going from broad to specific will help ensure you've checked the right resources and that you're closing in on the appropriate information.

❏ Use unique search terms. If you want to know how to install a sound card, searching for "computer" will get you a lot of hits—zillions of them, in fact. But that's too broad; "sound card" is better. Better still is the name of the manufacturer. Even better is "Sound Blaster AWC32 and installation." Use unique words and phrases as keywords.

❏ Use reference books to find keywords. Knowing what things are called is the key to finding them. Come as close as you can to the root of a word, and don't use plurals unless it changes the meaning of the word. If one keyword doesn't work, perhaps the search facility is set up to recognize another.

❏ Know your tools and when to use them. If you're looking for a program, it makes sense to use Archie or the Web first. If you know what your subject matter is and just need a general overview, go to a subject-indexed site like Yahoo (see the search site addresses later in this chapter). If you have to track down every bit of information about a subject, the place to go is AltaVista. Get to know your tools and how they're set up and organized. It makes a big difference to start out on the right foot.

❏ Search the top of the information pyramid whenever possible. There's no reason to tell some Archie or Web spider to go traipsing off across the Internet if the information's already been collected in one place. For example, why go searching for a software program on a general search page when you can go right to the source? If you're looking for a Mac file, most likely it's been archived at the MIT Hyperarchive (http:// hyperarchive.lcs.mit.edu/HyperArchive.html). If you're searching for a PC file, the OAK Software repository (http://www.acs.oakland.edu/oak/oak.html) probably has what you're looking for. Remember: your brain is your best search engine.

❏ Read the FAQs, help screens, and man pages (the online manual pages you can get on most UNIX systems). You'll get better results if you know where you can use wildcard searches and what kind of specifications you can put on searches.

❏ Don't forget geography. You might not find as much about French politicians on a Gopher in the United States as you would on one in France or, you might have a hard time accessing a server on a university site during the middle of a school day.

A SHORT GUIDE TO REALLY GOOD NET RESOURCES

Some of these resources are well known. Some of them are from our secret stash of helpful sites. Would you like to be the ultimate Internet information junkie? Keep up with everything presented in these lists, and you'll be all knowing and wise. (Then tell us how you do it, 'cause we sure can't.) Of course, you don't need to know everything, if you know how to get the goods on demand.

Mailing Lists for Power Searchers

Table 26-3 shows several mailing lists can that really help keep you informed on the latest news, information, and new Internet services. Ever wonder why some people seem to know everything that's going on in cyberspace before you do? They undoubtedly subscribe to some of these lists.

List Name	What it covers	How to subscribe
Gopher Jewels	Descriptions of better Gopher sites	LISTPROC@EINet.netput: SUBSCRIBE GOPHERJEWELS FirstName LastName in the body of the message
Edupage	Education and technology	listproc@educom.unc.eduput : subscribe updates.edupage FirstName LastName in the body of the message
Net-Happenings	Upcoming events and cool happenings on the Net	listserv@lists.internic.netput: subscribe net-happenings FirstName LastNamein the body of the message.
New-Nir	Network Information Retrieval	NEWNIR-L@ITOCSIVM.BITNETput: subscribe NEWNIR-L in the body of your message
Scout Report	New Internet services of special interest to educators and info-junkies	listserv@lists.internic.netput: info SCOUT-REPORT in the body of your message.
Seidman's Online Insider	Internet technologies and the companies that develop them, high-tech stock watch	listserv@peach.ease.lsoft.com put: Subscribe Online-L FirstName LastNamein the body of your message.

Table 26-3: Useful Mailing Lists for Power Users.

Newsgroups for Power Searchers

The following list of newsgroups are the top of the information pyramid, covering Internet services, archives of the computer groups, late-breaking news and announcements, and answers to frequently and infrequently asked questions.

- ❐ alt.internet.services
- ❐ comp.answers
- ❐ comp.archives
- ❐ comp.infosystems.www.announce
- ❐ comp.internet.net-happenings
- ❐ comp.society
- ❐ comp.society.futures
- ❐ news.announce
- ❐ news.announce.important
- ❐ news.announce.newsgroups
- ❐ news.answers
- ❐ news.lists

Gophers for Power Searchers

Table 26-4 lists some of the most useful Gopher sites we have found.

Gopher Site	Address
Peripatetic Eclectic Gopher	gopher://peg.cwis.uci.edu:70
Barron's Guide to Online Bibliographic Databases	gopher://vixen.cso.uiuc.edu:70/11/Libraries/Barron
Internet Library Catalog	gopher://libgopher.yale.edu:70/11/
SURAnet Network InfoCenter (FDIC)	gopher://fdic.sura.net:71/
Gopher Jewels	gopher://cwis.usc.edu/11/Other_Gophers_and_Information_Resources/Gopher-Jewels

Table 26-4: Useful Gopher sites.

Web Sites for Power Searchers

Here's a mega-list of useful Web sites. This list, although not exhaustive, should link you to just about every reference and information repository in Cyberspace. We tried to give you a little of everything, whether you're searching for information on current events, business and economics, government, computers, travel, pop culture, or digital culture.

Site Name	Address
Business Researchers	http://www.pitt.edu/~malhotra/interest.html
C.I.A. World Factbook	http://www.odci.gov/cia/publications/95fact/index.html
Clearinghouse for Subject-Oriented Internet Resources	http://www.lib.umich.edu/chhome.html
Computer Almanac, Interesting and Useful Numbers about Computers	http://www.cs.cmu.edu/afs/cs.cmu.edu/user/bam/www/numbers.html
Congressional Legislation- THOMAS	http://thomas.loc.gov/
Consumer Information Center	http://www.gsa.gov/staff/pa/cic/
Dylan Greene's Windows 95 Page	http:// www.dylan95.com/
E-Text Archive	http://www.etext.org/
e-zines list	http:// www.meer.net/~johnl/e-zine-list/
Federal Locator	http://www.law.vill.edu/Fed-Agency/fedwebloc.html
FedWorld Information Network	http://www.fedworld.gov/
Galaxy Gopher Jewels	http://galaxy.einet.net/GJ/
Global Network Academy Meta-Library	http://uu-gna.mit.edu:8001/uu-gna /meta-library
Global News Network (part of Global Network Navigator)	http:// gnn.com/
Government Printing Office	http://www.access.gpo.gov/su_docs/
International Business Resources	http://ciber.bus.msu.edu/busres.htm
Internet Patent Search	http://sunsite.unc.edu/patents/intropat.html
Internet Public Library	http://ipl.sils.umich.edu/
Internet Resources Meta Index	http://www.ncsa.uiuc.edu/SDG/Software/Mosaic/MetaIndex.html
InterNIC Directory of Directories	http://www.internic.net/ds/dsdirofdirs.html
Legal Information Institute	http://www.law.cornell.edu/

Site Name	Address
Library of Congress Internet Resource Page	http://lcweb.loc.gov/global/internet/internet.html
List of all Archie servers	http://pubweb.nexor.co.uk/public/archie/servers.html
National Library of Medicine	http://www.nlm.nih.gov/
Netsurfer Digest	http://www.netsurf.com/nsd/index.html
Online Computer Library Center	http://www.oclc.org/
NetPartners Company Site Locator — if you know part of a site name, try here for the rest.	http://netpart.com/company/search.html
Snoopie Internet File Finder	http://www.snoopie.com/
Stroud's Consumate Winsock Applications	http://www.enterprise.net/cwsapps/
The New York Times Navigator	http://www.nytimes.com/library/cyber/cynavi.html#about
The Salon	http://www.salon1999.com/
The Well	http://www.well.com/
Town Hall	http://www.town.hall.org/
U.S. Census Info Server	http://www.census.gov/

Table 26-5: Web search sites.

Various Helpful Services

Here are some other useful sites and services. If you're a business that needs to stay abreast of certain types of information and you don't want to spend a lot of time tracking down the data yourself, you might want to consider subscribing to one of the clipping services listed below. A clipping service hunts down articles with information on subjects you're interested in and sends the articles to you. If you're interested in being part of cutting-edge discussions on digital culture and just about everything else, consider joining the Well.

Mercury Center Newshound-San Jose Mercury News

This service will keyword-scan newspaper and wire services and e-mail you the results. $10 per month, e-mail: newshound-support@sjmercury.com, or call 800-818-6397 for information.

NewsPages "HeadsUp" Service

You can choose from among 1000 topics and get daily, two-sentence reviews e-mailed to you that match your subject choices. These topics are chosen from 500 different sources and 15,000 new articles daily. You get a 30-day free trial, after that it's $29.95 per month, $2.97 for each article after the first five per month. E-mail: heads-up@enews.com or phone 617-273-6000 for more information. Or go to http://www.newspage.com/.

Farcast

This is an electronic clipping service that lets you build your own information robots for tracking down only the information that's of interest to you. It ties into 8000 information services and offers access 24 hours a day for $10/month. Check out the Web site at http://www.farcast.com/ or, send e-mail addressed to info@farcast.com with the word *Hello* in the subject line to get more info on their services.

Stanford Netnews Filtering Service

This service is a free project of the Stanford Library. Once you subscribe, you'll receive the first few lines of newsgroups articles (posted messages) that match your search criteria. Once you find something you like, you can request that the full article be delivered to your mail box. See http://woodstock.stanford.edu:2000/ for more information.

The Well

The oldest extant virtual community on the Net, the Well is also the best place for online conversation. It's also the absolute best place to ask questions and (even better) get useful answers! You'll come for the professional contacts and megabytes of helpful information. You'll stay for the intense conversations and wonderful sense of place, something not easy to find online. Over 400 conferences demonstrate what Usenet could be if the noise level wasn't so high. And yet, the Well is dedicated to free speech tempered by personal responsibility for what you say. It's our favorite place to read, talk, ask questions, consult experts, soak up information, and (here comes the trite greeting card phrase) make new friends. See http://www.well.com for more information, or telnet well.com and follow the prompts.

One caution: the virtual residents of The Well don't take too kindly to "out-of-towners" coming in and strip mining the place for information. If you just want to cut and run, go someplace else. If you want to take up virtual residence in an online community that also functions as a new edge think tank, information archives, and expert system, by all means, give the Well a buzz.

MOVING ON

Stalking the wild data mushroom is a skill that takes time, practice, patience, and self-control to master. The good news is you have awesome tools available to you, most of them free: Web search facilities, Archie, Gopher, WAIS, Usenet newsgroups, FAQs, and mailing lists. Considering that only two years ago the section in some Internet books on Archie was twice as big as the one on the Web, it's entirely likely that within a year or two another interesting and useful way of storing, retrieving, and presenting information will come down the ol' info trail. Hopefully, more "intelligent" search robots and filtering services are on the horizon.

Now that we've looked at some of the tools and techniques of data searching, in the next chapter we'll move on to searching for people on the Net using a slightly different set of tools.

## Chapter 27

People Tracking

Looking for someone on the Net, whether it's your long lost friend from fourth grade or the name of the vice president of a company you're researching, can be a hit-or-miss proposition.

Long ago, when the Net was young and relatively small, people figured that there could be one directory for everything, but this soon proved to be unworkable. You'd think with all of the computing power out there that such a database would be easy to create and maintain. It isn't. All of those computers on the Net are not alike. They need protocols and interfaces to talk to each other. Developing and implementing standards to accomplish this has proven to be a daunting task. Many sites on the Net have created their own directories, tailored to their own purposes, but they are just different enough from other directories to cause problems when trying to tie them together.

In conventional phone books, your name and address appear in the geographic region in which you live and have phone service: purchase the service, get listed in the directory. In the wild, woolly world of the Net, no one knows you're online unless you tell them. Your service provider knows about you, but so far, no attempt has been made to tie individual providers' account databases into a Netwide white pages. Most directory efforts so far have been voluntary. You register with a directory of choice and hope that anyone who's going to be looking will check that particular directory. The other problem is Net transience. Lots of people change providers, use different e-mail addresses, and physically move without changing their directory listings or even remembering which directories they're registered with.

The good news is that there are some decent tools that can be used to search for people and organizations, and newer and better ones are popping up all the time. This chapter looks at some of the major (and minor) search technologies, including the following:

❏ **Finger**   An older Net utility used to find information about users on UNIX systems.

❏ **Whois**   Database services used to find information (mailing address, phone numbers, domains) about people and organizations associated with the Internet.

❏ **X.500**   A powerful, global Internet white pages directory that lets you search by name, country, organization, and department.

❏ **Web-based White & Yellow Pages**   Easy-to-use, forms-based searching tools for people, businesses, and organizations.

❏ **Netfind**   A Netwide searching tool that looks through multiple domains based on geographical information you provide.

❏ **CSO Name Servers**   Individual directories for schools, companies, organizations, and other groups.

TIP

Keep in mind that others might be looking for you: old friends, someone who owes you $20 from 10 years ago, colleagues from previous jobs. If you'd like to increase your chances of being found, you'll want to note the various white pages directories described in this chapter. They allow you to register for inclusion in them. You might find you're already in directories you didn't even know about. Make sure to update your information as needed. By the same token, if you don't want people tracking you down, *don't* sign up for listings in these directories, and if you find yourself listed, request that you be removed.

Accessibility vs. Privacy

Lots of people on the Net tend to value privacy and are not necessarily interested in a "One Book" for Cyberspace. Attempts to combine directories or make information readily available walks the line between accessibility and invasion of privacy. The heavy use of anonymous remailers, encryption, and, when possible, pseudonyms demonstrates just how seriously some people take their privacy.

There is a growing discussion about whether publicly listing e-mail addresses is a breach of privacy when it's done without the user's consent. Many sites deal with this by keeping their e-mail lists internal. This makes it hard for those looking for other people to conduct business or re-establish connections, but it is a protection against being spammed or getting junk mail. As the Net moves forward, it seems likely that voluntary registration with one of the public directories (and a single search interface to those directories) is going to win out over merging directories or getting the private ones to go public.

INTERNIC

The mother of all directories on the Net started in the same way Teflon, Jeeps, and the Internet did—with the military. At the time, anyone who was a site administrator, or responsible for some aspect of the Net, was automatically listed in the Defense Data Network's NIC directory. As the Net grew, the military decided to keep its listings in a separate directory. InterNIC, the Internet Network Information Center, became the master information clearinghouse for civilian Internet directories.

One of these directories is run by the Registration Services (RS) Department. It contains all of the Internet domains and information about their administrative personnel. The other directory, run by Directory and Database Services (DS), offers listings for people not directly involved with the Internet who wish to sign up for it. Unfortunately, not many people are accessible through the DS directory (at least not the people we're looking for).

You can access the InterNIC Directory Services at http://www. internic.net/. It offers Whois, Netfind, X.500, and pointers to other resources.

PEOPLE-FINDING TOOLS

Most of the tools used to find people and information about organizations are straightforward to use. They also are available through many different interfaces. You can use your Web browser, the programs available through your UNIX shell account, or stand-alone client software. Let's look at a few of these search services and the various options for connecting to them.

Finger

Finger allows you to get information about users registered on a specific UNIX system (accessing the /etc/passwd user login file). You can find information about a person's real name, his or her e-mail address, and whether that person's currently online. You can also use finger to get a list of who's logged on to a specific system.

All of this information availability is subject to the site administrator's discretion. Some administrators consider finger a security risk and/or an invasion of their users' privacy, and disable it altogether. Some sites let you see information about some users (those who have set global permissions) and not others, or info on all users but not the entire list of users.

You must know the domain name you're trying to contact in order to use finger. There are no wildcards and little flexibility. Since finger is picky about case, it's best to always use lowercase.

Using Finger on UNIX

To use finger on a UNIX shell account, you enter this:

```
finger <options> name...
```

Using finger without any options or a specific name gives you a list of people who are currently online, their usernames, real name, the domain they're calling from, how long they've been online, and other information.

If you specify a user, you get information even if that user is not online at the time. You can use either a real name or a username. While the amount of information available varies, you can often find these items:

- ☐ The person's home directory and which shell that person uses (if he or she is using a shell account)
- ☐ When the person last logged in
- ☐ What process the person does if online (e.g., reading e-mail, using IRC)
- ☐ The last time the person received mail and if it has been read
- ☐ A .plan file, if the person has created one

Among the options that can be used with finger are:

-m Match arguments only on username (not first or last name)

-l Force long output format (full finger file shown)

-s Force short output format (basic info only, such as login name, real name, log in time, etc.)

For more information about using finger on UNIX, enter **man finger** at the shell prompt to get the online manual.

.Plan Files

Finger looks for whatever information a site gives about its users. For some sites, additional information about users can be stored in what's called a .plan file. These files can contain biographical information about the user such as where he or she lives and the user's occupation. Plan files are optional.

Some people set their .plan files up as tiny servers, allowing Net-wide users to finger their file to access the information stored there. Joke pages, daily recipes, sports scores, top ten lists, hurricane/tornado reports, and trivia are some of the types of information people have "served" over their .plan files. As e-mail lists, Web pages, white pages, and more advanced information distribution technologies have emerged, .plan files have fallen out of favor.

Finger Clients

A number of programs provide a graphical interface to finger. They allow you to finger a UNIX host while running TCP/IP on your desktop. They provide the same finger information as if you were running the finger program on a shell account. Among these TCP/IP clients are WS-Finger for Windows and Finger for the Mac. See Figure 27-1.

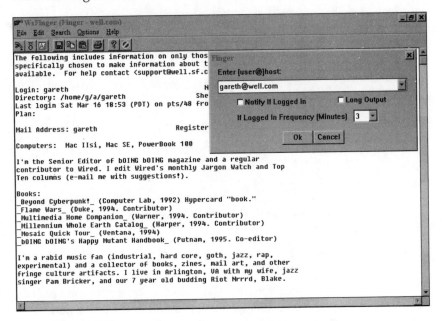

Figure 27-1: WS-Finger.

WS-Finger offers finger and Whois capability. (Whois is discussed in the next section.)

Using Finger on the Web

The Web doesn't actually offer a facility for using finger, but you can access a finger gateway. A Web-based finger gateway is simply an HTML form that lets you finger a user on a UNIX system from the Web. Try one of these URLs, or ask your ISP for one.

Brett's Web to Finger Gateway:
  http://www.rickman.com/finger.html
WWW Finger Gateway with Faces:
  http://www.cs.indiana. edu:800/finger/gateway

Whois

Whois ("Who is . . .") is a database system offering information on users, domains, and organizations on the Internet. The term Whois means a lot of different things, depending on how it's used. Sometimes it means white pages directories. Other times it refers to the database program that was used to build a given directory. It's important to understand that the term Whois is used in these different contexts.

Whois is most often associated with either the InterNIC directories or the UNIX command (whois <username>) that's used to access these directories. There are also client programs for Whois and Web interface pages that allow you to search through Whois directories without having to be on a UNIX system.

Using Whois from UNIX

To use Whois from a UNIX shell, you type this:

```
whois <-h host> identifier
```

Let's say we wanted to find the e-mail address of Cyberculture writer Howard Rheingold. We would enter the following at the UNIX prompt:

```
whois rheingold
```

And here's what we'd get back:

```
Rheingold, Howard (HR58)        hlr@WELL.COM
(415)XXX-XXXX
Rheingold, Jeff (JR460)         jeffr@CNS-NJ.COM
201-XXX-XXXX


The InterNIC Registration Services Host contains ONLY
Internet Information
```

```
(Networks, ASN's, Domains, and POC's).
Please use the whois server at nic.ddn.mil for MILNET Infor-
mation.
```

The [-h host] option allows you to specify which Whois directory you want to search (the default host is rs.internic.net). Let's say we wanted to look at the MILNET database (the Defense Department's Military Network) to see if Sean has a secret defense job that we don't know about. We'd type this:

```
whois -h nic.ddn.mil carton
```

And here's the result:

```
Carton, Sean (SC294)
Special Forces/Black Projects
666 Shuriken Way
McLean, VA 22205
```

Oh my God! No wonder he's always traipsing around in that silly Ninja costume. Actually, we're just foolin'. The Whois query only returned the name, address, and phone number of Jeff Carton (no relation).

Whois can also be used to search out domain names, the names of their administrators, and other information about the organizations that maintain Internet sites. Searching on eff.org, we find this:

```
whois eff.org

Electronic Frontier Foundation Inc. (EFF-DOM)
    1550 Bryant
    Suite 725
    San Francisco, CA 94103
    USA

Domain Name: EFF.ORG

Administrative Contact:
    Mccandlish, Stanton W.f. [Rev.]  (SM100)
    mech@NITV.NET
    202 861 7700 (FAX) 202 861 1258
```

```
Technical Contact, Zone Contact:
    Brown, Daniel H.  (DHB23)  brown@EFF.ORG
    415-436-9333 voice 415-436-3999 fax

Record last updated on 25-Nov-95.
Record created on 10-Oct-90.

Domain servers in listed order:

TOAD.COM                 140.174.2.1
NS.EFF.ORG               204.253.162.3
NS2.EFF.ORG              204.253.162.4
KEI.COM                  192.88.144.5
AUTH00.NS.UU.NET         198.6.1.65
AUTH01.NS.UU.NET         198.6.1.81
```

The InterNIC Registration Services Host contains ONLY
Internet Information
(Networks, ASN's, Domains, and POC's).
Please use the whois server at nic.ddn.mil for MILNET Infor-
mation.

For more information on using Whois on your UNIX account, enter **man whois** from the UNIX prompt.

Using Whois Client Programs

A number of Whois clients are available for Windows. WS-Finger, the PC client we discussed in the finger section, also includes Whois capability. NetScan Tools, which is included on the Companion CD-ROM available with this book, also includes a Whois client (see Figure 27-2). A Whois TCP/IP client works the same as on a UNIX host; you simply enter the person, organization, or domain you wish to search and you're presented with a list of any relevant information found in the database. Many Whois clients come with a list of Whois directories that you can access by switching to before beginning your search. If you're using a Mac, you'll need to use one of the Web gateways or Telnet to your shell account, and use UNIX Whois.

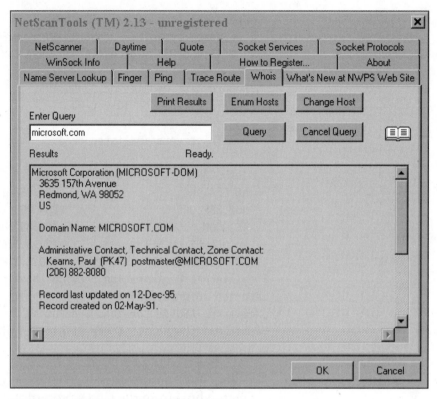

Figure 27-2: The Whois tool in NetScan Tools.

Whois by Telnet

You can use Telnet to access InterNIC's Whois database and other InterNIC services. Just enter **telnet internic.net** at the UNIX prompt, and follow the online instructions.

TIP

The big online services like AOL, CIS, and Genie have their own internal white page listings of users. If you're looking for someone you think is on one of these services and you don't have an account there, send e-mail to a friend that does and have your friend look up the person.

X.500

X.500 is a database technology for globally distributed directories. Many commercial, government, and educational organizations maintain X.500 directories. It is by far the most capable method of handling large directories and the nearest thing to a global white pages as can be found on the Net. Since it's so powerful, it's also very complex in terms of its command structure. Unless you're really into gruesome command syntax, you might want to put an interface between you and X.500, through Gopher or the Web.

X.500 via Gopher

Considering how powerful X.500 is, it couldn't be simpler to use via Gopher.

1. Using a Gopher client, go to the InterNIC X.500 location at gopher.ds.internic.net.
2. From there, choose InterNIC Directory and Database Services. (AT&T)
3. Choose InterNIC Directory Services: White Pages.
4. Choose X.500 Person/Organization Lookup (Gateway to X.500).

From this screen, you can look for organizations in the U.S. or other countries.

X.500 via the Web

Another way to use X.500 is via the Web at InterNIC's gateway, http://www.internic.net/ds/dspgx500.html. It's a Web interface to the same place you'll get to via Gopher access.

This directory is set up by country. Choose a country, and you'll be taken to the Gopher site there. From there, you can find whichever organizations are listed. See Figure 27-3.

Figure 27-3: An X.500 search via the Web.

X.500 via Telnet

You can also access X.500 via Telnet. Telnet to ds.internic.net, and enter **guest** as the login ID (don't enter a password, just hit return). Read Selection I, which contains the instructions on how to use the various modes:

S Simple Queries

P Power Searches

Y Yellow Pages

U Enter search string

Prompts and help abound, plus ways to tailor your search to zero in on who you're looking for.

OTHER WHITE PAGES & DIRECTORIES

A number of Internet white pages are just dying to have you register with them. They're all competing with one another, trying to become the definitive reference for looking up Net citizens. Table 27-1 lists (in alphabetical order) some of the more popular ones.

CMC Information Sources	Excellent links to all sorts of directories http://www.december.com/cmc/info/culture-people-lists.html
Finding an E-mail address	An extremely helpful guide with links to many directories http://sunsite.oit.unc.edu/~masha/
Four 11	5 million listings http://www.four11.com/
Lookup Directory Services	Name-to-e-mail address mapping http://www.lookup.com/
OKRA	Over 3.5 million listings http://okra.ucr.edu/okra/info.html
Switchboard	Claims 90 million listings http://www.switchboard.com/
Who's Online	A small directory that includes extensive bio information http://www.ictp.trieste.it/Canessa/whoiswho.html
WhoWhere?	Individuals and companies, street addresses http://www.whowhere.com/
World E-mail Directory	E-mail directory with estimated access to more than 9 million e-mail addresses http://worldemail.com/
Yahoo White Pages for Individuals	Links to many smaller and specialized white pages http://www.yahoo.com/Reference/White_Pages/Individuals/

Table 27-1: Other white pages and directories.

Knowbot Information Services (KIS)

Knowbot Information Services provides an interface for accessing various white page directory services. It's not a database like Whois but a service that lets you access several directories at once. It will choose which tool, such as finger or Whois, it thinks is best for the job and bring you the results. You need to know something about who you're looking for in order to find him or her. Telnet to info. cnri.reston.va.us, and choose man or help to guide your search.

Netfind

Netfind uses keywords to search various directories for people. It can be very inefficient and time-consuming, and it's something of a drain on Net resources. You can access Netfind on the Web at http://www.nova.edu/Inter-Links/netfind.html or http://ds.internic.net/ds/dspgwp.html. If you use Telnet, you can access Netfind through one of the hosts listed in Table 27-2. There is one at InterNIC, ds.internic.net. Gopher can also be employed for a Netfind search at ds.internic.net.

Host	Country
ds.internic.net	USA
bruno.cs.colorado.edu	USA
eis.calstate.edu	USA
hto-e.usc.edu	USA
mudhoney.micro.umn.edu	USA
netfind.oc.com	USA
redmont.cis.uab.edu	USA
archie.au	Australia
dino.conicit.ve	Venezuela
krnic.net	Korea
lincoln.technet.sg	Singapore
malloco.ing.puc.cl	Chile
monolith.cc.ic.ac.uk	England
netfind.anu.edu.au	Australia

Host	Country
netfind.ee.mcgill.ca	Canada
netfind.if.usp.br	Brazil
netfind.vslib.cz	Czech Rep.
nic.uakom.sk	Slovakia

Table 27-2: Netfind hosts.

TIP

If you use a Macintosh, there's a nice client program called (amazingly enough!) Netfind/Mac. It's got a simple-to-use interface that allows you to query multiple Netfind servers across the Internet just by entering a last name and some geographical information. See the section on Netfind/Mac in Chapter 15, "Mac Net Tools Gallery," for more info.

BUSINESS YELLOW PAGES

Several directories have turned their attention strictly toward businesses. These yellow pages do overlap with white pages directories to some extent. All of these sites are available on the World Wide Web.

BigBook

BigBook (http://www.bigbook.com) is an amazing directory (see Figure 24-4). Eleven million U.S. businesses are already listed with name, full address, and phone number. And, there's more here than just the typical phone book information. For many of the listings, there's a digital map (see Figure 27-5) that will pinpoint exactly where the business is located. You can zoom in to the street level or zoom out to the country level. You can search, for example, on all dry cleaners convenient to you. Powerful stuff . . . and reasonably fast.

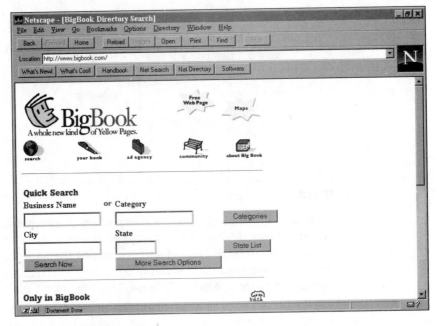

Figure 27-4: BigBook main page.

BigBook is free to consumers and businesses. In fact, BigBook would like any business to take advantage of a free Web page with audio messages or a link to an established business page.

Soon, consumers will be able to rate their experiences with businesses in terms of price, quality, and recommendations to others. Several guides to restaurants and travel guides are available on BigBook.

Consumers will also be able to build an address book that will reside on BigBook. If you see business listings that you want to revisit, you enter them into your address book instead of your browser's bookmark or hotlist function.

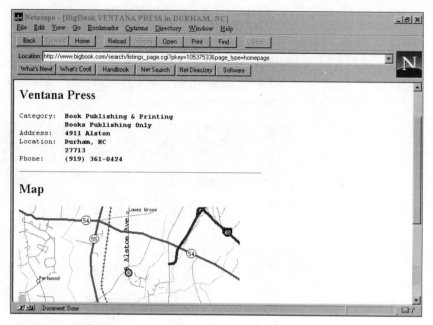

Figure 27-5: BigBook business map.

BigBook is partnered with some heavy hitters in Web development: Organic Online, Silicon Graphics, Informix Software, GeoSystems, Database America, Etak, Connect Inc., Progressive Network, and Yo Designs. It plans to include Canada and Mexico in 1996 and then expand to Asia, Europe, and South America by the latter part of 1996 and 1997.

This is a site to watch. If they continue to deliver, BigBook could become a significant Net yellow pages.

New Rider

New Rider (http://www.mcp.com/nrp/wwwyp/) produces the WWW Yellow Pages books. You can search by partial site names, URLs, or descriptive words and categories. New Rider uses WAIS technology as the basis for its directory. See Figure 27-6.

Figure 27-6: The main page in New Rider.

WebDirect

WebDirect (http://www.cfonline.com/cgi-win/wdirect.exe) allows you to search through over 1,000 categories and to limit the type of information you received. You can also search by keywords. See Figure 27-7.

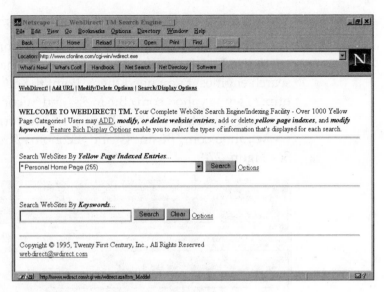

Figure 27-7: The main page in WebDirect.

Open Market Commercial Sites

Open Market (http://www.directory.net/) provides a directory of commercial services, products, and information on the Internet. See Figure 27-8.

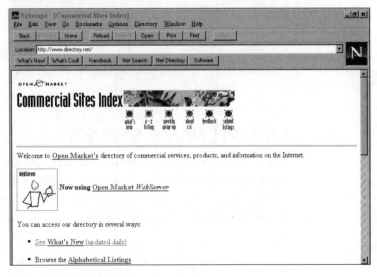

Figure 27-8: Open Market.

Yahoo List of Business Directories Links

Yahoo has a fairly comprehensive list of all sorts of smaller and specialized business directories. Yahoo also has links to other search engines if you need them. Point the ol' Web browser at http://www.yahoo.com/Business_and_ Economy/ Business_Directory/Other_Business_Directories/ and http:// www.yahoo.com/Business_and_Economy/Companies/Indices/. See Figure 27-9.

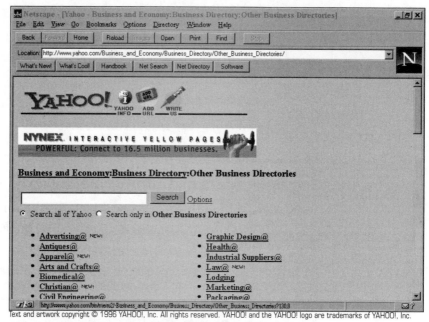

Figure 27-9: Yahoo's business directories categories.

CSO/PH NAME SERVERS

CSO name servers (also called Ph servers) are site-specific phone directories that use the Ph software. These directory listings can offer a lot of information about a person, everything from full name to birthday, depending on the server. Many name servers are for internal university and business use, while others allow outside searches. A major name server, gopher.nd.edu, is at the University of Notre Dame. This site contains lists of searchable CSO servers worldwide. See Figure 27-10.

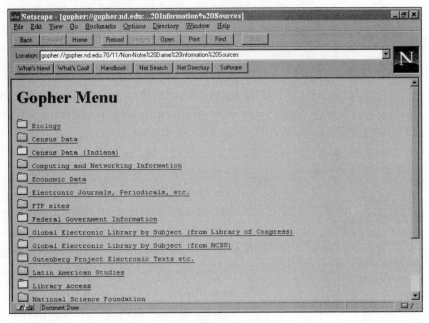

Figure 27-10: Notre Dame list of institutions.

- -

TIP

The e-mail program Eudora has Ph and finger clients built into it. See Chapter 7 for information on Windows Eudora and Chapter 12 for information on Mac Eudora.

- -

FINDING PEOPLE THROUGH USENET & MAILING LISTS

All those people posting to Usenet groups and various electronic mailing lists leave their marks in Cyberspace. If you're looking for someone's e-mail address and you think he or she might post to newsgroups, you can use one of the following in attempting to find that person:

❑ DejaNews is the best way to search Usenet (http://www.dejanews.com/). They've got indexes dating back several months, so if something's been posted, you should be able to find it.

❑ Go to one of the more comprehensive search engines, such as AltaVista or MetaCrawler (see Chapter 26, "Data Tracking"). You can do a Usenet-only search, indicating that you're looking for information from the header part of the newsgroup article.

❑ Excite! provides a great newsgroup-searching service. Hop on over to http://www.excite.com/ to check it out.

❑ Apparently people at MIT have lots of time on their hands, so they keep a list of everyone who posts on Usenet. It doesn't include local or restricted groups. Send e-mail to mail-server@rtfm.mit.edu. In the body of the message, type the following:

```
send usenet-addresses/search string
```

❑ The search string could be the last name of the person you're searching for, for instance. Remember that some people use alternative names or anonymous mailers, so they might not show up even if they're on Usenet.

❑ Read soc.net-people, the newsgroup that can be used for reconnecting with people you've lost track of.

❒ Join a mailing list that you think the person (or type of person) you're looking to connect with might be interested in. Many mailing lists will let you ask for who's registered on the list. If that fails, you could send e-mail to the list manager and ask for help. List managers are probably swamped with e-mail, so use this suggestion as a last resort.

MISCELLANEOUS

Here are a couple of additional resources that we couldn't figure out where else to put (hey, at least we're honest).

Contacting a Postmaster

Postmasters are the people in charge of e-mail for a site. The first thing to know about them is that they're super busy and get more e-mail in a day than most of us see in a month. Please don't bother them unless you're desperate to find someone you think is on their system. Send a message asking if they'd be willing to forward your message to the person in question. (It's unlikely that they'd give you someone's e-mail address outright.) There is no guarantee that they'll do it, but it's worth a try. The last thing you want to do is to antagonize a postmaster by complaining or making yourself annoying—postmasters talk to each other, and you could receive a request from your own ISP to cool it. You can usually reach a postmaster by sending e-mail to postmaster@*host.domain*.

TIP

If you're being harassed by someone online or getting spammed with unwanted junk mail, you can also e-mail a complaint to the appropriate postmaster.

Alumni

If you know where someone graduated from college or high school, you can contact the alumni office at that institution. Almost every college and university is on the Net, along with many other types of schools. Use a search engine to find the school's Web site. Then, try e-mailing the alumni office, or call them if a phone number is available.

TIP

Some e-mail programs, like Pegasus, make it easy for you to keep a list of who has sent you e-mail and who you've sent e-mail to. This way, if you need to reconnect with someone you've lost touch with, you can search his or her e-mail address from your own database.

MOVING ON

As the Net's growth continues to explode, there will be an increasing need for tools that manage where to find people and organizations. Privacy concerns have held back the push for centralized directories, but they are as inevitable as the local phone book. Despite the means already at your disposal for people searching, it takes some knowledge about who you're searching for to find them: a last name, a domain, an employer, or something else that gives a directory more to go on. If the search tools available now prove frustrating, you'll find that each year will bring more sophisticated search technologies. For now, we hope this survey of people-searching tools will tide you over.

In the next chapter, we look at some of the cutting-edge audio/ video and entertainment technologies that are part of the new wave of Net power tools. We'll look at video teleconferencing, Net telephone, and Net radio. That's right, you can now teleconference with your business associates, yak on the phone with your friends, and listen to the radio, all for free and without having to leave your desktop. Convergence here we come!

Part IX

Miscellaneous Power Tools

## Chapter 28

Audio/Video Power Tools

Can you imagine what it must have been like the first time radio was heard by the public, or film was shown, or television was broadcast? These media technologies have had a profound impact. The Net seems to declare tiny media revolutions on a monthly basis as cool new tools are constantly debuted. Whether they are just fun toys or represent entirely new ways of communicating is always debatable. While the Web gets all of the media attention, other Net innovations could evolve into something significant.

Several of these are live audio, desktop video teleconferencing, Net radio, and television. Everyone and their country cousins seem to know now about the Internet and the World Wide Web by now. But does everyone know about the thousands of people who are using the Net as a secondary phone service, or about how people from all over the world congregate in video chat rooms, or about how NPR, ABC News, CNN, and even special Net-based radio stations can be heard over a personal computer? While everyone is busy staring at their TV sets, waiting for the computer to merge with a television set, the audio and video broadcasting of TV is migrating onto your desktop. One of the more exciting things about all this is the global participation in developing these new technologies and finding ways of using them.

Of course, society (as well as commerce) is always giddy about technologies as they're introduced and over-hyped. Sometimes they're so over-hyped that they can't possibly live up to people's expectations. (Remember virtual reality?) Who knows if global video teleconferencing will bring the world closer together, or whether Internet phone service will give the phone companies a run for their money, or if netcast TV will pan out anytime soon. In the end, it might all end up looking like the '70s CB radio craze, but we'd be lying to you if we didn't tell you how much of a rush we got the first time we talked to someone in Hong Kong on our computer, or teleconferenced with six people at once, or used collaboration/whiteboard software. Give it a try yourself, and see if you don't get the feeling you're participating in the birth of new media.

In this chapter, we'll look at a number of emerging Internet audio and video technologies and how clever businesses, educators, and individuals are using this tech to push the envelope of Net-based communication and interactivity. The future face of the Internet (its eyes, ears, and mouth) can be glimpsed in the cutting edge technologies explored below.

HARDWARE CONSIDERATIONS

When some people first hear that you can listen to the radio and watch live(-ish) video over the Internet, they ask: "But don't you need to have a really great computer and monitor and an expensive connection to use that stuff?" Well, if you want to use real-time audio/video for business, you'll definitely want a top-of-the-line machine and an above 28.8 dial-up connection. But, if you only plan to use your Net phone and video teleconferencing for recreation, the occasional call to your wired grandma, and some video cruisin' on a Saturday night, you can get by just fine with an average multimedia-capable computer and a 28.8 modem. To use any of the Internet phones and video teleconferencing software, you're going to need a minimum of the following:

Windows

❏ A 486SX (ideally higher) and 8MB RAM (ideally much higher)

❏ 256-color monitor

❏ 28.8 modem (or better)

❏ A 16-bit or 32-bit sound card (either one board for half-duplex, two boards for full duplex, or one that supports full duplex)

❏ Speakers

❏ Microphone

❏ PPP or SLIP Net connections (or better)

❏ A camera, such as the Connectix QuickCam or a Camcorder (to send video)

❏ Video capture board (to sendvideo–although not always necessary)

Macintosh

❏ Any color Mac with 68030 processor (or higher)

❏ System 7.x

❏ Sound Manager 3.1, QuickTime 2.1

❏ Speakers

❏ Microphone (comes with all recent Macs)

❏ 28.8 modem (or better)

❏ PPP or SLIP Net connections (or better)

❏ A camera, such as the Connectix QuickCam (to send video)

NOTE: Earlier Mac models only support half-duplex sound. See Table 28-1 for a list of Macs that do not support full duplex.

PowerBook 1xx

PowerBook Duo 210, 230, 250, 270, 280, 280c

Mac LC, LC II, LC III

Mac LC475, LC630

Mac si, IIvx, IIvi

Quadra 605, 630

Performa 46x, 47x, 63x

Table 28-1: Macs that do not support full-duplex sound.

INTERNET TELEPHONY: "WATSON, COME IN HERE."

When we first heard Marc Fisher of Pacific Bell saying that they weren't scared about the growing popularity of Net phones, we could almost believe him. The first generation of these phones left much to the imagination and much of their audio someplace between the point of origin and the destination. These early models were nothing more than toys that looked like they could grow up to be tools. Well, they're still only in their adolescence, but they're definitely at the sit-up-and-take-notice age. The latest generation of full-duplex Net phones offers better compression, sound quality, and oodles of features like answering machines, conference calling, file transfer, and blocking. The sound quality is not even close to that of a regular phone service, but think of the trade-offs. You can place long distance, even international, calls for the cost of your network connection. If you only have a short message or need to check in with members of a project team, or you just want to nag Junior at college (every few hours), a Net phone is entirely adequate. Some businesses claim that they're now saving thousands of dollars a month in phone bills thanks to these crude phones. A sign that these phones might be a real threat to the phone companies is that they've changed their complacent tune. They've recently filed a petition with the FCC demanding that Internet phone services be subject to the same regulations and tariffs as conventional phone services. This could get interesting.

How do Net phones work? We're glad you asked. Basically they work in much the same way that all data transfer works over the Internet. You, the caller, speak into the microphone on your PC. The sound is digitized and compressed using compression software (called "codec" for compression/decompression). This compressed data (not the actual audio, but instructions for how to reproduce it on the other end) is sent as data packets over the Net to the person you're calling on the other end. Once received, the data is decompressed and used by the sound card to re-create the sound of your voice. If you have a half-duplex sound card, only one party can talk at a time. Full-duplex allows both parties to speak simultaneously as in an ordinary phone conversation.

TIP

Many Windows users are often shocked and dismayed to find out that you need two sound cards, or a newer sound card that uses full-duplex, to have simultaneous conversations over a Net phone. While lots of PCs are shipping with full-duplex cards, what do the rest of us do with yesterday's cards? Creative Labs is now offering a full-duplex sound driver that can be used with Sound Blaster 16 and AWE32 to get full-duplex sound out of these half-duplex cards. To get the Creative Labs drivers, go to http://www.creaf.com:80/wwwnew/tech/ ftp/ftp-beta.html. Most recently available Mac models come with full-duplex sound capability. See Table 28-1 for those models that are half-duplex.

The drawbacks to Net phones are typical: standards and bandwidth. There are currently no agreed-upon standards; subsequently, phones using different codecs cannot communicate with one another. The most popular compression scheme is called GSM (Global Standard for Mobile Communications). Others include True Speech and RTP (Real Time Protocol). GSM is becoming enough of a de facto standard that some interoperability is beginning to exist between different phones. Obviously, if Internet telephony is ever going to catch on, some agreed-upon codec standard is a must. The other drawback to Net phones is the bane of all data-hungry Net-based media: bandwidth. Regardless of what kind of stunning digital audio quality you might be able to get on either end of your connection, you can't cram enough data through the pipe to do it justice. The sound quality that you're used to with your conventional phone is equivalent to 8K of data per second. A Net phone on a 28.8 modem is only capable of *under* 3K per second. Many of the phone software packages try to make up for this by attempting to reconstruct some of the data that was lost during the transmission.

Televox (Formerly Cyberphone)

Televox/Cyberphone is a handsome, no-nonsense full-duplex Net phone that has surprisingly decent sound quality and some nice features, like text chat and the ability to exchange files with other users. A free full-functioning demo is available for downloading. The commercial version sells for $39. See Figure 28-1.

Figure 28-1: Televox (formerly called Cyberphone).

Macintosh		Windows	
PowerPC	68K	Windows 95	Windows 3.1
No	No	Yes	Yes

Where to get the latest version: http://www.voxware.com//

Internet Phone

This commercial Net phone is one of the best in its class. It offers discernible sound quality—you can actually hear what people are saying *most* of the time. While other Net phones' audio quality ranges from tin can telephone to shouting through a wall, Internet Phone provides good enough sound quality to make it a useful tool. Internet Phone has a clean, easy-to-use interface (see Figure 28-2) with lots of cool features, such as the ability to create hyperlinks for Internet Phone users in HTML documents. One drawback of the program is that it uses a proprietary codec, meaning that all your phone mates will have to use Internet Phone. Another drawback is the $69.95 price tag. The Mac version, due out any day now, will retail for $99. A demo version (which only allows 60-second conversations) is available from the VocalTec Web site.

Figure 28-2: The main "switchboard" in Internet Phone.

Macintosh		Windows	
PowerPC	68K	Windows 95	Windows 3.1
Planned	Planned	Yes	Yes

Where to get the latest version: http://www.vocaltec.com/

Maven

Unfortunately, there are not nearly as many phone programs for the Mac as for the PC. And it's doubly unfortunate that one of the main ones available is Maven. A bare-bones interface and . . . ah . . . "experimental" sound quality is what you get with Maven. We really can't recommend this program for anything other than as a curiosity. We certainly couldn't recommend it to anyone with a serious interest in Net telephony. One feature is that you can use Maven to communicate with UNIX's Vat (Video Audio Tool) program.

Macintosh		Windows	
PowerPC	68K	Windows 95	Windows 3.1
Yes	Yes	No	No

Where to get the latest version: ftp://sunsite.unc.edu/pub/ packages/infosystems/maven

NetPhone

NetPhone is the most popular phone software for the Macintosh. By the time you read this, the release of Internet Phone for the Mac may have changed that. Although we had heard good things about it, we were not impressed with NetPhone's audio quality. We found ourselves having to talk in such a stilted voice, it makes ham radio conversations sound like music. NetPhone sells for $39.95.

Macintosh		Windows	
PowerPC	68K	Windows 95	Windows 3.1
Yes	Yes	No	No

Where to get the latest version: http://www.emagic.com/

TIP

Electric Magic, NetPhone's creators, also sell Sound Advantage, a serial port device that turns half-duplex Macs into full-duplex. It sells for $99.

PowWow

This freeware program offers a number of nifty features not found in other phone programs. It actually began life as a text-based chat client and collaboration tool. Similar to the collaborate feature in Mosaic for Windows (see Chapter 9, "Windows Web Power Tools"), PowWow lets a group of people tour the Web with one person acting as the "cruise leader." As the leader chooses pages in a browser, the PowWow follows him or her. Unfortunately, PowWow's weakness is awful sound quality only available in half-duplex. If future versions dramatically improve, PowWow could become a very useful tool, especially for educators and distant work teams. And the product name "PowWow" and the company's name "Tribal Voice" are not just another co-option of the Indian mystique—the creators of PowWow designed the program to be a networking tool for Native Americans.

| Macintosh | | Windows | |
PowerPC	68K	Windows 95	Windows 3.1
No	No	Yes	Yes
Where to get the latest version:		http://www.tribal.com/	

Speak Freely

Speak Freely was created by John Walker, founder of the pioneering software company Autodesk (home, for a time, of Ted Nelson's infamous Xanadu project). Speak Freely is not compatible with any other phones, except Speak Freely for UNIX. This freeware program supports many different codecs, including GSM and the encryption standards DES and PGP. This is a program that really only works on a high-end PC with a connection above 28.8. Several notable features include the ability to send a bitmap image and the ability to connect (audio-only) to CU-SeeMe (see "Video Teleconferencing," later in this chapter). Many important features are missing from Speak Freely, such as notification that you've made a connection! Definitely a work in progress.

Macintosh		Windows	
PowerPC	**68K**	**Windows 95**	**Windows 3.1**
No	No	Yes	Yes

Where to get the latest version: http://www.fourmilab.ch/speakfree/windows/speak_freely.html

TIP

A word about evaluating Net telephony. We're surprised, in talking to Net telephony users and in reading reviews, how vastly different people's opinions of these programs are. Ones that we found terrible, others rave about. The one that worked best on Gareth's PC (WebPhone) got completely panned in one review. We were howling with laughter at the goofy sound quality of NetPhone on our Macs. It seems as though so many variables can affect quality, it's best to download several programs and try them out. Whatever you do, don't buy a Net phone without listening (on your own machine!) first.

WebPhone

Another popular commercial phone program is NetSpeak's WebPhone. It has a cool cell phone interface (see Figure 28-3) and a number of impressive features such as the ability to handle up to four simultaneous connections, encryption, caller ID, speed dialing, and even voice mail sending and receiving. The interface is not the easiest to use, but once you get the hang of it, the power features available make it worth the effort. The sound quality on

WebPhone is pretty good, but many users have complained about "drop out," losing portions of the audio data. The version you can download over the Net is fully functional, but it only allows you to use one line, talk for three minutes, and store three directory entries. An obnoxious ad billboard (called the "WebBoard") loads a new advertisement every time you make a connection in the demo version. When you register the software (for $49.95), NetSpeak will enable all of the full features and allow you to turn off the WebBoard, if you wish. WebPhone uses GSM compression.

Figure 28-3: WebPhone's "cell phone" interface.

| Macintosh | | Windows | |
PowerPC	68K	Windows 95	Windows 3.1
No	No	Yes	Yes
Where to get the latest version:		http://www.itelco.com/	

Hi Mom, It's Me . . . I'm Calling You From My Computer

While the phone companies may or may not be sweating over the current state of Internet telephony, they might start if Net calls start ringing on conventional phones. That's the idea behind Free World Dialup, a crusading effort in Net telephony. FWD is a grass-roots voluntary effort to provide completely free international net-to-phone services. That means that you could call anyone in the world from your PC, whether or not he or she had a PC.

How does it work? Using Internet Phone or other phone software, you place a call over the Internet (as described earlier in the chapter). The call is received on an FWD server in the area you're trying to reach. Once connected, the server patches the call into the local phone system. As we write this, a small test of this concept is being conducted. To find out more about it, go to the FWD Web site at http://www.pulver.com/fwd/). A company in New Jersey called International Discount Telecommunications (http://www.idt.net/) plans on offering a commercial version of the same thing. They hope their Net2Phone software will be able to provide quality international phone services for 80 percent of the current rate. We have no idea if they have what it takes to pull this off, but if they do, you can bet it will make the phone companies' current sweats turn into high fever.

VIDEO TELECONFERENCING

The Net offers so many different ways for people to experiment with communication. The MUD and MOO denizens create fantasy persona, the IRC chatters engage in all manner of text conversation, and the Net phone users talk to voices emanating from their PCspeakers. Then there are those, many in the educational community, who are bringing global video teleconferencing to the Net. Unlike the Internet phone, Net-based video teleconferencing has already proven itself. It is already being used, beyond the novelty stage, in grade schools, universities, research groups, and a growing Net video community. The Global SchoolNet (http://www.gsn.org/) is one such pioneering project, linking students in special virtual classrooms with scientists, writers, civic leaders, and other students worldwide.

As bandwidth increases (boy, ya hear that a lot, don't you?), Net video broadcasting and conferencing become effective ways of connecting to, and even working with, others at a distance. In at least one school experiment, students work at home connected to teacher and fellow students over the Internet, able to do research, writing, and conduct experiments together, sometimes from across the globe. If you think you might get a kick out of this kind of audio chat with jumpy pictures (at least that's how it behaves on a 28.8 connection), download one of the clients mentioned in this section, and check it out. To receive video and audio, all you need is a basic multimedia computer and a 28.8 modem. To send video, you'll need a video camera (and appropriate connections and boards) or the Connectix QuickCam, available for both Mac and PC.

CU-SeeMe was the first program to show the potential for video teleconferencing, even over slow modem connections. Over the years, new versions have been released, and new applications have been found by enterprising students and teachers. There are also lots of bored nerds who just want to look at what's going on at the Internet cafes late on a Friday night. Although CU-SeeMe is a freeware application developed at Cornell University (hence the "CU" part), they have recently licensed it to White Pine, a small software company. The commercial version (called "Enhanced CU-SeeMe") offers a number of improvements and innovations, especially the whiteboard feature for remote collaborations, Web browser support, text-based chatting, and full color. The commercial version is fully compatible with the freeware version and sells for $65. A demo can be downloaded from the White Pine Web site (http://www.wpine.com/).

TIP

If you want to see CU-SeeMe in action on a directly connected computer, check out the exhibits at the San Francisco Exploratorium and the Ithaca Sciencenter in Ithaca, New York. "What are the URLs," you ask? No, no, no, we mean in real life. You gotta come out of the house sooner or later.

A newer commercial package for the PC called CineVideo/ Direct offers video conferencing with decent audio and video quality (on days when the Net's in a good mood, anyway) at a reasonable price. You can download a 30-day demo from their Web site at http://cinecom.com/. The commercial version sells for $39.95. Cinecom's Web site also has a directory of other CineVideo users who are willing to be contacted so that you can check out how the program works.

TIP

Information about the video programs mentioned in this section can be found in Chapter 24, "WWW Multimedia Power Tools."

NET RADIO

The future of radio may be over the wires, not over the airwaves. The Internet has been a boon to many forms of media, and radio may prove to be no exception. Although the current network technology, especially for personal computers connected to the Net, is still not sophisticated enough to make delivery of digital radio commonplace, the basic components are already in place. Both commercial and noncommercial broadcasters (dubbed "net-casters") are already starting to create Net radio programming.

Radio first popped up on the Internet in the spring of 1993 when journalist and Net evangelist Carl Malamud began netcasting a professionally produced half-hour audio show, called "Geek of the Week." Using National Public Radio as a model, the show was produced in a conventional sound studio and mastered onto digital audio tape. The finished programs, interviews with notable members of the Internet community, were then "multicast" over the Internet. Users directly connected to the Net on workstations could play the audio files. Desktop users, connected via modems, could download the massive audio files (if they wanted to bear the expense and the long download time). The system was awkward by all accounts, but it demonstrated the potential for delivering radio-like programming in Cyberspace.

Since these humble beginnings, Net radio has begun to come into its own. Programs like RealAudio, StreamWorks, and IWave allow users to listen to audio programming in "real-time," while the programming is being transferred, without having to download it first. RealAudio turns your PC into a radio with the audio quality of a cheap AM unit. Further technical innovations and increasingly fast Net connections will eventually make netcasting an attractive alternative to both commercial and noncommercial radio programs. An increasing number of radio stations, from NPR to local FM stations, are creating their own Web sites and making their shows available for listening in "real time," using streaming programs like RealAudio, or for downloading and later playback. So far, owing to the rather low quality of sound technology over the Net and through the home PC, most of netcasting is spoken word, not music, but this will change with the next generation of Net and PC sound tools.

Net radio could provide the answer to a big problem in small commercial, community, and amateur radio. Currently, if you want to march out and buy a radio station, you need a truckload o' bucks, for the FCC licensing, the sophisticated, high-powered studio and broadcast equipment, the tower, and so on. Those who choose to invest in radio have to do so with an intense commitment to quick commercial success. Local communities, especially in poor urban and rural areas, simply cannot afford to buy their way onto the airwaves. Rascally kids and radio hobbyists who choose to pirate the airwaves, broadcasting as little as one mile from their houses, can face heavy fines from the FCC.

Now, think of how Net radio could change all that. For the moment, before government and the FCC stick their noses too far into the Internet, netcasting can provide free "radio" services worldwide.

Take KPIG from Freedom, California, as an example (see Figure 28-4). This small 2,850-watt station, south of San Francisco, is now able to reach a global audience. Using StreamWorks technology, the freeform music station, located at "107-oink-5" on the FM dial, simulcasts its programs on the Internet. Besides its audio offerings, the station's Web site (http://www.kpig.com) offers an in-studio camera (so you can see what the DJ looks like) and a walking tour of the station. Community groups wanting to be heard could use Net radio in a similar fashion. Of course, in poor areas radio programming on computer doesn't make much sense, but it could in the future. Community activist groups wanting to reach a more middle class audience are taking to the "netwaves." For amateurs, Net radio offers all aspects of the DJ fantasy (hasn't everyone wanted to be a DJ at least some point in life?) without the risks of unlicensed broadcasting.

Figure 28-4: Pig out on freeform Net radio at KPIG.

Net radio has also attracted large media organizations, the entertainment business, and the academic community. NPR, CBS News, ABC World News Now, Monitor Radio, and PBS all offer netcasts. Many art and sports events are now netcast as well. Just as with the current skirmish over Net telephony, one wonders how this is all going to shake out when the FCC realizes that radio has moved into Cyberspace in a big way.

To find out more about Net radio, a number of useful online resources are available. The Internet Town Hall (yes, the Internet *does* have one) is a good place to start. There you will find over 200 hours of audio programming that can be searched by keywords and categories. There is also a great list of links to other Net radio projects from around the world. The Town Hall is located at http://town.hall.org/. RealAudio maintains a guide to RealAudio offerings available on the Net at http://www.realaudio.com/. See Figure 28-5.

Figure 28-5: A page of the RealAudio program guide.

TIP

Information about the audio programs mentioned in this section can be found in Chapter 24, "WWW Multimedia Power Tools."

TV OR NETTV?

Video on the Internet began in 1992 with something called the MBone, or the Multimedia Backbone. The MBone was an outgrowth of several audio/video experiments conducted by the Internet Engineering Task Force. The idea was to create a multicast network through the Internet, which would allow for the transfer of live audio and video transmissions. The MBone is a virtual network of special routers (called *mrouters*) and point-to-point links, called *tunnels*. Using this multicast network, users on workstations can video teleconference or watch video and television netcasts. Over 1,000 networks are currently connected to the MBone, and more are joining all of the time. MBone netcasts have included full-length films, rock concerts, and NASA missions.

TIP

For more information on MBone, check out the MBone FAQ (http://www.research.att.com/mbone-faq.html) and the MBone Information Web (http://www. mbone.com/techinfo). Also, see the MBone sidebar in Chapter 3, "TCP/IP Primer."

Streaming audio/video works differently than the MBone multicast model. While the MBone works much like conventional broadcast TV (the transmission fans out over the network to be picked up by the sponsoring hosts and made available to anyone who's running the appropriate client software), streaming content is served up in much the same way that HTML and other Web content is. In a streaming setup, the site offering streaming audio/video must be running a streaming server that makes point-to-point contact with the client and then sends compressed stream data to be decompressed and played on the client end. Streaming technology is optimized for modems and ISDN connections, while MBone is still the province of workstations and direct Internet connections. StreamWorks and VDOlive are two popular packages, offering client software to users and server software to those wanting to serve streaming content on their sites.

Streaming audio/video is already being used in some innovative ways. Besides the audio content discussed in the Net radio section above, people are using it to create low-end Net TV programming. For instance, a series of Japanese public access programs called SimTV were simulcast over the Web using StreamWorks. Encouraging a "viewers as broadcasters" approach, the SimTV creators asked Net citizens to send in their own digital contributions: stories, video, and pictures. They created a show using all this material and simulcast it on the Web and Japanese television. Three different programs (SimTV1, SimTV2, and SimTV3) were broadcast. You can view the material that was submitted for the shows and reports of the events at http://www.nhk.or.jp/SimTV/warp/warp.html. See Figure 28-6.

Figure 28-6: SimTV brings people's TVs to an international audience.

The Web sites for VDOLive (http://www.vdolive.com), StreamWorks (http://www.streamworks.com), and other providers of Net TV technology maintain link lists and guides to netcasts that use their technology. Visit these sites to download the software, learn more about this emerging technology, and check out the programming guides.

TIP

Information about the video programs mentioned in this section can be found in Chapter 24, "WWW Multimedia Power Tools."

Beyond the current experiments in Net-based television and video conferencing lies the realm of truly interactive television (at least in the minds of media executives). Most people expect this kind of TV to arrive inside that big box in the corner of the living room. But maybe not. Two new technologies, HyperTV and Intercast, were recently unveiled. They will make use of the Vertical Blanking Interval of the broadcast signal (the digital portion of the signal reserved for things like closed captioning) to send things like HTML code. By combining a TV card with a computer, this will allow TV programming to contain other interactive material to go along with the broadcast. Allegedly, Intercast will require a special board, while HyperTV will use Java technology and will allow you to use a computer with a TV card or a conventional TV wired into your PC. More information about Intercast can be found at http://www.intercast.org/. EarthWeb, developers of HyperTV can be reached at http://www.ew.net/.

TIP

A great starting point for finding out more about the technologies and services discussed in this chapter (and new ones as they emerge) is Jeff Pulver's NetWatch (http://www.pulver.com/netwatch/). Jeff offers a site, updated weekly, with news, information, and links covering all aspects of video and voice over the Net.

MOVING ON

Well friends, it's time to move on—*really* move on. We're sorry to leave you like this, but our hands are tired from all this typing and our stomachs have been ravaged by too much coffee. We need a break. And aren't you tired from holding this big heavy tome in your lap? Time to get up, go for a walk, and think about all the cool things you can do with your newfound knowledge and the power tools we've stuffed onto that little silver disc in the back of the book. We hope we've given you a few skills that can help you stay on top of the big data wave. In emergencies, this book also serves as a handy flotation device.

The future of the Internet is deliciously unknown. We've been online daily since the late '80s, and we still can't get over how excited we remain (and we're cynical slacker types!). Sure, it's getting commercial and mainstream, and yes, big media is moving in and killing a lot of the early pioneering spirit we were so drawn to. But the beauty of the Internet is that it's not fixed; it's a universe of possibility waiting for unlikely constellations of people and technology to forge new alliances. Hopefully, regardless of what happens to big media in Cyberspace (do we really need an interactive version of Melrose Place?), the freedom of expression and association we now enjoy there will remain. If so, we're ever hopeful that creative, fun, and life-enriching experiences will continue to flower there. As long as they do, that's where you'll find us.

Appendices

About the Online Companion

To stay abreast of developments covered in this book, visit our *Internet Power Toolkit* Online Updates. There you'll find updates to the book and updates of the software contained on the Companion CD-ROM. Drop by and pay us a visit—we love the company. The address is http://www.vmedia.com/updates.html.

About the Companion CD-ROM

The CD-ROM included with your copy of *The Internet Power Toolkit* contains valuable software programs and example files from each chapter.

To view the CD-ROM:

❐ **Windows 3.1/Windows 95/Windows NT:** Double-click on the viewer.exe file from your Windows Explorer or File Manager.

❐ **Macintosh:** Double-click on the Viewer icon on your Macintosh hard drive.

You'll see a menu screen offering several choices. See "Navigating the CD-ROM" below for your option choices.

NAVIGATING THE CD-ROM

Your choices for navigating the CD-ROM appear on the opening screen. You can exit from the CD, get Help on navigating, look over the CD Contents (software), learn more about Ventana, or browse the Hot Picks.

If you click on the CD Contents button, you will see a list of all the software programs on the CD. You can choose to copy the programs one at a time to your hard drive or you can copy all of the programs at once. If you have a Windows 3.x or 95 computer, the viewer will create a C:\IPTKCD folder on your hard drive and place the programs you select there. If you have a Macintosh, the viewer will create an Internet PTK CD folder to put the selected programs in. To install the program, you will have to go to the appropriate folder on your hard drive. A complete listing of the programs follows:

Program	Description
Windows Software	
CRT	A 32-bit Winsock emulator supporting rlogin and Telnet, along with ZModem file transfer over Telnet.
Email Connection	Email Connection is an award-winning one-stop manager for your Internet mail.
Envoy Plug-in	A Netscape Navigator plug-in that enables viewing of Envoy Documents.
Lightning Strike Plug-in	The Lightning Strike plug-in allows Web-surfers to view Lightning Strike–compressed graphics through Netscape Navigator.
Mail Check	Mail Check, available in 32-bit and 16-bit versions, automatically checks your inbox for new mail.
Ncompass	Ncompass's ActiveX plug-in for Netscape Navigator allows Web authors and surfers to create and view ActiveX-based applications.
Netscan Tools	A collection of UNIX Internet tools ported to the Windows environment.
OpenScape	OpenScape is a tool for moving existing programs and software components across an intranet or the Internet.
The Palace	The Palace is a "multimedia chat architecture." By controlling a graphic representation of yourself, you can participate in multimedia chat, games, and more in an interactive environment.
RAS+	RAS+ is an improved interface for Windows 95's built-in Dial Up Networking that simplifies accessing the Internet.

Program	Description
TrueSpeech	The TrueSpeech Player lets you play any TrueSpeech-encoded sound files (.WAV) in real-time as you download them from the World Wide Web.
VDOLive Plug-in	A Netscape plug-in that allows surfers to view VDO-format video files directly within Web pages.
Shockwave	Shockwave allows Web-surfers to view interactive multimedia presentations created in Macromedia Director.
Web Arranger	Web Arranger for Windows was unavailable at press time. To download the latest 30-day demo version of Web Arranger, go to: http://www.cesoft.com/webarranger/webarrangerpage.html.
WebWhacker	WebWhacker downloads the HTML code and images for Web pages, allowing users to store pages locally and update them only occasionally, reducing connect time and costs.
WIRL Lite	WIRL Lite is a fully interactive VRML browser plug-in for Navigator.
WS Archie	WS Archie is a Winsock client (32- or 16-bit) that searches the Internet through Archie servers.
Wplany	Wplany is a helper application for playing sound files downloaded from the Net.
Internet PHONE	VocalTec's Internet PHONE allows you to speak with other Internet PHONE users anywhere in the world in real-time for just the cost of your Internet connection.
Internet Wave	Internet Wave allows you to hear live or recorded streaming audio over the Net.
Acrobat Reader 3.0	This prerelease version of Acrobat 3.0 (previously code-named "Amber") allows you to view Adobe Acrobat portable document format files inside Netscape.
VRScout Plug-in	VRScout is a VRML browser Netscape plug-in that provides the user with an "aircraft cockpit"-type control panel for navigation.
Pueblo	Pueblo is a multimedia Internet client meant to allow users to easily navigate rich multi-user environments.

➥

Program	Description
NewsXpress	NewsXpress is a Winsock Usenet newsreader.
PowerMedia	Visual multimedia authoring software for the Web and the Netscape plug-in that allows you to view PowerMedia presentations.
Eudora Light™	Eudora Light is the freeware version of the popular Eudora e-mail software.

Macintosh Software

MailSniffer	MailSniffer is a bare-bones POP client that's built to do one thing—tell you if you have mail waiting.
The Palace	The Palace is a "multimedia chat architecture." By controlling a graphic representation of yourself, you can participate in multimedia chat, games, and more in an interactive environment.
Video Mail Pro	VideoMail lets you record brief audio and video messages and mail them over the Net.
WebWhacker	WebWhacker downloads the HTML code and images for Web pages, allowing users to store pages locally and update them only occasionally, reducing connect time and costs.
Web Arranger	Web Arranger makes it simple to locate a page you visited yesterday or last month.
Lightning Strike Plug-in	The Lightning Strike plug-in allows Web-surfers to view Lightning Strike-compressed graphics through Netscape Navigator.
Eudora Light™	Eudora Light is the freeware version of the popular Eudora e-mail software.
Envoy Plug-in	A Netscape Navigator plug-in that enables viewing of Envoy documents.
Anarchie	Anarchie is an FTP and Archie client.
Daemon	Daemon is a general TCP server, implementing Finger, Whois, Ident, Daytime, and Time (but not NTP).
Finger	Finger allows you to finger other machines on the Internet.
MacTCP Watcher	MacTCP Watcher displays the internal data of MacTCP: the Mac's IP, DNS name, and all the internal information that MacTCP provides.

Program	Description
NetPresenz	NetPresenz turns your Macintosh into an FTP, WWW, or Gopher server.
Internet Logger	Internet Logger is a small utility for tracking time spent on your Internet account.
InterSLIP Timer	InterSLIP Timer works with InterSLIP to track your online time.
MacPPP Timer	MacPPP Timer is a sister utility to InterSLIP Timer, designed to function in concert with MacPPP.
Shockwave	Shockwave allows Web-surfers to view interactive multimedia presentations created in Macromedia Director.
Acrobat Reader 3.0	This prerelease version of Acrobat 3.0 (previously code-named "Amber") allows you to view Adobe Acrobat portable document format files inside Netscape.
Blue-Skies ver. 1.1	Blue-Skies provides access to real-time meteorological data via interactive imagery.
ShockTalk	ShockTalk allows Webmasters to create speakable Web sites and Macromedia Director Shockwave movies that contain spoken user interactions.
TurboGopherVR	TurboGopherVR allows you to view and navigate Gopher space in three dimensions.
Power Media	The Macintosh version of PowerMedia was not available at press time. To download PowerMedia, go to: http://www.radmedia.com.

SPECIAL OFFERS

Purchasers of *The Internet Power Toolkit* can take advantage of a special offer from VocalTec to purchase the Internet PHONE at 20 percent off the regular price. See the VREADME.TXT file in the Iphone folder for full details.

TECHNICAL SUPPORT

Technical support is available for installation-related problems only. The technical support office is open from 8:00 A.M. to 6:00 P.M. Monday through Friday and can be reached via the following methods:

Phone: (919) 544-9404 extension 81

FaxBack Service: (919) 544-9404 extension 85

E-mail: help@vmedia.com

FAX: (919) 544-9472

World Wide Web: **http://www.vmedia.com/support**

America Online: keyword *Ventana*

LIMITS OF LIABILITY & DISCLAIMER OF WARRANTY

The authors and publisher of this book have used their best efforts in preparing the CD-ROM and the programs contained in it. These efforts include the development, research, and testing of the theories and programs to determine their effectiveness. The authors and publisher make no warranty of any kind, expressed or implied, with regard to these programs or the documentation contained in this book.

The authors and publisher shall not be liable in the event of incidental or consequential damages in connection with, or arising out of, the furnishing, performance, or use of the programs, associated instructions, and/or claims of productivity gains.

Some of the software on this CD-ROM is shareware; there may be additional charges (owed to the software authors/makers) incurred for their continued use and registration. See individual programs' VREADME.TXT files for more information.

Field Guide to File Types

As you cruise the Net, you're bound to run into many different types of files. Some files will be compressed archives—groups of files "smooshed" by special compression software into packages. On the multimedia front, you'll certainly run into a host of graphic, sound, and video files.

The great thing about all these files is that each one provides its own special level of functionality. Compression types work on different kinds of computers and provide useful features for a variety of compression problems. Although all graphic files will provide you with a pretty (or not so pretty!) picture, each one has its own usage depending on what type of program is used to create the graphics and what kind of quality and features are needed. Likewise, the different types of sound files allow for varying levels of quality and portability to different kinds of computers.

However, all the flexibility provided by different types of files comes with a price—complexity. And all this complexity can make life very confusing for people wanting to view or listen or use these various types of files.

Well, friends—we're here to take the confusion out of your Netsurfing. In the following series of charts, we've tried to make dealing with files as simple as possible by providing a quick and not-so-dirty directory of what files are what and what programs you need to deal with them.

COMPRESSION & ENCODING

Compression lets you take a large file and make it smaller. Simple, huh? And while there are a few standard types of compression—ZIP for Windows and SIT for the Mac—not everyone uses the standard methods. Most often, compression is used for making program files smaller to allow for quicker transfer, so you'll be most likely to run into compressed files when you're cruising FTP sites or downloading files from the Web. This section provides a brief overview of the most common forms of program compression and encoding (translating files for transmission) used on the Net, and the programs you need to have in order to handle them.

		Player/Viewer/Decompressor	
Extension	Description	Macintosh	Windows
.arc	Old file compression format that is not often used these days.	StuffIt Expander ftp://ftp.aladdinsys.com/	StuffIt Expander for Windows ftp://ftp.aladdinsys.com/
.arj	Archiving and compression format, often used in DOS/Windows.	UnArjMac http://hyperarchive.lcs.mit.edu/HyperArchive/Archive/cmp/unarj-221.hqx	StuffIt Expander for Windows ftp://ftp.aladdinsys.com/
.cpt	Compact Pro, Macintosh-only compression and archiving format.	Compact Pro http://hyperarchive.lcs.mit.edu/HyperArchive/Archive/cmp/compact-pro-151.hqx	ExtractorPC ftp://mirrors.aol.com/pub/cica/pc/win3/util/ext-pc.zip
.exe	Windows self-extracting archive.	None	Application—needs no extractor.
.gz	UNIX GNU zip format. See also .z, .Z.	MacGZip http://hyperarchive.lcs.mit.edu/HyperArchive/Archive/cmp/mac-gzip-10.hqx	StuffIt Expander for Windows ftp://ftp.aladdinsys.com/

➡

Extension	Description	Player/Viewer/Decompressor	
		Macintosh	**Windows**
.hqx	BinHex format, most often used for ASCII encoding of Mac binary files.	BinHex http://hyperarchive.lcs. mit.edu/HyperArchive/Archive/cmp/binhex-50.hqx BinHex13 ftp://oak.oakland.edu/simtel/msdos/mac/	StuffIt Expander for Windows ftp://ftp.aladdinsys.com/
.image	Macintosh disk image.	http://hyperarchive.lcs.mit.edu/HyperArchive/Archive/disk/shrink-wrap-142.hqx	None.
.lha/.lzh	Amiga compression format.	MacLHA http://hyperarchive.lcs.mit.edu/HyperArchive/Archive/cmp/mac-lha-213.hqx	LHA 2.55 gopher://gopher.archive.umich.edu:7055/59/msdos/compression/lzh/lha255b.exe
MIME	(Multipurpose Internet Mail Extension) Mainly used for transferring binary files through e-mail and Usenet.	Mpack ftp://ftp.andrew.cmu.edu/pub/mpack/mpack-1.5-mac.hqx	Mpack ftp://ftp.andrew.cmu.edu/pub/mpack/mpack15d.zip
.shk	ShrinkIt, AppleII compression program.	None	None
.sea	Macintosh compressed self-extracting archive.	Self-extracting archive	None
.sit	StuffIt Macintosh compression program.	StuffIt Lite/StuffIt Expander ftp://ftp.aladdinsys.com/	StuffIt Expander for Windows ftp://ftp.aladdinsys.com/
.tar	UNIX tape archive, does not compress, merely combines many files and directories into one.	TAR 4.0 http://hyperarchive.lcs.mit.edu/HyperArchive/Archive/cmp/tar-40b.hqx	Wpack ftp://mirrors.aol.com/pub/cica/pc/win3/util/wpackd.exe
.uu	uuencode, used for encoding binary files into ASCII for e-mailing and posting to Usenet newsgroups.	Uuundo http://hyperarchive.lcs.mit.edu/HyperArchive/Archive/cmp/uu-undo-10.hqx	Wpack ftp://mirrors.aol.com/pub/cica/pc/win3/util/wpackd.exe
.Z/.z	UNIX compression format. See .gz.	MacGZip http://hyperarchive.lcs.mit.edu/HyperArchive/Archive/cmp/mac-gzip-10.hqx	StuffIt Expander for Windows ftp://ftp.aladdinsys.com/
.zip	PKZIP compression and archiving format, Premier DOS/Windows compression format.	ZipIt http://hyperarchive.lcs.mit.edu/HyperArchive/Archive/cmp/zip-it-135.hqx	WinZip ftp://mirrors.aol.com/pub/cica/pc/win95/miscutil/winzip95.exe
.zoo	Ancient file compression format that is not often used.	MacZoo http://hyperarchive.lcs.mit.edu/HyperArchive/Archive/cmp/maczoo-21.hqx	Zoo210 gopher://gopher.archive.umich.edu:7055/59/msdos/compression/zoo/zoo210.exe

GRAPHICS

Judging from the popularity of the alt.binaries.pictures newsgroup hierarchy, downloading and viewing graphics files is probably one of the most popular pastimes on the Net. For most folks, knowing how to view the two main types of graphics files—.GIF and .JPEG (or .JPG)—is probably sufficient for most uses. However, what do you do if you want to view a digital movie? What do you do if you want to view an encapsulated PostScript file? Well, wonder no more! The following handy guide to graphics file types will let you know what to do when you download a graphic file you don't know how to handle.

Extension	Description	Player/Viewer/Decompressor	
		Macintosh	Windows
.avi	Microsoft Video for Windows	AVI->QuickTime Converter http://hyperarchive.lcs.mit.edu/HyperArchive/Archive/gst/mov/avi-to-qt-converter.hqx	Windows 3.1 CompuPic ftp://ftp.photodex.com/cpic.exe Windows 95Built in. Just double-click the .AVI file.
.bmp	Windows Bitmap	Graphic Converter http://hyperarchive.lcs.mit.edu/HyperArchive/Archive/gst/grf/graphic-converter-24.hqx	Graphic Workshop ftp://ftp.north.net/pub/alchemy/ Alternatively, use Windows Paintbrush to open and view.
.cgm	Computer Graphics Metafile	Graphic Converter http://hyperarchive.lcs.mit.edu/HyperArchive/Archive/gst/grf/graphic-converter-24.hqx	Paint Shop Pro ftp://mirrors.aol.com/pub/cica/pc/win95/desktop/psp311.zip
.eps	Encapsulated PostScript	Graphic Converter http://hyperarchive.lcs.mit.edu/HyperArchive/Archive/gst/grf/graphic-converter-24.hqx [Note: Only works with bitmap .EPS files. For vector files, use the commercial program Macromedia FreeHand.]	Paint Shop Pro ftp://mirrors.aol.com/pub/cica/pc/win95/desktop/psp311.zip [Note: Only works with bitmap .EPS files. For vector files, use the commercial program Macromedia FreeHand.]
.flc/.fli	Animator Pro	MacAnimation Viewer http://hyperarchive.lcs.mit.edu/HyperArchive/Archive/gst/mov/mac-anim-viewer-11.hqx	Graphic Workshop ftp://ftp.north.net/pub/alchemy/
.fits	Flexible Image Transport System	None	Graphic Workshop ftp://ftp.north.net/pub/alchemy/
.gif	CompuServe Graphics Interchange Format	Graphic Converter http://hyperarchive.lcs.mit.edu/HyperArchive/Archive/gst/grf/graphic-converter-24.hqx	Graphic Workshop ftp://ftp.north.net/pub/alchemy/

➡

		Player/Viewer/Decompressor	
Extension	Description	Macintosh	Windows
.jpg/ .jpeg/.jfif	Joint Photographic Experts Group color graphic file	Graphic Converter http://hyperarchive.lcs.mit.edu/ HyperArchive/Archive/gst/grf/ graphic-converter-24.hqx	Graphic Workshop ftp://ftp.north.net/pub/alchemy/
.mac	MacPaint	Graphic Converter http://hyperarchive.lcs.mit.edu/ HyperArchive/Archive/gst/grf/ graphic-converter-24.hqx	Graphic Workshop ftp://ftp.north.net/pub/alchemy/
.mpg/ .mpeg	Motion Picture Experts Group digital video file	Sparkle http://hyperarchive.lcs.mit.edu/ HyperArchive/Archive/gst/mov/ sparkle-245.hqx	Graphic Workshop ftp://ftp.north.net/pub/alchemy/
.mov	QuickTime digital video	Sparkle http://hyperarchive.lcs.mit.edu/ HyperArchive/Archive/gst/mov/ sparkle-245.hqx	Graphic Workshop ftp://ftp.north.net/pub/alchemy/
.msp	Microsoft Paint	Graphic Converter http://hyperarchive.lcs.mit.edu/ HyperArchive/Archive/gst/grf/ graphic-converter-24.hqx	Graphic Workshop ftp://ftp.north.net/pub/alchemy/
.pcx	PC Paintbrush	Graphic Converter http://hyperarchive.lcs.mit.edu/ HyperArchive/Archive/gst/grf/ graphic-converter-24.hqx	Graphic Workshop ftp://ftp.north.net/pub/alchemy/ Alternatively, use Paintbrush (it comes with Windows).
.pdf	Adobe Portable Document Format	Adobe Acrobat Reader http://www.adobe.com	Adobe Acrobat Reader http://www.adobe.com
.pics	Macintosh PICT animation	MacAnimation Viewer http://hyperarchive.lcs.mit.edu/ HyperArchive/Archive/gst/mov/mac-anim-viewer-11.hqx	None
.pict	Macintosh bitmap picture file	Graphic Converter http://hyperarchive.lcs.mit.edu/ HyperArchive/Archive/gst/grf/ graphic-converter-24.hqx	Graphic Workshop ftp://ftp.north.net/pub/alchemy/
.ps	PostScript	Ghost Script http://hyperarchive.lcs.mit.edu/ HyperArchive/Archive/gst/grf/mac-ghostscript-252b3.hqx	Ghost Script ftp://mirrors.aol.com/pub/cica/pc/ win3/util/gs261exe.zip
.ras	Sun Rasterfile	Graphic Converter http://hyperarchive.lcs.mit.edu/ HyperArchive/Archive/gst/grf/ graphic-converter-24.hqx	Graphic Workshop ftp://ftp.north.net/pub/alchemy/
.scan	Thunderscan	GIF Converter http://hyperarchive.lcs.mit.edu/ HyperArchive/Archive/gst/grf/gif-converter-237.hqx	None

		Player/Viewer/Decompressor	
Extension	Description	Macintosh	Windows
.scan	Thunderscan	GIF Converter http://hyperarchive.lcs.mit.edu/ HyperArchive/Archive/gst/grf/gif-converter-237.hqx	None
.tga	Targa	Graphic Converter http://hyperarchive.lcs.mit.edu/ HyperArchive/Archive/gst/grf/ graphic-converter-24.hqx	Graphic Workshop ftp://ftp.north.net/pub/alchemy/
.tif/.tiff	Tagged Image File Format	Graphic Converter http://hyperarchive.lcs.mit.edu/ HyperArchive/Archive/gst/grf/ graphic-converter-24.hqx	Graphic Workshop ftp://ftp.north.net/pub/alchemy/
.wmf	Windows MetaFile	Graphic Converter http://hyperarchive.lcs.mit.edu/ HyperArchive/Archive/gst/grf/ graphic-converter-24.hqx	Graphic Workshop ftp://ftp.north.net/pub/alchemy/
.wpg	Word Perfect Graphic	Graphic Converter http://hyperarchive.lcs.mit.edu/ HyperArchive/Archive/gst/grf/ graphic-converter-24.hqx	Graphic Workshop ftp://ftp.north.net/pub/alchemy/
.wrl	VRML	See section onVRML in Chapter 24	

SOUND

Looking at graphics is nice, but some times you may want to put more "media" in your multimedia. Sound files allow you to hear, well, *sounds* (this ain't rocket science!) on your computer. These sounds can be anything from a simple "beep"-type alert to entire symphonies. And, as you've come to discover in this section, there are many different types of sound files on the Net. But don't worry—if you encounter a sound file you don't know how to deal with, just consult the handy chart on the next page.

		Player/Viewer/Decompressor	
Extension	**Description**	**Macintosh**	**Windows**
.aiff/.aif	Apple sound format	SoundApp http://hyperarchive.lcs.mit.edu/ HyperArchive/Archive/gst/snd/ sound-app-151.hqx	Windows Media Player Included with Windows
.au	NeXT sound format	SoundApp http://hyperarchive.lcs.mit.edu/ HyperArchive/Archive/gst/snd/ sound-app-151.hqx	Wplany ftp://ftp.netcom.com/pub/neisius
.mid/ .midi	MIDI	Arnold's MIDI Player http://hyperarchive.lcs.mit.edu/ HyperArchive/Archive/gst/midi/ arnolds-midi-player-251b.hqx	MIDI Gate ftp://mirrors.aol.com/pub/cica/pc/ win3/sounds/midigate.exe
.mod	Amiga	MacModPro http://hyperarchive.lcs.mit.edu/ HyperArchive/Archive/gst/snd/mac- mod-pro-415.hqx	MOD for Windows ftp://mirrors.aol.com/pub/cica/pc/ win3/sounds/m4w230sx.zip
.snd	Mac sound file	SoundApp http://hyperarchive.lcs.mit.edu/ HyperArchive/Archive/gst/snd/ sound-app-151.hqx	Wplany ftp://ftp.netcom.com/pub/neisius
.voc	SoundBlaster	SoundApp http://hyperarchive.lcs.mit.edu/ HyperArchive/Archive/gst/snd/ sound-app-151.hqx	Wplany ftp://ftp.netcom.com/pub/neisius
.wav	Microsoft Wave	SoundApp http://hyperarchive.lcs.mit.edu/ HyperArchive/Archive/gst/snd/ sound-app-151.hqx	Wplany ftp://ftp.netcom.com/pub/neisius

UNIX Boot Camp

Recruits! Attention! We know why you're here—you're in need of some serious brushing up on UNIX command-line skills. Years of clicking that mouse has made you soft. Point and click, click and point . . . it's a wonder some of you can even type your own names!

Well soldier, it's time you cut the mouse cord and learned how *real* power users do their computin'—with a keyboard! Don't look so scared! If it was good enough for Bill Gates, it's good enough for you, so listen up! When we're done, you'll wonder how you ever stood yourself and your mamby-pamby mouse-clickin' ways.

We're not going to lie to you—you might find some of this a bit tough. You won't find any pretty icons and cutesy screensavers here, friends. What you'll get is a no-nonsense, straight-to-the-gut introduction to the world of UNIX.

So let's get goin'. When you're done, you'll be of the few, the proud, the UNIX power users!

COMMAND-LINE CRASH COURSE

Using a command-line interface allows you to bypass a lot of the user-friendly but slower methods of inputting commands on a graphical interface. *Slag* is computer jargon for all the junk (graphics, banners, hyperlinked info, etc.) that one must shovel through to get to the intended information "ore." UNIX command-line Internetting allows you to bypass much of this annoying slag. On top of that, because many UNIX programs work together, taking information from one and putting it into another, you can often do all sorts of things that just aren't possible on your Mac or Windows system.

The right tool for the job—that's the importance of learning UNIX. So, let's get started.

Getting Around : The UNIX File Structure

Probably the most important thing you need to learn about UNIX is how to get around in the file structure. Most operating systems share many of the same features originally found in UNIX, so most of the concepts should be familiar to you. If you're used to DOS, learning UNIX will be easier. Even if you use a Mac, a lot of the concepts are the same.

■ ■

Like an Old Friend: DOS-Friendly UNIX

In fact, if you're using DOS and want to keep using many of the same commands in UNIX, you can! UNIX allows you to *alias* commands so that you can make up new names for old commands. If you want to keep the same commands in UNIX as you use in DOS, just add the following to the .login file in your UNIX account using the text editor on your system:

```
alias    copy     cp
alias    del      rm
alias    dir      ls -l
alias    edit     $EDITOR
alias    type     more
alias    ren      mv
```

■ ■

First and foremost, UNIX has a hierarchical file structure, which means that files can be placed in directories and directories can be placed inside of other directories. If you were to draw a schematic of a typical UNIX file structure, it would look very similar to a tree (See Figure D-1).

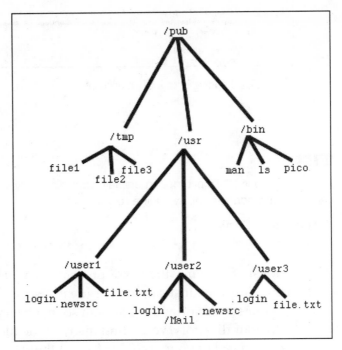

Figure D-1: UNIX hierarchical file structure.

When you first log in to your UNIX account, you will probably enter into your own "home" directory (see Figure D-2). From this directory, you can move to other directories, create your own directories, write your own files, and place files in the directories that you've created.

```
        o  Send Email to "help" for customer support
           Send Email to "billing" for billing
           Send Email to "report" for no reply notice of problem.
           Send Email to "faq@clark.net" for FAQ list

        o  see /share/clarknet/ for ClarkNet information

        o  Type "menu" or "help" for menus
           or "fmenu" for Fastmenu

      *  If possible please dont run WWW usage counter programs between
         9am and 11pm untill the new mail server is online to keep
         explorer loads down.

explorer:[/homec/elrod]
explorer:[/homec/elrod] █
```

Figure D-2: Logging in to a UNIX account.

■ ■

TIP

If you want your UNIX prompt to display what directory you're currently in, just add the following line to your .login file.

```
set prompt="%m:[%/] "
```

■ ■

Most of the time, the UNIX programs you use don't live in your
home directory. Instead, they reside in a special public directory
on your service provider's system so that everyone can use them.

In your directory, you'll find many of the files that control the
look and feel of your account. A lot of these are resource files—
files that contain information about how you want the different
programs you use to look. Resource files are much like the INI
files in Windows. Most of the time, the programs that use them
modify the resource files without your help. But, if you want to
customize things a bit, you can poke around in them yourself.

Let's take a look at what kinds of files you have in your account.

Listing Files

The command to get a directory listing in UNIX is ls. Type **ls** at the command line in your account, and you should see something like the directory listing in Figure D-3.

```
explorer:[/] ls
DEADJOE      core       homec      lost+found   proc        tftpboot
Mail         dev        homed      mail         readline    tmp
News         devices    homee      mnt          ree         ufsboot
allison      etc        homef      myjamie      root        usr
awk          export     homeg      net          root.cron   uucp.check
bin          forward    homeh      news         s           var
bkup         ftp        hsfsboot   opt          sbin        work
cdrom        home       kadb       opt2         share       wuarchive
charm        homea      kernel     opt3         sun1
clarknet     homeb      lib        opt4         tempfoo
explorer:[/] ▮
```

Figure D-3: A UNIX directory listing.

That's a lot of stuff! Basically, all ls does is give you a listing of the non-resource filenames. If you want a more detailed listing, you'll have to use one of the many modifiers for ls. See the summary section, "The UNIX Command Survival Kit," later in this chapter for a more detailed look at ls.

Changing Directories

Next, let's say that you want to change to a different directory. The command for changing directories is cd, which means, surprise, "change directory."

If you want to change to a directory "below" the one you're currently in (a directory whose name you can see in the directory listing), just type cd <directory name>, where <directory name> is the directory. Hey, I thought we told you not to type those brackets!

```
bin          forward     homeh        news      s          var
bkup         ftp         hsfsboot     opt       sbin       work
cdrom        home        kadb         opt2      share      wuarchive
charm        homea       kernel       opt3      sun1
clarknet     homeb       lib          opt4      tempfoo
explorer:[/] cd bin
explorer:[/bin] █
```

Figure D-4: Changing directories in UNIX.

If you want to move "up" a directory, just type cd. It'll move you back to the directory "above" your current location. If you want to move to a specific directory, say the alt.hackers directory in the News directory of your account, you can specify the path name using slashes. If you were in the top level of your account, you could type cd **News/alt.hackers/.** That's it!

TIP

If you ever get lost in all the directories, just type **cd** by itself. It'll send you home again.

TIP

If you get lost and want to find where you are, just type p**wd**, which stands for "print working directory." It'll give you your bearings.

Deleting Files

Working with files is easy. If you want to delete a file, just type **rm** <filename>. Your file will instantly be whisked away, never to return. Use this command with caution, though—unlike many personal computer systems, there's no way to get your files back once they're deleted! However, you can use some fancy tricks to avoid disasters. Unfortunately, we don't have time to go into them here. If you're curious about UNIX tricks, check out *Voodoo UNIX* by Charlie Russel and Sharon Crawford.

Voodoo UNIX

If all these UNIX basics are a little mundane for your taste, and you aspire to real UNIX wizardry, you'll want to delve into *Voodoo UNIX*. With 300 jam-packed pages of UNIX tricks and tips, you'll be a UNIX guru in no time.

Voodoo UNIX: Mastery Tips and Masterful Tricks by Charlie Russel & Sharon Crawford. Ventana, 1994. $27.95

Moving & Copying Files

When using UNIX, moving files from one place to another is easy. When you use the mv <filename> <destination> command, UNIX copies the file to the destination you've specified and then deletes the original file. This way, you don't have to copy a file to a new place and then delete it yourself. Great for getting your directory organized.

If you use mv to move a file in the directory you're in, it's great for renaming files. For example, if you have a file named carla, and you want to rename it netchick, you'd just use the command:

```
mv carla netchick
```

Piece of cake, eh?

If you want to make a copy of a file, just type **cp** <filename> <destination>, and UNIX will copy the file to the destination in a jiffy!

That's about it for the basics of getting around. Now that you know these commands, you can view a directory, move to other directories, delete files, move files, rename files, and copy files. Pretty simple stuff.

Of course, that's just the beginning. UNIX has a zillion other commands. In fact, some of these commands are so complex that whole books have been written about one single command.

Fortunately, you don't need to know that much (whew!). In fact, in an effort to get you up and running with UNIX in the absolute shortest possible time, we've come up with what we like to call . . .

The UNIX Command Survival Kit

Table D-1 lists 14 of the most useful UNIX commands.

Command	Description
man	display help information
ls	directory listing
cd	change directory
mkdir	make directory
rmdir	remove directory
mv	move a file
rm	delete a file
cp	copy a file
cat	display a file
more	display file with pauses
who	who is on the system
ps	display processes being run
kill	stop and delete a process
grep	search for a pattern in a file

Table D-1: The fourteen essential UNIX survival commands.

Let's take a look at these in depth. You don't have to memorize them now. Just tear off a piece of paper (no, not from this book—use your own paper!), and mark this section for future reference.

man

If have to make some brain space for only one UNIX command in your life, make it this one. Man is the closest thing UNIX ever gets to a help command. Since UNIX is an open system and is constantly being added to and improved on by people all over the world, users needed a way to find out how to use all the new features as they were added. Man was born.

Man makes special "manual pages" available online so that users can read them. We'll warn you that these manual pages were often written by and for hackers, so the syntax and writing is a little . . . um . . . terse to say the least. But, they also contain a huge amount of information on every aspect of the commands.

Let's try it out. If you want to find out more about the ls command (which, as you remember, fetches directory listings) just type the following, and press Enter:

```
man ls
```

You should see something similar to the man page shown in Figure D-5.

```
explorer:[/bin] man ls

ls(1)                        User Commands                        ls(1)

NAME
     ls - list contents of directory

SYNOPSIS
     ls [ -abcCdfFgilLmnopqrRstux1 ] [ names ]

AVAILABILITY
     SUNWcsu

DESCRIPTION
     For each directory argument, ls lists the  contents  of  the
     directory;  for  each file argument, ls repeats its name and
     any other  information  requested.   The  output  is  sorted
     alphabetically  by  default.  When no argument is given, the
     current directory is listed.   When  several  arguments  are
     given,  the  arguments  are  first sorted appropriately, but
     file arguments appear before directories and their contents.

     There are three major listing formats.  The  default  format
--More--(5%)
```

Figure D-5: The manual page for ls.

Uh, yeah. Like we said, it's not going to be exactly clear at first. But let's take a closer look. The word NAME tells you in the briefest way possible that the name of the command is ls and then what it does.

Next, SYNOPSIS gives you a description of the command, along with the syntax for using it and all the command-line modifiers. It might look like a bunch of technobabble right now, but it's all explained later on in the man page.

AVAILABILITY isn't too important. It just tells you where you can read this page if you actually had the manuals. (You don't.)

Finally, DESCRIPTION is where the meat of the manual page lives. In here, you'll find everything you could want to know about what the command is and how it works.

So, if you remember nothing else, remember man. It supplies the help function in UNIX. Table D-2 gives you a brief synopsis of the man command.

TIP

What do you do if you don't even know the name of a command but you know what you want the computer to do? You use appropos. Appropos allows you to search the manual pages for commands that are related to the keyword you've specified. For example, if you are looking for commands related to sorting, you'd just type **appropos sort**, and press Enter. UNIX will spit back all the commands related to sorting. Then, to get more information on the command, use your old friend man.

---

man [options] [command]

Provides online reference information about [command].

Option	Description
-a	Shows all manual pages matching title specified. man -a print
-b	Leaves all blank lines in output
-d	Allows user to specify directory to be added to the list of directories being searched for information. man -d /usr/man/newman [command]

Table D-2. man synopsis.

ls

As we saw earlier in the chapter, ls is the command for getting a directory listing. If all you want is a simple listing of the directory that you are in, no problem—just type **ls** by itself, press Enter, and you should see a simple listing of your files.

But, that listing doesn't tell you much, does it? In fact, unless you already know, you can't even tell which names represent directories and which represent files. Plus, ls by itself doesn't show you the hidden files that are in your account. Finally, what do you do if you want to know the size of your files? Simple! Type **ls -la**, and press Enter. You should see a directory listing like the one in Figure D-6.:

```
explorer:[/homec/elrod/Mail] ls -la
total 242
drwx------    2 elrod    ipusers      512 Nov  6 00:01 .
drwx--x--x    9 elrod    ipusers     2560 Nov  7 01:21 ..
-rw-------    1 elrod    ipusers     3508 Jun 15 15:41 ei-i
-rw-------    1 elrod    ipusers      743 Nov  6 00:26 posted
-rw-------    1 elrod    ipusers   105034 Oct 29 14:35 received
explorer:[/homec/elrod/Mail] █
```

Figure D-6: An ls -la directory listing.

Now that's information! Here's what we've got:
The first column shows the file permissions for each file and whether or not it's a directory. (Don't worry about file permissions—we'll cover that later.) For now, it's just important to recognize that the d in the first column indicates whether the item is a directory. The next three columns we can also skip for the time being. They just refer to the owners and group access for the file. The fifth column indicates the size in bytes of each file. This is important information if you want to know how much space a file is taking up. The next two columns indicate the date and time that a file was created or modified. The last column indicates the name of the file.

- -

TIP

If you've got a directory listing that's too long to see all at once, you can use a nifty UNIX feature called piping to get the output to pause. Just type:

```
ls -la |more
```

The output of ls will then be displayed using the more command, which causes the output to pause after every screenful. That way you won't miss a thing.

- -

Learning to use ls is vital. In fact, it's probably one of the commands you'll use most often. Table D-3 gives you a brief overview of the ls command.

ls [options] [directories]

Provides a file listing of the directories specified. If you don't specify a directory, ls will give you a listing of the current directory.

Option	Description
-A	Shows all files in the directory or directories specified. Listing includes all hidden files (those that start with a period). Using the -A option does not show the parent (..)or current (.) directory.
-a	Displays all files and directories including parent (..)and current (.) directory.
-C	Displays contents of directory in columns. Makes long directory listing easier to read.
-d	Shows a directory listing of directory names.
-l	Provides a long listing, with detailed information, about file permissions, owners, size, modification dates, and filenames.
-R	Shows a recursive listing of the current directory, its contents, and all directories and contents below.
-s	Gives a listing of all files along with their sizes in kilobytes.
-x	Lists files in rows.

Table D-3. ls synopsis.

cd

As you saw before, cd is used for changing directories. That's all.(See Table D-4) There's really no tricks to using it, except for bringing you home again by typing **cd** by itself and pressing Enter.

cd [directory]

Allows you to change your working directory. Changing directories by using the command cd will move you up one directory. Entering cd by itself will return you to your home directory.

Option
None

Table D-4: cd synopsis.

mkdir

Enough with changing directories—what if you want to make your own directory? Just use the **mkdir** command. Just type: mkdir [options] [new directory name]. UNIX will create a new directory for you with the name that you've specified. Most of the time, no options are necessary, but you can consult Table D-5 for ideas of how you might want to use them.

You'll probably use mkdir mainly to organize yourself. There's practically no limit to the amount of directories you can create, so try making new directories for saved e-mail, programs you've downloaded, news articles you've saved, and other items of interest.

However, don't just go creating directories willy-nilly. Some directory names are traditionally reserved for certain programs and information that your UNIX account uses. Consult Table D-6 for a description of these directory names and what they're used for.

mkdir [options][directory]

Allows you to create a directory with the name [directory].

Option	Description
-m	Allows you to set the access mode for the new directory. .
-p	Creates a directory and all directories in between. For example, if you wanted to create three nested directories named directory, directory1, and directory2, you'd use the command
	mkdir -p directory/directory1/directory2

Table D-5: mkdir synopsis.

Directory Name	Contents
bin	Programs and scripts
tmp	A temporary directory. Your system probably has its own /tmp directory for you to use if you just want to save something temporarily.
News	Saved Usenet news articles and kill files.
Mail	Used by the elm newsreader to store information.

➡

Directory Name	Contents
pub	The public directory. Most user account directories are actually subdirectories in the system /pub directory.
source	Program source code.
etc	Contains miscellaneous files.
dev	Contains ways of acccessing hard drives, printers, and other peripherals.
usr	Contains user-executable programs.
/dev/null	"Null" device directory, generally used as a "trashcan." When you hear someone say that something should be sent to/dev/null, it's a nice way of telling you that it should be trashed.

Table D-6: UNIX directory naming conventions.

rmdir

What if you want to remove a directory? If you want to delete a directory, use rmdir. However, you can only remove directories that don't contain any files. If you try to remove a directory containing files, you'll get an error that looks something like the one in Figure D-7.

```
explorer:[/homec/elrod] rmdir Mail
rmdir: Mail: Directory not empty
explorer:[/homec/elrod] █
```

Figure D-7: A rmdir error message.

Remember, however, UNIX is not too forgiving with deletions. If you delete a directory, you cannot get it back. Of course, since you can only delete directories that are empty, this shouldn't pose a problem. See Table D-7 for a quick overview of how to use **rmdir**.

mkdir [options][directory]

Allows you to delete a directory with the name [directory].

Option	Description
-p	This command does the opposite of the mkdir -p command. It removes the directory specified in [directory] and all the directories in between your current directory. For example, if you wanted to delete the directory we created in the mkdir example, you'd use the command: rmdir -pdirectory/directory1/directory2
-s	Often, using rmdir -p causes standard error messages to appear. Most of the time, these messages don't mean anything important. Using the -s option along with rmdir -p will keep those messages from appearing.

Table D-7: rmdir synopsis.

mv

If you want to move files, rename files, and even replace old files with new ones, use mv.

First, though, a word of caution. *Operations done with mv cannot be undone!* If you trash an important file by mving a file on top of it, it's gone forever. Trashed. Kablooey. And, UNIX doesn't ask nicely when you use mv. It just does the job—no questions asked. It doesn't care if you've just replaced that report you've been working on for weeks with a note you'd taken earlier. Once you use mv, the old file's gone. Note that UNIX isn't an idiot-proofed OS—it assumes that you know what you're doing.

On a happier note, mv can be an incredibly useful command depending on how you manipulate its simple options. Let's take a look.

If you want to rename a file, just use the command mv <existing filename> <new filename>. Your file will be renamed to whatever you specified in <new filename>. If you want to delete an already existing file and replace it with another file, just use the command mv <replacement filename> <old filename>. The old file will be replaced by <replacement filename>.

Mv works with directories, too. If you want to rename a directory, just use the command mv <existing directory name> <new directory name>. Or you can use mv to take a directory from somewhere else and make it a subdirectory of your current directory. For example, using mv /pub/beavis/nachorecipes beavisnachos will take the directory named nachorecipes from the /pub/beavis/ directory and make it a subdirectory of your account named beavisnachos.

One thing to remember, though. Just because you can snag directories from other places and move them into your own directory doesn't mean you can grab other people's directories and move them to your own. You can only move directories that you have permission to move. Finally, if you want to move a file from one directory and place it in another directory, mv will let you do it. Just use the command mv <filename> [directory], and the file called <filename> will be moved to the [directory] you specify. See Table D-8 for a quick review of the mv command.

mkdir [options] <source file> <target file>

mkdir [options] [source directory] [target directory]

Allows you to move, rename, or replace files and directory.

Option	Description
-f	Overwrites target with source, ignoring permissions. Use this option with caution. You can't delete or replace other people's files with this option, but if you've protected your own directories or files, this will wipe 'em out.

Table D-8: mv synopsis.

rm

If you want to wipe out a file, then use rm.

Rm is the delete function for UNIX. And when we say delete, we mean delete—gone forever. There's no "undelete" in UNIX (which may explain why Peter Norton hasn't released his utilities for UNIX).

If you want to delete a single file , just type **rm** <filename>. If you have a bunch of files you want to get rid of, you can use the UNIX wildcard character, an asterisk (*).

For example, let's say that you want to delete a bunch of saved news articles. If you've been methodical and have saved all the files with a .news ending, you can delete all the files by using the command:

```
rm *.news
```

Another powerful feature of rm is that you can use it to wipe out a slew of files in a directory as well as the directory itself by using the recursive option.

Let's look at how it works. Say you've saved all those .news files in a directory called /savednews. To delete all the files in the /savednews directory as well as the directory itself, type the following:

```
rm -r savednews
```

TIP

The authors of *Voodoo UNIX* have a great TIP for keeping rm under control. If you add the line:

```
alias rm='rm -i'
```

to your .login, .cshrc, or .kshrc (depending on what shell you use) file, rm will always ask for confirmation.

Obviously, you can do a lot of damage with the rm command. One way to avoid wiping out files and directories you didn't mean to delete is to add the -i option. -i stands for "interactive." UNIX will prompt you to answer Yes or No to confirm every deletion. For a quick review of the **rm** command, see Table D-9.

rm [options] <filename>

Deletes files specified in <filename>.

Option	Description
-f	Deletes files that have been write protected without asking for confirmation.
-I	Interactive mode. Asks for confirmation before deleting.
-r	Recursive mode. Deletes directory specified in <filename>as well as everything in the directory.

Table D-9: rm synopsis.

cp

This one's simple. If you want to merely copy a file from one place to another, you can use cp to do so. Unlike mv, cp doesn't delete the source file. As you might imagine, cp is short for "copy." Using this command is as simple as reading it. To copy a file from one location to another, use the following syntax:

```
cp <current file location> <new file location>
```

Easy, huh? So, if you wanted to place a copy of the nigel.txt file in the /boh directory , you'd type:

```
cp nigel.txt /boh/nigel.txt
```

However, if you wanted to give your new file a different name, that's okay, too. Say we wanted to make a copy of nigel.txt, name it donovan.dat, and put it in the same directory. We'd use the command:

```
cp nigel.txt /boh/donovan.dat
```

cp <source file> <destination file>

Copies <source file> to <destination file>

Option	Description
-i	When you use the -i option, cp will prompt you to confirm each copying procedure, which is good if you're copying a bunch of files with a wildcard character.

➡

cp <source file> <destination file>	continued
-p	When you use this option, cp will preserve all the modification date and file permission information from the <source file> and apply it to the <destination file>
-r	Recursive mode. If you use cp -r <source directory> <destination directory>, cp will copy the contents of the source directory and place them in the destination directory

Table D-10: cp synopsis.

more

Here's where things get a little juicier. The more command doesn't do anything to the files or directories in your account. Instead, more is used for displaying text files on your screen. But that's not all. More causes the text in a file to be displayed one screenful at a time. When you more a file, you'll see the contents of the file scroll up the screen until they reach the top. Then, you'll see a little box that says "—More—(2%)" at the bottom of the screen.

```
explorer:[/homec/elrod] more ufospell.txt
0HF
0UP
110th
114th
129th
12th
13th
1597038cc
17th
1993Mar19
1DX
20Chester
20From
20from
21st
288th
2AQ
2TL
34th
3DTerminology
46AQ
46amily
--More--(2%)
```

Figure D-8: The more command in action.

So what's that "—More—(2%)" mean? Well, it's an indication that the more command is waiting for you to give it the okay to display more text. The percentage indicates how much of the file you've seen. If you want to display another screenful of text, press the spacebar. If you just want to advance the display a line at a time, press the Enter key. Not too complicated. But remember, this is UNIX—there's a lot more than meets the eye. Let's look at a couple of options available to you.

First of all, that little "—More—(2%)" can be tricky. Not only can you page ahead with the spacebar and advance line-by-line with the Enter key, you can actually control just about any movement throughout the file you want. Take a look at Table D-11 for some examples:

Command	Description
x SPACE	Display one more screenful of text made up of x lines. If *x* is not specified, more will display the system default number of lines-per-screenful.
x RETURN	If you specify a number for *x*, more will display *x* number of lines.
x Ctrl+d	Scroll down half a screenful— 11 lines. If a number *x* is specified, more will scroll down *x* number of lines.
x d	Can be used in place of Ctrl+d.
x Ctrl+b	Skips backwards *x* screenfuls and then displays a screenful of text.
x b	Can be used in place of Ctrl+b.
q or Q	Quit more.
=	Shows current line number.
V	This is a very useful command. Using v while in more will transfer you (and the file you are looking at) into the default editor that's been specified on your account by the $EDITOR environment variable.
/pattern	Searches for the character pattern specified.
H	Help. Shows you help for all the more commands.

Table D-11: Text display commands while using more.

As you can see, more is a useful little command. In fact, it's used by nearly every UNIX program that displays text. Depending on your system, you may encounter more while reading your mail, checking out Usenet news, or just bumming around in the various informational sections of the system, when you want to read a file. See Table D-12 for a brief synopsis of the more command.

more [options] <filename>

Displays the file <filename> to the screen one screenful at a time.

Option	Description
-c	Clears the screen before displaying each screenful of data instead of scrolling information up the screen. Depending on your configuration, this may be a faster way to view text files. Experiment.
-d	Displays detailed error messages instead of beeping. Great if you're a beginner.
-l	Causes more to ignore form feed (Ctrl+L) characters for a smoother display.
-s	Squeezes multiple blank lines into one line. Great for viewing text files that have lots of blank lines.
-w	Waits before exiting more at the end of a file.

Table D-12: more Synopsis.

who

By its very nature, UNIX is a multiuser operating system. When you log onto your account, you're not using the whole computer as you would when you turn on your PC at home. Instead, you're just using a small portion of the resources that your host has doled out to you. By using the who command, you can find out who else is logged on to the system. You can also see when they logged in and where they logged in from. Figure D-9 shows you an example of using the who command.

```
explorer:[/homec/elrod] who
lscott      pts/10     Nov   7 07:49     (annex8.clark.net)
eclipse     pts/8      Nov   7 11:10     (annex4.clark.net)
papete      pts/9      Nov   7 10:27     (annex5.clark.net)
noel        pts/33     Nov   7 12:17     (annex8.clark.net)
ftjones     pts/2      Nov   7 12:16     (annex4.clark.net)
destry      pts/16     Nov   7 12:20     (annex5.clark.net)
rhuckste    pts/47     Nov   7 12:19     (annex3.clark.net)
bgood       pts/28     Nov   7 10:00     (annex8.clark.net)
jvt         pts/12     Nov   7 07:33     (unknown.tycho.ncsc.mil)
akonopka    pts/108    Nov   7 12:17     (annex1.clark.net)
mac         pts/67     Nov   7 12:20     (annex5.clark.net)
drezenr     pts/53     Nov   7 12:19     (annex9.clark.net)
gregw       pts/177    Nov   7 12:07     (204.245.172.108)
kolesar     pts/13     Nov   7 04:41     (annex8.clark.net)
pkilpe      pts/84     Nov   7 11:38     (pkilpe.clark.net)
mcoletti    pts/57     Nov   7 09:42     (resdgw17.er.usgs.gov)
zilla       pts/29     Nov   7 10:29     (atticus.nlm.nih.gov)
robertsj    pts/90     Nov   7 12:02     (annex6.clark.net)
tjordan     pts/27     Nov   7 07:42     (omaha.gsfc.nasa.gov)
eq          pts/17     Nov   7 06:22     (mail.bcpl.lib.md.us)
saucillo    pts/1      Nov   7 12:11     (annex6.clark.net)
elrod       pts/23     Nov   7 12:13     (elrod-ppp.clark.net)
cpaulus     pts/24     Nov   7 11:56     (annex5.clark.net)
```

Figure D-9: A user listing generated from the who command.

Let's take a look at what all this means. Starting from the far left column, who tells you the user name of the person on the account. In the next column, you'll see what "terminal line" they're logged in from. This isn't too important. Continuing to the right, the next two columns show the date and time that the user first logged in. Finally, the last column tells you where they logged in from.

You'll notice that a lot of the addresses in the far right column start with "annex." If you're dialing in to a large computer system by modem, you'll probably notice a similar listing when you do a who. That's because many dial-up service providers use low-powered annex computers to handle the details of modem calls.

who is useful when you want to see if a friend is online or if you want to check to see if someone else is using your account. If you do a who and see that someone you know is logged in, you can then use the UNIX talk or write commands to send the person a message.

TIP

If you log in, use who, and see that your username is listed more than once, you may want to contact your system administrator. Someone could have hacked into your account.

If you use multiple accounts, who is a useful and an existentially poignant option that you can use to find information about what account name you're using at the time. Just type **who am I**, and who will tell you what username you're using.

---

who [options]

Displays information about who is currently logged in to the system as well as other vital system information. Use who by itself if you just want to see who else is logged in.

Option	Description
-a	Displays all information about other users including terminal status.
-b	Tells you the last time the server was rebooted.
-q	Displays only a list of usernames and a count of users current online.
-T	Displays the state of the terminal and whether you can "write" to it.

Table D-13: who Synopsis.

---

ps

Not only is UNIX a multiuser system, but it's a multitasking system as well. That means that you can run more than one program or process from your account at the same time. Why would you want to do that? Well, one reason is if you're going to execute a program that takes a long time to run. With multitasking you can put that program in the background so that it doesn't hold up your account while you do other stuff.

Let's take a look at an example. We'll assume that your host has the Archie program installed on it so that you can search for files on the Net.

Say you want to find a file called somemacfile.hqx. If you don't mind waiting until Archie's finished searching, you can command Archie to search for that file by typing:

```
archie somemacfile.hqx
```

Within a few minutes, Archie will tell you what it found. In the mean time, you'll have to wait. But, since you're a power user, you don't want to wait, do you? What do you do? Let Archie search in the background while you get on with your life! To do that, type the following command, and press Enter:

```
archie somemacfile.hqx > filesfound.txt &
```

You should see something like this:

```
[1] 19227
```

19927 is the process ID of the job you've just started running in the background. It will crank along in the background until it's done, and then, when the process has finished, it will notify you with a message like:

```
[1]  + Exit 1     archie somemacfile.hqx > filesfound.txt
```

If you want to go look at what files Archie found for you, take a look at the filesfound.txt file using the more command (you didn't forget already did you!)

But let's step back a minute and look at what we just did. First, we told Archie to find the file called somemacfile.txt. Then, using the magic of UNIX redirection, we used > filesfound.txt to put the output from Archie into a file called filesfound.txt. Finally, using the & operator, we put the job in the background until it was finished.

Pretty cool, eh? You can use this trick to put just about as many jobs in the background as you want—search Archie, send files, and search databases without having to wait.

To keep track of all this backgrounding, you need the ps command (See Table D-14). Ps prints a list of processes so that you can see what's going on in the background. Take our previous example. While it was running, if you had typed ps, you would have seen a listing of all the process IDs and what processes they were running. If you know the process number, you can bring a process into the foreground, if you want to see how it's coming along, by typing:

```
fg [process ID]
```

ps [options]	
Option	Description
-a	Prints the most requested processes. Useful if you want to see what other programs people on your system are using.
-e	Shows you all the processes currently running on your host system.

Table D-14: ps Synopsis.

kill

Sorry to disappoint you, but this command's not a cure for that guy in the next cubicle who talks too much. Instead, you can use it to cancel a process that's running out of control or has been going on for too long. Let's say that you're doing an Archie search in the background (as in our last example). It's been ten minutes, and you still don't have your answer. Chances are, Archie's hung up or the server's down. In that case, when you've given up on your process ever finishing, issue a kill.

First, do a ps to get a list of processes that you're running. Let's say that our Archie process is Process ID number 19227. If you want to cancel it, just type the following, and press Enter:

```
kill 19227
```

The process will stop, and the system resources will be freed up.

One way that kill is particularly useful is if you're ever forced to quit a program you're running using a terminal break command. Often, this will kick you out of the program and back to the command line. You might think that everything's peachy, but when you try to log out, you can't. You're informed that you've got a process still running. Most likely, that process is the program that you forced yourself out of. If you want to log out, do a ps to get the process ID number and then kill it. Now you can log out.

grep

How many times have you *sworn* that you had an important bit of information in a file somewhere on your account but you weren't able to find it. It's grep to the rescue!

The grep command comes from an old line-editor command g/re/p meaning "globally search for a regular expression and print." In plain English, what grep does is simple: It searches a file for a regular expression or specially defined search pattern and then prints all the lines containing that search pattern.

So, what's it useful for? A heck of a lot. See, in UNIX, a file can be just about anything, including a stream of text. That means if you send the output of any program that outputs text to grep, you can use grep to search that output.

Say that you want to find all the files in your account that have been created in October. If you just use the old ls -l command, you'll have to search out those files yourself from the list on the screen. However, if you pipe the output of ls -l to grep, you can let grep do the searching:

```
ls -l | grep "Oct"
```

When you use this command, you'll just see a list of all the files that were created in October because grep looked for the pattern "Oct" in the output of ls -l. And just like we mentioned at the beginning, grep is great for finding information in files. For example, if you wanted to find any HTML files on your account, you could use the command:

```
grep "HTML" *.*
```

Because you've used the wildcard characters (*.*), grep will search any file on your account for the string "HTML" and output any line containing the string HTML, printing the name of the file along with the line containing the word:

```
test.html: <HTML>
web.doc.txt: HTML is a subset of the SGML markup language
```

The real power of grep lies in its ability to define searches with regular expressions—strings of text with special pattern-matching characters that allow you to define amazingly flexible searches. (See Table D-15 for a once-over on grep commands.) For more information on how to define searches, turn back to Part VIII "Netsearching: Unleashing Your Code Hound." But make sure you come back. We've got a lot more to cover before we're through with UNIX. Are we having fun yet?

grep [options] "pattern" <filename>	
Option	**Description**
-c	Shows only a count of the number of lines that match "pattern."
-i	Disables case-sensitive searches. If you use the -i option, the pattern "word" will match both word and WORD.
-l	Shows only the names of the files that contain a string matching the pattern.
-n	Prints line numbers along with the lines that match.
-v	Print all the lines that don't match the search pattern. This option is useful if you're trying to determine the differences between two files.

Table D-15: grep synopsis.

< > ? << & >> | * ~ !! or What Are Those Funky Characters for Anyway?

Along the way in your UNIX career, you're sure to encounter examples in books or on the Net that use strange characters. Don't worry—they weren't invented just to make your life more confusing. Many of these characters have special uses that can accomplish all kinds of interesting stuff.

Table D-16 shows most of the special symbols in UNIX and their uses. At this point, this table might not be too useful to you, but we're providing it as a way of setting the stage for what's to come. In this next section, we'll take a look at what they do.

Character	Use
>	Redirects output to a file.
<	Redirects input from a file.
>>	Appends to existing file.
|	Pipes to command.
!!	Repeats previous command. Also called "command history."
*	Serves as multi-character wildcard .
?	Serves as single-character wildcard.
[]	Matches characters in brackets.
&	Places process in background.

Table D-16: Special UNIX characters and uses.

> Redirect Output to a File

One great thing about UNIX is that it treats the text input and output from programs as streams of characters, which allows you to take that stream of characters and redirect it to someplace else.

Using the > symbol allows you to send the output of a program to a file on your account. By using it, you can, for instance, take the long, screen-filling output from a program and send it to a file for later reading. We've already looked at one example with using the Archie command. Archie spits back a long list of programs that it has found, and often this list can be kind of hard to read as it flies up the screen, especially if you don't have a way of scrolling backwards. If you wanted Archie to send its output to a file you could read later, use this command:

```
archie somefilename > archie.find.list.txt
```

Poof! All of Archie's output will go into the file archie.find.list.txt for later reading.

Or, say that you were working on a project involving lots of different files. If you wanted to send your friend a list of files that you were using, you could dump your directory listing into a text file with the following command:

```
ls -la > mydirectory.txt
```

The output from ls -la would go into the file named mydirectory.txt, which you could then send to your friend.

< Redirect Input from a File

Redirection can work the other way, too. By using < , you can take the contents of a file and redirect them so that they function as if you had typed them from the keyboard.

While we'll cover a lot more about using UNIX mail later on in this appendix, for now we'll at least assume that you know that the basic mail command on UNIX is mail. Remember how, in the previous example, you learned how to dump your directory listing into a text file so that you could send it to your friend? We saw how you could put the listing in a file but not how you could actually send it. Here's how:

```
mail yourfriends@email.address < mydirectory.txt
```

That's it! The command mail yourfriends@email.address invokes mail and tells it that the message you are going to send is going to yourfriends@email.address.

Here's where the magic comes in. By redirecting the file mydirectory.txt into the mail yourfriends@email.address command, you're putting the text of mydirectory.txt into an e-mail message and sending it off—all in one command line.

>> Append to an Existing File

We come to this operator by way of a caution. If you use the > redirection operator to redirect output to a file, UNIX clobbers any old file with the same name to make way for the new one. So, what do you do if you want to keep sending different information into the same file? You use the >> command to append each new chunk of text to the file you've already created.

Let's look at an example. Say your newbie friend sends you a message asking you to use Archie to find several files for him and then send him the searches. Ordinarily, we'd say "Tell your friend to buy this book!" but then we wouldn't have an example to show you. If the files that your friend was searching for were called area51.txt, roswell.txt, and abduction.guide.txt, the search would go like this:

```
archie area51.txt > mulder.search.txt
archie roswell.txt >> mulder.search.txt
archie abduction.guide.txt >> mulder.search.txt
```

The first line tells Archie to search for area51.txt and place it in a file called mulder.search.txt. The other two lines perform their own searches and then append the search findings to that same mulder.search.txt file. When you're finished, you can send your search results to your friend by using that other redirection command:

```
mail fmulder@fbi.gov < mulder.search.txt
```

| Pipe to Command

Besides sending output to files, you can send the output of one command to the input of another command by using the | or pipe operator. | sets up a pipe between two commands. Like a pipe, | functions as a conduit, moving output from the first command into the input of the second command. This might not seem too clear, so let's look at some examples.

First, suppose you had a directory that was chock-full of stuff. As soon as you type ls, the listing just goes flying up the screen into the ether, never to be seen again. You can get that directory listing to pause so that you can look at it by piping the output from the ls command into the more command. That way, as soon as ls outputs a screenful of information, more will pause the listing until you hit the spacebar. Here's how:

```
ls | more
```

The output from your listing will fill the screen, and then more will pause and wait for you to press the spacebar before giving you another screen of text.

If you've ever used ftp through UNIX to get a file, you know that sometimes it would be nice to be able to read some of the text files on the remote computer before downloading them. This is especially true if you're downloading files from an archive site that has a directory.txt file containing descriptions of all the files.

TIP

If you've never used ftp, you may want to brush up on it. Go to Chapter 19, "UNIX Net Tools Gallery," for a description of using ftp through UNIX.

Not a problem. From ftp, all you have to do is issue the following command:

```
get directoryfile.txt | more
```

Once you do this, ftp will transfer the file named directoryfile.txt to your more command, allowing you to read it one screenful at a time.

!! Repeat Previous Command

This one's different from the other commands we've looked at so far. It really doesn't have anything to do with input or output at all. Instead, ! ! can save you time. If you're at the command line and want to repeat a command that you just used, use ! !. Once you use it, the line that you had previously typed will appear on the screen.

Wildcards: * and ?

We're lumping these two together because they are just different ways of using a similar concept—wildcards. If you use DOS, you already know what wildcards can do. If not, here's a brief definition: wildcards are characters that can be used to stand for one or more characters when using commands that perform actions on a file or files. Using wildcards, you perform actions on a whole bunch of files with similar names. Here's an example.

Let's say that you've just written a book. Let's call it the *Internet Power Toolkit*. Now that you're finished, the time has come to put all the separate chapters into one file called book.txt. How do you do it? Using wildcards, of course. If you had named each chapter with its chapter number (chapter1.txt, chapter2.txt, chapter3.txt), you could use the following command to put them all together.

```
cat chap*.txt >> book.txt
```

The command cat tells UNIX to dump the contents of the file to the screen. But, if you'll notice, we used the redirect and append operators >> to redirect the output of cat to a file called book.txt. If you entered this command, UNIX would take all the files that contained the string "chap" (our chapter titles) and append them to the file called book.txt.

The * wildcard stands for any number of characters. If we had files called chapter1old.txt, chapter1.txt, and chapterfigures.txt, they all would have been put in the book.txt file. That would be a problem, since all we wanted were the numbered chapters.

To get around that problem, we could have used the ? wildcard character. It matches only one character. So, the improved command that just dumps the chapters to book.txt would be:

```
cat chap?.txt >> book.txt
```

Wildcards can be used in just about any situation in which you want to perform an operation on a number of files. However, using wildcards with commands that only expect one file, like mail, won't work. For example, the following command wouldn't work correctly:

```
mail editor@vmedia.com << chap*.txt
```

[] Match Characters in Brackets

If you want to just perform an operation on files that contain a certain character, you can use brackets to specify what characters have to exist in the filename in order for the file to be selected.

As in our previous example, what if you wanted to put absolutely everything containing the characters IPTK (Internet Power Toolkit) into a file called masterbook.txt? The problem is, some of the files have IPTK in the middle of the name, some at the beginning, some at the end. If you use the following command, you would put all the files that contain I, P, T, or K into the masterbook.txt file:

```
cat [IPTK]* >> masterbook.txt
```

& Place Process in the Background

If you've been diligently following along up until now, you've seen the & operator at work when we discussed job control, foregrounding, and backgrounding. If you've skipped ahead to this point (you slacker!) or have forgotten already, here's a little refresher.

One of UNIX's niftiest features is that it allows you to multitask, or run several programs (or processes) at once. You can search at the same time that you're spell-checking a file, grepping a file, and writing a letter. That is, you can if you know how to control your processes.

What the & operator does is allow you to start a job running and then put it in the background until it's complete. When a job is in the background, it cooks along at its own pace, accomplishing your work, all while you go off to do other things. When it's complete, it'll pop a message onto the screen so you'll know that it's finished.

Like we said—with &, you can search, grep, spellcheck, and do e-mail all at the same time if you want. Look at this example:

```
>archie redbox.txt > redsearch.txt&
 [1] 25611
>spell sean.txt >> seanserrors.txt &
 [2] 25639
>grep "JFK" gemstone.txt > jfksearch.txt &
 [3] 25666
>elm
```

In this example, we first did an Archie search for the redbox.txt file. We put the search in the background, and UNIX told us its process number. Next, we did a spellcheck on one of Sean's files, put it in the background, and got another process number. Finally, we searched the gemstone.txt file for the string "JFK," put it in the background, and got another process number. Finally, we started the elm mail program, went off, and sent a message. When we exit out of elm, we'd probably see something like this:

```
[1]   Done       archie redbox.txt > redsearch.txt
[2]   Done       sean.txt >> seanserrors.txt
[3]   Done       grep "JFK" gemstone.txt > jfksearch.txt
>
```

All of the jobs are done, completed while we did other stuff! Now, if you look in your directory, you'd see that the files redsearch.txt, seanserrors.txt, and jfksearch.txt are all in the directory, ready to be viewed.

The only drawback of using & to place jobs in the background is that you can't background jobs that require input from you unless you're redirecting a command file (using <), which takes care of your input. Also, any job that you put in the background that outputs to the screen will pop up and run as soon as it begins its output. That's why we redirected the output to a file.

Basic UNIX Troubleshooting

No matter how carefully you've been following along, chances are you may run into a problem or two. Here's some troubleshooting advice for the new UNIX user that may help:

❏ UNIX commands are case sensitive. The word MAN is not the same as the command man. In fact, almost without exception, UNIX commands are lowercase. It's best to get in the habit of just using lowercase.

❏ Make sure that you're trying to operate on a file you actually have in your directory. To see where you are, type **pwd**. It'll tell you your current working directory.

❏ If you are getting weird characters or you see ^H when you try to use your backspace key, make sure that you've used stty to set your terminal control characters correctly.

❏ Be absolutely sure that when you use rm or > that you are deleting or overwriting the correct file. UNIX has no way to undelete files, so when you've made a boo-boo, it's too late.

❏ Filenames are case sensitive, too. Trying to operate on a file named FILE when what you really want is file can be frustrating. Get in the habit of using lowercase!

❏ If your account is locked up and nothing happens when you try to type, you've got a few options. First, you can just turn off your modem, dial in again, and start over. Or, if you're in the middle of something important, you can try one of the following:

   a) Press the Enter or Return keys a few times. If you don't introduce Enter or Return key characters, UNIX doesn't know that you want it to execute your command.

   b) Type **Ctrl+Q**. You may have suspended a process by hitting Ctrl+S accidentally.

   c) Type **Ctrl+Z**, which will suspend the program you are in and give you a new prompt. Type **ps** to get a process list, and then try **fg [process number]** to re-enter your suspended process.

   d) Try typing **Ctrl+C**. This may quit you out of the program that has frozen your computer.

   e) Look at the modem. If you have lost your connection, you'll have to dial in again.

   f) If your terminal program can send a break character (such as Zterm for the Macintosh can), try it. You may have to log in again, but at least you won't have to go through the whole dial-up procedure again.

❏ If the system is running slowly, it may be that it is over-loaded. Remember, UNIX is a multi-user operating system. If you're using your account during prime time (usually between 6pm and 11pm on weekdays), there's nothing you can do.

❑ What do you do if you've forgotten your password? Not much. Call your system administrator, steel yourself for his or her wrath, and don't forget your password next time.

❑ If you can't find your .login or .profile file, or any other. files for that matter, remember to use the ls -l command. The ordinary ls command will not show you these hidden files.

❑ If none of these hints solve your problem, try the most useful troubleshooting tool of all: the telephone. Pick it up, call the person responsible for your system, and explain the problem. This method will probably work better than any other for solving your UNIX problems.

A Glossary of Common Internet Terms & Slang

alias   A shortcut or nickname that represents something else. For instance, in an e-mail program, you can assign the alias "IPTK" to represent the e-mail addresses of all the people involved in the Internet Power Toolkit project. To send mail to them all, you would put "IPTK" in the To: field of your e-mail program. In UNIX, you might assign the familiar DOS "copy" as an alias for the UNIX "cp" command.

applet   A Java program that can be included in an HTML document. *See also* **Java**.

anonymous remailer   A forwarding system on the Internet that lets you send anonymous messages to (and receive responses from) newsgroups and e-mail addresses, all without revealing your identity.

Archie   A Net-based service that allows you to locate files available for downloading via FTP. *See also* **FTP**.

AU sounds   A common audio file format. Other audio formats include WAV, AIFF, and MIDI.

AT commands   The series of commands used to program a Hayes-compatible modem. AT is short for attention.

bandwidth   In broadcasting, bandwidth is the measure, in hertz (Hz), of the spectrum between the highest frequency and the lowest. On the Net, bandwidth is used to refer to the amount of data that can fit through a network connection.

baud rate   In technical terms, the number of signal transitions per second of a modem transfer. In common usage, baud rate is considered the same as the number of bits per second that a modem can transfer, even though technically they are not the same. Bits per second (bps) is a better way of referring to the speed of a modem.

BinHex   A file conversion format that changes binary files into ASCII text files and vice-versa.

bookmarks   The term most prominently used in Navigator (and other Web tools) for the stored URLs of frequently visited Net locations. In Internet Explorer, the term is *favorites* and in Mosaic, *hotlists*.

bounce   E-mail that cannot be delivered to its intended recipient "bounces" back to your mailbox with a new message header that describes why the transaction didn't go through.

box   Techno-slang for any digital device, especially a computer. "I just got a new box, a screamin' Pentium 180 MHz." The term can also refer to a device that's used by phone phreaks to make free phone calls, tap a phone or something similarly illegal. The function of these boxes is indicated by their color (a red box, for instance, mimics the sounds of coins dropping into a payphone to fool it into thinking you've paid).

bozo.filter   Increasingly used as an alternative term for kill file (as it applies to filters on users' names and addresses). The first bozo.filter was written by Jef Poskanzer for the UNIX-based Well BBS. Once you encounter a posting from someone that you've put into your bozolist, the post is deleted and replaced by the message: <bozofiltered>. Also called a *twit filter*. *See also* **kill file**.

bridge   A hardware and software configuration used to link computer networks together.

chat   Conversations in IRC (Internet Relay Chat) and other text-based conversation areas of the Net are called *chats*. IRC programs are called *chat clients*. America Online calls its "People Connection" areas *chat rooms*. *See also* **IRC**.

client   A computer (or application) that has access to services over a network. The computer that can be accessed by the client is called a *server*. Once connected, the client can access the various services available on the server such as FTP, Gopher, and HTTP.

client/server   The client/server scheme involves a client program (such as Netscape) connected to a server program on a host computer. The client sends a request to the server, which then takes the request, processes it, and then reconnects to the client to send the requested info. This is in contrast to traditional Internet databases to which you connect remotely (via Telnet or some other form of connection) and then proceed to actually run the program from the remote site.

codec (compression/decompression)   Compression technique used to reduce the size of audio and video files for transfer. Codecs compress the analog input on the sending end and decompress it for output on the receiving end. Popular audio codecs (used in Net phones, for instance) include GSM, the European "Global Standard for Mobile Communications," TrueSpeech, and Lernout and Hauspie. Video codecs include Cinepak and Indeo.

connectoid   Slang in Windows 95 for a Dial-Up Networking (DUN) connection. *See also* **dial-up connection.**

cyberspace   Word coined by sci-fi writer William Gibson to refer to a near-future computer network on which users can mentally travel through matrices of data. The term is now often used to describe today's Internet.

cracker   A computer hacker with malicious or criminal intent. The mainstream media refuses to differentiate between benign hackers and malicious crackers, despite the computer community's attempts to clarify the difference. *See also* **hacker**.

cryptography   The creation, manipulation, and deciphering of coded messages.

decrypt   To undo or decipher an encrypted message.

daemon   (Pronounced "day-mon") A program that runs in the background to carry on certain tasks while other processes run in the foreground. The term derives from the word for helpful servant and does not refer to those more fiendish servants of Satan called *demons*.

Data Encryption Standard (DES)   A data encryption standard developed by NIST (National Institute of Standards and Technology).

datagram   A packet of information transmitted and received with networking protocols. A datagram can vary in size depending on the protocol being used.

dial-up connection   A connection from your computer to an Internet-connected computer over standard phone lines, using a modem. Dial-up connection types include shell accounts (dialing into a UNIX host) and SLIP and PPP type connections.

dial-in connection   This term is sometimes used to distinguish between a shell account in which you dial into a host machine and a SLIP or PPP connection in which you dial up a service provider who establishes a temporary direct connection for you to the Internet. In this book, we've used the term *shell account* instead of *dial in*.

Dial-Up Networking (DUN)   Microsoft's name for their suite of programs and utilities that allow you to connect your PC to another PC, a LAN, and/or the Internet.

digital signature   A document authentication scheme that amends an electronic document with a unique cryptographic "signature" that can alert the recipient if the document is a forgery or has been tampered with in any way.

direct connection   A permanent connection between a computer system (either a single CPU or a LAN) and the Internet. This is sometimes called a *leased line connection* because you are leasing the telephone connection from the phone company. A direct connection is in contrast to a *dial-up connection*.

DNS (Domain Name Service)   A database used for resolving hostnames and IP addresses. Allows users' machines to query the database for domain names so that users don't have to enter numeric IP addresses. *See also* **IP address**.

document   The term *document* is used generically to refer to any digital file type, whether text, graphic, sound, etc.

document window   In a Web browser, the scrollable window in which HTML documents can be viewed is commonly referred to as the *document window*.

DSP (Digital Signal Processor)   A microprocessor designed to handle audio and video signal processing. You'll find DSPs in sound cards, modems, and audio/video compression hardware.

duplex   A communications connection that allows you to send and receive data at the same time is said to be *full duplex*. A connection is *half duplex* if it can only handle sending or receiving one at a time. *Full duplex* capability is important if you want to use an Internet phone or video teleconferencing software.

encryption   The act of scrambling information so that only those with access to certain key information can unscramble (or decrypt) it.

Ethernet   Popular local area network technology.

external viewer   *See* **helper applications**.

e-zines   Electronic zines—publications with limited circulation, that are distributed over computer networks. The word *zines* comes from the print world where it's used to describe do-it-yourself publications.

FAQ (frequently asked questions)   Allegedly pronounced "fak," although we always say "F-A-Q." A text file on the Internet that answers commonly asked questions on a given subject. FAQs are a major source of Net-related knowledge and wisdom.

finger   A UNIX command that can access information about a user or group of users on a network. Finger queries are made either by using a finger client or by typing **finger** *user@host.domain* at a UNIX prompt.

firewall   A computer that acts as a security gateway between a local network and a larger network. The firewall monitors and restricts data traffic between networks according to various security criteria specified by the systems administrator/computer security person.

flame   An angry response to a Usenet posting or e-mail message. Protracted, argumentative exchanges sparked by an initial flame are called flame wars. New users who haven't read the appropriate FAQs, and virtual door-to-door salespeople who spam newsgroups, are often the target of flames.

frame relay   A network connectivity option that can provide Internet access at speeds between 56KB and 1.5MB.

freenet   Large community bulletin board system that provides free accounts to local residents. Many freenets provide full Internet access. Freenets are supported by the National Public Telecommunications Network (NPTN) based in Cleveland, Ohio.

freeware   Software that's distributed free of charge. Lots of freeware, much of it quite good, is available on the Internet. So much freeware, in fact, that frugal Netsurfers can get most of the software they'll need free-of-charge. *See also* **shareware**.

FTP (File Transfer Protocol)   A commonly used protocol for transferring files from one computer to another. FTP also refers to the act of transferring files (e.g., "I need to FTP Shockwave from TUCOWS").

gateway   A computer that transfers data between ordinarily incompatible applications or networks. Not to be confused with a router that transfers data between compatible networks.

GIF (graphic interchange format)   Pronounced "jiff." A file compression format developed by CompuServe for transferring graphics files to and from online services. Now a common Internet-wide graphic exchange program.

Gopher   A menu-driven system for searching online information resources on the Internet.

Gopherspace   Another term used to describe the entire Gopher network spanning the Net.

GSM (Global Standard for Mobile Communications)   *See* **codec**.

hacker   A computer enthusiast who enjoys pushing the limits of computer hardware and software, and their own knowledge. The original pioneers of the personal computer were hackers. *See* **cracker**.

helper applications   Programs used for presenting graphics, audio, video, and other external applications in a Web browser. Also sometimes called *external viewers*.

hit   Every time a Web page is contacted, it registers a *hit* (assuming it has the appropriate logging software installed). Many Web pages have counters at the bottom that indicate how many hits the page has received.

home page   The document that's displayed when you first open a Web browser. Also, commonly used to refer to the first document you come to in a collection of documents on a Web site.

host   A computer that users can log in to in order to run programs and access services.

hotlink   *See* **hyperlink**.

hotlist   *See* **bookmarks**.

HTML (HyperText Markup Language)   A system for marking (or tagging) the various parts of a Web document to tell the browser software how to display the document's text, links, graphics, and linked media.

HTML document   Any document tagged in the HTML format. HTML documents that are accessible on the Web are referred to as *Web documents*.

HTTP (HyperText Transport Protocol)   The communications protocol used to transfer documents from servers to clients over the World Wide Web.

hyperlink   Parts of a Web document that are linked to other parts of the same document, other documents, or external media files. *Hyperlink* is actually redundant; *link* works just fine.

hypermedia   The hypertext concept extended to include linked multiple media such as graphics, movies, and audio.

hypertext   Documents that are cross-linked in such a way that the reader can explore nonlinear information trails through them. For example, clicking on a word might take the reader to a definition of that word or to another document related to it.

inline media   Graphics or other media contained within a Web document. This media can be either loaded automatically when the page is accessed, or manually by clicking on an inline image icon.

IMHO   Online shorthand for "in my humble opinion." IMNSHO stands for "in my not so humble opinion." And then there's IMNERHO for "in my not even remotely humble opinion."

IP address   The 32-bit addressing standard used by the Internet Protocol. Every resource on the Net has a unique IP address, represented in dotted decimal notation (e.g., 198.72.13.150). Besides this numerical form, there's also a corresponding domain name in the form of: *subnetwork.network.domain* (e.g., *www.vmedia.com*).

IPX/SPX   A Windows local area network protocol for connecting to Novell's NetWare and recent versions of Windows NT.

IRC (Internet Relay Chat)   Real-time global text chatting over the Internet. Participants must have IRC chat software and be connected to an IRC server. Once connected, the users can choose various "channels" centered around different topics.

ISDN (Integrated Services Digital Network)   A digital phone connection technology that provides both voice and data services over the same connection. ISDN can provide high-speed Internet access at 56KB.

ISP (Internet Service Provider)   A company that provides Internet access and other Net-related services.

Java   A language designed by SunSoft (a division of Sun Microsystems). Java programs are stored on a server. Browsers that support the <APPLET> tag download Java applications and execute them. The applications are known as Java *applets*. Java can also be used to write stand-alone applications: the HotJava browser is one example.

JavaScript   A series of extensions to the HTML language used by Web browsers. It's an interpreted language designed for controlling the browser. It can open and close windows, manipulate form elements, adjust browser settings, and download and execute applets. Although JavaScript has a syntax similar to Java, it is distinct in many ways.

Jughead   No, not the goofy comic book character, this is Jughead the indexing tool that's used in Gopherspace. *See also* **Veronica** and **Gopher**.

JPEG (Joint Photographic Experts Group)   An image compression format used to transfer images over computer networks.

key   A quantity used in cryptography to encrypt or decrypt information. *See also* **private key** and **public key**.

Kermit   An older file transfer protocol. Still commonly included in communications software, Kermit is not used as much as Xmodem, Ymodem, and Zmodem.

kill file   A set of criteria that can be set to filter unwanted postings from a newsgroup or an e-mail mailbox. Most kill file schemes allow you to do very sophisticated pattern matching using UNIX's regular expressions. The opposite of killing is usually called *autoselecting*. *See also* **bozo.filter**.

links   *See* **hotlink** and **hyperlink**.

local area network (LAN)   Locally wired network usually consisting of coaxial cable or twisted pair telephone wiring (as in 10BaseT Ethernet). To gain Internet access, the LAN must be connected to the Internet and be configured so it is capable of handling TCP/IP data packets. *See also* **WAN**.

lurking   Users who read BBS, IRC, and Usenet postings but don't respond are said to be *lurking*. On CU-SeeMe video, some chats specify "No Lurkers."

MIDI (Musical Instrument Digital Interface)   A communications protocol and hardware specification for electronic instruments and computers.

MIME (Multipurpose Internet Mail Extensions)   A specification developed for attaching sounds, images, and other media files to electronic mail messages. Designated by a series of types/subtypes (e.g., image/gif, where image is the general type of file, and gif is the specific format). MIME file types are also used in World Wide Web browsers to activate helper applications.

mirror site   Some popular FTP and WWW sites create mirror sites on other systems to redirect traffic jams on their sites. These mirror sites contain an exact copy of the parent sites.

MOO   An acronym for MUD-Object Oriented. MOOs are multiuser, text-based environments where people can explore virtual worlds while interacting with other users. MOOs contain their own internal object oriented programming languages that people on the MOO can use to create their own objects and locations. *See also* **MUD**.

MPEG (Moving Pictures Expert Group)   MPEG is an international standard for video compression and desktop movie presentation. You need a special viewing application to run MPEG "movies" on your computer.

MUD (Multiuser Dungeon or Domain)   A MUD is a multiuser, text-based virtual world. Usually, people "on" a MUD assume a new identity (called a *character* or an *avatar*) while exploring the world and interacting with other characters. Many MUDs are based on fantasy role-playing or science fiction themes.

multicasting   A way of transmitting TCP/IP packets to many users at the same time. Ordinarily, TCP/IP is a point-to-point protocol, only allowing two computers to "talk" to each other at a time. Multicasting allows networking information to be broadcast to the Net where it can "picked up" by many different people.

NCSA   The National Center for Supercomputing Applications at the University of Illinois, Urbana-Champaign. Developers of Mosaic, NCSA Telnet, and a number of other Internet applications.

NetBEUI   A Windows local area network protocol for connecting to earlier versions of Windows NT servers and Windows for Workgroups. *See also* **IPX/SPX**.

Netiquette   The etiquette, or socially-constructed rules of online behavior. Practicing good Netiquette helps to integrate you into the various online communities.

Network Interface Card (NIC)   Hardware (e.g., an Ethernet card) that connects your computer to a local area network.

NNTP   (Network News Transport Protocol)   The protocol that defines how Usenet news traffic will be posted, distributed, retrieved, etc.

packet   A standard unit of data. On the Internet, data is broken down into small bundles called *packets*. These packets travel independently through the network and are recombined on the receiving end to present the data in its original form.

POP (Point of Presence)   The local node of an ISP who owns or leases an access point so that it can provide local dial-up service to its far-flung customers. Many large and medium-sized online services maintain POPs in major cities and other key access points.

POP (Post Office Protocol)   The protocol that is used to allow users to retrieve mail from a server. E-mail sent to you arrives at the server and waits for you to log in and retrieve it.

POTS (plain old telephone system)   What you're using when you pick up your telephone. Brought to you by Ma Bell and her babies.

PPP (Point-to-Point Protocol)   A type of Internet connection in which a computer can use phone lines and a modem to connect to the Internet (without having to connect to a host). PPP connections are rented from a local Internet service provider.

private key   In public key cryptography, this is the key you keep secret. *See also* **key** and **public key**.

public key   In public key cryptography, the key you make public so that others can encrypt messages to you using your public key. Your private key is the only key that can then be used to decrypt the message. *See also* **key** and **private key**.

QuickTime   A digital video standard developed by Apple Computer. QuickTime is now standard on all Mac and Windows systems.

reflector   A computer designed to "reflect" a single incoming message or data stream to several other computers. Mail reflectors take one incoming message and broadcast it to a group of subscribers. CU-SeeMe reflectors allow several users to view each other's video data.

Registry   In Windows 95, the Registry is a huge database that contains types of information that used to be contained in Windows 3.*x* INI files. The Registry also contains various application preferences, system-wide settings, and descriptions of all the installed hardware.

regular expression   A term from the land of UNIX, a regular expression is a string of characters that are used for text pattern matching. A regular expression is used in many e-mail and newsreader programs to define text strings that you want to ignore. *See also* **kill file**.

RJ11   The standard phone plug used in the United States and 50 percent of the world.

robot (or bot)   A computer program that can automatically search the Internet. Robots that are used on the Web to hunt information to build databases are called *spiders*. *See also* **Web spider**.

ROFL   Online shorthand for "rolling on the floor laughing."

RFC (Request for Comments)   The set of technical documents that describe the standards and protocols on which the Internet is based. These RFCs are readily available online.

router   A system that transfers data between compatible networks using the same protocols.

RTFM (Read The Friggin' Manual)   Online shorthand used to admonish someone for asking a question that could have been easily answered by reading documentation or an FAQ file.

server   A computer that offers various services (document viewing, file transfer, etc.) to other computers (called *clients*) over a network.

shareware   A "try before you buy" software distribution method. Shareware authors freely distribute their offerings. If you try out a program, like it, and plan on using it, you send the author a shareware fee (usually less than the cost of a comparable commercial package). *See also* **freeware**.

shell account   A dial-in account on a UNIX host machine.

signature file (or sig file)   A text document that serves as a sort of calling card that can be appended to an e-mail message or Usenet posting. Sig files often contain the user's name, address, phone number, e-mail addresses, Web page URLs, quotes, simple ASCII art, and anything else that the person wants to share with readers.

slag (or bit slag)   Internet slang for all of the "useless" data you have to wade through to get to the essential information. Slag includes routing headers and footers, commented text, sig files, and boring posts. Also called *cybercrud*.

SLIP (Serial Line Internet Protocol)   A type of Internet connection in which a computer can use phone lines and a modem to connect to the Internet (without having to connect to a host). SLIP connections are rented from a local Internet service provider.

SMTP (Simple Mail Transport Protocol)   The e-mail protocol used to transfer mail from one Internet server to another. The user then accesses the Post Office Protocol (POP) to download the mail to his or her local machine.

spamming   The act of flooding Usenet newsgroups with obnoxious commercial postings or unwanted propaganda. Netiquette dictates that the newsgroups are for conversation and information exchange, not advertising and leafleting. Although "spam" has come to mean all forms of USENET (and e-mail) advertising, it specifically refers to ads that have been posted individually to each newsgroup. A commercial posting that has been cross-posted to a number of groups is sometimes called Velveeta (for that other charming processed food product).

tags   Formatting codes used in HTML documents. These tags indicate how the parts of a document will appear when displayed by browsing software.

TCP/IP (Transmission Control Protocol/Internet Protocol)   A suite of network communications protocols used for specifying how packets of data will be constructed, transferred, error corrected, etc. Windows machines wishing to connect to the Internet need to use a TCP/IP protocol stack. The Macintosh uses MacTCP, a proprietary software package.

TCP/IP stack   Windows machines use what's called a TCP/IP stack to connect to the Internet. The TCP/IP stack consists of the TCP/IP software and sockets software, called a Winsock. *See also* **Winsock**.

Telnet   An application that lets you log in to another system using the Telnet protocol. If you have a Telnet program installed on your computer (and you have the Telnet client correctly linked to your browser software), you can dial in to other computers without having to leave your Web browser.

TIFF (Tagged Image File Format)   A graphic file format developed by Aldus and Microsoft. Originally intended to be used with scanners, TIFF is now used as an image transfer format on computer networks.

Token Ring   A LAN topology that often uses TCP/IP protocols and is connected to the Internet. A Token Ring LAN is configured in a ring configuration, with each computer in constant contact with the next node in the ring. A token control message is used by a node wishing to send a message over the network. *See also* **Ethernet**.

topology   The layout of a computer network.

timeout   When a computer attempts to make a connection but gets no response, it gives up, or timesout, after a certain interval (usually defined by the user).

UDP (User Datagram Protocol)   One of the protocols on which the Internet is based.

UNIX   A multi-platform, multiuser operating system developed by AT&T and widely used by the government, universities, and businesses. A large part of the Internet is built on UNIX systems.

URL (Uniform Resource Locator)   The addressing system used in the World Wide Web and a proposed addressing standard for the entire Internet. The URL contains information about the method of access, the server to be accessed, and the path of any files to be accessed.

UUCP (UNIX-to-UNIX Copy)   A utility for copying files between one UNIX machine and another. UUCP was also the technology on which Usenet news and e-mail was originally based.

Velveeta   Spam lite. *See* **spamming.**

Veronica   A service that allows you to search Gopherspace.

VRML (Virtual Reality Modeling Language, pronounced "ver-mul")   An ASCII-based graphics description language used for defining and rendering navigable 3D environments.

WAIS (wide area information service)   A Internet-wide system for looking up information in databases and libraries.

WAIS gateway   A computer that is used to translate WAIS data so that it can be made available to an otherwise incompatible network or application.

WAN (wide area network)   A network of computers that is connected over a distance, usually by conventional phone service. A WAN is the opposite of a LAN, which is connected through local wiring. *See also* **local area network.**

Web browser   Software that allows a user to access and view HTML documents as well as most other Internet services. Netscape Navigator and Internet Explorer are two popular Web browsers.

Web document   An HTML document that is browsable on the World Wide Web.

Webmaster   The person in charge of administrating a World Wide Web site.

Web page   An HTML document that is accessible on the Web.

Webspace   Another term used to describe the "space" created by the Web.

Web spider   Automated software that "crawls through" or checks the links of the Web and sends back a list of all the links it has traversed. A Web spider is used to create and maintain the databases on which Web search engines are built.

Web walking   The act of using a Web browser to move through the documents available on the World Wide Web. The casual browsing nature of navigating the WWW has given rise to many slang terms that have to do with walking, strolling, crawling, and jumping, as opposed to the more frantic metaphors (jacking in, data surfing, data mining, etc.) found on the rest of the Internet.

whiteboard   A program (or feature within a program) that allows teleconferencing users to draw on a screen that can be collectively viewed, just like a real world conference room whiteboard.

Whois   An Internet database technology that lets you query a database over the Net in search of information on users, networks, and domains.

WINS (Windows Internet Name Service)   A name/IP address lookup service on a Windows-based local area network.

Winsock (Windows Sockets)   A technical specification that interfaces a Windows TCP/IP application and the TCP/IP protocol stack used to connect to the Internet. The Winsock provides compatibility between TCP/IP applications. On your PC, Winsock appears as a DLL (dynamic link library) file.

white pages   Internet directories that allow you to search for people with Internet accounts.

World Wide Web (WWW or 3W)   The hypermedia document presentation system that can be accessed over the Internet using software called a *browser*.

yellow pages   Internet directories that allow you to search for organizations, businesses, and services on the Net.

YMMV (your mileage may vary)   Hacker shorthand meaning "the results you get may differ from the results I got because of different conditions."

Xmodem   *See* **Zmodem.**

Ymodem   *See* **Zmodem.**

Zmodem   The best of the popular serial file transmission protocols. Zmodem supersedes Ymodem and Xmodem. X, Y, and Zmodem protocols are ordinarily used when transmitting data over a telephone line using a modem-to-modem hookup. Zmodem is not an Internet protocol.

zines   *See* **e-zines**.

Index

A

O

P

X

Y

Z

Don't Miss Your Connection!

Are you sure you have the latest software?
Want to stay up-to-date but don't know how?

Ventana Online helps Net surfers link up to the latest Internet innovations and keep up with popular Internet tools.

- **Save money by ordering electronically** from our complete, annotated online library.

- **Explore Ventana's** *Online Companions*™—regularly updated "cybersupplements" to our books, offering hyperlinked listings and current versions of related free software, shareware and other resources.

- **Visit the hottest sites on the Web!** Ventana's "Nifty Site of the Week" features the newest, most interesting and most innovative online resources.

So check in often to Ventana Online. We're just a URL away!
http://www.vmedia.com

Explore the Internet

Internet Business 500

$29.95, 488 pages, illustrated, part #: 287-9

This authoritative list of the most useful, most valuable online resources for business is also the most current list, linked to a regularly updated *Online Companion* on the Internet. The companion CD-ROM features the latest version of *Netscape Navigator*, plus a hyperlinked version of the entire text of the book.

Walking the World Wide Web, Second Edition

$39.95, 800 pages, illustrated, part #: 298-4

More than 30% new, this book now features 500 listings and an extensive index of servers, expanded and arranged by subject. This groundbreaking bestseller includes a CD-ROM enhanced with Ventana's WebWalker technology; updated online components that make it the richest resource available for Web travelers; and the latest version of Netscape Navigator along with a full hyperlinked version of the text.

Quicken 5 on the Internet

$24.95, 472 pages, illustrated, part #: 448-0

Get your finances under control with *Quicken 5 on the Internet*. Quicken 5 helps make banker's hours a thing of the past—by incorporating Internet access and linking you directly to institutions that see a future in 24-hour services. *Quicken 5 on the Internet* provides complete guidelines to Quicken to aid your offline mastery and help you take advantage of online opportunities.

HTML Publishing on the Internet for Windows
HTML Publishing on the Internet for Macintosh

$49.95, 512 pages, illustrated
Windows part #: 229-1, Macintosh part #: 228-3

Successful publishing for the Internet requires an understanding of "nonlinear" presentation as well as specialized software. Both are here. Learn how HTML builds the hot links that let readers choose their own paths—and how to use effective design to drive your message for them. The enclosed CD-ROM includes Netscape Navigator, HoTMetaL LITE, graphic viewer, templates conversion software and more!

The Web Server Book

$49.95, 680 pages, illustrated, part #: 234-8

The cornerstone of Internet publishing is a set of UNIX tools, which transform a computer into a "server" that can be accessed by networked "clients." This step-by-step in-depth guide to the tools also features a look at key issues—including content development, services and security. The companion CD-ROM contains Linux™, Netscape Navigator™, ready-to-run server software and more.

The Windows NT Web Server Book

$49.95, 500 pages, illustrated, part #: 342-5

A complete toolkit for providing services on the Internet using the Windows NT operating system. This how-to guide includes adding the necessary World Wide Web server software, comparison of the major Windows NT server packages for the Web, becoming a global product provider and more! The CD-ROM features a hyperlinked, searchable copy of the book, plus ready-to-run server software, support programs, scripts, forms, utilities and demos.

 Books marked with this logo include a free Internet *Online Companion*™, featuring archives of free utilities plus a software archive and links to other Internet resources.

Web Pages Enhanced

Shockwave!

$49.95, 350 pages, illustrated, part #:441-3

Breathe new life into your Web pages with Macromedia Shockwave. Ventana's Shockwave! teaches how to enliven and animate your Web sites with online movies. Beginning with step-by-step exercises and examples, and ending with in-depth excursions into the use of Shockwave Lingo extensions, Shockwave! is a must-buy for both novices and experienced Director developers. Plus, tap into current Macromedia resources on the Internet with Ventana's *Online Companion*.

Java Programming for the Internet

$49.95, 500 pages, illustrated, part #: 355-7

Create dynamic, interactive Internet applications with Java Programming for the Internet. Expand the scope of your online development with this comprehensive, step-by-step guide to creating Java applets. Includes four real-world, start-to-finish tutorials. The CD-ROM has all the programs, samples and applets from the book, plus shareware. Continual updates on Ventana's *Online Companion* will keep this information on the cutting edge.

Exploring Moving Worlds

$24.99, 300 pages, illustrated, part #: 467-7

Moving Worlds—a newly accepted standard that uses Java and JavaScript for animating objects in three dimensions—is billed as the next-generation implementation of VRML. Exploring Moving Worlds includes an overview of the Moving Worlds standard, detailed specifications on design and architecture, and software examples to help advanced Web developers create live content, animation and full motion on the Web.

Macromedia Director 5 Power Toolkit

$49.95, 800 pages, illustrated, part #: 289-5

Macromedia Director 5 Power Toolkit views the industry's hottest multimedia authoring environment from the inside out. Features tools, tips and professional tricks for producing power-packed projects for CD-ROM and Internet distribution. Dozens of exercises detail the principles behind successful multimedia presentations and the steps to achieve professional results. The companion CD-ROM includes utilities, sample presentations, animations, scripts and files.

Internet Power Toolkit

$49.95, 800 pages, illustrated, part #: 329-8

Plunge deeper into cyberspace with *Internet Power Toolkit*, the advanced guide to Internet tools, techniques and possibilities. Channel its array of Internet utilities and advice into increased productivity and profitability on the Internet. The CD-ROM features an extensive set of TCP/IP tools including Web USENET, e-mail, IRC, MUD and MOO, and more.

The 10 Secrets for Web Success

$19.95, 350 pages, illustrated, part #: 370-0

Create a winning Web site—by discovering what the visionaries behind some of the hottest sites on the Web know instinctively. Meet the people behind Yahoo, IUMA, Word and more, and learn the 10 key principles that set their sites apart from the masses. Discover a whole new way of thinking that will inspire and enhance your own efforts as a Web publisher.

 Books marked with this logo include a free Internet *Online Companion*™, featuring archives of free utilities plus a software archive and links to other Internet resources.

TO ORDER ANY VENTANA TITLE, COMPLETE THIS ORDER FORM AND MAIL OR FAX IT TO US, WITH PAYMENT, FOR QUICK SHIPMENT.

TITLE	PART #	QTY	PRICE	TOTAL

SHIPPING

For all standard orders, please ADD $4.50/first book, $1.35/each additional.
For software kit orders, ADD $6.50/first kit, $2.00/each additional.
For "two-day air," ADD $8.25/first book, $2.25/each additional.
For "two-day air" on the kits, ADD $10.50/first kit, $4.00/each additional.
For orders to Canada, ADD $6.50/book.
For orders sent C.O.D., ADD $4.50 to your shipping rate.
North Carolina residents must ADD 6% sales tax.
International orders require additional shipping charges.

SUBTOTAL = $ _____

SHIPPING = $ _____

TOTAL = $ _____

Name _____

E-mail _____ Daytime phone _____

Company _____

Address (No PO Box) _____

City _____ State _____ Zip _____

Payment enclosed ____ VISA ____ MC ____ Acc't # _____ Exp. date _____

Signature _____ Exact name on card _____

Mail to: Ventana • PO Box 13964 • Research Triangle Park, NC 27709-3964 ☎ 800/743-5369 • Fax 919/544-9472

Check your local bookstore or software retailer for these and other bestselling titles, or call toll free: **800/743-5369**

MACROMEDIA ®
End-User License Agreement for Shockwave ™ Run-Time Software (*"The Software"*)

PLEASE READ THIS DOCUMENT CAREFULLY BEFORE FIRST USING THE SOFTWARE. THIS DOCUMENT PROVIDES IMPORTANT INFORMATION CONCERNING THE SOFTWARE, PROVIDES YOU WITH A LICENSE TO USE THE SOFTWARE, AND CONTAINS WARRANTY AND LIABILITY INFORMATION. BY FIRST USING THE SOFTWARE, YOU ARE ACCEPTING THE SOFTWARE AND AGREEING TO BECOME BOUND BY THE TERMS OF THIS AGREEMENT. IF YOU DO NOT WISH TO DO SO, DO NOT USE THE SOFTWARE.

1. Important Notice
Shockwave software is a unique addition to Macromedia's Run-Time software library, allowing End-Users to play applications created with Macromedia's authoring software, available on the World Wide Web. The Software is an object code package that is designed to run with and will run only with an Internet browser which is licensed to contain and contains Macromedia Player software. If your browser is not one of these, the Software may not function properly.

2. License
This Agreement allows you to:
    (a) Use the Software on a single computer.
    (b) Make one copy of the Software in machine-readable form for backup purposes.

3. Restrictions
Unless Macromedia has authorized you to distribute the Software, you may not make or distribute copies of the Software or electronically transfer the Software from one computer to another. You may not decompile, reverse engineer, disassemble, or otherwise reduce the Software to a human-perceivable form. You may not modify, rent, resell for profit, distribute or create derivative works based upon the Software.

4. Ownership
This license gives you limited rights to use the Software. You do not own and Macromedia retains ownership of the Software and all copies of it. All rights not specifically granted in this Agreement, including Federal and International copyrights, are reserved by Macromedia.

5. Disclaimer of Warranties and Technical Support
The Software is provided to you free of charge, and on an "AS IS" basis, without any technical support or warranty of any kind from Macromedia, including, without limitation, a warranty of merchantability, fitness for a particular purpose and non-infringement. SOME STATES DO NOT ALLOW THE EXCLUSION OF IMPLIED WARRANTIES, SO THE ABOVE EXCLUSION MAY NOT APPLY TO YOU. YOU MAY ALSO HAVE OTHER LEGAL RIGHTS WHICH VARY FROM STATE TO STATE.

6. Limitation of Damages
MACROMEDIA SHALL NOT BE LIABLE FOR ANY INDIRECT, SPECIAL, INCIDENTAL OR CONSEQUENTIAL DAMAGE OR LOSS (INCLUDING DAMAGES FOR LOSS OF BUSINESS, LOSS OF PROFITS, OR THE LIKE), WHETHER BASED ON BREACH OF CONTRACT, TORT (INCLUDING NEGLIGENCE), PRODUCT LIABILITY OR OTHERWISE, EVEN IF MACROMEDIA OR ITS REPRESENTATIVES HAVE BEEN ADVISED OF THE POSSIBILITY OF SUCH DAMAGES. SOME STATES DO NOT ALLOW THE LIMITATION OR EXCLUSION OF LIABILITY FOR INCIDENTAL OR CONSEQUENTIAL DAMAGES, SO THIS LIMITATION OR EXCLUSION MAY NOT APPLY TO YOU. The limited warranty, exclusive remedies and limited liability set forth above are fundamental elements of the basis of the bargain between Macromedia and you. You agree that Macromedia would not be able to provide the Macromedia Software on an economic basis without such limitations.

7. Government End-Users   RESTRICTED RIGHTS LEGEND
The Software is "Restricted Computer Software." Use, duplication, or disclosure by the Government is subject to restrictions as set forth in subparagraph (c)(1)(ii) of the Rights in Technical Data and Computer Software clause at DFARS 252.227-7013. Manufacturer: Macromedia, Inc., 600 Townsend St., San Francisco, CA, 94103.

8. General
This Agreement shall be governed by the internal laws of the State of California. This Agreement contains the complete agreement between the parties with respect to the subject matter hereof, and supersedes all prior or contemporaneous agreements or understandings, whether oral or written. All questions concerning this Agreement shall be directed to: Macromedia, Inc., 600 Townsend St., San Francisco, CA, 94103, Attention: Chief Financial Officer.

Macromedia is a registered trademark and Shockwave is a trademark of Macromedia, Inc.